POLITICS IN THE AMERICAN STATES

Politics in the American States

A COMPARATIVE ANALYSIS

SEVENTH EDITION

Editors

VIRGINIA GRAY, *University of Minnesota*

RUSSELL L. HANSON, *Indiana University*

HERBERT JACOB, *late of Northwestern University*

CQ PRESS
Washington, D.C.

Congressional Quarterly Books
1414 22nd Street, N.W.
Washington, D.C. 20037
(202) 822-1475; (800) 638-1710

http://books.cq.com

Printed in the United States of America

Library of Congress Cataloging-in-Publication Data

Politics in the American states : a comparative analysis / editors,
    Virginia Gray, Russell L. Hanson, Herbert Jacob. — 7th ed.
        p.   cm.
    Includes bibliographical references and index.
    ISBN 1-56802-342-1
        1. State governments—United States. I. Gray, Virginia
II. Hanson, Russell L.   III. Jacob, Herbert.
JK2408.P64   1999
320.973—dc21   99-11401

IN MEMORY OF HERBERT JACOB

Contents

Tables, Figures, and Boxes

(Asterisks indicate tables and figures that have entries for all states.)

TABLES

Preface

In 1965 the first edition of this book appeared, edited by Herbert Jacob and Kenneth Vines; in 1999 the seventh edition is being published, sadly without Herbert Jacob at the helm. Herb died on August 29, 1996, of cancer. Herb was a pioneer in the field of state politics, where in the 1960s he and Vines introduced the systematic empirical and comparative study of the fifty states. Herb was as well a pioneer in the field of judicial process, where he did the bulk of his research over the years and was one of the founders of the Law and Society Association. His fine chapters on state courts in this book exemplified his unique combination of scholarly interests. Herb furnished new conceptual approaches to the study of state courts as well as careful empirical analysis of their operation.

As an editor, Herb brought a sharp eye and a willingness to take the heat for tough decisions. Although he worked on this book for more than thirty years, for each edition he had new ideas about how to organize it, who the authors should be, and what new pedagogical features should be added. He was never satisfied that the book was perfect, and he never rested on his considerable laurels. It was his wish that the book continue into a seventh edition and that his name be associated with it one last time. I hope and trust that this edition brings honor to his memory.

Herb had wide-ranging scholarly and personal interests. He might call to get you involved in his latest political action project or to talk about the latest teaching technique he was trying in Introduction to American Government. For someone trained before computers were in widespread use, he was amazingly computer literate, usually the first to try a new machine or a new program. He loved to proselytize about computer technology and what it could do for you. You always learned something by talking to Herb Jacob.

Colleagues associated with this book and those throughout the profession greatly admired Herb Jacob and valued their association with him. We shall miss his fair-mindedness, his energy, his high standards, and his wisdom about many, many things. However, this book will continue as one of his most important legacies.

I was fortunate to have secured Russell Hanson as a new co-editor. A long-time author of the intergovernmental relations chapter, Russ has written on many topics within state politics, including political culture, welfare policy, health policy, economic development, and state-local relations. Russ also has published widely in political theory and brings a broad vision to this enterprise.

As has been true with each new edition, the seventh includes substantial changes. Two chapters have been passed on to a new generation of scholars. Keith Hamm and Gary Moncrief bring new scholarship and insights to the state legislatures chapter, as Samuel Patterson had so ably done before them. Each author has published widely on the legislature as a state institution and on campaign finance. Henry Glick takes over the courts chapter, bringing his expertise on judicial elections and on policy innovations in the judicial arena. As a former student of Vines, Glick provides fitting continuity with early editions of the book. The criminal justice chapter has been dropped from this edition so that more space could be devoted to other developments. The remaining chapters have been extensively revised to represent new scholarship and changed events, such as the 1996 elections, new court rulings, and new policy developments.

The goal of *Politics in the American States* continues to be both the instruction of students and the advancement of knowledge about state politics. As residents of many different states, the contributors to this volume provide nuanced understandings of individual states along with rigorous analysis of the fifty states as a whole. Thus readers can make systematic comparisons between states and also become sensitive to the many subtleties of political life at the state level. As the careful reader will notice, however, many gaps remain in our understanding. We hope that this edition, like previous ones, will stimulate future scholars to fill them.

Finally, we thank the staff at CQ: Brenda Carter and Gwenda Larsen, our sponsoring editors; Debbie Hardin, our copyeditor; and Nadine Steffan, our production editor. As always, it was a pleasure to work with such dedicated professionals.

Virginia Gray

Contributors

MARGERY M. AMBROSIUS received her Ph.D. from the University of Nebraska and is an associate professor emeritus from Kansas State University, where she taught for twelve years. She is the author of numerous articles on state politics and state economic policies.

THAD BEYLE is the Thomas C. Pearsall Professor of Political Science at the University of North Carolina at Chapel Hill and was board chairman of the North Carolina Center for Public Policy Research for ten years. He has worked in the North Carolina Governor's Office and with the National Governors' Association. He is editor of *Governors and Hard Times* (1992), *North Carolina DataNet*, and since 1985 has edited annual editions of *State Government: CQ's Guide to Current Issues and Activities*.

JOHN F. BIBBY is professor of political science at the University of Wisconsin–Milwaukee. A specialist in American political parties, he is the author of *Politics, Parties, and Elections in America* (third edition 1996); and coauthor of *Two Parties—Or More? The American Party System* (1998), and *Party Organizations in American Politics* (1984). He has also held leadership positions in national and state party organizations.

SUSAN E. CLARKE is professor of political science at the University of Colorado at Boulder. Her publications include *The New Localism* (with Edward Goetz) and *The Work of Cities* (with Gary L. Gaile) and articles on state and local economic development strategies, education reform, cultural politics, and gender and politics.

RICHARD C. ELLING is professor of political science at Wayne State University in Detroit. Much of his research has examined issues of state management and administrative politics and includes his book *Public Management in the States: A Comparative Study of Administrative Performance and Politics* (1992). His current research focuses on employee turnover in state bureaucracies; the attitudes of Michigan citizens regarding the privatization of public services; and the impact of term limits on the performance of the Michigan state legislature.

HENRY R. GLICK is professor of political science and research associate in the Pepper Institute on Aging and Public Policy at Florida State University. Much of his scholarly work and teaching has been on state court systems and judicial policy. Recently, he has been concerned with the development and evolution of government policy concerning the right to die, and he is the author of *The Right to Die: Policy Innovation and Its Consequences* (1992). He has authored numerous other books and journal articles on the judicial process and the impact and implementation of right to die policy.

VIRGINIA GRAY is professor of political science at the University of Minnesota. She has published widely on numerous topics in state politics and public policy, including interest groups, economic development, and policy innovation. Her most recent book is *The Population Ecology of Interest Representation* (1996), written with David Lowery.

KEITH E. HAMM is professor and chair of the Political Science Department at Rice University. He is the author or coauthor of several articles and book chapters on American state legislatures, interest groups, and political parties included in *The Encyclopedia of the American Legislative System* (1994) and *Changing Patterns in State Legislative Careers* (1992). He is currently co-editor of *Legislative Studies Quarterly*.

RUSSELL L. HANSON is professor of political science at Indiana University–Bloomington, where he has taught since 1980. He is interested in American federalism and has published articles on political culture and welfare policy making in the states. He is the editor of *Governing Partners: State-Local Relations in the United States* (1998), coeditor of *Reconsidering the Democratic Public* (1993) and *Political Innovation and Conceptual Change* (1989), and author of *The Democratic Imagination in America* (1985).

THOMAS M. HOLBROOK is associate professor of political science at the University of Wisconsin–Milwaukee, where he has taught since 1989 and serves as editor of *American Politics Quarterly.* He has written extensively on state politics with an emphasis on state elections and is the author of *Do Campaigns Matter?* (1996).

RONALD J. HREBENAR is professor of political science at the University of Utah. His research and teaching focus on interest groups, political parties, public policy, and Japanese politics. He has published several books and articles including *Interest Group Politics in America* (third edition 1997). He was a Fulbright scholar in Japan in 1982–1983.

DAN A. LEWIS holds a joint appointment at the Institute for Policy Research and School of Education and Social Policy at Northwestern University. He is interested in urban policies that attempt to reform public bureaucracies and revitalize communities, and has focused on community crime prevention, school decentralization, and mental health policy. His most recent books include *Worlds of the Mentally Ill* (1991), *The State Mental Patient and Urban Life* (1994), and *Race and Educational Reform in the American Metropolis* (1995). Lewis serves on a variety of civic and governmental boards and committees.

SHADD MARUNA is assistant professor in the School of Criminal Justice at the State University of New York at Albany. His research involves the rehabilitative effects of educational services in the correctional system and the relationship between education, skills training, and crime.

GARY F. MONCRIEF is professor of political science at Boise State University. He is the author or coauthor of numerous articles and book chapters on American state legislatures and Canadian provincial legislatures. He is the coeditor of *Changing Patterns in State Legislative Careers* (1992) and *Campaign Finance in State Legislative Elections* (1998).

MARK CARL ROM is associate professor of government and public policy and acting executive director of the Georgetown Public Policy Institute. He is the author of *Fatal Extraction: The Story Behind the Florida Dentist Accused of Infecting His Patients with HIV and Poisoning Public Health* (1997) and *Public Spirit in the Thrift Tragedy* (1996); he is coauthor of *Welfare Magnets: A New Case for a National Welfare Standard* (1990) and is working on books on welfare reform and behavioral risk policy.

MARTIN SAIZ is assistant professor of government at the University of Notre Dame. He has published articles on urban politics, state and local economic development, and the effects of voting turnout on state public policies. He recently published *Local Parties in Political and Organizational Perspective* (1999) with Hans Geser.

CLIVE S. THOMAS is professor of political science at the University of Alaska–Juneau. His publications include works on interest groups, legislative process, and state politics. He is director of the University of Alaska Legislative Internship Program, has been a volunteer lobbyist, and teaches seminars on lobby organization and tactics. In 1997–1998 he was a Fulbright senior research scholar in Brussels studying American interest groups operating in the European Union.

SUE THOMAS is associate professor of government and director of women's studies at Georgetown University. Her primary area of research interest is women in political office. Her books include *How Women Legislate* (1994) and *Women and Elective Office: Past, Present, and Future* (1998) She is working on *Legislative Careers: The Personal and the Political.*

SUSAN WELCH is professor of political science and dean of the College of the Liberal Arts at Pennsylvania State University. She has published widely in the areas of women and politics and African American and Latino politics. Her recent books include *Affirmative Action and Minority Enrollments: The Impact of Bakke on Medical and Law Schools* (1998, written with John Gruhl) and *Black Americans' Views of Racial Inequality: The Dream Deferred* (revised edition, 1993, written with Lee Sigelman).

BRUCE A. WILLIAMS is professor in the Department of Urban and Regional Planning and research professor in the Institute of Communications Research at the University of Illinois Champaign–Urbana. He does research on citizen participation in environmental policy making, the use of scientific and technical information in democratic societies, and the role of the mass media in shaping public discourse. His most recent book, *Democracy, Dialogue, and Environmental Disputes: The Contested Languages of Social Regulation* (with Albert Matheny), was named best book published on environmental politics in 1996 by the Science, Technology, and Environmental Politics section of the American Political Science Association.

RICHARD F. WINTERS is professor of government at Dartmouth College. He has published several articles on the making of taxing and spending policies in the American states. He is coauthor, with Denis G. Sullivan and Robert T. Nakamura, of *How America Is Ruled* (1980). Currently he is conducting a study of the conditions under which general taxes get adopted and changed in the states, the conditions under which taxes to pursue specific and particular ends are adopted, and the ways political leaders reduce the electoral consequences of these new tax burdens.

CHAPTER 1

The Socioeconomic and Political Context of States

VIRGINIA GRAY

State governments deal with many pressing issues: the costs of tobacco use, low test scores in public schools, early childhood development, affirmative action, and crime. They operate large public enterprises, such as prisons, hospitals, and universities; they build new highways and bridges; they respond to sports owners who want new stadiums. They regulate health maintenance organizations (HMOs), the Internet, animal waste, and campaign finance, even as they are deregulating electricity. They are important partners in the federal system, implementing many federal programs and inventing new programs that are later adopted by Congress. State government is the place where many national politicians get their start; thus the caliber of people attracted to state service has an impact on the quality of national leadership.

This is a particularly exciting time to learn about state politics and government. Nearly all states experienced boom times in the late 1990s, leaving their governments flush with cash by 1998. State policy makers were able to address a backlog of spending needs accumulated since 1980, the last boom in state finances; many states were able to cut taxes or build up hefty surpluses. In part this renaissance was a result of balancing the federal budget and reducing the scope of the national government. The reduction of the national government began with President Ronald Reagan, accelerated with the Republican takeover of Congress in 1995, and was aided and abetted by President Bill Clinton's keen desire to balance the federal budget and "end welfare as we know it." When the federal government cut back on its spending, state governments were forced either to bear the financial burden of some of the threatened programs or else drop them. This shift created new stresses on states, but it also generated new programs and

1

problem-solving activity. The combination of devolution of federal authority and robust state revenue growth means that states have a lot of room to maneuver. As West Virginia governor Cecil Underwood said in his 1998 legislative address, "I can't remember a time brimming so completely with optimism and opportunity" (quoted in Ryen 1998, xvii).

The 1980s modernization of state governmental institutions is another reason for the states' resurgence. A "new breed" of governors promoted significant reforms in education and championed economic development. State legislatures were better equipped to deal with the challenges of rising health care costs and increasing welfare populations. State-run experiments in getting welfare recipients back to work led the federal government to abandon a sixty-year-old welfare program, Aid to Families with Dependent Children (AFDC) and replace it with a new block grant program (see Chapter 2). State governments have a greater capacity to deal with their problems today than ever before.

The authors of this volume compare the fifty states in terms of their policy differences and explain these differences using the methods of political science. We find these political differences both fascinating and intriguing to analyze. The social and economic differences among states are also significant. This chapter will make you aware of some of the differences among states in population, natural resources, and wealth, differences that affect what policy makers can do, and the sort of problems they face.

Political and economic differences, in turn, relate to another way in which states differ. States offer different levels of services and benefits to their citizens and allocate costs for those benefits differently. In this book we explore these policy differences and some of the political reasons for them. Expect to learn how state government operates in general—that is, the similarities among the fifty states—and expect to learn how the politics of various states differ. As the authors develop these points, you will also see that state governments and their politics are different from the national government and its politics. States, for example, are subject to many competitive pressures from other states. These pressures constrain state actions on taxation and rachet up spending on economic development.

DIFFERENCES AMONG THE STATES

Differences among the states abound. If you pay attention to the news, you will begin to notice some of these differences. For instance, during the week of January 18, 1998, the news media presented several interesting stories about the operations of state governments. It was reported that Montana is seeking to emulate the success of Switzerland and the Caymans in attracting wealthy investors who want privacy. Montana has become the first state to be an "offshore" banking haven, allowing rich foreigners to park their money in secret accounts protected by its state constitution. A small tax on each account is projected to raise a lot of money for the state, perhaps enough to eliminate state taxes.

Also that week two important court trials began, the first being the legal show-down between talk-show personality Oprah Winfrey and Texas cattlemen. Texas and twelve other agricultural states have "veggie libel" laws that protect cattlemen and food producers from lies that might stop consumers from buying their products. Because food is perishable, the food industry argues that it needs special protection from lies. In 1996 Winfrey moderated on her show a discussion of beef safety in which it was suggested that U.S. livestock might be prone to "mad cow" disease, as happened in Great Britain. The prices of cattle futures plummeted, causing Texas beef ranchers to lose millions—so they sued Winfrey. The federal district court decided that Winfrey was not liable, but did not rule directly on the Texas law's constitutionality. Rather, the judge said that ordinary disparagement standards applied in this instance.

Meanwhile, in a Minnesota state court an important tobacco case went to a jury trial. In recent years the attorneys general of forty-one states have sued the tobacco industry, seeking to recover the costs of state-paid medical bills for treating smokers. Many of the states entered into a joint settlement agreement of all claims against the tobacco companies, an agreement that is awaiting congressional approval; Florida, Mississippi, and Texas reached their own financial settlements with the industry. But Minnesota's attorney general, over the objection of its governor, chose to go to trial, saying that the potential national settlement was not good enough. The state was joined in the lawsuit by Blue Cross/Blue Shield, the state's largest medical insurer. They hoped the trial would make heretofore secret industry documents public, force an end to advertising aimed at youth, and recover billions in damages for the state. An out-of-court settlement on the eve of the jury's verdict achieved all of these goals, including a $7 billion payment to the claimants.

These examples illustrate that states do things differently. In Montana and Texas the state legislatures chose to pass unusual laws—in Montana a novel tax source, in Texas a relatively unusual regulation. In the tobacco example no legislative action was required; an important change in behavior is being forced by the concerted effort of attorneys general in Minnesota and many other states. Public policies can come about in multiple ways.

A more systematic way to see the differences among states is to look at rankings of the states on various quantitative indicators. Table 1-1 presents state rankings on five indicators. The first is the average expenditure on each pupil in public school; per pupil spending ranges per year from more than $9,500 in Alaska, New Jersey, and New York to around $4,000 in Utah and Mississippi. More than twice as many financial resources are available to educate children in the top-ranked states as in the lowest ranked states. Education expenditures are an important dimension of total expenditures, which are ranked in column two on a per capita basis. Alaska and Hawaii lead the way, partly because of the high cost of living, whereas Texas and Missouri lag far behind. Expenditure rankings are usually influenced heavily by the wealth of the state: Wealthier states can afford to spend more on their citizenry.

Table 1-1 State Rankings on Selected Policy Indicators

Rank	Education expenditures	Total expenditures	Health ranking	Condition of children	Percentage of deficient bridges
1	Alaska	Alaska	Minnesota	New Hampshire	New York
2	New Jersey	Hawaii	Utah	Maine	Massachusetts
3	New York	Delaware	West Virginia	North Dakota	Hawaii
4	Connecticut	Wyoming	Hawaii	Vermont	Rhode Island
5	Rhode Island	New York	New Hampshire	Iowa	West Virginia
6	Delaware	Massachusetts	Massachusetts	Nebraska	New Jersey
7	Vermont	Rhode Island	Wisconsin	Utah	Pennsylvania
8	Pennsylvania	Connecticut	Connecticut	Massachusetts	Vermont
9	Massachusetts	New Mexico	Iowa	Wisconsin	Maine
10	Wisconsin	New Jersey	Colorado	Hawaii	Missouri
11	Michigan	Michigan	Virginia	Minnesota	Michigan
12	Maryland	Washington	Maryland	Connecticut	North Carolina
13	West Virginia	Minnesota	Nebraska	Montana	Washington
14	Maine	North Dakota	Washington	Rhode Island	Louisiana
15	New Hampshire	Vermont	Kansas	Kansas	Kentucky
16	Oregon	Louisiana	New Jersey	Washington	Mississippi
17	Hawaii	Oregon	Ohio	New Jersey	Utah
18	Indiana	California	Pennsylvania	South Dakota	Virginia
19	Minnesota	West Virginia	Indiana	Wyoming	Alabama
20	Wyoming	Maine	Vermont	Delaware	New Hampshire
21	Washington	Montana	California	Oregon	Connecticut
22	Kentucky	Wisconsin	Oregon	Virginia	Oregon
23	Virginia	Pennsylvania	Maine	Idaho	Maryland
24	Kansas	Iowa	North Dakota	Alaska	Oklahoma
25	Florida	Utah	Georgia	Ohio	California
26	Georgia	South Carolina	Illinois	Indiana	Tennessee
27	Montana	Kentucky	Texas	Pennsylvania	Ohio
28	Ohio	North Carolina	Michigan	Colorado	Florida
29	Iowa	Maryland	North Carolina	Michigan	Illinois
30	New Mexico	Ohio	Rhode Island	Maryland	South Carolina
31	Texas	Idaho	Arizona	Oklahoma	Georgia
32	Illinois	Kansas	Idaho	California	Delaware
33	Nebraska	Nebraska	South Dakota	Missouri	Iowa
34	Colorado	Mississippi	Montana	Nevada	Montana
35	Nevada	Indiana	Missouri	Illinois	Nevada
36	North Carolina	Alabama	Oklahoma	New York	Colorado
37	South Carolina	Georgia	Delaware	West Virginia	Idaho
38	Missouri	Illinois	Florida	Kentucky	Indiana
39	South Dakota	Arkansas	New York	Texas	Arkansas
40	California	South Dakota	Wyoming	Arkansas	Alaska
41	Louisiana	Nevada	Kentucky	Arizona	Wisconsin
42	North Dakota	Tennessee	Alabama	North Carolina	Kansas
43	Tennessee	Virginia	Tennessee	Tennessee	Texas
44	Oklahoma	New Hampshire	Alaska	New Mexico	Wyoming
45	Idaho	Arizona	Arkansas	Georgia	New Mexico
46	Alabama	Oklahoma	New Mexico	Alabama	Minnesota
47	Arkansas	Florida	South Carolina	Florida	Nebraska
48	Arizona	Colorado	Mississippi	South Carolina	South Dakota
49	Mississippi	Texas	Nevada	Mississippi	Arizona
50	Utah	Missouri	Louisiana	Louisiana	North Dakota

SOURCES: U.S. Bureau of the Census, 1997: education expenditures (average per pupil expenditures, 1996), 170; total per capita expenditures (as of July 1, 1995), 312. *Congressional Quarterly's State Fact Finder: Rankings Across America 1998:* Health Ranking, 1996, 224. Rankings reflect a composite of indicators including smoking, unemployment, and the availability of health services; percentage deficient bridges, 1996, 272; child well-being, 1997, 289. Rankings reflect indicators of health, income, education, and other factors.

Columns three and four present state rankings on outcome measures in health and the condition of children. Minnesota and Utah are the healthiest places to live, and Nevada and Louisiana have the least healthy populations. Children are best off in New Hampshire and Maine and worst off in Mississippi and Louisiana. Outcome measures such as these are explained by state expenditures and by the socioeconomic makeup of the citizenry. Note that New Hampshire is toward the bottom of the per capita expenditure rankings, but its citizenry is affluent, highly educated, and takes care of its health and its children. Thus government spending is not the sole cause of policy outcomes; the socioeconomic composition matters too.

The last column in the table is a bit different: It ranks the states on the proportion of bridges that are deficient. New York and Massachusetts have the highest percentage of bridges that need attention; Arizona and North Dakota have the least. This measure of infrastructure need can be explained by the relative emphasis states put on highway expenditures; in general, the rural states devote more of their resources to highways than do the urban states.

EXPLAINING POLICY DIFFERENCES

The preceding comparisons provide an idea of how state governments differ and how their policies may change our lives. The second half of this book focuses on a state government's many activities. These outputs of a government's activities are called *public policies,* which are usually defined as means to governmental ends. The public policies reviewed in this book deal with taxes, health and welfare, education, regulation, economic development, and family.

Scholars have spent years trying to understand the differences among states' public policies and the reasons for those differences. The intellectual task is to explain interstate patterns—that is, what conditions or characteristics of states lead to generous educational expenditure, low welfare expenditure, or innovation in health policy? In general these investigations focus on two broad sets of variables: political characteristics and socioeconomic factors. Among a state's political variables, researchers have found the following to be important: political party control and interparty competition, interest group strength, gubernatorial power, the political background of judges, professionalism of the legislature, public and elite opinion, and political culture. Subsequent chapters in this book examine the major governmental institutions, both in their own right and as policy makers. Other chapters focus on key political actors such as interest groups and political parties.

In this chapter I examine the set of socioeconomic factors that may affect patterns of state policy. Included in these factors are the following: population size and composition, migration and urbanization, physical characteristics and natural resources, types of economic activities stemming from a state's physical endowments, wealth, and regional economic forces. These factors structure a state government's problems and affect a state government's ability to deal with them. I also explore the broader political context that affects state governments, such as political culture, public opinion, and national political forces. An understanding of the broader

Table 1-2 State Population Contrasted with Similar Country Population Rank, 1996

State rank	State/Country	Population	State rank	State/Country	Population
1	California	31,878,000	24	Kentucky	3,884,000
	Canada	*28,821,000*	25	Colorado	3,823,000
2	Texas	19,128,000	26	South Carolina	3,699,000
	Australia	*18,261,000*		*Ireland*	*3,567,000*
3	New York	18,185,000	27	Oklahoma	3,301,000
	Chile	*14,333,000*	28	Connecticut	3,274,000
4	Florida	14,400,000		*Uruguay*	*3,239,000*
5	Pennsylvania	12,056,000	29	Oregon	3,204,000
6	Illinois	11,847,000	30	Iowa	2,852,000
	Zimbabwe	*11,271,000*	31	Mississippi	2,716,000
7	Ohio	11,173,000		*Jamaica*	*2,595,000*
	Somalia	*9,639,000*	32	Kansas	2,572,000
8	Michigan	9,594,000	33	Arkansas	2,510,000
9	New Jersey	7,988,000	34	Utah	2,000,000
10	Georgia	7,353,000		*Slovenia*	*1,951,000*
11	North Carolina	7,323,000	35	West Virginia	1,826,000
	Switzerland	*7,207,000*	36	New Mexico	1,713,000
12	Virginia	6,675,000	37	Nebraska	1,652,000
	Haiti	*6,732,000*	38	Nevada	1,603,000
13	Massachusetts	6,092,000		*Estonia*	*1,459,000*
	Israel	*5,422,000*	39	Maine	1,243,000
14	Indiana	5,841,000	40	Idaho	1,189,000
15	Washington	5,533,000	41	Hawaii	1,184,000
16	Missouri	5,359,000	42	New Hampshire	1,162,000
17	Tennessee	5,320,000	43	Rhode Island	990,000
18	Wisconsin	5,160,000	44	Montana	879,000
19	Maryland	5,072,000		*Cyprus*	*745,000*
	Croatia	*5,004,000*	45	South Dakota	732,000
20	Minnesota	4,658,000	46	Delaware	725,000
21	Arizona	4,428,000	47	North Dakota	644,000
	Norway	*4,384,000*	48	Alaska	607,000
22	Louisiana	4,351,000	49	Vermont	589,000
23	Alabama	4,273,000	50	Wyoming	481,000

SOURCES: U.S. Bureau of the Census, 1997, 28–29; 1996, 827–829.

context will aid in understanding the role of political players and each state's governmental institutions.

Understanding the magnitude of state differences also helps us to understand the existence of federalism. The states are so different it is hard to imagine they would get along within a single union. Only federalism could accommodate the cultural distance between, say, clean-living Utah and gambling-mecca Nevada. Federalism allows these differences to flourish.

THE PEOPLE

The first state resource that I examine is the human resource. What kinds of people live where? How does the movement of people back and forth affect states? Why are trends in population growth and economic competition important for a state's future?

Population Size

A fundamental fact influencing a state's policies is its population size. In Table 1-2, I list each state's population in 1996, and for comparative purposes, the populations of selected nations. The largest state, California, has about 32 million residents or one in eight Americans. California can be considered more the size of a major nation than of a state. In fact, California's population is slightly larger than that of Canada's, and California's provision for education, highways, hospitals, and housing is on the same scale as many large nations; its state legislative districts are the size of congressional districts in other states.

Some less populous states are also the size of major foreign countries. New York, for instance, ranks second in U.S. population and is about the size of Australia. Louisiana is a medium-sized state by U.S. standards, ranking twenty-second in population; yet it is the same size as Norway. We must appreciate the fact that American state governments are large enterprises.

There are also some small states; and again, size has its consequences. Alaska and Wyoming are among the most sparsely populated states, but they are huge in the number of square miles. Thus the unit cost of building highways and providing other services is high. Alaska and Wyoming cannot achieve economies of scale. Smaller democracies have difficulties and opportunities not found in California and New York.

Population Growth

Whatever the population size, a state's leaders develop ways to cope with that size. More difficult to manage in the short run are changes in population. States experiencing sudden population growth have difficulties providing schools, roads, bridges, waste management, law enforcement, and the housing needed for an expanding population. States experiencing population decline, on the other hand, have a different set of concerns. As people leave the state and businesses die, the tax base erodes; if a state government adjusts by raising taxes, more people may leave and initiate a vicious cycle. Obviously, states would rather be growing than shrinking.

Changes in population between 1980 and 1997 are shown in Figure 1-1. During this period when the national increase was 15.3 percent, the Sunbelt (from California to Florida) and the Mountain West states (Alaska, Arizona, Colorado, Idaho, Montana, Nevada, New Mexico, Utah, and Wyoming) experienced high growth. Nevada doubled in population; Arizona, Alaska, and Florida grew by a third. Population shifts among states are a result of different fertility rates and different rates of net migration (in other words, the difference in the number of people moving into a state and the number moving out of that state). Migration patterns, in turn, are a function of economic opportunities: People usually move to find better jobs and a better quality of life. State leaders, therefore, focus on economic growth and full employment as a means to retain old citizens and attract new ones.

Quality of life, by contrast, is in the eye of the beholder: Retirees have one set of preferences and young people another, although perhaps both may agree on the

Figure 1-1   State Population Growth, 1980–1997

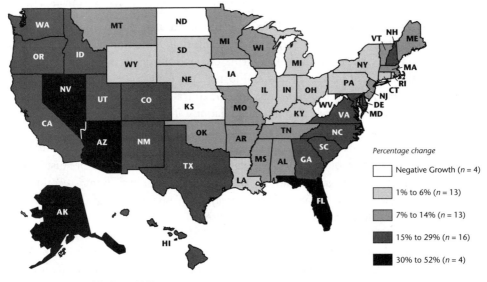

SOURCE: U.S. Bureau of the Census 1997.

virtues of a warm or moderate climate. For many people an important aspect of the quality of life is the opportunity to watch major league sports. Professional sports franchises have followed the regional demographic trends described previously: In 1960 there were forty U.S.-based pro teams in the four major sports (baseball, basketball, football, hockey), with 80 percent of the teams located in the Northeast and Midwest. By 1995 there were 102 U.S.-based teams, of which half were located in the South and West (De Vita 1996, 7). Teams follow people. In the 1990s bidding wars for teams broke out between states as sports owners demanded that state and city governments build stadiums for them.

The populations of Iowa, North Dakota, West Virginia, and Kansas decreased during the seventeen-year period (Figure 1-1). In the declining states a major issue is the necessity for school consolidation in sparsely populated rural areas. A school is often the focal point of a community, so its loss is a blow to community pride and identity. The loss of the sports teams associated with the schools is a further blow to a small town's esteem. For instance, in a decade North Dakota lost 9.2 percent of its public school population outside its few large cities. Some now refer to the state football championship as the Hyphen Bowl, in which one consolidated school plays another.

These descriptions point up the differences among states associated with the pace of population growth. Florida is illustrative of those states struggling to keep up with an expanding population and struggling to cope with the political values of new residents. Most states are in the middle of the two extremes, growing at a moderate rate. Even in cases of moderate population growth, state governments need to plan ahead to meet the needs of a growing population, because schools and roads are not built overnight, but the needs are rarely as critical as those found in states such as Florida.

Population Density

States also vary in the extent to which citizens live in densely populated urban areas or in more sparsely populated rural areas. As the U.S. population has grown, it has become more urbanized and less rural. Three quarters of Americans live in metropolitan areas; more than half live in large metropolitan areas with more than 1 million residents. But most of these metro residents live in the suburbs, not the inner cities. Growth in the 1990s was in "edge cities" and in suburban and exurban areas, not in central cities.

The most populous states tend to be among the most urbanized. There is a regional pattern as well. States on the East or West coast—California and New Jersey, for example—tend to be densely populated, and states in the South and Mountain West are clearly the least metropolitan. Even so, the growth of the metropolitan sector in the South has contributed to the rise of the Republican Party there.

The different interests of rural and urbanized areas often furnish the basis for sharp intrastate conflict. Illinois is a state with well-known metropolitan–downstate splits; about two-thirds of its population lives in the Chicago metropolitan area. As governed by the late mayor Richard J. Daley from 1955 to 1976, Chicago was the classic Democratic city machine. Its fiscal interests were often at odds with those in the rest of the state. In fact, columnist Mike Royko once suggested that the city secede from the state in order to free itself from the control of "downstate hayseeds and polyester-leisure suit suburbanites" (quoted in Peirce and Hagstrom 1984, 225).

Many other states manifest urban–rural splits or other sectional divisions. In heavily urbanized Florida, for example, there is a split between northern Florida and southern Florida. In the northern part of the state the traditional "southern" flavor pervades, whereas in southern Florida northern migrants furnish a "Yankee" flavor, and Latino immigrants provide their own flavor. In California since the 1970s the split has been between coastal and inland California, with the coast tending toward liberalism, and the inland areas tending toward conservatism. Such intrastate sectional differences influence and structure voting patterns and electoral outcomes.

Population Composition

States also differ in the composition of their populations—that is, in the types of demographic groups that are typical. States vary in the proportion of old people to young people, in the number of poor people, in the number of foreign-born people, and in the number of minorities. The increasingly diverse population mix presents challenges to government and often provides a basis for political conflict.

Age. Although the U.S. population as a whole is aging, the growth and concentration of seniors is quite variable at the state and local level. Retirement magnets in the South and Southwest attract relatively affluent retirees; other locations in the Midwest and Northeast have large elderly populations because of "aging in place" and the out-migration of younger persons. Iowa expects that in 2020 nearly one in six senior citizens will be at least 85 (De Vita 1996, 15). Thus there will be a greater demand for the number of nursing homes, doctors, and social services.

Other states, especially those growing rapidly, have a high proportion of children. Generally speaking, the southern and western states have more young people: More than one in three residents of Utah is under age 18, for example. These states have to worry about the demand for classrooms and youth services. A special stress is felt in those states with simultaneous rapid growth in both the elderly and the youth populations. Five states—Nevada, Arizona, Colorado, New Mexico, and Alaska—ranked in the top ten on both dimensions of age growth between 1990 and 1994 (De Vita 1996, 16). Their state leaders have to wrestle with questions of intergenerational fairness and equity in making trade-offs between different age segments.

Poverty. Altogether about 40 million people in the United States fall below the U.S. government's poverty line, but poverty is not equally distributed among the states. About 25 percent of New Mexico's population is poor, whereas only 5.3 percent of New Hampshire's population is poor. In Figure 1-2 the states are displayed according to the percentage of residents in 1995 with incomes below what is defined by the U.S. government as providing a minimal standard of living. Clearly, the rate of poverty is highest in the South and Southwest.

The size of the poverty population presents a direct challenge and burden to state governments. States, even with aid from the federal government, struggle to provide cash benefits, medical care, and housing to the poor within their borders. The states such as New Mexico and Mississippi that can least afford it are the states with the largest number of potential recipients. The states that can more easily afford to support the poor may exercise restraint because they fear generous benefits will attract poor people from out of state. The "welfare magnet" concept has been a popularly accepted one, although it receives only mixed support in scholarly literature. The perception by policy makers, however, that high welfare benefits act as a magnet can constrain the level of benefits (Peterson and Rom 1990, 80–81).

Poverty is associated with a syndrome of other social problems. People are often poor because they lack a good education and job skills; thus the need for education and training is greater in a state with significant portions of its population in poverty. Poverty is also often correlated with crime, especially in urban areas. The criminal justice system is, therefore, often more burdened in poorer states.

Immigrants. The United States is a nation formed by immigrants. Much of our nation's history can be told by reviewing the arrival of the different waves of immigrants—the Italians, the Irish, the Scandinavians, and so forth. Indeed, the entry of these ethnic groups into the political system formed the basis of many political cleavages. Today's immigrants are primarily from Latin America, the Caribbean,

Figure 1-2   Percentage of the Population in Poverty, 1995

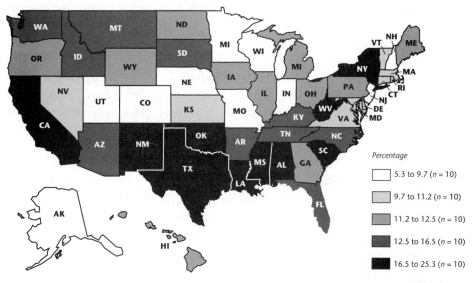

SOURCE: U.S. Bureau of the Census 1997, 477.

and Asia, not Europe. In the long run the country may reap substantial benefits from their arrival, just as it did from earlier immigrants. But in the short run the states in which refugees, "regular" immigrants (in other words, those who are not refugees or in this country with political asylum), and illegal immigrants locate experience difficulties in absorbing them. Between 1994 and 1996 about two-thirds of the immigrants settled in just six states: California, Florida, Illinois, New Jersey, New York, and Texas. And the wave continues: Approximately 1 million newcomers arrive each year (a net flow of 700,000 legal immigrants and refugees and 300,000 illegal immigrants; Martin and Midgley 1994, 4).

Today's immigrants differ markedly from native-born Americans in their ethnic origins, education, and skills. It is interesting to note that immigrants are both less likely to have a high school degree compared to native-born Americans and more likely to have an advanced degree (Martin and Midgley 1994, 2). In other words, there are two streams of immigrants arriving, which makes it more difficult to estimate their net impact. One stream will need extensive social services and language training, and the other stream will provide valuable workers for high-tech industries. For states the problem is that immigrants pay most of their taxes to the federal government, whereas more of the costs of caring for immigrants falls to state and local governments. For example, a study of Los Angeles County, where recently arrived immigrants make up 25 percent of the population, showed that immigrants paid a great deal more in taxes than they received in social services. However, so much of the taxes went to Washington, D.C., that Los Angeles County was left with a $808 million "immigration deficit" (cited in Martin and Midgley 1994, 33).

The magnitude, geographic concentration, and type of immigration has affected many state governments, even provoking a backlash in some states. One obvious impact is that many new arrivals do not speak English or do not speak it well. Between the 1980 and 1990 censuses there was a 40 percent increase in the number of people who speak a language other than English at home (De Vita 1996, 26). The prevalence of non-English speakers has provoked some to react by enacting laws making English the official language. More than twenty states have adopted English-only laws, though it is unclear what practical effect they have because most immigrants want to learn English.

The task of teaching English falls to the public schools, particularly to the large urban districts. Los Angeles had a herculean task: It had to educate more than 300,000 students with limited English proficiency in 1996–1997, just about half of its total school population. They spoke more than eighty different languages (Bathen 1998, 32). The success of California schools in teaching English became a divisive political issue, culminating in the adoption of Proposition 227 in 1998, which ended bilingual instruction in the public schools.

Even in America's heartland the educational challenge is daunting: In Minnesota's schools eighty native tongues are heard; in St. Paul, the capital city, more than 20 percent of the students are enrolled in English as a second language classes. Many St. Paul students were raised in refugee camps and lack basic skills in any language (Smith 1997, A17). Nearly all of the cost of English language instruction comes from state and local coffers; very little funding is given by the federal government.

In addition to the linguistic impact, immigrants may initially need a broad array of social services, including welfare, medical care, housing, and so on. Backlash against social service use has taken several forms. In the early 1990s several states, including Florida, Texas, California, New Jersey, and Arizona, filed lawsuits against the federal government to recover the costs of social services the states provided to illegal immigrants. The governors of these states argued that the national government had lost control of its borders; therefore, it should pay for the consequences. Their arguments were unsuccessful in court, however.

In 1994 California voters passed Proposition 187, an initiative to deny health care, education, and public services to illegal immigrants; most of its provisions have been invalidated by the courts or superseded by federal action. Under recent changes in federal welfare laws, illegal immigrants get no federal benefits; legal immigrants are ineligible for strictly federal programs such as food stamps and SSI (Supplemental Security Income), and states can choose to deny them benefits under joint federal–state programs such as welfare and Medicaid; refugees continue to be eligible for federal benefits. Thus the effect of federal reforms is to put the burden of immigration even more squarely onto the states.

Minorities. Because of immigration and differential birth rates, the United States has gradually evolved from a largely white, European society to an increasingly diverse one; today one in four Americans is a racial or ethnic minority. By the middle of the twenty-first century (and earlier in some states) minorities will equal the majority. The Hispanic and Asian populations are growing the fastest; by 2005 Hispanics are expected to become the largest minority group, outnumbering blacks (del Pinal and Singer 1997, 1).[1]

As our previous discussion of immigration would suggest, each minority population tends to be concentrated in certain states. More than half of all African Americans live in the South. Historically, the politics of individual southern states have varied according to the proportion of blacks. The Deep South states—Alabama, Georgia, Louisiana, Mississippi, and South Carolina—with the highest concentration of blacks were much more conservative than the peripheral South—Virginia, Tennessee, Florida, Arkansas, North Carolina, and Texas. Political behavior varied because where there were more blacks, whites were more likely to unite behind racial conservatism. Today blacks constitute about one quarter of the population in those five Deep South states.

Hispanics, in contrast, are highly concentrated in the Southwest, totalling a quarter of the population in California, New Mexico, and Texas. There are also significant Hispanic communities in New York (Puerto Ricans) and Florida (Cubans). Like blacks, Latinos are a disadvantaged minority, but unlike blacks many Hispanics lack fluency in English, which provides an additional obstacle in obtaining jobs.

More than half of all Asian Americans live in the West, primarily in California or Hawaii, with another significant portion in New York. As their numbers are much smaller than those of Hispanics or African Americans, Asian Americans do not constitute a significant fraction of the total population except in Hawaii. There the Asian American population is the majority. Hawaii has been successful in race relations for a long time and may provide a model for other states.

Native Americans are the smallest minority group; they primarily reside in the Southwest, especially California, New Mexico, Oklahoma, Arizona, and Alaska. About half live on tribal lands and about half are urbanites.

The rapid growth of minorities has increased their political clout, though they are still underrepresented among voters and among elected officials. Thus far Hispanics have achieved the governorship in Florida, Arizona, and New Mexico. Douglas Wilder in Virginia is the only African American to attain this office, and Gary Locke, elected governor of Washington in 1996, is the first Chinese American governor.

The close proximity of minority groups sometimes creates racial tensions over political issues. Several states have had challenges to congressional districts drawn along racial lines, and the U.S. Supreme Court is dealing with those affirmative gerrymandering cases. Chapter 5 describes in more detail the racial issues involved in

---

1. Hispanics are an ethnic group, not a racial group; Hispanics can be white, black, or other. The term "Hispanic" is a Census Bureau label that applies to all people from Spanish-speaking countries—that is from Spain or Latin America. Many Hispanics born in the United States prefer to be called Latino, which refers to people of Latin American descent living in the United States. Or they prefer to be known by their national origin—for example, Cuban or Mexican.

legislative reapportionment. In California backlash against minorities was expressed in 1996 by voters' adoption of Proposition 209, which says that state government cannot use racial quotas or preferences in education, contracting, and employment. The initiative proposition was particularly directed at race preferences in
the admissions policies of the University of California.

Overall the states' diversity in population composition—whether racial, age, or
poverty—leads to political diversity. Political parties are likely to be different in
California than in Iowa. They will be based on different political cleavages and different opinions about public policy needs. There are likely to be more groups representing a wider spectrum of interests in Florida than in Mississippi. In future
chapters we will see the consequences of states' population diversity.

THE PLACE

States also differ in terms of their physical characteristics. Some of these attributes are fixed and cannot be changed: the land area, the location, and the climate.
State leaders can try to compensate for the effects of a remote location, a cold or
unpleasant climate, or small size, but for the most part they are constrained by nature. Similarly, states are constrained by their natural resource endowments: Some
states have rich soil; others cannot grow much. Some states have plenty of water,
forests, minerals, oil, or coal. Others have to get their water from other states and
must rely on imported oil and coal. The net effect of the maldistribution of natural
resources is that states vary in the types of economic activities that can be conducted in them. The overall wealth of states, in turn, depends on the vigor of the economy. These natural economic advantages and disadvantages affect state government
a great deal.

Land

States vary enormously in their land area. We all know that Alaska is the largest
state, followed by Texas. What is less well known, however, is how big Alaska is in
relation to other states. It is more than twice the size of Texas. In fact, the twenty-
two smallest states could be combined before an area as large as Alaska is reached.

What difference to a state does its geographic size make? First, there are distinct
differences in a state's political style. In larger states, legislative districts are by necessity quite large. In some instances they are as large as the congressional districts
in some other states. In wide-ranging districts it is hard for legislators to keep in
touch with constituents; airplanes are frequently used for campaigning in Alaska,
for instance.

In Texas, rural districts are vast. In one House district the distance from one
corner to the opposite corner is more than 300 miles (Jewell 1982). Moreover, legislators must travel hundreds of miles from their homes and jobs to Austin, the
state capital. The travel burden affects the type of people who can afford to serve
in the legislature. In smaller states, such as New Hampshire and Vermont, districts
are small and compact. Legislators can run personal, almost one-on-one cam-

paigns. Once in office, they can commute to the capital on a daily basis, continuing in their regular occupations. The result is more of an amateur, small-town flavor in politics.

Second, geographic size has policy implications. In the provision of highways, for instance, geographic area and population density determine expense. Alaska, Montana, and Wyoming are large and sparsely populated states; their per capita highway expenditures are among the highest in the nation. Rhode Island is a small state with a compact population; its expenditure is among the lowest. The state's size affects the delivery of services in many other policy areas as well.

Third, land can be the basis of political conflict. Among the most divisive issues in the western states is that the federal government owns much of the land. Eighty-two percent of Nevada is owned by the federal government; more than 60 percent of Alaska, California, Idaho, and Utah is federal domain. This means that vast areas of the West are not under state jurisdiction; this land can be put only to the uses allowed by the federal government. Federal ownership, therefore, constrains urban growth and economic development in many western cities. Federal lands are often rich in mineral and other natural resources, assets unavailable to state governments. The federal government does, however, pay state royalties for the lost tax revenues. Occasionally, unrest over federal landholding rises, and outbreaks occur, such as the Sagebrush Rebellion in 1979. This symbolic revolution began when Nevada passed a law requiring the U.S. government to turn much of its land over to the state; several other states passed similar laws. Naturally, the federal government ignored these laws, and the rebellion gradually died out.

Location and Climate

In addition to the extent of a state's land, another physical characteristic is crucial: a state's geographic location. A state's location might be an asset because it is located on an ocean or on another waterway, or it might be an asset because of a favorable climate or because of its proximity to profitable markets. Unfortunately, other states have to deal with less desirable and more remote locations, where the costs of transportation to markets are higher.

States located near major markets have a natural economic advantage over states in more distant locations. Traditionally, access to markets and transportation has been among the more important factors in making decisions about where to locate a business. For example, Tennessee was victorious over thirty-seven other competitors in attracting the General Motors' Saturn plant (see Chapter 13 for more on the "car wars"). A key factor in General Motors' decision was Tennessee's central location: It was close to suppliers and markets. Other states, in fact, offered the company better financial incentives. Similarly, Japanese investment in a Tennessee Nissan plant was secured when the governor showed the potential investors satellite photographs of the United States taken at night, illustrating how many Americans live within a day's drive of Tennessee. Location was a feature that other states could not overcome with money.

Climate accompanies a state's location, and it is an important feature. Climate determines the length of the growing season and thus the type of agricultural crops that can be grown. For instance, oranges are an important crop in Florida and California, but not in the Dakotas. The climatic conditions in the Plains states—Iowa, Kansas, Minnesota, Missouri, Nebraska, North Dakota, Oklahoma, South Dakota, Texas—favor wheat instead. A state's climate is also a factor in where people choose to live. More people express a preference to move to a warmer area than to a colder one. Some of this preference relates to the greater economic opportunities in the Sunbelt than in the Frostbelt. The names *frost* and *sun,* however, reinforce the climatic aspect of the economic conflict among regions.

Natural Resources

Natural resources such as soil, water, minerals, and energy resources are attached to the land. The distribution of natural resources has great economic consequences: It allows states blessed with abundant water and rich topsoil to concentrate on crop production. Less fortunate states must import their water and some of their food. Some states receive income from the coal, oil, and minerals extracted from the land. Not only do these states have access to these nonrenewable resources, they can also derive tax revenue from their use. In essence, resource-rich states can tax the citizens of other states for consuming their oil, coal, and natural gas, thereby reducing their own tax burden.

To begin, first consider the rich topsoil that makes some states substantial agricultural producers. California is the top farm producer, as measured by gross state product (GSP),[2] followed by Texas, Florida, Washington, Iowa, Illinois, North Carolina, and Nebraska. Most of the other states in the Midwest rank fairly high, and the New England states rank low. Their state economies produce little agriculture. In no state, however, is agriculture the largest sector of the state's GSP. But agriculture looms large in other ways. For example, more than 10 percent of the acreage in Iowa, Kansas, Nebraska, North Dakota, and South Dakota is farmland. In the rural states there is a sense of pride and identification with the land. Iowa, for example, has on its billboards the slogan, "Iowa, a Place to Grow," suggesting simultaneously the growth of crops and the growth of sturdy young children. The floods that occurred in the summer of 1993 were devastating to the farm economy and to the rural lifestyle in Iowa; similarly, the floods of 1997 wiped out vast sections of Minnesota's and North Dakota's farming economy and damaged the towns that sustain it.

In addition to fertile topsoil, agriculture requires the availability of water. The Midwest is blessed with sufficient water, but the West is not. Nowhere is water a more important issue than in the Southwest. On the wall of the Colorado state capitol an inscription reads, "Here is the land where life is written in water." The same statement applies to Arizona, New Mexico, and Utah, where water is equally pre-

---

2. GSP is the gross market value of the goods and services attributable to labor and property located in a state. It is the state equivalent of gross national product (GNP).

cious. Historically, in these four states 90 percent of the water has been consumed by agriculture. But economic development, the rapidly increasing population, and some energy projects all require water. The allocation of water to agriculture rather than to other competing economic interests is a fierce and constant battle.

Finally, nonrenewable natural resources are unevenly distributed across the states. Minerals, coal, and petroleum are found only in some locations. Coal is found in large quantities in Kentucky, Pennsylvania, West Virginia, and the surrounding states, and in the West, particularly in New Mexico and Wyoming. Oil is located in the South and Southwest, primarily Louisiana, Oklahoma, and Texas, and in Alaska. The unequal distribution of natural resources has at least two major consequences for state governments. One favorable consequence for a state that has such resources is that the resources can be taxed. This tax is called a *severance tax,* and it is levied on the consumer located in other states. Oil-producing states can derive substantial revenues from the severance tax, thereby avoiding taxing their own citizens as heavily. The states in which the severance tax looms large are Alaska (63 percent of tax revenue in 1996) and Wyoming (30 percent of tax revenue; U.S. Bureau of the Census 1997, 315). These states do not use an income tax; in fact, for years Alaska even gave its citizens a rebate—$1,130 per one-year resident in 1996 (Barone and Ujifusa 1997, 75).

Reliance on the severance tax to the exclusion of other taxes, however, has an undesirable consequence. When the price of the nonrenewable resource drops, tax revenue plummets. Louisiana, in particular, experienced severe budget crises in the past decade when oil prices fell; energy produced 41 percent of state government revenues in 1982 but only 9 percent in 1996 (Barone and Ujifusa 1997, 618). A similar fate befell Alaska in 1994; oil revenues fell so much that budget cuts were implemented, and the imposition of an income tax was even contemplated. Thus, the reliance on the severance tax introduces an element of unpredictability into state budgeting.

THE ECONOMIC CONTEXT

States' economic performance depends on their natural resources, available human capital, national and international economic trends, and on the spending patterns of the federal government.

State Economic Activities

The land and its natural resources initially determine the type of economic activities that will prosper in different regions of the country. The regions' different resource bases mean they concentrate on different economic activities, and they enjoy different levels of prosperity. Table 1-3 relates some of these differences. As you see, California has by far the largest economy, followed by New York, Texas, Illinois, Florida, and Pennsylvania.

Historically, the largest single sector of the national economy has been the manufacturing sector. As can be seen in the table, however, in twenty-seven states man-

Table 1-3 Value of Gross State Product (in $ millions) and Size of Dominant Economic Sector, 1994

Rank	State	GSP	Dominant sector	Percentage of GSP
1	California	875,700	Finance, insurance, real estate	22
2	New York	571,000	Finance, insurance, real estate	29
3	Texas	479,800	Services	18
4	Illinois	332,600	Services	20
5	Florida	317,800	Services	22
6	Pennsylvania	294,400	Services	21
7	Ohio	274,800	Manufacturing	27
8	New Jersey	254,900	Finance, insurance, real estate	22
9	Michigan	240,400	Manufacturing	30
10	Massachusetts	186,200	Services	25
11	Georgia	183,000	Manufacturing	32
12	North Carolina	181,500	Manufacturing	31
13	Virginia	177,700	Government	20
14	Washington	143,900	Services	19
15	Indiana	138,200	Manufacturing	31
16	Maryland	132,700	Services	22
17	Missouri	128,200	Manufacturing	21
18	Tennessee	126,500	Manufacturing	25
19	Wisconsin	125,300	Manufacturing	29
20	Minnesota	124,600	Manufacturing	20
21	Connecticut	110,400	Finance, insurance, real estate	26
22	Louisiana	101,100	Manufacturing	17
23	Colorado	99,800	Services	20
24	Arizona	94,100	Services	19
25	Alabama	88,700	Manufacturing	22
26	Kentucky	86,500	Manufacturing	27
27	South Carolina	79,900	Manufacturing	28
28	Oregon	74,400	Manufacturing	20
29	Iowa	68,300	Manufacturing	25
30	Oklahoma	66,200	Manufacturing	17
31	Kansas	61,800	Manufacturing	17
32	Mississippi	50,600	Manufacturing	24
32	Arkansas	50,600	Manufacturing	25
34	Nevada	44,000	Services	34
35	Utah	41,700	Services	19
36	Nebraska	41,400	Services	16
37	New Mexico	37,800	Government	18
38	Hawaii	36,700	Finance, insurance, real estate	23
39	West Virginia	34,700	Manufacturing	17
40	New Hampshire	29,400	Manufacturing	22
41	Delaware	26,700	Finance, insurance, real estate	38
42	Maine	26,100	Manufacturing	18
43	Idaho	24,200	Manufacturing	19
44	Rhode Island	23,900	Finance, insurance, real estate	22
45	Alaska	22,700	Government	20
46	South Dakota	17,300	Finance, insurance, real estate	20
47	Montana	16,900	Services	18
48	Wyoming	15,700	Transportation, public utilities	17
49	North Dakota	13,500	Services	16
50	Vermont	13,300	Services	20

SOURCE: Calculated from data in U.S. Bureau of the Census 1997, 450–451.

ufacturing is now surpassed in value by some other economic sector. For example, the service sector is the single largest sector in fifteen states, including the industrial states of Illinois, Massachusetts, and Pennsylvania. Primarily, this sector is composed of business services, but in Florida tourism is important, and in Nevada, gambling. In other states the financial sector is the most important: New York, the established financial capital, has been joined in financial circles by seven other states, including California, New Jersey, Connecticut, Hawaii, Delaware, Rhode Island, and South Dakota. The latter state offers especially favorable regulatory conditions to the banking and insurance industries, so banks locate their subsidiary operations there. Three states rely mostly on government—Virginia (because of the spillover of federal government from D.C.), New Mexico, and Alaska. Finally, only one state—Wyoming—relies on transportation and utilities as the dominant economic sector.

In nearly all states, the manufacturing sector is very important, even when it is no longer the single dominant economic activity. Each state's natural resources heavily determine the type of manufacturing base. Midwestern states such as Illinois, Michigan, and Wisconsin focus on the production of machinery. In parts of the South—Georgia, North Carolina, and South Carolina—the manufacturing base rests on the textile industry. Food and food processing is the major manufacturing activity in other parts of the South—Arkansas, Florida, Kentucky—and in the Midwest—Nebraska, North Dakota, and South Dakota. The chemical industry is crucial to the economies of Alabama, Delaware, Louisiana, New Jersey, Tennessee, and West Virginia.

In summary, the states' economies vary in size, in which economic sector is most important (manufacturing, services, finance, and so on), and in the major goods produced. Many of the variations result from the natural resources of each state—that is, minerals, timber, soil, and access to waterways. These physical advantages give each state's economy a unique cast.

States, however, cannot rest on their natural resource advantages. Over time the sectors of the economy based on natural resources have declined in dollar value and in employment relative to the rest of the economy. The proportion of the population engaged in farming has decreased, as well as the proportion of the population engaged in manufacturing. These two occupations are heavily tied to the land. The proportion of the population engaged in services, in trade, and in finance has increased. These tend to be more mobile occupations, such as trading, servicing of business, and finance. Government work, of course, goes on everywhere. These occupations do not necessarily depend on particular natural resources, although they do depend on business activity in general. Thus the resource advantages and disadvantages of the states, although important, do not determine economic vitality as much as they once did.

These changes in economic circumstances are a part of larger changes in the national and international economies. We are now part of a world economy. The "globalization of capitalism" means that states increasingly feel the effects of surges and declines in prices, labor markets, and exchange rates thousands of miles away. Manufacturing's share of employment shrank from 26 percent in 1970 to 16 percent in 1996 (U.S. Bureau of the Census 1997, 415). This is referred to as the "deindustrialization of America." Manufacturing jobs have disappeared from New England, the Middle Atlantic states, and the Midwest. Some of the less skilled jobs have moved overseas.

At the same time, the service sector's share of employment has increased from 26 percent to 36 percent. These service jobs, however, are often in the growing regions, not in the stagnating regions. The shift in the U.S. economy from industrialization to postindustrialization has affected states unevenly and profoundly. Leaders in states whose economies were heavily industrialized have had to work especially hard to attract new types of economic activities. Some of their attempts at the courtship of capital are described in Chapter 13.

States' economies obviously depend on their ability to export products abroad and their capacity to attract direct foreign investment. Although Chapter 13 describes states' effort to attract foreign investors, as well as domestic investors, let us say a bit about exports. Exports account for about 10 percent of the U.S. economy, but states vary in their dependence on export markets. In recent years states have greatly increased their budgets for export promotion, for example establishing more trade offices overseas or sending governors abroad on trade missions. Utah has trade offices in Belgium, Japan, Korea, Mexico, and Taiwan, and Mississippi has offices in Canada, Chile, Germany, Korea, and Taiwan (Ryen 1996, 528–529). Tourism is an important industry for many states, and attracting foreign visitors is an essential element of tourism promotion.

States along the borders of Mexico and Canada have special ties to the international economy. Obviously immigration is a longstanding issue affecting local labor markets as well as reliance on social services. Trade relations have been and will be affected by NAFTA, the North American Free Trade Agreement; a series of other international agreements attempt to coordinate border policies on pollution, wildlife, fishing, disease, law enforcement, and so on. Texas is often cited for having good relations with its neighbor, Mexico; on being elected, new Texas governors often visit Mexico even before they visit Washington, D.C. In fact, in the past thirty years all Texas governors have visited Mexico in the first ninety days of their administration (Don Lutz September 1997, personal communication). Several international commissions and banks are located in south Texas, demonstrating the volume of international economic activity taking place along the border.

The globalization of the economy will continue, and experts think that the nation–state will become less relevant as an economic actor. The national economy may fracture into regional economies or smaller subnational economies, which is where the American states come in. One author even went so far as to say the fate of the United States depends on what the fifty states do in the international economy: "To a great extent, it will be state strategies and state alliances across a broad range of international issues that will determine our nation's relative success in the global marketplace of the future" (Ryen 1996, 525).

Spending by the federal government also greatly affects the economies of the states. The federal government can "prime the pump" of state economies through transfer payments (government payments to individuals, such as social security)

Table 1-4 Per Capita Personal Income by State, 1996

Rank	State	PCPI	Rank	State	PCPI
1	Connecticut	33,189	26	Georgia	22,709
2	New Jersey	31,053	27	Oregon	22,668
3	Massachusetts	29,439	28	Iowa	22,560
4	New York	28,782	29	Indiana	22,440
5	Delaware	27,622	30	Vermont	22,124
6	Maryland	27,221	31	Texas	22,045
7	Illinois	26,958	32	North Carolina	22,010
8	New Hampshire	26,520	33	Tennessee	21,764
9	Minnesota	25,580	34	South Dakota	21,516
10	Nevada	25,451	35	Wyoming	21,245
11	Hawaii	25,159	36	Arizona	20,989
12	California	25,144	37	Maine	20,826
13	Colorado	25,084	38	North Dakota	20,710
14	Virginia	24,925	39	Alabama	20,055
15	Washington	24,838	40	Louisiana	19,824
16	Michigan	24,810	41	South Carolina	19,755
17	Rhode Island	24,765	42	Kentucky	19,687
18	Pennsylvania	24,668	43	Idaho	19,539
19	Alaska	24,558	44	Oklahoma	19,350
20	Florida	24,104	45	Utah	19,156
21	Ohio	23,537	46	Montana	19,047
22	Kansas	23,281	47	Arkansas	18,928
23	Wisconsin	24,810	48	New Mexico	18,770
24	Nebraska	23,047	49	West Virginia	18,444
25	Missouri	22,864	50	Mississippi	17,471

SOURCE: U.S. Bureau of the Census, 1997, 457.

and defense spending. Other chapters in this book describe various federal transfer programs that provide aid to citizens. Often overlooked by state politics scholars is the stimulative effect of federal defense spending on states. Each $1 billion in defense spending adds about 35,000 jobs to the local economy ("After the Boom" 1987, 3197). Thus, how much Congress decides to spend and where it decides to spend it significantly affects state economies. In the 1990s, defense spending declined precipitously. Defense spending is concentrated: About half of all defense-related jobs are in just eight states—California, Florida, Massachusetts, New York, Ohio, Pennsylvania, Texas, and Virginia (Sylvester 1992, 64). So these states' economies were hurt in the early 1990s by the cuts in defense spending, though most states' economies recovered later.

State Personal Income

The net effect of states' natural resources, national and international economic trends, and the flow of federal funds is reflected in state wealth, usually measured in political science research by per capita personal income. This figure includes the income of individuals from all sources; a state's growth in personal income over time is a good index of how well its economy is doing. In Table 1-4 I list the average personal income per person in 1996 for each state. It is clear that there are significant disparities in income between states and between regions: Connecticut at $33,189 is significantly ahead of Mississippi at $17,471. In general, the southern states cluster at the bottom; the New England and Middle Atlantic states toward the top. The disparity, however, has lessened over the years, so the South does not lag as far behind the rest of the country as it once did.

Personal income is an important constraint on state programs because wealth determines what a state can afford to do on its own and what its people need or want from the state. States such as Mississippi do not have a lot of taxable income. States at the top of the income ranking, such as Connecticut, have a larger tax base and can afford to offer more generous benefits to their citizens. The irony is, of course, that Mississippi's needs are greater than Connecticut's. Federal aid reduces these interstate disparities to some extent. How states make their decisions in regard to taxing and spending is described in Chapter 9.

State leaders do not, however, simply "convert" economic wealth into expenditures for public programs. There are too many anomalies in state wealth and expenditure rankings for simple conversion to be a convincing explanation. Moreover, as we have seen, the economic performance of states changes over time. Some develop new fiscal capacities that might be tapped by government; the fiscal capacity of others shrinks, leaving them with overdeveloped public sectors. Politics shape how economic resources will be translated into public policies. In the next section I introduce some of the political dimensions that structure how states use their economic resources.

THE POLITICAL CONTEXT

Historical Differences

Many of the political differences in states today—differences in voter turnout and party competition, for example—are long-standing ones. The South in particular has had a different political history from the rest of the country. Some of the South's differences from other regions of the country are rooted in distinct economic interests. But another important historical difference is the South's political culture. It shapes the habits, perspectives, and attitudes that influence present-day political life.

Daniel Elazar (1984) has written extensively on how state political cultures have shaped the operations of state political systems. He has argued that the United States shares a general political culture that is, in turn, a synthesis of three major subcultures. The values of each subculture were brought to this country by the early settlers and spread unevenly across the country as various ethnic and religious groups moved westward. These migration streams have deposited their political values much like the Ice Age left permanent geological traces on the earth. Today's differences, according to Elazar, can be traced to the political values and perspectives of the earliest settlers.

Elazar has identified the three major subcultures as individualist, moralist, and traditionalist. The individualist subculture emphasizes the marketplace. Government has a limited role, primarily to keep the marketplace working properly. Politicians run for office out of material motivations in order to advance themselves professionally. Bureaucracy is viewed negatively as a deterrent to the spoils system. Corruption in office is tolerated because politics is conceived of as a dirty business. Political competition tends to be partisan and oriented toward gaining office rather than toward dealing with issues.

The individualist view of politics, Elazar has maintained, originated with English and German groups who settled the Middle Atlantic colonies. They were seeking individual economic opportunities and thus wanted a government that would advance, not inhibit, their materialistic interests. As their descendants moved westward into New York and Pennsylvania, the lower Midwest, Missouri, and the western states, they brought along the belief that government's role should be sharply limited.

In distinct contrast is the moralist subculture that emphasizes the commonwealth. In this view government's role is to advance the public interest or the good of the commonwealth. Thus government is a positive force in the lives of citizens. Politics revolve around issues, and politicians run for office on the basis of issues. Corruption is not tolerated because government service is seen as public service, not a business. The bureaucracy is viewed favorably and as a means to achieving the public good. Politics are a matter of concern to all citizens; it is therefore a citizen's duty to participate in elections.

The moralist view was brought to the New World by the Puritans, who settled New England in a series of religious communities. Their Yankee descendants transported these values as they moved westward across the upper Great Lakes into the Midwest and across the Northwest; later waves of Scandinavian and northern European groups with similar values reinforced their moralism. Politics in states settled by these groups tend to be participatory and oriented toward advancing the common good.

The third subculture, the traditionalist, is rooted in an ambivalent attitude toward the marketplace and the commonwealth. The purpose of government under this philosophy is to maintain the existing social and economic hierarchy. Politicians come from society's elite, who have almost a familial obligation to govern. Ordinary citizens are not expected to participate in political affairs or even to vote. Political competition tends to occur between rival factions within the elite rather than between class-based political parties. Bureaucracy is regarded as suspect because it interferes with personal relationships.

The traditionalist values were brought to this country by the people who originally settled the southern colonies. They were seeking economic opportunity through a plantation-centered agricultural system. Their descendants moved westward throughout the southern and border tier of states into the Southwest. In states settled by these groups fewer people participate in politics, and government's role is limited to maintenance of the existing social order, according to Elazar's theory.

Elazar classified the dominant political subcultures of each state, using the settlement patterns completed by the early twentieth century (Figure 1-3). Few states

Figure 1-3 Dominant Political Culture by State

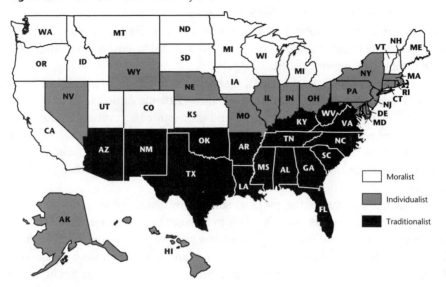

SOURCE: Adapted in part from Elazar 1984, 136.

are pure examples of one subculture, but usually there is a dominant culture that gives the state its particular political style. In general, the states of the South are dominated by the traditionalist subculture. The individualist states stretch across the country's middle section in a southwesterly direction. The states of the far North, Northwest, and Pacific Coast are dominated by the moralist culture. Sometimes two subcultures coexist in a single state, leading to political conflict between cultural groups. For example, Washington is moralist with a strong individualist strain; North Carolina is traditionalist with a strong moralist strain.

Contemporary migration patterns between regions may either reinforce or override the cultural base laid by the first settlers. For example, if people leave individualist states such as Pennsylvania and Ohio to seek better jobs in Texas, they will reinforce the individualism within the Texas political culture and move it away from traditionalism. Or if the population influx is quite large, as in Florida, the cultural base may be eroded. States with stable populations, such as Michigan, Minnesota, North Dakota, and Wisconsin, remain relatively pure examples of moralism.

Elazar's cultural theory has a great deal of intuitive appeal to many scholars of state politics. It is consistent with general impressions about state differences in political values, style, and tone. It also provides a historical explanation for differences. Many researchers, therefore, have subjected his thesis to empirical investigation—that is, they have tested his predictions about political and policy differences between the three subcultures and found some support for them. An investigation by Fitzpatrick and Hero (1988), for example, confirmed many of Elazar's hypotheses at the system level. They found that the competition between parties was stronger in moralist states than in other types of states and that this competition had greater relevance to public policy. Moralist states made greater use of merit systems than did other states. They demonstrated greater policy innovation and greater economic equality.

One interesting question is what happens to people who move from one political culture to another. Russell Hanson (1992) found that migrants' adjustment to different norms depended on their culture of origin. Persons raised as moralists were dutiful wherever they lived; traditionalists and individualists conformed to their new surroundings, becoming either more or less dutiful, depending on the new culture.

Further evidence that political attitudes are conditioned by local political culture or context is provided by Erikson, Wright, and McIver (1993). Because their *Statehouse Democracy* is a significant study that we refer to throughout the book, it is worthwhile to explain their methods. To get around the usual objection that there are no public opinion polls that are comparable across all states, they pooled 122 CBS News/*New York Times* telephone surveys from 1976 to 1988 to obtain measures of ideology and party identification by state.

They are able to show that state political context has a dramatic effect on individual attitudes. They control for the obvious demographic variables that explain individuals' attitudes (education, income, age, race, religion, gender, and size of place) and still find that the state of residence has a significant effect, approximately equal to the demographic effects. For example, the difference in party identification produced by living in Democratic Arkansas as opposed to living in Republican New Hampshire approaches the magnitude of the partisan differences produced by being Jewish instead of Protestant or being black instead of white.

Although the authors cannot account for the source of these state effects (cultural or otherwise), they conclude that "the political attitudes of American citizens vary in important ways on the basis of where in the United States they live" (Erikson et al. 1993, 72). Thus they demonstrate that something about a state's background affects its citizens' views; in further analyses they find strong support for Elazar's particular categorization of culture. State boundaries do make a difference.

Contemporary Differences

Others argue that historical differences are not as important as contemporary differences in explaining public policy. Rodney Hero and Caroline Tolbert (1996) argue that present-day patterns of racial and ethnic diversity are more influential than political subcultures derived from settlement patterns of the past. What is valuable about the Hero–Tolbert work is that they include the extent of the minority population (blacks, Latinos, and Asians) as well as the proportion of white ethnics (particularly those from southern and eastern Europe). Figure 1-4 plots the states on both dimensions, using 1990 census data. States along the horizontal dimension show increasing concentration of minority diversity as one moves to the right. States along the vertical dimension show increasing proportions of

Figure 1-4 State Breakdown of White Ethnic Diversity and Minority Diversity, 1990

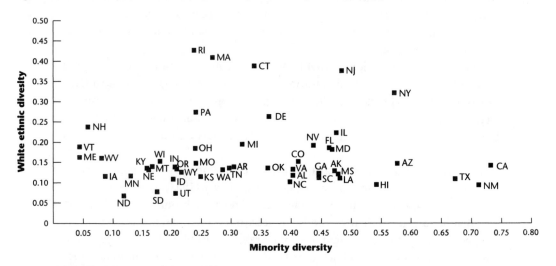

SOURCE: Calculated from data in Appexdix A, Hero, 1997.

white ethnic diversity as one moves upward. Those states falling into the lower left-hand corner have little diversity of any type—Utah, Iowa, and the Dakotas have very homogenous populations. In the upper right-hand cell are the most diverse states, such as New Jersey and New York. In the other cells states are diverse in terms of either white ethnicity or in terms of minorities but not both. Hero and Tolbert show that states vary in their policy choices according to the heterogeneity of their populations, but this research is quite preliminary and needs to be validated by further investigation before their categorizations will replace political subcultures as an explanation.

Another contemporary difference in states' political makeup is public opinion. Public opinion constitutes the attitudes of individual citizens toward public issues: Should their state spend more on welfare? Should their state allow abortions? Should a state lottery be established? The cultural thesis outlined previously suggests that public opinion on these and other issues should vary by state, and indeed it does. An even more important question, given our policy focus, is whether state policy differences are related to (or caused by) differences in public opinion.

Erikson, Wright, and McIver (1993) provided a persuasive demonstration that public opinion does matter. They combined a set of eight policy measures into a single index of policy liberalism; a high score on this measure indicates that a state spends more or intervenes more in a liberal direction than do other states. Their measure of public opinion was the standard ideology question: "How would you describe your views on most political matters? Generally, do you think of yourself as liberal, moderate, or conservative?" Because in every state conservatives outnumber liberals, their ideological scale (the percentage of liberals minus the percentage of conservatives) is always a negative number. They found that state opinion liberalism was highly correlated $(r = +.82)$ with state policy liberalism.

In addition to public opinion, states' political organizations are crucial in policy making. In this book we examine in detail two types of organizations: political parties, treated in Chapter 3, and interest groups, discussed in Chapter 4. The chapter authors describe how parties and groups function and how they differ from state to state. In this chapter I consider only the question of whether these political organizations affect public policy. Many scholars have examined this question, particularly the extent to which the party–policy relationship exists independently of economic causes.

One of the best examinations is that of Thomas Dye (1984), who related party competition to welfare policy. He was interested in the conditions under which the party in control has relevance for public policy—that is, whether policies change when parties change. He found that the party in power makes a difference where there is a high degree of competition between the parties and where each party is cohesive and focused on the issues. Brown (1995) later found that the specific nature of the party cleavage structure intensifies the impact of competition on policy.

Interest groups also have a major influence on public policy. They put issues on the policy agenda; they block the issues of the opposition; they shape legislation throughout its passage and its implementation. Gray and Lowery (1995) have shown that states with more interest groups pass fewer bills; in other words, interest groups lead to government gridlock. As shown in Chapter 12, groups are particularly powerful in the arena of regulatory policy. Although convinced of their importance, political scientists have not been able to analyze systematically the effect of groups on policy because they lacked comparable data from the fifty states. In Chapter 4, new data on group influence are presented, which may allow for such rigorous comparisons in the future.

National Forces

The states' political context is also conditioned by national political trends. These external forces do have an effect on the linkages between politics and policy within states. An article by John Chubb (1988) captures the statistical impact of external political and economic forces on state legislative and gubernatorial elections. Chubb found that presidential and senatorial coattails, voter turnout surges and declines, and national economic conditions have all affected the outcomes of state legislative races since 1940. Later research by Niemi, Stanley, and Vogel (1995) demonstrated that gubernatorial electoral outcomes are significantly affected by national political and economic forces. For example, in the 1994 elections when Republicans gained control of the U.S. Congress, they also picked up Republican strength in southern governorships and state legislatures, where Republican success had been slow to come. Thus national political and economic trends may indirectly affect state government through their impact on state elections.

Besides the electoral forces Chubb analyzed, other national political factors may affect the states. One such factor is the hierarchy of national offices that exists in the United States. As Schlesinger (1966, 1991) and Sabato (1983) have documented, there is a regular career progression from state legislative and other entry-level offices to the governorship to Washington-based positions such as senator, vice president, and president. Most people who achieve high office in Washington have "worked their way up" through this office hierarchy. Former governors Jimmy Carter, Ronald Reagan, and Bill Clinton are three examples of this phenomenon.

Because many politicians are ambitious people who want to top off their careers with service in Washington, they behave in response to their office goals, according to Schlesinger (1966). In other words, they take stands on issues with an eye on the next rung of their career ladder. The records of ambitious governors are scrutinized carefully by the voters; controversial decisions can come back to haunt them, as Massachusetts governor Michael Dukakis found in the presidential election of 1988. His prison furlough program seemed to attract more attention from the nation's voters than did his balancing of the state's budget. His rejection by the national electorate may lead other ambitious governors to avoid making tough decisions, even though making tough decisions is a daily requirement for governors.

Another nationalizing force is the power of the national Democratic and Republican parties. The two national parties have become more powerful relative to the 100 state parties, as is shown in Chapter 3. They have adopted rule changes limiting the autonomy of state parties and forced them to comply. This change is particularly apparent in the selection of delegates to the national nominating conventions. Similarly, the recent large-scale transfers of national party funds to state parties may be welcomed initially but do pose threats to state party autonomy in the long run.

These are but a few of the ways in which national political trends may affect state politics. Together with the historical and contemporary political differences among states, they structure how states handle their problems. Fiscal resources offer only the opportunity to solve problems; political means must still be used to confront the problems. In the final section of this chapter, I examine these problems and discuss the capacity of states to face them.

STATES' ABILITY TO GOVERN

Today the fifty states face a number of serious concerns. One is the issue of growth and decline. Some states, primarily in the Sunbelt, struggle with the problems accompanying rapid population growth. Some states cannot implement programs fast enough to cope with the influx of new residents. Other states are faced with the problem of decline in the economy and in the population, and they must adjust to a lower tax base and reduced public services. Both growth and decline require action from state government.

Another issue the states face is distribution and redistribution. All states have to distribute goods and services to their citizens. The mechanisms for doing this may differ in small, densely populated states from the arrangements used in large, sparsely populated states. The economies of scale are quite different in the two instances. All states also face the problem of redistribution—that is, they have to redirect resources from the rich to the poor. As discussed earlier, some states have demographic groups that require extra resources—the poor, minorities, and immigrants. Yet the well-off in some states—moralist ones, for example—seem more willing to support redistributive programs than the rich in other states. Too great an emphasis on redistribution may lead affluent citizens to relocate to states where the tax burden is lower. Thus the balance between distribution and redistribution is tenuous in the face of interstate competitive pressures.

A third issue confronting the states is the growing diversity of the population. The United States has experienced a demographic revolution since the 1970s. The shift from European to primarily Asian and Latin American immigration, as well as different birth rates between whites and racial minorities, alters the composition of the population into the next century. The workforce will be much more diverse, and the school-age population will be more heterogeneous. Meeting the needs of minorities will continue to challenge the school system and the welfare system, both of which are ultimately state responsibilities. Assimilating immigrants into communities and minimizing social conflicts will also be the province of state governments.

These broad issues, in turn, affect how states cope with their traditional responsibilities—education, welfare, hospitals, highways, corrections, and a myriad of smaller spending programs. As shown in Chapters 9 to 14, these responsibilities are the major objects of state expenditure. Population growth and decline certainly affect the demand for and cost of public services. The presence of refugees and other immigrants affects the provision of many services. The issues of distribution and redistribution come up in each policy area but loom especially large in welfare and regulation. Therefore, all traditional areas of state responsibility will undergo scrutiny as the economy and society change.

Relatedly, the "devolution revolution"—that is, the transfer of authority from the federal government to the states—intensifies state responsibility across the board. As will be explained in Chapter 2, the Reagan administration initiated a reassessment of the functional roles of each level of government and of the appropriate balance between the public and private sectors. The Republican Party's takeover of Congress in the 1994 elections accelerated the devolution, and President Bill Clinton went along with key parts of their devolution agenda, including returning more power over welfare to the states.

Fortunately, states seem to be ready to take on these challenges. They end the decade of the 1990s in far better shape than in any previous decade. For one thing, the states now have money to address their problems. In 1998 tax collections in nearly every state exceeded expectations, and federal budget cuts were not as severe as expected. The result is that states are in the best fiscal position since 1980, as measured by year-end fund balances ("The State of State Finances" 1997). Some states will use their surpluses to cut taxes, and others will catch up on spending needs deferred in the early 1990s.

As documented in Chapters 5 to 8, the states have vastly improved their capacity for dealing with problems. In the legislative arena, increased staffing, longer sessions, better pay for members, new committee structures, and other changes allow a greater capacity for effective decision making than in the past. Similarly, state executive branches have undergone many dramatic changes during the past decade or two. Much of this reform has been directed toward enhancing the governor's authority and centralizing the executive functions within fewer agencies. The improvement in the capacity of executive and legislative branches to solve problems has been accompanied by an improvement in the caliber of people willing to serve in these institutions. Most observers agree that there is a "new breed" of legislators and governors. In addition, state judicial systems have been modernized and improved in the same time period. Thus state governments now have the institutional capacity to address the challenges of the next century.

Improvement in the governance capability of states is good news, given the general concern about the "ungovernability" of advanced industrial societies. Much has been written in the past two decades about the impotence of national governments in the face of strong interests and under the pressure of fiscal crises. By taking a close look at smaller political systems such as the American states, ones that have undeniably improved their institutional capacities, we may be able to find cause for optimism about governance in general.

REFERENCES

"After the Boom." 1987. *National Journal,* December 19, 3193–3198.

Barone, Michael, and Grant Ujifusa. 1997. *The Almanac of American Politics, 1998.* Washington, D.C.: National Journal.

Bathen, Sigrid. 1998. "Los Angeles Unified School District." *California Journal,* January, 32–38.

Brown, Robert. 1995. "Party Cleavages and Welfare Effort in the American States." *American Political Science Review* 89:23–33.

Chubb, John. 1988. "Institutions, the Economy, and the Dynamics of State Elections." *American Political Science Review* 82:133–154.

De Vita, Carol J. 1996. "The United States at Mid-Decade." *Population Bulletin* 50:1–48.

del Pinal, Jorge, and Audrey Singer. 1997. "Generations of Diversity: Latinos in the United States." *Population Bulletin* 52:1–48.

Dye, Thomas R. 1984. "Party and Policy in the States." *Journal of Politics* 46:1097–1116.

Elazar, Daniel J. 1984. *American Federalism: A View from the States.* 3d ed. New York: Harper and Row.

Erikson, Robert S., Gerald C. Wright, and John P. McIver. 1993. *Statehouse Democracy: Public Opinion and Policy in the American States.* Cambridge: Cambridge University Press.

Fitzpatrick, Jody L., and Rodney E. Hero. 1988. "Political Culture and Political Characteristics of the American States: A Consideration of Some Old and New Questions." *Western Political Quarterly* 41:145–153.

Gray, Virginia, and David Lowery. 1995. "Interest Representation and Democratic Gridlock." *Legislative Studies Quarterly* 20 (November):531–552.

Hanson, Russell L. 1992. "The Political Acculturation of Migrants in the American States." *Western Political Quarterly* 45:355–384.

Hero, Rodney E., and Caroline J. Tolbert. 1996. "A Racial/Ethnic Diversity Interpretation of Politics and Policy in the States of the U.S." *American Journal of Political Science* 40:851–871.

Jewell, Malcolm. 1982. *Representation in State Legislatures.* Lexington: University Press of Kentucky.

Martin, Philip, and Elizabeth Midgley. 1994. "Immigration to the United States: Journey to an Uncertain Destination." *Population Bulletin* 49:1–47.

Niemi, Richard G., Harold W. Stanley, and Ronald J. Vogel. 1995. "State Economies and State Taxes: Do Voters Hold Governors Accountable?" *American Journal of Political Science* 39:936–957.

Peirce, Neal R., and Jerry Hagstrom. 1984. *The Book of America.* New York: Warner Books.

Peterson, Paul E., and Mark C. Rom. 1990. *Welfare Magnets.* Washington, D.C.: Brookings Institution.

Ryen, Dag. 1996. "State Action in a Global Framework." In *The Book of the States,* Vol. 31. Lexington, Ky.: Council of State Governments.

———. 1998. "These Are the Good Old Days: The State of Governance in the American States." In *The Book of the States,* Vol. 32. Lexington, Ky.: Council of State Governments.

Sabato, Larry. 1983. *Goodbye to Good-time Charlie.* 2d ed. Washington, D.C.: CQ Press.

Schlesinger, Joseph A. 1966. *Ambition and Politics.* Chicago: Rand McNally.

———. 1991. *Political Parties and the Winning of Office.* Ann Arbor: University of Michigan Press.

Smith, Maureen. 1997. "The Language Challenge." *Minneapolis Star Tribune,* May 24, A1, A16–17.

"The State of State Finances." 1997. *State Policy Reports* 15(23):2–7.

Sylvester, Kathleen. 1992. "Retooling for Peace." *Governing,* July, 63–67.

U.S. Bureau of the Census. 1997. *Statistical Abstract of the United States, 1997.* Washington, D.C.: U.S. Government Printing Office.·

SUGGESTED READINGS

Brace, Paul. *State Government and Economic Performance.* Baltimore: Johns Hopkins University Press, 1993. Treats the economic fortunes of the states in historical and comparative perspective.

Browne, William P., and Kenneth VerBurg. *Michigan Politics and Government: Facing Change in a Complex State.* Lincoln: University of Nebraska Press, 1995. Comprehensive treatment of Michigan state politics and government, written by a team of experts.

Elazar, Daniel J. *American Federalism: A View from the States.* 3d ed. New York: Harper and Row, 1984. An analysis of nation–state relations in the United States, stressing the political role of the states in the federal system. Describes and applies Elazar's theory of political culture.

Erikson, Robert S., Gerald C. Wright, and John P. McIver. *Statehouse Democracy: Public Opinion and Policy in the American States.* Cambridge: Cambridge University Press, 1993. A sophisticated study of public opinion in the states and its effect on public policy.

U.S. Bureau of the Census. *Statistical Abstract of the United States, 1997.* Washington, D.C.: U.S. Government Printing Office, 1997. The official source of statistics on many aspects of state demography, economy, and policy.

CHAPTER 2

Intergovernmental Relations

RUSSELL L. HANSON

The national government has been the driving force in American policy making since the Great Depression. Social security and Medicare, civil rights, and environmental protection are examples of far-reaching policies initiated by the national government and sustained by its resources. State and local governments' involvement in these programs is circumscribed, and they have ceded power to the national government in education and transportation. The national government used to play little or no role in these policy areas, but it has become the leader in many domestic undertakings.

This division of political labor is now changing. A "devolution revolution" is underway. Its partisans want to reduce the power of the national government and expand the authority of state and local governments. Ironically, these revolutionaries are political conservatives in Congress and the statehouses. They have already won several battles, including the fight to end Aid to Families with Dependent Children, a federal entitlement program dating from the New Deal. Now conservatives are setting their sights on affirmative action and environmental protection, policy areas in which liberals want to preserve a strong role for the national government.

The devolution revolution will probably not achieve all of its objectives; few revolutions do. But the devolutionary movement has already changed the terms of political discourse in the United States. No one is proposing bold new initiatives for the national government. The action is at the state level, where governors and legislators are discussing what to do about health care, educational reform, economic development, and a host of controversial issues, including the right to die, affirmative action, immigration, and the like.

The change is not confined to the realm of discourse. The structure of American government is being altered by the attack on "big government" launched by President Ronald Reagan in 1981. The power of the national government is being curtailed, creating new opportunities for state and local governments. State governments in particular have become more active in policy making. In the process they have been modernized, and states' capacity for effective administration has improved (Hedge 1998). The states' current fiscal situation is rosy, too, and elected politicians are eager to display their problem-solving skills in this new environment.

As the center of political gravity in our system of intergovernmental relations descends to the state level, there will be profound political consequences. Devolution will change what governments do, which governments do them, and for whom. There will undoubtedly be winners and losers in this process; indeed, that is what the devolution revolution is all about. Conservatives are determined to return power to their traditional state and local strongholds, and liberals are equally committed to the preservation of a national government that has been the principal agent of progressive policy making. The extent to which liberals lose and conservatives gain will depend on just how far devolution proceeds.

If devolution continues and states resume control of domestic policy, the pattern of winners and losers will vary geographically. So long as the national government dominates policy, there will be some uniformity: The rules are more or less the same in all areas of the country, so the range of policy outcomes is constrained. That will change if states become more powerful. States differ enormously in terms of their demographic composition, economic capacity, and political orientation. They will not reach the same answers to leading policy questions of the day; in fact the leading questions will not even be the same in all states. As a consequence, policies will develop unevenly and the resulting patchwork of outcomes will raise issues of equity, just as they did before the national government gained the dominant position in domestic politics during the Great Depression.

Thus American politics in the new millennium could look very different. A review of the current system of intergovernmental relations—in other words, the status quo that is the object of so much contention—will reveal the magnitude of these potential changes.

THE VARIETY OF INTERGOVERNMENTAL RELATIONS

The U.S. Constitution and fifty state constitutions define our system of intergovernmental relations. The U.S. Constitution sketches the relation between national and state governments, provides the basic guidelines within which interstate relations occur, and establishes the fundamental liberties of all American citizens. State constitutions establish state governments, determine the relation between state and local units of government, and specify the rights of people who live under their jurisdiction. Together these legal instruments define the role of governments in our political system and organize the field of intergovernmental relations.

The field of intergovernmental relations has different sectors. *Federalism* refers to the division of power between the national government (that is, the federal government in Washington, D.C.) and the governments of the states. In a federal system, national and state governments each have substantial authority to make important policy decisions. In certain areas (for example, foreign policy) the national government predominates. In other areas (for example, education) state governments have more power (except when civil rights are at risk). But in most areas of domestic policy, national and state governments share the authority to act. The sharing can be cooperative, but often it is competitive. Different levels of government vie with one another for control of policy and the affection of voters.

Relations between states are not federal. They are *confederal,* to use an older terminology that is still useful in conveying the importance of sovereignty in this sector of interactions. As constitutionally recognized entities, states are on equal footing; none has a higher status than any other state in the Union. There are differences in political power and influence, to be sure, but the symmetry of constitutional authority means that state governments must negotiate their differences, just as sovereign nations do. Therefore, intergovernmental relations in this sector proceed diplomatically, with the important difference that military options are not available to any of the parties. Also, some disputes between state governments may be decided by agencies of the national government, a situation that differs from world affairs, where no supreme authority exists (although the United Nations and World Court fill this role with varying degrees of success).

Relations between states and their local units of government are *unitary.* Localities do not enjoy sovereignty; they are creatures of state government. In this sector of intergovernmental relations the asymmetry of constitutional power is incontestable, although it is seldom displayed openly. Rather, it forms the backdrop for political relations that are much more balanced. The states vary tremendously in their treatment of local units of government, and so this sector of intergovernmental relations is further characterized by great diversity.

States also mediate the relation between national and local governments, carrying the goals and concerns of one to the other, while adding the preferences and resources of governors and legislators to the mix. Similarly, states increasingly regulate interactions between local governments, arbitrating conflicts and creating regional agencies for coordinating the actions of neighboring localities (Cigler 1998). State governments are at the center of an elaborate web of intergovernmental relations; they transmit political developments from one sector of the web to others, sometimes magnifying the impulses and sometimes dampening them.

CONFEDERALISM

It is appropriate to begin with an examination of relations between states, because federalism in the United States was itself a product of dissatisfaction with the Articles of Confederation (1781–1788). Under the articles each of the thirteen former colonies of Great Britain enjoyed full sovereignty. The confederal Congress was an assembly of states that addressed problems of mutual concern, chiefly their common defense. But the states were unwilling to give Congress power to act on these problems. Congress could not levy taxes, nor could it conscript citizens. It could only request assistance from state governments—and then only if an extraordinary majority of states agreed that such a request was valid. Individual states could and did refuse to honor these requests, just as nations in our time withhold money or troops from peacekeeping ventures of a modern confederacy: the United Nations.

Dissatisfaction with the Articles of Confederation led the Federalists to propose the establishment of a more energetic central government. Their Constitution, which was ratified in 1788, created a national government with powers of its own, powers that once belonged exclusively to state governments. The proud sovereignty of the states was thereby undermined; the residual "states' rights" were a far cry from the independence enjoyed by states under the Articles of Confederation.

The loss of autonomy was probably greatest in the area of economic regulation, which was left entirely to states in the Confederation. Under the Constitution, however, states are enjoined from passing laws that interfere with contractual obligations. Equally important is the ban on taxing imports and exports as a way of raising revenues for state governments. States may not coin money or issue credit; these powers belong only to the national government. Nor may states establish religion, limit expression, or otherwise infringe on liberties protected under the Bill of Rights.

States are also forbidden from entering into treaties, alliances, or confederations with other nations, although international agreements occasionally allow for the involvement of officials in states affected by them. For example, American states and Canadian provinces recently joined to halt the spread of zebra mussels in the Great Lakes basin and eastern spruce budworms in northern forests. Similarly, the North American Clean Air Alliance of northeastern states and provinces is promoting the commercial development of zero-emission vehicles to reduce air pollution in that region of the continent. Along the Rio Grande, southern U.S. and Mexican states jointly monitor the spread of tuberculosis across the border, and regulate the international trucking industry (Ryen 1996).

Treaty-making powers belong to the national government, but state actions may nullify or weaken them. For example, states and localities have enacted a significant amount of protectionist legislation to stem the flow of imported goods and services, which has caused problems for a national government seeking fair trade on the international front. In the Uruguay Round of talks on the General Agreement on Tariffs and Trade (GATT), the European Community pressed the U.S. government to eliminate "buy American" requirements in forty states and lower other trade barriers erected in 2,700 municipalities (Weiler 1993/1994). The North American Free Trade Agreement (NAFTA) brought similar requests from Mexico and Canada, over the objections of state and local officials who feared job losses in their districts. These officials have influence in Congress, which must approve legislation needed to implement such international agreements.

States act like sovereigns in other ways, too. With the emergence of a well-integrated global economy, every state now devotes considerable attention to foreign trade. Most state governments have offices in Japan, and thirty states conduct similar activities in Europe, building ties to the European Union (Levine 1994). Other states promote exports by exploring overseas markets, providing information and technical assistance to exporting firms, and even capitalizing their activities (Ryen 1996). Foreign investors are wooed by trade missions from many states, and the prospect of joint ventures with domestic firms, investment assistance, and incentives (Clarke 1986).

States not only interact extensively with foreign countries; they develop relations with other state governments, too. Some of these interactions are expressed in formal compacts, wherein states agree to address common problems. Other, less formal transactions have become frequent and thoroughly routine—a departure from earlier times when encounters were sporadic. Finally, a growing network of professional associations now links state officials in a web of information exchange, policy promulgation, political lobbying, and legal cooperation. (Coordinated challenges to the tobacco industry and Microsoft are examples of the latter.) As a result, the structure of intergovernmental relations in the United States has acquired a horizontal dimension to go with its vertical or hierarchical dimension.

The Constitution establishes the legal framework for these transactions. The most important provisions governing relations between the states are found in Article III, which stipulates that the Supreme Court shall resolve legal controversies between states. Often these controversies involve boundaries. For example, in 1993 New Jersey sued for control of Ellis Island, which has been part of New York since the two states signed an agreement in 1834. The agreement stipulated that the portion of Ellis Island above water (about three acres) was in New York, and the surrounding underwater area belonged to the Garden State (New Jersey). Over time the underwater areas were land-filled and the island grew to almost twenty-eight acres in size, with new buildings and a ferry slip. In May 1998 the Court ruled in favor of New Jersey, which now has the power to enact zoning measures, impose environmental restrictions, and collect taxes on most of Ellis Island.

States settle persistent disagreements by means of interstate compacts. The power to form compacts is implied in Article I, section 10, which requires that Congress must approve such "treaties between states." Before 1920 only three dozen compacts were signed by states. Since then more than 150 compacts have been established—100 of them since World War II. These compacts cover boundaries, conservation, navigation on interstate waterways, law enforcement, metropolitan development across state lines, pollution, transportation, energy, and natural resources. They may be concluded between two, several, or all fifty states, depending on the problem or policy area involved (Council of State Governments 1977). Bilateral compacts are the most common, but regional and national compacts have become increasingly important as states begin to cooperate on problems of mutual concern, such as economic development.

Some interstate compacts incorporate agencies of the national government as parties to the agreement, but most do not. Indeed, interstate compacts can preempt (or at least limit) national intervention in state affairs. For that reason such compacts represent what Elazar (1984) has called "federalism without Washington." The Delaware River Compact and the Colorado River Compact are two instances in which states make regional allocations of water without resorting to Congress. In fact, the upper-basin states in the Colorado River agreement have their own compact within a compact to allocate water from the Colorado River among themselves (Lord and Kenney 1993).

Interstate compacts allow states to oppose the national government, not simply preempt its involvement in activities traditionally left to state and local discretion. For example, at the suggestion of Congress, four areas of the country entered into compacts governing the disposal of hazardous waste and radioactive materials (Feigenbaum 1988). They took the lead in setting policy in this area, to the point of enforcing their standards on the national government. Cecil D. Andrus, governor of Idaho, stopped accepting radioactive materials generated by plants that manufactured nuclear weapons for the national government. The governors of Colorado and New Mexico threatened to follow suit, and the Department of Energy agreed to dispose of the waste in a safe, environmentally sound manner (Wald 1988).

Compacts are not the only means of ensuring interstate cooperation. Many states have reciprocal ties with neighboring states. Within the area of higher education, for example, neighbors may offer the equivalent of in-state tuition to residents of adjacent states in exchange for similar treatment of their own citizens. These and other routines make up an important part of interstate relations, although they lack the formality of compacts.

Then there are the national associations of governors, lieutenant governors, attorneys general, and other state officials, which exchange information and policy recommendations on matters relevant to state government (Freeman 1985). These associations, as well as professional organizations that link administrators and policy specialists, provide a well-developed communications network among the states, alerting them to emerging problems and, above all, to political developments in Washington.

Organizations of subnational officials act as interest groups at the national level, trying to influence the legislature and administration on behalf of state and local interests (Haider 1974). Public interest groups—for example, the National Governors' Association, National Conference of State Legislatures, National League of Cities, U.S. Conference of Mayors, and National Association of Counties—now make up a formidable lobby in national politics (Cigler 1995). The success of this lobby contributed heavily to the growth of social welfare spending in the United States, which now taxes the revenue-raising capacity of the national government, as one prominent scholar observed in the late 1970s (Beer 1978).

More recently, state and local governments have lobbied for greater control over the use of grants for social welfare programs and other purposes. In 1995 members of the National Governors' Association joined the Council of State Governments, the National Conference of State Legislatures, and the American Legislative Exchange Council in a "federalism summit" to discuss strategies for strengthening the power of state and local governments. A second summit in 1997 issued an eleven-point plan to "strengthen the federal-state partnership." Among other things, the plan called for an end to "federal conscription and coercion of state governments"; recommended the consolidation of categorical programs into block grants; and required "federalism impact statements" for any congressional action that might have an effect on the distribution of powers and responsibilities across levels of government (Council of State Governments 1997). Although these proposals did not become law, they had the desired effect: Congress became more attentive to the concerns of state politicians and their lobbyists in Washington.

FEDERALISM

Under federalism a national government and one or more subnational levels of government enjoy substantial powers, often in the same policy areas. In the United States the formal allocation of power between state and national governments is constitutionally prescribed. The Constitution gives some powers primarily or exclusively to the national government. Other powers are given to the states, which must exercise those powers within limits set by the Constitution and Bill of Rights. Still other unspecified powers are reserved to the states and the people under the Ninth and Tenth Amendments. Then there are powers concurrently exercised by national and state governments, including the authority to tax and borrow money, make and enforce laws, and so forth. Within this group of concurrent powers there are some—for example, the power of amendment—that must be exercised jointly.

A schematic representation of this distribution of authority at the time of ratification is shown in part (a) of Figure 2-1. The largest circle represents the power of the people, some of which was delegated to the national and state governments under a federal arrangement. As shown, a broad area of power was reserved to the people, reflecting the Founders' restrictive view of government. The overlap between the national and state circles of power symbolizes the range of concurrent powers just mentioned. State powers were large under this schema, again manifesting the Founders' belief in an expansive role for state governments in a federal arrangement. This role included complete constitutional authority over local governments, which stand in a unitary, rather than federal, relationship to their state governments.

Of course, federalism is not static. The boundaries of national and state powers shift as the different levels of governments try to expand their influence. The federal government has been particularly successful in gaining influence over the long run, as part (b) of Figure 2-1 suggests. To a significant extent the growth in federal power is the cumulative result of Supreme Court interpretations of the Constitution. As the umpire of our federal system, the Court has claimed the power of judicial review over state actions; increased the power of Congress to regulate interstate

Figure 2-1   The Distribution of Constitutional Authority in the United States

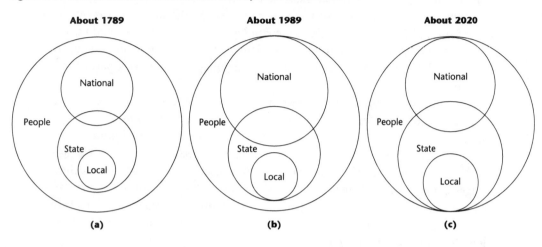

transactions, particularly those related to commerce; and enlarged executive powers it deemed necessary to the fulfillment of the Constitution. It has even allowed some degree of national control over local affairs, especially in matters pertaining to civil rights and public employment. At the same time the Court has been reluctant to interpret other clauses of the Constitution, including the reserved powers clause of the Tenth Amendment, in ways that could augment the authority of states.

Federal power grew over a long period of time, and the Supreme Court was not the only agent of change. Congress played a role by enacting legislation that gave rise to judicial challenges in the first place. The executive, or rather certain executives, tested the limits of federalism, pushing them back from time to time. Finally, the people themselves bestowed new authority on the national government by enacting amendments to the Constitution, including the power to tax income (which made it possible for the national government to fund a broad array of new activities, including entitlement programs).

Not all of the increase in national power came at the expense of states' rights. The national government mandates compliance with some of its objectives, but more often it relies on inducements to achieve its ends. These inducements or incentives generally take the form of financial assistance that is made available to governments willing to pursue national goals. These programs are voluntary, but in virtually all cases the amount of assistance is attractive enough to enlist state and local participation—under the supervision of national agencies, and subject to national guidelines, of course.

The use of incentives to bring about compliance by states with national objectives has generated a concomitant expansion of state powers. All levels of government have become more active in the twentieth century, not just the national government. State and local governments together employ more than 82 percent of all civilian government workers. That share increased steadily during the 1970s, 1980s, and 1990s, when the number of civilians employed by the national government hovered around 3 million. By 1996, state employment had risen to 4 million, and local employment to 10 million workers. Hence state and local governments are part of the "big government" we now have; in fact they are the largest part of that government.

State and local governments will become even more important if the devolution revolution unfolds any further. Conservative policy makers want to shift power and responsibility from the national government to the states and their localities. The welfare reform of 1996 was the first major step in this direction, but similar changes could affect environmental policy making, transportation, and education. If these changes come to pass, we will be in the situation portrayed in (c) of Figure 2-1, which shows a reversal in the domestic roles of national and state governments in the United States. Under that scenario states could dominate domestic policy making in the early years of the new millennium.

As Figure 2-1 suggests, the phenomenal growth of domestic government in the United States has not been smooth. It occurred in bursts of expansion, followed by more conservative eras of policy making. This cycle reflects the rising and falling influence of liberal political forces over national institutions (Nathan, Doolittle, and Associates 1987). Different phases of federalism may therefore be discerned, each characterized by distinctive relations between state and national governments.

Phases of Federalism

The increasing velocity of national government—its expansion of power—is recorded in patterns of government spending. By examining the expenditures of different levels of government, we can compare changes in the relative velocity of each and the combined velocity of all. Figure 2-2 shows spending by national, state, and local governments in selected years from 1927 to 1995. (To facilitate comparisons with state and local spending, only spending on domestic programs by the national government is shown; it is calculated by subtracting outlays for defense and foreign aid from total national expenditure.)

The velocity of national government has increased substantially in this century. Just before the Great Depression, direct spending by local governments was about 2 percent of the gross domestic product (GDP). This was only a little less than the national government spent on domestic matters. States played a much larger role, spending twice as much as the national government and three times as much as local governments. Clearly, states were the most important policy makers before the New Deal.

The minuscule involvement of the national government in domestic affairs reflected more than a century of dual sovereignty (Corwin 1934). According to this doctrine federalism entailed a sharp division of responsibilities. National responsibilities centered on defense and foreign policy, regulation of currency, and, to a much lesser extent, interstate trade. Property laws, civil rights, and the provision of

Figure 2-2 Velocity of Federal, State, and Local Governments, 1927–1995

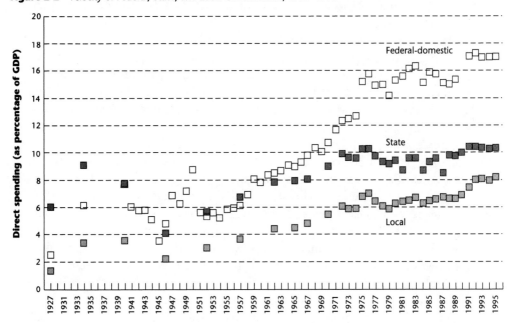

SOURCE: Calculated from U.S. Advisory Commission 1993a; U.S. Bureau of the Census, *Government Finances*, various; Office of Management and Budget, *Historical Tables*, various.

basic services were under the purview of state governments, and through them, local communities. The two spheres of responsibility were considered more or less distinct, and conflicts between governments over the right to make policy in specific cases were generally decided in favor of one or the other by the Supreme Court. The Court seldom recognized joint responsibilities; it preferred a system of constitutionally segregated powers, which scholars have likened to a layer cake.

Not surprisingly, the doctrine of dual federalism retarded the activity of the national government in domestic affairs, with several notable exceptions—for example, the Civil War, the disposition of western lands, and the trust-busting of the Progressive era. During the Great Depression, however, the velocity of national government accelerated rapidly; as a proportion of the GDP, national spending on the home front tripled by the onset of World War II. This was a period in which the foundations of the American welfare state were laid. Social security, unemployment insurance, and public assistance were all established at this time. Massive public works projects were also undertaken at the behest of President Franklin D. Roosevelt and advocates of the New Deal. The national government subsidized the construction of roads, dams, public buildings, and other projects undertaken by state and local governments, and it initiated wholly national programs—for example, the Works Progress Administration. The subsequent mixing of powers and re-

sources in programs for maintaining incomes and stimulating growth has been described as "marble cake federalism," to distinguish it from its "layer cake" predecessor (Grodzins 1966).

The federal partnership continued after World War II as veterans' benefits were
added to income security programs and new public works, such as the interstate
highway system, were constructed. The expansion of activities funded by the national government accelerated in the 1960s during the War on Poverty, a period of
"creative federalism." The velocity of all governments rose steadily in this period, as
is evident in Figure 2-2. Beginning in 1970, though, the national government began
to outpace state and local governments. Even the presidency of Ronald Reagan,
which was generally characterized by reductions in the role of federal government,
saw a burst of speed unmatched by any corresponding increase in the velocity of
state and local governments. This was followed by another sharp upturn in 1990,
when the so-called peace dividend (the savings in defense spending after the Cold
War ended) swelled the domestic side of the national budget and financed new
programs in health, education, and the conversion of defense industries. In subsequent years federal domestic spending stabilized around 17 percent of GDP.

How has the increased velocity of national government affected the velocity of
state and local governments? Has it come at their expense, as some argue? Or has it
stimulated them to become more active themselves, leading to an even larger public
sector?

Figure 2-2 shows that the velocity of state government increased during the
1930s, as states joined the efforts of the national government to combat the Depression. State activities also expanded during the War on Poverty in the 1960s. By the
mid-1970s state spending as a proportion of the GDP settled just under 10 percent.
In the early 1990s it grew to about 11 percent, and then receded to previous levels.
During the same period, local spending grew slowly and now represents about 8
percent of the GDP. Altogether, national domestic, state, and local spending consumed about 33 percent of the GDP in 1995, a considerably smaller portion than
most industrialized countries spend on domestic affairs.

If spending is the measure of energy, the national government has overtaken and
surpassed state and local governments. In fact, the true velocity of national government is understated in Figure 2-2, which does not take intergovernmental transfers or
grants-in-aid into account (Bahl 1990; Break 1980). In fiscal year 1995 the national
government spent almost $1.6 trillion; this included more than $229 billion in financial assistance to state and local governments. State governments passed a good portion of the federal funds to local governments and added an even larger sum of their
own monies to this subsidy. Without this twin subsidy, direct spending by local governments would have been much less, and the difference in the velocities of national
and local governments would have been greater than is indicated in Figure 2-2.

Because a sizable portion of national domestic spending is actually a transfer to
state and local governments, increases in the velocity of national government tend
to bring about increases in the velocity of subnational political units. The author of

one study (Chubb 1985) concluded that federal aid has been a leading cause of the growth of state bureaucracy. Similarly, state aid, some of which consists of national monies being passed on, has stimulated increases in employment by local governments. In short, the increasing activity of the national government has made subnational governments more energetic, leading them to expand their own efforts, albeit under national supervision. As former governor Richard A. Snelling of Vermont once complained, "Four out of ten state and local employees are actually federal employees in disguise, marching like a secret army to the guidelines and regulations of Washington" (Snelling 1980, 168).

Even this remark suggests that the growth of the national government has not occurred entirely at the expense of state and local governments. By Governor Snelling's own count, six of ten state and local workers remain loyal to the states and local communities that employ them, and many of them are new workers. In several policy areas, the power of state and local government has been enhanced by national funds that enable them to meet the increasing demands of citizens for public goods and services.

Certainly, there are areas of public policy in which national policy makers have displaced subnational governments, civil rights being a prime example. This displacement has fueled popular resentment of "big government," expressed so well by Reagan, who in 1980 launched his presidential campaign in Philadelphia, Mississippi, with a speech celebrating states' rights. According to Reagan, the imposition of mandates by the national government was an unwarranted intrusion in state and local affairs. Worse, it was an encroachment on powers protected by the Tenth Amendment, which stipulates that "the powers not delegated to the United States by the Constitution, nor prohibited by it to the States, are reserved to the States respectively, or to the people."

Of course, it is often difficult to know when mandates derive from powers usurped by Congress or the executive, or when they rest on firm constitutional ground. The Supreme Court decides these matters; during most of the twentieth century it has allowed the national government great leeway in levying mandates. Successively broader interpretations of the commerce clause of the Constitution have permitted Congress to regulate economic affairs quite generally, even when tangentially related to interstate commerce.

In 1976, however, the Court seemed to retreat from a permissive interpretation of the commerce clause. Minimum wage and overtime provisions of the National Fair Labor Standards Act did not protect most employees of state and local governments until 1974, when Congress amended the act to include them under the law. State and local governments, which had to pay the costs associated with this mandate, challenged the new law on the grounds that it infringed on powers reserved under the Tenth Amendment. In *National League of Cities v. Usery* (426 U.S. 833 [1976]), the Supreme Court ruled in favor of this challenge, holding that Congress did not have the authority to impose this requirement on state and local governments whose employees were carrying out "traditional governmental functions," such as fire and police protection, sanitation, public health administration, and the administration of parks and recreation.

The issue was not settled, though. In later decisions the Court decided that "traditional government functions" included licensing automobile drivers, operating a highway authority, and operating a municipal airport—but not the regulation of traffic on public roads or the regulation of air transportation. The difficulty of establishing a reasonable constitutional test for deciding which activities were traditional and which were not eventually led Justice Harry Blackmun to a change of heart. Blackmun, who had voted with the majority on *National League of Cities*, joined four others in overturning that decision. In *Garcia v. San Antonio Metropolitan Transit Authority* (469 U.S. 528 [1985]) the Court held that Joe Garcia, an employee of the transit authority, was entitled to overtime pay under the National Fair Labor Standards Act, and it rejected as unsound in principle and unworkable in practice a rule protecting "traditional governmental functions" from congressional regulation.

This decision was reaffirmed and broadened in 1988, when the Court decided that Congress was entitled to tax the interest on bonds sold by state and local governments. As in *Garcia*, the justices in the majority refused to shield state and local activities from congressional control. As Justice Brennan observed, "The states must find their protection from congressional regulation through the national political process, not through judicially defined spheres of unregulable state activity" (*South Carolina v. Baker*, 485 U.S. 505 [1988]). Only by exerting power and influence over representatives in Congress could state and local officials legitimately limit the imposition of mandates.

The Supreme Court's position is evolving, though (Schram and Weissert 1997). In 1995 a deeply divided Court invalidated a federal statute prohibiting the possession of firearms in school zones. Siding with the majority, Justices Anthony M. Kennedy and Sandra Day O'Connor wrote, "The Statute now before us forecloses the States from experimenting and exercising their own judgment in an area to which States lay claim by right of history and expertise, and it does so by regulating an activity beyond the realm of commerce in the ordinary and usual sense of that term" (*U.S. v. Lopez*, 514 U.S. 549 [1995]).

In 1997 conservative members of the Supreme Court issued an even stronger assertion of states' rights. The Court invalidated portions of the Brady Handgun Violence Protection Act, which required local law enforcement officers to conduct background checks on people purchasing handguns. "Such commands are fundamentally incompatible with our system of dual sovereignty," ruled the Court; "the federal government may neither issue directives requiring States to address particular problems, nor command State officers, or those of their political subdivisions, to administer or enforce a federal regulatory program" (*Printz v. United States*, 117 S. Ct. 2365 [1997]).

In the end it may not matter where the Court decides to draw the line on national power because Congress does not have to rely on mandates to get its way. It can achieve its objectives by other means: Congress can use grants-in-aid to "buy" cooperation from state policy makers who might otherwise be reluctant to endorse national legislation. Because states are not compelled to accept grants, there is no basis for intervention by the Supreme Court. The only limits on Congress's ability to set conditions for grant programs are political.

Fiscal Federalism

Although officials of state and local government do not welcome mandates from the national government, they willingly accept grants-in-aid, even those with strings attached. Grants allow officials to do more for their constituents without raising state and local taxes, or at least without raising taxes in proportion to spending increases. The political advantages of this financing arrangement undoubtedly explain the enthusiasm with which subnational policy makers have lobbied for the creation of new grants-in-aid and the expansion of programs already in existence.

Financial grants-in-aid are the chief incentives by which national policy makers induce state governments to enact programs and policies intended to serve national objectives. An extraordinary amount of money has been used to subsidize these activities, and an army of scholars has attempted to analyze "the politics of federal grants" (Brown 1984; Hale and Palley 1981). The political origins of grants, the different forms they assume, and the bureaucratic linkages they bring into existence are best described by Anton (1989), who views grants as the product of "vertical coalitions."

Vertical coalitions consist of widely dispersed individuals and groups who form alliances with other, similarly situated, groups across the country to gain a favorable hearing at the national level. By responding to vertical coalitions, national policy makers can seem to be addressing "societal needs and at the same time take credit for new program dollars that flow into their districts." Similarly, administrators can "appear to be responsive while simultaneously expanding budget and staff to deliver the new benefits." And lower level officials who receive the benefits "have new resources to be devoted in various ways to the problem or problems that originally motivated their search for assistance." Thus when vertical coalitions are successful, everyone seems to benefit (Anton 1989, 85).

Grant programs are well suited to the demands of vertical coalitions. Serious political differences can be sublimated under general, unobjectionable statements about policy goals, whereas important details of program design and implementation are left to the discretion of state and local policy makers. Grants are also highly resistant to attack; clients who receive services, government employees who provide them, administrators who oversee them, and politicians who claim credit for these programs regularly and effectively lobby to continue grants. Even in the face of rising deficits, created in part by the successes of many vertical coalitions, Congress and the president were reluctant to eliminate grant programs.

Aid programs typically originate as categorical project grants closely controlled by the national government. *Categorical grants* may be used only for narrow purposes approved by Congress. *Project grants* are awarded on a more or less competitive basis to governmental units that have submitted proposals for review and funding to an agency of the national government. A categorical project grant, then, allows the national government to determine which governments will receive money, and for which purposes.

Categorical grants spawn bureaucratic alliances that span levels of government. Administrative subsystems form around each grant program, as program specialists and professionals from different levels of government develop routines and forms of interaction that may be difficult to comprehend or influence, even for politicians who created the programs in the first place. This produces fragmentation of policy at the national level, because programs are both isolated and insulated from each other by the existence of distinct bureaucratic subsystems (Sundquist 1969). At state and local levels, it causes great consternation among elected officials, who discover that personnel in local agencies are strongly oriented toward patron agencies at the national level and either cannot or will not respond adequately to the preferences of subnational policy makers (Howitt 1984).

This development has been called *picket fence federalism,* because of the narrow ties that run between higher and lower levels of government (Wright 1988). State and local officials and their allies have long advocated reforms to eliminate the bureaucratic maze and reduce national control over the disposition of grant monies. These reforms have been accomplished in two ways. Categorical grants have been combined or consolidated into block grants, which permit recipients to determine, within broad limits, the uses to which aid will be put. Another way of reducing national control involves the distribution of aid according to some formula, rather than by project. Under formula grants, eligibility for assistance is automatic, so national agencies no longer determine which governments will receive aid. When block grants are awarded according to a congressionally approved formula, national influence is minimized, and state and local discretion is correspondingly enhanced.

This was the rationale behind the New Federalism of Richard Nixon's administration, which combined some categorical grants with block-formula grants (Conlan 1988). The latter were called *special revenue-sharing grants,* to distinguish them from general revenue-sharing grants, which awarded money to state and local governments on the basis of population, per capita income, levels of taxation, and several other factors. Subnational governments were virtually free to decide how funds would be used, and the amounts of money were not trivial: tens of billions of dollars were distributed between 1972 and 1986, when general revenue sharing ceased. Not coincidentally, the shift toward block-formula grants and general revenue sharing bestowed greater assistance on fast growing cities in the Sunbelt, as well as suburbs, small cities, and rural areas—all integral to the emerging Republican presidential coalition (Brown 1984).

In 1980 the same coalition elected Ronald Reagan, who sought to replace many categorical grants with a much smaller number of block grants in education, health, social services, community development, and transportation (Conlan and Walker 1983). Reagan's proposals were defeated, however (Fossett 1984). For all the

Figure 2-3   Intergovernmental Revenue Flows, 1955–1995

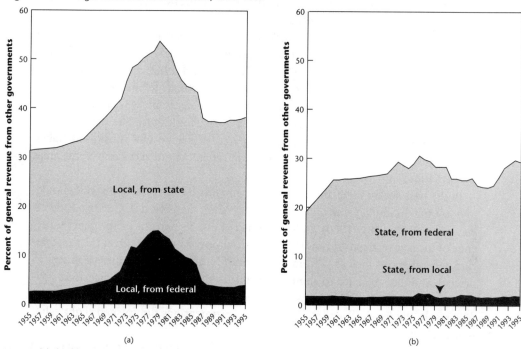

(a)   (b)

SOURCE: Calculated from U.S. Bureau of the Census, *State and Local Government Finances,* various years.

reasons identified by Anton (1989), categorical grants remained very popular with Congress. By fiscal year 1993, almost 600 grants-in-aid were in operation. The grants were worth $200 billion, but less than $20 million of that amount was provided through block grants. The rest was channeled into categorical grants, 419 of them awarded on a project basis.

When Republicans gained control of Congress in 1995, categorical grants came under renewed attack. Once again block grants were proposed to limit the involvement of the national government in state and local affairs. That way subnational policy makers could still enjoy financial support from the national government without having to meet many conditions. In some cases the block grants were formed by consolidating existing programs, but most new block grants were simply added to the long list of (mostly) categorical grants. The durability of vertical coalitions defeated Republican lawmakers' efforts to reform the system.

The existence of so many grants, and the availability of so much grant money, has made subnational governments dependent on federal aid. The extent of this fiscal dependency on higher levels of government is shown in Figure 2-3, from 1955 to 1995. The graphs in Figure 2-3 compare the size of intergovernmental subsidies with all general revenues raised by state and local governments. When intergovernmental revenues constitute a high proportion of general revenues, subnational governments are fiscally dependent—a condition of subjection into which local governments had fallen in the late 1970s.

As seen in Figure 2-3a, the dependence of local governments has abated since 1979, partly because the flow of funds from the national government has declined. The real value of grants fell in 1979, 1980, 1981, and 1982, when inflation outstripped spending increases. Nominal grant outlays actually fell in 1982, the year after states lost access to general revenue sharing, and again in 1987, when the program ended and localities lost general revenue-sharing funds. The demise of the Comprehensive Employment and Training Act, which heavily subsidized public work forces in many cities, also precipitated retrenchment of services in some areas (Fossett 1984).

In the past decade state aid to local governments has increased, but not enough to offset the declining value of federal grants. When the period of Creative Federalism began in the early 1960s, states supplied about 33 percent of the general revenue of local governments; now they provide almost 38 percent. Over the same period, federal grants increased from 3 percent of local general revenues to almost 15 percent, and then fell back to about 5 percent. To make up the difference, local governments have exploited their own revenue sources more intensively (Gold 1990). As a result, the fiscal dependency of local government has diminished slightly, but remains high.

State governments themselves are becoming more dependent on national grants, as may be seen in Figure 2-3b. Overall, a little less than 30 percent of all state revenues comes from Washington, D.C. Of course, the percentage is much higher in some states and much lower in others; the grant system is not geographically neutral, nor is it intended to be. One of its principal functions is to achieve some degree of equalization by redistributing resources to states and localities with great needs but few resources of their own. That is why a substantial portion of national grant monies goes to deprived areas, as measured by legislative formulas that incorporate various indicators of need and financial ability. To the extent that these formulas succeed in targeting aid, some states reap especially large shares of financial assistance from the national government, and other states receive smaller shares (Stein 1981).

The amount of redistribution can be approximated by estimating the amount of taxes paid by residents in each state to finance the national grant system (Tax Foundation 1998). This can be compared with the value of grants-in-aid received by governments in each state. Whenever residents of a state pay less than their governments receive in aid, they benefit from a redistributive grant system. Citizens who give more than they get are financing a disproportionate share of the system. In either case, the extent of redistribution is measured by the ratio of taxes paid for the purpose of maintaining a national grant system to grants received.

State ratios for fiscal year 1996 are depicted in Figure 2-4. A minority of states has ratios less than one, meaning those states receive more grant dollars than their citizens pay in taxes for grants. Some of these states are big winners indeed; small,

Figure 2-4 Ratio of Federal Grant Tax Burden to Grants, 1996

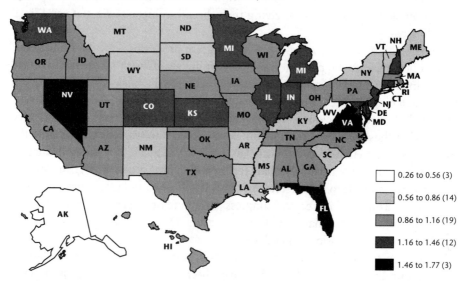

Legend:
- 0.26 to 0.56 (3)
- 0.56 to 0.86 (14)
- 0.86 to 1.16 (19)
- 1.16 to 1.46 (12)
- 1.46 to 1.77 (3)

SOURCES: Calculated from U.S. Bureau of the Census, *Federal Expenditures by State for Fiscal Year 1996*; and Tax Foundation, *Facts and Figures on Government Finances, 1997*.

rural states (for example, Louisiana, Mississippi, West Virginia, and Wyoming) pay roughly $0.50 for every $1.00 they receive in grants from the national government. In contrast, populous states (for example, Florida, Illinois, and New Jersey) pay about $1.50 for each $1.00 in grants received by state and local governments. Residents in these states are effectively subsidizing the operations of government in small, rural states (Peterson 1995).

Through grant formulas and administrative decisions about the distribution of grant funds, resources are redistributed on a rather large scale. Not surprisingly, losing states complain about this treatment; what counts as equalization for some is discrimination for others. This gives rise to pitched battles over the composition of formulas for distributing aid (Stanfield 1978). Representatives from states with divergent interests, each supplied with statistical analyses of the estimated impact of alternative formulas, must then resolve their differences (Dilger 1982). A dispute between northern and southern states delayed passage of welfare reform in 1996 until a compromise formula was discovered, one that did not disturb the existing distribution of matching funds. Similarly, the Census Bureau's methods for estimating population at the state level are a matter of contention in the legislature. Different statistical techniques yield different population estimates, and hence different grant allocations, and the members of Congress know it (DeVaul and Twomey 1989).

The budgetary impact of grants-in-aid is significant. Most grants require matching funds from states, and depending on the stringency of these requirements, states may have to commit a substantial portion of their own revenues to purposes served by the grants. States may also exceed matching fund requirements in some policy areas, if they want to enlarge on national policy objectives. As a result, grants have leverage beyond their size, giving them broad influence over state and local spending patterns.

In part, this is what Congress intends, but grant programs skew the priorities of state policy makers who concentrate on obtaining grants with low matching fund requirements. These programs give a bigger "bang for the buck" than programs in which matching fund requirements are high, or where national funds are not available at all. Budget-conscious policy makers may neglect important state and local concerns, if those concerns are not sufficiently general to warrant attention by the national government. Clever state officials, however, may discover methods that allow them to substitute national dollars for their own or those of local governments. This permits officials to divert state and local revenues to popular causes, or alternatively, to avoid tax increases. Congress has therefore begun to perfect other means of ensuring compliance with its objectives. One consequence has been the proliferation of congressional mandates.

According to the U.S. Advisory Commission on Intergovernmental Relations (1984), four different kinds of mandates have been employed by Congress (and the executive branch). A *direct order,* in the form of a law or regulation, may be issued in policy areas in which national power is well-established under the supremacy clause of the Constitution. Subnational governments must abide by the Equal Employment Opportunity Act, the Fair Labor Standards Act, and the Occupational Safety and Health Act, and they risk civil and criminal sanctions if they do not respond to orders of compliance.

Cross-cutting regulations are across-the-board requirements that affect all or most federal assistance programs. They involve provisions that prohibit the use of funds from any national source in programs that discriminate on the basis of race, ethnicity, gender, or religious practice, for example. Another familiar cross-cutting regulation requires the preparation of an environmental impact statement for any construction project involving national funds. State and local governments must provide evidence of compliance with these regulations, and they incur administrative costs for preparing the necessary scientific and technical reports.

National officials may terminate or reduce funding or aid in a specified program if state and local officials do not comply with the requirements of another grant-in-aid program. This is a *cross-over sanction.* National highway funds are often used in this way to force states to adopt policies preferred by Congress (Sevin 1989). Under a 1984 law states that refused to raise the minimum drinking age to twenty-one forfeited 5 percent of their national highway funds. The penalty increased by 10 percent for each subsequent year in which the states failed to act. All states eventually complied with this demand, although in 1988 the Wyoming legislature considered lowering the drinking age and risking the loss of funds as a show of independence but did not act on this inclination.

The fourth type of regulation is *partial preemption,* and often rests on the commerce clause of the Constitution. By engaging in this type of regulation the national government essentially sets national minimum standards by issuing appropriate regulations for, say, air or water quality, if a state refuses to do so. Should a state refuse to enforce standards issued by an agency of the national government, then the agency will assume jurisdiction for enforcement. States are entitled to adopt and implement more stringent standards, but weak or nonexistent standards are preemptively denied by Congress and its delegates (Zimmerman 1988).

Whatever the form, state (and local) government officials strongly resent mandates. In some notable cases they have gained satisfaction through the national political process, as the Court has said they must: Under pressure from the states Congress eventually agreed to rescind the fifty-five-mile-per-hour speed limit on rural interstate highways constructed with national funds, for instance. And in the spring of 1998 the Rules Committee of the House of Representatives killed a proposal to link highway funding with states' willingness to lower the blood alcohol threshold for drunk driving, although Congress maintained its insistence on a legal drinking age of twenty-one as a condition for aid.

In other cases, states and localities have not been successful lobbyists. Faced with demands to reduce the national deficit, Congress eliminated general revenue-sharing funds, first for state governments and then for local governments, too, despite sustained lobbying by officials from the affected governments. Similarly, state and local officials have not been entirely successful in persuading their representatives in Congress to compensate them for the expense of complying with national mandates. If anything, the members of Congress are inclined to shift more—not less—of the costs of compliance to lower levels of government, while retaining ultimate responsibility for establishing the goals of policy (Posner 1997).

Indeed, the political viability of Congress now rests heavily on its ability to meet the demands of interest groups by unfunded mandates (Kincaid 1994). Ironically, the expanding capacity of state governments invites Congress to conscript them for its own use. As Derthick (1986, 36) put it, Congress gives orders to states "as if they were administrative agents of the national government, while expecting state officials and electorates to bear whatever costs ensue." According to a study published in 1992, at least thirty-six significant mandates were in force as of 1980; another twenty-seven were added by 1990, and more than a dozen others were passed by the 102d Congress before it adjourned in 1992.

Few of the new mandates were accompanied by grants-in-aid, although the cumulative cost of mandates adopted between 1983 and 1990 alone was between $8.9 billion and $12.7 billion, according to one of the lower estimates of the burden on state and local governments (Conlan and Beam 1992). The projected cost of mandates at the end of the decade was much higher. That, plus the national intrusion into traditional areas of state responsibility, explains why subnational officials believed that "mandates are putting a stranglehold on state budgets" (Conlan and Beam 1992, 1). It also explains why many subnational governments observed National Unfunded Mandates Week as a way of calling attention to their plight.

The message took hold. After the Republican landslide of 1994, the 104th Congress quickly adopted the second plank of the Contract with America. With the support of many Democrats, including President Clinton, the Republicans passed legislation requiring the Congressional Budget Office to estimate the cost of all mandates proposed in Congress. Bills that impose new mandates in excess of $50 million on state and local governments must be approved by a majority of each chamber in a separate vote.

The Unfunded Mandates Reform Act of 1995 did not rescind any previous mandates, and it produced only a slight reduction in the number of mandates enacted in 1996. On the other hand, it has modified new mandates that have been adopted. They are less sweeping, less expensive, and less heavy-handed than before. Furthermore, passage of the act has probably deterred lawmakers from proposing mandates that are popular only with some interest groups and congressional constituencies (Posner 1997).

RELATIONS BETWEEN STATE AND LOCAL GOVERNMENTS

If policy-making authority is devolved to the states, local governments will become more important, too. Most states rely heavily on their local governments to maintain law and order, educate children, and care for the needy. States also work with local governments to build and maintain roads, attract businesses, and protect the environment. The extensive partnership means that any increase in state activity is bound to affect local governments in significant ways. Indeed, it already has.

For example, the 1996 welfare reforms replaced Aid to Families with Dependent Children with Temporary Assistance to Needy Families (TANF). TANF operates like a block grant: Participating states enjoy considerable leeway in designing public assistance programs for poor children and their families. States also decide how these programs will be administered and by whom. Some rely on branch offices of a state agency to implement TANF, but most assign day-to-day administrative responsibility to county or city welfare departments, which must make the reforms work. Other grant programs, whether federal or state in origin, operate in a similar fashion, with local governments carrying out the wishes of their senior partners. Public goods and services are typically delivered by an agency of local government.

In most cases, local governments cannot opt out of programs enacted by their state. This is a key difference between national–state relations, on the one hand, and state–local relations, on the other. Because they are sovereign, state governments have the capacity to resist national policy makers, who depend on substantial cooperation from state officials when implementing policy (Derthick 1986). But local governments are administrative conveniences of the state, and they find it harder to resist state officials determined to have their way. As a result, local governments labor under hundreds or even thousands of mandates from state governments (Zimmerman and Clark 1994).

Local opposition to state mandating has spread, and some states restrict the practice (perhaps because their own experience with congressional mandating has made state officials more sympathetic to local complaints). More than half the states now have constitutional limits or statutory restrictions on mandating; the latter have become especially popular in the past ten years. A few of these measures require approval of mandates by local governments, but most prohibit mandating unless the state legislature provides funding for the activity in question, reimburses local governments for the cost of mandates, or provides them with a new source of funding to cover those costs (Zimmerman 1994). There are ways around these restrictions, however, and many state legislators would rather mandate than raise taxes and face the wrath of voters.

The authority of states to issue mandates is challenged by supporters of the so-called county movement. Adherents of the movement want local sovereignty or self-determination, which they believe is the culmination of any devolution revolution worthy of the name. The movement enjoys a smattering of support in the East, Midwest, and South, but it is stronger in the West, where counties must contend with numerous state and federal mandates. The majority of those advocating local sovereignty pursue their goal through the political process, but the movement has extreme elements. The preamble to the Catron County, New Mexico, Comprehensive Land Use and Policy Plan insists that "federal and state agents threaten the life, liberty, and happiness" of county residents. Before their incarceration the Freemen in Montana issued "warrants" for the arrest of elected state officials, who were charged with "capital crimes" in "freemen's common-law courts." And in Texas, Richard McLaren and his fellow "officials" from the "Republic of Texas" resorted to kidnapping in their battle with state authorities, which resulted in an armed confrontation with 300 Texas Department of Public Safety Officers and the Texas Rangers.

These are unusual cases, but many law-abiding citizens are attracted to the idea of self-determination at the local level. Indeed, the popularity of local control offsets the constitutional supremacy of state government in most areas of the country, for reasons that deserve further scrutiny.

POLITICAL CONSIDERATIONS

Local governments' terms of existence are spelled out in charters of incorporation or special acts of the state legislature, which establish units of local government. According to Dillon's Rule (City of Clinton v. Cedar Rapids and Missouri River R. R. co., 24 Iowa 455, 1868) a doctrine adopted by federal and state courts alike, local governments may exercise only those powers expressly granted in the charter or act of incorporation, powers necessarily implied therein, or powers that are indispensable (not merely convenient) for carrying out the assigned responsibilities of local government. In contrast, state governments may, at their discretion, alter the functions, powers, and structures of local government as they see fit.

States may create special-purpose districts, stripping existing governments of previously held authority to make policy in certain policy areas—for example, mass transit, fire protection, water and sewer services—and providing for libraries, hospitals, and parks. This has been a common practice in the states: According to the Bureau of the Census, 33,555 special districts existed in 1992, about two and a half times as many as were in existence forty years earlier (Bureau of the Census 1994). Most of these districts perform a single function; as a consequence, the proliferation of districts has fragmented local policy making along narrow functional lines. The average citizen is now subject simultaneously to a half-dozen or more units of local government with taxing or regulatory authority—county government, city government, school district, transit authority, parks board, waste district, and so on.

When special districts improve services and reduce costs, citizens and local officials welcome their establishment, even if it reduces their control. Other reductions in local control are conceded only grudgingly. This is particularly true in the case of independent school districts. Immediately after World War II, many state governments consolidated local school districts by abolishing small rural districts and transferring their students to urban districts so that education could be provided more efficiently and inexpensively. State policy makers, who controlled state aid for transportation and schooling, overrode local objections. The power to create—and destroy—local governments was effectively used to bring about consolidation, and the number of school districts nationwide fell from 67,355 in 1952 to 14,422 in 1992, even though two new states were added to the Union and the number of children enrolled in public elementary and secondary schools climbed 40 percent during this same period.

The constitutional vulnerability of local governments is mitigated by political considerations. A commitment to local determination is central to Americans' political heritage. In the Northeast, state constitutions were adopted after the Declaration of Independence, when local governments formed under the authority of the Crown or other proprietors were already a hundred years old. Other areas of the country, too, were settled, and towns established, long before territories became states. As a result, strong traditions of localism exist, particularly in northern states (Elazar 1998). In these states, communities may be legally powerless to prevent states from limiting their autonomy, but in practice they enjoy substantial independence because tradition favors delegation of authority to the local level. Once delegated, this authority may be difficult to recover; and, indeed, some state courts have begun to protect local prerogatives in such areas as land use (Briffault 1987).

Furthermore, the same forces that make Congress responsive to states also make states responsive to local government. Representation in the legislature is by locale, and elected representatives often have prior experience in local affairs. They are sensitive to the desire of local policy makers for autonomy, and quickly learn of resentment over state mandating and other practices that infringe on local self-determination. Representatives are forewarned of opposition to pending legislation by lobbying associations of local governments and mayors, law enforcement officers, school superintendents, and the like. These associations are among the most powerful lobbies in the state capital and members of the state legislature are not inclined to enact measures that localities find too objectionable.

The major political consideration, therefore, is not whether states will be responsive to local governments but rather to which set of local governments they will be most responsive. Historically, the malapportionment of state legislatures gave rural counties a disproportionate voice in state policy making. Reapportionment strengthened the representation of urban and suburban areas in state legislatures, but in many states rural areas still elect a substantial number of members, some of whom occupy positions of leadership by virtue of their seniority. Consequently, the interests of urban areas are not always well-served, or at least not as well-served as their local governments might like.

It was precisely this situation that led Mike Royko, the late Chicago columnist, to suggest facetiously that Chicago secede from the state of Illinois because the city was not faring well at the hands of downstate Republican legislators in the General Assembly. A more serious case of secessionist sentiment is found in northern California, a major source of water for much of the southern part of the state. Tired of seeing water diverted by state government canals, and wary of uncontrolled development, some northern residents want to break away and become the nation's fifty-first state. In June 1993 an advisory referendum on secession was held in thirty-one of California's fifty-eight counties; secession was the preference in twenty-seven counties. The result vividly illustrates the tension between state governments and powerful local constituencies (north and south, in this case).

The political influence of certain locales may be enough to win favored treatment from state government. For example, big central cities, particularly those in otherwise rural states, commonly enjoy home-rule charters, designed to promote local autonomy. The amount of autonomy under home rule varies from state to state and even across cities within the same state, and home-rule charters may be withdrawn or set aside when state interests are deemed paramount. Nevertheless, home-rule charters give discretion to localities. So would state laws permitting sections of counties to break away and form new counties, which is why a group of people in Washington tried to enlist the aid of the United Nations in its battle to "secede" from Snohomish County (*Seattle Times* 1997).

A systematic examination of local autonomy in the American states shows that local governments enjoy different kinds of discretion (U.S. Advisory Commission 1981, 1993b). When the residents of a locale petition to establish a local government, they may in some states be able to draft their own charter of incorporation. In other states, they may be able to choose from a variety of alternative forms of government, depending on the size of the local population and type of government desired. Local powers to amend charters may also be broad, and local units may be given limited or broad powers of annexation, further affecting control over the structure of local government.

A second area of discretion involves the range of functions local units may undertake. The greatest discretion exists in states that devolve authority to local governments, which enjoy powers that are not specifically denied to them by the legislature or the constitution. At the other extreme are Dillon's Rule states, which insist on enumerating the powers and functions of local governments; powers not explicitly given are denied, although the legal understanding of granted powers may be fairly liberal. More subtle ways of affecting the level and kind of services provided by local governments include restricting revenues, or earmarking, to certain uses, and establishing performance standards.

Although garbage collection, fire protection, and even elementary education can be provided through contractual arrangements with private concerns, they are most often supplied by public employees, and the conditions of employment by local government are stipulated in detail by state governments. The most important requirements concern the extent to which merit informs hiring, promoting, and firing decisions. But states may also establish training, licensing, and certification standards for employees; define procedures for determining wage and salary levels (for example, collective bargaining and compulsory arbitration rules); set actual salary and wage levels for certain categories of employees; control hours of employment and working conditions; regulate disability benefits; and mandate retirement programs (MacManus 1983).

The exercise of local discretion in all three areas (structure, function, and personnel matters) is often limited by fiscal regulations. Although cities in Arizona, Illinois, Maine, and Texas have substantial latitude in fiscal matters, local units in other states do not. In most states the constitution or legislature determines which taxes may be levied by local units and what sort of exemptions must be granted. In addition, the magnitude of tax increases is often restricted by constitutional amendments enacted during the tax revolts of the late 1970s and early 1980s. Local borrowing is also tightly regulated in most states; overall debt loads are limited, and the type of debts that may be incurred, as well as the interest rates that may be paid on bonds, are typically controlled by the legislature. Similar restrictions affect spending practices, and in New Mexico, cities and counties must submit their entire budgets to an agency of the state government for approval.

Variations in the autonomy of local governments are the result of many factors. The political culture of a state shapes beliefs about the most appropriate relation between state and local government. The length of legislative sessions and the number of local governments in a state have an effect, too. Legislatures cannot closely supervise a large number of local units, especially if they meet infrequently and for short periods of time. Under these circumstances legislatures are more inclined to grant higher degrees of local autonomy, especially because the existence of a large number of governments is associated with strong associations of local officials capable of influencing legislators. (It is also associated with large public employee unions, which may persuade legislatures to mandate actions on their behalf, over the objections of local policy makers.)

Finally, the complexity of a state's constitution and the ease of amending it can influence the amount of discretion permitted local governments. The constitution of a state may make it extremely difficult for legislatures to exercise authority over local governments in a timely fashion, particularly if incorporation of the governments is by constitutional amendment; in that case, further amendments must be adopted for the legislature to have its way. The Alabama constitution is three times longer than any other state constitution, primarily because it spells out the status of specific county governments in detail. Constitutions in other southern states do the same, owing to the strength of political traditions that favor localism over centralism.

Even in states in which constitutions are not an impediment to legislative control, trends since the mid-1970s favor the expansion of local discretion and home rule (Zimmerman 1981; Zimmerman and Clark 1994). State legislatures have granted more statutory authority to local governments, and voters in many states have approved constitutional amendments that expand local autonomy. The pace of change is particularly quick in states that allow ballot initiatives, but amendments are frequent in other states, too. It is much easier to change state constitutions than it is to amend the U.S. Constitution; amendments and even constitutional conventions occur periodically in most states.

FISCAL RELATIONS BETWEEN STATE AND LOCAL GOVERNMENTS

Although the discretionary powers of local governments have increased in many states, the capacity to exercise discretion has not grown. As they are now constituted local governments often lack the resources needed to address problems on their own. Economic instability, weak infrastructure, environmental degradation, and inadequate school systems pose great challenges to local policy makers, not just in older, central cities, but in many boom towns, suburbs, and rural areas as well. Local governments cannot cope with these problems; their tax bases have stagnated, voters have imposed restrictions on taxing and spending powers, and the national government has decreased its support for grant programs aimed at local governments. Unable to discharge all of the responsibilities assigned them by state government or demanded by constituents, local policy makers have turned to state leaders for help.

A new breed of governors seems willing to provide leadership, and as a result policy making is becoming more centralized at the state level. Of course, centralization has not increased by the same amount in all states, nor is it the same across different policy areas within the same state. States generally take the lead in constructing highways, providing welfare, maintaining correctional institutions and mental health hospitals, and regulating natural resources. Municipal governments typically provide public safety, sanitation, and sewage disposal, and school districts manage educational services. Yet even these locally provided services are heavily influenced by state actions, insofar as many state governments provide huge sums of money to the responsible local units.

In fact, financial dominance can be an indicator of policy centralization because states use aid to influence local decisions. State aid to localities has grown rapidly since the early 1980s. From 1980 to 1995, total state spending for local governments increased from $82.8 billion to $232.8 billion—an increase of more than 180 percent. (Inflation increased by 85 percent during the same period.) This produced a higher degree of fiscal centralization, meaning that states became the principal financiers of many public services, even those provided by local governments. New legal requirements and general policy guidelines were imposed as state officials began to demand greater accountability from local governments seeking assistance. State governments now control or influence areas of policy making long dominated by local governments.

Increased state aid is only one path to fiscal centralization, however. As Stonecash (1985) has argued, states can achieve the same result by providing goods and services directly, without involving local governments. This requires substantial outlays by state governments, because local governments contribute nothing under this arrangement, but it does permit greater control over the formulation and implementation of public policy. Under this method, no intermediaries are needed— or rather, the intermediaries are agencies and employees of state government, whose actions are easier to regulate than those of local government officials. Social services sometimes fall under this heading; higher education typically does.

States differ in the extent to which they rely on direct or indirect methods of centralizing control over the provision of public goods and services. These differences are apparent in Figure 2-5, in which states are listed by region according to their overall or combined level of fiscal centralization. The most centralized states are at the top of each region's listing, and the least centralized states are toward the bottom. Small, rural states tend to be most centralized: State governments in North Dakota and New Mexico, for instance, directly and indirectly account for three quarters of all state and local spending there. Near the other extreme are several large, diverse states—for example, Florida and Texas— where direct and indirect state expenditure amounts to half of all state and local outlays.

Among the more highly centralized states there are clear differences on the two dimensions of centralization. Hawaii and New Mexico are almost equally centralized, but they arrive at this end by different routes. Hawaii provides almost no state aid at all; it funds services directly from the state treasury. In fact Hawaii is the only state in the Union that fully funds public education, and because education is the most expensive service provided by state and local governments, the state ranks high on the index of fiscal centralization.

New Mexico, by contrast, augments direct spending with a significant amount of state aid, mostly for local school systems. The use to which the money is put may be the same as in Hawaii, but the method of financing is indirect. In New Mexico, the importance of state aid in funding education allows the state government substantial control over this vital service.

Both state aid and direct spending by states have become more centralized over time (Stonecash 1985, 1995). States that were initially centralized on both dimensions have remained so, whereas those that emphasized state aid have begun to stress direct spending more. States with traditions of heavy direct spending have maintained them, but they have also shown more interest in indirect financing of

Figure 2-5 Centralization of State and Local Finances, 1995

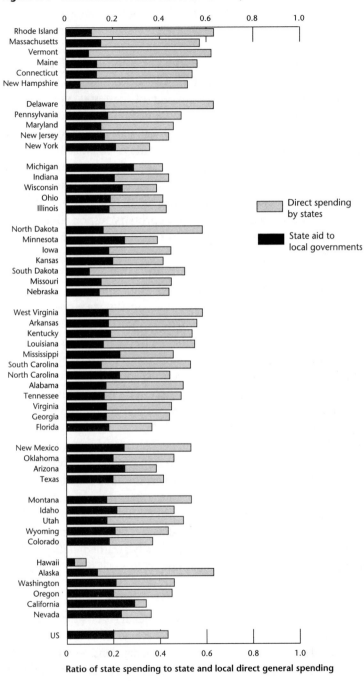

SOURCE: Calculated from U.S. Bureau of the Census, *State and Local Government Finances, FY1995.*

services. Finally, states not originally centralized on either dimension have become more centralized on both—even in Nebraska, state spending now accounts for more than 40 percent of all state and local outlays, when state aid and direct spending are combined.

The continuing importance of state aid in this process of fiscal centralization, especially in California, New York, Florida, and the Great Lakes states, is significant. In simple terms, it represents a political determination of these state governments to work with, rather than without, local governments in fulfilling basic functions. In part this reflects political realities: In these and similar states, local governments are powerful enough to persuade legislatures to assist them financially. Many of them are also capable policy makers, with long histories of service provision and relatively high levels of citizen satisfaction with local government. The idea of a partnership between state and local government is particularly strong in such states. Even though state governments have assumed primary responsibility for financing the activities of government, local governments still occupy an important position in this division of labor.

One reflection of the prominence of local governments under this form of fiscal centralization is the form in which state aid is given. The lion's share of state aid goes to categorical grants for education and public welfare. But state revenue sharing is next in importance; some states return a portion of sales and income taxes to the jurisdiction in which they were collected. Others reimburse local governments for property tax exemptions mandated by the state, or replace tax revenues lost because of general limitations on increases in property tax rates. State revenue-sharing funds are also distributed in some states on a per capita basis, although states are turning toward more complex formulas based on differences in need and ability to raise revenue (Peliserro 1985; Stein 1988).

State revenue-sharing funds are relatively unrestricted; local governments are free to decide how these funds will be used. The monies therefore preserve local discretion and serve local priorities. State policy makers do not control or strongly influence the use of revenue-sharing funds, as they often do where categorical grants are involved, and as they most certainly do when funds are spent directly by agencies of the state. To the extent that fiscal centralization occurs when state aid is increased, and to the extent that the aid is unconditionally awarded, policy making may remain decentralized, even if financing does not.

INTERGOVERNMENTAL RELATIONS IN THE 1990S

Fundamental changes in American intergovernmental relations have occurred in the past two decades. Congress is reluctant to undertake new domestic policy initiatives, especially expensive ones. This reflects budgetary considerations, and it also reflects deep divisions among the members of Congress, or between Congress and the executive branch. The resulting paralysis of national policy making leaves important needs unmet. By default, state governments have become policy leaders in many key areas, including industrial policy, child care, educational reform, hazardous waste disposal, and health insurance for those with low incomes, to name but a few. In the process, state governments have resumed their role as innovators in the federal system, displaying an improved capacity for action and changing public expectations about the function of state governments.

Republicans and New Democrats (in other words, moderate Democrats) alike support these changes. In fact, the National Performance Review, which was issued by Vice President Albert Gore in the fall of 1993, made several recommendations for "reinventing federalism." Shortly thereafter President Clinton authorized the establishment of community boards for coordinating national, state, and local efforts to promote economic development in specially designated enterprise zones. Clinton also insisted that the Office of Management and Budget begin regular consultations with state, local, and tribal officials for the purpose of eliminating unnecessary regulations. Perhaps most important, the president ordered executive agencies to reduce the number of unfunded mandates arising from administrative action and to provide subnational governments an opportunity to influence rules for implementing new mandates and regulations authorized by Congress. The Republican Congress went even further with its Contract with America. As a result, states now enjoy more flexibility in administering costly grant-in-aid programs—for example, Medicaid—and more freedom to experiment with reform measures. This devolution of power raises important questions about equity. Will state governments be as willing as the national government to protect the rights and interests of racial, ethnic, and religious minorities, or those of women and the poor? Even if they are willing (and many have not been in the past), will state governments have the resources to ensure equitable treatment, particularly if their economies falter? And how should the members of a democratic society view the inevitable differences in treatment that will arise, as some states act vigorously and others do not?

These questions will be answered in the next decade. As the national government shrinks (or at least stops growing), state governments will become the focal point of citizens' demands for public goods and services. Because most state governments work through local governments, any increase in the power of states necessarily means a larger role for local governments. The partnership will develop on both sides, and relations between the partners will become more complex and differentiated over time. In that sense, the distinction between state and local government is likely to blur as the system of governance evolves. The line between public and private sectors will become less distinct as the delivery of goods and services becomes selectively privatized (Cigler 1998).

Interactions between state and local governments will change, too. In most policy areas the trend is toward greater assistance for local governments. States are not taking over the functions of local government; they are trying to increase local governments' capacity for supplying public goods and services. Financial assistance is crucial, but so is technical advice on difficult policy issues. Restrictions on local governments are being lifted, and their powers are being increased. All of this underscores the enabling role of states, and the political preference for localized problem solving in American politics.

Indeed, relations between state and local governments are themselves becoming a policy issue. These relations developed incrementally in the past, and without much discussion between state and local authorities. Now intergovernmental relations are planned; they are the product of considerable discussion concerning the advantages and disadvantages of alternative forms of partnership. The reinvention of government has become a conscious, even self-conscious, exercise as we enter the twenty-first century. It is also a highly experimental process, and the result is likely to be great variation in the form of state–local relations in the United States. That has always been true, of course, but the extent of variation may increase and its significance will become more pronounced as the devolution revolution unfolds.

The adaptability of American federalism is impressive. In other contexts, the devolution of authority is associated with political disintegration. That is the situation in Canada, where the independence movement in Quebec may dismember the nation. But in the United States the devolution revolution may actually be a stabilizing development. It is a way of restoring balance to a system of governance that conservative voters found overly centralized. Liberals do not agree and they are fighting against devolution, but the fight is likely to remain within a familiar federal framework.

REFERENCES

Anton, Thomas J. 1989. *American Federalism and Public Policy: How the System Works.* New York: Random House.

Bahl, Roy. 1990. "Changing Federalism: Trends and Interstate Variations." In *The Changing Face of Fiscal Federalism,* edited by Thomas R. Swartz and John E. Peck. Armonk, N.Y.: M. E. Sharpe.

Beer, Samuel H. 1978. "Federalism, Nationalism, and Democracy in America." *American Political Science Review* 72:9–21

Break, George F. 1980. *Financing Government in a Federal System.* Washington, D.C.: Brookings Institution.

Briffault, Richard. 1987. "State-Local Relations and Constitutional Law." *Intergovernmental Perspective* 13(3/4):10–14.

Brown, Lawrence D. 1984. "The Politics of Devolution in Nixon's New Federalism." In *The Changing Politics of Federal Grants,* edited by Lawrence D. Brown, James W. Fossett, and Kenneth T. Palmer. Washington, D.C.: Brookings Institution.

Chubb, John E. 1985. "Federalism and the Bias for Centralization." In *The New Direction in American Politics,* edited by John E. Chubb and Paul E. Peterson. Washington, D.C.: Brookings Institution.

Cigler, Beverly. 1995. "Not Just Another Special Interest: Intergovernmental Representation." In *Interest Group Politics,* 4th ed., edited by Allen J. Cigler and Burdett A. Loomis. Washington, D.C.: CQ Press.

———.1998. "Emerging Trends in State-Local Relations." In *Governing Partners: State-Local Relations in the United States,* edited by Russell L. Hanson. Boulder, Colo.: Westview Press.

Clarke, Marianne K. 1986. *Revitalizing State Economies: A Review of State Economic Development Policies and Programs.* Washington D.C.: Center for Policy Research and Analysis, National Governors' Association.

Conlan, Timothy J. 1988. *New Federalism: Intergovernmental Reform from Nixon to Reagan.* Washington, D.C.: Brookings Institution.

Conlan, Timothy J., and David R. Beam. 1992. "Federal Mandates: The Record of Reform and Future Prospects." *Intergovernmental Perspective* 18(4):7–11.

Conlan, Timothy J., and David B. Walker. 1983. "Reagan's New Federalism: Design, Debate, and Discord." *Intergovernmental Perspective* 8(4):6–22.

Corwin, Edwin S. 1934. *The Twilight of the Supreme Court*. New Haven, Conn.: Yale University Press.

Council of State Governments. 1977. *Interstate Compacts: 1783–1977*. Rev. ed. Lexington, Ky.: Council of State Governments.

———.1997. "State Leaders Unveil Federalism Plan." Press release, available at http://www.csg. org/whatsnew/pr-07nov97pressrel.htm. November 7, 1997.

Derthick, Martha. 1986. "Preserving Federalism: Congress, the States, and the Supreme Court." *Brookings Review* 4(2):32–37.

DeVaul, Diane, and Heather Twomey. 1989. *Federal Funding Formulas and State Allocations*. Washington, D.C.: Center for Regional Policy, Northeast Midwest Institute.

Dilger, Robert Jay. 1982. *The Sunbelt/Snowbelt Controversy: The War over Federal Funds*. New York: New York University Press.

Elazar, Daniel J. 1984. *American Federalism: A View from the States*. 3d ed. New York: Harper and Row.

———.1998. "State-Local Relations: Union and Home Rule." In *Governing Partners: State-Local Relations in the United States*, edited by Russell L. Hanson. Boulder, Colo.: Westview Press.

Feigenbaum, Edward D. 1988. "Interstate Compacts and Agreements." In *The Book of the States, 1988–1989*. Lexington, Ky.: Council of State Governments.

Fossett, James W. 1984. "The Politics of Dependence: Federal Aid to Big Cities." In *The Changing Politics of Federal Grants*, edited by Lawrence D. Brown, James W. Fossett, and Kenneth T. Palmer. Washington, D.C.: Brookings Institution.

Freeman, Patricia K. 1985. "Interstate Communication among State Legislators Regarding Energy Policy Innovations." *Publius* 15(4):99–111.

Gold, Steven D. 1990. "State Finances in the New Era of Federalism." In *The Changing Face of Fiscal Federalism*, edited by Thomas R. Swartz and John E. Peck. Armonk, N.Y.: M. E. Sharpe.

Grodzins, Morton. 1966. *The American Political System*. Chicago: Rand-McNally.

Haider, Donald. 1974. *When Governments Come to Washington*. New York: Free Press.

Hale, George E., and Marian Lief Palley. 1981. *The Politics of Federal Grants*. Washington D.C.: Congressional Quarterly.

Hedge, David M. 1998. *Governance and the Changing American States*. Boulder, Colo.: Westview Press.

Howitt, Arnold M. 1984. *Managing Federalism: Studies in Intergovernmental Relations*. Washington, D.C.: CQ Press.

Kincaid, John. 1994. "Developments in Federal–State Relations, 1992–1993." In *The Book of the States, 1994–1995*. Lexington, Ky.: Council of State Governments.

Levine, Jerry. 1994. "American State Offices in Europe: Activities and Connections." *Intergovernmental Perspective* 20(1):44–46.

Lord, William B., and Douglas S. Kenney. 1993. "Resolving Interstate Water Conflicts: The Compact Approach." *Intergovernmental Perspective* 19(1):19–23.

MacManus, Susan A. 1983. "State Government: The Overseer of Municipal Finance." In *The Municipal Money Chase: The Politics of Local Government Finance*, edited by Alberta M. Sbragia. Boulder, Colo.: Westview Press.

Nathan, Richard P., Fred Doolittle, and Associates. 1987. *Reagan and the States*. Princeton, N.J.: Princeton University Press.

"New County Rebels Say They'll Ask U.N. to Help." 1997. *Seattle Times*. April 8, A1.

Peliserro, John P. 1985. "State Revenue Sharing with Large Cities: A Policy Analysis over Time." *Policy Studies Journal* 13:643–652.

Peterson, Paul E. 1995. *The Price of Federalism*. Washington, D.C.: Brookings Institution.

Posner, Paul L. 1997. "Unfunded Mandates Reform Act: 1996 and Beyond." *Publius* 27(2):53–71.

Ryen, Dag. 1996. "State Action in a Global Framework." *The Book of the States 1996–1997*. Lexington, Ky.: Council of State Governments.

Schram, Sanford F., and Carol S. Weissert. 1997. "The State of American Federalism, 1996–1997." *Publius* 27(2):1–31.

Sevin, Ali F. 1989. "Highway Sanctions: Circumventing the Constitution." *State Legislatures* 15(2):25–29.

Snelling, Richard A. 1980. "American Federalism in the Eighties." *State Government* 53:168–170.

Stanfield, Rochelle L. 1978. "Playing Computer Politics with Local Aid Formulas." *National Journal,* December 9, 1977:1981.

Stein, Robert M. 1981. "The Allocation of Federal Aid Monies: The Synthesis of Demand-Side and Supply-Side Explanations." *American Political Science Review* 75:334–343.

———.1988. "Explaining the Incidence of State Aid Transfers." A paper presented at the annual meeting of the American Political Science Association, Washington, D.C., September 1–4.

Stonecash, Jeffrey M. 1985. "Paths of Fiscal Centralization in the American States." *Policy Studies Journal* 13:653–661.

———.1995. *American State and Local Politics.* Ft. Worth, Texas: Harcourt Brace.

Sundquist, James L. 1969. *Making Federalism Work.* Washington, D.C.: Brookings Institution.

Tax Foundation. 1998. *Facts and Figures on Government Finance.* Washington, D.C.: Tax Foundation.

U.S. Advisory Commission on Intergovernmental Relations. 1981. *Measuring Local Discretionary Authority.* Washington, D.C.: U.S. Government Printing Office.

———.1984. *Regulatory Federalism: Policy, Process, Impact, and Reform.* Washington, D.C.: U.S. Government Printing Office.

———.1993a. *Significant Features of Fiscal Federalism, 1993.* Washington, D.C.: U.S. Government Printing Office.

———.1993b. *State Laws Governing Local Government Structure and Administration.* Publication No. ACIR M-186. Washington, D.C.: U.S. Government Printing Office.

U.S. Bureau of the Census. 1994. *1992 Census of Governments: Government Organizations.* Washington, D.C.: U.S. Government Printing Office.

———.1997. *Federal Expenditures by State for Fiscal Year 1996.* Washington, D.C.: U.S. Government Printing Office.

———.Various years. *Government Finances.* Washington, D.C.: U.S. Government Printing Office.

U.S. Office of Management and Budget. Various years. *Historical Tables.* Washington, D.C.: U.S. Government Printing Office.

Wald, Matthew L. 1988. "3 States Ask Waste Cleanup as Price of Atomic Operation." *New York Times,* December 17, I, 1:1.

Weiler, Conrad. 1993–1994. "GATT, NAFTA, and State and Local Powers." *Intergovernmental Perspective* 20(1):38–41.

Wright, Deil S. 1988. *Understanding Intergovernmental Relations.* 3d ed. Pacific Grove, Calif.: Brooks/Cole.

Zimmerman, Joseph F. 1981. "The Discretionary Authority of Local Governments." *Urban Data Service Reports* 13(11).

———.1988. "The Silent Revolution: Federal Preemption." A paper presented at the annual meeting of the American Political Science Association, Washington, D.C., September 1–4.

———.1994. "State Mandate Relief: A Quick Look." *Intergovernmental Perspective* 20(2):28–30.

Zimmerman, Joseph F., and Julie M. Clark. 1994. "The Political Dynamics of State-Local Relations, 1991–1993." In *The Book of the States, 1994–1995.* Lexington, Ky.: Council of State Governments.

SUGGESTED READINGS

The Book of the States. An annual publication of the Council of State Governments, the "bible" of research on state politics contains a wealth of comparative data and information, along with reviews of trends in all aspects of state politics and policy.

Publius: The Journal of Federalism. A scholarly journal devoted primarily to research on American federalism, although comparative studies are occasionally included. It is published quarterly, and one issue each year centers on the state of American federalism in that year.

Significant Features of Fiscal Federalism. The Rockefeller Institute at SUNY-Albany replaces the U.S. Advisory Commission on Intergovernmental Relations as publisher of an indispensable reference for taxing and spending by all levels of government. This is an annual publication and contains numerous measures of fiscal capacity and dependency, financial breakdowns by functional category, changes in national and state tax laws, and so forth.

Wright, Deil S. *Understanding Intergovernmental Relations.* 3d ed. Pacific Grove, Calif.: Brooks/Cole, 1988. This provides the definitive review of intergovernmental relations in the United States. David C. Nice and Patricia Fredericksen provide a more recent treatment in *The Politics of Intergovernmental Relations,* 2d ed. Chicago: Nelson-Hall, 1995.

CHAPTER 3

Parties and Elections

JOHN F. BIBBY AND
THOMAS M. HOLBROOK

The development of political parties in Western democracies has been closely linked to the extension of suffrage and the spread of the belief that governments derive their authority from the consent of the governed. Political scientists have for decades exhibited a strong commitment to political parties as the principal intermediaries between the people and their governments because of the parties' role in aggregating and mobilizing the interests of vast numbers of citizens, enhancing voters' capacity to hold public officials accountable for their performance in office, nominating candidates, contesting elections, acting as agents of political socialization, and organizing the decision-making institutions of government.

Although political scientists' commitment to parties has remained relatively constant (Epstein 1986, 9–39), the public's support for parties has withered as they have been buffeted in this century by a succession of threatening challenges: the loss of patronage traditionally used to sustain their organizations; a surrender of control over nominations as states adopted the direct primary and presidential primary; a loss of public support; and competition from political action committees (PACs), candidates' personal organizations, and campaign consultants. These party-weakening challenges have caused American politics to become less party-centered and increasingly candidate-centered. Yet despite the challenges, parties at the national, state, and local levels have demonstrated amazing adaptability and durability. Unlike traditional party organizations early in this century that controlled nominations and ran their candidates' campaigns, parties have found their niche in the current candidate-centered era as institutions in service to their candidates (Aldrich 1995, 269–274).

Political parties permeate every aspect of state government. It is, after all, Republicans and Democrats who "make the major decisions regarding who pays and who receives in the states" (Morehouse 1981, 29). Since 1950 only five persons have been elected to a governorship as independents or minor party candidates; and after the 1998 elections only twenty state legislators (.003 percent) out of a total of 7,375 were not Republicans or Democrats (excluding the nonpartisan legislature of Nebraska). Clearly, partisans are the movers and shakers of statehouse decision making, and understanding state politics requires attention to the role and status of parties as well as the nature of the electoral process.

Because the role and strength of state parties are directly affected by governmental policies toward parties, we begin by considering state public policy toward parties and the parties' changing legal status. We then focus on the changing nature of state party organizations, the role of parties in campaigns and elections including the integration of state parties into national party campaign strategies, nominating practices and their impact on state parties, the extent of interparty competition within the states, participation in state elections, and the pattern of election outcomes within the states. Of special concern throughout the chapter are the patterns of change occurring in state electoral politics and within American parties as they seek to adapt to changing conditions.

STATE PUBLIC POLICY TOWARD PARTIES

In most western democracies, political parties are considered to be private associations not unlike the United Way or Urban League. They are, therefore, permitted to transact business in private, largely unregulated by government. American political parties, however, are heavily regulated by state laws. They function in a manner similar to public utilities in that they provide essential public services (for example, nominating candidates, contesting elections, organizing the government) that have sufficient impact on the public to justify governmental regulation (Epstein 1986, 157).

State regulation of parties was encouraged by the introduction in the 1890s of the Australian ballot: secret general election ballots provided by the government with candidates designated by party labels. By granting official recognition to political parties on government-provided ballots, the states acquired a legal justification for engaging in the regulation of parties (Epstein 1986, 152–167). By far the most significant state regulatory requirement has been one requiring parties to nominate their candidates via the direct primary (discussed later in this chapter). State regulation of parties, however, extends well beyond nominating procedures.

Ballot Access and Form

State laws define what constitutes an officially recognized political party eligible for a line on the general election ballot. The requirements for parties gaining ballot access normally involve winning a specified percentage of the vote for governor in the last election (the percentage ranges from 20 percent in Georgia to a low of

1 percent in Wisconsin). New parties or independent candidates seeking ballot access must secure signatures from a designated percentage of the voters. Whatever the specific form statutes governing ballot access may take, their general effect is to protect the dominant status of the two major parties and serve as barriers to independent candidacies and the emergence of third-party movements. Thus Pennsylvania legislators in 1997, in an effort to erect a barrier for new parties to gain a line on the ballot, mandated that the party would be required to secure the signatures of 15 percent of the registered voters within a period of only fourteen weeks (the previous time limit was six months). Had this law been in effect in 1996, a new party would have had the daunting task of gathering 99,000 signatures—10,000 more than is required in California, the second most restrictive state, but a state with two and a half times the population of Pennsylvania (Seelye 1997, A8).

Through their regulation of the form of the ballot, states may either encourage straight-ticket party voting through use of the party column ballot or encourage voters to engage in split-ticket voting by using the office bloc ballot. The trend since the 1960s has been for states to switch from the party column ballot to the office bloc form of ballot so that in 1997 only a bare majority of states still used the party column ballot. Further encouraging a candidate-centered style of politics has been a companion trend of states to eliminate the ability of citizens to vote for all of a party's candidates with a single action in the polling booth. In 1997 only twenty states retained a ballot form containing a provision for expedited straight-ticket voting (Bass 1998).

Party Membership

In all but a handful of states, statutes provide a description of the requirements for party membership—that is, who is eligible to vote in partisan primary elections. Normally requirements include minimum age, state or local residence, citizenship, and depending on the type of primary election system employed in the state, party affiliation. By limiting participation in primaries to registered Democrats or Republicans, as is done in closed primary states, the law is in effect defining party membership. Party bylaws sometimes define membership in the party organization by making more substantial demands on voters and party activists. For example, the Democratic party of West Virginia requires people to register as Democrats in order to participate in party organizational activities. On the other hand, there are also numerous state parties that automatically issue legally meaningless "sustaining membership" cards to small contributors as a fund-raising incentive.

Organizational Structure

State regulations frequently extend to matters of internal party organization such as procedures for selecting officers, composition of party committees, dates and locations of meetings, and powers of party units. In each of the states, the two major parties have state central committees headed by a state chair. The state committees are normally composed of members elected by county committees, state and congressional district conventions, or party primaries. State committees range in size from about twenty in Iowa to more than 1,000 in California. The state committee's duties vary from state to state, but normally include calling the state convention, adoption of party policies, fund-raising, assisting with campaigns, aiding local party units, and serving as a party public relations agency. Most state parties have vested an executive committee with the same powers as the parent state central committee and authorized it to act for the party between the infrequent meetings of the central body.

More than three quarters (77 percent) of state party chairs are elected for two-year terms, and 23 percent have four-year terms. Turnover, however, is high, and tenure averages fewer than three years for chairs in both parties. State chairs or the party executive directors act as the operational heads of state party organizations responsible for fund-raising, candidate recruitment, campaign activities, party publicity, and liaison with local and national party organizations and elected officials. Both Republican and Democratic state chairs serve on their parties' national committees. State chairs are frequently handpicked by their party's governor and, therefore, are expected to advance and protect gubernatorial interests within the party. For the party out of power—lacking control of the governor's office—the state chair may be the real party leader and its principal spokesperson.

Congressional district, legislative district, county, city, ward, and precinct organizations constitute the remainder of the formal party structure. Each level of party organization is controlled by a committee that is headed by an elected leader. In reality, the state party organization is much more encompassing than this description would suggest. The party can be viewed as a network of individuals and organizations with an array of resources on which party candidates can draw. Included in this network are allied interest groups (for example, unions, teachers, and environmental groups for the Democrats; business groups and evangelical Christians for the GOP), PACs, fund-raisers, candidates' personal campaign organizations, political consultants, and the state legislative campaign committees controlled by legislative leaders (Schwartz 1990).

Campaign Finance

States have long set at least some minimal limits on campaign spending and activities. Most ban election-day expenditures; all prohibit bribery and vote buying; and each imposes some form of public disclosure and reporting of campaign receipts and expenditures. Since the Watergate scandals of the 1970s campaign finance legislation has been the most rapidly growing body of election law. As of 1996, thirty-five states had imposed some limits on individual contributions; forty-two placed restrictions on corporate contributions; thirty-eight had restrictions on direct labor union contributions; thirty-two states limited PAC contributions; and nineteen states restricted party expenditures (Malbin and Gais 1998, 14–19). However, there are states, such as Colorado, New Mexico, Texas, and Utah, with no restrictions on individual and PAC contributions or party spending. Despite the abundance of state campaign finance laws, the effectiveness of state regulation is severely limited by the fact that most enforcement agencies are understaffed and have inadequate resources. Indeed, there is a "near absence of any relationship" between the extent of the agencies' resources and the laws they are responsible for administering (Malbin and Gais 1998, 27).

In twenty-two states there are programs to provide some form of state financing of elections that channel public funds to candidates, political parties, or both. State funding, however, tends to be inadequate for financing campaigns at a level commensurate with candidates' needs. The evidence to date shows that public funding has not brought about the heightened electoral competition that was intended by this reform (Malbin and Gais 1998, 137). As the states have run up against antitax movements and fiscal constraints, the momentum for public financing has diminished and the reform movement has shifted its focus from replacing private money with public money toward attempts to restrict and disclose private sources of campaign money.

The Changing Legal Status of State Parties

As state statutes have given parties legal standing and special benefits (for example, ballot access and public funding), stipulated functions they will perform, and regulated how those functions will be carried out, the parties have become quasi-public agencies. As adjuncts of state government, their existence has been practically mandated by state law and their continued existence virtually assured. The legal status of parties is, however, in the process of modification as a result of a series of U.S. Supreme Court decisions. These decisions have extended First and Fourteenth Amendment freedom of association rights to political parties and struck down a series of state-imposed restrictions on parties.

In *Tashjian v. Connecticut* (479 U.S. 20 [1986]), the Court held that Connecticut could not prevent voters registered as independents from voting in a Republican primary if the state GOP wanted to permit independents as well as registered Republicans to vote in its primaries. This case has potentially long-term implications for state regulatory policy, but its short-term consequences have been limited. Only a few parties have actually used this court-granted power to modify the primary election procedures mandated by state law; for example, several state parties have opened their primaries to independents (Epstein 1989). However, an attempt by the Alaska Republicans to use the *Tashjian* precedent to circumvent the state's blanket primary law, which allows voters to vote for candidates of both parties so long as they vote for only one candidate per office, was invalidated by the U.S. Supreme Court in 1996 (reported in Appleton and Ward 1997, 10). The Alaska GOP had sought by party rule to restrict participation in the Republican primary to registered Republicans and unaffiliated voters. By holding that the state's blanket primary law did not violate the party's associational rights, the Court indicated that it is reluctant to tamper in any significant way with state primary laws that are an established part of a state's political system.

The Supreme Court in 1989 further limited state regulatory authority over parties in *Eu v. San Francisco County Democratic Central Committee* (49 U.S. 214 [1989]), when it threw out a California law that banned party organizations from endorsing candidates in primaries, limited the length of state party chairs' terms to two years, and required rotating the state chairs' position between northern and southern California every two years.

An additional expansion of parties' association rights occurred in 1996. The Supreme Court in *Colorado Republican Campaign Committee v. FEC* (520 U.S. 604 [1996]) freed parties from spending restrictions imposed by the Federal Election Campaign Act when parties are engaged in supporting candidates through independent expenditures (spending that is not coordinated with candidates). This decision opened the way for major increases in spending by state and national party organizations in federal elections.

In these cases, the Court has stated clearly that there are limits on the extent of regulation that states or the federal government may impose on political parties. However, even though the Court has indicated a willingness to relieve the state parties of burdensome regulations, it has also demonstrated a willingness to allow the states considerable leeway in determining the nature of their electoral and party system. Thus in 1997 it held in *Timmons v. Twin Cities New Party* (520 U.S. 351 [1997]) that although parties have an unquestioned right to nominate their own candidates, the states also have the constitutional right to regulate elections and prevent manipulations of the ballot and factionalism among the voters. The Court, therefore, ruled that Minnesota had the power to prevent the left-leaning New Party from engaging in the practice of "cross-filing" or "fusion" by nominating a candidate for the state legislature who had already accepted the Democratic nomination. This decision, of course, struck a severe blow against a struggling third party and, in effect, gave the Court's blessing to state efforts to promote a two-party system.

STATE PARTY ORGANIZATIONS: INSTITUTIONALIZED SERVICE AGENCIES

In the 1950s the leading student of American political parties, V. O. Key Jr., gave the following dismal assessment of state parties. The "common situation is the almost complete absence of a functioning statewide organization" and the "general impression that most . . . [state party committees] are virtually dead is probably not far from wrong" (1956, 271, 287). During the 1960s and 1970s prominent observers of American politics continued to express concern for the state of the parties, and there were even forecasts of their demise. Although it is indeed true that voters—the party-in-the-electorate—are now less guided by partisanship in making their choices in the polling booth, state parties have not collapsed. Instead state party organizations at the end of the twentieth century have become increasingly professional and stronger in the sense that most can provide campaign services to their candidates and assistance to their local affiliates. The once highly autonomous state party organizations are also now closely integrated with the national party organizations, which use them to implement their campaign strategies in presidential, senatorial, and congressional campaigns.

The institutionalization of state parties as campaign service organizations parallels the resurgence of the national party organizations, where a massive fund-raising capacity has transformed the once weak Republican and Democratic National Committees into major service agencies to candidates and state and local party organizations. There are also parallels between the substantial campaign roles being played by the parties' senatorial and congressional campaign committees at the national level with the emergence of state legislative campaign committees as a major party-based campaign resource for legislative candidates.

The Passing of the Traditional State Party Organization

Although state party organizations have gone through a resurgence since the early 1970s, they bear scant resemblance to the traditional party organizations that dominated state politics, particularly in the Middle Atlantic, New England, and lower Great Lakes states at the turn of the century (Mayhew 1986). These patronage-based organizations, which controlled nominations and ran their candidates' campaigns, had largely passed from the scene by the mid-1980s (Reichley 1992, 383–384). Patronage as a basis for building party organizations was severely weakened by civil service laws, by strengthened public employee unions, and by a critical public. In the 1970s the Supreme Court threw its might into the antipatronage movement. In a series of cases the Court hit at the heart of large-scale patronage operations run by both Democrats and Republicans in Illinois. It ruled that the Cook County Democratic organization could no longer fire people on the basis of their party affiliations (*Elrod v. Burns,* 427 U.S. 347 [1976]) and it followed this decision with one declaring that the state GOP could not use "party affiliations and support" as a basis for filling state jobs unless party affiliation was an "appropriate requirement" for filling the position (*Rutan v. Republican Party* 488 U.S. 1872 [1990]). In this once patronage-rich state, the Democratic chair observed that "the party no longer functions as an employment agency. More and more we must rely on the spirit of volunteerism that moves so many other organizations" (Reichley 1992, 385).

Even though patronage jobs no longer provide an important basis for party workers and money, other forms of governmental preferments remain important. Gubernatorial appointments to state boards and commissions that control professional licensing, gambling, higher education, hospitals, state investments, environmental and recreation policy, and cultural activities are assignments that are much sought after by persons seeking policy influence, recognition, and material gain. Partisan considerations can also affect state decisions regarding state contracts, bank deposits, economic development, and purchase of legal and consulting services. However, these types of preferments are useful primarily for party and candidate fund-raising and they do not provide campaign workers in the same way that patronage jobs once did (Reichley 1992, 385).

The Service-Oriented State Party Organization

Among the indicators of the strengthened nature of most state party organizations are permanent headquarters; professional leadership and staffing; and adequate budgets to maintain the organization and its programs of support for candidates, officeholders, and local units (Appleton and Ward 1997; Cotter et al. 1984; Reichley 1992, 386–391).

Permanent Headquarters. As late as the early 1970s state party organizations were frequently run out of the offices and homes of the state chairs. This ad hoc type of operation has now largely ceased to exist as the parties in the main now operate permanent headquarters stocked with high-tech equipment in modern office buildings located in state capitals. A notable example of this trend is the Wisconsin Republicans' three-story facility opened in 1995 containing a telemarketing center capable of contacting 400,000 persons in a single day, computers that link up with every media outlet in the state (with reporters' names listed by legislative and congressional district), a computer-based research facility, a finance center, and office space for political operatives.

Professional Staffing. Even into the 1970s many state party headquarters operated with small staffs consisting of only an executive director, secretary, and a few volunteers. Today virtually all state parties have professional leadership either in the form of a paid full-time chair (in approximately one-third of the states) or an executive director (Reichley 1992, 389). Although the level of staffing fluctuates between election and nonelection years and depends on the financial health of the party, the basic trend has been for an increased staff size and specialization because campaigning in the 1990s requires specialized skills and professionalism. These staffing patterns are apparent in Florida where in 1995 the state GOP had a staff of twenty-five plus several part-time workers and the Democratic state committee operated with a staff of sixteen and four part-time workers (Appleton and Ward 1997, 62). State parties, however, are plagued by high staff turnover. State chairs normally serve only two to three years and professional operatives tend to be transients who move from job to job with party organizations, candidates, and consulting firms, often on leads provided by national party organizations (Reichley 1992, 391–392).

Finances. Operating a professional headquarters requires an ability to raise significant amounts of money on a continuing basis. Most state parties have developed or are developing direct mail and telemarketing capabilities to reach small- and medium-sized contributors, while also having more traditional large donor programs. Complete data on state party expenditures is not available, but one indicator of the substantial financial resources of state parties can be seen in Figure 3-1 showing state party receipts reported to the FEC during the 1995–1996 election cycle. More than 75 percent of all state parties had reportable receipts in excess of $1 million and more than half had receipts of more than $3 million, with the California Republicans at $43.6 million and the California Democrats at $19.5 million. Most state party receipts actually are greater than the amounts reported because

Figure 3-1 State Party Receipts Reported to the Federal Election Commission, 1995–1996

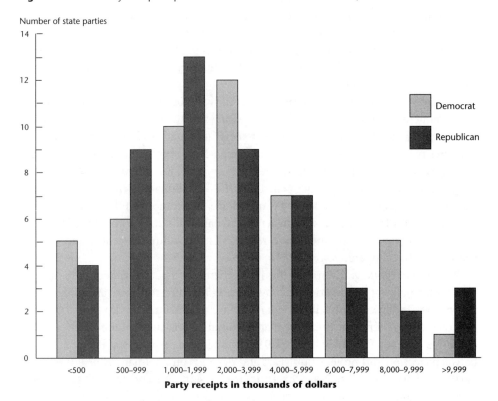

Number of state parties

Party receipts in thousands of dollars

SOURCE: Federal Election Commission (1997).

NOTE: Dollar amounts shown are state party receipts reported to the FEC, including funds transferred to state parties by national party committees, and do not include funds used exclusively in state elections.

the FEC does not require state parties to report funds used exclusively in state elections. It has been estimated, therefore, that a state party' receipts could total as much as 25 percent higher than in the FEC reports.

Although several of the state parties have shown an ability to raise prodigious amounts of money (for example, the New York state GOP committee raised $10 million in 1996; Dao 1998), it needs to be kept in mind that a significant share of some state party budgets was money transferred to them by national-level party committees. For example, the Florida Democratic party received $5.7 million from the Democratic National Committee (DNC) and the Florida GOP got $2.2 million for the Republican National Committee (RNC) in 1995–1996 (FEC 1997). As discussed later in this chapter, massive national party fund transfers during the 1995–1996 election cycle, totaling $66.3 million by the RNC and $74.3 million by the DNC, demonstrate that the national party organizations are using the state parties as vehicles to implement national campaign strategies.

Party Activities: Organization Building and Candidate Support

Most state parties now have well-developed fund-raising operations, get-out-the-vote programs, newsletters for contributors and volunteers, research and communications specialists, and programs to assist local affiliates. There are also candidate assistance programs—financial contributions, polling, fund-raising help (for example, coordinating and channeling PAC contributions), media services, and campaign seminars (Reichley 1992, 390). However, because their resources are limited, state parties must be selective in the services they offer, and there has been a tendency to concentrate efforts on labor intensive voter mobilization programs that have the potential to benefit party candidates up and down the ballot. For example, the New York Republican state committee has developed one of the most sophisticated voter databases in the country (Dao 1998). And in Washington state, which has permitted permanent absentee voting since 1993, the Republican Party has followed a strategy of focusing on absentee voters. In 1996 that strategy paid off with victories in two congressional districts in which Democratic candidates ran ahead of their GOP opponents based on ballots cast at the polls ("GOP Retains Hold on Washington State" 1996).

Although state parties have been strengthened in terms of their ability to provide services to their candidates, it must be kept in mind that their role is to supplement the activities of the candidates' own personal campaign organizations principally in the areas of voter mobilization and fund-raising. This restricted campaign role is an adaptation by the parties to the candidate-centered nature of state electoral politics in which candidates rely primarily on their own organizations, set up personal headquarters, and have nonparty groups providing campaign assistance. The candidates also often hire campaign consultants to work exclusively on their behalf.

Electoral Impact of State Party Organizations

Although in this era of candidate-centered politics, party organizations play a supplementary role to that of the candidates' own personal organizations, the level of party organizational strength can affect elections. Analyses of gubernatorial elections show that the state party with an organizational strength advantage gains increments of votes over the opposition party (Cotter et al. 1984, 100–101); and the parties' ability to turn out voters on election day is a factor in determining the extent of interparty competition within the states (Patterson and Calderia 1984). Clearly, the Republican emphasis on organization building in the South during the 1960s and 1970s provided the party with the infrastructure to take advantage of increasingly favorable conditions as the region's white voters realigned with the GOP. There is also evidence that strong and competitive party organizations within a state contribute to public attitudes supportive of parties (Coleman 1996).

The relationship between party organizational strength and electoral success, however, is complex and difficult to fully assess. Just because a state party develops itself into a sophisticated campaign service organization does not mean that it will automatically and simultaneously become successful electorally, as the southern GOP found during its years in the electoral wilderness. Yet, it is apparent that the maintenance of effective party structures has aided the continuing electoral success of the Minnesota and Michigan Democrats and the Ohio and Indiana Republicans. Even so, in states where a party has long enjoyed electoral dominance, there may be little incentive to build a strong party structure—for example, the Democrats in Massachusetts or the Democrats in the South during their time of hegemony. It appears, therefore, that the real significance of party organizational strength is not so much its impact in any given year, but rather that such strength provides the infrastructure for candidates and activists to continue to compete in the face of short-term defeats and even long-term minority status and to take advantage of favorable conditions when they occur (for example, an opposition incumbent's retirement, scandal, divisiveness within the other party, a shift in public mood).

Party Differences and the Heightened Involvement of Party-Allied Groups

Studies of state central committees have generally shown the Republicans to be organizationally stronger than their Democratic counterparts (Cotter et al. 1984; Reichley 1992, 387–391). This reflects a key difference between the parties: Republican state organizations tend to be a more important source of campaign support than do Democratic party organizations. This does not mean that Democratic candidates are necessarily lacking or unequal in resources, but it does mean that Democrats tend to rely more heavily for assistance from allied nonparty groups such as organized labor, especially teachers' unions. These organizations can engage in voter registration and get-out-the vote operations and also provide candidates with volunteers, money, media advertising, and in-kind services. Of course, the Republicans are not without allied group support of their own, often from business groups and in many of the states groups such as the Christian Coalition.

One of the most important trends in party politics is the heightened role that party-allied groups are playing in electoral politics. This is illustrated by the way in which party-allied groups descended on Oregon for the 1996 special senatorial election to replace Republican senator Bob Packwood. Representative Ron Wyden, the Democratic nominee, was aided by twelve full-time staff members from the AFL-CIO national office, and local unions provided twenty-five more; the League of Conservation Voters and the Sierra Club joined together in a $200,000 independent expenditure campaign; and the Human Rights Campaign (a gay and lesbian PAC) had a full-time operative in the state. Working with the state party and Wyden's own campaign, these organizations were engaged in a televised air war of commercials, door-to-door canvassing, direct mail, and neighborhood rallies. This pro-Democratic activity was countered by Christian Right, antiabortion, and property rights groups working on behalf of the unsuccessful GOP candidate (Edsall 1996).

In Oklahoma, a state that was once a stronghold for the Democrats, the Christian Right played a critical campaign role in helping elect a totally Republican delegation to the U.S. House of Representatives in 1996. Five of the state's six GOP House members were openly affiliated with the Christian Right and the other successful candidate was acceptable to it (Bednar 1997).

In California during the 1990s one of the most free-spending political organizations was the conservative California Independent Business PAC, which between 1992 and 1996 spent more than $9 million to become a major player in state politics. In 1994 its money helped the Republicans win control of the State Assembly for the first time in a quarter century (Bailey and Warren 1997). The use that state parties and their candidates make of allied group assistance—indeed, oftentimes their dependence on it—demonstrates the need to view parties in an inclusive and comprehensive manner that encompasses more than the formal legally sanctioned organizational structure. The state party organization is actually a network that includes the regular party structure, candidate organizations, party-allied groups, fund-raisers, and campaign consultants (Schwartz 1990). An additional, but often overlooked, element of the party network is the army of incumbent legislators' staffers, who are frequently and heavily involved in advancing their bosses' electoral interests as well as those of the party.

Parties as Networks of Issue-Oriented Activists

An emerging feature of American parties is that they are increasingly networks of "issue based participatory activists" (Shafer 1996, 73–76). The sources for this trend are found in a complex set of interacting forces: the development of a postindustrial society in which noneconomic social–cultural issues have gained heightened salience (for example, abortion, environmentalism, crime, gun control, women's and gay rights); sociological and economic change that resulted in heightened educational attainment, reduced blue-collar employment, and an expanding white-collar workforce; and decline in the availability of patronage as an incentive for political participation. Changes in the rules governing presidential nominating politics that have diminished the influence of party leaders have also enhanced the role of issue-oriented activists (Shafer 1988, 98–100).

Evidence of the extent to which parties are becoming networks of issue-based participatory activists can be seen in the gap between the issue positions taken by delegates from the states to national conventions and rank-and-file party voters (Shafer 1988, 100–107). As Byron Shafer, a seasoned and acute student of national conventions, noted, "One could find almost no anti-abortion delegates among the state delegations to the 1992 Democratic convention, while the pro-choice minority at the Republican convention felt constrained to hide its preferences despite the fact that this issue split the mass base of each party almost identically" (1996, 32).

Surveys of individuals participating in presidential nominating politics through attendance at state party caucuses and conventions similarly have shown that the largest share of these activists "have pronounced ideological tilt to them, far more so than primary voters or party identifiers" (Mayer 1996, 133). Liberals and moderates have become scarce at GOP state party conventions, and the center of gravity at Democratic party gatherings have a pronounced liberal bent. State party attendees show a strong propensity for interest group involvement, with the Democrats having higher levels of participation in education, social issue, and environmental organizations than their Republican counterparts (Francis and Benedict 1986, 105–110).

Policy-oriented activists are also well established within the parties' organizational and campaign structures at the county level. A study of local presidential campaign workers revealed that "true believers" significantly outnumbered the more pragmatic leaders concerned first and foremost with getting more votes than the opposition. Because a significant proportion of these "true believer" types were also serving as the chairs of the regular county party organizations, researchers concluded that "advocacy politics" had permeated into the parties' organizational structure (Bruce et al. 1991).

There is also mounting evidence that issue-based groups are becoming firmly ensconced in the organizational structure of the state parties. In 1994 *Campaigns and Elections* reported that the Christian Right was the dominant faction in eighteen state Republican organizations and that it had substantial influence in thirteen more (Wilcox 1996, 75–77). This influence was clearly revealed at the 1997 meeting of the RNC, which is composed of state party representatives. Ralph Reed, the former executive director of the Christian Coalition, played a major role in switching thirty Religious Right RNC members' votes on the third ballot to enable James Nicholson to be elected national chair (Broder 1997).

The Democrats, too, have been afflicted with issue-oriented group influence that has made it difficult to maintain the support of rank and file voters. An analysis of Democratic party–interest group relations concluded, "No one decided that the party would be the party of . . . liberal causes at the expense of middle class voters. The Democrats became the party of these causes because it was effectively lobbied" (Berry and Schildkraut 1995, 29).

The mounting involvement and domination of party organizations by individuals and groups whose motivation to participate in party affairs is based not on material rewards such as patronage but rather stems from issue-based concerns is creating not just conflicts between rank-and-file party voters and the activists. It is also causing rifts between officeholders and party organizations. Indeed, in some states an almost schizophrenic party structure has developed with elected officials needing broad-based electoral support to win existing side-by-side with a growing body of organizational activists mainly concerned about ideology and principles. Moderate Republican Sen. John Warner (Va.) decided in 1996 not to speak at his party's state convention because conservative party leaders did not want him there, thereby leaving his primary opponent to speak unrebutted to 3,000 convention delegates (Berke 1996, 11). Warner, however, went on to win both the primary and general election. In Minnesota, a Religious Right-dominated Republican state party convention endorsed one of its own for the gubernatorial nomination, in the process rejecting its incumbent GOP governor, moderate Arne Carlson. Like Warner, Carlson easily won the GOP primary and reelection.

Although Warner and Carlson fought off their more extreme intraparty rivals, there is a clear pattern emerging of ideological and issue-based groups taking an active role in party nominating politics. In Kansas, a state long noted for producing prominent moderate Republicans such as Senators Bob Dole, Nancy Kassebaum, Frank Carlson, and James Pearson, an alliance of Christian Right–conservative Republicans produced in 1996 "a full slate of abortion opponents and either full-fledged social conservatives or candidates clearly acceptable to the right wing of the party" (Cigler and Loomis 1998, 216). The growing involvement of issue-oriented activist groups in nominating politics was also on display in California during the 1998 U.S. House special election in the Santa Barbara, California, area. Groups on the Right and Left poured resources into the primary for television ads, mailings, voter guides, telephone banks, and leaflets. Among the groups heavily involved in this primary were on the political Left—the AFL-CIO, Planned Parenthood Action Fund, EMILY's List, and People for the American Way; and on the Right—the Campaign for Working Families, Catholic Alliance, Christian Coalition, National Rifle Association, Americans for Term Limits, and the Foundation for Responsible Government (Greenblatt 1998, 137).

To the extent that state parties become increasingly networks of issue-oriented activists, elected officials' conflicts with party organizational and allied group activists are likely to proliferate. In addition, the increasing influence exerted by issue-oriented activists within the parties and on their candidates will in all likelihood widen the policy differences between the parties. Indeed, the traditional conception of parties as "vote maximizers" appears to require some revision. Like interest groups, parties now contain an enlarged element that is mainly interested in achieving policy objectives—that is, the party structures are heavily influenced by "policy maximizers."

STATE LEGISLATIVE CAMPAIGN COMMITTEES

As is the case at the national level, the state party organizational structure is decentralized, with a variety of organizations focusing on different offices and activities. Although the RNC and DNC concentrate primarily on presidential politics and working with their constituent state organizations, the congressional and senatorial campaign committees are the principal party support agencies for U.S. House and Senate candidates, to whom they provide money (including assistance in securing PAC financing), polling, media advertising, and other technical assistance (Herrnson 1998, 72–102). At the state level, the state central committees tend to concentrate on statewide races, and the state legislative campaign committees focus their resources exclusively in legislative races and have emerged as the major source of party assistance to legislative candidates in a significant number of states.

Reasons for the Emergence of State Legislative Campaign Committees

Legislative campaign committees are composed of incumbent legislators in both chambers and are headed normally by legislative party leaders. These committees emerged as party support agencies for legislative candidates in response to intensifying partisan competition for control of legislative chambers, rising campaign costs, increased uncertainty about election outcomes, and the inability of many state central committees in the 1970s to provide meaningful assistance to legislative candidates (Gierzynski 1992, 11–14; Rosenthal 1993, 5). In addition, the development of strong legislative campaign committees is linked to increased legislative professionalism—full-time legislators who are paid a reasonable salary and backed by ample staff. Professionalism increases the value of legislative service, especially when accompanied by majority-party status. Legislative leaders, therefore, created campaign committees to protect and further their own and their party colleagues' interests. At the same time, a legislatively based campaign organization requires institutional capacity to operate—virtually full-time legislative leaders, legislative caucus staffs, and computer and media resources (Rosenthal 1993, 4–5).

Campaign Activities

Legislative campaign committees began as mechanisms to raise and distribute funds to candidates. However, they have developed into full-service operations for individual candidates, particularly in states with professionalized legislatures. The committees' involvement in candidate recruitment is particularly crucial. Recruitment of quality candidates is directly related to being able to raise campaign dollars, gain volunteer workers, and run truly competitive races for legislative seats. As state politics expert Alan Ehrenhalt noted,

> Every other year, Democrats and Republicans battle for legislative control . . . in what is advertised as a debate about which party best reflects the views of the electorate. Within in the corridors of the state capitol, however, the biennial legislative elections are recognized for what they really are: a competition to attract candidates who have the skills and energy to win and the desire and resourcefulness to stay in office. (1989, 29–30)

The scope of legislative campaign committee spending and services can be extensive. In Ohio, for example, the Republican Senate Caucus provides candidates with a structured package of in-house polling, campaign managers, telephone banks, media planning, and issues research that costs in excess of $3.5 million. The former Speaker of the Wisconsin Assembly described the range of services his Democratic Assembly Committee provided as follows:

> We raised [money] to help Democrats running in marginal seats. In most cases we recruited the candidate. We provide training through campaign schools. We provide personnel and logistical support, issue papers, press releases, speakers for fund raisers, fund raisers, and phone banks. We pay for the recount if it's a close race; we pay for the lawyer if it goes to court. . . . We do everything a political party is supposed to do. (Loftus 1985, 100)

Both the state committees and the legislative campaign committees have also proven to be adaptable to the growing role of PACs in funding elections. This adaptation has involved working with the PACs to channel PAC money into races in which additional dollars are thought to have the potential to affect outcomes. The legislative leaders provide PAC directors with political intelligence about where their contributions will have maximum impact. In the process, candidates benefit by having the campaign committees give them a stamp of legitimacy as good PAC investments. An assistant to the Speaker of the Indiana House observed, "For every one dollar we [the legislative campaign committee] raise, we direct two dollars of interest group money" (Gierzynski 1992, 55).

By channeling PAC money to candidates, as well as by soliciting PAC funds directly, the parties have infused campaigns with additional money that carries "the imprimatur of the party at no direct expense to party coffers" (Jones 1984, 197). State party organizations and allied PACs have also coordinated their efforts to provide in-kind services to candidates.

Electoral Strategies

Legislative campaign committees concentrate their resources on close or competitive races—either to maintain or gain control of a legislative chamber. Party money tends to flow either to vulnerable incumbents, viable challengers, or open-seat candidates. A recent multistate study of legislative campaign finance revealed parties are particularly generous with nonincumbent candidates. Slightly fewer than 50 percent of Democratic party funds went to nonincumbents, whereas the amount going to nonincumbent Republicans was 80 percent. This interparty difference reflected the fact that Democrats controlled more legislative seats than did the GOP at the time of the study (Gierzynski and Breaux 1998, 195–196).

Although party money can play a critical role in legislative races, one should not overstate the parties' involvement. The multistate study cited previously found that in 1992 the highest proportion of legislative candidates' revenues coming from party sources was approximately 16 percent. This constituted on average $48,148 for Democratic candidates in California, $15,802 for New Jersey Democrats, and $645 for Maine Republicans. The smallest share of candidate revenues coming from party sources was .3 percent for Mississippi Democrats, who received only $8 on average. The parties' share of candidate revenues is greatest in states with professionalized legislatures and where interparty competition is most intense (Gierzynski and Breaux 1998, 187–192).

Shared goals, party loyalty, and personal connections do encourage an element of cooperation and coordinated activity between legislative campaign committees and state committees. However, because legislative campaign committees are always led and dominated by legislative leaders, the committees tend to operate independently of state central committees. Campaign finance expert Frank J. Sorauf (1992, 120) has observed that legislative campaign committees are built and maintained by incumbents to serve primarily the agendas and priorities of legislative partisans and "insulate them from the pressure of other parts of the party. Collective action has helped to bring legislative parties freedom from the agencies of . . . gubernatorial parties."

GOVERNORS AND STATE PARTY ORGANIZATIONS

It is an unusual governor who actively seeks to direct the day-to-day affairs of the state central committee. In a nationwide study, fewer than 50 percent of the state party chairs reported that they believed it necessary to have the governor's approval before taking action. Most considered the governor's role in party affairs to be advisory rather than controlling (Cotter et al. 1984, 112). Governors do, however, expect their state parties to play a supportive and supplementary role to their own personal campaign organizations, which in a candidate-centered era of state politics carry the principal campaign load. Even governors such as Tommy Thompson (R-Wis.), who have been particularly supportive of their parties, carefully cultivate a personal following that transcends partisanship and engage in the extensive fund-raising required to maintain a well-oiled personal campaign apparatus.

Governors do frequently seek to influence and even control the selection of their state party's chair, lest the party structure fall into unfriendly hands. New York has had a long tradition of governors handpicking the party chair and expecting the designatee to follow gubernatorial directions. However, because the interests of the governor and the state party organizations are not necessarily identical, conflicts can arise. In 1992 Virginia governor Douglas Wilder's appointee as state chair was forced to share power with a steering committee of party leaders when he was accused of placing the governor's national political ambitions ahead of the electoral interests of the state Democratic party (Baker 1992, B4).

The range of gubernatorial–state party organization relationships varies from those in which the organization is dominated by the governor and closely tied to his or her political fortunes to those exhibiting the type of outright hostility described previously. A New England Democratic chair described a tightly linked relationship with his governor as follows: "I'm the governor's agent. If I look good, he looks good, because I'm his man. I don't bother him with messy stuff. He expects me to handle it my way. I meet with the [local] leaders on his behalf. I'm liaison to city and town leaders" (personal communication). Some governors also rely on their state party chairs to assist them in influencing state legislators to support the governor's legislative agenda. There are also those rare state chairs whose intraparty power base is sufficiently strong that they can operate with considerable independence from their party's governor. Since 1994 New York GOP chair William Powers has been this type of state leader, operating with unprecedented independence because he rebuilt the party structure while Democrats still controlled the governor's office. In addition, it was Powers who promoted an obscure state senator, George Pataki, to be the party's nominee for governor and then played a major role in getting him elected (Dao 1998).

The most common relationship, however, is one of coordinate responsibility. The governor and state chair consult with one another on appointments, candidate recruitment, fund-raising, and other major party activities. And the governor assists the party with fund-raising and candidate recruitment, but neither the governor nor his or her staff run the state central committee headquarters. Likewise, the state party chair does not seek to manage the governor's campaign or determine gubernatorial policy. A Republican chair in a midwestern state with a long tradition of professional party leadership summarized his relationship with his governor as follows: "I don't go to his office and he doesn't come over here. . . . A lot of people think he isn't interested in the party. But that's not true. He cares and he helps me. His attitude is 'What can I do to help.'" The governor corroborated these comments by saying that his state party chair "doesn't want to be governor and I don't want to be party chairman."

THE IMPACT OF STRENGTHENED NATIONAL PARTY ORGANIZATIONS: NATIONALIZATION AND HEIGHTENED INTRAPARTY INTEGRATION

Until the 1970s, political scientists emphasized the decentralized and confederate nature of American party organizations. The RNC and the DNC were considered so lacking in influence that a landmark study even characterized them as "politics without power" (Cotter and Hennessy 1964). Power within the party structure resided with state and local organizations, and the national committees were heavily dependent on the state organizations for their funds. The national committees, which once existed in a state of dependency on their state affiliates, have now been transformed into large-scale and well-heeled enterprises housed in party-owned modern offices. Through their ability to raise massive amounts of money through direct mail, large giver programs, and solicitation of unions, corporations, trade associations, and various groups for soft money (funds raised outside the restrictions of the Federal Election Campaign Act [FECA]), the national committees have been transformed into institutions capable of playing a major role in providing significant assistance to candidates and to their state affiliates. In the 1995–1996 election cycle, the DNC's combined hard money (dollars raised in compliance with the FECA) and soft money receipts totaled more than $210 million and the RNC total topped $304 million (FEC 1997). The increased resources and influence of the national party organizations has been accompanied by heightened integration and interdependence between national and state party organizations.

Centralizing Power through National Party Rule Enforcement

Since 1968 the national Democratic party organization has intensified efforts begun in 1948 to use its rule-making authority to ensure the loyalty of state party organizations to the national ticket. Starting with the McGovern–Fraser Committee in the late 1960s, the national party has developed elaborate rules that state parties are required to follow in the selection of national convention delegates. In addition, the National Democratic Charter, adopted in 1974, contains stipulations concerning the organization and operation of state parties. The national party's authority has been backed up by a series of Supreme Court decisions that ruled that national party rules governing delegate selection take precedence over state party rules and state statutes *(Cousins v. Wigoda,* 419 U.S. 450 [1975]; *Democratic Party of the U.S. v. Ex rel. La Follette,* 450 U.S. 107 [1981]).

Unlike the Democrats, the national GOP has not sought to gain influence over its state affiliates through tough rule enforcement. Instead, it has maintained the confederate legal structure of the party, and the RNC has assumed a relatively passive role in delegate selection and internal party organization. Nevertheless, party centralization and integration moved forward dramatically in the GOP through a process of providing assistance to state organizations and their candidates.

National Party Assistance Programs to State Parties and the Shift of Intraparty Influence to National Organizations

The Republicans were the first to use their ability to raise massive amounts of money to institute programs of financial, technical, and staff assistance designed to strengthen their state affiliates during the 1960s and 1970s. By the 1980s the Democrats were quite consciously copying the RNC's state party assistance programs. Among the programs provided to state parties by the national committees are cash grants, professional staff, consulting services for organizational development, data processing, fund-raising, campaigning, media communications, and redistricting. Both parties operate special programs to assist state legislative candidates, and there have been major investments of money and personnel in the development and maintenance of voter lists and efforts to get out the vote. Because they have been more proficient in raising national party money, the RNC has had a more extensive array of programs than has the DNC, which has sought to make up for this deficiency by encouraging state parties, state-level candidates, and allied interest groups (particularly organized labor) to pool resources with the national party and engage in "coordinated campaigns."

By providing an array of services to their state and local party organizations, the national committees have gained unprecedented intraparty influence and leverage. These assistance programs operate in a manner similar to federal grant-in-aid programs for the states in that before the state parties can receive aid they frequently have to accept conditions—albeit usually quite flexible conditions—imposed by the national party. Through these national-to-state party aid programs, the state parties have gained campaign assets—professionalized staffs, money, current voter lists and telephone banks for get-out-the-vote operations, and computers. However, an additional consequence of these aid programs has been that the national party organizations have gained unprecedented intraparty influence and leverage over their state and local affiliates.

Political scientist Alexander Heard foresaw the implications of a shift of financial and campaign resources to the national party organizations in 1960 when he observed that "any changes that freed the national party committees of dependence on state organizations could importantly affect the loci of party power" and enable the parties to develop "a more cohesive organizational structure" (294). The conditions that Heard predicted have now come to pass as the national parties have vastly increased their financial resources and freed themselves from dependence on the state parties for their revenues. With the shift in the direction of the flow of resources that now runs from national to state parties instead of the other way around, intraparty power is increasingly being centralized in the national parties, and the state parties have become increasingly dependent on the national parties for resources. Indeed, organs of the national party have even become major players in state races. For example, a DNC-sponsored group spent $80,000 on a 1996 special state senate election that caused a shift of party control in the Wisconsin state senate (Bice 1996); and in 1997 the RNC pumped $1 million into the Virginia governor's race and spent $750,000 supporting Governor Christine Whitman in New Jersey (Greenblatt 1997).

Strengthened Intraparty Integration

Using their considerable financial resources, the national party committees have been able to achieve an unprecedented level of intraparty integration as the state parties have become integral elements in implementing national campaign strategies. In this process, large scale transfers of funds from the national committees, particularly in the form of soft money, have played a critical role. In the 1995–1996 election cycle, the RNC and DNC combined transferred $140.6 million to their state parties. Of the $74.3 million sent to state parties by the DNC, $54.2 million was soft money; and of $66.3 million transferred by the RNC $48.2 million was soft money (FEC 1997).

These transferred funds were used to defray general party overhead and pay for voter mobilization programs and state and local campaigns. Under current interpretation of the FECA these general "party-building" activities are not considered direct contributions in support of federal candidates and hence are not restricted by FECA expenditure limits. State party-building activities, such as get-out-the-vote drives, however, can in reality provide crucial assistance to federal as well as state campaigns.

The national party organizations allocate funds to state parties in a manner that is intended to implement a national campaign strategy geared toward winning key states in the presidential race and maximizing the parties' seats in the House and Senate. An illustration of the scope of joint national–state party campaign activity was the RNC's Victory '96 direct-voter contact operation. It included candidate-specific mail, slate mail (84 million pieces of targeted mail), absentee ballot programs, voter identification and turnout telephone calls (14.5 million calls to Republican households), volunteer phone centers, and collateral materials. The Victory '96 program was funded by $15.3 million in RNC money and $48.3 million in state party funds (Republican National Committee 1997, 9–10). The Democrats also had major national–state party voter mobilization projects.

A particularly dramatic example of a national party using its state organizations to carry out a national strategy occurred when the DNC in 1996 transferred $32 million to state parties in twelve battleground states. These state parties in turn paid for television advertising that had been developed and placed in the media by the DNC's media production company (Abramson and Wayne 1997).

Coordinated national–state party campaigns, which result in a flow of funds into state parties and the creation of tangible assets such as voter lists, professional personnel, and high-tech equipment, can strengthen state organizations' campaign capacity. In the process, however, state parties can suffer a loss of autonomy and become dependent on national party largess. In some instances, state parties' headquarters quite literally may be taken over by the national party or presidential campaign operatives as the state party becomes little more than a check-writing mechanism for the national party to avoid restrictions of the FECA.

Moreover, when these takeovers occur, national party priorities prevail, often with resources devoted to the presidential or other high-profile races to the detriment of contests lower down on the ballot such as state legislative candidates. This was one of the consequences of the Democrats' coordinated campaign in 1992 in New Jersey and in Ohio in 1996 (Blumberg et al. 1997; Heldman 1996).

Nor do national parties treat all of their state affiliates equally. Parties in key states such as California, Florida, and Ohio are showered with national party largess. But others lacking national priority status can receive virtually no help from the national party. During 1995–1996, the DNC transferred no money to its affiliates in New York, Rhode Island, and West Virginia, and the RNC sent a mere $6,000 to the West Virginia GOP (FEC 1997). Furthermore, national party resources can be pulled out of a state mid-campaign when it appears that these resources could be more effectively used in another state.

PARTY NOMINATIONS

The nomination process is crucial for parties because selecting a quality candidate can bring victory on election day, whereas a weak nominee can doom the party to defeat. In addition, control of the party is at stake, because nominations go a long way in determining which party factions will gain ascendancy, who receives the rewards that elected offices bestow on their supporters, and a party's policy orientation.

In most Western democracies, party candidates are selected by party organization leaders. Operating largely without government regulation, these party leaders designate the party nominees and there is no appeal of their decisions to the voters. Rank-and-file voters participate only in the general election—a contest between parties—not in intraparty contests to select nominees. By contrast, the widespread use of the direct primary election in the American states involves not only party activists, but also ordinary voters in the nomination process. Because it gives rank-and-file voters a deciding voice in nominations, the direct primary has weakened the capacity of party hierarchies to control candidate selection. Among Western democracies, the American direct primary is unique not only for the amount of popular participation it permits but also for the wide variety and extensive state-level regulation that accompanies it.

Early in the twentieth century the direct primary gradually replaced nominations by party conventions and caucuses as a part of the Progressive Era reform movement, whose leaders decried bossism and corrupt party machines and believed that ordinary voters should have a direct say in selecting party candidates. The absence of real two-party competition in much of the country also furthered the spread of the direct primary. In one-party states, nomination by leaders of the dominant party was tantamount to election. As a result, instituting primary elections to nominate candidates constituted a means of ensuring meaningful popular participation in election. As V. O. Key, Jr., concluded, the direct primary was "an escape from one-partyism" (1956, 81).

Types of Direct Primaries

The constitutional principle of federalism permits the states wide latitude in regulating the nominating process. They can specify the circumstances under which a primary must be used and the type of primary to be used for a party's candidates to secure a slot on the general election ballot. Thus state laws regulating party nominating procedures vary significantly in terms of the degree of public disclosure of party preference required of voters, and whether voters are allowed to participate in the primary of more than one party (see Table 3-1).

Open Primary Systems. Thirteen states have an open primary system, in which a public declaration of party preference is not required to vote in the primaries. In nine of these states, voters receive a ballot containing the names of all parties' candidates and then decide in the secrecy of the voting booth in which party's primary they wish to vote. An even more open system is the blanket primary pioneered by Washington and now used in three states, including California since 1998. This type of primary permits the voter to take part in more than one party's primary, switching back and forth between parties from office to office. Another wide-open type of primary is Louisiana's "nonpartisan" primary. In this system all of the candidates for each office are placed on the ballot with candidates' party affiliation listed on the ballot. If a candidate receives a majority of votes cast in the primary, he or she is elected, as occurred in the gubernatorial primaries of 1975 and 1983. But if no candidate receives a majority of the primary votes, the two top finishers, irrespective of party, must face each other in the general election. Louisiana's unique primary, instituted in 1975, was a project of a Democratic governor, the roguish Edwin Edwards, and was designed to aid his party's candidates because at the time of its adoption the Republican party was weak and its candidates were not assured of even making it into the general election runoff. However, as Macolm E. Jewell, a distinguished student of state politics, observed "the major consequence of the nonpartisan primary has been to blur differences between the parties" (personal correspondence, 1997). Thus in 1991 the losing Republican gubernatorial candidate had been elected to the post as a Democrat four years earlier; and the Republican governor elected in 1995 had been a Democrat until six weeks before the election.

Table 3-1 Types of Direct Primaries

Closed[a]	Semiclosed[b]	Semiopen[c]	Open[d]	Blanket[e]	Nonpartisan[f]
Arizona	*Voters may change*	*Voters must*	Hawaii	Alaska	Louisiana
Connecticut	*registration on*	*openly state in*	Idaho	Washington	
Delaware	*primary election day*	*which party*	Michigan	California	
Florida	Iowa	*primary they wish*	Minnesota		
Kentucky	Ohio	*to vote*	Montana		
Maryland	Wyoming	Alabama	North Dakota		
Nebraska		Arkansas	Utah		
Nevada	*Independents may*	Georgia	Vermont		
New Mexico	*register with a party*	Illinois	Wisconsin		
New York	*primary election day*	Indiana			
North Carolina	Massachusetts	Mississippi			
Oklahoma	New Hampshire	Missouri			
Oregon		South Carolina			
Pennsylvania	*Voters who have not*	Tennessee			
South Dakota	*previously voted in a*	Texas			
West Virginia	*party primary may*	Virginia			
	change registration				
	Colorado				
	Kansas				
	Maine				
	New Jersey				
	Rhode Island				

SOURCE: The authors are indebted to Professor Malcolm E. Jewell for providing updated information on voter qualifications for participating in partisan primaries in the state.

[a] Party registration required.
[b] Voters may register or change registration on election day.
[c] Public selection of a party required.
[d] Voter may vote in any party's primary.
[e] Voter may vote in more than one party's primary, but one candidate per office.
[f] Top two primary votegetters, regardless of party, are nominated for general election.

In the eleven mainly southern states, a semiopen system is used in which voters are not made to register with a party to vote but are required to declare openly at the polls in which party's primary they wish to vote. This system is only slightly less restrictive than the open primary.

Closed Primaries. Sixteen states operate closed primary systems, in which voters must be registered as party affiliates to vote in partisan primaries. They are permitted to vote only in the party in which they are registered. A voter who wishes to switch party registration must do so in advance of the primary, normally twenty to thirty days before the primary. As is shown in Table 3-1, ten states have created loopholes in their closed primary laws that permit voters either to register or change party registration on election day. These arrangements tend to make these states' primaries into virtual open primaries.

The Effect of Open and Closed Primaries. Open primary systems encourage crossover voting—partisans of one party voting in the primary of the other party—whereas closed primary systems largely preclude this type of behavior. Crossover voting tends to occur in the party's primary in which there is a meaningful nomination contest, and those voters who cross over typically are engaging in sincere rather than strategic crossover voting. That is, they are voting for their most preferred candidate rather than crossing over to "raid" the opposition party's primary by voting for its weakest candidate. Because sincere crossover voting can affect primary outcomes, the candidates with policy positions closest to the median voter's views are more likely to be selected in open primary systems than in closed primaries (Gerber and Morton 1994).

Runoff Primaries. Usually the candidate who receives the most votes (a *plurality)* in the primary gains the nomination, even if that individual receives less than a majority of total votes cast. In nine southern and border states, a majority of the vote in the primary is required for nomination (40 percent in North Carolina). If no candidate receives a majority, then a second, or runoff, primary is held between the top two finishers in the first primary. This system was instituted in the South when the Democratic party was so dominant that winning its primary was equivalent to being elected. To ensure that the person nominated in the Democratic primary and therefore "elected" had the support of a majority of Democrats, the runoff primary was instituted. It has been found that (1) runoffs are required in about 10 percent of the races; (2) the leader in the first primary goes on to win in the runoff 70 percent of the time, although the success rate falls to 50 percent for African American candidates; and (3) women are not at a disadvantage in the runoff system (Bullock and Johnson, 1992).

Nominating Conventions and Preprimary Endorsements

Although the direct primary is the predominant method of nomination, thirteen states either permit or require conventions for the nomination process. Four states (Alabama, Georgia, South Carolina, and Virginia) permit parties to nominate either by party convention or primary. There are also seven states that by law provide for preprimary endorsements by party conventions (Colorado, Connecticut, New Mexico, New York, North Dakota, Rhode Island, and Utah). In Connecticut, New Mexico, New York, and Utah, primaries are not mandatory and are held if two or more candidates receive a specified share of the delegate vote (25 percent in New York, 15 percent in Connecticut, and 20 percent in New Mexico). In Utah, the convention designates for each office two candidates whose names are placed on the primary ballot, although if one receives 70 percent of the convention vote that person is automatically declared the nominee. Colorado law makes it possible for a candidate to become the nominee and avoid a primary by receiving the support of 50 percent of the convention delegates. In several of the states with statutorily required preprimary conventions, candidates may also get on the ballot by securing a requisite number of signatures on a petition.

Some state party organizations use informal or extralegal preprimary endorsement in an effort to influence the selection of nominees. For example, both parties in Massachusetts and Minnesota regularly endorse candidates at state party conventions; and in New Jersey county party committees endorse gubernatorial candidates in an effort to influence who will enter and win the primary. Behind the scenes, it is not at all unusual for party leaders to assist favored and quality candidates, while discouraging others from entering the race. The various methods that party organizations may use to influence primaries demonstrate that parties can be a critical factor in the nomination process. A frequent pattern in states that by law require preprimary conventions is for nonendorsed candidates to drop out of the race. However, the trend since the 1980s has been one of declining primary victories for party-endorsed candidates. Thus in 1994, six of eleven endorsed gubernatorial candidates lost their parties' primaries, even in Connecticut where the Democrats have had a tradition of strong party organizational influence over nominations (Jewell and Morehouse 1995).

Although preprimary endorsements appear to have declined in influence in recent years, Sarah McCally Morehouse, in a comprehensive study (1998, 199), has concluded that preprimary endorsements reduce the impact of money on the outcome of primary contests for governor. Candidates who succeed in securing party convention endorsements normally become as well known as their challengers because the endorsement process requires them to engage in face-to-face meetings with about a thousand party activist delegates from across the state. The public visibility achieved in the endorsement process helps to compensate for any campaign spending advantage their challengers may have. Further offsetting the impact of campaign spending in gubernatorial primaries are the resources of time and effort that parties confer on endorsed candidates. By contrast, in states that do not use preprimary endorsing conventions, Morehouse found that candidate spending was the overwhelming predictor of the outcome of primary contests for governor (1998, 121, 199).

Consequences of the Direct Primary

Just as the Progressive reformers had hoped, the direct primary has undercut the influence and control that parties can exert over nominations. With nominations ultimately in the hands of voters, party organizations cannot unilaterally designate party nominees. Primaries therefore encourage a candidate-centered style of politics, because without parties capable of controlling nominations, candidates have an incentive and need to set up their own personal campaign organizations. As the weak showing of endorsed candidates in 1994 demonstrates, endorsement by state or local party organizations does not eliminate the need for candidates to have an effective personal organization.

Although succeeding in breaking the party organization's grip on the selection of nominees, direct primaries have never fulfilled the expectations of their reform-minded sponsors. Voter turnout is typically much lower than in general elections. Between 1962 and 1994 in states holding primaries, the average turnout in midterm election years, when most of the nation's governors are elected, was only 23.9 percent of the voting age population (Center for the Study of the American Electorate 1994). In addition, the extent of vigorous competition in primaries has been limited, with incumbents either running unopposed or with only token opposition. More than 90 percent of incumbent governors and U.S. representatives win renomination. Contests occur most often within the party that has the greatest opportunity of winning the general election and when there is no incumbent seeking renomination.

Implications of the Primary for the General Election

The outcome of the primary, of course, has implications for the general election. In addition to narrowing the field of candidates and choices available to voters, the primary results can enhance or demolish a party's general election prospects, depending on which candidates are victorious. Party leaders frequently strive to avoid contested primaries on the assumption that divisive primaries will undermine the party's prospects in the general election. However, there is no consistent pattern demonstrating that contested primaries are necessarily damaging (Kenney 1988). One reason for this is that contested primaries are most common in the stronger of a state's two parties. Contested primaries may also generate publicity for a candidate. In addition, the winner may emerge as a more seasoned campaigner with a battle-tested organization and campaign momentum.

POLITICAL COMPETITION

Since V. O. Key's seminal work on southern state politics (1949), scholars have recognized the importance political competition can have on the nature of politics in the states. First, it is generally recognized that competition can affect state public policy, with competitive states tending to spend more on social programs than do those with weak interparty competition. Second, strong interparty competition is associated with higher levels of voter turnout.

An analysis of political competition in the states requires an examination of (1) why electoral competition is essentially restricted to competition between Republican and Democratic candidates; and (2) analysis of two different aspects of competition: interparty competition for control of state government (the governorship and legislature) and electoral competition (percentage of votes won in state elections).

Barriers to Third Parties

The environment of the American states has not proven hospitable to sustaining viable third parties. The institutional barriers they must overcome are substantial and are likely to remain in place, because most are firmly established in the American political culture.

The Single-Member District System Combined with Separation of Powers. The standard method of electing state legislators is via the single-member district system in which the person who wins a plurality of the votes is elected. Because there are no legislative seats awarded for coming in second, third, or fourth in this system, as there is in proportional representation systems, there is an incentive to create two broad-based parties, each capable of winning district-level pluralities and majorities in legislative chambers. In the single-member district system, third and minor parties are condemned to almost perpetual defeat, hardly a recipe for longevity. Electing the states' governors separately with terms that overlap those of the upper and lower chamber legislators creates an additional incentive to create broadly based parties capable of winning a grand prize of state politics—the governorship.

The Direct Primary. One of the reasons for electoral dominance of the Republican and Democratic parties for more than 140 years has been the direct primary system of nominations. The direct primary has the effect of channeling dissent into the two major parties. It thereby creates highly permeable parties that are easily penetrated by dissidents and insurgents who do not find it necessary to go through the difficult and usually frustrating exercise of forming an alternative party. Instead, insurgents can adopt a "burrowing from within" strategy to achieve electoral gains. The impact of the direct primary is not without its paradoxes. On the one hand, it weakens the party organizations and makes the party susceptible to external influences; but on the other hand, the electoral looseness it imposes on the parties also acts as a preservative by enabling them to absorb protest movements and dissidents. Voters become used to choosing among individuals competing for the Republican and Democratic label. In addition, a majority of the states require voters to register as Republicans or Democrats to vote in primaries, thereby giving the parties a ready-made list of adherents (Epstein 1986, 244–245).

State Regulations and Ballot Access Laws. Over and above primary election laws, other aspects of state regulation of elections tend to work to the disadvantage of third parties. As was noted previously, state ballot access laws can impose severe barriers to third parties and independent candidates trying to secure a place on the ballot. Statutory bans on "cross-filing" or "fusion" tickets, which prevent candidates from running simultaneously as the nominee of more than one party, make it virtually impossible for small parties to form electoral alliances to gain public office. However, where this practice is permitted, as in New York, third parties such as the Conservative and Liberal parties, can frequently play a crucial role in elections. A large number of states also have "sore loser" laws designed to keep those who lose primary elections from turning around and running in the general election as independents. In effect, state election law has tended to create an "institutionalized duopoly" (Epstein 1986, 173).

National Electoral Alignments Overwhelm State Multiparty Systems. There have been several viable third parties at the state level that have temporarily overcome the institutional barriers, most notably in Minnesota and Wisconsin during the 1930s and 1940s. Minnesota's Farmer–Labor party and Wisconsin's Progressives temporarily displaced the Democrats as one of their states' major parties as both states operated with three-party systems. Both of these third parties achieved substantial electoral success—electing governors, controlling legislative chambers, and sending representatives and senators to Washington. However, as impressive as these third-party successes were, their demise after a viable existence of only about twenty years is of much greater significance. These multiparty systems collapsed in the 1940s as voters increasingly aligned themselves along national party lines. The tides of national politics overwhelmed the Farmer–Labor and Progressive parties and they were forced to merge with the major parties (Epstein 1986, 124–126).

The Recent Increase in Minor Party Candidates. Although electoral success and longevity are rare for minor parties, there has been a sharp increase in the number of such candidacies in the 1990s. In the 1992–1994 election cycles, 910 minor party candidates were on the ballot for statewide and federal offices—more than 3.5 times as many as in the 1964–1966 cycle; and 2,800 minor party candidates ran for state legislatures between 1992 and 1994 (Collett 1998, 104). The surge and decline of minor parties has been associated throughout American history with the performance of the major parties and the public's perception of the major parties, which has not been high of late.

It is interesting to note that two of the minor parties that succeeded in posting gubernatorial victories in the 1990s were led by prominent officeholders who left one of the major parties. In Alaska, former Republican governor Walter Hickel was elected in 1990 running as the Alaska Independence nominee, and former Republican senator Lowell Weicker won as the candidate of A Connecticut Party. In neither instance, however, did the parties survive when their well-known founders were no longer heading the ticket.

Competition for Control of Government

A measure of interparty competition developed by Austin Ranney constitutes a widely used and long-standing indicator of competition for control of government (1976, 59–60). The Ranney index has several different components.

> *Proportion of success:* the percentage of votes won by the parties in gubernatorial elections and the percentage of seats won by the parties in each house of the legislature;
> *Duration of success:* the length of time the parties controlled the governorship and the length of time the parties controlled the legislature;
> *Frequency of divided control:* the proportion of time the governorship and the legislature has been divided between the two parties.

Ranney used these three dimensions to calculate his index of interparty competition, which we have updated for 1995–1998.[1] The index is actually a measure of

---

1. We calculated the average percentage of the popular vote won by Democratic gubernatorial candidates; the average percentage of seats held by Democrats in the state senate, in all legislative sessions; the average percentage of seats held by Democrats in the state house of representatives, in all sessions; and the percentage of all gubernatorial, senate, and house terms that were controlled by the Democrats. For each state we averaged these four percentages to create an index value representing the degree of interparty competition. Because of its use of nonpartisan state legislative elections, no index value was calculated for Nebraska.

control of government, with a score of 0 indicating complete Republican control and a score of 1 indicating absolute Democratic control. At its midpoint (.5000), control of government is evenly split between the two parties, indicating a highly competitive environment. Ranney used this index to classify states by party control, using the following categories and definitions:

- .8500 or higher: one-party Democratic;
- 6500 to .8499: modified one-party Democratic;
- 3500 to .6499: two-party;
- 1500 to .3499: modified one-party Republican;
- 0000 to .1499: one-party Republican.

The values of the Ranney party control index calculated for the period 1995–1998 are presented in Table 3-2, where several patterns emerge. First, no state now qualifies as a one-party state. This is a major change from previous years, when usually several states could be considered one-party Democratic states. Second, although the majority of states can be classified as two-party states, the Republicans hold a slight advantage over the Democrats (twelve modified Republican states to nine modified Democratic states). This too represents a real change in the balance of power in state politics and reflects the impact of the 1994 elections. Third, party control of states exhibits a distinct regional pattern. The Democratic party is strongest in the South, whereas the Republican party is strongest in many Mountain West states (Arizona, Idaho, Montana, Utah, and Wyoming) and Plains states (Kansas, North Dakota, and South Dakota). This regional pattern, however, is not as strong as it has been in the past.

The Ranney index can be recalculated to indicate the level of competition between the parties for control of government, rather than the degree of Democratic or Republican control.[2] Consider the most competitive states in Table 3-2, Texas and Washington, which have Ranney party control index values of .507 and .493, respectively. As you move away from Texas and Washington, in both directions, the states are less and less competitive. For instance, even though Massachusetts and Wisconsin display different partisan leanings, their party control values (.634 and .364, respectively) make them almost equally noncompetitive: Massachusetts is .134 and Wisconsin is .136 units away from the point of perfect competition, .500.

The Ranney competition index is derived from the original Ranney index and represents how close the states are to perfect competition between the parties for control of government.[3] The Ranney competition index ranges from .500 (no competition) to 1.000 (perfect competition). The data in Table 3-2 indicate that the least competitive states are located in the South and, to some degree, in the Mountain West region. Although the states in the Midwest and Northeast have tradition-

2. In the professional literature, this is called the *folded Ranney index.*
3. The formula for the Ranney competition index is 1 - |(.5 - Ranney)|. This index measures how close a state's level of interparty competition is to "perfect" competition on the Ranney index.

Table 3-2 States Classified According to Degree of Interparty Competition for Control of Government, 1995–1998

State	Ranney party control index	Ranney competition index	State	Ranney party control index	Ranney competition index
Modified one party: Democratic					
Hawaii	0.775	0.725	Georgia	0.681	0.819
Arkansas	0.774	0.726	Louisiana	0.680	0.820
Maryland	0.720	0.780	Kentucky	0.672	0.828
West Virginia	0.689	0.811	Missouri	0.665	0.835
Rhode Island	0.688	0.812			
Two-party competition					
Vermont	0.648	0.852	Washington	0.493	0.993
Massachusetts	0.634	0.866	Florida	0.487	0.987
Alabama	0.629	0.871	Connecticut	0.486	0.986
Mississippi	0.625	0.875	Maine	0.464	0.964
Oklahoma	0.579	0.921	South Carolina	0.461	0.961
New Mexico	0.578	0.922	New York	0.461	0.961
Delaware	0.572	0.928	Indiana	0.448	0.948
Tennessee	0.566	0.934	Colorado	0.425	0.925
North Carolina	0.562	0.938	Oregon	0.413	0.913
Minnesota	0.540	0.960	Alaska	0.374	0.874
Virginia	0.536	0.964	Iowa	0.371	0.871
California	0.532	0.968	Michigan	0.369	0.869
Nevada	0.516	0.984	Wisconsin	0.364	0.864
Texas	0.507	0.993	Illinois	0.363	0.863
Modified one-party: Republican					
Pennsylvania	0.325	0.825	Kansas	0.264	0.764
New Jersey	0.307	0.807	Ohio	0.261	0.761
New Hampshire	0.304	0.804	North Dakota	0.245	0.745
Arizona	0.298	0.798	Wyoming	0.242	0.742
Utah	0.290	0.790	Montana	0.225	0.725
South Dakota	0.287	0.787	Idaho	0.199	0.699

SOURCE: Calculated by authors.

NOTE: Nebraska is excluded from this table because it has nonpartisan state legislative elections.

ally been the most competitive, the data in Table 3-2 do not show a clear regional pattern among the most competitive states.

Although the classifications in Table 3-2 are useful, it is important to realize the limitations of such an index. First, the Ranney index is based exclusively on state offices and does not reflect the strength of the parties at other levels. For instance, until the 1992 election, the Democratic presidential ticket had not won more than a single southern state (Georgia in 1980) since 1976, when a southerner, Jimmy Carter, headed the ticket. This is exactly the opposite of what would be expected, based on the degree of Democratic Party strength as measured by the Ranney index. Also, the significant gains made by Republicans in U.S. House and Senate elections in the South in recent years are not reflected in the Ranney index.

Table 3-3 Changes in the Ranney Index of Interparty Competition, 1948–1998

	1948–1960	1962–1973	1974–1980	1981–1988	1989–1994	1995–1998
Mean level of Democratic control (Range: 0–1)	0.56	0.58	0.64	0.60	0.55	0.48
Mean level of interparty competition (Range: .5–1)	0.78	0.83	0.81	0.84	0.87	0.86

SOURCES: Compiled from data in Patterson and Caldeira 1984; Bibby et al. 1990; Bibby and Holbrook 1996; and Table 3.2, this volume.

Second, the Ranney index gives more weight to some state offices than to others. The way the index is constructed, the state legislature is given much more weight than the governorship. This may also result in underestimating the strength of the Republican Party in southern states, because many of the party's gains have been made in the governorships. It is also worth noting that the Ranney index does not include other statewide offices, such as lieutenant governor (where separately elect-ed), attorney general, state auditor, and state treasurer. Not all states elect these of-fices, but most of them do.

Third, this measure of interparty competition is "a snapshot of an object mov-ing in time and hence does not always capture change that may be occurring when the measurement is taken" (Ranney 1976, 60–61).

Although interparty competition is a long-term phenomenon and, as such, should be relatively stable, significant change in the nature of competition for con-trol of government has taken place. The changes from 1948 to 1998 in the mean level of Democratic control, as measured in Table 3-2, and the mean level of inter-party competition, based on the Ranney competition index, are presented in Table 3-3. In these two measures there are signs of both stability and change. First, the mean score of Democratic control in the Ranney index tilted toward the Democra-tic side throughout most of the period, only to tip slightly Republican in the most recent period. Second, the Democratic party grew in strength from 1948 to 1980 and steadily lost strength from 1981 to 1998. Much of the decline in Democratic strength in the 1980s and 1990s has occurred in southern states, where Republicans have been making inroads. Third, in terms of the level of competition for control of government, the least competitive period was from 1948 to 1960, and the most competitive period was from 1989 to 1998. In large part, Republican gains in southern states account for the increase in competition in recent years.

Many of the recent changes in party control and interparty competition shown in Table 3-3 reflect the impact of the 1994 elections. Prior to the 1994 elections, the Democrats controlled twenty-five state legislatures and the Republicans controlled eight; following the 1994 elections the Democrats controlled eighteen legislatures and the Republicans controlled nineteen. A similar change occurred in governorships: The Democrats went into the 1994 election with a twenty-nine to nineteen advantage in governorships and came out with nineteen governorships to the Republicans' thirty. Thus the 1994 elections represent a true reversal of fortunes for the two major parties.

Electoral Competition

One of the limitations of the Ranney index is that, because it is based on control of government, it is not an ideal measure of electoral competition. This is especially disconcerting because many of the hypotheses concerning the effect of competition on state politics are about how electoral competition affects state politics and policy making. To measure electoral competition in the states more accurately, an index based on district-level state legislative election outcomes from 1982 to 1986 has been developed by Holbrook and Van Dunk (1993). In the Holbrook–Van Dunk index, a value for each state is derived from several different indicators: the average margin of victory, the average percentage of the vote going to the winning candidate, the percentage of seats uncontested, and the percentage of seats considered "safe" (won by five percentage points or more).[4] The crucial difference between this index and the Ranney index is that the Holbrook–Van Dunk index is based entirely on election outcomes, whereas the Ranney index is based primarily on partisan control of state government. Another important difference is that this index is based solely on state legislative elections, whereas the Ranney index is based on control of both the state legislature and the governorship.

Although there is wide variation in the level of electoral competition in the states, there is, to some extent, a familiar regional pattern: Most of the least competitive states are from the south, and there is no clear regional pattern among the most competitive states. This regional pattern bears some resemblance to the Ranney competition index. Although the two are conceptually distinct, the relationship between the Ranney competition index from the late 1980s and the original Holbrook–Van Dunk index is moderately strong $(r = .68;$ Bibby and Holbrook 1996).

Many of the limitations of the Ranney index also apply to the Holbrook–Van Dunk index. First, the Holbrook–Van Dunk index is based only on state legislative elections and does not necessarily say anything about competition at other levels of office. Second, this index is also only a snapshot in time of a phenomenon that could be in a state of flux. Indeed, although the state values of the Holbrook–Van Dunk index are highly correlated over time (the correlation between values from 1972 to 1976 and 1982 to 1986 is .89), there have been changes in the index. Although the analysis of the Ranney index in Table 3-3 indicated an increase in com-

---

4. The formula for the index is

Competition = 1 - [(average margin of victory + average winning percentage + percentage uncontested + percentage safe seats)/4]

The original index is based on district-level state legislative election outcomes from 1982 to 1986 and does not include multimember free-for-all districts.

petition for control of government, there was actually a slight decrease in the level of electoral competition from the mid-1970s to the mid-1980s.

Consequences of Competition. As mentioned earlier, it is widely expected that competition has an influence on public policy and voter turnout. Specifically, it is expected that competitive states will produce more liberal public policies and have higher rates of voter turnout than noncompetitive states. To a large extent, the data bear out these propositions, especially for the Holbrook-Van Dunk index. The Ranney competition index is moderately related to policy outcomes and voter turnout, but the relationship is inconsistent and, in many cases, disappears when the effects of other important variables, such as state wealth, political ideology, and partisanship are taken into account (Holbrook and Van Dunk 1993). The results are much stronger for the Holbrook–Van Dunk index, however. Holbrook and Van Dunk examined a broad range of policies and found that electoral competition has a strong influence on policy outcomes, even when there is a control for other important influences. The same results are found when the effect of electoral competition on voter turnout is examined (Holbrook and Van Dunk 1993).

Determinants of Competition. As we pointed out earlier, competition follows a regional pattern; on both measures of competition, southern states are distinctly less competitive than the rest of the country. To a large extent, this demonstrates the long-lasting effect of the Civil War and Reconstruction on southern politics.

Beyond the effects of region, several other variables help explain state differences in competition. First, states with diverse populations have more competitive political systems than do states with homogeneous populations (Barrilleaux 1986; Patterson and Caldeira 1984). Second, some states have lower levels of competition because they have higher levels of partisan bias in the electorate. If a state's electorate is overwhelmingly Democratic, then it makes sense that the Democrats would face little competition at the polls and would be able to establish control of state government (Barrilleaux 1986; Holbrook, Mangum, and Garand 1994). Finally, incumbency and the use of multimember districts have been found to suppress electoral competition, and minority party strength (percentage of seats held) and highly populous legislative districts have been found to enhance electoral competition (Holbrook et al. 1994; Van Dunk and Weber 1997). Note that both incumbency and district size can be manipulated to increase competition. Term limits, of course, could minimize the effect of incumbency, and reducing the size of the legislative body would result in larger electoral districts.

POLITICAL PARTICIPATION

Political participation in the United States takes many different forms: contributing to campaigns; attending rallies or protest events; writing letters to elected representatives; working for a campaign or community cause; attending town meetings or school board meetings; and, of course, voting in elections. Although voting is the most commonly practiced form of political participation, the degree to which citizens across the states take advantage of their right to vote varies widely.

Patterns of Turnout across the States

For a variety of reasons some people decide not to take advantage of their right to vote in elections. Although individual attributes have a lot to do with whether or not a person votes, turnout rates can also be affected by the type of election being held and by certain aspects of the state political environment. The traditional way of measuring turnout is to take the total number of votes cast as a percentage of the voting-age population in the state. In Table 3-4 this method is used to calculate the level of turnout in all states for presidential, gubernatorial, and congressional elections, from 1994 to 1997. The first column in Table 3-4 presents the average rate of turnout across all four types of elections for each state. Once again, we see the emergence of a regional pattern: Seven out of the ten lowest turnout states are southern or border states. At the other end of the scale we do not find a clear regional pattern, but most of the highest turnout states are small, sparsely populated states.

Besides differences across the states, it is clear in Table 3-4 that there are substantial differences in turnout in different types of elections. From 1994–1997, turnout was the highest in presidential elections, then in Senate elections, and lowest in House and gubernatorial elections. One of the reasons gubernatorial turnout is lower overall is that most gubernatorial elections are held in nonpresidential election years. However, as the data in Table 3-5 illustrate, in any given election year (midterm or presidential) turnout is usually higher for gubernatorial elections than for the other types of elections. This helps illustrate an important point: Turnout is always higher in presidential election years. Turnout was roughly 13 to 15 percentage points higher for all offices in the presidential years of 1992 and 1996 than in the midterm election years of 1990 and 1994. This is because presidential elections are high-visibility events that generate a lot of interest and bring out a lot of voters who do not turn out to vote in elections for lower offices.

The turnout data in Tables 3-4 and 3-5 need to be interpreted with some caution. Because turnout is expressed as a percentage of the voting-age population, the numbers are probably slightly different from what they would have been if turnout had been expressed as a percentage of the eligible voting-age electorate. The voting-age population of a state includes significant numbers of people who are not eligible to vote because they are not citizens or are institutionalized in correctional or mental health facilities. Nevertheless, there is every reason to believe that the patterns of turnout found in Tables 3-4 and 3-5 would not be substantially different if all ineligible voters were excluded.

What Determines Turnout?

Many factors help explain differences in voter turnout across states and individuals. For the individual voter, a variety of important demographic and attitudinal variables are related to turnout (Rosenstone and Hansen 1993; Wolfinger and Rosenstone 1980). For example, middle-aged people with high levels of income and education have a high probability of voting. People with a strong sense of po-

Table 3-4 Average Rates of Voter Turnout in the States by Office, 1994–1997

State	Total	President	Governor	U.S. Senate	U.S. House
Montana	61.2	62.9	62.6	59.6	59.5
South Dakota	60.4	61.1	59.7	61.2	59.8
Maine	59.5	64.5	54.9	59.8	59.0
Wyoming	59.3	60.1	58.8	60.0	58.5
Minnesota	58.1	64.3	52.5	58.4	57.4
Idaho	55.6	58.2	51.5	58.8	53.8
Oregon	55.2	57.5	52.8	56.8	53.7
North Dakota	54.0	56.3	55.9	50.7	53.0
Vermont	53.8	58.6	53.6	49.3	53.6
Alaska	53.3	56.9	49.8	54.6	51.8
Iowa	53.1	57.7	46.3	57.3	51.3
New Hampshire	52.4	58.0	47.4	57.3	46.9
Nebraska	52.1	56.1	48.6	52.3	51.4
Kansas	51.4	56.6	43.5	56.1	49.3
Missouri	50.7	54.2	53.8	45.5	49.2
Massachusetts	50.5	55.3	47.4	51.6	47.7
Washington	49.7	54.7	54.3	42.5	47.5
Michigan	48.7	54.5	44.2	48.4	47.7
Connecticut	48.4	56.4	46.1	43.4	47.7
Rhode Island	48.1	52.0	47.3	46.8	46.4
Colorado	47.6	52.4	41.1	51.7	45.2
Utah	47.0	50.3	50.8	41.7	45.4
Wisconsin	46.9	57.4	41.4	41.5	47.4
Delaware	46.4	49.6	49.6	43.8	42.7
Louisiana	46.1	56.9	49.4	54.2	23.9
Ohio	45.5	54.3	40.3	41.3	46.1
Oklahoma	45.3	49.9	41.6	45.0	44.7
North Carolina	44.2	45.8	46.7	46.5	37.7
Indiana	43.8	48.9	48.3	35.9	42.1
Arkansas	43.8	47.5	39.5	45.5	42.7
Illinois	43.6	49.2	35.7	48.5	41.0
Alabama	43.3	47.7	38.4	46.6	40.5
New Jersey	43.2	51.2	39.9	41.2	40.3
New Mexico	43.0	46.0	40.8	42.6	42.5
Pennsylvania	41.9	49.0	38.9	38.1	41.8
Tennessee	41.6	47.1	38.0	41.0	40.3
Virginia	41.5	47.5	33.8	43.8	40.8
Mississippi	41.3	45.6	41.8	38.4	39.4
Arizona	40.8	45.4	38.6	38.3	40.7
Hawaii	40.3	40.8	41.0	39.7	39.7
Kentucky	40.2	47.5	33.7	44.7	34.9
Maryland	40.1	46.7	37.6	36.5	39.5
Florida	39.7	48.0	38.7	37.8	34.4
West Virginia	39.7	45.0	44.5	36.2	33.1
New York	39.3	46.5	38.2	35.1	37.4
California	38.9	43.3	37.3	36.7	38.5
South Carolina	38.1	41.5	34.1	41.8	34.9
Georgia	37.3	42.6	30.0	41.9	34.6
Texas	36.4	41.2	33.2	36.5	34.8
Nevada	36.4	39.3	34.9	35.0	36.4
Average	46.0	50.8	43.9	45.7	43.8

SOURCE: Calculated from data in various sources.

Table 3-5 Mean Percentage of Voter Turnout in the States by Year and Office, 1989–1997

Year	President	Governor	U.S. Senate	U.S. House
1990	—	40.9	38.6	37.8
1992	58.3	59.2	55.2	54.3
1994	—	41.4	41.8	40.2
1996	50.8	52.6	51.5	48.9
Presidential year increase (%)	—	14.7	13.2	12.6

SOURCE: Calculated from Table 3-4, this volume, and from Bibby and Holbrook 1996.

NOTE: The turnout rates for the 1989 and 1991 gubernatorial elections are included in the 1990 figure, and the turnout rates for the 1993, 1995, and 1997 gubernatorial elections are included in the 1994 figure.

litical efficacy and strong ties to political parties are also very likely to vote. Many of these variables also help explain the pattern of turnout in the states. Socioeconomic differences across the states, for instance, are strongly related to differences in voter turnout; wealthy states and states with well-educated citizens generally have the highest rates of voter turnout (Kim, Petrocik, and Enokson 1975).

But state politics also have an effect on voter turnout. First, turnout is higher in states with high levels of electoral competition. In noncompetitive environments the elections are less likely to generate much interest and voters are less likely to vote. The correlation between electoral competition and overall voter turnout (r = .36) demonstrates the strength of this relationship. Turnout can also be influenced by the level of campaign spending in particular races (Jackson 1997; Patterson and Caldeira, 1983). As more money is spent in a campaign, voters are provided with more information about the candidates, which increases the likelihood that they will vote.

Another important determinant of turnout is the stringency of state voter registration laws (Wolfinger and Rosenstone 1980). In states in which it is difficult for voters to register or to stay registered, fewer people will register and voter turnout will be lower than it would be if registration laws made it easier to register. One example of such a law is the closing date for registration, or the number of days before the election that one must register to vote. The closing date ranges from zero (Election Day registration or, in North Dakota, no voter registration) to fifty days before the election. The difference in turnout between states with a closing date of ten or fewer days before the election and states with a closing date of thirty or more days before the election illustrates the effect registration laws can have: The average overall rate of turnout in the former is 52 percent, and the average turnout in the latter is 44 percent.

Class Bias in Turnout

Recent research on voter turnout has focused on the role of class bias in shaping public policies for the poor (Hill and Leighley 1992; Hill, Leighley, and Hinton-Anderson 1995). Class bias is defined in this research as the extent of overrepresentation (or underrepresentation) of higher (or lower) socioeconomic status voters in the electorate. The results of this research indicate that there is wide variation in the extent of class bias in state electorates and this bias is related to the provision of policies for the poor. Specifically, states in which the level of upper-class bias is relatively low (the poor are better represented in the electorate) tend to provide more generous welfare benefits than do states in which the level turnout bias is more severe. This research has also found that class bias tends to be most extreme in poor, racially diverse states (Hill and Leighley 1994).

DIRECT DEMOCRACY

In addition to choosing between candidates in elections, voters in some states are given the opportunity to vote directly on matters of public policy. This process is sometimes referred to as direct democracy because it allows the people to legislate directly, through the ballot box, rather than indirectly, through elected representatives. Several different forms of direct democracy are available to the voters, depending on where they live. In many cases the ballot propositions do not originate with the people but are submitted by the legislature for the approval of the people. Forty-nine states (Delaware is the exception) require voter approval of constitutional amendments through *constitutional referendums;* nineteen states require that certain types of legislation, usually bond issues and debt authorizations, be approved by the voters in a *constitutionally mandated referendum;* twenty-four states authorize the legislature to submit measures to the people for their approval in a *legislative referendum;* twenty-three states permit the people, after gathering a required number of signatures, to use a *petition referendum* to force an issue passed by the legislature onto the ballot, where it must gain a majority approval before taking effect.

Other forms of direct democracy are much more direct, with the proposition originating from the people. Twenty-three states permit the *legislative initiative,* which takes two forms: direct and indirect. The *direct initiative* forces a proposed statute onto the ballot on the petition of a specified number of voters. In three of these states, however, the *indirect initiative* is used, which requires that all such measures be submitted to the legislature first, allowing it an opportunity to approve the measure. In such cases, if the legislature does not approve the measure, it can then be submitted to the voters for their approval. Five states allow the use of both the direct and indirect legislative initiatives. Seventeen states use the *constitutional initiative,* which provides for direct placement of constitutional amendments on the ballot after a petition has been signed by a specified number of voters (Council of State Governments 1998; Magleby 1988, 601).

Every election year there are several instances in which voters use the machinery of direct democracy to make important public policy decisions. Many of the issues addressed through direct democracy have far-reaching policy consequences. One example of this is Proposition 13, which was a constitutional initiative placed on the ballot in California in 1978. Proposition 13, which rolled back property taxes, was approved by the voters and is frequently cited as the impetus for antitax movements in several other states. Another important issue that has recently been addressed through the initiative process is term limits for elected officials. The use of the initiative process to limit legislative terms is an example of how direct democracy can be used to accomplish national policy objectives when the objectives are unlikely to be satisfied by the national government. Another example of this phenomenon can be found in California and several other states that had proposals on the ballot for the 1998 elections that would significantly hamper the ability of labor organizations to use union dues for political purposes. Other issues that are routinely addressed through the initiative process are limits on taxing and spending, the rights of the accused, the regulation of industries, campaign finance, and certain public morality issues such as abortion, gay rights, and gambling.

The use of direct democracy was popular in the early part of this century, but from 1940 through the 1970s it waned in the public favor. Since then, it seems to have experienced a resurgence in popularity. From 1981 to 1986, there were 144 initiatives placed on the ballot. From 1987 to 1992, there were 202 items on the ballot, representing a 40 percent increase in use over the early 1980s (Kehler and Stern 1994); and in 1996 a single year peak of 106 was reached (Broder 1998). During the 1980s, more initiatives appeared on the ballot than at any time since the 1930s (Magleby 1988).

One criticism of direct democracy is that it may not, in fact, be democratic because of the low levels of turnout in referendum elections. Turnout in referendum elections is usually measured by how much the level of voting drops off from that in candidate elections occurring at the same time (that is, presidential, congressional, gubernatorial). For a variety of reasons, turnout in referendum elections tends to be much lower than turnout in other types of elections. As a result the active electorate for ballot propositions is severely biased because the poor and uneducated, who have low turnout rates anyway, are even less likely to vote on ballot propositions than in other types of elections (Magleby 1984). Several factors can, however, influence the rate of drop-off in referendum elections. First, drop-off is lower when the ballot measure comes directly from the people, through the initiative process, than when it is referred by the legislature. Second, drop-off is higher in constitutional referendums than in statutory referendums. Finally, drop-off is lower when more money is spent on the referendum campaigns (Bowler, Donovan, and Happ 1992).

ELECTION OUTCOMES

Although presidential elections generate a great deal of attention every four years, other important elections are being contested in the states in almost every year. Of course, the most visible of these elections are gubernatorial and state legislative elections. But there are also elections for other important statewide officials, such as the lieutenant governor, attorney general, state treasurer, secretary of state, and state auditor. These officials are appointed in some states, but a majority of the states elect at least some of them. In addition, in twenty-five states, judges are elected directly by the people.

Determinants of Election Outcomes

What determines these election outcomes? No single variable determines who wins these elections. Instead, state election outcomes are the result of many different variables.

Partisanship. One of the most important variables in determining voting behavior in American elections has been party identification. People tend to identify with a political party and vote for that party's candidates in elections. Although partisanship still plays an important role in elections, it has lost much of its impact. Some have argued that state elections are becoming more and more like presidential and congressional elections, where the influence of party has been diminished by increasingly candidate-oriented campaigns. Indeed, the evidence is undeniable that party is no longer as strong a voting cue in state elections as it once was. One indicator of the decline of party can be found in the increasing willingness of individuals to split their ticket and vote for candidates of different parties for different offices. In the late 1940s more than 70 percent of all state governments were unified along party lines, indicating that people tended to vote for the same party in both the gubernatorial and state legislative races. By the late 1980s, however, fewer than 45 percent of all state governments were unified along party lines (Fiorina 1992). This percentage has held fairly constant: Following the 1998 elections, only twenty-four states had one-party control of the governorship and state legislature.

Despite growing evidence that the influence of partisanship in elections is declining, there are still ample indications that it has not disappeared. Studies of state legislative, gubernatorial, and other statewide elections continue to find that party strength in the electorate is an important determinant of election outcomes (Gierzynski and Breaux 1991; Holbrook 1991; Squire 1992).

Incumbency. One variable that may be supplanting partisanship as an influence on election outcomes is incumbency. It is now widely known that incumbent members of Congress are almost certain to get reelected if they choose to run. Members of the U.S. House, for instance, have long had an incumbent reelection rate of more than 90 percent (Jacobson 1997). As the data in Table 3-6 illustrate, the same type of electoral advantage accrues to elected officials in the states. Among state officials, governors face the greatest chance of losing their reelection bids, although roughly 80 percent of those who run do win. State legislators and statewide constitutional officers (attorneys general, lieutenant governors, secretaries of state, treasurers, and auditors) have an incumbency advantage that approaches that of members of the U.S. House. With more than 85 percent of all incumbent state legislators and statewide officers winning reelection, potential challengers can find lit-

Table 3-6 Incumbent Success Rates of Those Who Sought Reelection in State Elections, 1968–1996 (in percentages)

Years	Governor	State representative	State senator	Statewide officer[a]
1968–78	74	89	85	88
1979–89	81	91	87	93
1990–96	87	90[b]	92[b]	85
Average	81	90	88	89

SOURCES: Stanley and Niemi 1994; *State Legislative Election Returns in the United States, 1968–1989* (ICPSR #8907); Monardi 1994; Monardi, personal communication, December 1994; *Congressional Quarterly Weekly Report,* November 12, 1994, and November 9, 1996; and the National Conference of State Legislatures Web site: http://www.ncsl.org.

[a] Statewide officers include lieutenant governors (where separately elected), attorneys general, secretaries of state, state auditors, and state treasurers. Data available only through 1993.

[b] Data for 1994 only.

tle cause for optimism. Even in gubernatorial elections, where the incumbent is most vulnerable, the odds are against a challenger's winning.

Incumbents have an advantage over challengers for several reasons. First, because incumbents are much more visible than challengers, voters are more likely to recognize the incumbent's name and therefore more likely to vote for the incumbent. Second, incumbents have already been elected once, so they have a base in the electorate. Third, and perhaps most important, incumbents have an easier time raising money (Moncrief 1992), which becomes more important as campaigning becomes more expensive.

Campaign Spending. Campaign spending is an extremely important determinant of state election outcomes. Money buys resources, organization, and exposure. Money can also scare off potential challengers. If an incumbent governor, for instance, raises a campaign war chest of $2 million during the first couple of years of his or her term, the governor is likely to scare off potential challengers who do not want, or are unable, to raise that kind of money.

Although it is difficult to get accurate information on all state races, the costs of campaigning have clearly gone up. Gierzynski and Breaux (1991) examined campaign spending in state legislative races in five states and found that from 1978 to 1986 campaign spending increased, on average, more than 200 percent. Moncrief (1992) controlled for inflation in his study of spending patterns in nine states from 1980 to 1988 and found that the average increase in spending, in constant dollars, was 78 percent, still a substantial increase.

Beyle (1994) has documented the increase in the cost of gubernatorial campaigns (see Chapter 6). Although spending increases in gubernatorial races leveled off in the 1990s, they increased substantially during the 1980s. From the late 1970s (1977–1980) to the early 1990s (1990–1993), the costs of gubernatorial campaigns, in constant dollars, went up 48 percent. Some recent races stand out as particularly expensive. A total of $25 million dollars was spent on the 1990 gubernatorial race in California, and more than $11 million were spent in the 1990 races in Texas and Illinois.

Although campaign spending has been shown to be an important influence in both state legislative (Gierzynski and Breaux 1991; Van Dunk 1997) and gubernatorial races (Svoboda 1995), the effects of spending are different for challengers and incumbents. The amount of money spent by challengers is much more important to the overall outcome than the amount spent by incumbents. In general, challengers get many more votes per dollar spent than do incumbents. Unfortunately for the challengers, they are usually unable to raise enough money to overcome the advantage of incumbency. This is not to say that challengers would always be able to beat incumbents if they were able to spend more money than the incumbents. Incumbency carries more electoral advantages than just being able to raise more money.

Candidate Quality. The candidates, of course, have something to do with election outcomes. A challenger with little political experience usually poses little threat to a sitting governor. In contrast, a challenger with political experience, especially elected office experience, poses a much more serious threat, because he or she may have greater visibility and will probably have an easier time raising money than most other challengers. One reason why governors have a somewhat lower reelection rate than other state officials is probably because of the experience level of the challengers they face. Whereas members of the U.S. House of Representatives face candidates with elected office experience about 25 percent of the time (Jacobson 1997, 35), governors face experienced challengers about 75 percent of the time (Holbrook 1991; Squire 1992). Many of these challengers are the electorally secure members of the state legislature or other statewide elected constitutional officers. Studies of both state legislative (Van Dunk 1997) and gubernatorial races (Holbrook 1991; Squire 1992) have found that challengers with significant political experience stand the best chance of defeating incumbent candidates.

National Politics. In addition to the factors associated with the state or the candidates, national politics also influence state elections. Studies of gubernatorial and state legislative elections have revealed that the state of the national economy and the popularity of the sitting president can have an effect on how his party does in state elections (Campbell 1986; Chubb 1988; Holbrook 1987). Salmore and Salmore (1993) suggested, however, that this relationship may be becoming weaker as fewer and fewer states hold their gubernatorial elections in presidential election years. One need look no further than the 1994 elections, however, to see that national politics can influence state elections, even in midterm election years. At a time when the president's popularity was relatively low and the public was still skeptical about the health of the economy, the president's party paid a heavy price at the polls, in both state and congressional elections.

State Economy. But state elections are not purely national events. What happens in the states during the gubernatorial term also has some impact. In particular, there is growing evidence that the condition of the state economy influences voting behavior in state elections. Although the evidence from aggregate studies is somewhat weak, there is evidence from individual-level studies (based on public opinion surveys) that perceptions of state economic performance are closely tied to support for incumbent gubernatorial candidates (Niemi, Stanley, and Vogel 1995; Partin 1995; Svoboda 1995). Specifically, people who perceive of the state economy as doing well or improving are more likely to support the incumbent gubernatorial party than are those who view the economy in more negative terms, all else held constant. In addition, Niemi et al. (1995) found that tax increases also reduce the likelihood of individuals voting for the incumbent governor or the candidate from the governor's party.

Referendum Election Outcomes

Besides voting for candidates, voters in many states also have the opportunity to vote in statutory or constitutional referendums. Many of these ballot proposals originate from the direct initiative, but some of them are also referred to the voters by the legislature. Generally, the odds are against most referendums getting voter approval. Between 1981 and 1992 only 44 percent of initiatives on the ballot won voter approval (Kehler and Stern 1994). Part of the reason for the difficulty in getting ballot propositions passed is that they almost always threaten the status quo, so there is a natural tendency to oppose them. Certain factors can, however, influence the odds that a measure will be passed (Bowler et al. 1992; Magleby 1984). First, spending is important; proponents can increase the probability of winning by outspending opponents. Spending levels in initiative campaigns can be quite high. In 1988, a total of $129 million was spent on initiative campaigns in California alone (Kehler and Stern 1994). Second, ballot location can also affect the likelihood that an initiative will pass. Items at the top of the ballot are more likely to pass than those found farther down on the ballot. Third, measures submitted to the voters by the legislature are more likely to be approved than those that originate in the direct initiative process.

PARTY ADAPTABILITY AND DURABILITY IN AN ERA OF CANDIDATE-CENTERED POLITICS

The theme of change runs consistently through this survey of state political parties and elections. Since the 1960s and 1970s, state party organizations have developed into increasingly professional service agencies assisting candidates and local parties. State parties have also come into the orbit of the national party organizations that through massive transfers of funds plus supplying personnel and expertise now use the state parties to implement national campaign strategies. This nationalization of the parties with its heightened national–state party integration has brought organizational benefits to the state parties, but it has also meant that they have lost some of their traditional autonomy.

Within the states, autonomous state legislative campaign committees have emerged as major party support agencies for legislative candidates. Campaign costs have escalated as candidates have sought to take advantage of the latest techniques and technologies. State regulation of campaign finance has tightened, and an increasing number of states provide some form of public financing of elections. Candidates now rely primarily on their own personal campaign organizations rather than the party machinery. State electoral politics thus focuses more and more on the candidate rather than the party.

Parties, however, remain a major force in state electoral politics. Interparty competition has intensified since the 1970s, as intense battles rage for control of legislative chambers and governorships. On Election Day partisanship continues to be a major determinant of voter choice. In the face of an increasingly candidate-centered style of politics, both state central committees and legislative campaign committees have become more sophisticated and capable of providing an array of services to their clienteles. They have also adapted to the growth of PACs by soliciting and channeling this special interest money. The story of state parties since World War II is thus an impressive record of adaptability and durability. Although state parties on the eve of the millennium neither control nominations nor run campaigns, they nevertheless remain the principal agencies for making nominations, contesting elections, recruiting leaders, and providing a link between citizens and their government.

REFERENCES

Abramson, Jill, and Leslie Wayne. 1997. "Democrats Used State Parties to Bypass Limits." *New York Times* (national edition), October 2, A1, A8.

Aldrich, John H. 1995. *Why Parties? The Origin and Transformation of Party Politics in America.* Chicago: University of Chicago Press.

Appleton, Andrew M., and Daniel S. Ward, eds. 1997. *State Party Profiles: A 50 State Guide to Development, Organization, and Resources.* Washington, D.C.: CQ Press.

Bailey, Eric, and Peter M. Warren. 1997. "Power PAC Steps out of Spotlight." *Los Angles Times,* June 15, A3, A23.

Baker, Donald P. 1992. "Va. Democratic Chief Survives Bid to Oust Him." *Washington Post,* June 10.

Barrilleaux, Charles. 1986. "A Dynamic Model of Partisan Competition in the American States." *American Journal of Political Science* 30:822–840.

Bass, Harold F., Jr. 1998. "Partisan Rules, 1946–1996." In *Partisan Approaches to Postwar American Politics,* edited by Byron E. Shafer. Chatham, NJ: Chatham House, chap. 6.

Bednar, Nancy L. 1997. "Christian Right Candidates Win Again: The 1996 Congressional Elections in Oklahoma." A paper prepared for the Annual Meeting of the American Political Science Association, Chicago, August 28–31.

Berke, Richard L. 1996. "Rifts in G.O.P. Are Widening in Many States." *New York Times* (national edition) May 26, 1, 11.

Berry, Jeffrey M., and Deborah Schildkraut. 1995. "Citizen Groups, Political Parties and the Decline of the Democrats." A paper prepared for the Annual Meeting of the American Political Science Association, Chicago, September.

Beyle, Thad L. 1994. "The Governors, 1992–1993." In *The Book of the States, 1992–1993.* Lexington, Ky.: Council of State Governments.

Bibby, John F., Cornelius P. Cotter, James L. Gibson, and Robert J. Huckshorn. 1990. "Parties in State Politics." In *Politics in the American States,* 5th ed., edited by Virginia Gray, Herbert Jacob, and Robert B. Albritton. Glenview, Ill.: Scott, Foresman.

Bibby, John F., and Thomas M. Holbrook. 1996. "Parties and Elections." In *Politics in the American States,* 6th ed., edited by Virginia Gray and Herbert Jacob. Washington, D.C.: CQ Press.

Bice, Daniel. 1996. "Unions and State Kept Low Profile in Plache's Effort to Beat Petak." *Milwaukee Journal Sentinel,* June 9, 5B.

Blumberg, Melanie, Willing Binning, and John C. Green. 1997. "The Grassroots Matter: The Coordinated Campaign in a Battleground State." A paper prepared for the State of the Parties: 1996 and Beyond conference, Ray C. Bliss Institute of Applied Politics, University of Akron, October 9–10.

Bowler, Shaun, Todd Donovan, and Trudi Happ. 1992. "Ballot Propositions and Information Costs: Direct Democracy and the Fatigued Voter." *Western Political Quarterly* 45:559–568.

Broder, David S. 1997. "Two Called to Serve." *Washington Post,* January 29, A21.

———. 1998. "The Ballot Battle: Collecting Signatures for a Price." *Washington Post,* April 12, A1.

Bruce, John M., John A. Clark, and John H. Kessel. 1991. "Advocacy Politics in Presidential Parties." *American Political Science Review* 85:1089–1105.

Bullock, Charles S., III, and Lock K. Johnson. 1992. *Runoff Elections in the United States.* Chapel Hill: University of North Carolina Press.

Campbell, James. 1986. "Presidential Coattails and Midterm Losses in State Legislative Elections." *American Political Science Review* 80:45–65.

Center for the Study of the American Electorate. 1994. *Primary Turnout Low.* Washington, D.C.: Center for the Study of the American Electorate.

Chubb, John. 1988. "Institutions, the Economy, and the Dynamics of State Elections." *American Political Science Review* 82:133–154.

Cigler, Allan J., and Burdett A. Loomis. 1998. "Kansas: The Christian Right and the New Mainstream of Republican Politics." In *God at the Grass Roots, 1996: The Christian Right in the 1996 Elections,* edited by Mark J. Rozell and Clyde Wilcox. Lanham, Md.: Rowman and Littlefield, 207–222.

Coleman, John J. 1996. "Party Organizational Strength and Public Support for Parties." *American Journal of Political Science* 40:805–824.

Collett, Christian. 1998. "Taking the 'Abnormal' Route: Backgrounds, Beliefs, and Political Activities of Minor Party Candidates." In *Multiparty Politics in America,* edited by Paul S. Herrnson and John C. Green. Lanham, Md.: Rowman and Littlefield, 103–124.

Cotter, Cornelius P., James L. Gibson, John F. Bibby, and Robert J. Huckshorn. 1984. *Party Organizations in American Politics.* New York: Praeger.

Cotter, Cornelius P., and Bernard Hennessy. 1964. *Politics without Power: National Party Committees.* New York: Atherton.

Council of State Governments. 1998. *The Book of the States, 1996–1997.* Lexington, Ky.: Council of State Governments

Dao, James. 1998. "A Political Kingmaker Takes No Prisoners." *New York Times* (national edition), January 18, 23.

Edsall, Thomas B. 1996. "Candidate's Backers Hope to Make Oregon a Liberal Proving Ground." *Washington Post,* January 27, A3.

Ehrenhalt, Alan. 1989. "How a Party of Enthusiasts Keeps Its Hammerlock on a State Legislature." *Governing,* June, 28–33.

Epstein, Leon D. 1986. *Parties in the American Mold.* Madison: University of Wisconsin Press.

———. 1989. "Will American Political Parties Be Privatized?" *Journal of Law and Politics* 52:239–274.

Federal Election Commission. 1997. "FEC Reports Major Increase in Party Activity for 1995–1996." Press release, March 19.

Fiorina, Morris. 1992. *Divided Government.* New York: Macmillan.

Francis, John G., and Robert Benedict. 1986. "Issue Group Activists at Conventions." In *The Life of the Parties: Activists in Presidential Politics,* edited by Ronald B. Rapoport, Alan I. Abramowitz, and John McGlennon. Lexington: University of Kentucky Press, 105–110.

Gerber, Elizabeth, and Rebecca B. Morton. 1994. "Primary Elections Laws and the Nomination of Congressional Candidates." A paper presented at the Annual Meeting of the American Political Science Association, New York, September 1–4.

Gierzynski, Anthony. 1992. *Legislative Party Campaign Committees in the American States.* Lexington: University of Kentucky Press.

Gierzynski, Anthony, and David A. Breaux. "Money and Votes in State Legislative Elections." *Legislative Studies Quarterly* 16:203–217.

———. 1998. "The Financing Role of the Parties." In *Campaign Finance in State Legislative Elections*, edited by Joel A. Thompson and Gary F. Moncrief. Washington, D.C.: CQ Press, 185–206.

"GOP Retains Hold on Washington State." 1996. *New York Times* (national edition), November 20, A16

Greenblatt, Alan. 1997. "'Soft Money' Helps Propel GOP to Victory in Key Races." *Congressional Quarterly Weekly Report,* November 8, 2784–2788.

———. 1998. "California House Race Shapes up as a Duel of Interest Groups." *Congressional Quarterly Weekly Report,* January 17, 137–138.

"Guru in Ohio." *Congressional Quarterly Weekly Report,* November 4, 2977.

Heard, Alexander. 1960. *The Costs of Democracy.* Chapel Hill: University of North Carolina Press.

Heldman, Caroline E. 1996. "The Coordinated Campaign: Party Builder or Stumbling Block?" A paper prepared for the Annual Meeting of the Midwest Political Science Association, Chicago, April 18–20.

Herrnson, Paul S. 1998. *Congressional Elections: Campaigning at Home and in Washington.* Washington, D.C.: CQ Press.

Hill, Kim, and Jan Leighley. 1992. "The Policy Consequences of Class Bias in State Electorates." *American Journal of Political Science* 36:351–365.

———. 1994. "Mobilizing Institutions and Class Representation in the U.S. State Electorates." *Political Research Quarterly* 47:137–150.

Hill, Kim, Jan Leighley, and Angela Hinton-Anderson. 1995. "Lower-Class Mobilization and Policy Linkage in the U.S. States." *American Journal of Political Science* 39:75–86.

Holbrook, Thomas M. 1987. "National Factors in Gubernatorial Elections." *American Politics Quarterly* 15:471–483.

———. 1991. "Candidates, Economics, and Gubernatorial Elections." A paper presented at the annual meeting of the American Political Science Association, Chicago, August 29–September 1.

Holbrook, Thomas M., Maurice Mangum, and James Garand. 1994. "Sources of Electoral Competition in the American States." A paper presented at the annual meeting of the American Political Science Association, New York, September 1–4.

Holbrook, Thomas M., and Emily Van Dunk. 1993. "Electoral Competition in the American States." *American Political Science Review* 87:955–962.

Jackson, Robert. 1997. "The Mobilization of the U.S. State Electorates in the 1988 and 1990 Elections." *Journal of Politics* 59:520–537.

Jacobson, Gary C. 1997. *The Politics of Congressional Elections.* 4th ed. New York: Longman.

Jewell, Malcolm E., and Sarah M. Morehouse. 1995. "What Are Party Endorsements Worth? A Study of Preprimary Gubernatorial Endorsements in Ten State Parties in 1994." A paper presented at the Annual Meeting of the Midwest Political Science Association, Chicago, April 6–8.

Jones, Ruth S. 1984. "Financing State Elections." In *Money and Politics in the United States*, edited by Michael J. Malbin. Washington, D.C.: American Enterprise Institute.

Kehler, David, and Robert Stern. 1994. "Initiatives in the 1980s and 1990s." In *The Book of the States, 1992–1993.* Lexington, Ky.: Council of State Governments.

Kenney, Patrick J. 1988. "Sorting out the Effects of Primary Divisiveness in Congressional and Senatorial Elections." *Western Political Quarterly* 41:756–777.

Key, V. O., Jr. 1949. *Southern Politics in State and Nation.* New York: Knopf.

———. 1956. *American State Politics: An Introduction.* New York: Knopf.

Kim, Jae-on, John R. Petrocik, and Stephen Enokson. 1975. "Voter Turnout among the American States: Systemic and Individual Components." *American Political Science Review* 69:107–123.

Loftus, Thomas. 1985. "The 'New Politics' Parties in State Legislatures." *State Government* 58:108–109.

Magleby, David. 1984. *Direct Legislation.* Baltimore: Johns Hopkins University Press.

———. 1988. "Taking the Initiative: Direct Legislation and Direct Democracy in the 1980s." *PS* 11:600–611.

Malbin, Michael J., and Thomas L. Gais. 1998. *The Day after Reform: Sobering Campaign Finance Lessons from the American States.* Albany: Rockefeller Institute Press.

Mayer, William G. 1996. "Caucuses: How They Work, What Difference They Make." In *In Pursuit of the White House: How We Choose Our Presidential Nominees,* edited by William G. Mayer. Chatham, N.J.: Chatham House.

Mayhew, David R. 1986. *Placing Parties in American Politics.* Princeton: Princeton University Press.

Monardi, Fred M. 1994. "Election Outcomes at the Sub-Gubernatorial Level." A paper presented at the annual meeting of the Midwest Political Science Association, Chicago, April 14–16.

Moncrief, Gary. 1992. "The Increase in State Legislative Campaign Expenditures: A Comparison of Four Northeastern States." *Western Political Quarterly* 45:549–689.

Morehouse, Sarah McCally. 1981. *State Politics, Parties, and Policy.* New York: Holt, Rinehart and Winston.

———. 1998. *The Governor as Party Leader: Campaigning and Governing.* Ann Arbor: University of Michigan Press.

Niemi, Richard, Harold Stanley, and Ronald Vogel. 1995. "State Economies and State Taxes: Do Voters Hold Governors Responsible?" *American Journal of Political Science* 39:936–957.

Partin, Randall. 1995. "Economic Conditions and Gubernatorial Elections: Is the State Executive Held Accountable?" *American Politics Quarterly* 23:81–95

Patterson, Samuel, and Gregory Caldeira. 1983. "Getting out the Vote: Participation in Gubernatorial Elections." *American Political Science Review* 77:675–689.

———. 1984. "Etiology of Partisan Competition." *American Political Science Review* 78:691–707.

Ranney, Austin. 1976. "Parties in State Politics." In *Politics in the American States: A Comparative Analysis,* 3d ed., edited by Herbert Jacob and Kenneth Vines. Boston: Little, Brown.

Reichley, A. James. 1992. *The Life of the Parties: A History of American Political Parties.* New York: Free Press.

Republican National Committee. 1997. *1996 Chairman's Report.* Washington, D.C.

Rosenstone, Steven J., and John Mark Hansen. 1993. *Mobilization, Participation, and Democracy in America.* New York: Macmillan.

Rosenthal, Cindy Simon. 1993. "Partners of Solo Players: Legislative Campaign Committees and State Parties." A paper presented at the Ray C. Bliss Institute of Applied Politics, Akron, Ohio, September 23–24.

Salmore, Stephen, and Barbara Salmore. 1995. "The Transformation of State Electoral Politics." In *State of the States,* 2d ed., edited by Carl Van Horn. Washington, D.C.: CQ Press.

Schwartz, Mildred A. 1990. *The Party Network: The Robust Organization of Illinois Republicans.* Madison: University of Wisconsin Press.

Seelye, Katherine Q. 1997. "Parties Team up to Protect Their Turf." *New York Times* (national edition), June 24, A8.

Shafer, Byron E. 1988. *Bifurcated Politics: The Evolution and Reform of National Party Conventions.* New York: Russell Sage.

———. 1996. "The United States." In *Postwar Politics in the G-7: Order and Eras in Comparative Perspective,* edited by Byron E. Shafer. Madison: University of Wisconsin Press, 12–46.

Sorauf, Frank J. 1992. *Inside Campaign Finance: Myths and Realities.* New Haven, Conn.: Yale University Press.

Squire, Peverill. 1992. "Challenger Profile and Gubernatorial Elections." *Western Political Quarterly* 45:125–142.

Stanley, Harold, and Richard Niemi. 1994. *Vital Statistics on American Politics.* 4th ed. Washington, D.C.: CQ Press.

Svoboda, Craig. 1995. "Retrospective Voting in Gubernatorial Elections: 1982 and 1986." *Political Research Quarterly* 48:135–150.

Van Dunk, Emily. 1997. "Challenger Quality in State Legislative Elections." *Political Research Quarterly* 50:793–807.

Van Dunk, Emily, and Ronald Weber. 1997. "Constituency-Level Competition in the U.S. States: A Pooled Analysis." *Legislative Studies Quarterly* 22:141–159.

Wattenberg, Martin P. 1991. *The Rise of Candidate-Centered Politics: Presidential Elections of the 1980s.* Cambridge, Mass.: Harvard University Press.

Wilcox, Clyde. 1996. *Onward Christian Soldiers: The Religious Right in American Politics*. Boulder, Colo.: Westview Press.

Wolfinger, Raymond E., and Steven J. Rosenstone. 1980. *Who Votes?* New Haven, Conn.: Yale University Press.

SUGGESTED READINGS

Appleton, Andrew M., and Daniel S. Ward. *State Party Profiles: A 50-State Guide to Development, Organization, and Resources*. Washington, D.C.: Congressional Quarterly, 1997. A description of party organizations in each of the states along with a guide to resources for further research.

Cotter, Cornelius P., James L. Gibson, John F. Bibby, and Robert J. Huckshorn. *Party Organizations in American Politics*. New York: Praeger, 1984. An analysis of the status, activities, and impact of state and local parties, based on a nationwide survey.

Esptein, Leon D. *Political Parties in the American Mold*. Madison: University of Wisconsin Press, 1986. A comprehensive treatise on American parties by a distinguished scholar, with significant insights concerning state parties in Chapters 5 and 6.

Gierzynski, Anthony. *Legislative Party Campaign Committees in the American States*. Lexington: University of Kentucky Press, 1992. Analysis of the development and role of legislative campaign committees.

Malbin, Michael J., and Thomas L. Gais. *The Day After Reform: Sobering Campaign Finance Lessons from the American States*. Albany: Rockefeller Institute Press, 1998. A survey of campaign finance reforms in the states and an assessment of their impact.

Mayhew, David R. *Placing Parties in American Politics*. Princeton: Princeton University Press, 1986. An exhaustive survey of party organization in each of the fifty states, with an analysis of the factors influencing organizational development.

CHAPTER 4

 Interest Groups in the States

CLIVE S. THOMAS AND
RONALD J. HREBENAR

If we want to understand the major changes that have taken place in state politics—particularly changes in power relationships—interest groups and lobbying are among the best elements of state politics to study. This is because lobbyists quickly sense the changing needs of state officials and adapt their operations accordingly. They are among the first to detect changes in power relationships and direct their efforts toward these power points. Furthermore, changes in the number and types of groups active in state politics, the rise of some and the decline of others, are indicators of the changing importance of issues in a state.

Although state interest groups are a political bellwether for political scientists, the general public sees them from a different perspective. The public sees some positive elements in them, but generally their attitude is negative, particularly toward lobbyists (Benedict, Hrebenar, and Thomas, 1996). Over the years, much of this negative attitude has been shaped by interest group activity in the states. Such activities include states being dominated by one or a few powerful interests, events involving groups thwarting the public will, and scandals involving lobbyists. All states have gone through eras in which one or a handful of interests dominated state politics to the extent that they could determine what state government did and—often of more importance—did not do. During the late nineteenth and early twentieth centuries all forty-eight contiguous states experienced politics dominated by railroad interests. And as late as the 1960s, for example, Montana was captive to the Anaconda Copper Company and Delaware to the DuPont Corporation. The nefarious activities of railroad lobbyists in states such as Wyoming and Nevada at the turn of the century contributed to the

negative image of lobbyists, an image reinforced by recent scandals involving lobbyists in Arizona and South Carolina in the 1990s.

Although these abuses did occur, today they are less extensive than is generally
believed. There remains considerable variation across the states in the power of
groups, and what are and are not acceptable operating techniques for interest
groups and their lobbyists. In all but a few states the power of the railroads has long
since waned, and many of the old manufacturing, agricultural, mining, and
forestry interests have seen their political power eroded. Although some states still
have one or more prominent interests (the Mormon Church in Utah, Boeing in
Washington state, agriculture and agribusiness in Arkansas, the coal companies in
West Virginia, for example), the days of states being dominated by one or a few interests are likely gone forever. In addition, interest groups perform functions essential to the democratic process, including representation, providing information to
policy makers and the public, and offering opportunities for people to acquire political training.

In this chapter we explore these three elements of interest group activity: (1)
their significance as a bellwether of state politics, including the types of groups operating past and present, their strategies and tactics, and their power in the public
policy process; (2) how and why state interest group systems vary from state to state
and the consequences of this; and (3) the pros and cons of interest groups as they
affect the democratic process in the states. First, however, we need to define some
key terms.[1]

KEY TERMS

An *interest group* is an association of individuals or organizations, usually formally organized, that attempts to influence public policy. There are, however, many
definitions of *interest group* (Baumgartner and Leech, 1998, 25–30), and often the
term is more narrowly defined in studies of state groups. Most often the legal definition is used, confining the focus of study to those groups required to register under state laws and excluding those not required to do so. Yet many groups and organizations engage in lobbying but are not required to register. The most
important are those representing government itself, particularly state government
agencies. Most states do not require public officials at any level of government to
register as lobbyists.

---

1. The data in this chapter come mainly from studies on various aspects of state interest groups
undertaken by the authors over the past twenty years. In particular is the Hrebenar–Thomas study of
interest groups in all fifty states conducted between 1983 and 1988 and two updates of that study in
1993–1994 and 1997–1998. The results of the original project, which involved eighty political scientists, can be found in Hrebenar and Thomas 1987, 1992, 1993a, and 1993b; syntheses can be found in
Thomas and Hrebenar, 1990 and 1996. Research for the two updates of the study, also involving all
fifty states, focused on changes in interest group power, expansion in the range of groups, and changing group strategies and tactics.
    Those contributing data to the 1997–1998 update, which provided much of the new material used
in this chapter, are listed at the end of the text of this chapter.

It is also important to study interest group activity in the entire state capital—not just in the capitol building. Some studies focus only on the legislature, which is certainly the major target of lobbying for many groups. But the executive branch has always been lobbied, particularly the bureaucracy where major policy and regulatory decisions are made that affect a host of interests, and this target of lobbying is increasing (Nownes and Freeman 1998b, 96–97). Although less prominent, lobbying through state courts is also on the rise.

The terms *interest, lobby,* and *sector* are often used synonymously and interchangeably with the term *interest group;* but each is a more general term and they are used in a variety of ways. The term *lobby* always has political connotations (usually referring to a collection of interests such as business groups); but *interest* and *sector* may or may not. They may refer to a part (a sector) of society with similar concerns or a common identity that may or may not engage in political activity, such as farmers or minorities. It is from these similar concerns and common identities of interests and sectors, however, that interest groups and lobbies are formed. Furthermore, the distinction between an interest or lobby and an organized interest group is sometimes difficult to make in practice. This is partly because organized groups such as antitax groups often act and are perceived as representing a broader political interest than their official membership.

Interest groups operate in the state public policy-making process mainly by using one or more lobbyists. A lobbyist is a person who represents an interest group in an effort to influence government decisions in that group's favor. The decisions most often targeted by lobbyists are those concerning public policies, but they also include decisions about who gets elected and appointed to make those policies. Lobbyists include not only those required to register by law but also those representing nonregistered groups and organizations, particularly government.

Finally, we need to explain the concept of a *state interest group system.* This is the array of groups and organizations, both formal and informal, and the lobbyists who represent them working to affect public policy within that state. As one element of the socioeconomic and political life of the state, it is this interest group system's characteristics—size, development, composition, methods of operating, and so on—in its relationship to the economy, society, and government in a state that is particularly important. The idea of a state interest group system is an abstraction, of course, because even though there are relations between various groups and lobbyists representing various interests, never do all the groups in a political system act in concert to achieve one goal.

TYPES OF INTEREST GROUPS ACTIVE
IN THE STATES PAST AND PRESENT

Interest Groups Active in the States before 1970

Before the 1900s there were few organized interests operating in state capitals and what ones there were, mainly business and agriculture, were usually intent on killing legislation, particularly regulations, rather than promoting policies. The fact that most states were dominated by one or a few interests until World War II, and in some cases much later, reflected their usually underdeveloped economies and their minimal role of government (Gray and Lowery 1996, 13–31). The most wide-ranging power within the contiguous forty-eight states was that of the railroads like the Northern Pacific in North Dakota, Montana, Idaho, and Washington and the Pennsylvania Railroad and Baltimore & Ohio in the Middle Atlantic states.

By the 1930s five broad categories of interests had established themselves across the then forty-eight states: business, predominantly business associations and some individual businesses; labor, both federations and individual unions; education, mainly teachers unions and school boards; agriculture, both general organizations and commodity groups; and local government, associations, elected officials and employees. These five interests have been called the traditional interests in state politics as they were the major ones active in the states for more than two genera-tions until the 1970s (Zeigler 1983, 99). However, with the minimal role of state government, entire legislative sessions would go by without any activity by some of the groups that composed these interests.

Explaining Increased Interest Group Activity since 1970

All this began to change in the late 1960s and the change continues today. Not only has there been a marked increase in the number of groups lobbying in state capitals, the variety or range of groups operating has also expanded. A host of new groups and organizations, from individual businesses to social issue groups (for the poor, the handicapped, victims of crime, and so on) to minority groups to religious organizations to good government groups (Common Cause and the League of Women Voters) began to establish a presence as lobbying forces in the states. Five major factors appear to be at the root of this expansion over the past thirty years.

The first is the increase in the level and range of economic activity in the states, resulting in a diversification of business and other interests, though again to differ-ing degrees across the states. Many southern states, for example, benefited from businesses moving from the Rustbelt of the Northeast; high technology has come to states such as Washington, Oregon, and Colorado; and so on. With the expan-sion of economies comes an increase in the middle-class, which has important con-sequences for group formation, as we will see. Second, as state governments became more involved in the economic and social life of their states in areas such as busi-ness regulation, environmental protection, and health, more and more interests were affected. They became politically active either to protect their interest from government or to take advantage of some new state program or benefit. Third, the expanding range and complexity of issues dealt with by government meant that the old general interest organizations, such as trade associations, were not able to deal with many of the specific needs of their members. The result has been a fragmenta-tion of certain traditional interests. Fragmentation has been particularly evident within the business and local government lobbies. Individual corporations and businesses and individual cities and special districts (especially school districts) have increasingly lobbied on their own. Although they usually remain part of an umbrella organization (state chamber of commerce, municipal league), they see their specific interests as best served by a separate lobbying operation. Fourth, a combination of factors—heightened political awareness (resulting from such events as the Vietnam War and the civil rights movement), an increase in the size of the middle class, the transition of America into a postindustrial society—has propelled the rise of many social issue and public interest groups, from environmentalists to gay rights groups to abortion groups. And fifth, although there is less hard evidence for this, changes in the role and competition of political parties has had an effect. On the one hand, the decline of parties has apparently led many people to join an interest group in an attempt to achieve their specific goals. On the other, increased party competition is also seen as increasing the number of groups.

The Interest Group Scene in the States in the Late 1990s

The latest research from the Hrebenar–Thomas study reveals an expansion in both numbers and variety of groups since the mid-1990s. The increasing prominence of several interests that are active in virtually all states is worthy of special mention. The most prominent of state agencies in all states are the departments in charge of education, transportation, and welfare and state universities and colleges. Associated with this rise in government lobbying has been the increased prominence of public sector unions, particularly unions of state and local employees, including police and fire fighters, as well as teachers' unions. Ideological groups, which are often single-issue groups such as antiabortionists and the Religious Right, have also become quite active in recent years. Good government, environmentalist, and senior citizens groups are other forces that now have a significant presence in almost all state capitals.

Interests that do not have a presence across all the states tend to be newly formed groups, such as school choice (favoring vouchers or charter schools), children's rights groups, and family value groups, or those representing an interest concentrated in certain states, such as Native Americans, commercial fishing interests, and professional sports franchises. The general trend for most interests is to expand to more and more states. Since 1990 several interests have emerged that were not politically active before, such as victims' rights groups and organizations concerned with responding to environmental disasters. Still other groups, particularly gaming interests, Hispanics, and pro- and antismoking groups, have expanded their presence in the states. And more groups, senior citizens, and Native Americans, for example, are active in virtually every legislative session.

According to work by Gray and Lowery, expansion of the number of interests in state capitals tells only one side of the story. Although many groups enter the lobbying scene, others leave it largely because the groups cease to exist. Mortality, the authors have argued, is much more likely to occur with membership groups and associations than with institutions (businesses, state agencies, and so on). In general, they have argued that the state interest group scene is more fluid in composition than has hitherto been believed (Gray and Lowery 1996, 124–125, 243; Lowery and Gray 1998).

Besides the greater number and variety of groups, the groups that already exist are lobbying more intensively than was the case in the mid-1970s or even in the mid-1980s. They have more regular contact with public officials and use more sophisticated techniques. In addition, ad hoc coalitions of groups come together to promote or fight issues more often than ever before.

This overview of changes in the number and types of interests active in state capitals is a good illustration of one way in which interest group activity is a bellwether of changes in state politics in recent years. The rise in the number of groups was both partly responsible for and a reflection of the increased role of state government, particularly from the 1970s onward. And the changing role of state government as the "Reagan revolution" affected the states also brought some groups into state capitals that had not been active before, such as antitax groups, individual local governments, groups promoting the arts, and the like. Similarly, the increase in the variety of groups both generated and reflected the much broader range of issues dealt with by state government, including issues about what responsibilities state government should shed as a result of the Reagan revolution.

It is important not to assume that a group's presence or high visibility automatically translates into political power. Just because a group or interest is active in state politics does not by itself ensure its success in achieving its goals. This will become clear when we consider the power of interest groups.

THE PRIVATE GOALS AND THE PUBLIC ROLES OF INTEREST GROUPS

Unlike political parties, which originate and exist primarily for political purposes, most interest groups are not primarily political organizations. They usually develop from a common economic or social interest, as, for example, workers forming a trade union, gays forming a self-help association, or model railroad enthusiasts forming a club. Such organizations promote programs and disseminate information to enhance the professional, business, social, or avocational interests of their members. Much of this activity is nonpolitical, as when the American Dental Association publishes its journal or provides cut-rate life insurance for its members. However, many nonpolitical interest groups are forced to become politically active because there is no other way to protect or promote their interests. In promoting their private goals in the public arena, interest groups perform some indispensable public roles, the most important of which will be discussed in turn.

The Aggregation and Representation of Interests

Together with political parties, interest groups are a major means by which people with similar interests and concerns are brought together, or aggregated, and their views articulated to government. Interest groups are an important vehicle of political participation; they act as major intermediaries between the governed and the government by representing the views of their members to public officials, especially between elections.

Facilitating Government

Groups contribute to the substance of public policy by being significant sources of both technical and political information for policy makers. In most instances groups help to facilitate the process of bargaining and compromise essential to policy making in a pluralist system. And in some cases they aid in the implementation of public policies, as, for example, when the Iowa Farm Bureau distributes information about a state or federal agricultural program.

Political Education and Training

To varying degrees, interest groups educate their members and the public on issues. They also provide opportunities for citizens to learn about the political process and to gain valuable practical experience for seeking public office.

Candidate Recruitment

Groups often recruit candidates to run for public office, both from within and outside their group membership.

Campaign Finance

Increasingly these days, groups help to finance political campaigns, both candidate elections and, at the state and local level, ballot measure elections (initiative, referendum, and recall).

Certainly, each of these five functions is subject to abuse by interest groups, particularly campaign finance. But that does not make them any less essential to the working of democracy or lessen the importance of the public role of interest groups. What is contradictory about the relationship between these private political goals and public roles of interest groups is that the positive public roles are purely incidental. With the minor exception of good government groups, such as Common Cause and the League of Women Voters, and some think tanks, in their private capacity interest groups do not exist to improve democracy or to improve the functioning of the political process. The positive public role of interest groups is a paradoxical byproduct of the sum of their selfish interests.

THE POLITICAL PARTY–INTEREST GROUP CONNECTION IN THE STATES

Three aspects of the party–group relationship are particularly important for understanding the role and influence of interest groups in the states. First is the tension between the competitive and cooperative elements of the party–group relationship (Cigler, 1993, 408–410). On the one hand, interest groups compete with parties. Their competition centers around performing three overlapping functions: acting as vehicles of political representation and influence in securing policy objectives; as providers of information, both technical and political, to public officials; and as sources of electoral support, particularly the provision of campaign funds. At the same time, parties and groups cooperate in several ways. This includes working together to build broad coalitions at elections or to enact policies; interest groups providing funding for party organization operations as well as financial and other support during elections; and parties adopting group policy goals into a party platform to enhance the policy's chances of success. On this last point, association with a political party may be the only chance of success for small or new groups with few resources such as poverty action groups.

Second is the effect of party competition (or lack of it) and of party control on interest group activity and on state politics. Party competition raises political uncertainty because with changes of party control all types of groups may find their vital interests adversely affected. So more groups mobilize to protect their causes (Gray and Lowery 1996, 204, 244; Lowery and Gray 1995). As a consequence, party-competitive states often produce a nonpartisan or bipartisan lobbying community. Lobbyists and group leaders need to support each party, not to the extent that they antagonize the other but enough to ensure access after an election.

Party control affects interest group activity in two ways: by creating policy uncertainty in some instances and clear policy direction in others (Morehouse 1997). When moderate or liberal Democrats control a legislature or executive, their heterogeneity and their support for reform policies often causes policy uncertainty and increased group activity. Party control is also important in giving certain groups an advantage in access and influence. Moderate and liberal Democrats, and sometimes moderate Republicans, tend to favor liberal causes and unions. These interests lose prominence when there are strong conservative Republicans or conservative Democrats in control. The most recent update of the Hrebenar–Thomas study clearly shows that since 1994, when Republicans swept into many governorships and legislatures, business and prodevelopment interests and those favoring privatization of many government services have risen in prominence at the expense of traditional and public sector unions and liberal causes.

Third is the power relationship of parties and groups. This relationship is complex, however, and only partly understood by political scientists. In general, the stronger the party, the more control it has in determining the policy agenda and ensuring its passage. Strong parties also control the access of interests and interest groups to the policy-making process. The weaker a party, the more leeway is given to other elements of the political system to fill the power vacuum. The trend in the states since the 1960s has been that groups have gained strength and parties have gotten weaker (see Morehouse 1981, 101–118; Thomas and Hrebenar 1990, 147–148).

Interest groups have gained strength at the expense of parties for three reasons. First, groups have been more effective in securing policy goals for many organized interests, and this has put them in the ascendancy in relation to parties. Second, they have been more effective sources of information and so gotten the ear of public officials much more than parties. Access often leads to the leveraging of influence. Third, groups play an increasing role in the financing of elections—probably the single most important explanation for their greater prominence and power in recent years.

It was once believed that there was an inverse relationship between the relative power of parties and groups: Strong parties, such as in the Northeast, meant weak interest groups; and weak parties, such as in the South, resulted in strong interest groups (Key 1964, 154–165; Zeigler 1983, 111–117; Zeller 1954, 190–193). Although this may once have been the case, this inverse relationship does not stand up to scrutiny in the states today. Often (but not always) weak parties do produce strong interest groups as in parts of the South and West; but strong parties often go hand in hand with strong interest groups, as New York, Illinois, and Michigan attest. Several lines of research have undermined this two-dimensional, inverse relationship (if, indeed, it ever was valid), including a greater understanding of the relationship and access of individual groups to parties; the fact that strong and effective party organization is not necessarily a constraint on group access and influence and, for certain groups, may even enhance it; and that other factors may affect this party–group power relationship or fill power vacuums such as a strong governorship or a political culture. For example, both South Dakota and Vermont have moderate to weak interest group systems that, according to the old theory, would lead to the assumption that they have strong parties. South Dakota, however, has a weak party system and Vermont a moderate one with increasing party competition. In South Dakota what fills this void is a strong governorship and in Vermont a strong executive branch, plus a socially regarding political culture (Burns 1998; Christy 1998).

Although parties may have declined in power and as vehicles of representation since the 1960s, they are not going to disappear. Both parties and interest groups are here to stay in the states. The symbiotic relationship between parties and interest groups and the unique functions of parties—such as organizing legislatures—will dictate that. However, the party–group relationship does undergo constant change both across the states and within particular states. For instance, the move to the Republicans in many states since the mid-1990s has seen a party reassertion of power—at least for the GOP—in relation to many interest groups.

EXPLAINING DIFFERENCES IN STATE INTEREST GROUP SYSTEMS

The party–group relationship is just one of many variations in state group systems. There are, in fact, variations of some type in all fifty state group systems. Why do such differences exist and what are their lessons for understanding state interest group activity?

At the most general level, there is agreement among scholars that the socioeconomic and political environment shapes interest group systems and that differences in this environment produce variations in group system development and operation. There is both agreement and debate, however, as to the importance of the effects of the various elements in producing such variations. Wide agreement exists on the importance of the level of economic development and on the role of government. There is less agreement on such things as the role of political parties, political culture, and regional and interstate influences. One aspect of this debate revolves around whether the major factors that shape interest group systems are internal to the state, as Gray and Lowery in essence have argued, or whether there is a combination of internal and external factors as the Hrebenar–Thomas study has argued. In the absence of any definitive answers, it is most useful to combine the two perspectives to explain differences in group systems. This is done in the analytical framework set out in the box on pages 123–124.

This framework sheds light on such key aspects of group activity as the development of state group systems; the types of groups that are active; the methods they use in pursuing their goals; the power they exert; and short-term variations resulting from electoral changes and shifts in policy priorities. Not only can the framework be used to understand differences in the interest groups systems, it also sheds light on the particulars of the operation of individual systems. The five categories of factors and their components in this framework are very much interrelated. A change in one may reflect or lead to a change in one or more of the other factors.

INTEREST GROUP STRATEGIES AND TACTICS: TIME-HONORED METHODS AND NEW TECHNIQUES

Interest groups employ a much wider range of strategies and tactics in their never-ending quest to gain access to and influence public officials than they did in the 1970s or even the 1980s. Although modern technologies such as computers and television have expanded their options, group strategy and tactics are still very much an art rather than a science. The essence of this art is interpersonal communications from an advocacy perspective between group members and leaders on one side and policy makers on the other. Effective personal contacts are the key to lobbying success and form an enduring element of any group's involvement in politics, despite the development of modern techniques. In fact, the new techniques are simply more sophisticated tools for increasing the effectiveness of group contacts in the policy arena.

Choosing a Group Strategy and Deciding on Specific Tactics

The essence of any group strategy is the ability to marshal group resources to achieve the goal at hand. Exactly how these resources should be marshaled and managed varies according to the nature of the group, its available resources, the way it is perceived by policy makers, the issue it is pursuing, and the political circumstances at the time. As a consequence, no one strategy is a guarantee of success for all groups or for any one group at all times. This is what makes lobbying an art and not a science and provides a continual challenge to lobbyists and group leaders and gives interest group politics its variety and fascination.

Box 4-1 Five Major Categories of Factors Affecting the Development, Makeup, Operating Techniques, and Influence of Interest Group Systems in the American States

---

Available resources and extent of socioeconomic diversity

Key Elements
Level of economic development and state wealth
Governmental expenditure and taxing levels
Extent of social development and social/demographic diversity

Significance
The more resources available and the greater the level of social development and social and demographic diversity (for example, higher percentage of the middle class and minorities) the wider the range or diversity of groups, but not necessarily the density of groups—the number per capita. The level of state economic development and wealth (measured by Gross State Product, GSP) and the level of government spending makes more resources available for the organization and maintenance of groups, though high state taxation can restrain both. Generally, however, this factor produces a more diverse and competitive group system; a decline in the dominance of one or an oligarchy of groups; use of more sophisticated techniques of lobbying; and a rise in the professionalization of lobbyists.

State political environment

Key Elements
Political attitudes: political culture, political ideology, and public opinion
Political party–interest group relations
Level of campaign costs and sources of electoral support

Significance
Political attitudes influence the types and extent of policies pursued; the strength/weakness of political parties; the level of integration/fragmentation of the policy-making process; what are and what are not acceptable influence or "lobbying" techniques; and the general context in which interest groups will operate and the attitudes toward them. Political party–interest group relations affect avenues of access and influence; group strategies and tactics; in the short run, the specific policies pursued and enacted, among other things. An increase in campaign costs puts increased pressure on candidates to raise funds. The more support coming directly to candidates from groups and their PACs, the more candidates are beholden to them.

Governmental institutional capacity

Key Elements
State policy domain/areas of policy jurisdiction
Level of integration/fragmentation of the policy process: extent to which this process is centralized or dispersed
Level of professionalization of state government
Stringency and enforcement of public disclosure laws including lobbyist registration, ethics, and campaign finance laws

Significance
State policy domain will determine which interests will attempt to affect state policy. As the area of policy authority expands, the number and types of groups lobbying will increase. The level of integration/fragmentation of the policy process will have an impact on patterns of group access and influence. Generally, the more integrated the system (strong parties, strong executive including appointed cabinet, no or little provision for direct democracy, and so on.) the fewer the options available to groups. Conversely, the more the system is fragmented, the larger is the number of access points and available methods of influence. The level of professionalization (including state legislators, the bureaucracy and the governor's staff) makes more varied sources of information available to policy makers. It also creates a higher demand for information by policy makers, including information from groups and lobbyists. Public disclosure laws increase public information about lobbying activities. This affects the methods and techniques of lobbying, which in turn affects the power of certain individual groups and lobbyists, though not necessarily system group power.

Box 4-1 *Continued*

Intergovernmental and external influences

Key elements
 Intergovernmental spending and policy making authority
 The "nationalization" of issues and intergovernmental lobbying

Significance
   The distribution of intergovernmental spending and policy authority refers to the policies exercised and the amount of money spent by state governments versus policies and spending by federal and local governments. Changes in responsibilities between levels of government will affect the types of groups that lobby federal, state, and local governments and the intensity of their lobbying efforts. The "nationalization" of issues such as antismoking, term limits, and stiffer penalties for drunk driving have spawned similar groups across the states; increased out-of-state funding for group activity, especially on ballot propositions; and generally increased intergovernmental contact by all groups, including traditional interests.

Short-term state policy-making environment

Key elements
 Political party effectiveness in government
 State public policy and spending priorities

Significance
   Changes in party control of government, in either the legislative or executive branch, especially when this is accompanied by party, caucus, or ideological cohesiveness, can affect the access and effectiveness of certain groups and interests. Spending and policy priorities, which may change as the result of an election or other event such as a financial crisis, refer to the policies and spending that state governments emphasize at a particular time, as opposed to their general constitutional/statutory responsibilities. Groups directly concerned with and affected by the areas of policy priority will often be given preferential access by government. The extent of this preferential access is related to the degree to which the group is needed by policy makers for advice in policy development and implementation. Thus, shifts in policy and spending priorities will also affect both the access and influence capability of certain groups and the relative power of groups within specific policy areas.
   SOURCES: Developed by the authors from the fifty state chapters of the Hrebenar–Thomas study (Hrebenar and Thomas, 1987, 1992, 1993a and 1993b) and the two updates of the study, 1994 and 1998, and by reference to: Anderson (1997); Brace (1993); Elazar (1984); Erikson, Wright, and McIver (1993); Gray and Lowery (1996); Lowery and Gray (1995, 1998): Hunter, Wilson and Brunk (1991); Morehouse (1981, 1997); Olson (1982); Rosenthal (1996, 1993); Thomas and Hrebenar (1991a); Wilson (1990); Zeigler (1983); Zeigler and Baer (1969); and Zeller (1954).

Two other basic factors about a group's choice of a strategy are important to bear in mind. First, particular strategies are largely determined by whether the group is currently involved in a defensive, maintenance, or promotional situation. A group trying to stop the passage of a law need only halt it at one point in its tortuous journey to enactment. Therefore, it is likely that the group will concentrate on a particular point in the system—such as a sympathetic committee chair. In contrast, to achieve enactment, the group must clear all the hurdles in the process, and thus a more broadly based strategy is required. Between these two situations are those groups that are simply working to maintain good relations with policy makers for the time when they will need to fight for their interests. Maintenance lobbying requires yet another strategy, which varies from group to group. Paralleling the increased activism of state government, one major change in state capital lobbying since 1960 has been the increase in the number of groups pursuing promotional strategies. Before 1960 most lobbying was defensive. In general, more resources and greater sophistication in their use are required to promote something than to kill it.

Second, most lobbying campaigns require a multifaceted approach. Few lobbyists today deal solely with the legislature. This is because a successful lobbying campaign, especially one that seeks to promote something, requires the cooperation and often the active support of one or more executive agencies. Without this support the chances of even partial success are considerably reduced. Moreover, passing legislation is only the first step in effective law making. Implementation of a law is the job of the bureaucracy and in many cases, such as with health care and environmental legislation, this involves writing regulations before the law can be effectively enforced. Lobbyists and group leaders must closely monitor this implementation process as it can make or break the effectiveness of a law.

Deciding on Tactics: Direct and Indirect Approaches

It has become common in academic writing about group tactics to divide them into direct (sometime called *insider)* and indirect *(outsider)* tactics. Although the division is not always a clear one (and not a distinction made by lobbyists and group leaders), direct tactics are those involving direct contact with public officials to influence their decisions, such as lobbying the legislature and executive and using the courts. Indirect lobbying includes activities aimed at getting access to and influencing the environment in which officials make decisions, such as working on election campaigns and contributing money to them, trying to influence public opinion through public relations campaigns, and even mounting demonstrations, boycotts, and sit-ins.

In their contact with the public policy process, according to a recent three-state study, the major activity in which interest groups engage is not directly contacting public officials but monitoring—keeping tabs on the activities of policy proposals and the activities of public officials and other groups that may affect their interests (Nownes and Freeman 1998b, 89). When it comes to direct involvement, by far the most common and still the most effective of group tactics is the use of one or more lobbyists. In fact, until very recently it was the only tactical device used by the vast majority of groups; and it remains the sole approach used by many. Since the 1960s, however, increased competition between groups as their numbers expanded, the changing needs of public officials, an increased public awareness of both the activities and potential of interest groups, plus the fact that certain issues affect many groups have spawned other tactical devices. These include mobilizing grassroots support through networking (sophisticated member contact systems); building coalitions with other groups; and, as we shall see, intergovernmental lobbying activities. It is important to note, however, that such tactics are not viewed as a substitute for lobbying. Rather they are employed as a means of increasing the ability of the group's lobbyists to gain access to public officials and to influence them. Shrewd and experienced group leaders and lobbyists choose the most cost-efficient and politically effective method that they can to achieve their goals. This is particularly evident in the increased use of three tactics: money, the courts, and ad hoc issue coalitions.

Over the past twenty years or so there has been a significant increase in spending by certain interest groups both in their lobbying efforts in the state capital and in contributions of group members, lobbyists, and political action committees (PACs) to state-level candidates. PACs, in particular, have become major campaign fund providers in the states. Although scholarly evidence is mixed regarding the effect of PAC contributions on the voting behavior and actions of elected officials, evidence from the Hrebenar–Thomas study strongly suggests that those organizations that make the biggest contributions to campaign chests also wield most of the influence. There also appears to be a strong relationship between the overall amount of money spent by a group on lobbying and its success in the political process in the states. Money is not the only reason why groups are successful, but it does appear to be an important—probably the most significant—factor. Regardless of the strength of party in a state, the money triangle of elected official, lobbyist, and PAC is becoming increasingly significant.

Because of the role state courts play—like their federal counterparts—in interpreting their respective constitutions, some interest groups have increasingly turned to the courts to achieve their goals. The business community often challenges the constitutionality of regulations. And groups that cannot get the legislature to act or the administration to enforce mandated functions, such as certain mental health provisions, also often use the courts. One of the most publicized uses of the courts in recent years was their overthrow of a statewide initiative passed in Colorado in 1992 to limit the rights of gays and lesbians (Thomas and Hrebenar 1994).

Increasingly these days, viewing state lobbying efforts as being conducted by individual groups can be misleading. Coalitions of groups and particularly ad hoc issue coalitions are increasingly important. To be sure, groups with long-term common goals and a similar philosophy have been natural allies for years—business and professional groups, social issue and public interest groups, and so forth—and have always used coalitions when it was to their advantage. But today certain issues, such as tort reform, economic development, health care costs, and education quality, affect a wide range of groups, sometimes cutting across philosophical boundaries and dividing traditional allies, and have produced a new type of coalition—the ad hoc coalition. This usually consists of a number of groups and may last for no more than the life of a legislative session or for the life of an initiative or referendum campaign. The campaign to deal with increasing health care costs is a good example. In many states it brought together business groups (particularly small business), farm groups, universities, local governments, and social issue and poverty groups.

Lobbyists

Few, if any, occupations are held in such low regard by the general public as that of the lobbyist. For 100 years following the Civil War the flamboyance and flagrant abuses of many lobbyists gave ample justification for this attitude. Although the images linger, the reality has changed drastically. The fundamental changes in American government and politics since 1970 have had a significant effect on the types of people who make up the lobbying community, the skills required of them, and their styles and methods of doing business—as well as an increasing number of women in the field. Overall, developments in the state capital lobbying community have been even more dramatic than those in Washington, D.C.

An in-depth understanding of the state capital lobbying community requires that we distinguish between categories or types of lobbyists. Different types of lobbyists have different assets and liabilities and are perceived differently by public officials. Such perceptions will determine the nature and extent of the lobbyist's power base. In turn, the nature and extent of this power base will affect the way a lobbyist approaches his or her job of gaining access to and influencing officials (Thomas and Hrebenar 1991b). Today's state capital lobbying community is composed of five categories of lobbyists: contract, in-house, government, volunteer, and private individual or self-appointed lobbyists.

Although they only constitute about a quarter of the state capital lobbying community it is the contract lobbyist, sometimes referred to derisively as a "hired gun," about whom the public hears most through the press. This is partly because some contract lobbyists earn six- or seven-figure incomes (although by our estimates these sorts of salaries make up less than 15 percent of the total) and partly because most of them represent the interests that spend the most money and have the most political clout—mainly business and professional associations. Often they represent more than one client at a time, approximately 25 percent of them representing five or more clients. Their percentage in the makeup of the state capital lobbying community has increased steadily since contract lobbyists began to appear in the 1930s; and it has increased markedly since the late 1960s.

In-house lobbyists are the executive directors, presidents, and employees of a host of organizations and businesses from environmental groups, state AFL-CIO affiliates, school board associations, and trade groups to telecommunications companies and large corporations such as General Motors and Boeing. These were the first type of lobbyists to appear on the political scene beginning in the mid-nineteenth century, when big business and especially the railroads became a significant part of the American economy. As a group they have probably always constituted the largest segment of the state capital lobbying community, and today account for about a third of all lobbyists. Probably because of the negative connotations raised in the public's mind by the word *lobbyist*, in-house lobbyists are often given a euphemistic title by their organizations, such as *representative, agent, advocate, government relations specialist,* or, more often, *legislative liaison.*

Possibly for the same reason lobbyists have a negative image—in addition to the fact that governments attempt to maintain at least a facade of unity—no state officially refers to those lobbying for government agencies as *lobbyists.* Instead they most often use the designation *legislative liaison* as well. As we noted earlier, however, in practice they are very much lobbyists. They include heads and senior staff of state government agencies, representatives of state universities, both elected and appointed officials of local governments, and some federal officials. Government lobbyists constitute between a quarter and a third of the state capital lobbying community, more in states, such as those in the West, that are more dependent on government economically. About half of all government lobbyists are women.

Citizen, cause, or volunteer lobbyists tend to represent small nonprofit organizations, social welfare groups, or community organizations. Because they usually receive reimbursement only for their expenses, if that, as a group they tend to be personally committed to their causes. These constitute about 10 percent of the state lobbying community; about 75 percent of them are women.

Private individuals, "hobbyists," or self-appointed lobbyists, who constitute only 1 or 2 percent of the state lobbying community, lobby for pet projects or direct personal benefits or against a policy or proposal they find particularly objectionable. In Florida, for example, one such "hobbyist" stalked the capitol for thirty-seven years. Armed with the concept that "knowledge is power," Nell Foster "Bloomer Girl" Rogers (so named for her distinctive attire) took up issues that affected the lives of "ordinary folks" (Kelley and Taylor 1992, 134). In addition, the category of individual lobbyist has seen a "return of the moguls" in the mid- and late-1990s, as prominent, often very wealthy individuals such as Peter Angelos, owner of the Baltimore Orioles baseball franchise and a prominent trial lawyer, work state government to benefit their economic interests (Gimpel 1998).

The common denominator of lobbyists is that they provide information. Different types of lobbyists, however, frequently have different types of political assets and different methods of access and influence.

Technical knowledge is often not the greatest asset of contract lobbyists, who, as political insiders, are hired primarily for their knowledge of the system and their close contacts with public officials. What they usually possess is special knowledge of certain parts of the governmental process—for example, the budget or a particular department—and so they may be used by legislators and other officials to assist in the policy-making process. In most cases they are facilitators of dialogue between their clients and public officials. Often, they have a great influence on the disbursement of campaign funds on behalf of their clients. Many contract lobbyists also organize fund-raisers for candidates and work to help them get elected or reelected. They usually represent clients with important economic influence, and this fact is not lost on public officials.

The major political asset of many in-house lobbyists is their unequaled knowledge of their particular interest. This knowledge is often supplemented by campaign contributions from their association or business in cash and in kind and by their ability to mobilize their membership. Government lobbyists, in contrast, have only one important tool—information—although they can, and often do, use their constituent groups to their advantage. For example, state departments of education often work, unofficially, with state parent–teacher associations and other client groups, such as those for handicapped or gifted children, to secure increased funding or to promote legislation. As voters and members of the public, these constituent groups can add political clout to the department's attempt to achieve its policy agenda. Volunteer lobbyists usually rely on moral persuasion to sell their causes to public officials. They may also provide information not available elsewhere, but they usually lack the status of political insiders or access to big campaign contributions and sophisticated organizations. Self-appointed lobbyists have the fewest political assets of all, unless they have been major campaign contributors and are major economic forces in their state. These differing assets and liabilities very much shape the way that public officials view these lobbyists, and that view in turn partly determines their power base.

Overall, the state capital lobbying community has become much more pluralistic and has advanced greatly in its level of professionalism since the early 1960s. Although the level of professionalism varies from state to state, its general increase among contract lobbyists is evidenced by several developments. These include an increase in the number of those working at the job full-time, the emergence of lobbying firms that provide a variety of services and represent as many as twenty-five clients, and an increase in the number of specialists among contract lobbyists in response to the increasing complexity of government. One California contract lobbyist, for example, specializes in representing California high tech interests. Other contract lobbyists specialize in representing such interests as agriculture, health care, education, and local governments.

As mentioned earlier, lobbying is no longer a male-dominated occupation in state capitals. Women now make up about 20 percent of state capital lobbyists compared with less than 5 percent twenty years ago. Differences still exist, however, in the activities males and females perform as lobbyists. Women tend to have less experience than men at the job and are more likely to represent religious, charitable, or citizen groups, and less likely to represent business and unions than men. Nevertheless, women use the same methods as men in trying to affect public policy. Furthermore, in many cases women are consulted more often by public officials on some policy issues—mainly social issues, because they offer a contrasting perspective (Nownes and Freeman 1998a).

Do all these developments mean that the old wheeler-dealer has passed from the lobbying scene in state capitals? In the raw form in which he used to exist, as with Artie Samish, the legendary "boss" of California in the 1940s, the answer is probably yes. Today's issues are more complex than they were in Samish's time, and many more campaigns are promotional. The old wheeler-dealer was not much of a technical expert and was more adept at killing than promoting legislation. Still, under a more sophisticated guise, wheeler-dealers do exist today and are very successful lobbyists. Like the old wheeler-dealers, they realize the need for a multifaceted approach to establishing and maintaining good relations with public officials. This includes everything from helping in election campaigns to aiding officials with their personal needs. In addition, the modern-day wheeler-dealer is aware of the greater importance of technical information, the higher degree of professionalism in politics, and the increased public visibility of lobbying. The result is a low-key, highly skilled, effective professional who is a far cry from the old public image of a lobbyist.

THE INTERGOVERNMENTAL CONNECTION AND THE NATIONALIZATION OF STATE INTEREST GROUP ACTIVITY

So far we have discussed state interest group activity largely as though it was isolated from other levels of government. Yet, as indicated in the box on pages 123–124, one important aspect of state group activity is interaction with affiliate and like-minded organizations at other levels of government and in other states. This interaction has always been important as epitomized by the Anti Saloon League at the turn of the century; but it has become increasingly important since the early 1980s (Anderson 1997). Scholars have disagreed on the effect of intergovernmental and external influences on individual state interest group systems. However, a recent study demonstrates that their effect is considerable (Anderson 1997, 214–217). Although differences continue to exist between the levels of the American interest group system, a nationalization or homogenization of interest group activity is taking place. The trend is especially evident in state group systems. There are several, interrelated reasons for this development.

Many state groups are, and always have been, federations operating at more than one level of government and often in all fifty states such as the National Education Association, the Farm Bureau, and the National Federation of Independent Business. Numerous businesses have also had operations at two or three levels of government and in many states. These federations and businesses benefit from the experience and experiments of their affiliates. Added to this is the nationalization of issues such as tobacco, abortion, term limits, and antitax attitudes brought about by the increased communications ability offered by television, computers, fax machines, fiber optics, and greater media attention to politics, and, on the political front, the expanding role of states in policy making and implementation. The result is increased cooperation between groups at the three levels of government and thus the exchange of ideas and techniques. This often leads to interstate and federal, state, and local cooperation between like-minded groups, including out-of-state funding for lobbying campaigns, particularly referenda and initiative drives.

As a result of these developments, few organizations today confine their activities to one level of government alone. More and more, groups and organizations as diverse as the AFL-CIO, American Telephone and Telegraph (AT&T), the League of Women Voters, and the American Legion are finding it necessary to have a presence at more than one level of government. In many cases, largely because of greater overlapping of jurisdictional authority among levels of government, they must be active at all three levels. For example, many national groups that once operated only in Washington, D.C., find themselves having to operate in states and communities. This is the case for the tobacco industry as it tries to ward off antismoking provisions across the country. Such needs have spawned a new breed of political consultant in Washington, D.C.: firms such as Multistate Associates and Statewide who set up lobbying operations in state capitals for out-of-state organizations and firms.

THREE PERSPECTIVES ON INTEREST GROUP POWER IN THE STATES

To be successful in the policy process an interest group and its lobbyist must possess influence or power. It is important to be aware, however, that the term *group power* as used in interest group studies can mean one of three things. First, it may refer to the ability of a single group or coalition to achieve its policy goals. Second, it may refer to the most effective interest groups and interests overall in the state over a period of time such as five years. Third, it may refer to the strength of interest groups as a whole within a state in relation to other organizations or institutions, particularly political parties. We refer to the first as *single group power*, to the second as *overall individual interest power*, and to the third as *group system power.*[2] Political scientists have long realized that power is not the simple phenomenon that the press and the public often believe. In particular, scholars have found power to be one of the most elusive aspects of interest groups to study, particularly the measurement of overall individual interest power and group system power. Single group power is much easier to assess definitively.

Single Group Power

Single group power is defined as the ability of a group or coalition to achieve its goals as it defines them. As a consequence, the only important assessment of the degree of success is an internal evaluation by the group. Some groups can be very successful in achieving their goals but keep a low profile in a state and not be singled out as powerful by public officials. This could be the case for several reasons. It might be because the group is only intermittently active when they have an issue such as an association of billboard owners working to defeat restriction on the size of highway billboards. It could be an ad hoc group coming together on one issue and then disbanding when success is achieved, such as a coalition to defeat an anti-smoking ballot initiative in California or one to defeat a proposal for school vouchers. Or it could be that the group's issue is far from public view and of minor public concern, such as working with a department to write regulations as might be the case with dentists interested in the occupational licensing process. Rarely are dentists listed as among the most effective groups in a state; but they may be among the most successful groups in achieving their limited goals. Many groups involved in the regulatory process are very successful because they have captured their area of

---

2. This is a slight change of terminology from our previous studies. Our recent research strongly indicates that this change more accurately explains group power. We have introduced the *single group power* category because it is an important element in considering group effectiveness but has so far been ignored by most researchers. The overall individual interest category is identical to our former individual group power designation, and the system group category designation remains the same.

concern (in other words, gotten control of policy making) through dependence of bureaucrats on their expertise. The last thing most of these groups would want is public attention and to be singled out as an "effective group."

What do we know about the bases and exercise of single group power? Research has identified certain elements as essential to the foundation and exercise of political power by groups. The three most important elements are the possession of resources (money, members, and so forth), the ability to mobilize these resources for political purposes, and political acumen or leadership (Stone, Whelan, and Murin 1986, 196–208). In terms of the two single most important practical factors the Hrebenar–Thomas study singles out the degree of necessity of the group to public officials and good lobbyist–policy maker relations (Thomas and Hrebenar, 1991b).

Overall Individual Interest Power

This is the aspect of group power that most interests the press and the public who are less concerned about the minutiae of government and more with high profile issues and questions such as, "Who is running the state," or, "Who has real political clout." Whereas the only important assessment of single group power is internal to a group, overall interest power is based on external assessments of informed observers.

There are several problems involved in such assessments, however. First, political scientists agree that the acquisition and exercise of power encompass many factors. Second, it is hard to compare groups whose activity varies over time and from issue to issue. Given these problems, researchers have used three methods, singly or in combination, to assess overall interest power: sending questionnaires to public officials and sometimes conducting interviews with them; drawing on the expertise of political scientists; and consulting academic and popular literature on the states. Our assessment uses the Hrebenar–Thomas study, which combined quantitative and qualitative techniques employing the first two methods. This study has assessed overall interest power in all fifty states on three occasions (1989, 1994, and 1998). The 1998 assessment is set out in Table 4-1. The three assessments, in addition to an earlier fifty-state assessment conducted in the late 1970s (Morehouse 1981, 108–112), enable us to compare trends over twenty years.

First, however, we must be clear on exactly what these assessments (particularly Table 4-1) do and do not reveal. They do reveal the interests that are viewed by policy makers and political observers as the most effective in the states over a five-year period prior to the assessment. For this reason they tend to be the most active groups or those with a high profile. The assessment should not be viewed as indicating that the groups near the top of the list always win or even win most of the time; in fact, they may win less often than some low-profile groups not listed. The place of an individual interest in the ranking, however, does indicate its level of importance as a player in state politics over the period assessed and the extent of its ability to bring political clout to bear on the issues that affect it. The factors contributing to the overall power of an interest are the same as those for a single group.

Comparing the listings over the years, what comes though most of all is the relative stability both of the types of groups that make the list and their ranking. When changes in ranking do occur or new groups appear on the list, the changes appear to be very much influenced by the prominence of issues at the time and partisan control and the ideological persuasion of state government. Gaming, health, and insurance interests, for example, have steadily increased in perceived influence as lotteries and casinos, health care, and tort reform became issues in the states. Environmental and other liberal causes, as well as senior citizens' groups, wax and wane in strength according to who is in power in government. This is also true of business and development interests, which have seen a boost in their rankings since the GOP successes in state elections in 1994. The biggest loser over the past twenty years is traditional labor, though white-collar unions—particularly state and local employees—have risen to prominence and held on even as partisan control has changed.

Today, as over the past twenty years, two interests far outstrip any others in terms of their perceived influence and continue to vie for the top ranking. These are general business organizations (mainly state chambers of commerce) and schoolteachers (mainly state affiliates of the National Education Association—NEA). Despite the major expansion in group activity, however, what Table 4-1 and previous surveys reveal is that relatively few interests are considered to be effective in a large number of states. Only the top thirteen ranked interests are mentioned as effective *(most effective* and *second level of effectiveness)* in more than half of the fifty states. This survey also confirms once again what we have known since the first study of the power of state interest groups, conducted by Zeller (1954): Business and the professions remain the most effective interests in the states (as they do in Washington, D.C.).

Interest Group System Power in the States

Whereas the power of single groups and the overall impact of individual interests is observed in their political mobilization and their ability to achieve their goals, group system power is much more abstract. It is also even more difficult to assess than overall interest power because of the multiplicity of variables involved. The method most frequently used has been to garner the observations of political practitioners and political scientists regarding the importance of the players involved in the policy-making process in each state (Morehouse 1981, 107–117; Zeller 1954, chap. 13 and 190–193). This was the method used over the past decade by the Hrebenar–Thomas study, though this study fine-tuned the way of categorizing and understanding changes in group system power.

What, then, can we say about what factors determine group system power? Reference back to the analytical framework presented in the box on pages 123–124 will help. It was observed in the Hrebenar–Thomas study that there is likely a connection between the political culture of a state and the extent of group system power (first

Table 4-1 Ranking of the Forty Most Influential Interests in the Fifty States in the Late 1990s [a]

		Number of states in which interest ranked among:		
Ranking	Interests	Most effective	Second level of effectiveness	Less/not effective
1	General business organizations (state chambers of commerce, and so on)	40	12	4[b]
2	School teachers' organizations (predominantly NEA)	41	8	1[c]
3	Utility companies and associations (electric, gas, water, telephone/ telecommunications, cable TV)	26	26	5[d]
4	Lawyers (predominantly trial lawyers and state bar associations)	26	14	12
5	Hospital associations/health care organizations (excluding physicians)	17	26	11
6	Insurance: general and medical (companies and associations)	21	16	13
7	General local government organizations (municipal leagues, county organizations, elected officials)	20	18	14
8	Manufacturers (companies and associations)	22	12	21
9	General farm organizations (mainly state farm bureaus)	17	18	16
10	Physicians/state medical associations	18	13	19
11	State and local government employees (other than teachers)	15	19	19
12	Traditional labor associations (predominantly the AFL-CIO)	14	21	15
13	Bankers' associations (includes savings and loan associations)	16	16	19
14	Contractors/builders/developers	11	13	28
15	Realtors' associations	11	12	27
16	K–12 education interests (other than teachers)	11	12	30
17	Gaming interests (race tracks, casinos, lotteries)	11	11	28
18	Individual banks and financial institutions	10	13	27
19	Environmentalists	7	19	25
20	Universities and colleges (institutions and personnel)	6	19	26
21	Truckers and private transport interests (excluding railroads)	6	17	27
22	Individual cities and towns	9	8	36
23	State agencies	9	7	37
24	Agricultural commodity organizations (stockgrowers, grain growers)	8	7	36
25	Taxpayers' interest groups	8	5	37
26	Retailers (companies and trade associations)	7	6	37
27	Individual traditional labor unions (Teamsters, UAW)	6	8	37
28	Sportspersons/hunting and fishing (includes antigun control groups)	5	8	37
29	Liquor, wine, and beer interests	4	10	36

Table 4-1 *Continued*

| | | Number of states in which interest ranked among: | | |
		Most effective	Second level of effectiveness	Less/not effective
Ranking	*Interests*			
30	Religious interests (churches and Religious Right)	3	12	35
31	Mining companies and associations	6	5	40
32	Forest product companies/associations	5	6	39
32	Tourist/hospitality interests	5	6	39
33	Oil and gas (companies and associations)	4	6	41
34	Senior citizens	1	11	38
35	Public interest/good government groups	1	11	40
36	Railroads	2	7	41
37	Tobacco interests	2	6	42
37	Prolife groups	2	6	42
38	Criminal justice lobby (victims' rights groups)	3	3	45
39	Women and minorities	2	5	44
40	Miscellaneous social issue groups (anti–drunk driving, antismoking, antipoverty groups)	1	7	43

S O U R C E :   Compiled by the authors from the 1998 fifty state update of the Hrebenar-Thomas study.

[a] This table is based on a ranking of individual interests in the fifty states conducted by political scientists during the spring of 1998. Each researcher was asked to rank groups into two categories: a most effective and a second level of effectiveness category. Rankings were calculated by allocating two points for each most effective ranking and one point for each second level placement and adding the totals. Where a tie in total points occurs, where possible, interests are ranked according to the number of most effective placements or the overall number of states in which they are effective. See note 1 for a list of those participating in the study.

In some cases the totals for an interest add up to more than fifty. This is because groups within an interest category sometimes appear within both the *most effective* and the *second level* category in a state. For example, utilities are ranked in both categories in North Dakota. Therefore, they are counted once for each category.
[b] These four states are Georgia, Maryland, Nevada, and West Virginia.
[c] The only state in which school teachers are not ranked at all is Georgia.
[d] These five states are Hawaii, Illinois, Louisiana, North Carolina, and Ohio.

element of category 2 in the box). States that have moralistic political cultures, such as Maine and Vermont, generally have less powerful group systems than states that have more individualistic cultures, such as Nevada and New Mexico. Socioeconomic development (first element of category 1 in the table) also has its effects, usually by increasing the number of groups and reducing the likelihood that the state will be dominated by one or a few interests. One factor, however, appears to affect group system power more than any other. This is the relationship between the group system and the strength of political parties (second element in category 2) as explained in the earlier section on the interest group–political party connection in the states. It is probably true that in measuring group system power we may not be measuring the strength of all groups, but only the most powerful ones in a state (Gray and Lowery 1996, 246). But assessing group system power is still important because of what it reveals about the relationship and relative power of political institutions in a state.

Earlier assessments of group system power used only three categories: *strong, moderate,* and *weak* (Morehouse 1981, 116–118; Zeller 1954, 190–193). These are rather general and do not convey the gradual movement between categories. The five categories developed by the Hrebenar–Thomas study improve on this categorization. Table 4-2 presents these new categories and lists the fifty states according to the strength of their group systems in the late 1990s. States listed as *dominant* are those in which groups as a whole are the overwhelming and consistent influence on policy making. Groups in states listed as *complementary* tend to work in conjunction with or are constrained by other aspects of the political system. More often than not this is the party system; but it could also be a strong executive branch, competition between groups, the political culture, or a combination of all these. A *subordinate group system* is one that is consistently subordinated to other aspects of the policy-making process. The fact that there are no entries in the *subordinate* column indicates that groups were not consistently subordinate in any state. This was also true in 1994 and 1989. The *dominant/complementary* and the *complementary/ subordinate* columns include those states whose group systems alternate between the two situations or are in the process of moving from one to the other.

Comparisons between the 1989, 1994, and 1998 surveys using these categories reveal three major things about group system power in the states. First, the changes that do take place are gradual. Two-thirds of the states (thirty-four) have remained in the same category during this period. And the sixteen that have moved have moved only one category at a time: Eight states have moved up in strength and eight moved down, with only one state, Connecticut, moving up two categories over the past fifteen years. Group system power changes more gradually than does individual group power, because changes on a large scale take longer than changes on a small one. Second, most activity involved the dominant/complementary category, which showed the only increase in the number of states (from eighteen in 1989 to twenty-five in 1998). The dominant category dropped from nine to five states, the complementary category from eighteen to sixteen, and the complementary/subordinate category from five to four. Overall, the general movement has been to stronger but not dominant interest group systems. Part of the reason for this since the 1994 survey likely reflects short-term changes because of the close unison between many probusiness and prodevelopment groups and the Republicans who now control many state legislatures and governorships. Third, over all three surveys the South remained the region with the most powerful interest group systems, followed by the West and the Midwest; the Northeast remains the region with the least powerful interest group systems. These regional rankings are all unchanged from 1989.

One final point needs to be made about interest group power in the states in general. Although there are some common influences across the states—namely those identified in the analytical framework shown in the box on pages 123–124—the impact of groups in a particular state is a product of the unique ways in which these influences interact and change. In some states the power of certain single groups and the perception of the power of individual interests may hold firm or even increase at a time when the same groups and interests are declining in other

Table 4-2 Classification of the Fifty States According to the Overall Impact of Interest Groups in the Late 1990s

Dominant (5)	Dominant/ complementary (25)	Complementary (16)	Complementary/ subordinate (4)	Subordinate (0)
Alabama	Arizona	Colorado	Minnesota	
Florida	Arkansas	Delaware	Rhode Island	
Nevada	Alaska	Indiana	South Dakota	
South Carolina	California	Hawaii	Vermont	
West Virginia	Connecticut	Maine		
	Georgia	Massachusetts		
	Idaho	Michigan		
	Illinois	Missouri		
	Iowa	New Hampshire		
	Kansas	New Jersey		
	Kentucky	New York		
	Louisiana	North Carolina		
	Maryland	North Dakota		
	Mississippi	Pennsylvania		
	Montana	Utah		
	Nebraska	Wisconsin		
	New Mexico			
	Ohio			
	Oklahoma			
	Oregon			
	Tennessee			
	Texas			
	Virginia			
	Washington			
	Wyoming			

SOURCE: Compiled by the authors from the 1998 update of the Hrebenar–Thomas study. See p. 141.

states. The number of states that have seen increases in group system power in the past fifteen years is equal to the number in which group power has declined. So although some common denominators do exist across the states, changes in single group power, overall interest power, and group system power often depend on the individual circumstances in a state.

REGULATING INTEREST GROUP ACTIVITY IN THE STATES

Over the years, a combination of concerns about undue influence and corrupt practices of interest groups plus a desire to reach some better state of democracy has been at the root of moves to regulate interest groups. Today, four types of legal provisions provide for the regulation and public disclosure of lobbying activity in the states. Lobby laws are the most important, but these are supplemented by three other types of provisions. We briefly describe the other three provisions first and then focus on lobby laws.

Conflict of interest and personal financial disclosure provisions required of public officials are intended to make public the financial connections that government officials have with individuals, groups, organizations, and businesses. Sometimes these laws also prohibit certain types of financial relations or dealings. In several states, in an attempt to reduce corruption of administration officials, public ethics laws prohibit certain officials from being employed by an interest group within a specified period of time after having been involved in governmental decisions that directly affected that interest (COGEL 1990, 129–148).

Campaign finance regulations provide for public disclosure, to a varying extent, of campaign contributions from individuals and organizations. These laws often impose limits and prohibitions on contributions and sometimes also restrict the period during which such funds can be contributed. For example, some states prohibit contributions being made during the legislative session (COGEL 1990, 87–128).

The regulation of political action committees is another aspect of campaign finance. All states now have laws relating to the activities of PACs. As with campaign finance regulations, states often impose limits and sometimes prohibitions on the contributions of PACs. Many states, for example, limit the contributions to PACs that can be made by corporations, labor unions, and regulated industries, particularly public utilities.

Lobby laws now exist in all fifty states and provide for the registration of lobbyists, their clients or employers, as well as the reporting of the amounts spent on lobbyists and lobbying activities. These laws sometimes prohibit certain types of lobbying activities, such as contingent fee lobbying where a lobbyist agrees to be paid only if he or she is successful in obtaining what the client seeks. Lobby laws often impose restrictions, but their major purpose is to provide public information and throw light on group activities rather than to restrict or control them. Indeed, because of the provisions relating to the right to "petition government" in the First Amendment to the U.S. Constitution and similar provisions in many state constitutions, direct restrictions on lobbying would run into serious constitutional problems.

State lobby laws vary considerably, however, in their inclusiveness, their reporting requirements, and the stringency with which they are enforced (Crain, Haven, and Horner 1995; COGEL 1990, 149–171; Opheim 1991). For example, although all states include contact with the legislature within their definition of lobbying, only a handful include contact with administrative officials within that definition. Similarly, some states require public officials (state or agency personnel) to register when they lobby, but most do not. States also vary in their reporting requirements and in the stringency with which they enforce lobby laws.

How do we explain such differences across the nation among lobby laws? Morehouse has argued that states with the most stringent lobby laws tend to be those with weaker interest group systems (Morehouse 1981, 130–131). This is more or less confirmed by the Hrebenar–Thomas study. It is ironic that these are the states that have suffered relatively few abuses at the hands of interest groups over the years, and thus have less need of such laws. The weakest laws exist in the South, where some of the greatest abuses have taken place. The South's traditionalistic and individualistic political culture and the corresponding ability of powerful, entrenched interests to block such laws is likely the major explanation for this. Still, a state such as North Dakota, which has a predominantly moralistic political culture, also does not have extensive public disclosure provisions. In this case, however, it is probably for the opposite reason. That is, a political culture that looks with strong disapproval on unsavory and illegal activities by interest groups may not want such extensive regulations and, indeed, may not need them.

Given variations among the states in the extent and in the stringency of enforcement of lobby laws, can we make any generalizations about their effect on interest group activity in the states? The greatest value of lobby laws and other lobby regulations is in providing information on who is lobbying whom. Disclosure increases the potential for public and, particularly, press scrutiny of lobbying. Increased public information has probably been the element of lobby regulation that has had the most significant effect on state politics and government.

According to regulatory officials, however, it is not the general public but rather the press, candidates seeking election, and interest group personnel and lobbyists who make the most use of lobby registration and related information. The bulk of the information about lobbyist expenditures and activities is disseminated by the press. So although the public has benefited from these provisions, the extent of these benefits is largely determined by the press. What might be termed *outsider interests* may also have benefited from lobby regulations. Public information has made the activities of their entrenched opponents more visible and as a result more restrained in many instances.

This brings us to the effect that these regulations have had on the established interests and lobbyists in the states. Restraint in dealings with public officials, greater concern for their group's public image, and increased professionalism of lobbyists appear to be the three major effects. Lobbyists, especially those representing powerful interests, are much less likely to use blatant strong-arm tactics. This is, in part, the reason for the apparent disappearance of the old wheeler-dealer lobbyist from state politics and the increased professionalism of lobbyists in general. Even dominant interests, such as the Boeing Aircraft Company in Washington, prefer to use low-key approaches, buttressed by public relations campaigns. The more public are disclosures of lobbying in a state and the more stringently these laws are enforced, the more open is the process of group attempts to influence public policy.

INTEREST GROUPS AND THE DEMOCRATIC PROCESS IN THE STATES

One very important element in evaluating a political institution in a liberal democracy is to assess its contribution to the democratic process. More specifically, to what extent does any particular institution—the legislature, political parties, the governorship, and so on—promote or hinder a level political playing field for all citizens? Because interest groups have long been accused of thwarting democracy, in this concluding section we briefly examine the question, "Have the various developments in state interest group activity over the past twenty-five years enhanced, stymied, or had little effect on the democratic process in the states?" The answer is far from definitive.

There can be no doubt that today more citizens in every state are involved in interest groups than ever before and these groups cover the gamut from traditional conservative business interests to newer middle-of-the road and liberal interests such as senior citizen, environmental, women, minority, and poverty action groups. Development of networking and grassroots techniques aided by new electronic technology has made access to state elected and appointed officials by both group leaders and members easier and much more efficient than ever before. Small groups with minimal resources do sometimes succeed. Public disclosure laws give the press, the public, and potential candidates much more information about the activities of groups and make it less likely that lobbyist–public official relations will involve or give the appearance of corruption. And public opinion can and often does matter much more so than it did twenty-five years ago when it comes to affecting interest group goals, even when a strong opposing interest is involved. This was the case across the country with Mothers against Drunk Driving (MADD) in the late 1980s and early 1990s. But it is also sometimes the case in which strong opposition exists to a majority stance among the public. For example, most states have passed restrictions on smoking despite the well-financed opposition of the tobacco lobby.

Against this we can list many points on the minus side. Interest groups, even in the late 1990s, are still organizations that have a bias toward representing the middle- and upper-middle classes. The mere presence of a group does not mean that it will be effective, and in the end it is influence that will determine success. Moreover, the increase in the number of groups has likely undermined the chances of political success in some ways. The "hyperpluralism" that has often resulted in many states has made success in the process less predictable and even less likely for groups without substantial resources. Public disclosure laws cannot and do not restrict the power of "insider interests" or promote the power of "outsider interests." These laws have a much more modest effect—to create a more open scene for the lobbying game. And public opinion is still often thwarted by powerful interests. This was the case in 1997 when the Milwaukee Brewers baseball franchise was able to secure state aid to build a new stadium despite the fact that a statewide poll in Wisconsin showed that 70 percent of the public opposed such aid (Wegge 1998). Finally, although major changes have occurred in the state interest groups scene in the past twenty-five years, those groups considered powerful have changed very little.

This last point illustrates the crux of why the contribution of interest groups to the democratic process has and likely always will be riddled with contradictions. Resources are the major determinant of long-term success, and often short-term effectiveness, of interest groups, and resources are likely to be unevenly distributed in America for decades to come. In this regard, business and other well-financed lobbies are unsurpassed. In fact, in state after state our research indicates that business has consolidated and in many places expanded its power. An important reason for this is that it has "the advantage of the defense" (Zeigler and van Dalen 1976, 125–127). Another reason, however, is the political experience of business groups and the resources they can employ, which have enabled business groups to adapt more easily than the new interests to the changing circumstances and demands of state political systems. Predictions of many writers a decade or so ago that increased political pluralism brought about by socioeconomic diversity and other advances would result in a general diminution of group power (and especially the power of business) in the states, have only partially materialized (Zeigler 1983, 129).

In one sense public skepticism of interest groups is justified: Money does count, and the more a group has the more likely it is to be successful. Although less so than it once was, the state political playing field is still tilted in favor of moneyed and insider interests.

CONTRIBUTORS TO UPDATE OF HREBENAR-THOMAS PROJECT

Alabama: David L. Martin (Auburn University); *Alaska:* Clive S. Thomas (University of Alaska, Juneau); *Arizona:* David R. Berman (Arizona State University); *Arkansas:* Arthur English (University of Arkansas at Little Rock); *California:* Beth Capell (Contract Lobbyist) and John H. Culver (California Polytechnic State University); *Colorado:* John A. Straayer (Colorado State University); *Connecticut:* Richard C. Kearney (University of Connecticut, Storrs); *Delaware:* Janet B. Johnson and Joseph A. Pika (University of Delaware); *Florida:* Anne E. Kelley (University of South Florida); *Georgia:* Charles S. Bullock III (University of Georgia); *Hawaii:* Anne Feder Lee (freelance writer, Honolulu) and Norman Meller (Professor Emeritus, University of Hawaii, Manoa); *Idaho:* James Weatherby and Stephanie Witt (Boise State University); *Illinois:* David H. Everson (University of Illinois, Springfield); *Indiana:* David J. Hadley (Wabash College); *Iowa:* David Yepsen (*Des Moines Register*); *Kansas:* Allan J. Cigler (University of Kansas); *Kentucky:* Penny M. Miller (University of Kentucky); *Louisiana:* Wayne T. Parent (Louisiana State University); *Maine:* Kenneth T. Palmer (University of Maine, Orono); *Maryland:* James Gimpel (University of Maryland, College Park); *Massachusetts:* John C. Berg (Suffolk University); *Michigan:* William P. Browne (Central Michigan University); *Minnesota:* Craig H. Grau (University of Minnesota, Duluth); *Mississippi:* David A. Breaux (Mississippi State University); *Missouri:* James W. Endersby and Gregory Casey (University of Missouri, Columbia); *Montana:* Jerry W. Calvert and Kenneth L. Weaver (Montana State University); *Nebraska:* John C. Comer (University of Nebraska, Lincoln); *Nevada:* Eric B. Herzik (University of Nevada, Reno); *New Hampshire:* Robert Egbert and Michelle Anne Fistek (Plymouth State College); *New Jersey:* Stephen A. Salmore (Eagleton Institute, Rutgers University); *New Mexico:* Gilbert K. St. Clair (University of New Mexico); *New York:* David L. Cingranelli (Binghamton University, SUNY); *North Carolina:* Jack D. Fleer (Wake Forest University); *North Dakota:* Theodore B. Pedeliski (University of North Dakota); *Ohio:* Cyril Kleem (University of Akron) and Brian B. Anderson (Pennsylvania State University); *Oklahoma:* Jason F. Kirksey, Vincent Burke, Jonathan Winfrey, Robert E. England (Oklahoma State University) and David R. Morgan (University of Oklahoma); *Oregon:* William M. Lunch (Oregon State University); *Pennsylvania:* Patricia McGee Crotty (East Stroudsburg State University) and Brian B. Anderson (Pennsylvania State University); *Rhode Island:* Edgar Leduc (University of Rhode Island); *South Carolina:* Robert E. Botsch (University of South Carolina at Aiken); *South Dakota:* Robert V. Burns (South Dakota State University); *Tennessee:* David M. Brodsky (University of Tennessee, Chattanooga); *Texas:* Keith E. Hamm (Rice University); *Utah:* Ronald J. Hrebenar (University of Utah); *Vermont:* Rodney Christy (Saint Michael's College); *Virginia:* John T. Whelan (University of Richmond); *Washington:* Stephen F. Johnson (Washington Public Utilities Districts Association); *West Virginia:* James R. Oxendale (West Virginia Institute of Technology), Brian B. Anderson (Pennsylvania State University) and Alfred Olivetti (West Virginia University); *Wisconsin:* David G. Wegge (St. Norbert College); *Wyoming:* James D. King (University of Wyoming).

REFERENCES

Anderson, Brian B. 1997. "Interest Group Federations: A View from the States." Ph.D. Dissertation, Pennsylvania State University.

Baumgartner, Frank R., and Beth L. Leech. 1998. *Basic Interests: The Importance of Groups in Politics and in Political Science*. Princeton, N.J.: Princeton University Press.

Benedict, Robert C., Ronald J. Hrebenar, and Clive S. Thomas. 1996. "Public Perceptions of Interest Groups: Varying Attitudes to Business, Labor and Public Interests." A paper presented at the annual meeting of the Western Political Science Association, San Francisco, March.

Brace, Paul. 1993. *State Government and Economic Performance*. Baltimore: Johns Hopkins University Press.

Burns, Robert E. 1998. *South Dakota: Update to Thomas–Hrebenar Study*. Unpublished manuscript.

Christy, Rodney. 1998. *Vermont: Update to Thomas–Hrebenar Study*. Unpublished manuscript.

Cigler, Allan J. 1993. "Political Parties and Interest Groups: Competitors, Collaborators and Uneasy Allies." In *American Political Parties: A Reader*, edited by Eric M. Uslaner. Itasca, Ill.: F. E. Peacock.

COGEL (Council on Governmental Ethics Laws). 1990. *Campaign Finance, Ethics, and Lobby Law Blue Book, 1988–1989: Special Report*. Lexington, Ky.: COGEL, through the Council of State Governments.

Craine, Susan, Russ Haven, and Blair Horner. 1995. *Taming the Fat Cats: A National Survey of State Lobby Laws*. New York: Public Research Interest Group/Common Cause.

Elazar, Daniel J. 1984. *American Federalism: A View from the States*. 3d ed. New York: Harper and Row.

Erikson, Robert S., Gerald C. Wright, and John P. McIver. 1993. *Statehouse Democracy: Public Opinion and Policy in the American States*. New York: Cambridge University Press.

Gimpel, James. 1998. *Maryland: Update to Thomas–Hrebenar Study*. Unpublished manuscript.

Gray, Virginia, and David Lowery. 1996. *The Population Ecology of Interest Representation: Lobbying Communities in the American States*. Ann Arbor: University of Michigan Press.

Hrebenar, Ronald J., and Clive S. Thomas, eds. 1987. *Interest Group Politics in the American West*. Salt Lake City: University of Utah Press.

———. 1992. *Interest Group Politics in the Southern States*. Tuscaloosa: University of Alabama Press.

———. 1993a. *Interest Group Politics in the Midwestern States*. Ames: Iowa State University Press.

———. 1993b. *Interest Group Politics in the Northeastern States*. University Park: Pennsylvania State University Press.

Hunter, Kennith G., Laura Ann Wilson, and Gregory G. Brunk. 1991. "Societal Complexity and Interest Group Lobbying in the American States." *Journal of Politics* 53:488–502.

Kelley, Anne E., and Ella L. Taylor. 1992. "Florida: The Changing Patterns of Power." In *Interest Group Politics in the Southern States*, edited by Ronald J. Hrebenar and Clive S. Thomas. Tuscaloosa: University of Alabama Press.

Key, V. O., Jr. 1964. *Politics, Parties & Pressure Groups*. 5th ed. New York: Thomas Y. Crowell.

Lowery, David, and Virginia Gray. 1995. "The Population Ecology of Gucci Gulch, or the Natural Regulation of Interest Group Numbers in the American States." *American Journal of Political Science* 39:1–29.

———. 1998. "The Dominance of Institutions in Interest Group Representation: A Test of Seven Explanations." *American Journal of Political Science* 42:231–255.

Morehouse, Sarah McCally. 1981. *State Politics, Parties, and Policy*. New York: Holt, Rinehart and Winston.

———. 1997. "Interest Groups, Parties and Policies in the American States." A paper presented at the annual meeting of the American Political Science Association, Washington, D.C., September.

Nownes, Anthony J., and Patricia Freeman. 1998a. "Female Lobbyists: Women in the World of 'Good ol' Boys.'" *Journal of Politics*, 60:1181–1201.

———. 1998b. "Interest Group Activity in the States." *Journal of Politics* 60:86–112.

Olson, Mancur. 1982. *The Rise and Decline of Nations' Economic Growth, Stagflation, and Social Rigidities.* New Haven: Yale University Press.

Opheim, Cynthia. 1991. "Explaining the Differences in State Lobby Regulation." *Western Political Quarterly* 44:405–421.

Rosenthal, Alan. 1993. *The Third House: Lobbyists and Lobbying in the States.* Washington, D.C.: CQ Press.

———. 1996. *Drawing the Line: Legislative Ethics in the States.* Lincoln: University of Nebraska Press, A Twentieth Century Fund Book.

Stone, Clarence N., Robert K. Whelan, and William J. Murin. 1986. *Urban Policy and Politics in a Bureaucratic Age.* 2d ed. Englewood Cliffs, N.J.: Prentice-Hall.

Thomas, Clive S., and Ronald J. Hrebenar. 1990. "Interest Groups in the States." In *Politics in the American States: A Comparative Analysis,* 5th ed., edited by Virginia Gray, Herbert Jacob, and Robert B. Albritton. Glenview, Ill: Scott, Foresman/Little, Brown.

———. 1991a. "The Nationalization of Interest Groups and Lobbying in the States." In *Interest Group Politics,* 3d ed., edited by Allan J. Cigler and Burdett A. Loomis. Washington, D.C.: CQ Press.

———. 1991b. "A New Look at Lobbyists and the Lobbying Community in the American States." *American Review* 1 (Fourth Quarter):2–15.

———. 1994. "Lobbying through the Courts by State Interest Groups: A Fifty State Comparison." A paper presented at the annual meeting of the Western Political Science Association, Albuquerque, N.M., March.

———. 1996. "Interest Groups in the States." In *Politics in the American States: A Comparative Analysis,* 6th ed., edited by Virginia Gray and Herbert Jacob. Washington, D.C.: CQ Press.

Wegge, David G. 1998. *Wisconsin: Update to Thomas–Hrebenar Study.* Unpublished manuscript.

Wilson, Graham K. 1990. *Interest Groups.* Oxford: Basil Blackwell.

Ziegler, L. Harmon. 1983. "Interest Groups in the States." In *Politics in the American States: A Comparative Analysis,* 4th ed., edited by Virginia Gray, Herbert Jacob, and Kenneth N. Vines. Boston: Little, Brown.

Zeigler, L. Harmon, and Michael Baer. 1969. *Lobbying: Interaction and Influence in American State Legislatures.* Belmont, Calif.: Wadsworth.

Zeigler, L. Harmon, and Hendrik van Dalen. 1976. "Interest Groups in the States." In *Politics in the American States: A Comparative Analysis,* 3d ed., edited by Herbert Jacob and Kenneth N. Vines. Boston: Little, Brown.

Zeller, Belle. 1954. *American State Legislatures.* 2d ed. New York: Thomas Y. Crowell.

SUGGESTED READINGS

Cigler, Allan J., and Burdett A. Loomis, eds. *Interest Group Politics,* 5th ed. Washington, D.C.: CQ Press, 1998. A collection of essays presenting the latest thinking on interest group formation and influence in America.

Gray, Virginia, and David Lowery. *The Population Ecology of Interest Representation: Lobbying Communities in the American States.* Ann Arbor: University of Michigan Press, 1996. Results of a major ongoing empirical study on the development of interest communities in the states and how their composition influences politics.

Hrebenar, Ronald J., and Clive S. Thomas, eds. *Interest Group Politics in the Northeastern States.* University Park: Pennsylvania State University Press, 1993. This is one of four books that analyzes interest group systems in each of the fifty states in the late 1980s and early 1990s.

Nownes, Anthony J., and Patricia Freeman. "Interest Group Activity in the States." *Journal of Politics* 60 (1998):86–112. Compares the types of interests operating, what groups do, and the techniques they use in three states (California, South Carolina, and Wisconsin) and extrapolates to provide insights on recent developments in interest group operations across the states.

Rosenthal, Alan. *The Third House: Lobbyists and Lobbying in the States.* Washington, D.C.: CQ Press, 1993. Good descriptive account of the role and techniques of contract and in-house lobbyists in the states.

CHAPTER 5

 Legislative Politics in the States

KEITH E. HAMM AND
GARY F. MONCRIEF

State legislatures provide a fascinating series of topics both for students of institutions and students of individual behavior. As institutions, state legislatures present an array of organizational and structural arrangements. It is probably safe to say there is more variation between state legislatures than any other institutions of state government. For example, some legislatures are quite large (the New Hampshire House, for example, consists of 400 members), and others are small bodies (there are twenty senators in the upper chamber in Alaska, and twenty-one in the Nevada and Delaware senates). The size of the districts represented by individual legislators is quite varied; each member of the Vermont House of Representatives has fewer than 4,000 constituents, whereas members of the Arizona, Florida, New Jersey, New York, Ohio, and Tennessee lower chambers each represent more than 100,000 people. A state senator in Texas has more than 550,000 people in his or her district, and each California state senator represents about 750,000 constituents.

Political scientists often categorize state legislatures by their degree of professionalization, a concept that summarizes the differences between legislative institutions in terms of session length, size of legislative operations, and salary. There are substantial differences between the state legislatures in regard to these and other dimensions (see Table 5-1 for some comparisons). For example, some state legislatures (California and New York) meet virtually full-time, much like the U.S. Congress. Others (North Dakota and New Mexico) meet only a few months each year.

Obviously, compensation for legislators is likely to be tied to the time commitment required of those legislators. In 1998 California state legislators were paid more than

Table 5-1 Classifying State Legislatures

	Average annual salary, 1997–1998	Average annual duration of session, 1996–1997[a]	Total staff during 1996 session
Professional legislatures			
California	$75,600	264	2,610
New York	57,500	193	3,899
Pennsylvania	57,367	347	2,702
Michigan	51,895	351	1,357
Illinois	47,039	133	1,057
Massachusetts	46,410	363	782
Ohio	42,427	360	552
Wisconsin	39,211	365	691
New Jersey	35,000	364	1,514
Hybrid legislatures			
Hawaii	32,000	105	742
Oklahoma	32,000	129	415
Maryland	29,700	90	737
Minnesota	29,675	105	841
Washington	28,800	82	902
Delaware	27,500	177	164
Missouri	26,803	128	524
Florida	24,912	66	2,173
Alaska	24,012	128	405
Iowa	20,120	110	366
Virginia	17,820	53	823
Colorado	17,500	119	260
Louisiana	16,800	119	524
Connecticut	16,760	119	623
Tennessee	16,500	123	283
Arizona	15,000	96	567
North Carolina	13,951	125	464
Oregon	13,104	87	484
Nebraska	12,000	131	250
South Carolina	10,400	162	493
Mississippi	10,000	109	180
Kansas	8,711	135	363
Texas	7,200	70	2,420
Kentucky	4,900	52	583
Alabama	1,040	103	414
Citizen legislatures			
West Virginia	15,000	60	356
Arkansas	12,500	55	456
Idaho	12,360	68	155
Indiana	11,600	133	326
Georgia	11,348	72	742
Rhode Island	10,250	256	228
Maine	9,000	152	180
Vermont	8,186	139	58
New Mexico	5,580	45	94
South Dakota	4,000	67	94
Nevada	3,900	84	490
Utah	3,825	44	225
Montana	3,138	54	229
Wyoming	2,400	36	125
North Dakota	2,160	48	172
New Hampshire	200	165	159

SOURCES: Margaret Ferguson, Indiana University-Indianapolis; Karl Kurtz, National Conference of State Legislatures; Donald Ostdiek, Rice University; Peverill Squire, University of Iowa.

[a] Numbers refer to calendar days in session. If the legislature meets only every other year, the days in session are divided by two.

$70,000 each year. (As of January 1999, they are now paid $99,000.) On the other hand, state legislators in South Dakota receive $4,000 per year for their work.

The magnitude of legislative operations also differs considerably. One commonly used measure is the number of legislative staff personnel. Although the New York and California state legislatures each employ several thousand people as staff, there are fewer than 100 full-time staff members in the New Mexico legislature.

All of these differences matter, in terms of the ability of the state legislature to be an effective and independent component of the policy-making arena. And they matter in terms of the types of people who are attracted to service in the state legislature. To put it another way, the incentives and the costs of legislative service are different in different states. When the discussion turns to state legislatures, the first question to be asked is, "Which state legislature are we talking about?" The capacity, personnel, and to some extent the issues of the South Dakota legislature are simply not the same as those of the Michigan legislature, for example.

These differences, although interesting in their own right, may become even more important as we enter a new century. There are important changes at work in the nature of the federal relationship. As power over certain issues, such as welfare, shifts from the national government to the states, the state legislatures become increasingly important policy makers. At the same time, shifts in fiscal responsibility accompany shifts in policy-making power. Even traditional areas of state responsibility, such as prisons and education, seem to require more and more state legislative involvement these days.

Although it is true that there is marked variation in the professionalization of state legislatures, it is also true that all state legislatures are more professional (based on the dimensions of salary, staff, and session length) today than they were a generation ago. For example, many state legislatures met only every other year (in other words, they held biennial sessions) until the 1960s. Today all but five or six hold annual sessions. If one thinks of legislative professionalization as a continuum, from "low professionalization" to "high professionalization," the fifty state legislatures are spread out along this line. But at the same time, all fifty state legislatures have moved (some only slightly, some a great deal) along the continuum in the past thirty years.

In part, these changes were brought about because state legislatures were thought to be inadequate institutions in the 1950s and 1960s. They were often viewed as unrepresentative of the general public, controlled by "good old boys"— older, white males from rural areas. They met for only brief periods of time and were poorly staffed, ill-equipped, and were generally perceived as being dominated by the governor or a handful of powerful interest groups.

Just as there are important institutional differences today between legislatures, there are also significant differences that bear on the individual legislators state to state. The incentive structure for the individual legislator is different in a part-time, low-pay, low-staff legislature than in the more professional ones. There are also differences in what is known as the "opportunity structure." In some states, for those legislators who are politically ambitious, there is ample opportunity to develop a political career by serving in the state legislature for a few years, then moving on to statewide or congressional office. In other states, such opportunities are extremely rare.

The prospects for state legislators to advance to higher office vary significantly among the states (Squire 1988a). For example, the eighty members of the California Assembly have an abundance of other electoral positions for which they may run, including forty state senate seats, fifty-four seats in the U.S. House, six state constitutional offices, and the mayor's office in several large California cities. Advancement prospects are much bleaker for the 400 members of the New Hampshire House of Representatives, because there are only twenty-four state senate seats, two seats in the U.S. House, and the only elected statewide office is that of the governor.

Although the individual costs and benefits of legislative service vary in different states, it is also true that almost all state legislators behave more like professional politicians today than they did a generation ago. The new breed of legislator displays a distinctive careerist behavior. What differentiates today's legislator from those of an earlier era? One recent study concluded that "most state legislators today spend more time raising campaign funds, are more concerned with district concerns than statewide issues and less likely to spend time learning the norms and paying their dues" (Thompson, Kurtz, and Moncrief 1996, 351). At the same time, the extent of change is not uniform across all legislatures. As one might expect, the behavioral changes seem to be greatest in the more professional, careerist legislatures. Although many of the changes and improvements made to the state legislative institutions in the past generation are positive, it is clear that legislatures are not held in particularly high regard by the general public. There are many reasons for this situation, including a lack of public understanding about how legislatures operate. They are, indeed, complex institutions, charged with solving very difficult societal problems.

Another reason is that candidates who run for legislative office often find it easy to campaign against the legislature itself. Candidates for governor rarely attack the *office* of governor but instead focus on the other candidates who are running for governor. Candidates for judicial positions (in many states, judges are elected) do not rail against the judicial system but instead promote their own qualifications for the office. But candidates for the legislature often campaign against the "do-nothing" legislature, characterizing it as "controlled by special interests," and urging the voters to "throw the bums out." Over time, this cannot help but drag down the public image of the state legislature.

Finally, Americans have never been fond of the idea that politics should be a career. It is clear that it *has* become more of a career in many state legislatures in the past twenty or thirty years. By the late 1980s, legislators in some states were staying in office for longer periods of time than ever before (although probably not for as long as the general public seems to think). The electoral system appeared to be so heavily biased in favor of incumbents that challengers seemed to have little chance to win. The public reaction in many states was to support the movement to limit the number of terms a legislator could serve. Term limits are now the law in eighteen states. The term limit phenomenon is discussed in detail later in this chapter; for now it is sufficient to note that term limits present a significant new challenge to the legislative institution—an institution that is already complex and quite different from one state to another.

THE ELECTORAL ARENA

The nature of the electoral system can have an effect on how legislative politics are played out. Two important characteristics of the electoral system are the *electoral formula* and *district magnitude*. All states use a plurality (also known as first-past-the-post) electoral formula for choosing legislators.[1] It is the simplest of all electoral formulas: Whoever gets the most votes wins. District magnitude (the number of legislators chosen from each district) varies a bit from state to state. Most states employ single-member districts (SMDs) exclusively. However, some states use multimember districts (MMDs) in the lower chamber. Within the multimember districting arrangement, there are further variations. The most common multimember arrangement is the two-member district, although there are a few states with three- or four-member districts (Niemi et al. 1991).

Most of the multimember districts are free-for-all districts, in which all candidates in the district run against one another and the two (in a two-member district) candidates receiving the highest vote counts are declared the winners. Some states employ *post-designate* (also known as *position-designate* or *seat-designate*) multimember districts, in which the candidates must declare for which seat in the district they are running (for example, seat A or B). In effect, such systems operate as a series of single-member elections within the same district.

To some extent, these characteristics of the electoral system make a difference. The role of political parties is probably greater in campaigns and elections in multimember districting systems, as members of the same party tend to run as a team. Historically, women were more likely to be elected in multimember districts than in single-member districts (see Moncrief and Thompson 1992b), although this distinction is probably diminishing as more and more women run for state legislative office. On the other hand, minorities (racial, ethnic, or the minority political party) are less likely to be elected in multimember districts. Because of the potential to discriminate against minorities, many states (especially southern states, under court mandate) eliminated most of their free-for-all multimember districts during the 1960s and 1970s. Today roughly 87 percent of all state legislators are elected in

---

1. This is true for general elections only. In some states, primary elections require a candidate to receive a true majority of votes cast. If no candidate receives a majority in the primary, a second primary election, called a *runoff*, is held between the two top vote getters from the original primary.

single-member (or seat-designate multimember) districts, with a plurality rule. These conditions encourage candidate-centered campaigns and elections.

Redistricting

The terms *reapportionment* and *redistricting* are often used interchangeably in the United States, although technically they are not synonymous (Scher, Mills, and Hotaling 1997, 4). *Apportionment* refers to the allocation of seats within the polity; *reapportionment* suggests a change in the number of seats allocated to subunits within the polity. *Redistricting* is simply the redrawing of the electoral boundaries, without a change in the actual number of seats or districts. At the congressional level, reapportionment does occur after each census, as the 435 seats in the U.S. House are reallocated so that some states gain House seats and some lose seats, based on population shifts within the country. At the state legislative level, the number of seats in each chamber is usually held constant, so the task is not one of reapportionment but rather one of redistricting.

The question of apportionment of legislative bodies is ultimately a question of how we view the concept of representation. In what way do we intend to represent the various interests and components of society? Do we wish to allocate seats to represent social class (as the French once did by allocating seats in their parliament to three "estates," made up of the nobility, clergy, and bourgeoisie)? By religious affiliation (as the Lebanese did, by allocating seats in the Chamber of Deputies and the Council of Ministers among different religious sects)? Do we wish to allocate seats by political units (as we do in the U.S. Senate, wherein each state is equally represented with two senators)?

With the exception of the U.S. Senate, the decision in this country has been resolved in favor of population equality as the basis of representation. The idea is that each person's vote should be of equal value, and in the context of the American system that has translated into equal populations per legislative district. Thus each district must contain roughly the same number of people.[2]

One of the most dramatic changes in the electoral system occurred in what has come to be known as the "reapportionment revolution" of the 1960s. Prior to 1962, the U.S. Supreme Court took a hands-off approach to the issues of state legislative reapportionment and redistricting. The constitutions of most states mandated that their lower chambers be apportioned according to equal population standards, but this requirement was simply ignored in some states. Moreover, many state constitutions provided for equal representation of counties in the state senates (usually one senator per county, regardless of population). The result of the county rule in the senates and the disregard for the population rule in many lower chambers was that many state legislatures were severely malapportioned according to population stan-

---

2. The Court does permit some latitude at the state legislative level. Generally, an overall population deviation of as much as 10 percent between the most populous and least populous districts is permissible.

dards. For example, in both Connecticut and Florida in 1962, more than 50 percent of the seats in the lower chamber were controlled by a mere 12 percent of the state population. In Alabama, 26 percent of the total population could elect a majority of house members (Scher et al., 1997, 23).

The situation changed dramatically when the U.S. Supreme Court decided a series of cases in the 1960s and early 1970s.[3] First, the U.S. Supreme Court reversed its previous position and decided that reapportionment issues were a justiciable matter, and that the courts could (and would) intervene in reapportionment matters. This had the effect of forcing states to honor their own constitutional requirements that lower chambers be apportioned by population. Second, the Court determined that state senates also must be apportioned according to population standards, effectively eliminating the standard of county representation in state upper chambers. The effect of these decisions was dramatic; it greatly increased the number of state legislators from urban and suburban areas and sharply reduced the number of legislators from rural areas. Along with other changes in society (for example, the implementation of the Voting Rights Act of 1965 and the increasing political participation of women in the late 1960s), these reapportionment decisions helped pave the way for significant increases in the number of women and minorities serving in state legislatures today.

The Issue of Minority Representation

Although population equality among districts has been the principal concern of the courts, considerable attention has been given to the protection of racial and ethnic minority groups. The case law in regard to minority interests is complex, convoluted, and still evolving. During the 1960s and 1970s the concern of the U.S. Supreme Court was to ensure that minority voting strength was not diluted. In particular, the Court struck down some state districting plans that had included multimember districts (MMDs). In some places African American populations were sufficiently large and geographically compact so that the creation of single-member districts would likely lead to the election of African Americans to the state legislature. However, by creating MMDs, states were able to "dilute" the voting strength of blacks, subsuming the minority population into larger multimember districts. This practice was particularly common in the southern states. Although never claiming that MMDs were by nature unconstitutional, the Court rejected their use in cases in which multimember districts would have the effect of reducing the potential influence of racial and ethnic minorities.[4]

During the 1980s and 1990s, however, the approach became different. Based in part on case law,[5] but largely on directives from the U.S. Department of Justice, em-

---

3. There are many important cases bearing on state legislative reapportionment–redistricting issues, but early cases of significance include *Baker v. Carr* (369 U.S. 186 [1962]); *Reynolds v. Sims* (377 U.S. 533 [1964]); *Lucas v. Forty-Fourth General Assembly of Colorado* (377 U.S. 713 [1964]); *Whitcomb v. Chavis* (403 U.S. 124 [1971]), and *White v. Regester* (412 U.S. 755 [1973]).

4. See, for example, *Whitcomb v. Chavis* and *White v. Regester*.

5. See, in particular, *Thornburg v. Gingles* (478 U.S. 30 [1986]).

phasis was placed on maximizing the number of districts in which racial minorities constituted a majority. Many state legislatures engaged in "affirmative gerrymandering," drawing district lines in such a way as to maximize the number of districts in which minorities constitute a significant majority of district voters. This often led to the convention of oddly shaped districts.

It also had potential partisan consequences. The creation of "majority–minority districts" (wherein the district lines are drawn in such a way that the targeted minority group makes up a majority of the population in the district) means that fewer members of the minority group will exist in other districts. Some minority groups, especially African Americans, tend to vote overwhelmingly for candidates from the Democratic party. Although majority–minority districts may be heavily Democratic, that party's strength in the remaining districts may be weakened in favor of the Republican party. The extent to which the creation of majority–minority districts actually enhanced the Republican party's fortunes in the southern states is a matter of some debate, but it probably was a contributing factor to the GOP surge in southern state legislatures in the 1990s.

Regardless of the potential partisan effects, it is clear that the effort to maximize the number of majority–minority districts contributed to the increase in the number of minority legislators in some states. However, the U.S. Supreme Court, in a series of cases in the mid- to late-1990s, indicated an unwillingness to continue the move toward "affirmative gerrymandering."[6] At this point the issue is unsettled, but it is likely that the approach taken by most states in the next reapportionment cycle will not be one that seeks to maximize majority–minority districts.

The Legislative Consequences of the Electoral System

Electoral systems are often judged in terms of the manner in which they translate electoral votes into legislative seats. The issue is the extent to which a particular percentage of votes (say, 40 percent) yields a commensurate percentage of seats in the legislative chamber. A system in which the votes-to-seats ratio is 1 (for example, 40 percent of the votes and 40 percent of the seats, or 40:40 = 1.00) is said to be proportional. The dominant system in the United States, single-member districts with plurality, tends to be *disproportional* (Cox 1997, 58). Specifically, the party that receives the most votes statewide will almost always receive an even higher percentage of seats in the legislature. Thus the party that receives, say 55 percent of the popular vote statewide will usually command 60 to 65 percent of the legislative seats. This results in what Patterson (1995, 165) has called "manufactured majorities," by which the electoral majority party will usually have a comfortable governing majority.

Moreover, the relative weakness of party loyalty among American voters means that individual candidates have a strong incentive to cultivate a "personal vote" among the electorate. The upshot is that American elections, both at the national

---

6. See, for example, *Abrams v. Johnson*, (No. 95-1425 [1997]); *Shaw v. Hunt* (116 S. Ct. 1894 [1996]); *Johnson v. DeGrandy* (512 U.S. 997 [1994]).

and state levels, are basically candidate-centered (rather than party-centered) contests. Running for the legislature puts a premium on personal ambition and drive, devotion to the local district and its needs, and attention to the political issues that can help mobilize voter support in the district.

On the other hand, the role of the legislature in governing the state requires a much different set of skills. First of all, it requires collective action, which in turn requires bargaining, negotiation, and compromise. This dilemma of legislative representation—serving the constituency and making policy for the state—provides the strain and conflict that makes legislative life both interesting and frustrating. This tension between the electoral needs of individual legislators and the policy-making needs of the legislative institution appears to be particularly great today (Rosenthal 1998).

RUNNING FOR THE LEGISLATURE

It is surprising that so little is known about the candidates for state legislative office. There has not been a systematic study of candidate recruitment at the state legislative level in more than twenty years. Such studies were relatively commonplace in the 1960s and even into the 1970s. But so much has changed in the campaign and electoral environment of state politics that we do not know if the findings from those earlier studies are still relevant.

In particular, there are three trends that may have changed the context of candidate recruitment in many states. First, as explained in Chapter 2, one of the significant political forces in American politics today is devolution—the transfer of some political power from the federal government to the states. Second, within the policy-making arena of the states, the legislatures have become more important. Beginning in the late 1960s, state legislatures underwent a modernization movement designed to increase their capacities to perform the tasks of policy making, oversight, and constituent service. These efforts led to "what is perhaps the most dramatic metamorphosis of any set of U.S. political institutions in living memory" (Mooney 1995, 47). Third, there is a belief that as the *institution* of the state legislature changed, so did the *individuals* serving as legislators. Much has been written about the "new breed" of American politician who sees politics as a career (Ehrenhalt 1991; Loomis 1988; Rosenthal 1998). This latter point is particularly relevant, because it suggests that the type of people recruited into the state legislatures today are somehow different than those who previously served. Whether there is a "new breed" or not is unclear. But what is certain is that the cost–benefit structure for serving in the state legislature has changed in many states and this probably has contributed to changes in the nature of recruitment.

Factors Affecting Candidacy

Candidate recruitment is a product of many factors, including the nature of the state political system *(systemic variables)*, the political conditions in the specific legislative district *(district variables)*, and the individual attributes and decision-making calculus of the potential candidates themselves *(personal variables)*. All these factors will enter, to varying degrees, into the determination of who runs for state legislative office.

Systemic Variables

THE NOMINATING SYSTEM.   In most countries, the political party structure is crucial in determining who among potential candidates will serve as the party nominee. But the adoption of the direct primary election in the American states complicates the recruitment role of parties. For example, research has shown that open, blanket, and nonpartisan primaries hamper the ability of the political party to nominate the candidate of its choice (Tobin and Keynes 1975). On the other hand, in those states in which closed primaries or district conventions are used as nominating devices the party maintains more control over the process. A few states still have a procedure allowing the party to endorse a specific candidate prior to the primary election. As one would expect, the endorsed candidate wins most of the time (Jewell and Olson 1988), and this strengthens the role of the party in the nomination process.

LEGISLATIVE PROFESSIONALIZATION.   It is widely understood that state legislatures vary in terms of factors such as salary, staffing, and session length, and that these factors define some relative degree of professional or amateur status of the legislature. The sorts of people attracted to legislative service vary with the legislature's level of professionalization, as mentioned in the beginning of this chapter (see Squire 1992).

Recently, several observers have suggested that professional state legislatures may have a differential effect on the recruitment patterns of Democrats compared to Republicans (Ehrenhalt 1991; Fiorina 1996). The argument is that Republicans find full-time legislative service less enticing because they must give up more lucrative positions in the private sector to serve in a full-time, professional state legislature. For Democrats in more professional legislatures, "legislative service now becomes an attractive career, probably better compensated and more highly regarded than their present careers" (Fiorina 1994, 307).

THE ELECTORAL OPPORTUNITY STRUCTURE.   Political ambition is channeled through the opportunity structure available in each state (Schlesinger 1966). And this opportunity structure may be quite different in one state compared to another. It is dependent, in part, on the nature of party competition and the number of political offices available in the state. Squire (1988a) has shown that career patterns and turnover in state legislatures are related to this opportunity structure. Specifically, different types of state legislatures are associated with different types of political ambition.

CAMPAIGN FINANCE SYSTEM.   The financial investment required to run a credible campaign for a state legislature varies dramatically between the states, ranging from several thousand dollars in states such as Montana, to several hundred thousand dollars in states such as California (Hogan and Hamm 1998; Moncrief 1998). Moreover, the campaign finance regulations differ among the states in terms of availability of public funding and in terms of the ceiling (or lack thereof) on contribution limits. Such regulations may affect the prospective candidate's assessment of how competitive he or she can be in the election. In some states, the regulations limit the role of political parties in "hard money" contributions, and therefore may limit the influence the party can have on the outcome of the election.

Changes in campaign finance laws may have consequences for candidate recruitment. For example, it has been suggested that Maine's new campaign finance law, which allows for full public funding of state legislative candidates, may lead to many more candidates filing for state legislative office—including more independent and third-party candidates (Maisel and Ivry 1997, 35).

COMPETITIVENESS OF THE POLITICAL PARTIES. It is likely that recruitment patterns vary depending on the competitiveness between the political parties within a state (Wahlke et al. 1962). A competitive party system means both parties have a legitimate chance to organize the government, depending on the outcome in any given election year. A legislative seat is more attractive if one's party controls the chamber.

The role played by either the state party leadership or the legislative leadership appears to be growing in some states, as the seat margins between majority and minority party status have narrowed, particularly in the South. Today there are many fewer one-party dominant chambers in state legislatures than there were a generation ago. For example, in 1960 there were fifty-eight state legislative chambers in which the majority party held at least 65 percent of the seats; by 1996 such a dominant majority existed in only thirty-one chambers.

There is evidence that the Republican Party, in particular, has been actively recruiting state legislative candidates in some southern states (Bullock and Shafer 1997; Cassie 1994). State legislative leaders also appear to be more active in seeking quality candidates (Gierzynski 1992; Jewell and Whicker 1994; C. S. Rosenthal 1995; Shea 1995).

TERM LIMITS. Almost 40 percent of the states now limit the time an individual legislator can serve in the office. The specifics of the limits vary from state to state (see later discussion), but there is considerable speculation that term limits may alter recruitment patterns in some states. For example, in those states in which legislators will be restricted to just a few years in office, ambitious politicians may bypass state legislative office altogether in their quest for a secure political career. In some instances, term limits may encourage more minorities and women to become candidates, because incumbents—most of whom are white males—will be barred from running again. Preliminary empirical analysis does not find much evidence to support this assertion (Carey, Niemi, and Powell 1998). However, limits are not yet fully implemented in most term-limited states, so it is too early to accurately assess the effect.

Legislative District Characteristics.

INCUMBENTS, CHALLENGERS, AND OPEN SEATS. One of the important determinants of the field of contestants in any given election is whether or not there is an incumbent in the race. The advantages of incumbency in state legislative elections are well documented (see later discussion). The percentage of uncontested races is greatest when an incumbent is running; as many as 40 to 60 percent of such races are uncontested in some states (Breaux and Jewell 1992, 103).

ROLE OF LOCAL SUPPORT GROUPS. In addition to the recruitment role played by state political parties or legislative campaign committees, the local political organization may be an important factor (Gibson, Frendreis, and Vertz 1989; Frendreis et al. 1996, 160). The recruitment role of local party organizations differs greatly from state to state. For example, in New Jersey—a state known for strong local party organizations—more than 45 percent of nonincumbent legislative candidates recently reported that they were recruited by the local party, whereas only 25 percent of the candidates in Virginia made the same claim (Moncrief, Squire, and Kurtz 1998).

DISTRICT MAGNITUDE. Several studies find that the incumbency advantage in multimember districts (MMDs) is somewhat smaller than in single-member districts (Carey, Niemi, and Powell 1997; Cox and Morgenstern 1995). If incumbents in MMDs are indeed more vulnerable, then we may expect that candidates are more likely to emerge as challengers in multimember districts than in single-member districts. Moreover, because of electoral self-interest, incumbents in MMDs are likely to take an active role in recruiting candidates to run with them as part of the "team" in the district.

DISTRICT MARGINALITY. It is the case that many state legislative districts are safe for one party or the other. The safeness or competitiveness of the district is often based as much on the distribution of party voters within the district as it is on the presence or absence of an incumbent. For example, as much as 50 percent of the open seats (in other words, no incumbent was running) for the Kentucky General Assembly were uncontested (Breaux and Jewell 1992). In cases in which one party is decidedly advantaged in a district, the recruitment process is likely to be much different in the majority party compared to the minority party.

The combination of local party strength and incumbency advantage means that many state legislative districts are uncontested. For example, 48 percent of the General Assembly seats in the 1996 Rhode Island election (Moakley 1997, 107), and more than 50 percent of the house seats in Idaho in 1998 were uncontested.

Personal Attributes.

PERSONAL RESOURCES. Such resources include the time available to commit to both the campaign and legislative service. Obviously, the prospective candidate's assessment of time available will depend on both their personal situation and the relative professionalization of the legislature (especially the length of the session). Personal financial resources may also be a consideration, both in terms of the ability to help finance the campaign and in terms of the salary inducements available through legislative service.

GENDER AND RACE. It is possible that recruitment patterns differ by gender or race, at least in some states. We have already noted that the electoral structure may have an effect on the likelihood that women or minorities will be elected. It is also possible that the social network, which can be important in the recruitment process, will differ to some extent. Several recent studies find that women serving in today's state legislatures exhibit a different set of background characteristics than women who served several decades ago (Dolan and Ford 1997; Williams 1990).

ELECTIONS

State legislative elections have been the subject of intense study in the past decade. The consequence is that our understanding of state legislative electoral patterns has been significantly expanded. The following discussion focuses on the extent to which Democrats and Republicans contest elections, are competitive, and win. Attention is then turned to explanations for these outcomes.

Electoral Contestation, Competition, and Winning

The first step in the electoral process involves selecting candidates by the major parties. In most states this decision is made in a party primary. Key issues involve who may vote in the primary and what percentage of the vote determines the winner. In most states, the primary winner is determined by a simple plurality. For example, if candidates *X, Y,* and *Z* contest the Republican primary for a specific state legislative seat, and they receive 25 percent, 36 percent, and 39 percent of the vote, respectively, then candidate *Z* would receive the Republican nomination. However, some states require the primary winner to receive a majority of the vote. In this example, a runoff primary would then be held between the two top vote getters *(Y* and *Z)* to determine who would receive the party's nomination for the general election contest.

The general election is typically a contest between Democrats and Republicans, although a smattering of third-party candidates (for example, the Libertarian Party) and independents are sometimes on the ballot. How frequently does a contest between Democrats and Republicans occur?[7] Table 5-2 provides information to help answer this question (see Anderson 1997). The states are divided into two groups. The first group, labeled *competitive,* consists of states that have a long history of electoral competition. The second group, labeled *transforming,* consists of states that moved from one-party status in the late 1960s to a more competitive position in the 1990s. The group consists of ten southern states plus Oklahoma, Maryland, Kentucky, Nevada, New Mexico, and Missouri.

In the traditionally competitive group, more than 75 percent of the general election races were contested by both Democrats and Republicans. But this average masks substantial differences between the states. In five states—New Jersey, California, Connecticut, Michigan, and New York—a candidate for each party entered in

---

7. As defined in this study, a contested race is one in which the losing party received at least 10 percent of the vote.

Table 5-2 Level of Two-Party Contestation and Two-Party Competition in State Legislative Houses: 1968–1995 (in percentages)

States with competitive chambers	Two-party contestation	Two-party competition
New Jersey	99	47
California	93	25
Connecticut	92	44
Michigan	91	26
New York	90	22
Ohio	90	27
North Dakota	89	66
Washington	87	43
Oregon	86	44
Alaska	84	50
Pennsylvania	82	27
Utah	82	43
Indiana	81	46
South Dakota	80	56
Iowa	79	46
Colorado	78	41
Maine	77	39
Montana	77	47
Wisconsin	76	32
Delaware	74	38
Wyoming	73	47
Kansas	71	37
Rhode Island	70	27
West Virginia	69	40
Idaho	64	35
Hawaii	63	22
New Hampshire	58	30
Arizona	56	29
Illinois	54	23
Massachusetts	44	17

States with transforming chambers	Two-party contestation	Two-party competition
Nevada	77	37
Maryland	63	26
North Carolina	63	37
New Mexico	60	30
Missouri	46	19
Virginia	44	26
Oklahoma	38	17
Florida	37	20
South Carolina	36	16
Kentucky	33	17
Tennessee	33	17
Texas	29	13
Alabama	26	10
Mississippi	22	10
Georgia	19	9
Arkansas	8	3

SOURCE: Adapted from Anderson, 1997.

at least 90 percent of the races, but in Massachusetts, Illinois, and Arizona it only occurred in approximately one in two races. In the transforming states, the mean level of contestation is about 43 percent, indicating that in a majority of cases only one party, typically the Democrats, fielded a candidate. As expected, the states in the South have tended to have the lowest level of contestation. The most extreme case is Arkansas in which only 8 percent of the races were contested, whereas in Georgia, Mississippi, Alabama, and Texas fewer than one in three general election races had two candidates.

Has contestation for state legislative office increased or decreased since the late 1960s? The general trend in the thirty competitive chambers is a decrease in two-party contestation for legislative seats. In Wisconsin, Indiana, Rhode Island, Iowa, and Delaware, the change is dramatic. For example, in the 1968 election 92 percent of the seats for the Iowa House were contested; in 1994 this figure dropped to 60 percent. Only Illinois shows a strong upswing in seat contestation, most likely the result of a change in the state's electoral system. Most southern chambers also show increases in two-party contestation over time.[8] This increase in contestation is a result of a greater number of Republicans challenging Democrats. The most significant Republican increases occur in Alabama, Texas, Oklahoma, and Florida. Over time, Democrats have contested significantly fewer seats in several states—Texas, Virginia, South Carolina, Alabama, Mississippi, Florida, and North Carolina (Anderson 1997).

It is one thing for a party to simply contest a legislative seat; it is quite another thing to be truly competitive—that is, to have a reasonable chance to win the seat. Some legislative districts are so dominated by one party that the opposition party has little chance of winning even when they contest the election. Such a situation makes it more difficult to recruit quality candidates for the losing party. How competitive are the two parties in the states? If we define "competitive" as the case in which the loser received at least 40 percent of the vote, we again see substantial differences among the states. The greatest proportions of competitive races are in North Dakota (66 percent), South Dakota (56 percent), and Alaska (50 percent). In some states, especially those labeled "transforming" in Table 5-2, we find a much lower incidence of competitive races. Only 10 percent of the races in Alabama and Mississippi are truly competitive; in Georgia and Arkansas the figure is less than 10 percent.

By averaging the figures over the 1968–1995 time period, Table 5-2 masks some important trends over time. In most of the states in the competitive category, the percentage of competitive races has actually declined since the late 1960s.[9] On the other hand, in many of the transforming states, the percentage of competitive races has increased as the Republican Party has made significant gains in some southern and border states (Anderson 1997).

8. This change is statistically significant only for seats in the Georgia House.
9. This trend is statistically significant in eighteen states.

Contestation and competition are important, but winning is ultimately what counts. An examination of the share of state legislative seats won by the two parties since 1960 underscores several trends. First, the greatest change has occurred in the southern states. In 1960, the Democrats won 94 percent of all races in the South, but by 1996 this figure had fallen to just 62 percent. In 1999 the Republicans claimed majority control in five southern chambers—Florida Senate and House, North Carolina House, South Carolina House, Texas Senate, and Virginia Senate. Second, in nonsouthern states the percentage of seats won by the two parties has fluctuated. Republicans won 62 percent of the seats in 1968, but tumbled to 41 percent in 1974, probably as a result of the effects of the Watergate scandal. Third, since 1962 the president's party had always lost seats in mid-term elections until 1998, when Democrats actually gained about three dozen seats; losses average 253 seats in state houses and fifty-four seats in state senates. In the past nine presidential elections, the president's party has won seats in six elections and lost them in three. President Clinton's coattails have not been long. The Democrats lost eighty-eight state house seats and sixty-two state senate seats in 1992; in 1996 they lost twenty-one senate seats but gained seventy-four house seats (National Conference of State Legislatures 1996c).

What Affects Legislative Election Outcomes?

In analyzing state legislative elections, one can view the contests in either of two ways. One perspective sees state legislative elections as battles between Democrats and Republicans; thus the focus is on trying to explain the percentage of the vote received by each party. A second perspective conceptualizes the battle as one between incumbents versus challengers. This view is more candidate-centered and focuses on what influences the percentage of the vote received by each type of candidate, regardless of party. From either perspective, election outcomes are conceptualized as a function of some combination of incumbency, campaign expenditures, past party strength, and, to a lesser extent, characteristics of the challenger (for example, quality of the challenger) and officeholder (for example, voting record).

Party Strength. In states in which political parties are competitive, election outcomes are often affected by the partisan makeup of the district. Studies of Iowa, California, and Washington demonstrate the importance of party strength in the district on election outcomes (Caldeira and Patterson 1982; Tucker and Weber 1987). The impact of party strength, however, varies across the states. It is apparently more important in Michigan and New York than in California (Gierzynski and Breaux 1993, 522–523). In addition, the electoral impact of district party strength is greater in some years than in others (Tucker and Weber 1987).

The tumultuous events of the 1994 election point out the potential volatility of the electorate and initially call into question the impact of party strength. In 1994 the Republicans captured not only the U.S. House of Representatives but took control of seventeen state chambers, gaining a total of 354 lower house seats and 106 state senate seats (Van Dunk and Holbrook 1994). Outside the South, the Democratic share of seats won was the lowest since the 1968 election. Nonetheless, an analysis of the pattern of control of lower house seats during 1992–1996 in eight states shows that 82 percent were won by the same party in all three elections (Frendreis and Gitelson 1997). Part of the reason for this outcome is that only one in three seats was contested in all three elections. At the same time we should not underplay the extent of change in some states.

Incumbency. State legislators, if they seek reelection, have a high probability of winning. In 1994, the last year for which we have complete data, incumbents won 92 percent of the time in the state senates and 90 percent in the state houses. Even in the states in which incumbents were least successful, they won more than two-thirds of the races (National Conference of State Legislatures 1996d). The incumbency advantage has grown in recent years, increasing by about half a percentage point per election cycle from 1970 to 1986 (Cox and Morgenstern 1993, 503).

The probability of reelection varies across states. What factors account for this variation? Two studies (Berry, Berkman, and Schneiderman 1998; Carey et al. 1997), covering elections from 1970–1989 and from 1992–1994, respectively, find that the probability of reelection is higher when: (1) the length of term is two years (as opposed to four years); (2) the legislator is a member of a more professional legislature; (3) redistricting is under the control of the incumbent's own party (rather than divided control or control by the opposite party), and (4) the incumbent was unopposed in the previous election (rather than being contested).[10]

Why is the level of legislative professionalism such a strong influence on incumbency, and thus on electoral outcomes? The argument is that by providing more institutional resources to members, professional legislatures serve to reduce the impact of other variables (for example, presidential coattails or a poor economy) on election outcomes. "Because members of professional legislatures can focus attention on themselves through both their legislative and campaign activities, they can make themselves less susceptible to factors that render incumbents in less professionalized bodies more vulnerable" (Berry et al. 1998, 12).

Effects of Campaign Spending. It is clear that money matters in American elections, including state legislative elections. Research convincingly shows that the candidate who spends the most money usually wins (Cassie and Breaux 1998, 101). Incumbents generally have a substantial advantage over challengers in their ability to attract campaign contributions, and therefore incumbents enjoy a similar advantage in their ability to outspend challengers. This spending disparity between incumbents and challengers is particularly great in the states with more professional legislatures. For example, only about one in ten challengers in California, Illinois, New Jersey, and Pennsylvania are able to spend at least 75 percent as much as the incumbent they face in the election. But in some citizen legislatures (for example, Montana, Utah, and Wyoming) at least half of the challengers are able to spend at

10. The last two variables were included only in the Berry, Berkman, and Schneiderman (1998) study.

this level (Cassie and Breaux 1998, 105). The reason for this disparity is clear; it simply does not cost much to run for the state legislature in the rural states with citizen legislatures, and a challenger is more likely to be able to muster the $5,000 or so it takes to be competitive. On the other hand, it may cost $100,000 or more to run a competitive campaign in Illinois or California, and most challengers simply cannot raise that amount of money.

Does the amount of money spent on the campaign directly affect the share of votes that a candidate receives? Generally, the answer is yes. It seems to be especially true in primary elections, where candidates are able to increase their vote share by spending larger amounts of money (Breaux and Gierzynski 1991). In general elections, the impact of expenditures on the percentage of the vote won appears to vary from state to state and from year to year (Gierzynski and Breaux 1993, 524).

State Legislative Campaigns. Over the past few decades, electioneering practices in the United States have undergone dramatic changes. Political campaigns have become more candidate-centered as grassroots campaigning and party organizational support have been replaced by mass media contact and professional consultants (Agranoff 1976; Salmore and Salmore 1989). Modern electioneering practices are certainly used by some state legislative candidates who enlist the assistance of political consultants, conduct polls to gauge the preferences of voters, target tailored messages to specific segments of the population, and contact voters via radio and television. Although more state legislative candidates use these techniques than in previous years, their use is not pervasive, and huge variations often exist across states. A few examples of modern campaign characteristics will highlight these points. A survey of candidates running in seven states during the 1994 general election showed that only about 29 percent reported hiring a professional campaign consultant (Hogan 1998). However, there was variation across states with only 6 percent of candidates in Wyoming but more than 50 percent of candidates in Oregon and Texas reporting their use (Hogan 1998). An analysis of expenditures made by these same campaigns found that spending for television and radio advertising made up a limited portion of a campaign's budget. Candidates spent anywhere between 5.5 percent (Connecticut) and 21.2 percent (Illinois) of voter contact spending on television and radio advertisements combined. A large majority of candidates in the state legislative setting do not even make expenditures for radio and television advertising (considered to be the most modern forms of campaign communication). Voter contact spending in state legislative races is allocated primarily to such things as mailings and signs (Hogan 1998).

THE STATE LEGISLATORS

Who Are They?

Throughout most of the twentieth century state legislators were seen as "local boys who made good," meaning that most were well-off white males who were native to the state and long-time residents of their districts (Dye 1981, 125; Thomp-

son and Moncrief 1992, 23). Although that characterization fits some current legislators, the composition of most state legislatures is more diverse today. In this section we explore changes in four characteristics of state legislators (nativity, gender,
race–ethnicity, and occupation) that have resulted in more diverse legislatures.

Nativity. On attending a session of the Florida legislature one is struck by the
variety of accents heard during floor debate. Perhaps this is to be expected, given
the significant influx of people into that state. But it does raise the question as to
whether the legislative institutions are as homogenous as sometimes depicted.
About one-third of today's state legislators were not born in the state they represent. The old characterization still seems to fit in states such as Oklahoma, Nebraska, and Mississippi, where only slightly more than 10 percent are nonnatives. On
the other hand, nonnatives made up a majority of the state legislatures of Nevada
(83 percent), Alaska (73 percent), Arizona (69 percent), Florida (59 percent), and
Oregon (57 percent; Thompson and Moncrief 1992b, 26–27). These legislatures are
generally in states undergoing significant population growth and immigration.
These nonnative legislators are not really 'outsiders' but simply reflect the makeup
of the states' changing population.

Gender. Although women make up a majority of the voting population, they
have never been a majority in any U.S. state legislature. In 1894 the first three
women to serve in a state legislature were elected to the Colorado House of Representatives (Cox 1996, 16). In 1925, 141 women were serving in state legislatures
(Cox 1996, 24). By the early 1970s, this number had grown to 344 women, but this
still constituted only 4.5 percent of the total number of state legislators. By 1997,
however, there were 1,588 women serving in state legislatures (21 percent; Center
for the American Woman and Politics 1998). The number of women legislators was
five times greater than it was just one generation earlier. In 1997 women held at
least 31 percent of the legislative seats in seven states (Washington, Arizona, Colorado, Minnesota, Nevada, Vermont, and New Hampshire), and less than 13 percent in only six states (Alabama, Kentucky, Mississippi, Pennsylvania, Oklahoma,
and Louisiana; see Figure 5-1). In general, higher percentages of women are found
in the less professional legislatures and in liberal states outside the South (Squire
1992, 72).

Although it is important from the point of view of symbolic representation that
more women now serve in legislatures, ultimately we want to know if their presence makes a difference behaviorally and in terms of public policy. Recent research
suggests that it does, but only after a sufficient number of women are elected to
reach a critical mass. In those state legislatures with the highest proportion of female legislators, women are more likely to exhibit policy priorities related to issues
of women, children, and family. In states with the lowest levels of female representation, these gender differences in terms of legislative priorities are absent (Thomas
1991, 1994). Stated differently, "women representatives are more willing to 'act for'
women when they are in the presence of other women" (Mezey 1994, 266). The
presence of a formal organization such as a women's political caucus appears to

Figure 5-1   Women in State Legislatures, 1998

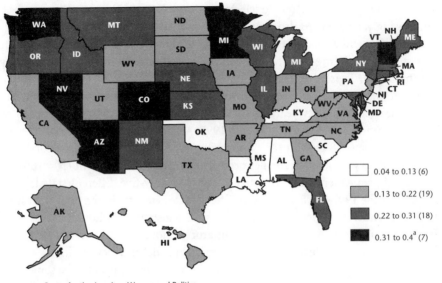

0.04 to 0.13 (6)

0.13 to 0.22 (19)

0.22 to 0.31 (18)

0.31 to 0.4[a] (7)

SOURCE: Center for the American Woman and Politics.
[a] Entries are proportion of state legislators who are women

help in the passage of legislation intended to help women, children, and the family (Thomas 1994, 100).

It also appears that the types of women serving, and the attitudes they bring to the legislature, have changed over the years. One recent study compared women elected to state legislatures in 1992 to those elected in 1972 and 1982. It concluded that "women serving in the 1990s are younger, better educated, come to the legislature from more professional occupations and more varied political backgrounds, and experience different legislative careers once in office than women serving in previous decades" (Dolan and Ford 1997, 147). The authors did not find similar changes in the basic characteristics of men over the same twenty-year period.

Legislators have their greatest impact through the organizational positions they hold—the committee and leadership posts. In the 1970s women were typically assigned to and chaired committees dealing with those issues traditionally thought of as "women's concerns" (health and welfare), and they were underrepresented on rules, fiscal, and business affairs committees (Diamond 1977, 45; Kirkpatrick 1974, 126). By the late 1980s, although women were still more often assigned to and chaired health and welfare committees, they had significantly increased their representation on budget committees but were still underrepresented on business committees in most states (Thomas 1994, 66–67). In terms of chairing committees, by 1993–1994 women were still overrepresented as chairs on education, health, and social and human service committees, and underrepresented on banking and financial institutions, energy, insurance, and rules committees (Darcy 1996, 894).

Nonetheless, one recent study concluded that "women are not discriminated against when committee chairs are selected" (Darcy 1996, 892).

Increasingly, women are also assuming the most powerful positions in state legislatures. They held a total of twenty-four top leadership positions, including four house speakerships, three senate presidencies, and seventeen majority or minority posts in the 1997 legislative session ("Statestats" 1997, 5).

Race–Ethnicity. Another area of diversification has been in terms of racial–ethnic characteristics. Fifty years ago, there were almost no African Americans or Hispanics serving in state legislatures. By 1997, African American legislators constituted approximately 8 percent *(N =* approximately 600) of all state legislators. Hispanic legislators were a much smaller proportion, roughly 2.2 percent *(N =* 169). At least one African American was elected to serve in forty-five different state legislatures during the 1997–1998 sessions. In fifteen states (mostly in the South), at least ten African Americans were serving in the state legislature. Although at least one Hispanic is serving in twenty-six state legislatures, more than two-thirds are found in just five states: New Mexico, Texas, California, Florida, and New York.

The recruitment patterns for black and white legislators appears to be somewhat different. For example, black legislators received their start in politics outside of government (the civil rights movement, churches, or unions), whereas white legislators were more likely to start in state or local government (Button and Hedge 1996). African American legislators usually represent majority black urban districts, whereas white legislators tend to represent white rural or suburban districts. In terms of whether or not African American state legislators face discrimination within the legislature, there is some disagreement. One recent study found that white legislators were less likely to perceive any discriminatory practices within the legislature, whereas the black legislators themselves were more prone to believe that some discrimination did occur (Button and Hedge 1996). Black lawmakers report the greatest amount of discrimination in the Deep South legislatures, and the least amount of discrimination is perceived in the Rim South, probably because of the fact that blacks in this area represent a sizable number of white constituencies (Button and Hedge 1996, 215). Comparable information for Hispanic legislators is not available.

Occupation. Historically, the two largest occupation groups represented in the legislature were farmers and lawyers. This pattern has changed, however, during the twentieth century. A century ago, farmers constituted the largest group of state legislators (31.0 percent), followed by lawyers (21.7 percent; Haynes 1900a, 1900b, 1900c, 1900d). By 1950 the proportion of farmer–legislators had dropped to 20 percent (Zeller 1954). Lawyers remained a significant factor in state legislatures through the mid-1990s, making up 16 percent of all state legislators, whereas the proportion of farmers declined to just 8 percent (National Conference of State Legislatures 1996a, Table 1).

A major change in the composition of state legislatures has occurred with the emergence of the full-time legislator. When legislatures met for only a few months every other year, legislators could treat their office as a part-time vocation. The advent of longer sessions, higher pay, and more complex legislation, coupled with the availability of more technical and political information, has meant that legislators are forced to devote more time to their elected position. A former Washington state representative recently commented, "Anyone who thinks legislating anywhere in this country is a part-time commitment is nuts" (quoted in National Conference of State Legislatures 1996a, 3). As legislatures have professionalized, the number of members who claim that their legislative occupation is their full-time job has also increased. According to the National Conference of State Legislatures, in 1972 fewer than 3 percent of the members listed their occupation as full-time legislator. By 1995, 14 percent reported they were full-time legislators (1996a, Table 1).

As one might expect, the distribution of occupations is not the same in all state legislatures. In seven of the nine professional legislatures the largest occupation category is full-time legislator, reaching a high of 82 percent in Pennsylvania. Ironically, in the California legislature, often considered to be closest to the model of the U.S. Congress, only a handful of members considered themselves full-time legislators in 1995. How do we account for this anomaly? A significant part of the answer involves the impact of term limits. Two years earlier in 1993, before the implementation of term limits, roughly 38 percent of the members of the California legislature designated themselves full-time legislators. Today, given the short legislative career and the public's unhappiness with professional legislatures (Squire 1993), few legislators in California describe themselves this way. Attorneys and businesspersons are also well represented in most professional legislatures. A case can be made that as the percentage of full-time legislators increases, the percentage of businesspersons in the chamber decreases.

A greater mix of occupations exists in citizen legislatures. Business-related occupations are most consistently represented in these fifteen state legislatures. Farmers still constitute a sizable percentage of the membership in several citizen legislatures, such as North Dakota (33 percent). Professionals other than lawyers—including accountants, consultants, doctors, clergy, and engineers–scientists—add to the mosaic of the citizen legislature, constituting more than 10 percent of all but one citizen legislature. Finally, in New Hampshire, arguably one of the least professional legislatures in the country, more than 40 percent of its members consider themselves retirees, students, or homemakers. This is quite a contrast to Pennsylvania or New York, where only 1 percent of the members designate themselves as fitting these categories.

The occupational structure of hybrid legislatures is more complicated to describe. Legislators who are in business-related occupations are represented reasonably well in the hybrid legislatures. Lawyers are quite prominent in some southern legislatures, constituting at least 20 percent in Florida, Louisiana, Texas, South Carolina, Virginia, and Mississippi, but are a relatively small contingent in some western states including Washington, Arizona, and Alaska. Full-time legislators constitute more than one in ten legislators in six hybrid legislatures. At the other end of

Table 5–3 State Legislative Turnover, 1987–1997
(in percentages)

Level of professionalism	Mean	Standard deviation	Range	Turnover[a]
Professional				
Senate	64.78	12.19	52–85	0/9
House	75.22	10.96	62–100	1/9
Hybrid				
Senate	74.46	9.79	58–93	11/28
House	77.60	9.84	46–92	11/25
Citizen				
Senate	74.67	13.29	52–100	7/15
House	80.93	9.17	64–99	9/15

SOURCE: National Conference of State Legislatures, May 1, 1997.

NOTE: Values are percentages.

[a] Value given is the number of chambers with turnover over of 80% or more.

the spectrum, fewer than 1 percent of the state legislators in Tennessee, Virginia, and Mississippi claim they are full-time legislators.

The chamber memberships include a smattering of doctors, accountants, consultants, engineers, and scientists. As expected, those with an agriculture occupation are most frequently seen in states in the Middle West region, including Kansas, Missouri, Minnesota, Nebraska, and Iowa. Educators are more prevalent in Delaware, Maryland, Minnesota, Iowa, Arizona, and Alabama. In summary, membership in the hybrid category of legislatures defies easy summation.

Legislative Turnover and Legislative Careers

Few state legislators make a lengthy career out of service in the chamber (Luttbeg 1992; Moncrief, Thompson, Haddon, et al. 1992; Opheim 1994). Recently the National Conference of State Legislatures calculated the percentage of members serving in a legislative chamber in 1997 who were not in that chamber for the 1987 session. Overall, chamber turnover was 72 percent in the state senates and 84 percent in the state houses. The mean, standard deviation, and range are shown by level of professionalism in Table 5-3. The first observation is that turnover rates are quite high in both the houses and senates, regardless of the level of professionalism, although it is lowest in the most professional states. In only two chambers (the Delaware House and the New York Senate) is the turnover rate for the decade less than 50 percent, whereas it exceeds 80 percent in thirty-nine of the ninety-nine chambers. Mean turnover is highest in citizen legislatures, where it exceeds 80 percent in a majority of the chambers. In contrast, turnover reaches such levels in only one of the eighteen professional chambers.[11]

11. The exception is the California Assembly, where term limits had already run a full cycle such that turnover was 100 percent.

Why do members leave the legislature at such a relatively high rate? The answer is complicated. The first set of factors is institutional. Peverill Squire has shown that membership stability in the pre–term-limit period is best explained by two variables: pay and advancement prospects (1988a). In states in which advancement from the lower chamber to higher office (for example, state senate, statewide office, or U.S. Congress) is somewhat remote and legislative pay is high, membership stability is also high (for example, in New York). In other words, members in these legislatures are more likely to be career legislators, serving for longer periods in the same chamber. In "dead-end" legislatures, where both legislative pay and chances for advancement are low, membership is less stable. The greatest membership instability exists in "springboard legislatures," in which the pay is comparable to that in a career legislature, but the chances for advancement to higher office are also high.

The second reason, and one often overlooked, is that some members leave office involuntarily. The obvious example is the legislator who is forced out of office as a result of electoral defeat. As noted earlier, most incumbents win reelection, but at least a few incumbents lose in each election. Death accounts for about one-fourth of those instances in which a legislator vacates the office before completing the term (Hamm and Olson 1992). The third reason for involuntary departure involves the individual being arrested, indicted, or convicted of a crime, or otherwise being forced from the legislature for some unethical behavior. Again, we are not accounting for the bulk of the departures, but in some states the effect is quite noticeable. The most extreme cases in the early 1990s occurred in South Carolina where sixteen legislators went to jail in an FBI sting operation (Rosenthal 1998, 93) and in Kentucky where fifteen legislators were convicted on corruption charges (American Society of Legislative Clerks and Secretaries 1998, Table 96-6.4).

State legislatures, through their state constitution, statute, or chamber rules, have a wide variety of options available to discipline members, including expulsion, censure, sanctions, and reprimands. The power to expel a member is rarely used. Only seventeen of ninety-one state legislative chambers that responded to a questionnaire indicated that they have taken this most serious action (American Society of Legislative Clerks and Secretaries 1998, 6-2). This does not mean that state legislatures are unwilling to investigate serious charges. Rather, in the most serious cases members simply resign rather than be expelled. The upsurge in ethics laws and codes has not only clarified what actions are impermissible, but has also increased the frequency with which legislative chambers must investigate its members for a violation.

A fourth reason for involuntary departure now exists in many states: term limits. Until the early 1990s, legislators in the fifty states could serve as long as they wanted or until they were defeated. That situation began to change in the early 1990s when voters in nineteen states, using the initiative process, approved limiting legislators' tenure in nineteen states.[12] In addition, legislators in Utah voted to place limits on

12. Only in Mississippi and North Dakota did a majority of the citizens vote no on term-limit legislation.

Table 5-4 Term Limits of State Legislators[a]

Type of ban	Limit in years: House	Limit in years: Senate	Affects House	Affects Senate
Lifetime ban				
Oklahoma	12 total		2004	2004
California	6	8	1996	1998
Michigan	6	8	1998	2002
Oregon	6	8	2002	2002
Missouri	8	8	2002	2002
Arkansas	6	8	1998	2000
Nevada	12	12	2008	2008
Consecutive years				
Idaho	8 in 15-year period		2002	2002
Colorado	8	8	1998	1998
Montana	8	8	2000	2000
Maine	8	8	1996	1996
Arizona	8	8	2000	2000
Florida	8	8	2000	2000
Ohio	8	8	2000	2000
South Dakota	8	8	2000	2000
Utah	12	12	2006	2006
Wyoming	12	12	2006	2006
Louisiana	12	12	2007	2007

SOURCE: Adapted from National Conference of State Legislators, "Term Limits of State Elected Officials." http:/www/ ncsl.org/programs/legman/about/ term lim.html. March 30, 1998.

[a] Term limits were declared unconstitutional in Nebraska, Massachusettts, and Washington.

themselves, and in Louisiana the legislature placed the term limit issue on the ballot and the voters approved it. Subsequent court actions have overturned term limits in Massachusetts, Nebraska, and Washington, leaving eighteen states with term limits, as of January 1999. The term limit laws' main impact will be felt in the next few years (see Table 5-4 for an overview of in-place term limits).

Although a variety of states have term limits, the content of the term limits differs in two key criteria: (1) the particular limit on the number of years of continuous service allowed, and (2) whether there is a lifetime ban on subsequent service. Based on these two criteria, term limits will be most severe in the California Assembly, Arkansas House, Michigan House, and Oregon House where a lifetime ban exists after serving six years. On the other hand, in both chambers in Utah and Louisiana members may serve 12 years of continuous service, sit out a term, and then return. Thus in Utah one can actually serve a total of twenty-four years in a twenty-six-year time span.

The adoption of term limits has led to numerous predictions as to the potential impact on legislators and the legislative process. Early evidence, drawn from a survey of 3,000 legislators in 1995, indicates that term limits have not affected the composition of legislatures in terms of the background characteristics or ideology of those elected. In terms of redistributing power, the major beneficiary appears to be the governor and possibly legislative staff members, and majority party leaders have lost influence (Carey et al. 1998). Because term limits are not yet fully in effect in most term-limited states, the evidence to date is preliminary. Further research will be necessary to document whether these initial effects are long lasting.

Representing Constituents

In a representative democracy, the assumption is that legislators represent their constituents. This simple statement hides a complex political phenomenon. What do the terms "constituency" and "representation" mean? Legislators use the term "constituency" in several different ways. From this perspective, one views the constituency not as a single entity but as a "nest of concentric circles" (Fenno 1978, 1). The largest circle represents the *geographical constituency,* the entire population living within the legal boundaries of the district. Occupying a smaller circle are the legislator's supporters, the *reelection constituency.* A subset of the reelection constituency is composed of the legislator's strongest supporters or the loyalists, their *primary constituency.* The smallest circle is confined to the political confidants and advisors, or those whom the legislator sees as good friends, otherwise known as the *personal constituency* (Fenno 1978, 1–25). At any one time, a legislator may be focusing on one or more of these constituencies.

The concept of representation is also difficult to grasp (Loewenberg 1972, 12). One useful way to conceptualize representation is to think of it in terms of the legislator being "responsive" to the constituents in terms of policy, service, and allocation of public goods (Eulau and Karps 1977; Jewell 1982).

Policy responsiveness involves the relationship between the constituents' preferences and the behavior of the elected official. Alan Rosenthal has noted that "it is much more difficult, however, for representatives to act as agents of their constituency on policy matters" (Rosenthal 1998, 19). Why? First, some legislators, sometimes called *trustees,* use their own judgment because they do not have confidence in the views of organized groups in their district or they believe that voters want their legislator to lead on critical issues (Jewell 1982, 105–109). Second, as noted previously, the relevant constituency is not always obvious. Should the member be concerned with the total population, those who voted, or those who cast their vote for the legislator? Third, for those legislators who want to follow the wishes of their constituents, labeled *delegates,* the problem is that most people do not have an opinion, save for the major issues (Rosenthal 1998, 20). The result is that "most legislators are comfortable with the general policy viewpoints that they perceive as dominant in their districts; they believe that their own views are typical of those in the district. Consequently their role orientation does not usually lead trustees and delegates to vote differently on legislation" (Jewell 1982, 115).

Service responsiveness refers to the advantages and benefits that the representative is able to obtain for particular constituents (Eualu and Karps 1977, 243). Legislators are, in effect, asked to help attain a divisible resource for particular individuals. Requests may cover an almost infinite number of subjects. For example, the legislator may be asked to help citizens obtain governmental assistance in the form of jobs or unemployment compensation, or help a business that has a disagreement with a state agency over licensing, taxes, or paperwork (see Jewell 1982). The most common reasons constituents contact their state legislators are for information or help with bureaucratic red tape, and to a lesser extent in requests for jobs. Constituents contact their legislators less frequently about easing government regulations, intervening in local disputes, and helping with nongovernmental organizations (Freeman and Richardson 1996, 50–51). The common term for this type of activity is *casework.*

What role does casework play in the job of the average legislator? Veteran legislators perceive that constituent demand for services has significantly increased and, as a consequence, they are spending more time on casework (Moncrief, Thompson, and Kurtz 1996, 62). It is interesting to note that "legislators in all types of legislative institutions find tremendous increases in the pressures of the job, as well as in the demand for and time spent on constituent service" (Moncrief et al. 1996, 68). What affects the amount of time that a legislator and his or her staff devote to casework? The most recent research demonstrates that several factors appear to have an impact. At the individual level, legislators who place a high value on casework, who favor greater government spending, and who perceive that they will benefit electorally are more likely to devote more time, including that of the staff, to casework (Freeman and Richardson, 1996). Conversely, legislators who place a low value on casework, who believe in a more limited role for government, and do not see any electoral benefit from casework are less inclined to devote time to these activities. The type of legislature in which one serves also has an impact. Legislators who serve in a legislature with a tradition of supporting constituency service, offer career incentives for members, and provide personal staff or district offices are more likely to devote more time to casework (Freeman and Richardson 1994).

"Allocation responsiveness concerns the legislator's efforts to gain governmental goods and services for the district. They are general rather than individual benefits, but they frequently benefit one part of the district or one group more than others" (Jewell 1982, 135). This type of responsiveness is often associated with "pork barrel" projects, which provide a benefit to a specific district but are paid for by everyone. Unfortunately, state legislative scholars have all but neglected the study of allocation responsiveness (but see Rosenthal 1998, 18; Thompson 1986; Thompson and Moncrief 1987). Proponents of term limits argue that such limits will reduce allocational responsiveness, because legislators will not have the incentive to pursue pork barrel projects as a reelection tool. Preliminary results from one empirical study of term limits find evidence that this may indeed be the case. Legislators in term-limited states report spending less time securing government money and projects for their district, and they report placing higher priority on the needs of the state as a whole rather than the narrower interests of their own district (Carey et al. 1998).

THE LEGISLATURES

Organizational Features

A comparative analysis of state legislatures would uncover numerous differences in these organizations. Six important factors are the number of chambers, size, chamber leadership patterns, party caucuses, committees, and staff, each of which will be discussed in turn.

Number of Chambers and Size. In forty-nine of the fifty states, the legislature (also called the *general assembly* or *general court* in some states) is composed of two chambers. The upper chamber is called the *senate* in all states; the lower chamber is typically called the *house of representatives* (although in some states it is referred to as the *assembly, house of delegates,* or *general assembly*).

The Nebraska legislature is a unicameral body with just one chamber, a senate. State senates range in size from a low of twenty members in the Alaska Senate to a high of sixty-seven in the Minnesota Senate. The lower houses evidence greater variability, the smallest being the Alaska House of Representatives with only forty legislators, and the largest is the New Hampshire House of Representatives with 400 members. The size of the legislative body affects both structural and procedural aspects of life in the legislature. For example, the greater the number of members in the chamber, the greater the degree of hierarchical organizational structure, the more limited the floor debate, and the greater the specialization among members (see Hedlund 1984, 89–90, for a summary).

Chamber Leadership. In the forty-nine lower houses the chamber leader, referred to as the *speaker,* is elected by the members of the house. Greater variation exists among the state senates. The membership elects a president in twenty-three state senates and a speaker in one. The lieutenant governor presides in twenty-six. However, since the lieutenant governor is actually an executive branch official, his powers within the legislature are usually quite limited, and real power resides with the president pro tempore, who is chosen by the senate members themselves.

Although examples exist of legislative leaders who have served in that capacity for a number of terms, a recent study found that 86 percent of senate presidents, house speakers, and majority and minority leaders changed between 1990 to 1997 (Hansen 1997, 16). Until at least the early 1990s the career path to the top leadership position was becoming more institutionalized as the legislature itself institutionalized (Freeman 1995). Although the path to the top post varied, an apprenticeship in another leadership position (such as majority leader or chair of an important committee) was very common. This trend will probably continue to be the norm in those state legislatures not faced with term limits. If an apprenticeship norm is to be followed in the legislatures with term limits, future chamber leaders will have to be given major leadership positions (for example, committee chair or majority leader) early in their legislative careers—usually in their second or third terms at the latest (Hodson et al. 1995, 15).

The job of the legislative leader is more complex today than in the past. Internal responsibilities include acting as the chief administrative officer, building legislative coalitions, and providing services and information to individual members, to name only a few. Leaders also have external responsibilities, including being party spokesperson, interacting with the executive, serving as the interchamber representative, holding press conferences, and preparing for campaigns (Little 1995, 271–272).

Analyzing legislative leadership patterns in twenty-two states, Malcolm Jewell and Marcia Whicker (1994) have provided a framework for subsequent researchers. They contend that legislative leadership is, to a certain extent, dependent on context. A key factor is the structure of the institution, including the power of the legislature relative to other key state political actors, its level of professionalization and representativeness, the nature of legislative rules, and the degree of party polarization. The legislative setting also affects the leader's power. For example, the fewer the restrictions on leadership tenure the greater the leader's ability to affect policy. The larger the size of the party majority and the greater the degree of party cohesion and loyalty, the greater the impact of power of the leader. Leaders also have available to them a range of tools and techniques. For example, leaders will find their power to influence public policy outcomes increases as their power to appoint committee members increases, as the size of the professional leadership staff increases, and as the techniques for controlling the party caucuses also increase. Finally, personal leadership style and goals are hypothesized to affect the leader's power.

Party Caucus. In most state legislatures, members of the same political party belong to a party caucus. Although these groups dominated the state legislative process in the years after the Civil War and into the twentieth century (Campbell 1980), their role today is somewhat diminished. Caucuses may perform a multiplicity of functions: choosing the party leadership, keeping members informed, discussing policy to help leaders assess membership opinion, building cohesion, and mobilizing votes (Jewell and Whicker 1994, 100).

The importance of party caucuses varies among the state legislatures. In general party caucuses will be most important in the legislative process in small chambers with evenly matched parties. They are least important in large chambers with one dominant party (Francis 1989, 45). The importance of caucuses can change over time. According to one study, as many as one-fourth of the strong-party caucuses in the 1950s were not important by the early 1980s (Hamm, Hedlund, and Anderson 1994, 968). A recent analysis of party caucuses in formerly one-party legislatures, mostly in the South, found that when the minority party (in this case the Republican Party) is more competitive in the electoral realm, the party caucuses become more complex in terms of meeting more frequently, having formal leadership and formal rules, providing information and acting in formulating policies (Anderson 1997).

Committees. State legislatures face a daunting problem. There is not enough time in a legislative session to have each proposed bill adequately discussed and debated by the entire legislative membership. To solve this workload problem, legislatures create smaller working groups called *committees* to initially review, analyze, and rewrite bills that have been introduced. Because it is inefficient to assign a group of legislators to review only one bill or one specific issue and then break up, these small work groups usually exist for the life of the particular legislative session. To further enhance the division of labor, each committee generally has jurisdiction over a given policy area (for example, education or health). Jurisdiction is more likely set by the chamber leadership or a management committee rather than being set by rule (American Society of Legislative Clerks and Secretaries 1998, 4–6). Membership on committees is usually restricted to just those legislators serving in the particular chamber. However, in at least twenty-nine state legislatures, and especially in Maine, Massachusetts, and Connecticut, some joint committees, which are composed of members from both chambers, exist (Hamm and Hedlund 1994, 675).

Committee systems at the state level have undergone extensive changes over time. A recent study chronicles the development of committee systems in thirty-eight chambers during the twentieth century (Hamm and Hedlund 1995). At the beginning of the century, the typical standing committee system in a state legislature consisted of a relatively large number of committees; the size of each committee was relatively small; and each legislator had a significant number of committee assignments. Committee names were stable from session to session and jurisdiction was generally quite narrow, sometimes limited to a single institution or problem. An extreme case was the Michigan House in which there was a standing committee for each specifically named state asylum, one for each state prison, a separate committee for the school for the blind and one for the deaf, plus one for the employment institution for the blind. This description of the committee system was accurate through the 1930s. Starting in the 1940s, we begin to see a reduction in the total number of committees, committee positions, and mean number of assignments per member, with the nadir hit in the 1970s, followed by a slight increase since then. Indications are that the number of committees or the average size of committees is a function of the size of the legislature, whereas the degree of committee specialization at the individual level is a function of the stability of the legislative membership (Francis 1989; Hamm and Hedlund 1995).

The role that standing committees play today in the legislative process varies among the ninety-nine state legislative chambers. In one set of legislative chambers, the key decision-making power is lodged mainly in the committees; in a second set of legislatures, the critical decisions are made by either the majority party leadership or the majority party caucus; in a third set power is shared between the standing committees and the leadership or the caucus. According to a study conducted in the early 1980s, in nearly two-thirds of the chambers, the shared committee–leadership/caucus model prevails (Francis 1989, 44). It is interesting to note that committees are generally most important in chambers in which one party dominates (Francis 1989, 45–46). An unexplored research question is whether committees have remained as important in the decision-making process in those chambers that have moved in recent years from being one-party dominant to a more balanced two-party system (for example, South Carolina House, Georgia Senate, Nevada House).

The ability of committees to play a meaningful role in the legislative process can also be affected by the rules governing the operation of the legislature. These rules are found in state constitutions, state statutes, and the formal rules and regulations of legislative chambers. For example, committees in the Oregon House have significant influence over policy content because the rules permit them to introduce bills with the committee listed as the author; offer substitute bills in place of the original; have committee amendments automatically incorporated into the bill rather than have each amendment accepted or rejected by the floor; and make it very difficult to amend legislation on the floor by requiring unanimous consent to accept the amendment. The committees also are important in the lawmaking process because all bills must be referred to committee and bills reported from committee go directly to the calendar. In other words, the rules carve out a central role for committees in the legislative process. Committees do not have such favorable rules in most state legislatures (Hamm, Hedlund, and Martorano 1998).

Staff. A major change in state legislatures during the past thirty years has involved the growth of legislative staff. "State legislatures have moved away from dependence on external sources for information in favor of in-house staff resources" (Neal 1996, 24). The consequence of this change has not been studied systematically, although some research focuses on the addition of a particular type of staff (Sabatier and Whiteman 1985) or evaluates the adequacy of certain types of information (Jones, Guston, and Branscomb 1996).

Legislative staff are not equally distributed among the state legislatures. During the 1995–1996 legislative session, 3,899 staff were employed in the New York legislature, whereas there were only fifty-eight staff positions in the Vermont legislature (National Conference of State Legislatures 1996b). Because staff is a component of professionalism, it is not surprising that in the mid-1990s professional legislatures had more staff (mean = 1,798) than either the hybrid legislatures (mean = 640) or the citizen legislatures (mean = 256). In professional legislatures there are, on average, eleven staff members for each legislator; this figure drops to fewer than five in hybrid legislatures and to two in citizen legislatures. The greatest difference occurs between California, with almost twenty-two staff members per legislator, and Vermont, with three legislators for each staff member.

Between 1979 and 1996, total staff positions increased from slightly fewer than 27,000 to more than 34,400, with the total number of staff employed increasing in thirty-six legislatures. Permanent staff increased by almost 10,000 positions, with session-only staff decreasing by 2,500. Permanent staff increased in all but five state legislatures, with the greatest increase generally occurring in professional legislatures and the smallest in citizen legislatures. On the other hand, session-only staff decreased in all three categories, falling most precipitously in the professional legislatures (a loss of 58 percent). Because the professional legislatures are in session a

considerable number of months during the year, it is not surprising that permanent staff constitute between 88 to 100 percent of all staff in these legislatures. In
citizen legislatures, which meet much less frequently, only about one-half of the
staff are employed on a year-round basis; the other half work only when the legislature is in session.

Numerous types of legislative staff exist (National Conference of State Legislatures 1996b; Neal 1996, 24–27). In all state legislatures, the chief parliamentary officers and staff are involved with the lawmaking and administrative processes of state
legislatures. They deal with such issues as bill introductions, preparation of calen-
dars, tracking amendments offered during debate, and posting hearing schedules.
Leadership staff work directly for legislative leaders or for party caucuses. They are
typically involved in policy research, constituent services, and administrative duties. In the most systematic treatment of state legislative leadership to date, Jewell
and Whicker argued that "the ability of leaders to be effective depends in no small
part on the size, professional skills, and experience of their staffs" (1994, 97). According to these authors, staff provide a variety of services, but

> the most important function is communication: staff are the eyes and ears of the
> leadership. They keep the leadership informed about the concerns and needs of the
> members. Staff members supplement the work of assistant leaders or party whips in
> keeping members informed about what is going on in the chamber and in commit-
> tees. Prior to an important roll call, they help to poll the party membership. They
> keep the membership informed about the wishes of the leadership, the scheduling of
> legislation, and the status of members' bills. Staff members frequently represent the
> leadership in behind-the-scenes negotiations on bills, either in the committee stage
> or when bills are pending on the floor (1994, 98).

Research staff compile background information on bills, respond to members'
requests for information, and sometimes staff committees. The legal services staff,
composed of individuals with legal experience, draft bills, conduct legal research,
and may be involved in administration and enforcement of ethics codes. Legislative
program evaluation staff engage in program evaluation and performance auditing.
Legislative fiscal staff are involved in fiscal analysis, budget review, and revenue review for state legislatures. These staff usually examine budget requests made by
state agencies and make suggestions to the state legislators about these requests.
Personal staff who work for individual legislators are usually found in legislatures
that are closer to full-time.

Choosing Leaders and Subgroups

Once legislators have been chosen in district elections, the legislative chamber
must be organized to conduct business. In effect, three processes, sometimes inter-
secting, are occurring: choosing chamber leaders, choosing legislative party leaders,
and choosing committee chairs and members.

Chamber Leaders. In most state legislatures the majority-party caucuses determine which of their members will serve as the presiding officer. In these state legis-

latures significant politicking takes place before the caucus meets as candidates try to line up votes. In some cases it becomes apparent that one candidate has captured a majority of the vote and the losing candidate withdraws before the caucus meets. Another variant is to have a short meeting at which only one ballot is necessary to elect the party's nominee. The third pattern is to have a protracted battle in which no one is initially able to assemble a winning coalition. The Arizona House Republicans in the 1997 session provide an illustration of just such a process. It took more than fifty secret ballots cast over more than fifteen hours in two closed caucuses to elect one of the four contenders (Willey 1997).

There is no guarantee that the members of the majority party caucus will abide by the caucus decision. In that case, at least five scenarios are likely, ranging from little or no impact to a complete restructuring of the legislature. First, a few members may vote for the minority party candidate, but their defection is not significant enough to change the outcome. A second possibility is that several party dissidents may simply withhold their support, making it impossible for the majority party candidate to win the position, and ultimately forcing the candidate to withdraw. This fate befell Representative Sam Leake (D) in his quest for Missouri House Speakership in 1996 (Dewhirst 1996).

A third scenario involves a dissident faction of the majority party teaming up with the minority party to elect one of the dissidents as speaker, without there being any long-term impact.

A fourth possibility has more lasting consequences, but still has a member of the majority party as Speaker. For example, in 1989, twenty of the seventy-four North Carolina House Democrats teamed up with forty-five of the forty-six Republicans to oust a long-time Speaker and install another Democrat as Speaker. In this process, the dissident Democrats signed a "contract" with the Republican governor in which the governor would encourage House Republicans to vote for the Democratic challenger, the Republicans would be appointed chairs of several subcommittees, and the committee system would be completely revamped (Christensen 1989). The final scenario is more unusual in that the leadership is acquired by the minority party with the help of a few votes by disgruntled members of the majority party. The Democratic Speaker of Vermont from 1985–1991 (Ralph Wright) came to power this way.

What happens if the two parties have an identical number of seats? This is a possibility in sixty-one chambers, because there are an even number of seats and it has actually occurred ten times in the past twenty years. To resolve the situation, several solutions have been adopted. The most common is to have co-Speakers, either alternating daily or monthly in running the floor session and co-committee chairs (1979 and 1999 Washington House; 1989 Michigan House; 1989 Indiana House; 1995 Nevada House). A variant of this approach involves the Speakership changing partisan control at the end of the first year of a two-year session (1993 Florida Senate). Another way is to elect the Speaker from one party, but to give the bulk of the committee chairs to members of the other party (1978 Minnesota House). Sometimes the issue is settled by state law. For example, the fifty to fifty tie vote in the Indiana House at the start of the 1997 session was decided in favor of the Democrats because a recently passed state law gives the speakership and organizational control to the party elected to the governorship, in this case the Democrats ("On First Reading" 1998). Examples exist in which the speaker selected in this manner gave the speaker's party a majority on all committees and all committee chairs (1997 Indiana House) or split the chairs and assigned equal numbers of each party to committees (1985 Montana House). After the 1995 elections, the Democrats and Republicans were split twenty to twenty in the Virginia Senate. In this case the tie would be broken by the lieutenant governor, a Democrat. The only problem was that one of the Democrats abandoned the Democratic caucus and insisted that there be a more equal sharing of committee assignments. The result was that the Republicans were able to gain control of four committees (Baker 1996).

We have discussed the organization of the legislature as if it only involved the decisions of the members of that chamber. Although that is generally true today, in past years the governor, particularly in some southern states, was the kingmaker (Jewell 1962). In Louisiana it is still customary for the Speaker to be the governor's preferred candidate (Perkins 1996).

Party Leaders. The second selection process involves choosing the political party leadership. The formal legislative party organization varies among the state legislative chambers. Legislative party organizations can be placed on a continuum from simple to relatively complex (Hamm et al. 1994). At one extreme, there is no formal party organization (Mississippi). The simplest organization is where each party has a floor leader (majority or minority party) responsible for leading debate on the floor, and working with the speaker in setting the agenda (Alaska Senate). More complex organizations (New York Assembly) have a more detailed leadership structure, including positions such as assistant majority leader, whip, and majority caucus chair.

The actual selection of the key party leaders usually takes place in the party caucus in which the legislators from that party vote for their officers. In essence, the leaders are chosen by their peers. This, however, is not always the case because the elected chamber leader, who is also the party leader, does appoint the majority leader and other party officials in a few chambers (Connecticut Senate). In addition, in a few legislative bodies the elected chamber leader also carries the title of majority leader, thus fusing power in one person (Illinois Senate and New York Senate). Another option is to not have a majority leader designation but instead to simply have the elected chamber leader serve as the party chair. In the Ohio Senate, for example, there is no majority leader, and the Senate president, the elected chamber leader, presides over the majority party caucus.

Committee Chairs and Members. A third process, after the selection of the chamber and party leadership, involves designating the standing work groups for the legislature. The committee assignment process is a key organizational decision in which members are allocated for the duration of the legislative session to concentrate their time on certain policy areas. The leader's ability to control appointments is crucial to governing the chamber. Leadership is enhanced if they are able to appoint committee chairs. As Jewell and Whicker noted, "The ability of the majority-party leadership to appoint, and if necessary to remove, committee chairs is one of its greatest sources of power" (1994, 95). The elected chamber leader (speaker, president, or president pro tempore) selects committee chairs in about 70 percent of the state legislative chambers. In other states, committee chairs may be selected by the majority leader (Wisconsin Senate), by a chamber committee (California Senate), by substantive committee members (South Carolina House), by the entire chamber (Nebraska Senate), by chamber seniority (South Carolina Senate), or by committee seniority (Virginia Senate).

Across all state legislatures, the most frequently mentioned criteria considered when appointing committee chairs are political party, competency or talent of the member, and preference of the member, followed by seniority in the chamber, tenure on the committee, and support in the leadership election. Less important are occupation, geographic location of the member's district in the state, gender, and ethnic representation (American Society of Legislative Clerks and Secretaries 1998, Table 96-4.5). A recent study found that roughly 95 percent of the committee chairs appointed in the 1989–1990 legislative sessions belonged to the majority party, reaching 100 percent in two-thirds of the chambers. Almost 40 percent of the exceptions were found in eleven of the twenty-two southern state legislative chambers (Hedlund and Hamm 1996).

Legislators are appointed to committees in a variety of ways. In about one-half of the legislative chambers, legislators of the majority political party are appointed by the top leader (speaker, president), and in about one in four chambers this responsibility falls to the president pro tem, speaker pro tem, or majority leader. In roughly one in ten chambers, a committee-on-committees or a rules committee performs this task. Seniority is the rule in only a few chambers (Arkansas Senate, Utah Senate; American Society of Legislative Clerks and Secretaries 1998, Table 96-4.7). Even greater control is possible if the majority party leaders are able to dictate which minority-party members will be appointed to specific committees. In several states, the minority leader has some influence over which members of her party will be assigned to the various committees (American Society of Legislative Clerks and Secretaries 1998, 4-20–4-21).

THE LEGISLATURE AT WORK

As governmental institutions, state legislatures perform several important functions. First, they *make policy*. Legislatures are not the only policy-making institutions in the states, but they are at the center of the process. Thus when most people are asked, "What do legislatures do?" their first response is usually "They pass bills" or "They make laws for the state."

But legislatures perform other tasks as well. One of the most important is *appropriation*. Legislatures must approve the budget for the state. Technically, this can be considered part of the lawmaking function, because budgets are constructed through appropriation bills passed by the legislature. But budget setting is such an important issue, and so dominates many state legislative sessions, that we treat it as a separate function from the regular, substantive lawmaking process. State budgets today are billion-dollar documents. Not only does the state budget allocate funds for the various state agencies, but increasingly local governments (especially cities and school districts) command substantial appropriations from the state budget.

Governors have a powerful influence over the state budgetary process, because in most states it is the governor's office that first makes revenue estimates and then submits a proposed budget to the legislature, based on the projected revenue. Moreover, the governor can claim to represent the fiscal interests of the entire state, whereas legislators have a natural tendency to look out for the budgetary interests of their individual districts first. Nonetheless, few legislatures today are willing to abdicate the appropriations function entirely to the executive branch. As Rosenthal noted, "Over time legislative involvement has increased practically everywhere" (1998, 315). Most legislatures have added their own revenue estimation and budget review staff to provide themselves with an independent analysis of the budget needs of the various state agencies.

A third function of state legislatures is *administrative oversight*. Because they have primary responsibility for passing legislation, but not for administering these laws, the legislature seeks a check on the way the various state agencies are operating. This is a difficult task for state legislatures, many of which meet only part-time and have limited staff assistance. Moreover, for most legislators, the personal incentive to invest vast amounts of time in oversight is generally not very great. Nonetheless, legislatures, in varying degrees, make an effort to perform oversight. One way legislators seek oversight of state agencies is through budget hearings. Moreover, in most states the legislatures exercise some control by reviewing administrative rules and regulations. This review, which is now an institutionalized routine in many states, is a way to ensure that the administrative agencies are following legislative intent in the way the laws are executed.

Finally, legislatures perform *constituent service*. In truth, this function is more closely associated with the individual legislator than with the legislative institution, but legislators use institutional resources (for example, staff personnel) to perform this service. One form of constituent service is casework. Such service is often in the form of interceding on the constituents' behalf with a state agency, handling requests from constituents for information, or even helping them find a job (Freeman and Richardson 1996). In contrast to the oversight function, legislators have a strong incentive to perform casework and believe it aids in their efforts at reelection (Freeman and Richardson 1996).

Another form of constituent service is securing particularistic benefits to the district—a new road or airport, for example. Sometimes referred to as *pork* or *pork barrel projects,* these benefits are particularistic because they benefit a specific segment of the population (the legislators' district) but the costs are borne universally (the entire state foots the bill through the state budget). Obviously, this particular type of action is closely tied to the appropriations process.

The Legislative Process

The basic process of passing a bill into law is generally the same in all state legislatures (see the box on pages 181–183 for a summary of the legislative process), but there are differences in the details from one state to another. Moreover, the formal process is only part of the story. Personalities, outside events, and timing are all factors that affect the likelihood that any particular proposal will wend its way through the process to become law.

Most bills do not become law. The success rate varies greatly from one state to another. In 1997, for example, 9 percent of the bills introduced in the Hawaii state legislature ultimately became law, whereas the figure in the Colorado Legislature was a little more than 50 percent. There are many factors that account for this variation, but one recent study finds that more professional legislatures and those chambers that impose a limit on the number of bills a legislator can introduce tend to pass fewer proportions (Squire 1998). Another study found that both the number of bills and the proportion of bills enacted is inversely related to the number of interest groups in the state. In other words, the more interest groups, the more difficult it is to get legislation passed (Gray and Lowery 1995).

One reason that so many bills fail to become law is that the legislative process includes numerous obstacles, all of which must be overcome. To put it another way, the forces that oppose a bill only need to be successful at any one stage to block the proposed legislation, whereas the proponents must win at each step. A bill can be effectively killed (and many are) in committee. It may be gutted through floor amendments. It might be defeated on the floor vote. It might even be passed on the floor and defeated on a reconsideration motion. The bill can lose at any of these stages, in either chamber. Or it may die because a conference committee cannot produce an acceptable compromise. The governor may veto it. Some bills die simply because time runs out. It is not uncommon for a few bills to pass one chamber, be reported favorably out of committee in the second chamber, and yet be left to languish on the second or third reading calendar because the legislature adjourns the session.

Nor is it unusual for a specific piece of legislation to be introduced several years before it ultimately passes. Some proposals are so different from the status quo that it takes several years for the legislators to become "educated" about the issue, or for public opinion to become sufficiently solidified on a proposed solution. Interest groups, in particular, often take a long-term view, knowing a bill will not pass this year or perhaps even next year, but eventually "its time will come" (a common phrase in the legislative halls).

Influences on Legislative Policy Making

There are many factors involved in the policy-making process. Some of these factors have to do with the nature of the legislative institution. For example, the

Box 5-1 The Legislative Process

The Bill is drafted

The ideas for bills come from a variety of sources, including interest groups, administrative agencies, the governor's office, constituents, or the legislator herself. A bill may be drafted by an individual legislator, but more likely she will use the drafting service provided by the legislative staff. A proposal may go through several drafts before the legislator is satisfied that this is the particular proposal she wishes to carry. After the legislator approves the draft, she may seek cosponsors for the proposal.

Introduction and first reading

The draft becomes a bill when the sponsoring legislator "drops" the bill—in other words, gives it to the clerk of the chamber, who assigns the bill a number. The bill is given its first reading at this point.

In an effort to keep the institutional workload manageable, a few state legislatures limit the number of bills an individual legislator can introduce each year. In 1996 members of the Florida House were limited to six bill introductions during the legislative session; in the North Carolina House the limit was ten. In most states with such rules, exceptions are permitted for certain types of bills (for example, local bills).

Another method of containing the workload is to impose bill introduction deadlines, which many state legislatures now employ. Under such rules individual legislators cannot introduce bills after a specified day (for example, the 25th day of the session).

Committee referral

The bill is assigned to one of the substantive standing committees of the chamber. Because different committees are made up of different legislators, the decision about which committee should get the bill can sometimes be an important determinant of the bill's ultimate fate. In most states, the power of referral rests with the presiding officer.

Subcommittee

Some state legislatures make extensive use of subcommittees as a way to divide the workload within the committee. Some states make use of subcommittees only infrequently, usually to consider a particular issue such as reapportionment.

Committee hearings

Generally, the most extensive discussion and review of a bill occurs in hearings before the committee (or subcommittee). It is here that most public input will occur. This input, in the form of public testimony, is often dominated by lobbyists for interest groups, who testify in favor or opposition to the bill, or who argue for specific changes in the bill. Control over the hearing process (including, in many states, the decision of whether to schedule hearings) is usually in the hands of the committee chair. In many states, fewer than half of the bills introduced will actually be considered by the committee; the remaining bills simply die a quiet death. However, the rules of some state legislatures require all bills to receive a public hearing.

Committee action

After the bill has been reviewed and considered, the committee may report the bill out with one of several recommendations. The committee action at this stage is critical to the potential success of the bill. . The possible recommendations include "Do Pass," "Do Not Pass," "No Recommendation," "Refer to Another Committee," "Withdraw from Consideration," "Amend," "Substitute," or "Table."

Because the committee has had the chance to review the bill in detail, most legislators who are not members of this committee give serious weight to the committee's report. Thus, perhaps 90 percent of the bills that receive a favorable ("Do Pass") recommendation from the committee will ultimately pass when the bill comes up for floor vote. An unfavorable recommendation ("Do Not Pass") is rare in most states; if the committee does not favor the bill it will simply not hold hearings, or it will vote to put the bill aside ("Table"). However, a few states require all legislation to be reported from committee to floor. In

Box 5-1 *Continued*

Committee action (continued)

these states, a "Do Not Pass" recommendation is common, because the committee does not have the option of killing the bill through inaction.

Committees often recommend amendments to a bill. If substantial changes are needed, the committee may offer a substitute bill for the original one. In the case of committee amendments and substitute bills, the full membership of the chamber will have the opportunity to accept or reject the proposed changes in a separate vote prior to voting on passage of the bill itself.

Once the bill is reported from committee, it is placed on the Second Reading Calendar. If committee amendments were reported, the legislature, operating as the Committee of the Whole, will consider whether or not to adopt the proposed amendments. Amendments offered by other members (floor amendments) are usually in order at this stage as well. If amendments to the bill are adopted, the bill must be rewritten to reflect the changes. This is known as engrossment.

Third reading and floor vote

In most state legislative chambers, the floor debate and floor vote occurs at this stage. Many legislatures, especially in the lower chambers, use an electronic roll-call device to record each legislator's vote. For a bill to pass, a simple majority of those present and voting is required in most states. Thus, if there are one hundred members, and on a given bill the vote is forty-five "yeas," forty "nays," and fifteen "not present" or "abstaining," the bill would pass. However, a few states require a true majority of the chamber to vote in favor of a bill in order for it to pass. If a true majority is required, the above vote of 45–40–15 would mean the bill fails, because a true majority in a chamber with one hundred members is fifty-one. Under these circumstances, "taking a walk" on a bill has the same effect on the vote outcome as voting "nay."

Reconsideration

In keeping with the deliberative nature of legislatures, there is usually a provision that a vote on a bill can be reconsidered within a specified period of time (usually twenty-four to forty-eight hours, depending on the rules of the chamber). A call for reconsideration must be made by someone who voted on the prevailing side of the issue (in other words, if the bill passed, only someone who voted in favor of the bill can call reconsideration). Occasionally a bill will pass one day, be reconsidered and fail the next day. Or it may fail and subsequently be reconsidered and passed. This is a relatively rare occurrence, but it does happen.

Action in the second chamber

The steps in the second chamber are generally identical to those listed previously, from introduction through third reading and floor debate. Most states require sequential action, meaning that the bill is not referred to the second chamber until it has worked its way through the chamber in which it was originally introduced. However, some states permit concurrent introduction, meaning that the bill is introduced in both chambers at the same time.

Conference committees

To become law, a bill must pass both chambers in precisely the same form. If a bill passes each chamber, but in different form (for example, amendments were added in one chamber), a resolution of these differences is necessary. If neither chamber is willing to accede to the changes made by the other chamber, then a conference committee will be created in an effort to work out an acceptable compromise. In most cases the presiding officers appoint three or four members of each chamber to serve as the conferees. If a majority of the conference committee can negotiate an agreement, this new version of the bill is submitted for approval via floor vote in each chamber. If the conference report is accepted by the floor in both chambers, the bill passes. If either chamber rejects the conference report, or if the conferees cannot agree on a compromise version of the bill, the bill dies.

Box 5-1 *Continued*

Conference committees (continued)

Conference committees are more prevalent in some state legislatures than in others. In some states, they have become a very significant part of the legislative process.

Governor's action

Once a bill is passed in identical form in both chambers, the bill is sent to the governor. He may sign it into law or veto the bill. Vetoes are most common under conditions of divided government (the governor is from one party and the legislative majority is from the other party), but they occur in almost all legislative sessions. The provisions for overriding a gubernatorial veto vary a bit state to state; the most common rule is that a legislature must muster a two-thirds majority in each chamber to override the governor's veto. Only about 5 percent of gubernatorial vetoes are overwridden.

Implementation date

Once a bill is passed and signed by the governor, usually it does not immediately become law. In most states, there is a lag time of several months between passage of a bill and the date of its implementation into law. This allows the agency charged with administering the new law time to develop the procedures necessary for implementing the law.

need to develop a majority coalition at both the committee and floor vote stages means that compromise is a valued commodity. Moreover, the bicameral structure of state legislatures (except Nebraska's) means that negotiation between the chambers is often necessary.

Another consideration is the time dimension (Loomis 1994). Time is important in state legislatures in several ways. First, most state legislatures meet in session only part-time (two to four months per year). As the end of the session approaches, time becomes a critical consideration. Because there is not enough time to process all the proposals, leadership often takes control of the legislative agenda in the last few weeks of the session, deciding which bills will come to the floor for a vote and which will die on second or third reading calendar.

Second, because it takes time for legislation to be drafted, introduced, and go through the committee hearing process, the workflow of legislatures is different in the beginning of the session than at the end. In the first month or so, legislators spend most of their time in committees, and less time debating and voting on the floor. The pace appears to be slow and deliberative, even ponderous. As the session progresses, action on the floor picks up as more and more bills flow out of the committees. In the last few weeks, most of the committee work is complete and the floor activity often becomes frenetic, with perhaps dozens of roll-call votes occurring in a single day. Time, as Burdett Loomis noted, "may become more valuable the longer the legislative process runs. Two weeks at the beginning of the session may be worth less than two hours near the end" (1994, 10).

Third, legislators (and legislation) are affected by electoral cycles. Some types of policies (for example, tax increases and perhaps highly emotional issues such as abortion) are less likely to be considered during an electoral year, as legislators fear the consequences for their own careers.

Most of the legislation that comes to floor vote is relatively noncontroversial. These are often bills that make minor changes in existing law; the decision-making process on such legislation is rather routine and the roll-call votes are often unanimous or nearly unanimous. Over the course of the entire session, there may be only 100 or so bills that reach the floor and generate considerable debate and controversy. Of course, these are the bills that are most salient to the general public and the media and that may cause considerable angst for the legislators as they cast their votes.

The focus on how legislators vote on final passage of bills can mask the importance of behavior at earlier stages. Committee votes, for example, are less visible to the general public. There is evidence that roll-call votes on the floor (which are recorded) are not necessarily accurate predictors of the position taken by the legislator on the same bill in committee, where votes are often not recorded (Hamm 1982). Procedural votes (for example, a vote to recommit a bill to committee, or to hold a bill on second reading calendar) sometimes allow legislators to "kill" a bill without a formal roll call.

There are numerous "cue sources" used by state legislators in the policy-making process. Some of these sources, such as legislative staff, may be more influential at the bill formulation or the committee stage than at the floor vote stage. The committee report itself is often an important cue.

The extent of party voting varies by state legislature and circumstance. When a party holds a slim majority of seats in the chamber, legislators are more likely to feel pressure to "toe the party line" than when the party commands a large majority (more than 60 percent of the seats). In states in which the party plays an important role in nominating candidates, members are also more likely to vote with the party on important votes (Morehouse 1996).

Interest groups exert substantial influence over the legislative process in many states. In part this is because lobbyists are important sources of information for legislators, particularly in states with limited staff and time. In states in which there is a dominant economic interest (for example, agriculture in Kansas) legislators are often predisposed toward protecting that group's status. Recognizing the importance of the state legislature in policy making, many interest groups are increasingly active in state legislative elections. This often takes the form of campaign contributions to selected candidates who are supportive of the group's agenda.

Governors are also important players in the legislative process. Through the State of the State address and the budget message, both delivered at the beginning of the legislative session, the chief executive is able to help shape the policy agenda. The ultimate weapon in the gubernatorial arsenal, of course, is the veto. Because fewer than 10 percent of vetoes are successfully overridden by state legislatures, the governor can sometimes negotiate for the inclusion (or exclusion) of specific details in a bill before it is passed. Not surprisingly, the legislature is particularly pre-disposed to approve the executive's legislative package when the governor's party constitutes a legislative majority.

Ultimately, the most important cue source for most legislators is their own per-ception of constituent opinion. When public opinion in the district is clearly on one side of a specific issue, the legislator will rarely vote against it. However, very few issues provide a clear and unified voice from one's constituency. On the vast majority of bills, legislators are relatively unconstrained by constituent opinion. They may, however, feel constrained by the opinion or wishes of specific segments of their constituency. Legislators are particularly attentive to those individuals or groups within their district who have the ability to mobilize enough voters to po-tentially affect the outcome of the legislator's next election.

CONCLUSION

Legislatures are complex organizations. In part this complexity stems from the fact that to be productive legislatures must reach some consensus among a majority of its members. But the members are elected from different electoral districts, rep-resenting constituencies that are often very different from one another. This is a fact of legislative life, but one not fully appreciated by the general public.

There are numerous similarities among the legislatures in the states. For exam-ple, all state legislatures are expected to carry out the same functions: policy mak-ing, budget appropriation, administrative oversight, and constituent service. But there are also many ways in which the legislatures differ from one state to another. Many of these differences are captured in the concept of "professionalization," which reflects the differences in time commitment, monetary incentives, and staff support that one finds across the state legislatures. Other differences include the size of the legislative districts represented, the costs of campaigning for legislative office, and the degree of diversity among the legislators themselves. Further differ-ences emerge when we examine the way the legislatures are organized and the spe-cific rules under which they operate. It is these differences, and their consequences, that make state legislatures so interesting.

As a group, state legislatures face immense challenges in the years to come. Some of these challenges stem from the ongoing changes in federalism; states (and there-fore state legislatures) are again emerging as important partners in the federal rela-tionship. Other challenges stem from economic and social changes within the par-ticular state—changes that bring both opportunities and problems that must be addressed by the legislatures. Still other changes, such as term limits, are aimed di-rectly at the legislative institution itself. State legislatures under term limits will be forced to adapt in many ways.

This issue of adaptation and change in state legislatures will be a particularly in-teresting one to follow in the coming years. In the past thirty years, state legislatures have undergone many reforms aimed at "modernizing" the legislative institution. These reforms include an upgrade in physical facilities, larger staff, longer sessions, and increased salary for the legislators. Although these changes were important in extending the capacity of the legislative institution to do its job, they had the additional consequence of altering the incentive structure for those who serve in state legislatures. Because many legislatures now meet for longer periods, it becomes increasingly difficult for the individual legislator to juggle her private career and public service. Moreover, the increased staff and improved physical facilities have made the legislature a more attractive place to be. Thirty years ago many legislators served only one or two terms and then left public service because the benefits (both psychological and economic) simply did not outweigh the costs (in terms of time away from family and business). This is no longer the case in many states. Thus the changes wrought to improve the legislature also had an effect on those who serve in the legislatures. Dissatisfaction with what the public increasingly perceives as "career" legislators have created a reaction against the legislators, which in turn affects the institution itself. This is one of the important dilemmas that legislators and the public must face in the years to come: Can we build effective legislative institutions while at the same time discouraging legislators from long-term service?

REFERENCES

Agranoff, Robert. 1976. *The New Style in Election Campaigns.* Boston: Holbrook Press.

American Society of Legislative Clerks and Secretaries. 1998. *Inside the Legislative Process.* Denver, Colo.: National Conference of State Legislatures.

Anderson, R. Bruce. 1997. *Electoral Competition and the Structure of State Legislatures: Organizational Complexity and Party Building.* Unpublished Ph.D. dissertation, Rice University.

Baker, Peter. 1996. "Maverick Va. Democrat Lands in Senate Spotlight." *Washington Post,* January 22, 1996, D1.

Barber, James David. 1965. *The Lawmakers.* New Haven, Conn.: Yale University Press.

Berry, William D., Michael B. Berkman, and Stuart Schneiderman. 1998. "Explaining Incumbency Reelection." A paper presented at the annual meeting of the Midwest Political Science Association, Chicago, April 23–25.

Breaux, David, and Anthony Gierzynski. 1991. "'It's Money that Matters': Campaign Expenditures and State Legislative Primaries." *Legislative Studies Quarterly* 16:429–443.

Breaux, David, and Malcolm E. Jewell. 1992. "Winning Big: The Incumbency Advantage in State Legislative Races." In *Changing Patterns in State Legislative Careers,* edited by Gary F. Moncrief and Joel A. Thompson. Ann Arbor: University of Michigan Press.

Bullock, Charles III, and David J. Shafer. 1997. "Party Targeting and Electoral Success." *Legislative Studies Quarterly* 22:573–584.

Button, James, and David Hedge. 1996. "Legislative Life in the 1990s: A Comparison of Black and White State Legislators." *Legislative Studies Quarterly* 21:199–218.

Caldeira, Gregory, and Samuel C. Patterson. 1982. "Bringing Home the Votes: Electoral Outcomes in State Legislative Races." *Political Behavior* 4:33–67.

Campbell, Ballard. 1980. *Representative Democracy: Public Policy and Midwestern Legislatures in the Late Nineteenth Century.* Cambridge, Mass.: Harvard University Press.

Carey, John M., Richard G. Niemi, and Lynda W. Powell. 1997. "Incumbency and the Probability of Reelection in State Legislative Elections." A paper presented at the annual meeting of the American Political Science Association, Washington, D.C., August 28–31.

———. 1998. "The Effects of Term Limits on State Legislatures." *Legislative Studies Quarterly* 23:271–300.

Cassie, William E. 1994. "More May Not Always Be Better: Republican Recruiting Strategies in Southern Legislative Elections." *The American Review of Politics* 15:141–155.

Cassie, William E., and David Breaux. 1998. "Expenditures and Election Results." In *Campaign Finance in State Legislative Elections,"* edited by Joel A. Thompson and Gary F. Moncrief. Washington, D.C.: Congressional Quarterly.

Center for the American Woman and Politics. 1998. "CAWP Fact Sheet: Women in State Legislatures 1998." Available at http:/www/rci/rutgers/edu/~cawp/stleg98/html.

Christensen, Rob. 1989. "Growing Republican Ranks Help Topple Speaker in North Carolina." *State Legislatures* (April):16–19.

Cox, Elizabeth. 1996. *Women State and Territorial Legislators, 1895–1995: A State-by-State Analysis, with Rosters of 6000 Women.* Jefferson, N.C.: McFarland Press.

Cox, Gary W. 1997. *Making Votes Count.* Cambridge: Cambridge University Press.

Cox, Gary W., and Scott Morgenstern. 1993. "The Increasing Advantage of Incumbency in the American States." *Legislative Studies Quarterly* 18:495–514.

———. 1995. "The Incumbency Advantage in Multimember Districts: Evidence from the U.S. States." *Legislative Studies Quarterly* 20: 329–349.

Darcy, Robert. 1996. "Women in the State Legislative Power Structure: Committee Chairs." *Social Science Quarterly* 77:889–898.

Dewhirst, Robert. 1996. "The Missouri House Finally Elects a New Speaker." *Comparative State Politics* 17:1–3.

Diamond, Irene. 1977. *Sex Roles in the State House.* New Haven, Conn.: Yale University Press.

———. 1997. "Change and Continuity among Women State Legislators: Evidence from Three Decades." *Political Research Quarterly* 50:137–151.

Dolan, Kathleen and Lynne Ford. 1997. "Change and Continuity Among Women State Legislators: Evidence from Three Decades." *Political Research Quarterly.* 50:137–150.

Dye, Thomas. 1981. *Politics in States and Communities.* Englewood Cliffs, N.J: Prentice-Hall.

Ehrenhalt, Alan. 1991. *The United States of Ambition.* New York: Times Books.

Eulau, Heinz, and Paul D. Karps. 1977. "Representation: Specifying Components of Responsiveness." *Legislative Studies Quarterly* 2:233–254.

Fenno, Richard. 1978. *Homestyle.* Boston, Mass.: Little, Brown.

Fiorina, Morris P. 1994. "Divided Government in the American States: A Byproduct of Legislative Professionalism." *American Political Science Review* 88:314–316.

———. 1996. *Divided Government.* 2d ed. Boston: Allyn and Bacon.

Francis, Wayne. 1989. *The Legislative Committee Game: A Comparative Analysis of Fifty States.* Columbus: Ohio State University Press.

Freeman, Patricia. 1995. "A Comparative Analysis of Speaker Career Patterns in U.S. State Legislatures." *Legislative Studies Quarterly* 20:365–375.

Freeman, Patricia, and Lilliard Richardson, Jr. 1994. "Casework in State Legislatures." *State and Local Government Review* 26:21–26.

———. 1996. "Explaining Variation in Casework among State Legislators." *Legislative Studies Quarterly* 21:41–57.

Frendreis, John, Alan Gitelson, Gregory Fleming, and Anne Layzell. 1996. "Local Political Parties and Legislative Races in 1992 and 1994." In *The State of the Parties,* 2d ed., edited by John C. Green and Daniel M. Shea. Lanham, Md.: Rowman and Littlefield.

Frendreis, John, and Alan Gitelson. 1997. "Shifting Partisan Fortunes in Electoral Politics: Winning and Losing in the 1992, 1994, and 1996 State Legislative Elections." A paper presented at the annual meeting of the Southern Political Science Association, Norfolk, Va., November 5–8.

Gibson, James, John Frendreis, and Laura Vertz. 1989. "Party Dynamics in the 1980s: Changes in County Party Organization Strength, 1980–1984." *American Journal of Political Science* 33:67–90.

Gierzynski, Anthony. 1992. *Legislative Party Campaign Committees in the American States.* Lexington: University of Kentucky Press.

Gierzynski, Anthony, and David Breaux. 1993. "Money and the Party Vote in State House Elections." *Legislative Studies Quarterly* 18:515–534.

Gray, Virginia, and David Lowery. 1995. "Interest Representation and Democratic Gridlock." *Legislative Studies Quarterly* 20:531–552.

Hamm, Keith E. 1982. "Consistency between Committee and Floor Voting in U.S. State Legislatures." *Legislative Studies Quarterly* 7:473–490

Hamm, Keith E., and Ronald D. Hedlund. 1994. "Committees in State Legislatures." In *The Encyclopedia of the American Legislative System,* edited by Joel J. Silbey. New York: Charles Scribner's Sons.

———. 1995. "The Development of Committee Specialization in State Legislatures." A paper presented at the annual meeting of the American Political Science Association, Chicago, August 31–September 3.

Hamm, Keith E., Ronald D. Hedlund, and R. Bruce Anderson. 1994. "Political Parties in State Legislatures." In *The Encyclopedia of the American Legislative System*, edited by Joel J. Silbey. New York: Charles Scribner's Sons.

Hamm, Keith E., Ronald D. Hedlund, and Nancy Martorano. 1998. "The Evolution of Committee Structural Powers and Procedures in State Legislatures." A paper presented at the annual meeting of the Southwestern Political Science Association, Corpus Christi, Texas, March 18–21.

Hamm, Keith E., and David M. Olson. 1992. "Midsession Vacancies: Why Do State Legislators Leave and How Are They Replaced?" In *Changing Patterns in State Legislative Careers*, edited by Gary F. Moncrief and Joel A. Thompson. Ann Arbor: University of Michigan Press.

Hansen, Karen. 1997. "Living within Term Limits." *State Legislatures* (June):13–19.

Haynes, George H. 1990a. "Representation in the Legislatures of the North Atlantic States," *Annals of the Academy of Political and Social Science* 15:208–235.

———. 1990b. "Representation in the Legislatures of the North Central States," *Annals of the Academy of Political and Social Science* 15:405–425.

———. 1990c. "Representation in State Legislatures III: The Southern States," *Annals of the Academy of Political and Social Science* 16:93–119.

———. 1990d. "Representation in State Legislatures IV: The Western States," *Annals of the Academy of Political and Social Science* 16:243–273.

Hedlund, Ronald D. 1984. "Organizational Attributes of Legislative Institutions: Structure, Rules, Norms, Resources." *Legislative Studies Quarterly* 9:51–121.

Hedlund, Ronald D., and Keith E. Hamm. 1994. "The Evolution and Role of Committee Specialization in the Legislative Process: Developing and Testing a Cross-System Model." A paper presented at the International Political Science Association Meeting, Berlin, Germany, August 21–25.

———. 1996. "Political Parties as Vehicles for Organizing U.S. State Legislative Committees." *Legislative Studies Quarterly* 21:383–408.

Hodson, Timothy, Rich Jones, Karl Kurtz, and Gary F. Moncrief. 1995. "Leaders and Limits: Changing Patterns of State Legislative Leadership under Term Limits." *Spectrum: The Journal of State Government* 68 (Summer):6–15.

Hogan, Robert. 1998. *The Role of Political Campaigns in State Elections.* Unpublished Ph.D. dissertation, Rice University.

Hogan, Robert E., and Keith E. Hamm. 1998. "Variations in District-Level Campaign Spending in State Legislatures." In *Campaign Finance in State Legislative Elections*, edited by Joel A. Thompson and Gary F. Moncrief. Washington, D.C.: Congressional Quarterly.

Jewell, Malcolm E. 1962. *The State Legislature: Politics in Practice.* New York: Random House.

———. 1982. *Representation in State Legislatures.* Lexington: University of Kentucky Press.

Jewell, Malcolm E., and David M. Olson. 1988. *Political Parties and Elections in the American States.* Chicago: Dorsey Press.

Jewell, Malcolm E., and Marcia Whicker. 1994. *Legislative Leadership in the American States.* Ann Arbor: University of Michigan Press.

Jones, Megan, David H. Guston, and Lewis M. Branscomb. 1996. *Informed Legislatures: Coping with the Science of a Democracy.* Cambridge, Mass.: Center for Science and International Affairs Harvard University.

Kirkpatrick, Jeane. 1974. *Political Woman.* New York: Basic Books.

Little, Thomas H. 1995. "Understanding Legislative Leadership beyond the Chamber: The Members' Perspective." *Legislative Studies Quarterly* 20:269–289.

Loewenberg, Gerhard. 1972. "Comparative Legislative Research." In *Comparative Legislative Behavior: Frontiers of Research*, edited by Samuel C. Patterson and John C. Wahlke. New York: Wiley.

Loomis, Burdett A. 1988. *The New American Politician: Ambition, Entrepreneurship, and the Changing Face of Political Life.* New York: Basic Books.

———. 1994. *Time, Politics, and Policies: A Legislative Year.* Lawrence: University of Kansas Press.

Luttbeg, Norman. 1992. "Legislative Careers in Six States: Are Some Legislatures More Likely to Be Responsive?" *Legislative Studies Quarterly* 17:49–69.

Maisel, Sandy, and E. Ivry. 1997. "If You Don't Like Our Politics: Wait a Minute." *Polity* (Special Supplement):15–36.

Mezey, Susan Gluck. 1994. "Increasing the Number of Women in Office: Does It Matter?" In *The Year of the Woman: Myths and Realities*, edited by Elizabeth Adell Cook, Sue Thomas, and Clyde Wilcox. Boulder, Colo.: Westview Press.

Moakley, Maureen. 1997. "Political Parties in Rhode Island: Back to the Future." *Polity* (Special Supplement):95–112.

Moncrief, Gary F. 1998. "Candidate Spending in State Legislative Races." In *Campaign Finance in State Legislative Elections*, edited by Joel A. Thompson and Gary F. Moncrief. Washington, D.C.: Congressional Quarterly.

Moncrief, Gary F., and Joel A. Thompson. 1992a. *Changing Patterns in State Legislative Careers.* Ann Arbor: University of Michigan Press.

———. 1992b. "Electoral Structure and State Legislative Representation." *Journal of Politics* 54:246–257.

Moncrief, Gary F., Joel A. Thompson, Michael Haddon, and Robert Hoyer. 1992. "For Whom the Bell Tolls." *Legislative Studies Quarterly* 17:37–47.

Moncrief, Gary F., Joel A. Thompson, and William E. Cassie. 1996. "Revisiting the State of U.S. State Legislative Research." *Legislative Studies Quarterly* 21:301–335.

Moncrief, Gary F., Joel A. Thompson, and Karl Kurtz. 1996. "The Old Statehouse, It Ain't What It Used to Be." *Legislative Studies Quarterly* 21:57–72.

Moncrief, Gary F., Peverill Squire, and Karl Kurtz. 1998. "State Legislative Candidate Recruitment." A paper presented at the 1998 annual meeting of the Western Political Science Association, Los Angeles, March 19–21.

Mooney, Christopher. 1995. "Citizens, Structures, and Sister States: Influences on State Legislative Professionalism." *Legislative Studies Quarterly* 20:47–67.

Morehouse, Sarah McCally. 1996. "Legislative Party Voting for the Governor's Program." *Legislative Studies Quarterly* 21:359–381.

National Conference of State Legislatures. 1996a. *State Legislators' Occupations: 1993 and 1995.* Denver, Colo.: National Conference of State Legislatures.

———. 1996b. "Size of State Legislative Staff: 1979, 1988 and 1996." Available at http://www. ncsl.org/programs/legman/about/stf3.htm. June 30, 1996.

———. 1996c. "Fate of President's Party in State Legislative Elections, 1960–1996." Available at http:/www.ncsl.org/programs/legman.elect/presprty. html. November 11, 1996.

———. 1996d. "Incumbent Reelection Rates in 1994 State Legislative Elections." Available at http:/www/ncsl.org/programs/legman/elect/incumb.html. October 30, 1996.

———. 1997. "State Legislative Turnover: 1987–1997." *State Legislatures* (June):18.

———. 1998. "Term Limits of State Elected Officials." Available at http:/www.ncsl.org/programs/legman/about/termlim.html. March 30, 1998.

Neal, Tommy. 1996. *Lawmaking and the Legislative Process: Committees, Connections, and Compromises.* Denver, Colo.: National Conference of State Legislatures.

Niemi, Richard G., Simon Jackman, and Laura R. Winsky. 1991. "Candidacies and Competitiveness in Multimember Districts." *Legislative Studies Quarterly* 16:91–109.

"On First Reading: Close Chambers Yield Chaos, Rifts, and Power Sharing." *State Legislatures* (April):9.

Opheim, Cynthia. 1994. "The Effect of U.S. State Legislative Term Limits Revisited." *Legislative Studies Quarterly* 19:49–59.

Patterson, Samuel C. 1995. "Legislative Politics in the States." In *Politics in the American States*, 6th ed., edited by Virginia Gray and Herbert Jacob. Washington, D.C.: CQ Press.

Perkins, Jay. 1996. "Toeing the Line in Louisiana." *State Legislatures* (July/August):24–27.

Rosenthal, Alan. 1998. *The Decline of Representative Democracy: Process, Participation, and Power in State Legislatures.* Washington DC: CQ Press.

Rosenthal, Cindy Simon. 1995. "New Party or Campaign Bank Account? Explaining the Rise of State Legislative Campaign Committees." *Legislative Studies Quarterly* 20:249–268.

Sabatier, Paul, and David Whiteman. 1985. "Legislative Decision Making and Substantive Policy Information: Models of Information Flow." *Legislative Studies Quarterly* 10:395–421.

Salmore, Stephen A., and Barbarba G. Salmore. 1989. *Candidates, Parties, and Campaigns: Electoral Politics in America.* 2d ed. Washington, D.C.: CQ Press.

Scher, Richard, J. L. Mills, and J. J. Hotaling. 1997. *Voting Rights and Democracy.* Chicago: Nelson-Hall.

Schlesinger, Joseph A. 1966. *Political Parties and the Winning of Office.* Ann Arbor: University of Michigan Press.

Shea, David M. 1995 . *Transforming Democracy: Legislative Campaign Committees and Political Parties.* Albany: State University of New York Press.

Squire, Peverill. 1992. "Legislative Professionalization and Membership Diversity in State Legislatures." *Legislative Studies Quarterly* 17:69–79.

———. 1993. "Professionalization and Public Opinion of State Legislatures." *The Journal of Politics* 55:479–491.

———. 1998. "Membership Turnover and the Efficient Processing of Legislation." *Legislative Studies Quarterly* 23:23–32.

"Statestats: More Women Legislators and Leaders." 1997. *State Legislatures* (April):5.

Thomas, Sue. 1991. "The Impact of Women in State Legislative Policies." *Journal of Politics* 53:958–976.

———. 1994. *How Women Legislate.* New York: Oxford University Press.

Thompson, Joel A. 1986. "Bringing Home the Bacon: The Politics of Pork Barrel in the North Carolina Legislature." *Legislative Studies Quarterly* 11:91–108.

Thompson, Joel A., Karl Kurtz, and Gary F. Moncrief. 1996. "We've Lost that Family Feeling: The Norms of the New Breed of State Legislators." *Social Science Quarterly* 77:344–362.

Thompson, Joel A., and Gary F. Moncrief. 1987. "Pursuing the Pork in a State Legislature: A Research Note." *Legislative Studies Quarterly* 13:393–401.

———. 1992. "Nativity, Mobility, and State Legislators." In *Changing Patterns in State Legislative Careers,* edited by Gary F. Moncrief and Joel A. Thompson. Ann Arbor: University of Michigan Press.

———, ed. 1998. *Campaign Finance in State Legislative Elections.* Washington D.C.: Congressional Quarterly.

Tobin, Richard J., and Edward Keynes. 1975. "Institutional Differences in the Recruitment Process: A Four State Study." *American Journal of Political Science* 19:667–682.

Tucker, Harvey, and Ronald E. Weber. 1987. "State Legislative Election Outcomes: Contextual Effects and Legislative Performance Effects." *Legislative Studies Quarterly* 12:537–553.

Van Dunk, Emily, and Thomas M. Holbrook. 1994. "The 1994 State Legislative Elections." *Extension of Remarks, Legislative Studies Section Newsletter* (December):8–12.

Wahlke, John C., Heinz Eulau, William Buchanan, and Leroy C. Ferguson. 1962. *The Legislative System.* New York: John Wiley.

Willey, Keven. 1997. "Arizona Heats Up." *State Legislatures* (February):26–29.

Williams, Christine. 1990. "Women, Law and Politics: Recruitment Patterns in Fifty States." *Women and Politics* 10:103–123.

Zeller, Belle. 1954. *American State Legislatures.* New York: Thomas Y. Crowell.

SUGGESTED READINGS

Loftus, Tom. *The Art of Legislative Politics.* Washington, D.C.: CQ Press, 1994. An anecdotal, "inside" look at politics in a state legislature, written by the former Speaker of the Wisconsin State Assembly.

Rosenthal, Alan. *The Decline of Representative Democracy.* Washington, D.C.: CQ Press, 1998. A thoughtful review of the changes in state legislatures over the past generation.

Thomas, Sue. *How Women Legislate.* New York: Oxford University Press, 1994. Based on a survey of women legislators in twelve states, Thomas analyzes the increasingly important role of women in state legislatures.

Thompson, Joel A., and Gary F. Moncrief, eds. *Campaign Finance in State Legislative Elections.* Washington, D.C: CQ Press, 1998. Based on an extensive research collaboration involving eight political scientists, this book analyzes contribution and spending patterns in state legislative races in eighteen states.

CHAPTER 6

The Governors

THAD BEYLE

Greatest job in the world, as most Governors, I suspect, tell you.
—Michael Dukakis, governor of Massachusetts, 1975–1979, 1983–1991 (NGA 1981, 81)

At the top of each state's political and governmental hierarchy is the governor—the person who personifies the state to many. He or she is seen as the most powerful political personality in most states; the state's legislature, bureaucracy, press, politics, and policies are affected by or bear the imprint of the governor.

These major actors in our states are supposed to fill a long roster of roles. A handbook written just for governors lists the following: head of the executive branch, legislative leader, head of party, national figure, family member, and ceremonial chief (National Governors' Association [hereinafter NGA] 1978). Other roles are equally broad in responsibility, such as those of intergovernmental actor and policy leader, and some appear to be narrower in scope, such as those of manager and chief crisis manager (Morehouse 1981; NGA 1981).

How a governor responds to and handles unexpected crises greatly influences how we perceive his or her overall performance as a governor. As former governor Scott M. Matheson (D-Utah, 1977–1985) argued, "[T]he public expects the governor to take a lead . . . and a governor found wanting in a crisis situation rarely recovers politically" (Matheson 1986, 200).

How a governor performs in day-to-day administrative actions can also influence how we perceive his or her performance in office. Most governors perform admirably and their administrations are well-respected; others do not perform well and they struggle as they govern.

Governors have not always been at the top of the pecking order in their states, nor have they always been at the center of most state activities. The negligible powers and responsibilities given to the earliest state governors reflected the basic antipathy the citizens of the colonial period felt toward executive power—a dislike carried over from their relations with imposed colonial governors. Over the next two centuries, the governors gradually gained more power, and many of the early restrictions placed on them were removed or greatly reduced. This did not happen in an orderly fashion; rather, it happened in a series of incremental steps and in varying degrees across the states. And in many states, new restrictions or new problems and challenges faced the governors as state governments evolved.

Beginning with the democratization movement in the early nineteenth century, the selection of governors moved from the legislature to the people. This "pursuit of representativeness" also added new restrictions on the governor as other state administrative officials came to be selected by direct popular election (Kaufman 1963, 36). Thus some of the administrative functions were placed outside the control of the governor and into the hands of others directly responsible to the people.

As it became apparent following the Civil War that legislative bodies could not run the states or administer programs, and as patronage and corruption increased, more changes occurred. Restrictions were placed on gubernatorial and legislative powers, and a drive began to raise the competence of state government—like governments at all levels—through the use of merit systems and civil service personnel procedures in which "what you know" became more important than "who you know." Further, as new problems and responsibilities arose, agencies, boards, and commissions were established to handle them—again, often outside the direct control of any executive official. These efforts to obtain something called "neutral competence" in running government were an attempt to separate politics from administration. The governors and legislators were obviously on the political side, and these reforms were meant to maintain that separation.

In the twentieth century, constitutional revision and executive branch reorganization have changed state governments and clarified lines of authority. Governors now have longer terms of office, can succeed themselves, and have more staff for assistance. In addition, they have been given considerable budget authority to help control the executive branch and more veto power to use in their legislative negotiations. At the same time, however, the strength and reach of the civil service and merit systems have increased, providing state employees with a degree of protection and even insulation from the governor.

In this chapter, I examine the current status of the American governorship and discuss the following questions. First, who are the governors and how do they become governors? What is the nature of gubernatorial politics? Second, what powers do our states provide to the governors so they may fulfill their roles? To what extent do these powers vary across the fifty states and by individual governors? Third, what are the major roles that all governors must perform? How do these roles provide governors with greater informal powers to achieve their goals? Fourth, what do governors do after the governorship? What are the options available to these key state actors following their tenure in office? In a sense, I follow the trajectory of the

Table 6-1 Entry-Level or First Office of a Governor's Career (in percentages)[a]

	1900[b]–1949	1950[c]–1980	1981–1997	1900–1997
n =	501	324	108	933
Legislative	29	35	41	33
Law enforcement	19	23	17	20
Statewide elective	5	4	6	4
Congress	0.4	2	3	1
Administrative	15	15	4	14
Local elective	10	11	14	11
No prior office	8	10	13	10
Other	13	1	4	8

[a] Percentages do not add to 100 because of rounding.

[b] From Sabato (1983, 36–37).

[c] From Sabato (1983, 38–39).

individuals who seek to be governor, win the election, serve as governors, and move on from the governorship. Each step influences what happens on the next, and as we shall see, these are not discrete steps.

Throughout the chapter I present the differences between states, governorships, and governors to point out the diversity inherent in the fifty-state federal union. This should not overshadow the larger point of understanding, which is how similar these actors, their offices, and their responsibilities are, despite the diversity.

BECOMING GOVERNOR

Where You Have Been Makes a Difference

A basic clue to what a particular public office is all about, and its position within any political power hierarchy, is who seeks and fills that office. Of interest are some of the career steps governors pursue prior to the governorship. The first step of interest is their entry level onto the gubernatorial ambition ladder. Where did they start their elective political career? Table 6-1 indicates that more than half the governors serving between 1900 and 1997 began their careers either as state legislators or in law enforcement.[1] This has been especially true since 1950 when nearly three out of five governors used these offices as their entry points. And the importance of the state legislature as the first step is increasing as four out of ten governors entering office since 1981 began their elective career there.

Note also the growing number of governors for whom the first elective office is being elected governor—one of eight elected governors since 1980 had held no previous elected position. With the ability to translate a well-known name from another part of society along with being able to afford the "spend your way into office" type of politics so prevalent today, it is no surprise that this category should be on the rise. Also showing some increasing importance as first steps are local elective

---

1. County and city attorneys, district attorney, U.S. attorney, judges at all levels, CIA and FBI personnel, and state attorney general (even if elected by statewide vote).

positions[2] and serving in the U.S. Congress.[3] On the other hand, starting out in administrative positions en route to the governorship has declined sharply since 1981.[4]

The second step of interest is their last step prior to becoming governor, the penultimate or stepping stone office in their elective careers. Table 6-2 indicates that although three-fifths of the twentieth-century governors' penultimate offices were either other statewide elective offices, the state legislature, or law enforcement—in about equal rates—since 1981 there has been a considerable shift in their launching pads. Other statewide elective offices now account for nearly three of ten of the governors and law enforcement positions have declined considerably to only one in ten. Also rising in importance is U.S. congressional and senatorial seats and, as noted previously, those who have held no previous elective office.

Elective statewide positions—whether lieutenant governor, secretary of state, state treasurer, state attorney general, or state auditor—obviously can provide a strong jumping-off position for candidates for the governorship. Also included in this category are former governors who run and win the office again. Probably the most interesting former governor winning office in recent years is Cecil Underwood (R-W.V.) who rewon the office in 1996, the office he first won in 1956! In 1956 he was the youngest governor ever to be elected governor in that state; in 1996 he was the oldest.

Of the 1998 incumbent governors, sixteen moved up from a statewide elective position, four others were former governors, and two were former U.S. senators. Another, Gov. Christine Todd Whitman (R-N.J.), had run a nearly successful U.S. Senate campaign against Sen. Bill Bradley (D-N.J.) in 1990 prior to her successful gubernatorial run in 1993. Nearly half of the fifty governors serving in 1998 had had statewide elective and service experience prior to their successful run for the governor's chair. Seven of the other incumbents had had no prior elective office experience, four were former U.S. congressional representatives, eight had moved up from the legislature and four from local government positions, and one each came from a law enforcement or an administrative position. Three of these governors succeeded to the office on the removal or resignation from office of the elected governor.[5]

There has been a change in the number of governors moving from the U.S. Congress to the state house, from about 10 percent between 1900 and 1980 (Sabato

---

2. All elective offices at the local level except county and city attorneys or district attorneys.

3. Seats in the U.S. House of Representatives or U.S. Senate.

4. All public offices on local, statewide, and federal levels that are not elective. These are sometimes appointive and other times career positions. No law enforcement offices are included in this category. At the state level, elective offices in some states (such as the state auditor) are administrative in others.

5. In Arizona, Secretary of State Jane Hull become governor in 1997 on the conviction of incumbent governor Fife Symington on bank fraud; in Arkansas, Lt. Gov. Mike Huckabee became governor in 1996 on the conviction of incumbent governor Jim Guy Tucker on fraudulent business practices counts; and in Massachusetts, Lt. Gov. Paul Cellucci became governor in 1997 when incumbent governor William Weld resigned to accept a presidential appointment as the U.S. Ambassadorship to Mexico—an appointment that failed to be considered by the U.S. Senate, so Weld returned to private life.

Table 6-2 Penultimate or Stepping Stone Office of a Governor's Career (in percentages)[a]

	1900[b]–1949	1950[c]–1980	1981–1997	1900–1997
n =	501	324	108	933
Legislative	18	24	19	20
Law enforcement	19	19	11	18
Statewide elective	19	22	29	21
Congress	10	9	16	10
Administrative	14	10	7	12
Local elective	7	5	6	6
No prior office	8	10	13	10
Other	6	0	0	3

[a] Percentages do not add to 100 due to rounding.

[b] From Sabato (1983, 36–37).

[c] From Sabato (1983, 38–39)

1983, 40) up to 16 percent between 1981 and 1997. In the most recent period, those candidates using this avenue tended to be in the South and the Northeast, with forty-six of the sixty-three congressional candidates who ran (73 percent). Their success rate in these two regions was 28 percent, whereas only three of the seventeen congressional candidates running in the Midwest and West won (18 percent). It is better to run from the base of an U.S. senate seat, as four of the six candidates who did won.[6] The two losing U.S. senatorial candidacies were by the same individual in 1982 and 1986, Adlai Stevenson, III, the son of the former governor and Democratic presidential candidate of the 1950s.

A part of the political calculus involved in making this type of move is the ability to do so without jeopardizing one's current congressional seat. Some states have off-year gubernatorial elections, which allow some members of Congress to campaign while retaining their federal seat. In some other states, such as Connecticut, the timing of the party nominations permits a member of Congress to hold the congressional seat until the nomination is won and then resign in time for the election campaign (Sabato 1983, 41).

By and large, the evidence suggests that previous electoral experience (with the attendant visibility) at the statewide, congressional, or state legislative levels is one of the most important steps to the governorship. Most governors have had such electoral experience as their penultimate office. The career ladders of those who ran and failed to win the governorship are missing in this context. Would their paths to defeat be substantially different from the paths of those who won? It is an interesting question to consider.

There are a few hints if we look at the unsuccessful rates for some specific elective positions in the 1981–1997 elections. In this case we would not only see that 70 percent of the lieutenant governors who ran lost, but then should add in all those

6. Henry Bellman in Oklahoma (1986); Pete Wilson in California (1990); Lowell Weicker in Connecticut (1990); and Lawton Chiles (1990).

other lieutenant governors who decided not to seek the office even though they were only a heartbeat away from being governor while holding that office. Other statewide offices had similar unsuccessful rates of moving up to be governor: state auditors (83 percent unsuccessful rate); attorneys general (77 percent unsuccessful rate); secretaries of state (69 percent unsuccessful rate); and state treasurers (67 percent unsuccessful rate).

The Election Campaign: It Costs Money

Will Rogers once said, "Politics has got so expensive that it takes a lot of money to get beat with." During the past few decades, the costs of running for and winning the governor's seat have escalated rapidly.[7] In 1956 the average cost of a gubernatorial campaign was estimated to be $100,000 (up to $300,000 in the more populated states); any "political skull-duggery" would be on top of that (Ransone 1956, 105–106). Those 1956 dollars would be equal to about $.6 million and nearly $1.8 million, respectively, in 1997 dollars.

The rise in the costs of gubernatorial elections is clearly demonstrated in Figure 6-1. Each data point represents the candidates' expenditures in the most recent four-year bank of elections, normalized into 1997 dollars for comparison purposes. In this way we are able to see the comparative costs of gubernatorial elections across all fifty states between 1977 and 1997. The year 1977 is selected as the starting point because that is when the reporting of such campaign data began to be required across the states, although in varying ways.

As can be seen, the cost of these elections has been rising steadily, and at times sharply, over the twenty-one year period. In the earliest 1977 to 1980 bank of elections, the total cost was $422.7 million; by the most recent 1994 to 1997 bank of elections the total cost was $611.8 million, a 45 percent increase. The largest jumps in the level of expenditures are tied to those years in which thirty-six states held their gubernatorial elections (1982, 1986, and 1990). In the 1980s these jumps were probably tied to the adoption of new and expensive campaign techniques and technologies in gubernatorial campaigns across the fifty states. Since the late 1980s, the cost of these elections has leveled off in the $600 million range, but that could change with 1998 being a banner year with thirty-six gubernatorial elections.

Some of the most expensive gubernatorial races have been where you might expect them to be: in the largest states. The past four gubernatorial races in California through 1994 averaged nearly $51 million per election, and in Texas the average was more than $44 million. In New York's last four elections through 1994 the average was lower (just under $26 million) mainly because incumbent governor Mario Cuomo was being reelected in two of them. However, cost of the 1982 election when he was initially elected governor was more than $39 million and the 1994

---

7. All dollar figures and amounts in this section are in 1997 equivalent dollars based on the Consumer Price Index (CPI-U). The CPI-U is based on 1982–1984 = 100. The 1977 CPI-U was equal to 60.6 of that index base, the 1997 CPI-U was equal to 161.3 of that index base.

Figure 6-1   Costs of Gubernatorial Elections, 1977–1997[1]

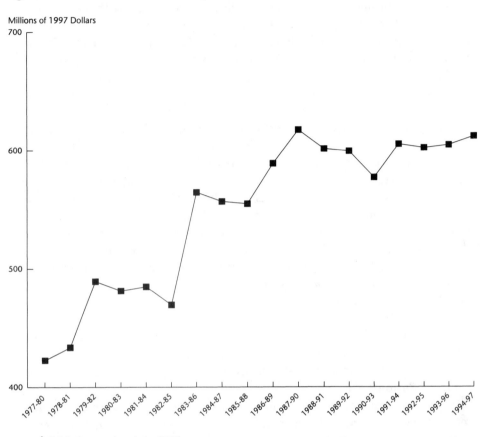

Millions of 1997 Dollars

[1] All dollar figures are in equivalent 1997$.

election when Republican challenger George Pataki unseated him cost $35 million. This New York history illustrates several points about the costs of these elections: Electing a new governor and unseating an incumbent governor that may include a change in party controlling the governorship costs a lot of money; the cost is less when incumbents successfully seek reelection (Beyle 1996).

Although large states might be expected to have expensive gubernatorial races, some of the most expensive races have been in southern states, where one-party Democratic dominance is being replaced by costly candidate-oriented campaigns in a two-party setting. The high $44 million average cost of the Texas elections was already noted. Louisiana, Florida, and Kentucky have seen their governors' races average between $21 million to $26 million, with Tennessee, Virginia, and North Carolina races averaging between $16 million to $20 million. Arkansas's gubernatorial races have averaged around $4 million over the period, a relatively low cost in good part because Bill Clinton was running for election or reelection in many of the state's seven elections over the 1977–1997 period.

The reasons for such costs and their continuing escalation are many. Changes in the style of campaigning are the most significant among them. With the transformation of state political parties and the decline of party identification among voters, candidates cannot afford to sit back and work with the party regulars to deliver the votes needed for winning. Going from county to county and meeting with the local politicos may solidify some votes and bring together part of a winning coalition, but doing so takes time, hits too few people, and does not deliver enough votes.

The most direct path to the potential voters is through the mass media, and that costs a lot of money. Opinion polls, political consultants, media consultants, direct-mail persuasion and fund-raising, telephone banks, and rapid travel throughout the state are all expensive, but all are needed in contemporary campaigns. The 1988 gubernatorial election in Utah provides a good example of the cost of media in a campaign. The four major candidates spent nearly $5.9 million in 1997 dollars, of which more than 46.5 percent, or nearly $2 million, was spent for communications media. For the not-so-well-known candidate in a party primary or the general election, "electronic advertising [television and radio] is the only way to gain visibility" (Morehouse 1987). As one political consultant noted, "[E]veryone knows that half the money spent in a political campaign is wasted. The trouble is that nobody knows which half" (North Carolina Center 1989).

What, in effect, all this money adds up to is the cost of building a winning coalition. As Sabato has suggested, this involves the creation of a party "substitute," through which the candidate constructs his own campaign organization for his or her race (Sabato 1978).

Why do so many candidates spend so much of their own and other people's money to become governor? One reason might be the salary a governor receives, a proposition suggesting that a candidate does so for the money he or she can make while being governor. In the mid-1990s, gubernatorial salaries averaged more than $100,000, ranging from $130,000 in New York to $60,000 in Arkansas (CSG 1998, 20–21). Adjusted for inflation, this average is not too different from the average salary governors made in 1955 (Beyle 1995). These may be goodly sums, but they scarcely warrant the amounts spent in the campaign to become governor.

Salary is not the only monetary reward a governor can receive: On leaving office, some former governors can obtain high-paying positions in the private sector. Those who are lawyers often open or join a law firm in the state capital and receive large retainers to serve as legal representatives or lobbyists for various interests that purchase the former governor's unique access to state officials and agencies. Thus some candidates may spend the money in campaigns for the money they can make after being governor.

A third reason is tied to the political ambitions of the gubernatorial candidates. The governorship can serve as a launching pad for the individual to seek other offices, such as a seat in the U.S. Senate or even the presidency. In the twentieth century, more than 120 governors moved on to the U.S. Senate; in the 105th Congress

(1997–1998) thirteen former governors held a seat in the U.S. Senate, and one former governor was sitting in the House of Representatives. Sixteen former governors have become president, and governors have been candidates for either the presidency or the vice presidency in forty-five of the nation's fifty-two presidential elections. Most governors, however, go no further than the governorship: More than 2,000 have served in the office, and for most it is the final elective office they hold (Beyle 1988, 134–135).

Of course, any listing of the reasons for spending large amounts of money in a political campaign must include the desire to perform public service for the good of the state and its citizens. Even so, it still costs a great deal to become a statesperson.

If we control for the cost per general election vote in each state, however, another picture appears. The most expensive gubernatorial election per vote cast in the past five general elections is Alaska ($42.10), followed by Hawaii ($23.54), Kentucky ($23.20), West Virginia ($16.58), Louisiana ($16.23), and Wyoming ($11.51). Three of these six states are in the South, but the other three—Alaska, Hawaii, Wyoming—have small populations spread about in some unique ways. It costs more to reach the voters in these states. Geography also plays a considerable role in the cost of gubernatorial elections.

Which of these factors is the most significant probably varies not only by state but also by candidate and by circumstances. Individual governor's races are generally more expensive when political parties are weak, an open seat is up, the race is highly contested from nomination to general election, there is a partisan shift as a result of the election, or an incumbent is unseated (Beyle 1988b, 21–22; 1996, 10–14; 1998, 26–30).

Opportunity to Become Governor

Another constraint on individuals wishing to become governors is the availability of opportunities to do so.[8] Just how often do the governors' chairs have new occupants?

The twentieth century has seen a decline in the number of such opportunities. One of the causes is obviously the executive reform movement, which has increased most gubernatorial terms from two years to four and has allowed more governors to seek reelection. In fact, several recent governors have effectively made the office their career, thereby closing off opportunities for others for more than a decade.

To demonstrate this change, the data in Table 6-3 indicate that there was a much greater opportunity to become governor after the Civil War, when the thirty-seven states averaged 4.2 governors per state in the 1870s, compared with the 1980s when the fifty states averaged 1.1 new governors per state. In the 1980s only two states—Kentucky and Mississippi—had three new governors, and four—Idaho, Massachusetts, Minnesota, Oklahoma—did not see a new governor in the decade (Beyle

---

8. Portions of this section are taken from Beyle 1992, "Term Limits".

Table 6-3 Number of New Governors: Selected Decades, 1800–1997[a]

Decade	States	New governors	Average number per state
1800–1809	17	56	3.3
1820–1829	24	92	3.8
1850–1859	31	124	4.0
1870–1879	37	154	4.2
1900–1909	46	154	3.3
1920–1929	48	185	3.9
1950–1959	48	108	2.3
1960–1969	50	102	2.0
1970–1979	50	93	1.9
1980–1989	50	55	1.1
1990–1997[b]	50	56	1.1

[a] Adapted from Beyle (1992, 164), updated through 1997.

[b] Results of the 1990–1997 elections only.

1992, 164, 166). In the 1990s through the 1997 elections there have been only 1.1 new governors per state—but that will increase with the results of the 1998 and 1999 elections. In the 1998 gubernatorial elections, there were seven governors who were term-limited and could not seek reelection; two other incumbent governors were defeated in their attempt to seek reelection; and three long-serving governors and one who had only served one term retired. That meant that there were thirteen new individuals elected as governor in 1998—one quarter of the fifty governors. Longer terms, the ability to succeed one's self to another term, and former governors reentering the office have greatly reduced the opportunities for outsiders to be elected to governorships.

This state of affairs is significant for politically ambitious individuals in various states, because it suggests a further tightening of electoral opportunities at the top of the states' political ladders. An earlier study by Schlesinger (1966) indicated that only the U.S. Senate seats tended to be career offices and that congressional seats and the offices of state attorney general, secretary of state, and state auditor were intermediate offices (held for more than four years). Now, with the governorship in some states becoming, at a minimum, an intermediate office, if not a career office, political opportunities are being restricted.

Important is the concept of *political time* or *window of opportunity*—that moment in a person's political career when he or she can or should move to run for a higher office. It is not easy to define exactly when one's political time occurs, how long it lasts, or for whom it really does exist. It is much easier to define when it is not the right political time for someone to seek a higher office: The person is too young and his or her time will come, or the person is too old and his or her time has passed. For some, there will be a time for such an upward political move, for others there may never be. Clearly, the concept of an individual's political time varies from state to state and from individual to individual.

In general, political time is relatively short from the individual's perspective. There are several reasons for this. As already noted, longer terms and succession have cut back the number of times available. Term limits on how long someone can hold an office, where they exist, create periodic openings for those seeking an office and a time schedule of when these openings will occur. But the political time of others on the ladder may conflict with a person's own political time. In addition, the new variable of money in the political process allows political interlopers to interrupt an otherwise ordered process of political advancement by buying their way into the system at the very top.

With the average number of new governors per state per decade dropping to 1.1, there are very few openings. What do ambitious politicians do when this happens? Many move their ambitions elsewhere, even if it means leaving the political arena. The reform goal of longer terms for governors, with governors being able to succeed themselves for another term, may have led to the unanticipated result of shunting off into other careers potential candidates for governor or some other higher office. This shift is difficult to measure, but the cries that there are too few good candidates in many states suggest that something like this may be happening (Beyle 1992, 172–173).

Although the term limits movement of the 1990s has been aimed mainly at state legislatures and Congress, some of the states have also included provisions restricting how long their governors may serve. Of the twenty-one states that adopted term limits through 1997, twelve placed limits on their governors. All went from no limits on how long a governor might serve to either two four-year terms or eight years in a specific time period (Beyle 1995; Beyle and Jones 1994). These limits should now produce more openings in these states.[9]

Sometimes idiosyncratic political situations can either severely restrict an individual's access to office or overly enhance it. Alabama is an example. For three decades gubernatorial politics revolved around George C. Wallace (D). After his unsuccessful campaign for governor in 1958, his successful candidacies in 1962, 1970, 1974, and 1982 gave him sixteen years in office. In addition, his first wife, Lurleen, ran in his stead in 1966 and won, but she died after serving less than sixteen months, thereby short-circuiting his attempt to govern through his wife. In 1993 Jim Folsom, Jr. (D) succeeded to become the Alabama governor when his predecessor was ousted because of a felony conviction. The junior Folsom is the son of former governor "Big Jim" Folsom who served from 1955–1959. In the 1994 elections, Folsom was narrowly defeated in his bid for a full term by former governor Fob James who had served his first term as a Democrat (1979–1983) but in 1994 was running as a Republican.

In addition to the rule that money can buy the best campaign for the winners (it is obviously wasted or ill-spent in the campaign of a loser), another political rule

---

9. The states are Arizona, Arkansas, California, Colorado, Idaho, Massachusetts, Michigan, Montana, Nevada, Utah, Washington, and Wyoming.

has gained importance in the past decade: Incumbency provides the best campaign platform. Even in the anti-incumbent mood of the 1994 elections, seventeen of the twenty-three incumbent governors running won, and in the 1995, 1996, 1997 elections every incumbent seeking reelection won (Beyle 1998), and only two of the twenty-five incumbents running in 1998 lost.

From Campaigner to Governor

A major hallmark of our political system is the concept of an orderly transition of power from one elected official to another once the election results are known. Even when an incumbent governor is beaten in a bitter and personally acrimonious campaign, the reins of power are turned over at the appointed time—although not always easily or with complete grace. There are no *coups d'état* led by colonels of the state's highway patrol or members of the state National Guard; the vehicle of change in our executive chairs is the vote of the electorate.

The keys to a successful transition are planning and communication. When both sides have thought ahead to the transition period and the potential problems of leaving or entering office, many of the difficulties can be reduced. When both sides strive to communicate rather than continue the election campaign or start another conflict, we seldom hear of difficulties during this period (NGA 1990a, 1990b). The National Governors' Association (NGA) has developed a series of materials to assist in gubernatorial transitions and holds a "New Governors' Seminar" in the even years to let incumbent governors pass on their accumulated wisdom to those who are about to enter office (NGA 1978, 1990b).

But there are always some deviations from any general rules, and the Blanton–Alexander transition in Tennessee in 1978–1979 is an example. Federal law enforcement officials had reason to believe that the outgoing Democratic governor, Ray Blanton, was "about to release some state prisoners who [were believed to have] bought their way out of prison." One of the prisoners allegedly involved in the governor's pardon-selling scheme was James Earl Ray, the convicted assassin of Martin Luther King, Jr. The newly elected Republican governor, Lamar Alexander, agreed to be sworn in three days early without the knowledge of the incumbent Blanton and the locks to the governor's office were changed so that Blanton could not gain access. Blanton was later convicted of selling pardons and served time in prison (Alexander 1986, 22, 24).

When a governor is forced from office by an adverse judicial decision, planning for a gubernatorial transition is more difficult. First, the incumbent is being forced from office and the new governor was not elected by the vote of the people to be governor. Second, the timing for such a transition is not written in the constitution or statute as being date specific—it just happens on the verdict of a judge or jury in a criminal trial. For example, we can cite the 1996 Arkansas transition between Gov. Jim Guy Tucker (D), convicted of two felony counts in federal court, and Lt. Gov. Mike Huckabee (R). This quick transition was thrown into momentary chaos when Tucker refused to give up the office until the question of whether he had received a fair trial was answered. Huckabee then called for Tucker's impeachment if he refused to resign, which Tucker did four hours after his earlier refusal to do so (English 1997, 18).

THE POWERS OF THE GOVERNORS: A COMPARISON

As Schlesinger (1965, 1971) has shown, some governors are strong, some are weak, and some fall in between. Reasons for strength can derive variously from personality, personal wealth, electoral mandate, party or interest group structure, state statute, or the formal powers of the office itself. The ability to be strong can vary within a particular state; for example, a governor may have considerable power over the executive branch but little in working with the legislature. A governor may have little power with either of these but have a close relationship with the president, which confers some significant power in the intergovernmental arena and even in the state.

The governors of the most populous states—California, New York, Texas—are important and powerful in political circles. They have greater influence in national political conventions with their large state delegations and in Congress with their larger congressional delegations. They are often elevated to potential presidential candidacy just because they are the governors of these states. The national press covers them closely, giving their state activities a national tinge. In short, these governors have national power because of the states they head. In the 1980s former governor of California Ronald Reagan won the presidency twice while in 1996 current Governor Wilson tried but failed. Texas governor George W. Bush is projected as a potential Republican candidate for president in 2000 as this book goes to print.

In this section we are more interested in the powers the governors have within their own state: those powers they bring to the office themselves and those powers provided them by state constitution, state statute, and the voters. Let us turn first to those powers the governors bring with them.

The Personal Power of Governors

Each individual serving as governor has his or her own set of personal attributes that can be turned into either strength (power) or weakness, depending on the situation. We will look at four separate indicators of the personal strength of the governors serving as of the summer of 1998.

Electoral Mandate. The margin of victory by which the governor won the seat is an indicator of the size of the electoral mandate. The premise is that the larger the margin of victory, the stronger the governor will be in the view of other actors in the system. Governors with a wide margin can use that margin politically by declaring that the people overwhelmingly wanted him or her in office so that a particular goal could be achieved. Governors who won by a narrow margin or by a plurality in a three- or four-way race and those who succeeded to office on the death, removal, or resignation of the elected governor cannot use this argument.

In the calculations of the extent of a governor's mandate, a five-point scale is used, ranging from those governors who won in a relative landslide on the high side to those who succeeded to office and thus were not elected on the low side. As

Table 6-4 Personal Powers of the Governors, 1998

State	EM	AL	PF	GP	GPP
Alabama	2	4	4	4	3.5
Alaska	2	2	4	3	2.8
Arizona	1	5	2	5	3.3
Arkansas	1	5	2	5	3.3
California	5	5	1	2	3.3
Colorado	5	5	1	4	3.8
Connecticut	2	3	4	5	3.5
Delaware	5	3	3	5	4.0
Florida	2	5	1	4	3.0
Georgia	2	5	1	5	3.3
Hawaii	2	5	4	1	3.0
Idaho	4	3	1	4	3.0
Illinois	5	5	1	5	4.0
Indiana	3	5	5	5	4.5
Iowa	5	5	1	5	4.0
Kansas	5	5	4	5	4.8
Kentucky	2	5	4	5	4.0
Louisiana	5	1	4	5	3.8
Maine	2	1	4	5	3.0
Maryland	2	2	4	3	2.8
Massachusetts	1	5	2	5	3.3
Michigan	5	3	4	5	4.3
Minnesota	5	5	1	4	3.8
Mississippi	5	1	1	4	2.8
Missouri	5	5	3	4	4.3
Montana	5	5	3	5	4.5
Nebraska	5	1	1	5	3.0
Nevada	5	5	1	4	3.8
New Hampshire	5	3	4	5	4.3
New Jersey	2	2	3	3	2.5
New Mexico	4	1	4	2	2.8
New York	3	3	4	5	3.8
North Carolina	5	4	3	5	4.3
North Dakota	5	1	5	4	3.8
Ohio	5	5	1	4	3.8
Oklahoma	5	3	4	5	4.3
Oregon	4	3	4	5	4.0
Pennsylvania	2	3	4	5	3.5
Rhode Island	2	1	4	4	2.8
South Carolina	2	3	4	4	3.3
South Dakota	5	4	4	3	4.0
Tennessee	4	3	4	4	3.8
Texas	4	1	4	5	3.5
Utah	5	1	5	5	4.0
Vermont	5	5	4	5	4.8
Virginia	5	5	3	5	4.5
Washington	5	2	5	4	4.0
West Virginia	3	4	5	4	4.0
Wisconsin	5	3	4	5	4.3
Wyoming	5	3	4	5	4.3
50 state average	3.8	3.4	3.1	4.3	3.8

EM: Governor's electoral mandate: 5 = landslide win of eleven or more points; 4 = comfortable majority of six to ten points; 3 = narrow majority of three to five points; 2 = tight win of zero to

Table 6-4 *Continued*

two points or a plurality win of under 50 percent; 1 = succeeded to office. [SOURCE: Barone and Ujifusa (1997)]

AL: Governor's position on the state's political ambition ladder: 5 = steady progression; 4 = former governors; 3 = legislative leaders or members of Congress; 2 = substate position to governor; 1 = governorship is first elective office. [SOURCE: NGA (1998a)]

PF: The personal future of the governor: 5 = early in term, can run again; 4 = late in term, can run again; 3 = early in term, term limited; 2 = succeeded to office, can run for election; 1 = late in final term. [SOURCE: CSG (1996) and NGA (1998)]

GP: Gubernatorial job performance rating in public opinion polls: 5 = more than 60 percent positive job approval rating; 4 = 50 to 59 percent positive job approval rating; 3 = 40 to 49 percent positive job approval rating; 2 = 30 to 39 percent positive job approval rating; 1 = less than 30 percent positive job approval rating. [SOURCE: Author's data]

GPP: Governor's personal powers' index score, the sum of the scores for EM, AL, PF, GP divided by 4 and rounded to nearest tenth of a point.

indicated in the EM column of Table 6-4, a majority of the governors (twenty-six) won their most recent election rather handily, another five comfortably. At the other end of the spectrum are the governors who won by less than 2 points or were plurality winners (thirteen), or succeeded to office (three). The average score for the 1998 governors is 3.8 on the five-point scale.

The governor with the greatest margin of victory was Marc Racicot (R-Mont.), who won by 60 points in his 1996 reelection bid! Mike Leavitt (R-Utah) won by 52 points and Howard Dean (D-Vermont) won by 49 points in their 1996 reelection bids. The squeakers were Govs. Parris Glendening (D-Md.), who won by 0.4 percent (5,993 votes) in a contested outcome, and Fob James (R-Ala.), who won by 0.8 percent (10,757 votes) in their 1994 elections (Barone and Ujifusa 1997). Does it make a difference? In a summer 1994 survey, one Virginia respondent said of then newly elected governor George Allen: "The reason [his legislation passed] is not that Assembly members liked him, but that they can count votes and understand Allen's mandate." [10]

Position on the State's Political Ambition Ladder. A political ambition indicator places the 1998 governors on the state's political ambition ladder in relation to their previous positions. The premise is that a governor progressing steadily up from substate to statewide elective office to the governorship will be stronger than those who start at the top with the governorship as their first office. They have worked their way through each level and have learned en route what to expect and what is expected of them. They also have developed friends and allies who will support them (as well as enemies and ingrates who will not). The governor for whom it is the first elective office must build such understanding and relationships on the job.

A five-point scale is used, running from those who moved upward in a steady progression from substate to statewide office to governor on the high side, to those

10. In the summer of 1994 I conducted a fifty-state survey of nearly 400 political scientists, working journalists, and others with experience in the states on how they viewed the performance of their state's governor. That survey will be cited as the summer 1994 survey in this chapter.

for whom the governorship was their first elective office on the low side. As shown in the AL column in Table 6-4, two-fifths of the governors (twenty) did follow a steady progression up the rungs on their state's political ambition ladder, and at the other extreme nearly one-fifth of them (nine) started at the top. Former governors, those who moved up from legislative leadership or congressional posts and those moving up from substate positions (mayors and legislators) fall between these two end points. The average score for the 1998 governors is 3.4 on the five-point scale.

The four former governors who regained their seats and are now serving indicate the advantage former governors have in seeking the office again. They have name recognition, a record of performance, and a political organization that has worked well before. James B. Hunt (D-N.C.) jumped from the lieutenant governorship to the higher office in 1976, and after an eight-year break is now serving his fourth term. The advantages that former governors bring to the office were summed up in the summer 1994 survey by two observers of Hunt: "[H]e returned to office with a very focused agenda" and "is a competent, polished chief executive [who] understands the issues and how to make the system work."

The Personal Future of Governors as Governors

Governors who are near the beginning of their terms and who have the ability to run again have more power than do governors who are nearing the end of their terms in office or are retiring or are term-limited. Governors up for reelection are able to go out to the voters again and seek the electoral mandate voters can provide and at the same time possibly help supporters and hurt detractors. Governors who cannot run again become lame ducks with little political potential remaining.

A five-point scale—ranging from those, on the high side, who are early in their terms and can seek reelection to those, on the low side, who are late in their final terms—was used to indicate the personal future of governors as governors. As shown in the PF column in Table 6-4, in 1998 most governors (twenty-nine) were able to run again and therefore still had some political potential. Three others who succeeded to office on the resignation of their successor can also run for reelection in their own right. Eighteen, however, were lame ducks in their final terms, twelve of them late in those terms. The average score for the 1998 governors is 3.1 on the five-point scale.

Being a lame duck is a frustrating malaise for governors. They have the trappings and formal powers of office but lack the political power and wallop they once had. In the summer of 1994 Gov. Edwin Edwards (D) announced his exit from Louisiana's politics a year and a half before his fourth term would end. According to one observer in the summer 1994 survey, he then found an immediate change in the political environment around him as the decision "left him a lame duck and largely ineffective in the legislature with no political clout to speak of and no money with which to reward loyal legislators with projects and patronage." Another observer in the survey stated that he would be surprised if Edwards "were able to get anything important through the legislature during the rest of his term."[11] Being a lame duck cuts both ways: You not only lose the potential wallop needed to convince those who are not necessarily your friends and allies, you also lose the support of your friends and allies.

Gubernatorial Performance Ratings. Their performance as governor is another aspect of the personal power of governors. There are several ways to measure the performance of the governors of the fifty states. Two of them rely on asking people—involved observers and the public—just how well they think the governor of their state is performing. The premise is that those governors who are seen as performing in a relatively positive way add to their own personal power and will be more effective than will those who are not performing well. But what constitutes a good performance by a governor? On what basis do observers make their judgments?

One factor in some evaluations is that the governor has achieved some level of success in economic development efforts. This can be especially important when a state has experienced a weak economic period during or just before the governor's term in office and thus successes in seeking and obtaining new businesses and new jobs would be important. Or it could be that the governor is just serving during good economic times and is receiving good marks for that.

A second factor is how well the governor compares to his or her predecessors. Clearly, if a governor is under some type of dark cloud for what he or she may have done (or not done), or what someone in his or her administration has done, this comparison will be negative. In the summer 1994 survey one governor was nominated as the "poorest governor in a long time." In another state with a history of serious ethical, moral, and legal problems among its elected leaders, an observer indicated that state's governor had "been a strong governor in a state that desperately needed political and governmental leadership of the highest ethical standards and of noble purpose."[12]

Another factor was the governor's ability to keep things on an even keel and to be in tune with what the voters wanted. For example, in the summer 1994 survey one governor was cited for running "a tight fiscal ship and that is what [citizens] want"; another was called "consistent and competent"; and still another was "elected to be a custodian and he has done this better [this] term." The assessment of some governors' performance was rather lukewarm: "average, which means good for [this state]" and "could have done more, but mostly status quo." Finally, there were the wholly negative assessments of some governors: "a disaster" and "lack of ethics."[13]

The second way to measure gubernatorial performance is by the proliferating state-level public opinion polls, which have led to some fairly consistent results be-

11. Summer 1994 survey.
12. Summer 1994 survey.
13. Summer 1994 survey.

ing published on how well the citizens, registered voters, or likely voters feel their governor is performing. These results are usually made public by the media paying for the polls or by a university center conducting the polls.

In such polls the reasons for the respondents' assessments are obscure, but how they rate their governor's performance becomes part of the politics around the governor. The categories of responses used vary from "approve, disapprove" to "excellent, good, average, fair, poor." What everyone looks for is the percentage of positive responses in the ratings of the governor, although most political consultants believe that the negative assessments are more meaningful in political terms.

To compare these performance ratings across the fifty states, we used a five-point scale, ranging from those governors with a positive rating of 60 percent or higher to those who had a rating of less than 30 percent. These are all snapshot ratings taken at one point in time. Most of these polls were taken between October 1997 and October 1998. The results presented in the GP column in Table 6-4 indicate that forty-three governors had a positive job approval rating of 50 percent or higher in their state, with twenty-eight of these governors having a rating above 60 percent and fifteen between 50 and 59 percent. At the lowest end of the scale were two governors with ratings in the 30 percentiles and one governor with a performance rating below 30 percent. The average score for the 1998 governors is 4.3 on the five-point scale. This compares to a 3.3 average among the fifty state governors in the summer of 1994 (Beyle 1995, 227), so as judged by their constituents governors are performing well, even better than four years ago. Why? The economy is growing, unemployment rates are down, state revenues are up, and state taxes are being cut. The times are better.

Although the reasons for these ratings are not always clear, their impact is. For those at the low side of the scale, their administrations are jarred, and their political future is unclear, if not damaged beyond repair. For those at the high side of the scale, these public opinion poll ratings become part of their political and personal arsenal in their attempt to achieve results. But, as an observer in the summer 1994 survey noted about Governor Whitman of New Jersey, "As long as she has 70 percent approval ratings, they [the old boy network] need her and will never bring her down. But once those ratings drop, watch out! The knives will be out."[14] Over the next few years her ratings did fall into the 40s and she narrowly won reelection in 1997, 47 percent to 46 percent.

The Personal Power of Governors: Summary. To make an assessment and comparison of how the fifty state governors fare in their personal power, the scores of each of the previously mentioned indicators were brought together into one index. I totaled each state's scores in the four separate indicators and then divided the total score by four to keep within the framework of the five-point scale.

As indicated in the GPP column in Table 6-4, thirty-three of the governors fell in the 3.5 to 5.0-point range, with an average score of 3.8. The five governors with the

---

14. Summer 1994 survey.

most personal power on this scale of 4.5 or more were Frank O'Bannon (D-Ind.) midway through his first term, Bill Graves (R-Kans.), at the end of his first term, Marc Racicot (R-Mont.) midway through his second term, Howard Dean (D-Vt.), at the end of his third two-year term, and James Gilmore (R-Va.) in the first year of his only term. At the other end of this index—in other words, with the least personal power on this scale—was Gov. Whitman (R-N.J.), who had narrowly won reelection the pervious year and was in her final term.

In summary, it would appear that most governors do bring, and continue to hold, their own brand of personal power to the governorship. Although there are some who fall toward the weaker side, there are considerably more on the stronger side.

The Institutional Powers of Governors

The institutional powers of the governorship are those powers given the governor by the state constitution, state statutes, and the voters when they vote on constitutions and referenda. In a sense, these powers are the structure into which the governor moves on being elected to office.

Separately Elected State-Level Officials. The concept of a plural executive is alive and well in many of the states. Instead of following the presidential model, which we see at the national level with a president and vice president as the only elected executive branch officials, the states have opted to allow voters to select a range of state officials.[15] Over the course of the twentieth century, however, one of the most consistent reforms advocated for the states has been to reduce the number of separately elected executive branch officials. The results of such reforms, however, are not impressive, nor do they look promising in the future. Between 1955 and 1994, the number of separately elected officials at the state level has dropped from 514 in the then forty-eight states to 511 in the now fifty states. The average has only dropped from 10.7 per state to 10.2 per state (Beyle 1995).

Each of these separate offices has its own political support network that is quite resistant to any changes in how leadership is selected. And as noted earlier, some of these offices serve as launching pads for individuals seeking higher elective offices, such as the governorship, and are tightly woven into the state's political ambition ladder. It is often just not worth the struggle to change how they are selected; too much political effort and capital would be expended for too little real political gain all in the name of reform.

As shown in the SEP column of Table 6-5, only five states come close to mirroring the presidential model. The remaining states have a variety of other elected officials, ranging from a few process-type offices (attorney general, secretary of state, treasurer, and auditor), to some major policy offices (K–12 education, university boards, and public utility authorities). On this five-point scale, the average score is 2.8.

---

15. Some still argue for the plural executive model in the states. See Robinson (1998) for a recent argument based on a study of several of these separately elected officials in Wyoming.

Table 6-5 Governor's Institutional Powers

State	SEP	TP	AP	BP	VP	PC	GIP
Alabama	1	4	2	3	4	2	2.7
Alaska	5	4	3.5	3	5	2	3.8
Arizona	1.5	4	2.5	3	5	4	3.3
Arkansas	2.5	4	2.5	3	4	1	2.8
California	1	4	3	3	5	2	3.0
Colorado	3	4	4	3	5	3	3.7
Connecticut	4	5	3	3	5	2	3.7
Delaware	2	4	3	3	5	3	3.3
Florida	3	4	1.5	3	5	2	3.1
Georgia	1	4	0.5	3	5	4	2.9
Hawaii	5	4	2.5	3	5	5	4.1
Idaho	2	5	2	3	5	5	3.7
Illinois	4	5	3	3	5	3	3.3
Indiana	3	4	4	3	2	3	3.2
Iowa	3	5	3	3	5	4	3.8
Kansas	3	4	3	3	5	4	3.7
Kentucky	3	4	3	3	4	4	3.5
Louisiana	1	4	3.5	3	5	2	3.1
Maine	5	4	3.5	3	4	1	3.4
Maryland	4	4	2.5	5	5	4	4.1
Massachusetts	4	4	1	3	5	1	3.0
Michigan	3	4	3.5	3	5	3	3.6
Minnesota	4	5	2.5	3	5	2	3.6
Mississippi	1	4	2	3	5	2	2.8
Missouri	2.5	4	2.5	3	5	4	3.5
Montana	3	4	2.5	3	5	4	3.6
Nebraska	3	4	3	4	5	3	3.7
Nevada	2.5	4	3.5	3	2	3	3.0
New Hampshire	5	2	3	3	2	2	2.8
New Jersey	5	4	3.5	3	5	4	4.1
New Mexico	3	4	4	3	5	2	3.5
New York	4	5	3.5	4	5	3	4.1
North Carolina	1	4	3	3	2	3	2.7
North Dakota	3	5	2.5	3	5	4	3.8
Ohio	4	4	4.5	3	5	4	4.1
Oklahoma	1	4	1	3	5	2	2.7
Oregon	2	4	2.5	3	5	2	3.1
Pennsylvania	4	4	4.5	3	5	4	4.1
Rhode Island	2.5	4	4	3	2	1	2.8
South Carolina	1	4	2	2	5	3	2.8
South Dakota	3	4	3.5	3	5	4	3.8
Tennessee	4.5	4	4	3	4	2	3.6
Texas	1	5	3.5	2	5	3	3.3
Utah	4	4.5	3.5	3	5	4	4.0
Vermont	2.5	2	4	3	2	4	2.9
Virginia	2.5	3	3.5	3	5	3	3.3
Washington	1	4	2.5	3	5	2	2.9
West Virginia	2.5	4	4.5	5	5	2	3.8

Table 6-5 *Continued*

State	SEP	TP	AP	BP	VP	PC	GIP
Wisconsin	3	5	2	3	5	4	3.7
Wyoming	2	4	3.5	3	5	4	3.6
50 state average	2.8	4.1	3.0	3.1	4.5	3.0	3.4

SEP: Separately elected executive branch officials: 5 = only governor or governor/lieutenant governor team elected; 4.5 = governor or governor/lieutenant governor team, with one other elected official; 4 = governor/lieutenant governor team with some process officials (attorney general, secretary of state, treasurer, auditor) elected; 3 = governor/lieutenant governor team with process officials, and some major and minor policy officials elected; 2.5 = governor (no team) with six or fewer officials elected, but none are major policy officials; 2 = governor (no team) with six or fewer officials elected, including one major policy official; 1.5 = governor (no team) with six or fewer officials elected, but two are major policy officials; 1 = governor (no team) with seven or more process and several major policy officials elected. [SOURCE: CSG, (1996, 33–39)].

TP: Tenure potential of governors: 5 = four-year term, no restraint on reelection; 4.5 = four-year term, only three terms permitted; 4 = four-year term, only two terms permitted; 3 = four-year term, no consecutive reelection permitted; 2 = two-year term, no restraint on reelection; 1 = two- year term, only two terms permitted. [SOURCE: CSG, (1996, 17–18)]

AP: Governor's appointment powers in six major functional areas: corrections, K-12 education, health, highways/transportation, public utilities regulation, and welfare. The six individual office scores are totaled and then averaged and rounded to the nearest .5 or for the state score. That average score is then rounded to the nearest .5 between 0 and 5. 5 = governor appoints, no other approval needed; 4.0 = governor appoints, a board, council, or legislature approves; 3 = someone else appoints, governor approves or shares appointment; 2 = someone else appoints, governor and others approve; 1 = someone else appoints, no approval or confirmation needed. [SOURCE: CSG (1996, 35–39)]

BP: Governor's budgetary power: 5 = governor has full responsibility; legislature may not increase executive budget; 4 = governor has full responsibility; legislature can increase special majority vote or subject to item veto; 3.0 = governor has full responsibility; legislature has unlimited power to change executive budget; 2 = governor shares responsibility; legislature has unlimited power to change executive budget; 1 = governor shares responsibility with other elected official; legislature has unlimited power to change executive budget. [SOURCE: CSG (1996, 228–229; NCSL (1998a)]

VP: Governor's veto power: 5 = has the item veto and a special majority vote of the legislature is needed to override a veto (three-fifths of legislators elected or two-thirds of legislators present); 4 = has item veto with a majority of the legislators elected needed to override; 3 = has item veto with only a majority of the legislators present needed to override; 2 = no item veto, with a special legislative majority needed to override it; 1 = no item veto, only a simple legislative majority needed to override. [SOURCE, CSG (1996, 22–23, 98–99)]

PC: Gubernatorial party control: the governor's party is: 5 = has a substantial majority (75 percent or more) in both houses of the legislature; 4 = has a simple majority in both houses (less than 75 percent), or a substantial majority in one house and a simple majority in the other; 3 = split party control in the legislature or a nonpartisan legislature; 2 = simple majority in both houses, or a simple minority (25 percent or less) in one and a substantial minority (more than 25 percent) in the other; 1 = substantial minority in both houses. [SOURCE: NCSL (1998b)]

GIP: Governors' institutional powers score: The sum of the scores for SEP, TP, AP, BP, VP and PC divided by 6 to stay within the 5-point format. Overall power score rounded to nearest tenth of a point.

For the governor, this means working with other officials who have similar claims to a statewide political constituency. And although process-type officials seem to be more innocuous by definition, they can cause a governor considerable problems. For example, tensions between governors and lieutenant governors have led to bizarre political situations in which governors have been wary of leaving their states lest their lieutenant governor sabotage their programs while serving as acting governor. In another situation, the Republican governor of North Carolina once found himself being sued by the separately elected Democratic attorney general in one case while nearly simultaneously being represented by the same attorney general in another case (CSG 1992, 29).

Tenure Potential. How long governors can serve and whether they can succeed themselves for more than one term are important factors in determining just how much power they have. One argument is that those having the possibility of a longer stay in the office are able to carry out their programs. But this can cut both ways: If limits were put on gubernatorial terms, governors might move faster and more decisively to achieve their goals and not be afraid of the voters' retribution at the ballot box when a necessary yet unpopular decision had to be made.

Initially, ten of the governors of the thirteen original states had one-year terms, another a two-year term, and two had three-year terms. Gradually, states moved to either two- or four-year terms, and one-year terms finally disappeared early in the twentieth century.

Another significant shift has been taking place since 1960: the borrowing by the states of the presidential succession model, as embodied in the Twenty-second Amendment to the U.S. Constitution, adopted in 1951, which states, "No person shall be elected to the office of President more than twice." This was a direct reaction to the four terms to which President Franklin D. Roosevelt was elected. In 1960 only six states restricted their governors to two four-year terms (Schlesinger 1965, 220). By 1969 this number had increased to eleven states (Schlesinger 1971, 223); and by 1988 to twenty-five states. With the rise of the term-limits movement, more states acted to impose such a restriction, and by 1998 a total of thirty-seven had done so (see the TP column of Table 6-5). On this five-point scale, the average score is 4.1.

The Power of Appointment. One of the first sets of decisions facing governors-elect on the morning after their election is the appointment of personnel to key positions in their administration. This power of appointment is fundamental to a governor's administration, especially in relation to the state bureaucracy. But the appointive power also extends to the governor's legislative role, for promises of appointments to high-level executive positions and to the state judiciary are often the coin spent for support for particular legislation.

The history of state governors' appointment powers is one of growth from weak beginnings. The increase of separately elected officials during the nineteenth century and the ad hoc proliferation of state agencies, often headed by boards and commissions, added to the problem of gubernatorial control. This diluted gubernatorial power was the background for twentieth-century reforms to increase gubernatorial appointive power. The assumption underlying these reforms is that governors who can appoint officials without any other authority involved can be held accountable for these officials' actions. Such governors are more powerful than those who must have either or both houses of the legislature confirm an appointment. Governors who only approve appointments rather than initiate them have even less appointive power. Weakest are those governors who neither appoint nor approve but have a separate body do so and those who have no opportunity to appoint because the officials who head agencies are elected.

The AP column in Table 6-5 presents the scores for the governor's appointment power. To gain this measure, who selects the heads of the agencies providing the six major functions in each state—corrections, K–12 education, health, highways or transportation, public utilities regulation, and welfare—were examined, and then the score was averaged for all six. Obviously, governors face constraints in their appointment power. A majority of the states are in the middle of the scale—that is, someone else appoints these individuals to their positions with the approval of the governor or the legislature, or both. On this five-point scale, the average score is 3.0.

On the high side are Pennsylvania and West Virginia, where the governor appoints all six of these officials with some of the appointments subject to the confirmation process. Ohio follows closely, with five of the six as gubernatorial appointees not needing any confirmation, but a board selects the head of K–12 education. At the other end of the scale is Georgia, where two of these officials are elected separately, boards appoint two other boards, and an agency head appoints two others.

One caveat on this appointive power index: A politically shrewd governor with an efficient political operation in the governor's office can probably orchestrate many of the selection decisions made by boards, commissions, and agency heads. Thus the governor might not be as powerless as the constitutional or statutory language might suggest.

Control over the Budget. The executive budget, centralized under gubernatorial control, is a twentieth-century response to the chaotic fiscal situations found in state government at the turn of the century. An executive budget in one document seeks to encompass under the chief executive's control all the agency and department requests for legislatively appropriated funds; it also reflects the governor's own policy priorities. This document is then transmitted to the legislature for its consideration and ultimate passage. By putting governors at the top of this process in the executive branch and making them the chief lobbyist for the budget in the legislature, the centralized budget places much power in their hands.

What the governor can do in developing and presenting the state budget as the fiscal road map for the next fiscal year or biennium, however, the legislature can often undo as the budget bill works its way through the legislative process. In some states the governor's proposed budget is described as DOA (dead on arrival) because the legislature intends to build the state's next budget on their own. Moreover, when there are conflicts over the budget within the executive branch agencies and between the agencies and the governor, the legislature is where agency grievances can be heard and gubernatorial decisions changed. The greater the power to make changes in the governor's proposed budget and the willingness of the legislature to do so, the less potential budget power for the governor. I use the word *potential* advisedly, because not all gubernatorial–legislative relationships are adversarial in nature, and what the governor proposes usually does set the agenda for debate and decision.

State legislatures have been seeking even more involvement in the budgetary process to regain some of the budgetary powers lost to governors. They have developed legislative oversight procedures, tried to require legislative appropriation or approval of federal grant funds flowing into the state, and sought to have legislative committees involved in administrative budgetary shifts made during the fiscal year.

But there are some limitations on the budgetary powers of both these executive and legislative branch actors. For example, most states earmark their gasoline taxes for highway or mass transportation uses, and some earmark taxes on alcohol for various purposes or allot a fraction of their sales taxes to local governments. Tolls and fees for bridges, highways, and other state-established public authorities are retained by the agencies collecting them to finance their activities and projects. In recent decades, states have been facing more and more federal mandates on how much they should be spending on Medicaid, certain environmental problems, prisons, and disabled individuals. A governor's budgetary power is thus reduced when appropriated funds are earmarked or otherwise diverted by legislative prescription, when public authorities raise or expend independent income, or when federal mandates direct state expenditures.

A five-point scale is used to measure the budgetary power given to each governor. It consists of two measures: the extent of the governor's responsibility to develop the budget and the extent of the legislature's power to change the governor's budget once it is sent to the legislature. At the top of the scale are the states whose governors have full responsibility for the executive budget and the legislature is constrained in how much change they can make in the governor's proposed budget. At the bottom of the scale are the states whose governors share responsibility for developing the executive budget with others and whose legislatures have unlimited power to change any proposed budget.

It can be seen in the BP column in Table 6-5 that most states provide their governors with full budget power and their legislatures with unlimited power to change a governor's proposed budget. The average score for the fifty states is 3.1.

The Veto Power. Governors have been provided the formal power of being able to veto bills, and in most states parts of bills, passed by the legislature. This is the most direct power the governor can exercise in relation to the legislature. There are many differences in the veto power extended to governors: total bill veto, item veto of selected words, and item veto to change the meaning of words (NASBO 1997, 29–31).

The veto, although a direct power over the legislature, also provides governors with some administrative powers because it gives them the ability to stop agencies from gaining support in a legislative end run around their governor's or their budget office's adverse decision. As noted earlier, this is especially true in those forty-three states in which the governor can veto particular items in an agency's budget without rejecting the entire bill (Benjamin 1982, 11; Moe 1988, 4). Several states have gone further by allowing the governor to condition his or her approval of a full bill with amendments to the bill or rewording of the lines (Moe 1988, 3–5).

The veto and its use involve two major actors: the governor and the legislature. It is a legislative act that a governor must sign or veto; however, the legislature has the opportunity to vote to override the veto and thus make a law without the governor's signature. In fact, more than a few states even allow their legislatures to recall bills from the governor prior to his or her action, thereby creating a negotiating situation—sort of an informal alternative to the veto (Benjamin 1982). This latter tactic can allow the governor to become part of the legislative process with de facto amendatory power as the governor and the legislature negotiate over the bill's contents (Benjamin 1982, 12; Moe 1988, 13–14).

The requirements for legislative override range from only a majority of members present and voting to a special majority, such as a three-fifth's vote. Although the threat of a legislative override has not been great in the past, the number of gubernatorial vetoes overridden by legislatures has grown somewhat. In 1947 governors vetoed approximately 5 percent of the bills passed by legislatures and were overridden on only 1.8 percent of them (Wiggins 1980, 1112–1113). In the early to mid-1990s, governors vetoed about 3.7 percent of the bills and resolutions passed by legislatures and only had 2.3 percent of these vetoes overridden (CSG 1996, 105–106). But this overall rate masks some of the extremes. In 1992–1993 Governor Ned McWherter (D-Tenn.) signed all 1,262 bills presented to him into law, whereas Governor Wilson (R-Calif.) vetoed more than 21 percent of the 2,681 bills presented to him—and none of these vetoes were overridden (CSG 1994, 148–150).

Some would argue that the use of the veto is a sign of gubernatorial weakness rather than strength because strong governors win the battle through negotiation rather than confrontation with the legislature. In a slightly different vein, one governor argued that a governor should "avoid threatening to veto a bill. You just relieve the legislature of responsibility for sound legislation" (Beyle and Huefner 1983, 268–269). Moreover, a governor using a veto risks embarrassment at the hands of the legislature. It is a power to be used sparingly (NGA 1987, 8).

A study done in the late 1980s suggests that there are at least four consequences following the use of a line-item veto in any of its variants: It profoundly alters the relationship of the legislature to the governor to the benefit of the latter; it increases the number of formal confrontations between the two branches; it spawns procedures to neutralize its impact; and it precipitates litigation between the two branches, thereby introducing the third branch of state government, the courts, into the lawmaking process at an early stage in its role as umpire (Moe 1988, 1–2).

The battle in Wisconsin over the governor's partial veto demonstrates most of these points. The Republican governor Tommy Thompson startled the Democratic legislature in 1987 by creatively using the partial veto to change legislative intent: He excised isolated digits, letters, and words to the point of creating new words and meaning. The legislative leaders sought relief from the state's Supreme Court only to have the court back the governor's actions in a four-to-three decision (*State ex. rel. State Senate v. Thompson* 144, Wis.2d 429, 424 N.W.2d 385, 386, n.3 [1988]; see also *Hutchison* 1989). The legislature placed a constitutional amendment on the ballot in 1988 prohibiting such vetoes; it was approved by a 62 percent vote. In 1991 a federal appeals court, in upholding a lower court decision, found the partial veto "quirky" but not unconstitutional. By mid-1993, Thompson had executed more than 1,300 vetoes (Farney 1993, A16).

The governors' veto power is measured on a five-point scale whose high side has governors with an item veto requiring an extraordinary legislative vote to override it (three-fifths or two-thirds), and whose low side has a governor with no item veto power and the legislature only needing a simple majority vote to override a veto. In between are variations on the type of veto and the size of the majority needed to override a governor's veto. As indicated in the VP column in Table 6-5, most states do provide their governors with considerable veto power, with nearly four-fifths of the states in the top category. No states are in the lowest category, although in six states the governor has no item veto at all. On this five-point scale, the average score is 4.5.

The veto can also be used in what might be called an affirmative way. During the 1991 legislative session, Gov. Lowell Weicker of Connecticut, an Independent, had no one of his party in the legislature; yet he was able to use the veto over the state's budget as a positive weapon. By continually vetoing the budget bill because it did not contain an income tax, he assisted those who favored the imposition of a state income tax and opposed those who would rather have turned to an increase in the state sales tax as a way to balance the state's growing budget deficit. In the end, an income tax was adopted, the first in the state's history (Murphy 1992, 69).

Party Control. Partisanship is a key variable in the governors' relationship with the legislatures. If the governor's party also controls the legislature, then partisan conflicts can be minimized and the governor's ability to achieve his or her agenda is more likely to be successful. Cooperation should be the style of their relationship. If the governor and the legislative leadership are not of the same party, then partisan conflicts all too often become the style of the relationship, and the ability of the governor to achieve his or her goals is lessened. Because there are two houses in the legislatures of each state except in Nebraska, it is quite possible that at least one house will be controlled by the opposition party.

Recent decades have seen a growing trend toward a "power split" in state governments (Sherman 1984). In 1984, sixteen states had a power split; in the summer of 1998 there were thirty-one. V. O. Key Jr., called this power split a "perversion" of separation of powers allowing partisan differences to present an almost intractable situation (Key 1956, 52), but not all view this situation with alarm. In 1984 Gov. Alexander of Tennessee indicated that "it makes it harder, sometimes much harder; but the results can be better, sometimes much better" (Sherman 1984, 9). But, as in many things, it depends on how individual leaders handle a power split (van Assendelft 1997). At least three factors help to determine just how harmonious the power-split relationship will be: how great a majority the opposition party has in the legislature; the style and the personalities of the individuals involved—the governor and the legislative leaders; and whether an election year is near (Sherman 1984, 10).

When the governor's party is in the minority but controls a sizable number of seats, it is more difficult for the opposition majority to change the governor's budget or override his or her veto. However, open and easy-going personalities can often overcome partisan differences or, as Alexander said, "If you have good, well-meaning leaders, it's likely to be much better than any other process" (quoted in Sherman 1984, 12).

These variations in the governor's party control were measured on a five-point scale. The highest score is for states in which a governor's party controls both houses by a substantial majority, and the lowest score is for states in which the governor faces a legislature controlled by a substantial majority of the opposing party in both houses. Given the fact that there were thirty-one states in which a power split existed in 1998, it is no surprise to see in the PC column in Table 6-5 that only two governors have a legislature in which their party has a substantial majority. Nebraska's governor faces a unicameral (one-house) legislature elected on a nonpartisan basis. Four governors, three Republicans, and one Independent faced a legislature controlled by a substantial majority of the opposition party.

On this five-point scale, the average score is 3.0, down slightly from the average score of 3.2 in the summer of 1994. The difference is tied to the increasing strength of Republican candidates in winning gubernatorial elections. In 1994 there were nineteen Republican governors serving in the states; with the results of recent elections moving in the Republican direction, in 1998 there were thirty-two Republican governors. Although the legislatures have been moving in the same Republican direction, there is still considerable Democratic strength there.

The Institutional Powers of the Governors: Summary. To make an assessment and comparison of how the fifty governors fare in their institutional powers, the scores of each of the previously mentioned indicators were brought together into one index. I totaled the scores in each of the six indicators for each state governor and then divided the total by six to keep within the framework of the five-point scale. As can be seen in the GIP column in Table 6-5, the average score was 3.4. The seven governorships with the most institutional power on this scale at 4.0 or higher were mainly in the urban Northeast (four). At the lower end of this index were ten governorships scoring 2.9 or less, located mainly in the South (six) and New England (three). The main weaknesses in the formal, institutional powers for these states lay in the presence of other statewide separately elected officials, reduced appointive power, and restricted veto power.

Overall Gubernatorial Powers in the Fifty States. Finally, the two sets of gubernatorial powers were combined into one overall ten-point index. The results, presented in Table 6-6, show an average score of 7.2. At the high side of this combined index with scores of 8.0 or greater are eight states, with most in either the Midwest (four) or the West (three), plus New York. At the low end of the scale with scores under 6.0 are three states, with two of them from the South. Of course, these ratings may change as incumbents are replaced with a new group of men and women carrying with them their own personal styles and strengths or weaknesses.

BEING GOVERNOR

The true measure of governors and their administrations is how well they actually perform the various roles for which they are responsible. Are they able to translate their potential powers into effective action? What additional informal powers must they use to achieve the goals of their administrations?

Table 6-6 Summary of Personal and Institutional
Powers of Governors by State, Summer 1998

States	Score	Number of governors
Kansas	8.6	1
	8.4	
Montana	8.2	1
Michigan	8.0	6
New York		
Ohio		
Utah		
Wisconsin		
Wyoming		
Indiana	7.8	7
Iowa		
Missouri		
South Dakota		
Vermont		
Virginia		
West Virginia		
Colorado	7.6	4
Kentucky		
North Dakota		
Pennsylvania		
Connecticut	7.4	5
Delaware		
Illinois		
Minnesota		
Tennessee		
Hawaii	7.2	3
New Hampshire		
Oregon		
Louisiana	7.0	5
Maryland		
North Carolina		
Oklahoma		
Washington		
Idaho	6.8	4
Nebraska		
Nevada		
Texas		
Arizona	6.6	3
Alaska		
New Jersey		
California	6.4	4
Maine		
Massachusetts		
New Mexico		
Alabama	6.2	4
Arizona		
Florida		
Georgia		
	6.0	
South Carolina	5.8	1
Mississippi	5.6	2
Rhode Island		

Average score = 7.2

SOURCE: Tables 6-4 and 6-5. Each state's summary score is the
sum of its scores on Tables 6-4 and 6-5.

As governor of Tennessee, Lamar Alexander argued that a governor's role was to "see the state's few most urgent needs, develop strategies to address them, and persuade at least half the people that he or she is right" (Alexander 1986, 112). To Alexander the governor's main role concerns policy. A former governor of Vermont, Madeleine Kunin (D, 1985–1991), agreed and asserted that "the power of a governor to set the tone and define the values of a state administration is enormous." She also felt that "as governor, I had the incredible luxury to dream on a grand scale" (Kunin 1994, 11–12).

The Governor as Policy Maker

The goals of a gubernatorial administration are those policy directions a governor wishes to emphasize during his or her tenure in office. The types of policy priorities vary greatly across the activities of state government and depend on several factors, including the governor's own personal interests and outside events.

In a series of interviews with former governors, several themes emerged concerning how they believed they exerted policy leadership. Most saw their role as that of an issue catalyst, picking the issue up from the public, focusing it, and seeking to take action on it. Some others saw their role as that of a spectator viewing policy issues arising out of conflicts between actors on the state scene, whether they were special interest groups, the bureaucracy, or the mayor of the state's largest city. Finally, a few saw the governor as a reactor to accidents of history and other unanticipated events. In the eyes of these governors, leadership was more a process of problem solving and conflict resolution than agenda setting (NGA 1981, 1).

Obviously, issues and policy needs flow from many sources and provide governors with both flexibility and restrictions on the choices available. The events of the late 1980s and the early 1990s demonstrated just how governors can be forced to address issues and concerns not of their own choosing. The national recession of those years hit almost every state budget hard and some states, such as California, extremely hard. The main issues facing governors then were how to keep the state budget balanced in the face of falling revenues and how to provide the services people needed in such a down economy and that were normally provided in the states. The options available to the governors, and by extension the state legislatures, were to increase taxes, cut services, or both. Many states had to follow the third option, which was not a pleasing prospect for these leaders and the citizens of the states (Beyle 1992).

By the mid-1990s, as the economy recovered in the country and in most every state, governors were freer to post their own agendas on the wall. Among the issues on the current agendas are economic development, education quality and reform, health cost containment, welfare reform, children's policies, and crime control. In fact, because some of the issues that seemed to bedevil our national leaders threatened to bankrupt the states or cause even greater problems, governors and other state leaders in many of the states were already taking steps to address them.

The results of the 1994 elections served to place some governors (Republicans) in a position to push the new national Republican congressional leadership to help the states. Some state leaders feared this new national leadership might seek to balance the federal budget at the expense of the states. But it was some of the long-serving Republican governors who took a leadership role in trying to shape new federal initiatives to benefit the states, or at least not to hurt the states.

In the late 1990s everyone involved in state policy making was helped by a very strong economy that provided almost every state with a surplus of tax revenues. From the dark fiscal days of the early 1990s, the states moved into the gravy days of the late 1990s where the policy questions revolve around what to do with all those excess revenues: spend it (where?); save it for a rainy day; or cut taxes (which?).

But some other basic changes have aided governors in exerting policy leadership. The first level of change has taken place in the governor's office itself. In recent years the office has increased greatly in size, ability, functions, and structure. What used to amount to a few close associates working together with the governor has now been transformed into a much larger and more sophisticated bureaucratic organization in many of the states.

There have also been changes in the governor's extended office, the budget and planning agencies, which are increasingly being moved closer to the governor. In the most recent changes, governors have developed more aggressive offices of policy management, often following the federal model by creating a state-level Office of Management and Budget. One of the most critical roles of these agencies is "to provide the governor an independent source of advice on a broad range of state policy issues" (Flentje 1980, 26). They can also assist by reaching into the departments and agencies to help them implement policy directions and decisions.

These changes, and others, highlight the basic fact that governors have had to improve their policy capacity substantially to govern, especially in administering their state's executive branch. But governors can vary on how they use this capacity, how much they believe it really helps them, and how well they perform in this role. In the summer 1994 survey respondents were asked how they would characterize their governor's overall administrative abilities, from "excellent" to "poor" on a five-point scale. The average score on the five-point scale was 3.2, with almost three quarters of the governors given scores of "average" to nearly "excellent" for their administrative efforts (Beyle 1996, 240). Clearly those governors were focusing on their administrative duties and getting good grades for their efforts.

The Governor and the Legislature

A governor's relations with the legislature and success in dealing with legislators often determine how successful his or her administration will be. Although the governor takes the lead, it is still the legislature that must adopt the state budget, set or agree to basic policy directions, and, in many cases, confirm major gubernatorial appointments. A governor and legislature at loggerheads over a tax proposal, budget, policy direction, or a major department head's confirmation can bring part or all of state government to a standstill.

Added to the constitutional separation of powers are the political facts of life in many states in which the governor is of one party and another party controls one or both the legislative houses. Ideological factions can splinter a majority party's control of the legislature and be just as debilitating to a governor. And Governor Michael Dukakis (D-Mass.) found himself under greatest fire from his own party members: "And when you've got majorities of four to one in the Legislature—I'm sure you recognize that is by no means an unmitigated blessing—you've got conservative Democrats, you've got liberal Democrats, you've got moderate Democrats, you've got suburban Democrats, you've got urban Democrats, and you don't have any Republicans." He also noted that he was beaten in his 1978 reelection bid by a Democrat who was "philosophically miles away from him" (NGA 1981, 65).

The members of each of these two major branches bring quite different perspectives to state government. In terms of constituency, the governor represents the whole state; the legislature is a collection of individuals representing much smaller parts of the state. The governorship is a full-time job, and complete responsibility is placed on the shoulders of one person; the legislature is not a full-time job, although the time involved varies among states, as is discussed elsewhere in this book, and responsibility is diffused widely among many leaders and many more members. The governor's chair sits atop the state's political ambition ladder; legislative seats are some of the rungs available in climbing the ladder.

Most new governors face their legislatures within the first month of their administration. The state of the state address, the governor's budget message, specific programmatic legislation, special messages on high-priority programs, oversight of agency bills, and responses to bills introduced by individual legislators are high on the governor's agenda. Over the course of an administration, the governor gradually reduces his or her relations with the legislature to a routine to lessen the personal burden and the burden on the governor's office in general.

The resources available to governors in their relations with the legislature can be formidable. Gubernatorial patronage appointments can be attractive to legislators either for themselves or for an important ally or constituent. Attractive, too, can be the allocation of certain state contracts for services and facilities or support for local projects. These political plums or "gifts" can be provided by a governor as payment for support, either already rendered or anticipated later, in the form of legislative votes for gubernatorial priorities.

Many governors develop elaborate legislative efforts under the direction of a legislative liaison. The governor's program is watched over by the liaison from its formative stages through its introduction as a bill or bills, legislative consideration in committee and on the floor, debate, and vote. Meetings with individual legislators and breakfast sessions at the governor's mansion with the governor serve to keep legislators aware of the governor's position and interest in issues.

But the governor should never try to be the chief legislator, according to those who have sat in the chair. This advice captures a very simple point: The governor can do much to set the agenda of the legislature, can try to direct the legislature's consideration and action on bills of concern to him or her, and can use the veto and other tools to redirect a legislative decision. But the governor should never intervene in purely legislative political processes such as leadership selection.

First, if the governor attempts to do this and loses this key legislative political decision at the outset of the legislative session, the governor's political power is often irretrievably diminished well before the key policy and budgetary issues are considered. Thus this step should never be taken unless the governor is certain to win. Second, such an intrusion is perceived as a step across the separation of powers line set in most state constitutions and in most state government practices. Third, and most important according to those who have been there, "a governor successful in managing the leadership selection gains a Pyrrhic victory" (Beyle and Huefner 1983, 268). All those on the losing side will be looking for a chance for revenge, and those on the winning side will not have their own strong political coalition on which they can count to run the legislature without the governor's support. Fourth, whatever negative situations occur in the legislature can be traced back to the governor and that political intrusion. Most governors find there are enough problems and explosive issues in the executive branch and elsewhere for them to cover and that there is no need for the added burden.

How well do governors perform their crucial legislative role? Are they able to handle both their own agenda and that of the many legislators who come to the capital to serve? In the summer 1994 survey, respondents were asked how they would characterize their governor's relations with the state legislature on a five-point scale ranging from excellent to poor. Although the fifty-state average on the five-point scale was right in the middle at 3.0, there was a much greater spread of gubernatorial abilities in this legislative relationship than in other areas analyzed in this chapter. Although the ratings for twelve governors were "good" to "excellent," those for eleven were "poor" to "fair" (Beyle 1996, 243).

Previous service in a state legislature did not necessarily seem to be a positive factor in how well a governor's legislative relations were perceived (average score: 3.1), nor did service in the U.S. Congress (average score: 3.0). Having been a legislative leader did seem to be an experience that assisted governors in this role (average score: 3.3)—but it was not a benefit to all of them. According to one respondent, one governor who had been a legislative leader was characterized as someone who "did not seem to remember her time in the legislature, and how that body operates" (summer 1994 survey).

In the Middle of Intergovernmental Relations

The world that a governor must address is not constrained by the boundaries of the state. In an earlier time, out-of-state efforts made by governors were limited to occasional trips to attract industry, to attend the more socially oriented governors' conferences, and to participate in the presidential nominating conventions every four years. In recent decades, however, the states and the governors have found a need to focus on the issues, problems, and governmental activities that are part of the larger intergovernmental system in which individual states are lodged. Some of these issues concern several states at once, such as a pollution problem with a common river. Others are regional in scope, such as higher education in the South following World War II. Still others, such as health and welfare reform, are national in scope and thus all states and governors have a stake in the actions of Congress and the national executive branch as noted earlier.

Governors were slow to move in these circles, tightly limiting their concerns and interests to their own states and leaving national government concerns to the state's congressional delegation. But since the 1960s, governors and states have been forced to develop their intergovernmental relations roles at varying levels of government: national, regional, state, substate, and local. This development has generally coincided with the rapid expansion in national programs since the administration of President Lyndon B. Johnson (1963–1969), and it is also tied to the increasingly articulated demands of state citizens and interests for the government to do more about a wider range of concerns. Most recently, in the face of a reduced federal domestic effort, governors have worked to lessen or cushion the impact of federal cutbacks, unfunded federal mandates, and the devolution of federal programs down the federal system on their states and citizens. Why? The consequences of such cutbacks and programmatic shifts often land on their own desks as problems to be solved.

During the past few decades, governors have taken several significant steps to enhance their intergovernmental role. One was the establishment of a joint gubernatorial presence in Washington in the form of the National Governors' Association (NGA). By the mid-1980s the NGA was considered one of the major public interest associations on Capitol Hill, with a lobbying, research, and state service staff of ninety—a marked increase from its staff of three in the late 1960s (Weissert 1983, 52). It is ironic to note that governors and other state officials have also had to increase their representation on Capitol Hill as it became increasingly clear that state congressional delegations often did not have the state government's overall interest in mind as they passed budgets and policy initiatives. So the states joined the crowd of interest groups pressing their needs on their own states' representatives.

Gubernatorial relations with a state's congressional delegation are complex and subject to different types of difficulties. At the purely political level, a governor can be seen as a potential challenger for a U.S. senator's seat or even a congressional seat, and we have seen that more members of Congress are eyeing gubernatorial chairs. On policy matters, a governor may have interest in particular issues for his or her own state or for states in general. Congressional delegation members also have their own interests—both of a national, specific, or constituent nature—that may or may not coincide with the governor's expressed interests. Therefore, the degree of cooperation between these two sets of political actors can vary greatly; some governors find their delegations remote, inaccessible, and suspicious of any joint venture, and others find camaraderie.

But in politics changes can occur almost without warning. Following the election of 1994, the partisan ratio of the governors who are the constituency and bosses of the NGA shifted from a long period of Democratic dominance to Republican dominance. Ray Scheppach, the executive director of the NGA, indicated that "when you get a two-thirds change in your membership after an election, it changes things dramatically" (Mahtesian 1997, 24). The NGA staff, long attuned to working with the federal agencies to increase federal programs and largess to the states, suddenly found themselves being directed by a strong majority of governors wanting less government. It was an ideological shift of considerable proportions.

Suddenly the common cause of all governors represented by the NGA was shaken deeply as governors took a different look at their joint organization and its goals. Scheppach observed that "(s)ome Democrats think we're conservatives and some Republicans think we're liberals" (quoted in Mahtesian, 1997, 24). And as already noted, some of the longer serving Republican governors began working directly with the new Republican congressional leadership on major policy concerns, leaving the NGA—and the Democratic governors—shut out of the negotiations. Republican governor James of Alabama decided to leave the NGA with its $100,000 annual dues because it "is useless, irrelevant and ideologically out of sync with the Republican ideal of smaller government" (Mahtesian 1997, 23).

In recent years a new factor entered the politics of intergovernmental relations. Longer tenure is important in the governor's intergovernmental role. The relations need time to mature and the activities undertaken are complex and take time to perform effectively. Furthermore, leadership in intergovernmental organizations provides a platform for views to be made known and the opportunity for governors actually to affect policy. Term limitations, therefore, restrict governors in their ability to fulfill this intergovernmental role, especially in holding leadership positions. Thus states may be shortchanging themselves by limiting the tenure they allow their governors (Grady 1987). As one observer suggested, "Our state changes the team captain and key players just about the time we get the opportunity and know-how to carry the ball and score" (Farb 1977, 18). As the movement to limit terms of public officials grows and succeeds, this particular role of governors may also be curtailed.

Working with the Media

Probably the most significant source of informal power available to governors is their relationship with the public through the media and through other modes of contact. Most of the governors used media contact with the people to gain election to office, so they are well aware of the potency of this informal power. However, once in office the governor's relationship with the press undergoes a subtle yet important change. The governor is no longer the head of the army of attack but is the head of the army of occupation, the new administration in the state capital.

Although the media's attention to state government and its activities has waned in recent years, the media still watches the governor with a keen eye, often evaluating his or her performance not only against the promises but against previous gubernatorial efforts and the needs of the state. Furthermore, the media can suddenly become very interested in the activities and conduct of some of those whom the governor has brought into the administration. Stories of official misconduct sell newspapers and make the evening news more exciting—or so many in the media believe.

Governors have the opportunity to dominate the news from the state capital by carefully planning when press conferences are held during the day and when press releases are distributed. If they time it right, their story is on the evening television news programs and in the morning papers, where there are greater audiences to reach. A governor's communications or press relations office (every governor has one) can in large part determine a portion of the news the citizens of a state receive about a gubernatorial administration.

Governors do vary, however, in their approach to and openness with the media. Some hold press conferences routinely and others hold them only on specific occasions. Individual interview sessions with members of the press are regular fare for some governors, whereas others are more protective of their time and interactions with the media.

The advice provided new governors by incumbents indicates just how sensitive they are to this relationship: "The media expects you to do well. Thus, doing well isn't news"; "When you hold a press conference and are going to face the lions, have some red meat to throw them or they'll chew on you"; "Never make policy at a news conference"; and "Never argue with a person who buys ink by the barrel" (Beyle and Huefner 1983, 268).

How well do governors actually do in this relationship? Do the new governors heed the advice of their more experienced peers? Are they able to make that switch from campaigner to governor in a manner that helps to continue their relationship with the media, voters, and other constituencies? In the summer 1994 survey, respondents were asked about their governor's relations with the media on a five-point scale ranging from excellent (5) to poor (1).

The results indicated that the governors were working well with the media. The fifty-state average on the five-point scale was 3.3, and one-third of the governors (seventeen) were rated as having good to excellent relations with the media. Those with the top ratings come from all over the country—three in the West, two in the South, and one each in the Northeast and the Midwest (Beyle 1996, 246).

But of the six governors in the poor to fair range, four decided not to run for reelection in 1994 or in 1995, another was beaten in his bid for his party's nomination in the primary after succeeding to the office on the death of the governor, and the sixth could not run because of a term-limit restriction. Governors seeking reelection do not need poor media relations, which are hard to overcome. After all, the media is one of the primary vehicles by which voters get a reading on how their governor is performing.

Another part of a governor's public role is primarily reactive. The governor's office receives many letters, visits, and telephone calls, each with a request, a critical comment, or question of some kind. Most of these must be answered. Each response probably affects two to five people among the extended family and friends of the recipient. Thus the number of contacts between the governor or the governor's staff with the public, either directly or indirectly, is very high. How well the governor's office handles these letters and requests can become an important part of the public's perception of the governor's performance.

Some governors take an activist stance with regard to the public and generate citizen contacts through a variety of approaches. Some capitalize on their ceremonial role by appearing at county fairs, cutting ribbons at shopping centers, attending dedication ceremonies, and crowning beauty queens. These activities often can require a considerable investment of time.

Not the least of a governor's relations with the media and their statewide constituency is responding to an emergency situation. This can range from calling out the National Guard to helping to keep control when a disaster such as an earthquake, hurricane, or tornado has occurred. It is clear that when the governor makes a personal visit to the site of a disaster to see the damage and to talk with the people who have suffered in the calamity it is a necessary step to be taken—and one can also reap political rewards. In fact, it is probably a liability for any governor to fail to appear under such circumstances.

The governor, through this public role, has the potential to set the state's public agenda and focus attention on it. A governor's priorities can become the state's priorities unless unforeseen crises or problems arise or the media itself is inadequate to the task.

Priorities on the Job: The Personal Factor

Being governor is a time-consuming and busy undertaking. Many who have been governors or served with governors find that discussions and analyses of gubernatorial roles, power, and responsibilities do not provide the sense of what being a governor really means. In an attempt to capture the pace of a governor's life and show how time, or lack of time, affects gubernatorial actions, the NGA developed a case study called "A Day in the Life of a Governor" for newly elected governors (Beyle and Muchmore 1983, 32–42). That case cannot be recreated here, but based on a survey of those who scheduled gubernatorial time and from the estimates of sixteen incumbent governors, some indication can be given about where they spend their time (Beyle and Muchmore 1983, 52–66). And time "is one of the Governor's scarcest and most valuable resources" (NGA 1990c, 1).

Both governors and their schedulers basically agreed on how much time was allocated to the various roles a governor performs. Including recruiting and appointing personnel to positions in the executive branch, half their time was taken up just in running state government and working with the legislature. Another large segment of time was spent in their public roles, either directly interacting with the public, participating in ceremonial functions, or indirectly working with the media. Their schedulers estimated that more than one-third of the schedule was devoted to these public roles; the governors had a lower estimate of one-fifth of their time. The governors' intergovernmental activities, divided equally between federal and local governmental issues, took up slightly more than one-eighth of their time (Beyle and Muchmore 1983, 52–66).

In sum, we find what most of us would hope to find—governors serving primarily as chief executives and working with the legislature, relegating their public roles to second place, and giving their intergovernmental concerns less but not inconsiderable attention. They spend less time on politics by these estimates, although much that is politics is present in ceremonial, legislative, and other activities.

What gets squeezed in these official priorities is the governor as a person and his or her ability to maintain some semblance of a private life. As the NGA case study suggests, a governor in those few, short moments of reflection when alone with family "may find that his campaign did not result in his capturing the office, but in the office capturing him" (NGA 1978, 115). Nearly half of the fifty-one former governors responding to a 1976 NGA survey cited interference with their family life when asked what they considered the most difficult aspects of being governor. Being governor exacts a personal toll on the individual (Beyle and Muchmore 1983, 23–27).

LEAVING THE GOVERNORSHIP

Former Vermont governor Kunin suggested that "[t]here are two climaxes in political life: rising to power and falling from it" (Kunin 1994, 19). At the end of a gubernatorial term, a governor usually has several options available for the future. Many can and do choose to seek reelection to the governor's chair. In recent decades, we have seen some governors virtually turn a gubernatorial chair into their own private property as they served for several terms. Although seeking reelection as an incumbent usually provides a major campaign advantage, winning reelection (sometimes renomination) is not always an easy task, as was noted earlier.

The Unplanned Departure

Why do incumbent governors lose? In a few situations a single issue can be pinpointed as the cause of a governor's defeat, and that issue may be something that the governor has little control over, such as a souring economy. In other cases, a defeat is the result of an accumulation of several issues and concerns about the governor's administration. Scandals and incompetence—administrative, political, or personal—are also significant factors in the defeat of an incumbent governor.

There have been situations in which incumbents just overstayed their welcome and were blocking others from the office; or the voters in the party primary or general election wanted someone new in the office. And as we have watched the Republican resurgence across the nation and in the South specifically, changing politics and voter preferences can be the cause.

Between 1970 and 1998, there were 414 separate gubernatorial elections and 250 incumbent governors sought reelection to another term. Although most of these incumbents won (75 percent), sixty of them lost, fifteen in their own party primary and forty-seven in the general election. Several governors have not had the luxury to seek reelection as they were removed from office by a criminal court decision or impeachment (or the threat of it).

In sum, governors seeking to stay in office, or to regain office, are vulnerable to the ambitions of others within their party and the state; to a desire on the part of voters for a change to someone new; to issues directly affecting the electorate's wallets (taxation) or lives (jobs, the economy, the environment); and to allegations of misconduct or poor performance.

Onward and Upward

Staying in office is only one of several options that an incumbent governor may weigh. As noted earlier, for some governors the position is one step on a ladder that they hope leads to a higher office, such as the U.S. Senate or even the presidency, as in the cases of three of the past four presidents: Jimmy Carter, Ronald Reagan, and Bill Clinton.

Some move on to appointed national-level positions, such as cabinet offices, as Interior Secretary Bruce Babbitt (D-Ariz., 1978–1987) and Education Secretary Richard Riley (D-S.C., 1979–1987) did in the Clinton administration. Two New Hampshire governors became the president's chief of staff: Sherman Adams (R, 1949–1953) for Dwight Eisenhower and John Sununu (R, 1983–1988) for George Bush. Why did New Hampshire governors do so well in these presidential administrations? The early New Hampshire presidential primary is crucial to the presidential nomination process; winning candidates remember the help given them by the governor.

Some other governors move into leadership positions in the corporate world or in higher education, as did the former governor of North Carolina Terry Sanford (D, 1961–1965), who became president of Duke University; Lamar Alexander, who became president of the University of Tennessee; and former New Jersey governor Tom Kean, who became president of Drew University. However, we must be impressed most with the large number of governors for whom the governorship was their ultimate elected public office. They sought the office, served, and returned to their private lives—often to a lucrative law practice that may have included representing clients before the state legislature, state agencies, or state courts. Unfortunately, some governors were prosecuted for their misconduct while in office or prior to becoming governor, and some later served terms in prison.

Leaving

Most governors find a good life after being governor. But as former Michigan governor William Milliken (1969–1983) observed, they must take pains in planning their departure and "take advantage of the lessons learned by those who have already gone down the path." This means taking steps to prepare for the new administration while winding down the old and preparing for their own new life (Weeks

1984, 77). The NGA has developed a "worst case scenario" to alert them to what can happen without such planning and to suggest some strategies to follow to avert such problems (NGA 1990a).

This sounds most rational, but in the white heat of politics, and especially in the worst of all situations—being unseated as governor—these steps are not easy to take, nor does there seem to be enough time to plan them. Although states generally make provisions for their incoming governors, they tend to ignore their outgoing governors. The exiting governors suddenly lose all the perquisites of being governor: staff, cars, drivers, schedulers, office equipment, telephones, and so forth. This is seen in the lament of former governor Calvin L. Rampton (D-Utah): "I never realized how much of a man's life he spends looking for a parking place" (quoted in Weeks 1984, 73).

CONCLUSION

The American state governorship is the highest elective office in a state and, in some cases, the stepping stone to an even higher office. The governor symbolizes the state to many, and when state government falters or errs, the public often holds the governor accountable. The states have refurbished their governments, bidding "Goodbye to Goodtime Charlie" and in doing so have generally obtained a new breed of very capable people to serve as governor (Sabato 1978). But there are still signals that although there are few Goodtime Charlies, there are still a few who have lost their moral or ethical compass either in seeking or in holding the office.

This chapter has provided a view of the governorship through the eyes of the governors themselves and of those who watch what governors do. In it are described the politics of becoming governor, the tools available to the governor—both personal and institutional—the major roles now being performed by governors, and how, in performing these roles, governors have informal powers of considerable magnitude. Governors not only sit atop the state governments and the state political system, but through their informal powers, they can set and dominate the state's policy agenda and have an impact on regional and national agendas as well.

REFERENCES

Alexander, Lamar. 1986. *Steps along the Way: A Governor's Scrapbook*. Nashville, Tenn.: Thomas Nelson.

Barone, Michael, and Grant Ujifusa. 1997. *The Almanac of American Politics 1998*. Washington, DC: National Journal.

Benjamin, Gerald. 1982. "The Diffusion of the Governor's Veto Power." *State Government* 55:99–105.

Beyle, Thad L. 1988. "The Governor as Innovator in the Federal System." *Publius* 18(3):131–152.

———. 1992. "Term Limits in the State Executive Branch." In *Limiting Legislative Terms*, edited by Gerald Benjamin and Michael Malbin. Washington, D.C.: CQ Press.

———. 1995. "Enhancing Executive Leadership in the States." *State and Local Government Review* 27(1):18–35.

———. 1996. "Governors: The Middlemen and Women in Our Political System." *Politics in the American States*, 6th ed., edited by Virginia Gray and Herbert Jacob. Washington, D.C.: CQ Press.

———. 1998. "Reading the Tea Leaves?" *State Government News* 41(8):26–30.

Beyle, Thad, and Rich Jones. 1994. "Term Limits in the States." In *The Book of the States, 1994–1995*. Lexington, Ky.: Council of State Governments.

Beyle, Thad L., and Robert Huefner. 1983. "Quips and Quotes from Old Governors to New." *Public Administration Review* 43:268–270.

Beyle, Thad L., and Lynn Muchmore. 1983. *Being Governor: The View from the Office*. Durham, N.C.: Duke University Press.

CSG (Council of State Governments). 1992. *The Book of the States, 1992–1993*. Lexington, Ky.: Council of State Governments.

———. 1994. *The Book of the States, 1994–1995*. Lexington, Ky.: Council of State Governments.

———. 1996. *The Book of the States, 1996–1997*. Lexington, Ky.: Council of State Governments.

———. 1998. *The Book of the States, 1998–1999*. Lexington, Ky.: Council of State Governments.

English, Arthur. 1997. "The Political Style of Jim Guy Tucker." *Comparative State Politics* 18(2) (April):18–28.

Farb, Robert L. 1977. *Report on the Proposed Gubernatorial Succession Amendment, 1977*. Chapel Hill, N.C.: Institute of Government.

Farney, Dennis. 1993. "When Wisconsin Governor Wields Partial Veto, the Legislature Might as Well Go Play Scrabble." *Wall Street Journal*, July 1, A16.

Flentje, H. Edward. 1980. *Knowledge and Gubernatorial Policy Making*. Wichita, Kansas: Center for Urban Studies, Wichita State University.

Grady, Dennis. 1987. "Gubernatorial Behavior in State–Federal Relations." *Western Political Quarterly* 40:305–318.

Hutchison, Tony. 1989. "Legislating via Veto." *State Legislatures* 18 (January):20–22.

Kaufman, Herbert. 1963. *Politics and Policies in State and Local Governments*. Englewood Cliffs, N.J.: Prentice-Hall.

Key, V.O. , Jr. 1956. *American State Politics*. New York: A. A. Knopf.

Kunin, Madeleine. 1994. *Living a Political Life*. New York: Alfred A. Knopf.

Mahtesian, Charles. 1997. "Ganging up on the Governors." *Governing* (August):23–25.

Matheson, Scott M. 1986. *Out of Balance*. Salt Lake City, Utah: Peregrine Smith Books.

Moe, Ronald C. 1988. *Prospects for the Item Veto at the Federal Level: Lessons from the States*. Washington, D.C.: National Academy of Public Administration.

Morehouse, Sarah M. 1981. *State Politics, Party, and Policy*. New York: Holt, Rinehart and Winston.

———. 1987. "Money Versus Party Effort: Nominating the Governor." A paper presented at the annual meeting of the American Political Science Association, Chicago, September 4–7.

Murphy, Russell D. 1992. "Connecticut: Lowell P. Weicker, Jr.: A Maverick in 'The Land of Steady Habits.'" In *Governors and Hard Times*, edited by Thad Beyle. Washington, D.C.: CQ Press.

NASBO (National Association of State Budget Officers). 1997. *Budget Procedures in the States*. Washington, D.C.: Author.

NCSL (National Conference of State Legislatures). 1998a. *Limits on Authority of Legislature to Change Budget*. Denver, Colo.: Author.

———. 1998b. *Partisan Composition of State Legislatures*. Denver, Colo.: Author.

North Carolina Center for Public Policy Research. 1989. *Report on Campaign Financing in North Carolina*. Raleigh: Author.

NGA (National Governors' Association). 1978. *Governing the American States*. Washington, D.C.: Author.

———. 1981. *Reflections on Being Governor*. Washington, D.C.: Author.

———. 1987. "The Institutional Powers of the Governorship, 1965–1985." *State Management Notes*. Washington, D.C.: Author.

———. 1990a. "The Governor's Final Year: Challenges and Strategies." *State Management Notes*. Washington, D.C.: Author.

———. 1990b. "Organizing the Transition Team." *State Management Notes*. Washington, D.C.: Author.

———. 1990c. "Use of the Governor's Time." *Management Brief*. Washington, D.C.: Author.

———. 1998. *Governors of the American States, Commonwealths, and Territories, 1998 Directory*. Washington, D.C.: Author.

Ransone, Coleman B. 1956. *The Office of Governor in the United States.* University: University of Alabama Press.

Robinson, Julia E. 1998. "The Role of the Independent Political Executive in State Governance: Stability in the Face of Change" *Public Administration Review* 58:2 (March/April):119–128.

Sabato, Larry. 1978. *Goodbye to Good-Time Charlie: The American Governorship Transformed.* Lexington, Mass.: Lexington Books.

———. 1983. *Goodbye to Good-Time Charlie: The American Governorship Transformed.* 2d ed. Washington, D.C.: CQ Press.

Schlesinger, Joseph A. 1965. "The Politics of the Executive." In *Politics in the American States,* edited by Herbert Jacob and Kenneth N. Vines. Boston: Little, Brown.

———. 1966. *Ambition and Politics: Political Careers in the United States.* Chicago: Rand McNally.

———. 1971. "The Politics of the Executive." In *Politics in the American States,* 2d ed. edited by Herbert Jacob and Kenneth N. Vines. Boston: Little, Brown.

Sherman, Sharon. 1984. "Powersplit: When Legislatures and Governors Are of Opposing Parties." *State Legislatures* 10(5):9–12.

Van Assendelft, Laura A. 1997. *Governors, Agenda Setting, and Divided Government.* Lanham, Md.: University Press of America.

Weeks, George. 1984. "Gubernatorial Transitions: Leaving There." *State Government* 57(3):73–78.

Weissert, Carol S. 1983. "The National Governors' Association: 1908–1983." *State Government* 56(3):44–52.

Wiggins, Charles W. 1980. "Executive Vetoes and Legislative Overrides in the American States." *Journal of Politics* 42:1110–1117.

SUGGESTED READINGS

Blair, Diane. *Arkansas Politics and Government.* Lincoln: University of Nebraska Press, 1988. One of the best single-state studies of a state political and governmental system masquerading as a textbook.

Herzik, Eric B., and Brent W. Brown, eds. *Gubernatorial Leadership and State Policy.* Westport, Conn.: Greenwood Press, 1991. A multiauthored book focusing on the governors' policy roles. Case studies on both the policy processes around the governor and specific policy areas that concern governors.

Rosenthal, Alan. *The Governor and the Legislature.* Washington, D.C.: CQ Press, 1988. A fifty-state analysis of the relationship of the two major governmental actors in the states. Based on extensive interviewing and participant observation.

Thompson, Tommy G. *Power to the People: An American State at Work.* New York: Harper Collins, 1996. The longest serving governor's perspective on his administration and successes.

Van Assendelft, Laura A. *Governors, Agenda Setting, and Divided Government.* Lanham, Md.: University Press of America, 1997. A four-state case study of the problems governors have in setting and achieving their policy agendas when there is divided partisan control of government.

CHAPTER 7

Courts: Politics and the Judicial Process

HENRY R. GLICK

Courts rarely come to mind when thinking about state politics. Instead, we are more likely to envision a legislative session, a governor running for reelection, or interest groups making campaign contributions and lobbying on public policy. In contrast, most judicial elections are invisible, with incumbents seldom facing opposition, and most judicial decisions seem to have little to do with public policy. We expect courts to be governed according to law and to rise above politics. News reporting also limits our awareness of courts as important political institutions. Most news deals with lurid crimes and jury trials or occasional "ridiculous" lawsuits that focus on bizarre personal problems, not on broader social or economic concerns that underlie most court cases. As a consequence, news stories about state courts are more like entertainment and "human interest" than public affairs.

This image of courts is neither accurate nor complete. State courts frequently make controversial decisions that are equally or even more consequential than the policies of legislatures and governors. Examples include the death penalty, the liability of tobacco companies for cigarette-caused illnesses, taxation and spending on public education, regulation of businesses, professions and labor unions, employment discrimination, abortion, child custody and support, the rights of individuals to end life-prolonging medical treatment, and many others. Courts also make decisions that affect the rules of the political process, including disputed elections, conflicts among government agen-

I would like to acknowledge the helpful comments and suggestions made on an earlier draft by Lawrence Baum and Craig F. Emmert.

cies, removal of corrupt officials, and others. A consequence of their policy-making role is that interest groups and various public officials are acutely aware of the kinds of policies judges have or likely will pronounce on important public issues. Judges sometimes wage hotly contested elections—funded heavily by private groups—or controversy erupts over a particular judicial appointment. Besides these highly visible decisions, state courts annually make thousands of less visible decisions that settle the problems and disputes that most people are likely to encounter, such as divorce, traffic accidents and personal injury, dealings with businesses and government, and crime. Courts often make similar decisions in like cases, so numerous repeated decisions add up to policies for managing many common social problems. Therefore, how courts operate and what they produce are important social and political concerns.

DUAL IMAGES OF COURTS: LEGAL AND POPULAR POLITICAL CULTURE

Social scientists employ the term *culture* to refer to basic values and beliefs and expectations that people hold about social institutions. Our views of courts are ruled by two seemingly incompatible images: legal and popular political culture (Richardson and Vines 1970).

Legal Culture

Legal culture maintains that courts *ought* to be separated from partisan politics and personality as much as possible and that the rule of law should govern all that courts and judges do. Even courtrooms reflect the majesty and aura of law: They usually are decorated more ornately than most other government structures; judges wear black robes that distinguish their exalted status, and they sit on raised platforms facing everyone else; juries are symbolically separated in a boxed enclosure; and spectators sit in the rear sealed off by a low railing.

The judicial process also emphasizes "equal justice under law," not "by politics," and persons (litigants) with genuine disputes have the right to a trial and to one appeal. In trials, attorneys for each side establish their versions of the facts by closely questioning their own and opposing witnesses. Then a judge or jury "renders a verdict," which determines the guilt or innocence of criminal defendants or defendants' liability in a civil dispute, such as whether a person is responsible for an accident and has to pay compensation. Appeals allow for no witnesses and rarely any discussion of the facts. Instead, attorneys for each side have perhaps twenty to thirty minutes to summarize their position concerning the proper application of law and procedure at the trial. In all courts, judges behave as neutral umpires unaffected by their own beliefs or public opinion, and they refrain from using cases as opportunities to expand the law or insert the courts into policy making.

To ensure that judges are neutral and keep to the law, legal culture maintains that we must carefully select the best qualified judges. Instead of prior political experience, candidate appeal, partisanship, and elections, which are important elsewhere, legal culture emphasizes *merit* appointment of judges, which is expected to select people with quality law school educations and achievement, significant prior legal and judicial experience and knowledge, and possessing personal fairness and a calm judicial temperament.

In sum, the legal culture underscores the need to remove and insulate courts from the political and policy-making process. Legal culture affects the way that courts are organized, their procedures, the proper way to select judges, law-based decision making, and the proper scope of judicial decisions.

Popular Political Culture

Legal culture distinguishes courts from other governmental institutions, but it overlooks how courts also are affected by state and local politics and that law itself guarantees that politics affects courts. As mentioned earlier, probably the clearest link between courts and politics involves judicial elections in which groups organize campaigns or make contributions to elect judges with the "proper" attitudes. State and local politics also affect court organization. Elected state legislatures, state constitutional conventions, and popular referenda all are used to create new courts or to modify older ones. They also determine the kinds of cases courts may hear and the geographic boundaries of a court's authority. Most courts are placed in local communities, and each state has its own court system, which means that the social and economic context in which courts are situated influences the opportunities they have to decide cases. For example, New York City and Los Angeles courts are likely to get many more cases involving large businesses and corporations and more serious cases of crime than courts in rural upstate New York and northern California. Appellate courts in large, complex urban states also are likely to have more opportunities to decide controversial cases containing novel issues. Finally, the influence of state and local politics is paramount because nearly all state court cases begin and end in the states. State supreme courts decide 10,000 or more cases annually, but U.S. Supreme Court review occurs in fewer than 1 percent of them.

Judges and courts also are linked to state politics through law, which seems like a contradiction, but there are many sources of law and no two cases are identical, so trial and appellate judges always have leeway to interpret and apply law in particular cases. Most trials are held before judges alone (bench trials), so they determine the facts *and* apply the law. In jury trials, juries decide the facts and judges instruct the jury on applying the law. Fact finding seems straightforward, but there are many facts that can be raised. Determining which ones are crucial shapes the basis of a court's decision. For example, an out-of-work father who does not pay required child support offers the facts that he cannot find a job, is partially disabled, and has other financial responsibilities. But the other side wants to know how hard he has looked for a job; if there were jobs he refused to take; and if he regularly drinks alcohol or takes illegal drugs. In addition, the judge asks if the father is wearing gold jewelry, owns a car, or has money in his wallet.

Connecting facts to law appears easy, especially because judges usually give juries limited options to decide what crime has been committed (for example, first- or second-degree murder or manslaughter), but juries often consider whether applying the law would be fair in their particular case, and jury nullification—deciding to acquit defendants or convict on lesser charges, despite a cold reading of the facts and the law—is fairly common. Sometimes, despite clear evidence, juries have acquitted white Ku Klux Klan members of murdering blacks, or police of beating blacks, and other juries have freed antiwar and other protestors and drug users. Therefore, law and facts become mixed together to produce distinctive brands of local, popular justice (Abramson 1994).

Losers in the trial courts may ask appellate courts to review decisions for legal errors. Review may involve four main bodies of law: previous court decisions (precedents), also known as common law, legislative law (state statutes and city and county ordinances), administrative rules of various government agencies, and state and federal constitutions.

But problems develop quickly in using these sources of law. Regarding precedents, judges may choose among recent or old cases, cases from their own state or from others, or cases in which similar facts or legal principles seem most compelling. They also may decide that no precedents fit properly or reach the correct result, leading them to impose their own judgment. For example, the Missouri Supreme Court rejected factually similar precedents and consistent policies from nearly every other state supreme court when it decided that the families of patients who are permanently comatose may not stop unwanted life-prolonging medical treatment unless patients previously had made their wishes perfectly clear, preferably in writing.

Relying on the intentions of a legislature or the writers of an amendment to a state constitution is equally confounding because legislators often do not agree on a single clear intent, or they mask their intent in lofty, general rhetoric to avoid political controversy and opposition. Some laws intentionally allow judges to make choices, such as state criminal codes that provide a range of sentences that can be imposed in each case according to the facts and defendants' history and prospects.

Constitutions are the most general sources of law. The U.S. Constitution is a short document filled with broad, general principles and rights that courts have interpreted differently since the nation's early history. State constitutions are much longer and more specific. In addition to outlining the structure and basic powers of state governments, they impose precise limitations on state legislatures regarding, for example, the kinds and levels of taxes states may use, regulation of corporations and professions, relations between state and local governments, as well as individual rights that are not mentioned in the national constitution, such as a right to privacy and gender equality. Therefore, state constitutions would appear to be much more concrete guides for state courts than the U.S. Constitution, but specific provisions frequently become outdated and are difficult to apply to new circumstances, and many amendments added over the years sometimes are inconsistent and contradictory, which gives state courts great powers of interpretation and law making (Tarr 1997).

These many sources of law and their different possible meanings makes it inevitable that courts have substantial leeway or discretion to select and interpret law. In turn, discretion guarantees, first, that judges on many state supreme courts disagree on decisions, leading them to produce both a binding decision and written opinion by a majority of the judges as well as dissenting votes and opinions cast by those who come to the opposite conclusion. Second, discretion guarantees that the states have different judicial policies regarding similar issues. In addition to the Missouri right to die case just mentioned, state supreme courts currently disagree on very important and sensitive public policies, including the application of the death penalty and the constitutionality of relying on local property taxes to fund public education. State courts also disagree on current social and morals issues, including whether mothers can be criminally prosecuted for injuring their fetus because the women used drugs during pregnancy, crime victims or their families may testify before juries regarding a crime's impact, gays and lesbians may marry or have custody of children, biological parents may recover custody from adoptive parents, and more. The discretion to fit facts to law and to choose, interpret, or create new law means that many forces other than formal law—in other words, politics—are at work in the courts.

COURT ORGANIZATION

State government brings to mind the capital city and the few buildings that house the legislature, the governor's office, and perhaps the state supreme court. But there are many state courts, arranged in levels or a hierarchy from the highest appellate to the lowest trial courts. In some states, trial courts and intermediate appellate courts are located at the city, town, county, or district (multicounty) level. When courts at any level are created or changed, they also are given authority (jurisdiction) to hear certain types of cases. Therefore, court organization and jurisdiction are joined together and they have several political consequences.

Types of Courts

Most of the states have four basic types of courts at different levels: At the top of the hierarchy are state supreme courts (sometimes known by other names) located in the capital city; intermediate courts of appeal also located in the capital or with several divisions or panels sited in various cities to serve sections of the state, and, at the local level, one or two trial courts of general (major) jurisdiction and one or more trial courts of limited (specialized) jurisdiction (State Court Caseload Statistics 1997). Appeals from trial courts of limited jurisdiction get a new trial in a trial court of general jurisdiction, and appeals from trial courts of general jurisdiction go to intermediate appellate courts or state supreme courts, depending on the subject of the case. (Jurisdiction is discussed more fully in the next section.) A single judge presides over a trial court, intermediate appellate courts generally are com-

Figure 7-1 Florida Court System

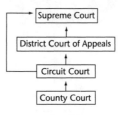

SOURCE: Derived from *State Court Caseload Statistics* 1996; 1997. Williamsburg, Va.: National Center for State Courts.

posed of three or more judges, and half the state supreme courts have seven members whereas the others have either five or nine judges.

State population partly explains the size of court systems because branches and new types of courts sometimes are added to serve growing populations or deal with new problems. Large states frequently have hundreds of trial and dozens of intermediate appellate court judges. But each state has its own distinctive set of courts. A few states have two intermediate appellate courts rather than one, and Texas and Oklahoma each have two supreme courts, one for criminal cases and another for civil cases. In contrast, a dozen less populous states in New England and the northern plains do not have intermediate appellate courts, so supreme courts hear all appeals in these states. Not only does structure vary, similar courts often have different names. Most of the highest appellate courts are termed *supreme courts,* but in New York, the highest appellate court is called the *court of appeals* and the trial courts of general jurisdiction are called *supreme courts.* In most states, trial courts are termed either *district* or *circuit courts,* but intermediate courts of appeals also may be called *district, circuit* or *superior courts,* or *courts of appeals.*

Court systems range from very simple and streamlined sets of a few courts to very complex and confusing arrangements of many courts. Consider the differences between the Florida and Indiana court systems (Figures 7-1 and 7-2). Florida's courts are easy to understand, and there are few courts at each level. There is one type of trial court of limited jurisdiction (county court), one type of trial court of general jurisdiction (circuit court), five regional divisions of a single intermediate appellate court (district courts of appeals), and one state supreme court. Appeals from county court go to circuit court and appeals from that court go either to the district or supreme court. In contrast, Indiana's courts are complicated. Indiana has a supreme court and intermediate appellate court (court of appeals), two types of trial courts of general jurisdiction (superior and circuit), and six trial courts of limited jurisdiction, including a special tax court, all with various avenues of appeal.

Jurisdiction

Jurisdiction has two elements: the geographic boundary of a court's district and the subject matter of cases that courts are permitted by state law to hear. For the

Figure 7-2   Indiana Court System

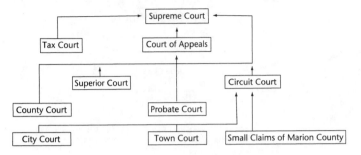

SOURCE: Derived from *State Court Caseload Statistics* 1996; 1997. Williamsburg, Va.: National Center for State Courts.

state supreme court and intermediate appellate courts in some states, the geographic boundary is the entire state. For trial courts, districts may include a single city or county or a few counties in rural parts of a state, and for intermediate appellate courts in other states, the geographic boundary includes contiguous counties in a region of the state. Subject matter jurisdiction is more complex. Cases are either criminal or civil matters. Criminal cases involve a violation of state law punishable by a fine payable to the government or imprisonment. Civil cases concern all other disputes. They sometimes involve individuals or groups versus government, as in government regulation of particular businesses or professions, but most civil cases are conflicts between private parties involving traffic accidents, divorces, contract disputes, property and landlord–tenant disputes, personal injury, inheritance, and others.

Trial courts of general jurisdiction hear cases involving the most serious crimes (felonies) and civil disputes involving large amounts of money—for example, $15,000 or more. Minor criminal offenses (misdemeanors), such as traffic violations and public drunkenness and smaller civil disputes, for instance, landlord–tenant conflicts and complaints against businesses regarding poor service or products, go into one or more specialized trial courts of limited jurisdiction, such as small claims or county court.

States frequently create or eliminate courts with specialized jurisdiction in response to political demands for new solutions to social problems. For example, spurred by federal grants-in-aid and innovative policies, various states recently have created special urban drug courts that impose probation and rehabilitation rather than incarceration on defendants facing minor charges and with few or no previous convictions. At the same time, some politicians and judges have called for dismantling special courts for juvenile offenders, which have been in operation for nearly 100 years, because these courts are overloaded with cases of violent juvenile crime, and many people believe that trying juveniles as adults and imposing harsh prison terms is the only way to stem what they see as a juvenile crime wave (Butterfield 1997, A1; McNaught 1997, 1B).

Appellate courts also have varying jurisdictions. In states with intermediate appellate courts, supreme courts have been given considerable discretion or latitude to hear or reject appeals, although they have some mandatory jurisdiction as well—for example, over all death penalty appeals and complaints that require disciplining attorneys or other judges. In a few other states, supreme courts receive all appeals, but they are permitted to send most of them to intermediate appellate courts and to keep others they wish to decide. Generally, state supreme courts with intermediate appellate courts below decide criminal cases carrying the most severe penalties, civil cases involving the greatest amounts of money, and appeals from government agencies. Intermediate appeals courts hear thousands of other appeals involving divorce judgments, criminal cases carrying sentences of a few years in prison, and smaller financial claims.

As in court organization, jurisdiction can be simple or complex. An important issue in many states is overlapping jurisdiction in which more than one court has the power to hear the same type of case. It occurs when legislatures add new courts without examining the structure and powers of existing courts or because legislative language about new court jurisdiction is vague. Over time, most court systems tended to become complex, and about half the states still have complicated and overlapping court systems. However, the trend is for states to reorganize their courts into more streamlined and simple systems, to give state supreme courts more discretion to select their own cases and the authority to make statewide rules governing judicial procedure. Some states also limit the kinds of cases that busy intermediate appellate courts must hear, thereby diverting cases to other specialized courts (*State Court Caseload Statistics* 1997).

It is difficult to account fully for why certain states have complex or simple court systems, because both types are found in all regions of the country and in large and small states, although supreme courts with the greatest control over their caseloads (dockets) tend to be in the more populous, urban, and socially and economically diverse states. Another explanation is that court reorganization often is a partisan and interest group issue that produces political deadlock. Prominent business people and their lawyers and many appellate judges believe that reorganized courts are more efficient, easier to use, and achieve a better public image. But many trial lawyers, judges, and court clerks sometimes resist change because they are satisfied with courts as they are, do not want to upset their routines, or lawyers see advantages over others in knowing how a complex court system works. Those who favor greater efficiency and a businesslike approach tend to be Republicans, but many trial lawyers, who bring personal injury and other lawsuits against businesses, are Democrats. In addition, changing court structure often has been tied to changes in judicial selection. Local politicians usually are wary about giving up their influence in electing or appointing judges, so comprehensive court reform proposals do not gain acceptance. New York state has one of the "most tangled" court systems in the country, and political battles have been fought for decades to simplify it. Reformers recently have agreed to abandon efforts to change how judges are selected in hope of persuading their traditional opponents to support a simplified court system (Hoffman 1997, B7)

Important political consequences flow from the organization and powers of state courts. First, in complex court systems, attorneys sometimes are uncertain which court to use, and judges dismiss some cases "for lack of jurisdiction," which may make the judiciary appear arbitrary and unfair. Second, overlapping jurisdiction allows attorneys and litigants to shop for courts where they believe they will find an advantage as a result of particular attitudes and decisional tendencies of judges and prosecutors, familiar court procedures, or through backlogs of cases that postpone criminal cases, leaving lucky defendants out of jail on bail, or that delay awarding compensation in civil cases.

But the most sweeping impact of court structure and jurisdiction concerns the policy-making role of state supreme courts. Reducing the types of cases that supreme courts are required to hear frees them to select cases they believe are the most important. With a reduced case load, supreme court judges acquire the time to write legal opinions that evaluate the arguments raised by both sides and explain the interpretation and direction that the court gives to the law—in other words, they make judicial policy. Trial courts rarely produce written opinions and intermediate appellate courts, which are loaded with cases, usually have time only to announce the winner and loser and issue a brief order to carry out their ruling. They cannot have much impact through an individual case.

As mentioned, supreme courts with the greatest control over their dockets are in the urban and socially diverse states in which there are many more opportunities to decide new issues that are important to business, labor, civil liberties, religious, and other organizations and state government and to individuals. As discussed later, their decisions often become models for courts in smaller states that have not yet had the same type of litigation. Since the U.S. Supreme Court may hear only cases involving federal issues, and they do not agree to hear most cases that are appealed, state supreme courts have the final word in nearly every important conflict they are asked to decide. Therefore, state supreme courts are becoming more and more important policy-making institutions.

SELECTING STATE JUDGES

Because state courts, especially supreme courts, have increasing opportunities to make policy, determining who becomes judges also is becoming more important. Except for the occasional drama that surrounds the selection of a new justice for the U.S. Supreme Court, most Americans pay little attention to how lawyers become judges. But the stakes are very high. There are more than 28,000 trial court and nearly 1,300 appellate court positions in the fifty states. Many states pay $80,000 and more to trial court judges and about $100,000 or more to appellate court judges (Council of State Governments 1996). There is no lack of qualified applicants, because many lawyers hope to get one of these secure and prestigious jobs.

Representing the legal culture, most judges, bar association leaders, and elite lawyers believe that judges ought to be chosen for their legal skills and distance from partisan politics. They prefer merit selection, which provides lawyers and sitting judges special influence in choosing new judges. However, many politicians and various interest groups believe that judicial selection is precisely the place where the popular political culture should apply: Because judges' personal values or attitudes influence decisions and judicial selection has policy-making implications, judges ought to be held directly accountable to the people through elections or be appointed by governors who represent the people.

Five Methods for Choosing Judges

The fifty states use five methods to select judges. They are *partisan election, nonpartisan election, gubernatorial appointment, legislative appointment,* and *merit selection* (also known as the *Missouri Plan* after the first state that adopted it more than fifty years ago). Table 7-1 presents the methods of selection and how they are used in the fifty states. The choice of a particular method has followed broader political trends throughout U.S. history. With independence, some states adopted legislative appointment as part of growing legislative supremacy and hostility to colonial executive rule, which included the governors' appointment of judges. Soon thereafter, partisan election became popular as democratic ideals spread, but in reaction to political corruption, nonpartisan elections for many offices, including courts, became popular in the early twentieth century. Recently, merit selection has become prominent as part of the effort to make courts more professional and removed from politics. Because each method emphasizes different ideals and goals, we might expect them to operate very differently, but the five methods have more in common than we might think.

Judicial Elections. About half the states use either partisan or nonpartisan elections to choose all or most of their judges. But most of these elections are uncontested, with incumbents easily winning reelection. Winning against incumbents is difficult in any election, but especially in judicial elections in which the legal culture dissuades potential challengers from campaigning against judges who are doing an adequate job. Judicial vacancies draw many candidates, but even then most campaigns are sedate and cordial. As a consequence, voting in most judicial elections is low, with turnout of 10 or 15 percent or heavy ballot fall-off when judges are elected with other officials (Dubois 1980).

An important consequence of uncontested judicial elections is that half or more "elective" judges actually are appointed initially by governors. Usually incumbents hold office term after term until they resign or die midterm, which gives governors the opportunity to fill vacancies on an interim basis until the next scheduled election. By then, however, the appointed judge is the incumbent who faces no serious opposition. Sometimes a judge who plans to retire does so

Table 7-1 Judicial Selection in the Fifty States

Partisan election	Nonpartisan election	Gubernatorial appointment	Legislative appointment	Merit selection (Missouri plan)
		All or most judgeships		
Alabama	Florida	California	South Carolina	Arizona
Arkansas	Georgia	Maine	Virginia	Alaska
Illinois	Idaho	New Hampshire		Colorado
New York	Kentucky	New Jersey		Connecticut
North Carolina	Louisiana			Delaware
Pennsylvania	Michigan			Hawaii
Tennessee	Minnesota			Indiana
Texas	Mississippi			Iowa
West Virginia	Montana			Kansas
	Nevada			Maryland
	North Dakota			Massachusetts
	Ohio			Missouri
	Oklahoma			Nebraska
	Oregon			New Mexico
	South Dakota			Rhode Island
	Washington			Utah
	Wisconsin			Vermont
				Wyoming
		Some judgeships		
Connecticut	Arizona	Montana	Rhode Island	Florida
Georgia	California	New York		New York
Indiana		North Carolina		Oklahoma
Maine				South Dakota
Missouri				Tennessee
South Carolina				

SOURCE: Derived from *The Book of the States 1996–1997*. Council of State Governments, Table 4.4.

midterm to give a governor of his or her own political party the chance to replace the judge with another loyal party supporter, thereby continuing party dominance on the courts.

Exceptions to this pattern occur most often in partisan elections in two-party competitive states. There, judicial elections are held in November along with elections for many other offices, and each party has a good chance of winning these contests. Voters frequently take cues from party leaders and interest groups, and if the out party sweeps elections for governor, legislature, or president, incumbent judges may lose their offices too. This occurs less frequently in nonpartisan elections, which generally are held at times other than the November partisan elections (Jacob 1996). However, other unusual election arrangements produce distinctive outcomes. For example, Ohio uses nonpartisan general elections preceded by partisan primaries but with partisan campaigning evident in *both* elections. Recent Ohio Supreme Court campaigns costing millions of dollars have emphasized economic issues, with some voters taking their cues from labor unions, which supported the most liberal candidates (Hojnacki and Baum 1992).

Heavily contested judicial elections still are the exception, but the trend seems to be toward more competition and intense political campaigns. In the past, most contributors to judicial elections were lawyers who probably hoped to maintain good rapport with sitting judges, but a variety of mainly business political action committees (PACs) are beginning to make significant contributions even to candidates who face no opposition and have no need for the money (Champagne and Cheek 1996; Nicholson and Nicholson 1994; Reid 1996). In three recent Texas elections, PACs contributed nearly $1.5 million to state supreme court candidates, judges sometimes endorsed interest groups favorably in PAC literature, and certain large contributions have been made just before big cases involving millions of corporate dollars have been argued before the Texas Supreme Court.

This trend worries legal reformers who fear that elections increasingly taint the judicial process. There probably is reason for concern, because we look to courts for the most impartial justice available in humanmade political institutions. Some reforms probably are possible, but imposing contribution limits is difficult, because giving money is considered a form of free speech, and laws impose few limits on contributions for issue-oriented advertising as distinguished from direct candidate contributions. Elections also are supported by those who believe the public ought to be able to hold judges accountable and replace them if their decisions veer too far from public opinion.

Legislative and Executive Appointment. The key to winning a judicial appointment in the few states that use legislative appointment is to have been a member of the state legislature, which rewards its own members. Getting appointed by the governor is more complicated mainly because the governor cannot personally know everyone who might be appointed to dozens of vacant judgeships. In general, governors place members of their own political party on the courts, particularly as patronage to reward people who have contributed money or other support to political parties and campaigns or who have held other offices. Also, awarding court positions to members of particular groups—for example, women, minorities, prosecuting attorneys (law enforcement)—attracts broader political support to a politician's or political party's voting base. Governors also sometimes use appointments as trade-offs with key legislators to get support for their programs. For trial and intermediate appellate courts, governors often rely on political allies for recommendations, including legislators, mayors, and local leading lawyers and friends. For the supreme court, governors are more likely to choose lawyers they know personally. Gubernatorial appointment is more prevalent than the distribution of states in Table 7-1 suggests because, as discussed earlier, many elective judges also are appointed initially. Governors also play an important role in merit selection.

Merit Selection. Merit selection is the most recent innovation in choosing judges. It is designed to reduce the influence of partisan politics by having local, regional, and statewide panels of lawyers, nonlawyers and, in some states, judges screen and nominate several candidates for each trial and appellate court vacancy.

Governors make the final choice, but they usually are limited to three nominees put forward by each selection panel. Once the governor makes an appointment, the new judge typically serves for one year and then runs in a retention election in which there is no other candidate. The voters are asked only whether Judge X should remain in office. If retained, the judge serves for life or a very long term.

Lawyers are expected to play a major role in influencing panel decisions because presumably they know what it takes to be a good judge. Local bar associations sometimes organize the election of lawyers to the panels, and the lawyer members tend to come from larger partnerships and law firms. The nonlawyers are appointed by the governor and generally are business and professional people such as doctors, accountants, and teachers (Henschen, Moog, and Davis 1990). In some states, judges serve as panel chairs and are chosen according to their seniority.

Although merit selection relies on experienced people and the mechanism is designed to protect courts from partisanship and interest group influence, the process produces outcomes that are not far different from the results of elections or appointment by the governor. First, as indicated earlier regarding court reorganization, lawyers in many states divide into two general camps: those representing individuals who sue insurance companies, hospitals, and other businesses and organizations for injuries or other damages (plaintiffs' lawyers), and lawyers who defend these organizations from lawsuits (defendants' lawyers). The plaintiff's position is closest to the Democratic Party, which receives much of its support from social and economic "underdogs," and business defendants are closest to Republicans. Each group works to elect its allies and supporters to the nominating panels. The legal attributes of good judges, such as fairness, integrity, moral courage, knowledge of the law, and so on, are vague and open to interpretation and can be used to support almost any candidate. Therefore, both sides tend to disagree on who would make the best judge, and group and party loyalties shape their choices. Partisanship occurs too because the governor appoints nonlawyer commissioners with political and civic group experience who also are aligned with the governor and her or his party. As a consequence, panels usually give governors lists of names that include at least one person the governor wants to appoint to the court vacancy (Watson and Downing 1969).

Because merit-appointed judges face no opposition during their retention election, almost all of them are retained by very wide vote margins (Hall and Aspin 1987). Rare exceptions occur, particularly when judges are involved in personal scandals or make visible and controversial court decisions, such as in California in the 1980s when the liberal chief justice and two others were voted off the state supreme court because they consistently reversed death penalty sentences. Law enforcement and conservative business groups organized a multimillion dollar campaign against them. The new Republican governor appointed conservatives in their place (Wold and Culver 1987). Similar campaigns have been waged in Florida and recently again in California. (California uses merit-type retention elections following gubernatorial appointment, but without merit screening.)

Despite claims for the superiority of merit selection, there is no evidence that a particular method of selection makes much difference in producing judges with different personal characteristics or abilities (Glick and Emmert 1987). This is probably a result of the similar influence of governors, political parties, and various groups in all selection systems. In addition, no one involved in the selection process is motivated to choose unqualified people for the courts, because that would reflect badly on them. Therefore, most state judges have credible educations and relevant legal, judicial, civic, and governmental experience.

White males still hold most judicial positions (Glick and Emmert 1986; Henry et al. 1985), but the number of women and blacks has increased substantially in the past fifteen years, from ten women and two blacks on state supreme courts in 1980 to fifty women and twenty blacks in the 1990s, including five black supreme court chief justices (Alozie 1996; Alozie forthcoming). However, there is some evidence that merit systems are somewhat less likely to produce judges who reflect the state's population or the pool of lawyers (Alozie forthcoming; Graham 1990). This may be a result of the domination of merit selection panels mostly by white males and lawyers from larger partnerships and law firms so that women and racial minorities are less likely to be considered. In the 1980s, merit also produced an underrepresentation of religious minorities for state supreme courts (Glick and Emmert 1987). Some observers speculate that the pool of black and Hispanic lawyers nationwide may decrease even more because judicial and other official support for affirmative action is weakening, and fewer minorities have been admitted to certain law schools.

Some election systems also have placed black judicial candidates at a disadvantage (Jacob 1996). In multijudge, at-large elections—many candidates stand for election in a single large district for more than one court position—white majorities usually elect few black judges. At-large districts have been challenged in court as discriminatory and a violation of the 1965 Voting Rights Act, and the U.S. Supreme Court has agreed that the act applies to judicial elections as well as those for legislatures and city councils (*Chisolm v. Roemer* [501 U.S. 380, 1991]; *Houston Lawyers v. Texas Attorney General* [501 U.S. 419, 1991]). About a dozen states have faced legal challenges, and some have created smaller districts with black majorities, guaranteeing an increased number of black trial judges. However, because appellate judges are chosen statewide or in larger districts, where blacks rarely constitute a majority, fewer blacks are elected.

Recently, affirmative action has been heavily attacked, and the U.S. Supreme Court has banned specially created majority black congressional and state legislative districts in which race was the only consideration in making the change and no overt attempts to discriminate against blacks was evident (*Shaw v. Reno* [509 U.S. 630, 1993]; *Johnson v. Miller* [515 U.S. 900, 1995]). Reacting to this change in Supreme Court policy, opponents have recontested judicial redistricting. In Arkansas—where thirteen black judges were elected after 1992—opponents have challenged previous Supreme Court rulings as well as the entire Voting Rights Act

(Smothers 1996). In Wisconsin federal trial and appellate judges found no need to change from at-large to smaller single member districts because some black judges had been elected, and civil rights plaintiffs in Georgia abandoned a suit spanning nine years after Supreme Court policy shifted. Overall, blacks and other minorities in elective states may find that their chances of getting court positions are greatest when governors make interim appointments to cement their links to minority voters.

LAWYERS, LITIGANTS, AND INTEREST GROUPS

Courts are passive institutions, which means they do not create their own workload but must wait for others to bring cases to them. Therefore, lawyers and their clients are crucial for determining which disputes or cases of crime get to court and how they shape the issues for judges and juries. However, most cases are dropped or settled through negotiation before they reach the trial stage, which makes lawyers and litigants doubly important for determining how disputes are resolved.

Lawyers

Except for small claims courts, where litigants might try to go it alone, lawyers are essential in the judicial process. Lawyers know each step for taking a case to court and possibly to trial, and they can translate ordinary disputes from anger and accusations into the proper legal language that makes it possible for courts to rule on them. Lawyers also know the clerks and judges who run the courts, the informal workaday routines for processing the paperwork, and the attitudes and inclinations of judges and opposing lawyers. No one else has this kind of knowledge and access.

Law Work. Although we think mostly about lawyers in court, lawyers do many different kinds of law work. Most of it is invisible and does not concern litigation, because trials represent less than 1 percent of all disputes that lawyers file as cases (Miller and Sarat 1980–1981). Most people are eager to avert trouble, and lawyers mainly research law and advise clients on how to avoid expensive and time-consuming lawsuits through negotiation, specifying agreements, and cooperating with government regulators.

Many other lawyers work for government and have a wide variety of jobs, for example auditing the budgeting and spending practices of state agencies, gathering and analyzing information for legislative committees, and advising university administrators. Others work for the attorney general, the state's leading lawyer, and represent the state when an agency is involved in litigation.

The most visible government attorneys are prosecutors and public defenders. The prosecutor represents "the people" or the state in criminal cases and public defenders represent criminal defendants who are too poor to hire their own lawyers. Chief prosecutors and public defenders employ a number of lawyers as assistants who directly handle the caseload. Prosecutors have almost unlimited power to decide whether to charge a defendant and what charges to bring, negotiate guilty pleas and the terms of settlements, or go to trial (Eisenstein, Fleming, and Nardulli 1987).

Prosecutors drop as many as a quarter or more of all cases and about 90 percent of the remainder are settled through negotiated guilty pleas. In most cities, prosecutors, defense attorneys, and judges interact regularly in stable work groups, so they soon reach understandings about acceptable sentences for different types of crimes (Eisenstein and Jacob 1977). Reelection politics sometimes influences prosecutors' decisions as well, and they sometimes seek publicity for temporary crackdowns against writers of bad checks, shops that rent X-rated videos, or pregnant teenagers and their partners who have violated old fornication statutes. In an unusual twist, an elected New York prosecutor recently attempted to use his discretion never to seek the death penalty, but the governor, supported by the Court of Appeals, removed him from a murder case in which the victim was a police officer.

Most criminal defendants are poor and are represented by public defenders. Some communities also use court-appointed lawyers who are paid a set fee for each case. Other defendants usually obtain a lawyer whose practice consists mostly of handling a large volume of criminal cases for modest fees. Given their large case-loads and the high odds that their clients are guilty of some violation, defense attorneys usually advise their clients to plead guilty to a negotiated settlement that will get defendants probation or shorter jail or prison sentences than if they are convicted at a trial. However, public defenders are willing to go to trial when they believe their clients are innocent or face charges that do not fit the facts (Eisenstein and Jacob 1977).

Lawyers in private (nongovernment) practice generally specialize in either business or personal law; and they opt either for law office work (research, communications, and negotiation) or a trial or appellate court practice. There is little overlap between each of these fields. However, lawyers in small towns and rural states usually cannot specialize (Curran 1986; Heinz and Laumann 1982). Business law involves doing work for large corporations or other businesses on antitrust matters, taxes, stocks and bonds, banking, public utilities, defending against lawsuits for injuries and property damage, and other commercial law. These lawyers usually are salaried staff of corporations or work in large private law firms that are hired by businesses for various transactions or cases. Personal law, sometimes called "personal plight," involves divorce, automobile accidents and other personal injury, house purchases, taxes, and criminal defense work.

There is an important link between law work and politics. Highly paid business law office lawyers have the most prestige because their work brings them into regular and long-term contact with wealthy, upper-class individuals, and the work avoids overt human conflict and distasteful personal problems. These lawyers also usually have high-status backgrounds themselves, and some of them become presidents or officers of large corporations. As discussed earlier, because these lawyers are closely connected to business, they are likely to be conservatives and Republicans and allied with defendants' lawyers who represent businesses and professions in court. Prosecuting attorneys frequently become business lawyer allies because of their shared conservative and law-and-order posture. At the bottom are lawyers who usually earn much less and handle the personal problems of clients who need lawyers only occasionally. These lawyers often have to search for new clients to maintain a stream of income, and they are more likely than others to favor lawyer advertising to bring in new business. Advertising generally is controversial and deplored by prestigious business lawyers because it detracts from the law's professional image (Seron 1993). Personal plight lawyers represent people with modest or low incomes who sue businesses for injuries, and these lawyers are likely to be liberals and Democrats. As we have seen, divisions among lawyers affect the politics of court reorganization and judicial selection, but they also divide lawyers in state legislatures on lawyer advertising and solicitation of clients, limits on the opportunities to sue (tort reform), liability law involving manufacturers of retail goods, hospitals and nursing homes and insurers, and similar issues.

Getting Representation. It often seems that we have enough or even too many lawyers. The number of lawyers has greatly increased during the past four decades. In 1960 the total number of lawyers in the United States was about 286,000 or one lawyer for each 627 people. By 1997 the number of lawyers had increased to nearly 925,000 or one lawyer for each 278 people (American Bar Association files; Council of State Governments 1996).

With so many lawyers and a variety of practitioners, it would seem that no one would have trouble finding a lawyer. But lawyers are not so widely available as one might think. First, lawyers are not distributed equally throughout the country. New York state has more than 100,000 lawyers—one for every 172 people—but Arkansas and North Dakota have approximately 6,500 and 1,300 lawyers or one lawyer for every 373 and 474 people, respectively. Most important, lawyers are concentrated in large cities, commercial centers, and state capitals. Second, few people have legal insurance, so hourly fees of $100 or more are steep for most individuals. Also, because few people use lawyers regularly or move in business circles, they have few ways of finding a suitable lawyer.

The very poor have some opportunities to get free legal help through clinics supported by various law schools and local charities, but most legal aid societies are connected to the Legal Services Corporation, a nonprofit organization supported by federal, state, and local government grants-in-aid. Legal services lawyers were especially aggressive regarding public policy during the 1960s when they took on local governments and businesses to try to improve housing, working conditions, and hospital and jail conditions for the poor. But this was so unpopular with businesses and state and local governments that conservative congresses and Republican presidents have reduced the program's budget and limited these organizations to helping the poor only in individual personal disputes. Even so, many of the poor are unaware of legal aid or are reluctant to seek help. Legal aid lawyers, especially in small towns and rural areas, also have felt pressured to get along with local business and law elites and to settle disputes without litigation (Kessler 1986; Lawrence 1990). As a consequence, both the poor and the middle class have less access to lawyers than the sheer number of lawyers would indicate.

Litigants

Courts are available to anyone, but not every group in society uses courts equally, and most people who start the process usually settle out of court. With the exception of divorce cases, where a formal court decree is required to end a marriage, strangers, such as those involved in automobile accidents or landlords and tenants, who do not plan to have future business, are more likely to use courts. Because going to court kills close ties, family members, friends, and many businesses, which have long lasting relationships with each other, usually try to work out their differences.

One comprehensive survey disclosed that a sizeable 40 percent of all households in the United States had grievances against others involving $1,000 or more during the previous three years. But fewer than 25 percent of these hired lawyers, only 11 percent filed court cases, and only 10 percent of these cases actually went to trial. This means that only about 1 percent of all grievances resulted in trials (Miller and Sarat 1980–1981). Instead, most people contacted the other party personally or through lawyers and received an acceptable settlement. Others abandoned their claims and took their lumps.

The main way that civil disputes are settled is through private negotiation, mediation, or arbitration. In successful negotiation, individuals try to put their emotions and disappointments aside and narrow their complaints to specific issues to which the other side can respond. Individuals often fare much better with lawyers than they could on their own, especially in disputes involving large amounts of money, such as insurance claims for personal injuries, or where the law is not so clear and understandable, as in a job discrimination claim (Ross 1970).

Mediation occurs when two opposing sides voluntarily ask a neutral third party to hear both sides and attempt to bring opponents to an agreement. Mediation is available through various volunteer and social agencies. It is informal and may cover the pertinent facts and the law as well as the broader relationship among the parties. However, it has not been as successful as many groups had hoped because businesses have little incentive to negotiate or settle clear-cut claims against individuals, such as in debt collections (National Institute of Justice 1980). Arbitration is more formal—like a mini-trial—and decisions of an arbitrator are legally binding. Arbitration is required by various business groups—for example, professional sports and securities sales and certain others. Many courts, especially small claims and family (divorce) courts, *require* litigants to try mediation as an alternative to trial as a way to reduce caseloads. Most litigants prefer mediation's less formal procedures and seem satisfied with the outcomes (McEwen, Mather, and Maiman 1994; Wissler 1995).

Although state courts deal with the kinds of disputes that most people are likely to encounter, most individuals appear in court as defendants. Much research shows that, other than divorce, most civil cases involve businesses and organizations, such as banks, loan companies, hospitals, and home construction firms filing cases against individuals to collect debts and unpaid bills. Governments file similar suits for nonpayment of property and other taxes. When individuals file suits against other individuals, it also mostly is to collect debts or compensation for accidents and other property damage and contract violations.

Business plaintiffs have huge advantages in these cases because there usually is no doubt that the debt is owed and, unlike defendants, they have the money, lawyers, and experience necessary for using the courts. Businesses win many of their cases by default because defendants do not appear for trial. Similar problems plague some individuals who have valid financial claims against others, but who are reluctant to file cases because they are inexperienced and wary of court procedures or they cannot afford to pursue collection of relatively small amounts of money (Yngvesson and Hennessey 1975).

Criminal cases also involve selective groups of individuals. Most crimes are committed by young men: More than 80 percent of those arrested are males and about the same percentage are younger than thirty-four; nearly half are younger than twenty-four. Whites are nearly 70 percent of those arrested, but because blacks are a small percentage of the total population, they are very disproportionately represented among criminal defendants and prisoners. Most arrests are for drunk driving and public drunkenness or disorderly conduct, larceny and theft, possession of drugs, and assaults. Arrests for the most serious offenses such as murder, rape, and manslaughter are less than 1 percent of all arrests, but these crimes receive the most attention because they inflict much more damage to victims and the public psyche.

A recent concern in the United States has been the very sharp increase in violent juvenile crime. Juvenile arrests overall are up nearly two-thirds from the mid-1980s, and of the nearly 2.75 million juvenile arrests in 1995, nearly 15 percent were for murder, manslaughter, rape, robbery, and serious assaults (U.S. Department of Justice 1997). Juvenile crime became especially salient to the public and politicians also because the increase involved black offenders much more heavily than whites, increased use of firearms, and more victims who were strangers or acquaintances rather than family members (Butterfield 1996). The lurid image of the predatory young black male became much more prominent in the news and in public fears even though most victims also were young black males.

In the 1990s the states reacted to this disturbing trend through harsher juvenile criminal justice policies. As mentioned earlier, some states considered getting rid of their juvenile courts entirely, but most others made changes in court jurisdiction that resulted in stiffer sentences for violent juvenile offenders. More than forty states allow for violent juvenile offenders to be tried in adult court, and half the states gave juvenile courts greater sentencing options for dealing with violent offenders. Pressures also exist to house juvenile offenders in adult prisons. The overall result is that nearly all states have compromised on the ideal of rehabilitation in favor of harsher punishments for violent juveniles.

Interest Groups in Court

In addition to individuals and particular businesses, organized groups use courts to benefit their members or others who share the organization's goals. Lobbyists are unlikely to contact a judge about a pending case because legal culture expects judges to wall themselves off from groups and individuals who are involved in litigation, but there are other ways to exert influence.

One of the best ways to influence government policy is through the selection of decision makers. Therefore, various interest groups, particularly lawyers and businesses, try to influence judicial recruitment. As discussed earlier, they appear to be making substantial campaign contributions to various court candidates, and they undoubtedly try to get the attention of key legislators or the governor's office to influence appointments.

Influencing the courts through decision making is more complicated. Cases must be filed by those who directly have suffered some wrong or damage, which prevents groups or associations from routinely filing cases themselves. But groups sometimes look for promising cases and pay the expenses and provide lawyers to individuals whose lawsuits closely represent the group's policy designs. Examples include cases filed by citizens who object to new types of taxes, claim they have suffered discrimination in obtaining a job or getting admitted to a university program, object to government-approved construction of radio towers, incinerators, and new garbage dumps, or planning for new residential subdivisions.

The major way that groups become involved in the courts is by filing *amicus curiae* or friends of the court briefs, mostly in state supreme courts. These are formal written documents that make legal and policy arguments similar to those submitted by one or the other main litigants in a case. Groups and their briefs are not the main focus in court, but judges can be expected to give the briefs some level of consideration. Cases that attract several *amicus* briefs on both sides project the real taste of interest group conflict in court.

Interest group lobbying has been important in the federal courts for many decades, but groups are becoming more active in state courts as well. Group participation as *amici* has increased since 1980, with a sharp upward trend into 1990 (Epstein 1994). On average, each state had nearly thirty-five cases that contained at least one *amicus* brief, compared to only ten in 1980. The variety of groups filing briefs also has grown. Now government and groups representing business, civil liberties and education organizations, and lawyers' associations are the most active. Because only sixteen states were studied, it is risky to generalize to all of the states, but it appears that the large, urban, socially complex states such as California, New Jersey, Illinois, and Michigan had the largest amount of interest group involvement. Increased interest group participation also indicates the growing role of state courts as important policy makers.

Is There Too Much Litigation?

The amount of litigation has increased sharply during the past fifty years, leading to what many have termed a "litigation explosion." In the late 1970s the total number of cases filed in the fifty states was about 67 million, but this increased to about 100 million in the early 1990s, although it has declined to about 88 million recently. Certain states have had even steeper climbs, such as Michigan, which went from 167,000 to nearly 700,000 civil cases per year and stood recently at nearly 581,000 cases (*State Court Caseload Statistics* 1993, 1997). To some extent increases in litigation parallel population growth, but that does not account for all of it. As a consequence, many critics claim that Americans have become enormously.litigious, meaning they react with lawsuits whenever they feel they have been wronged by some person, business, or public institution.

However, we should be cautious about sweeping statements regarding American litigiousness. First, research shows that rates of litigation (number of cases per 100,000 people) are not much different from rates in other developed, industrial countries. Second, although litigation has increased overall in the United States, the amounts vary widely among the states. New Jersey and Massachusetts, for example, recently have had nearly 140 and 105 cases per 100,000 people respectively, but California, which is another urban state, had less than 70. Figure 7-3 portrays the rates of tort (mostly personal injury) filings in eight states, for which data is most reliable, from 1975 to 1995 (Yates et al. 1998). Not only does the amount of litigation vary widely among the states, looking over the long and short haul also affects judgments we might make. Most states experienced huge increases in litigation after World War II (not shown in Figure 7-3), but since 1975 some states continue to have increases and others have leveled off or decreased except for a spike or two up or down.

Differences also exist in particular types of cases. For example, automobile liability cases are up in many states, but other liability cases, such as lawsuits against doctors and businesses, have decreased. There also is evidence that doctors are not sued routinely, as many believe, but face lawsuits only in the most grievous cases of negligence and injury. Trial lawyers also turn away as much business as they accept because many potential clients do not have good cases (Galanter 1993; Kritzer 1997; Sloan and Hsieh 1995).

The number of people per square mile (population density) is the most powerful explanation for differences in rates of litigation. For example, if North Dakota had the same population density as Maryland, it would have 40 percent more cases per 100,000 people than it does. This seems to point more to major changes in living and working relationships occurring over the past several decades than to a fundamental change in national personality. After all, going to court is not fun for most people. Most people no longer live in small towns and rural areas, but rather in large and growing cities where relationships with neighbors, employers, and businesses are likely to be much more complex—and also remote and temporary—and, as mentioned earlier, strangers are more likely to go to court.

Besides urban living, the size and scope of government and commerce have grown tremendously in the past fifty years. Business and technology have produced a growing flood of consumer products and services that sometimes cause harm or loss with legitimate claims for compensation. Government policies and regulations also affect individuals, businesses, and groups much more than ever before, not only in regulating business and labor practices but also through a huge expansion

Figure 7-3   Rates of Tort Litigation Filings in Eight States, 1975–1995

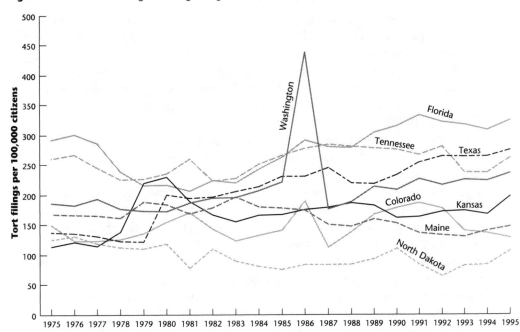

SOURCES: Derived from Yates et al., 1998, and National Center for State Courts.

of individual rights and liberties that give individuals and groups lawful opportunities to challenge the behavior and policies of government and public organizations. Even policies that seem to have no direct connection with litigation may have an effect. For instance, research on the eight states suggests that, in addition to population density, state government welfare policies that keep payments low and large gaps between rich and poor (income inequality) also are related to higher rates of litigation. This does not mean that the poor use the courts to get money; rather it suggests that wide internal economic differences within a state's population may reflect a conflictual and strained social setting with a greater likelihood for people generally to use courts. Finally, although it normally is not considered part of the litigation explosion, increases in the overall workload of state courts also is partly a result of recently rising crime rates and the increasing amount of criminal law produced by the states.

Additional possible explanations for differences in rates of litigation include court reforms that encourage mediation and arbitration, placing monetary limits on awards to discourage litigation, as well as localized population shifts (*State Court Caseload Statistics* 1996). But complete explanations elude us for now, and more research is needed. It seems clear, however, that it is a mistake to make sweeping conclusions about the litigious nature of American society or even to conclude that litigation forever increases.

MAKING JUDICIAL DECISIONS

For lawyers, politicians, and litigants, making decisions is the crux of the judicial process. Legal culture expects judges to be limited by the facts and the law, but the popular political culture conceives that many forces influence decisions, including the social and political context in which courts are embedded, the structure and operating rules of court systems, and judges' personal backgrounds, experiences, and political attitudes. Trial and appellate judges are affected by many similar forces, but studying appellate courts composed of a number of judges is especially informative because all of the judges have access to the same facts and law and they decide the same case. When they disagree on decisions, we can analyze who is in the majority or in dissent and why.

The extent that appellate judges register their disagreement by dissenting and writing separate opinions depends partly on institutional arrangements in each court system. In states where supreme courts have intermediate appellate courts below them to handle the large volume of mostly ordinary appeals, supreme court judges have more time to carefully consider a smaller number of other more important cases and to express possible disagreement about the law and the decision. Rules that allow for open and random interaction among the judges as they consider their votes and opinions also promotes dissents, as does elective judicial selection, which probably recruits judges experienced in rough and tumble electoral politics who are more independent and likely to accept the risk of speaking out (Brace and Hall 1990).

Although institutional arrangements permit or encourage dissenting behavior, certain "unofficial" political and social forces influence the direction of judges' decisions. The most important impact on judges' decisions is their political party affiliation (Dubois 1980). Like fellow partisans elsewhere, Democratic judges tend to be more liberal than Republicans. They favor labor unions, poorer litigants, women, racial minorities, those who have been injured by the negligence of others, and social underdogs in general. Republicans favor business interests and social upperdogs. This is not a hard and fast rule, for some cases do not raise issues that allow much leeway, such as when debtors clearly owe a bill, and a few state courts have traditions of bipartisanship, but when the law can be interpreted to favor either side, the political party affiliation of judges often makes a difference. Because the states are becoming more politically competitive with higher stakes riding on judicial elections, party affiliation probably will become even more important.

Additional personal characteristics also affect judges' decisions. For instance, compared with males, women judges more heavily support women's rights involving sex discrimination, child support collection, and others, and they are more likely to impose longer sentences on rapists. However, on other issues, for example, business regulation and criminal sentencing in general women judges, like males, divide mostly along party lines. On state supreme courts with very high levels of dissent, women judges have tended to be extreme partisans, possibly to avoid being seen as weak tokens by their assertive male counterparts (Allen and Wall 1993).

Judges also are affected by their environments. The public gives little notice to most court decisions, so judges' backgrounds and attitudes are foremost in decision making. However, in death penalty and other prominent cases, the public and active groups do pay attention, and judges respond. For example, one study revealed that trial judges changed their sentences for drug possession to make them more compatible with local views when public opinion became clear through a local referendum (Kuklinski and Stanga 1979). In death penalty cases, Republican judges, older judges, and judges who have served previously as prosecuting attorneys are more likely to uphold death sentences. Judges who have served the longest are the most partisan. But both Democratic and Republican judges in states with conservative ideologies and that use partisan judicial elections are likely to uphold death sentences. A smaller subset of judges at the end of their elective terms, who win reelection by narrow vote margins, are elected in smaller single-member districts, and who have had electoral experience before becoming a judge, lean very heavily toward death sentences. Overall, it appears that judges who are most easily held accountable are most likely to respond to public opinion in these most visible cases. Nevertheless, even in states that do not use elections, ideologically oriented governors influence death penalty decisions as well by appointing liberal Democrats or conservative Republicans who take decidedly different but predictable partisan positions on the death penalty.

What is the influence of law in applying the death penalty? Case facts and legal issues make some difference, but Democratic and Republican judges also rank the importance of case facts differently. Republican judges are more likely to uphold a death sentence in cases involving rape or multiple victims and Democrats favor the death penalty when the victims have been children or the elderly (Hall and Brace 1996; Traut and Emmert forthcoming).

This death penalty research has a number of important implications for understanding and evaluating state courts. First, it shows that a combination of familiar political forces are crucial in judicial decision making and that whether a defendant will be executed is contingent less on formal law than on which state supreme court makes the decision, who the judges are, and the method of judicial recruitment. Earlier we saw that the method of selection made little difference in who became a judge; but seeking reelection seems to make judges vulnerable to public preferences on hotly contested issues. As discussed earlier, some would conclude that judges ought to be further removed from politics, but others might argue that judges should be responsive to issues on which the public feels very strongly, especially because the law permits judges to decide which facts are most compelling in individual cases. However we evaluate the meaning of this research for debate over the death penalty and the proper role of courts, it clearly shows us that judicial decision making is a political process.

JUDICIAL POLICY MAKING

High rates of litigation and the large number of lawyers contributes to the view that courts are judicial "factories," in which one case endlessly follows another.

Clearly, state courts are busy, but concentrating on individual cases and their isolated results overlooks the courts' contributions to policy making. Although judicial decisions usually are less visible than a new budget or a governor's veto, courts nevertheless have an impact on the bigger picture of how state governments cope with social, economic, political, and moral issues.

Supreme courts have many more opportunities than other state courts to make policy. The most visible way is through decisions in which courts innovate or produce new solutions to social problems in a single prominent case. Not all supreme court judges embrace an energetic lawmaking role. Precedent is important to all judges, and many believe that courts should defer to state legislatures. However, as discussed earlier, law frequently is unclear or one source of law conflicts with another; therefore, appellate judges inevitably must innovate to deal with new issues or new twists on old problems.

Supreme courts have some opportunities to make policy in addition to deciding cases. First, in many states supreme courts may issue advisory opinions when asked by the governor, attorney general, or other high-level state officials. These opinions usually concern an area of law that is unclear, and executive officials want guidance from the highest court before taking action that could lead to litigation and uncertain outcomes. Second, supreme courts make legal rules of procedure for other state courts and they oversee the practice of law, including disciplining and disbarring attorneys. Rules of procedure affect the details of filing and processing cases, including filing deadlines, rules of evidence, and criminal procedure. Particular rules can favor one side or another in a court case, so some rules are controversial among attorneys and judges (Jacob 1996).

In contrast to supreme courts, trial and intermediate appellate courts deal with thousands of similar cases annually, which provides judges on these courts little time for developing innovative policy or writing opinions. Occasionally, trial judges produce novel decisions, such as criminal sentences that require public penitence, service in the emergency room or attending high school or community college rather than jail, but these are rare. Therefore, some observers see lower-level courts mainly as appliers or enforcers of locally accepted values and law in routine disputes and cases of crime (Jacob 1984). However, because they repeatedly make decisions in factually similar cases, lower court judges often reveal a consistent pattern for dealing with certain kinds of problems. This constitutes a cumulative form of policy making because it builds up gradually over time and reveals how courts contribute to the way that states and communities respond to particular problems and groups of litigants. Examples abound in criminal sentences such as reports that racial minorities are treated more harshly as criminal defendants by some state court systems or that court enforcement of "three strikes and you're out" laws results in heavier imprisonment of marijuana users as opposed to those convicted of murder, rape, and kidnapping combined. Others are that HIV sufferers lose most lawsuits against insurance companies for coverage or against employers in health care settings. As discussed earlier, the power of businesses in commercial cases against individuals portrays local trial courts contributing to policy that maintains dominant economic relationships in society.

Because the trend in state government is to reduce the mandatory jurisdiction of state supreme courts, the policy-making role of these courts likely will increase. Therefore, this chapter concludes by examining the policy-making role of state supreme courts further. This includes illustrations of innovative judicial decisions; policy making through judicial review of legislation; and possible shifts in policy-making opportunities from the U.S. Supreme Court to the state courts—termed the new judicial federalism.

Innovation

Examining policy innovation identifies those states and government institutions that produce new solutions to thorny problems. In general, the most populous and socially complex states produce greater amounts of new litigation and opportunities for judicial innovation. Also, when a state supreme court innovates, it probably encourages additional litigation on novel issues as well as additional policy making throughout the state political system as groups arrayed on both sides of an issue seek to expand or limit the policy through legislation and administrative rules. Therefore, judicial innovation can have far-reaching consequences beyond a court's decision in a single case. Finally, certain state supreme courts have attained national reputations for being early adopters or leaders in creating new solutions to society's modern problems. They frequently provide the policy models that other state supreme courts embrace.

The state supreme courts likely to be leaders in policy innovation are listed in Table 7-2. The list was compiled by combining the policy leadership rankings of all state supreme courts found in four studies of policy innovation, with extra weight given to each court that ranked high in two or more studies. The California, New Jersey, and New York supreme courts stand out from the rest and rank very high in all estimates of judicial policy leadership, followed by others mostly in large and growing states in the midwest and northeast. Three other courts (in New Hampshire, Florida, and Michigan) are policy leaders somewhat less often. These rankings do not mean that all of these courts are leaders in every new policy field, but the odds are high that they, rather than other courts, will provide policy models for other states.

An illustration of the intricate policy relationships of courts to state politics is found in the emergence of what is termed "right to die" litigation (Glick 1992). A modern social problem is that high-tech medicine has the ability to prolong the lives of terminally ill individuals or those in a permanent unconscious or vegetative state. Traditional medical ethics encourages preserving life, and physicians sometimes worry about legal liability if they do not do everything possible to save a patient. Conflicts occur when individuals or their families do not want treatment that only prolongs the process of dying or when patients' wishes are unclear but they no longer can communicate what they do or do not want. Numerous court cases have been fought over such unwanted treatment.

Table 7-2 The Top Innovating State Supreme Courts

Rank[a]	State
1	California
2	New Jersey
3	New York
4.5	Massachusetts; Washington
6	Pennsylvania
7.5	Illinois; Minnesota
9	New Hampshire
10.5	Florida; Michigan

SOURCE: Composite rankings constructed from Canon and Baum 1981; Caldeira 1983; Domino 1989; Glick 1992.

[a] States are rank-ordered according to their composite innovation scores. States with the same scores receive a ranking midway between the ranks determined by their scores. Massachusetts and Washington are tied and receive an average rank of 4.5 as are Florida and Michigan, which receive an average rank of 10.5.

The first innovative government decision in this policy area was made by the New Jersey Supreme Court in 1976 (*In re Quinlan* [355 A.2d 647]). Karen Quinlan was a young women who mixed alcohol and drugs at a party and fell into a permanent vegetative condition. Her breathing was maintained by a respirator and she was fed through implanted stomach tubes. Her parents sued to have the artificial breathing apparatus removed, although they did not contest the feeding tubes. The New Jersey Supreme Court ruled that Karen's parents had the right to act as guardians and could order nursing home staff to remove the respirator. (She was able to breathe on her own and lived for another ten years.)

From 1976 to 1991, seventeen state supreme courts made at least one decision (nine courts made several) concerning the rights of individuals to express their wishes regarding treatment and the duties of others to honor those wishes. Most of these decisions were made before state legislatures made new laws, mainly because state Catholic Conferences successfully lobbied most legislatures not to enact laws that would expand individual rights to curtail medical treatment at the end of life. In time, however, the rising volume of court cases and favorable public opinion convinced many legislatures that new laws were needed. Then Catholic lobbyists worked for law and nursing home regulations that limited supreme court rulings, which in turn often stimulated advocates of the right to die to go back to court. In some states, neither the supreme court nor the legislature nor the executive branch has had the last word.

Since the late 1980s the right to die has expanded to include a right to assisted suicide, and the issue has involved state courts, legislatures, public referenda, as well as the U.S. Supreme Court. For decades, about half the states have had laws criminalizing assisting in a suicide. Nearly a dozen more adopted similar laws in the 1990s, following the highly publicized assisted suicides by Dr. Jack Kevorkian, a retired Michigan pathologist. In 1997 the U.S. Supreme Court ruled that assisted suicide is not a constitutional right (*Washington v. Glucksberg* [521 U.S. 702]; *Vacco v.*

Quill [521 U.S. 793]), but it also said the issue was important and permitted the states to consider their own policies. Only the Florida Supreme Court has heard a case on assisted suicide since the U.S. Supreme Court decision, and it adopted the Supreme Court's position (*Krischer v. McIver* [697 So.2d 97, 1997]). Public opinion is sharply divided and the policy is much too controversial to get through most legislatures in cases in which conservative religious groups are prominent, but because the right to die is so important in general, and the U.S. Supreme Court has invited the states to act, it will reappear on legislative and judicial agendas for years to come.

A second illustration of judicial innovation concerns state taxing and spending for public education, which is the largest public program in the states. It has been common in the fifty states since the early 1900s for government to pay for public education largely with money raised locally through taxes on real estate property. Early in the 1970s, several state supreme courts ruled that since local property taxes produce unequal amounts of revenue because of variations in value, the tax also produces inequality in public education, which is forbidden by the U.S. Constitution. However, in 1973 the U.S. Supreme Court disagreed, saying that tax and education policies were unrelated (*San Antonio School District v. Rodriguez* [411 U.S. 1]). Nevertheless, citizens continued to bring cases to state courts relying on provisions in state constitutions. With both state and federal constitutions and a U.S. Supreme Court precedent available to them, forty state supreme courts have made education policy decisions. Twelve, mostly with reputations for liberal policies and a willingness to declare legislative acts unconstitutional (Swinford 1991), have ruled that relying on the property tax to fund public education is unconstitutional, twenty-one others have agreed with the U.S. Supreme Court that the two policies are unrelated or that legislatures should have broad discretion to determine education policy, and seven others have made decisions in both directions. The ten courts without cases are mostly in conservative and sparsely populated states.

Courts that have ordered a change in policy have led state legislatures to redistribute property tax revenues from rich to poor districts, reduce reliance on property taxes, and create other new taxes. Legislatures often have acted reluctantly and piecemeal, sometimes requiring additional litigation to get them to comply with state supreme court rulings. Undoubtedly, the considerable public conflict that exists over funding public education will continue, and courts will be involved.

Judicial Review of Legislation

Judicial review is the most visible part of a 200-year debate over the proper role of courts, particularly whether they should be activist or make policy by overturning legislation judges see as unconstitutional or exercise restraint by supporting laws passed by democratically elected legislatures. In general, when we think of judicial review, the U.S. Supreme Court comes to mind, but state supreme courts also have the power to review legislation, and together they examine more than 600 laws each year to assess whether they square with state and national constitutions (Emmert and Traut 1992).

State judicial review cases involve a wide range of issues. The largest percentage concerns rules of criminal procedure (40 percent) brought by defendants hoping to get out of jail, but courts overturn laws in fewer than 10 percent of these cases. Additional cases involve government regulation of businesses, professions and labor, civil rights and liberties, relationships among agencies of government, and various private disputes. In contrast to the criminal cases, courts overturn a quarter or more of the laws contested in these cases.

Unlike judicial innovation, in which courts in a handful of mostly populous and socially complex states stand out as leaders, the volume of judicial review cases depends more on the structure of legal and political systems that present supreme courts with opportunities to review cases (Emmert 1992; Wenzel, Bowler, and Lanoue 1997). Supreme courts that have heavy caseloads and little control of their dockets and where constitutions are long and complex (mostly in the South) generally have many more cases involving constitutional questions than courts in other states, and they overturn a larger number of state laws. However, courts that have greater control of their dockets and fewer cases often overturn a similar or greater percentage of laws than other courts. For example, Georgia leads the states with 165 laws challenged over five years and the court overturned twenty-five, or about 15 percent. New York had eighty challenged laws and the court overturned twenty, or about 25 percent, and California had fifty challenges, with the court overturning thirteen laws or about 26 percent. Therefore, judicial review can be an important component of supreme court policy making even in states that have fewer cases. Like the U.S. Supreme Court, state supreme courts with discretionary jurisdiction probably select cases they consider more important and with a greater probability of overturning a law.

New Judicial Federalism

An important issue regarding state supreme court judicial review concerns whether state courts are striking out on their own to create new constitutional rights. Since the 1950s the U.S. Supreme Court has been perceived as preeminent in judicial policy making primarily through its revolutionary liberal decisions expanding civil rights, civil liberties, and the rights of criminal defendants. However, with the appointment of conservative justices since the Reagan presidency of the 1980s and the general cooling of support for liberal policies, the justices appointed since 1986 have reversed more state supreme court cases in the conservative direction (Brisbin and Kilwein 1994). The Court also hears fewer cases and allows state governments more freedom to deal with social problems. Therefore, some legal analysts believe that this trend creates a new Supreme Court relationship with the states—a new judicial federalism—that will lead state supreme courts to become more active and independent policy makers. Under settled law, the states may create more, but not less, expansive interpretations of rights than those given by the U.S. Supreme Court. Believers in a new judicial federalism speculate that because minority and other underdog groups have lost much of their favorable access to the

U.S. Supreme Court, they will persuade state supreme courts to rely on Bill of Rights type provisions in state constitutions to continue the expansion of individual rights.

From time to time, particular new state supreme court decisions give the impression that the new judicial federalism is on the march. For example, in the 1970s supreme courts, most prominently in California, New Jersey, Alaska, and Michigan, as well as in a few other states, created standards for police interrogation and search and seizure that went beyond the weakened requirements produced by the increasingly conservative Supreme Court, as did the supreme courts of Illinois and Pennsylvania regarding sexual discrimination. In 1980 the California Supreme Court expanded the right to free speech on business premises that went beyond previous U.S. Supreme Court rulings, and Justice Rehnquist and other Supreme Court justices lauded the state court's use of state constitutions to support the decision (Stumpf and Culver 1992).

But more comprehensive study of state supreme court decisions leads to a different conclusion. First, state supreme courts rely on state constitutions as the sole basis of their decisions in one-sixth or fewer of their cases involving state legislation, preferring mostly U.S. Supreme Court precedents or a combination of state and national constitutions in these cases (Emmert and Traut 1992; Kramer 1996). Moreover, judicial review cases mostly involve state government issues in which the U.S. Constitution does not apply, including, for example, jurisdictional disputes among government agencies in state administration and rule making, and various state tax and spending issues. State constitutions are used in fewer than 10 percent of criminal and 15 percent of civil liberties cases, with some states never relying on state law of any sort (Emmert and Traut 1992; Esler 1994). Finally, many state supreme courts that rely on state constitutions or other state law do not use them to advance civil liberties but interpret rights about the same way as the U.S. Supreme Court, and a few state supreme courts that moved in a liberal policy direction in the 1980s were curtailed by state constitutional amendments that required the courts to conform to more conservative federal interpretations (Tarr 1997).

There are several explanations of why state supreme courts have not led toward a new judicial federalism. First, the U.S. Supreme Court is the preeminent court in the nation, and it has a long history of policy making in civil rights and liberties and provides many precedents for the state courts. Second, many state constitutional provisions are similar to federal law, and few law school courses emphasize state constitutions. Third, most state political environments are conservative and judges have few incentives to make liberal policies in the face of judicial elections or conservative public opinion, and police and prosecutors and other law and order interest groups that oppose greater constitutional protections (Esler 1994; Kilwein and Brisbin 1997). The few states that have been leaders in the new judicial federalism generally are in ideologically liberal states in the northeast, where public opinion and other political groups and institutions are more likely to promote or accept expansive decisions.

If the new judicial federalism means only that state supreme courts will expand personal liberties beyond U.S. Supreme Court rulings, there does not seem to be much to this anticipated trend. However, this definition of the new judicial federalism is too narrow. First, state supreme courts rely on their own constitutions not only to rule on state legislation but to review actions of the executive branch and local government as well. For example, the Florida Supreme Court recently upheld as constitutional a Miami ordinance requiring job applicants to swear they had not used tobacco products during the previous year. The court said there is no right to smoke under the state constitutional provision protecting against "governmental intrusion." We do not know how extensively state supreme courts use state constitutions in these kinds of cases. Second, besides relying on state or federal constitutions in state court decisions, state courts have opportunities to rule on matters potentially involving both state and federal statutes in cases in which litigants, for strategic purposes, choose to file cases in state court rather than federal court and rely on state law exclusively. An example concerns state fair-employment practices acts, which ban employment discrimination. Compared to federal law, many state employment discrimination laws allow much broader definitions of bias, have more generous or no caps on the amount and types of damages (compensatory and punitive) that can be awarded, do not require plaintiffs to use preliminary administrative hearings before they may file lawsuits, and state judges appear less likely than their federal counterparts to dismiss cases. Therefore, there appears to be a shift of litigation from federal to state court (Wolff 1997).

Recent tobacco litigation also demonstrates the importance of state law and courts as alternatives in litigation with potentially enormous impacts on policy. The U.S. Supreme Court has ruled that federal regulations do not exempt tobacco companies from lawsuits based on state products liability statutes and other long-standing state common law. Other federal judges have ruled that a national class action suit, in which thousands or millions of people would be represented at the same time, is too unwieldy. Therefore, a few separate class actions have been filed in various federal courts on behalf of citizens in individual states, but the recent success of individual litigants against tobacco companies in state court has focused more attention there as a likely location for additional litigation. More important, the state attorneys general have settled cases in state courts worth many billions of dollars for the cost of treating thousands of smoking-related illnesses paid for by government programs. These state cases have a great impact because they involve huge amounts of money and the future of a major industry. Moreover, unlike most previous individual plaintiffs who have been exhausted financially and emotionally by protracted tobacco defense tactics, the states have the staying power to weather drawn out and costly lawsuits. These settlements do not necessarily end state litigation for the tobacco industry because individuals and other organizations, such as labor union insurance funds, may continue to sue to recover damages for illnesses and the costs of medical treatment.

Regardless of how we might expand the definition of the new judicial federalism, searching for signs of a rebirth of state judicial power may lead us to undervalue the independent policy-making role that state supreme courts have always had. State judges are not mere subordinates in a hierarchical federal system; rather, they interpret state and federal law by applying their own values and assessments of state political conditions to their decisions. As it happens, most of their recent civil liberties and criminal justice decisions are in the conservative direction, which is consistent with recent Supreme Court policy. But in years past, conservative state court decisions ran contrary to liberal Supreme Court policy and provided the high court with the cases that allowed it to vastly expand personal freedoms and individual rights. And as discussed, judicial decisions include more than individual rights and protections from unlawful police conduct, and state courts rely mainly on state constitutions in many areas of state government administration, taxation, and spending, where the U.S. Constitution and the U.S. Supreme Court have little to say or have deferred to the states. These are important areas of state politics and policy, as the other chapters attest. Finally, not all court decisions have equal importance. Certain innovative state supreme court decisions based on state constitutions have been crucial in various areas of policy, notably equalizing state spending for education, the right to die, zoning and land use, as well as the right to an abortion in the face of limiting state legislation.

Finally, state supreme courts may achieve even greater importance in interpreting and applying state statutes in cases where litigants choose to use state rather than federal courts.

CONCLUSION

This chapter began by suggesting that courts usually are not seen as important governmental or political institutions. But state supreme courts have many opportunities to make important innovative policy decisions, and all state courts have substantial impacts on many people because they deal with most of the disputes and crime that people are likely to encounter. The patterns of decisions or cumulative policies courts produce and how their decisions relate to the policies of other government institutions places courts at the center of government and politics. Politics also affects other aspects of courts, including their organization and jurisdiction, judicial selection, and the effects of ideology and partisan politics on judicial decision making. As society becomes more complex, state courts will have an ever widening impact on social, economic, and political issues.

REFERENCES

Abramson, Jeffrey. 1994. *We, the Jury.* New York: Basic Books.

Allen, David W., and Diane E. Wall. 1993. "Role Orientations and Women State Supreme Court Justices." *Judicature* 77:156–165.

Alozie, Nicholas O. 1996. "Selection Methods and the Recruitment of Women to State Courts of Last Resort." *Social Science Quarterly* 77:110–126.

———. forthcoming. "The Recruitment of Blacks to State Courts of Last Resort." *National Political Science Review.*

Brace, Paul, and Melinda Gann Hall. 1990. "Neo-Institutionalism and Dissent in State Supreme Courts." *Journal of Politics* 52:54–70.

Brisbin, Richard A., Jr., and John C. Kilwein. 1994. "U.S. Supreme Court Review of State High Court Decisions." *Judicature* 78:33–46.

Butterfield, Fox. 1996. "Study Examines Race and Justice in California." *New York Times*, February 13, A12.

———. 1997. "With Juvenile Courts in Chaos, Critics Propose Their Demise." *New York Times*, September 21, A1.

Caldeira, Gregory A. 1983. "On the Reputation of State Supreme Courts." *Political Behavior* 5:83–108.

Canon, Bradley C., and Lawrence Baum. 1981. "Patterns of Adoption of Tort Law Innovations: An Application of Diffusion Theory to Judicial Doctrines." *American Political Science Review* 75:975–987.

Champagne, Anthony, and Kyle Cheek. 1996. "PACs and Judicial Politics in Texas." *Judicature* 80:26–27.

Council of State Governments. 1996. *The Book of the States, 1996–97*. Lexington, Ky.: Council of State Governments.

Curran, Barbara A. 1986. "American Lawyers in the 1980s." *Law and Society Review* 20:19–49.

Domino, John C. 1989. *State Supreme Court Innovation in the Policy Area of Privacy: A Comparative Analysis*. A paper presented at the annual meeting of the Law and Society Association, Madison, Wisconsin, June.

Dubois, Philip. 1980. *From Ballot to Bench*. Austin: University of Texas Press.

Eisenstein, James, Roy B. Fleming, and Peter Nardulli. 1987. *The Contours of Justice: Communities and Their Courts*. Boston: Little, Brown.

Eisenstein, James, and Herbert Jacob. 1977. *Felony Justice*. Boston: Little, Brown.

Emmert, Craig F. 1992. "An Integrated Case-Related Model of Judicial Decision Making: Explaining Supreme Court Decisions in Judicial Review Cases." *Journal of Politics* 54:543–552.

Emmert, Craig F., and Carol Ann Traut. 1992. "State Supreme Courts, State Constitutions, and Judicial Policymaking." *Justice System Journal* 16:36–48.

Epstein, Lee. 1994. "Exploring the Participation of Organized Interests in State Court Litigation." *Political Research Quarterly* 47:335–351.

Esler, Michael. 1994. "State Supreme Court Commitment to State Law." *Judicature* 78:25–32.

Galanter, Marc. 1993. "News from Nowhere: The Debased Debate on Civil Justice." *Denver University Law Review* 71:77–103.

Glick, Henry R. 1992. *The Right to Die*. New York: Columbia University Press.

Glick, Henry R., and Craig F. Emmert. 1986. "Stability and Change: the Characteristics of State Supreme Court Judges." *Judicature* 70:107–112.

———. 1987. "Selection Systems and Judicial Characteristics." *Judicature* 70: 228–235.

Graham, Barbara Luck. 1990. "Do Judicial Selection Systems Matter?" *American Politics Quarterly* 18:316–336.

Hall, Melinda Gann, and Paul Brace. 1996. "Justices' Responses to Case Facts: An Interactive Model." *American Politics Quarterly* 24:237–261.

Hall, William K., and Larry T. Aspin. 1987. "What Twenty Years of Judicial Retention Elections Have Told Us." *Judicature* 70:340–347.

Heinz, John P., and Edward O. Laumann. 1982. *Chicago Lawyers*. New York: Russell Sage Foundation and American Bar Foundation.

Henry, M. L., Jr., Estajo Koslow, Joseph Soiffer, and John Furey. 1985. *The Success of Women and Minorities in Achieving Judicial Office*. New York: Fund for Modern Courts.

Henschen, Beth, Robert Moog, and Steven Davis. 1990. "Judicial Nominating Commissions: A National Profile." *Judicature* 73:328–343.

Hoffman, Jan. 1997. "Chief Judge Offers a Plan to Consolidate the Court System." *New York Times*, March 20, B7.

Hojnacki, Marie, and Lawrence Baum. 1992. "'New Style' Judicial Campaigns and the Voters: Economic Issues and Union Members in Ohio." *Western Political Quarterly* 45:912–948.

Jacob, Herbert. 1984. *Justice in America*. 4th ed. Boston: Little, Brown.

———. 1996. "Courts: The Least Visible Branch." In *Politics in the American States*, 6th ed., edited by Virginia Gray and Herbert Jacob. Washington, D.C.: CQ Press.

Kessler, Mark. 1986. "The Politics of Legal Representation: The Influence of Local Politics on the Behavior of Poverty Lawyers." *Law and Society Review* 8:149–167.

Kilwein, John C., and Richard A. Brisbin. 1997. "Policy Convergence in a Federal Judicial System: Application of Intensified Scrutiny Doctrines by State Supreme Courts." *American Journal of Political Science* 41:122–148.

Kramer, Paul A. 1996. *Waiting for Godot?—The New Judicial Federalism 1987–1992: Reality or Hoax?* A paper presented at the annual meeting of the American Political Science Association, San Francisco, August 29–September 1.

Kritzer, Herbert M. 1997. "Contingency Fee Lawyers as Gatekeepers in the Civil Justice System." *Judicature* 81:22–29.

Kuklinski, James H., and John E. Stanga. 1979. "Political Participation and Government Responsiveness: The Behavior of California Superior Judges." *American Political Science Review* 73:1090–1099.

Lawrence, Susan. 1990. *The Poor in Court.* Princeton, N.J.: Princeton University Press.

McEwen, Craig A., Lynn Mather, and Richard J. Maiman. 1994. "Lawyers, Mediation, and the Management of Divorce Practice." *Law and Society Review* 28:149–187.

McNaught, Catherine. 1997. "Court Is a Success Story in Drug War." *Tallahassee Democrat,* September 15, 1B.

Miller, Richard E., and Austin Sarat. 1980–81. "Grievances, Claims and Disputes: Assessing the Adversary Culture." *Law and Society Review* 15:525–565.

National Institute of Justice. 1980. *Neighborhood Justice Centers Field Test: Final Evaluation Report.* Washington, D.C.: U.S. Department of Justice.

Nicholson, Marlene Arnold, and Norman Nicholson. 1994. "Funding Judicial Campaigns in Illinois." *Judicature* 77:294–299.

Reid, Traciel V. 1996. "PAC Participation in North Carolina Supreme Court Elections." *Judicature* 80:21–29.

Richardson, Richard J., and Kenneth N. Vines. 1970. *The Politics of Federal Courts.* Boston: Little, Brown.

Ross, H. Laurence. 1970. *Settled out of Court.* Chicago: Aldine.

Seron, Carroll. 1993. "New Strategies for Getting Clients: Urban and Suburban Lawyers' Views." *Law and Society Review* 27: 399–419.

Sloan, Frank A., and Chee Ruey Hsieh. 1995. "Injury, Liability, and the Decision to File a Medical Malpractice Claim." *Law and Society Review* 29:413–435.

Smothers, Ronald. 1996. "Arkansas Plan to Promote Election of Black Judges Brings a Familiar Challenge." *New York Times,* April 8, A10.

State Court Caseload Statistics: Annual Report 1991. 1993. Williamsburg, Va.: National Center for State Courts.

State Court Caseload Statistics: Annual Report 1995. Supplement to Examining the Work of State Courts, 1995. 1996. Williamsburg, Va.: National Center for State Courts.

State Court Caseload Statistics: Annual Report 1996. Supplement to Examining the Work of State Courts, 1996. 1997. Williamsburg, Va.: National Center for State Courts.

Stumpf, Harry P., and John H. Culver. 1992. *The Politics of State Courts.* White Plains, N.Y.: Longman.

Swinford, Bill. 1991. "A Predictive Model of Decision Making in State Supreme Courts: The School Funding Cases." *American Political Quarterly* 19:336–352.

Tarr, G. Alan. 1997. "The New Judicial Federalism in Perspective." *Notre Dame Law Review* 72:1097–1118.

Traut, Carol Ann, and Craig F. Emmert. forthcoming. "Expanding the Integrated Model of Judicial Decisionmaking: The California Justices and Capital Punishment." *Journal of Politics.*

U.S. Department of Justice, Office of Justice Programs, Office of Juvenile Justice and Delinquency Prevention. 1997. In *Juvenile Offenders and Victims: 1997 Update on Violence,* edited by Melissa Sickmund, Howard N. Snyder, and Eileen Poe-Yamagata. Washington, D.C.: U.S. Government Printing Office.

Watson, Richard A., and Rondal G. Downing. 1969. *The Politics of the Bench and the Bar.* New York: John Wiley Sons.

Wenzel, James P., Shaun Bowler, and David J. Lanoue. 1997. "Legislating from the Bench: A Comparative Analysis of Judicial Activism." *American Politics Quarterly* 25:363–379.

Wissler, Roselle L. 1995. "Mediation and Adjudication in the Small Claims Court: The Effects of Process and Case Characteristics." *Law and Society Review* 29:323–358.

Wold, John T., and John H. Culver. 1987. "The Defeat of the California Justices." *Judicature* 70:348–355.

Wolff, Robert M. 1997. "Making the Leap to State Courts." *National Law Journal* (June):38.

Yates, Jeff, Richard Fording, Belinda Davis, and Henry R. Glick. 1998. *State Litigiousness: An Empirical Examination of State Tort Litigation Rates.* A paper presented at the Annual Meeting of the Law and Society Association, Aspen, Colorado, June 4–7.

Yngvesson, Barbara, and Patricia Hennessey. 1975. "Small Claims, Complex Disputes: A Review of the Small Claims Literature." *Law and Society Review* 9:235–243.

SUGGESTED READINGS

Dubois, Philip L. *From Ballot to Bench.* Austin: University of Texas Press, 1980. A comprehensive analysis of state judicial elections that also considers the major criticisms of electing judges.

Eisenstein, James, and Herbert Jacob. *Felony Justice: An Organizational Analysis of Criminal Courts.* Boston: Little, Brown, 1977. A classic in the study of criminal courts that provides basic theory and in-depth understanding of the informal workings of local justice and the content of judicial decisions.

Glick, Henry R. *The Right to Die: Policy Innovation and Its Consequences.* New York: Columbia University Press, 1992. A study of the development and emergence of new social policy in the face of technological change that also illustrates the policy-making role of state supreme courts and the dynamic interaction of courts, legislatures, and the state policy-making process.

Janosik, Robert L., ed. *Encyclopedia of the American Judicial System.* New York: Charles Scribner's Sons, 3 vols. Includes eighty-eight original essays on legal history, substantive law, legal institutions and personnel, judicial process and behavior, constitutional law, and methodology in the study of the judicial process. A good place to start for more reading on a wide range of subjects.

Tarr, G. Alan, and Mary Cornelia Aldis Porter. *State Supreme Courts in State and Nation.* New Haven, Conn.: Yale University Press, 1988. An introduction to the political role of state supreme courts with detailed illustrations drawn from three states.

CHAPTER 8

*Administering State Programs:
Performance and Politics*

RICHARD C. ELLING

Beyond the governor's State of the State messages, beyond the bill signings and the veto messages, there is the state bureaucracy. After the legislative committee hearings and the roll-call votes, there is the administrative apparatus of state government. The actions of state administrative agencies may matter as much as any of the foregoing so far as the goals of elected officials are concerned. With responsibilities ranging from agriculture to zoos, state bureaucracies do much of what state governments do.[1] For most citizens, state government is as often a state agency and its employees as the governor or the legislature.

Citizens interact most frequently with lower level state bureaucrats. Welfare caseworkers, conservation officers, probation and parole agents, college financial aid officials, public health inspectors, state police officers, unemployment compensation clerks, workplace safety inspectors, and tax collection officials can significantly affect the fortunes of those with whom they deal. Higher-level administrators make less routine decisions, determine standards to guide the actions of subordinates in accomplishing agency objectives, and supervise the performance of those subordinates. They also interact with numerous external institutions, officials, and groups.

---

1. Here I am using the term *bureaucracy* as a synonym for a large complex organization, such as a government department. Later in the chapter I provide a more precise definition of the concept of bureaucracy. In this chapter I also use the terms *administer* and *implement* as synonyms that refer to the processes by which formal policies and programs are applied to the problems that those policies or programs were designed to address. Some scholars view implementation as a broader concept than administration, but for the purposes of this chapter treating the two terms as synonyms seems acceptable.

State administrative agencies matter because they implement state programs. The model of a single agency receiving the authority and the funding from the legislature to employ the personnel needed to carry out a given set of programs on its own is less and less common, however. Instead, implementing state programs increasingly involves several state agencies working together, sometimes in collaboration with nonprofit or for-profit organizations providing services under contract.

Equally important are the intergovernmental linkages involved in state administration. The federal government relies on state bureaucracies and their implementation structures to achieve the purposes of federal programs funded to varying degrees by its several hundred grant-in-aid programs. The administration of social welfare and environmental protection programs are but two of the more important examples of complex intergovernmental administrative configurations. Major changes in 1996 in federal programs for poor families that gave much greater responsibility to states and their public welfare agencies are but one example of increased federal reliance on state bureaucracies. State governments may, in turn, forge linkages with local units of government, and, increasingly, with nonprofit entities, to carry out programs funded in part by federal grant dollars.

State bureaucracies also matter because their role in state politics extends well beyond "administration" narrowly defined. After a policy has been established, many questions remain about how best to deliver services, or how to secure the compliance of those affected by a policy. Decisions on these matters are largely in the hands of state bureaucrats. Moreover, elected officials are often made aware of problems, or of deficiencies in existing programs, by the administrators who regularly deal with those problems or programs. Administrators help develop solutions to problems on the policy agenda and provide information to elected officials who formally adopt policies as those officials debate the merits of policy options.

The various roles played by state administrators, as well as the intergovernmental dimensions of state administration, are suggested by the following comment by Dr. Kristine Kelly, head of the Program Development and Services Section of the Air Resources Division of the New York State Department of Environmental Conservation:

> We work with division management to secure enough resources to ensure that we can meet our responsibilities under the *federal* Clean Air Act Amendments of 1990 *and* the New York State Clean Air Compliance Act of 1993—that is, controlling air pollution. We establish work plan priorities, oversee the hiring and recruitment of personnel, develop the state budget (for the division), *prepare new legislative programs* and conduct program evaluation (personal communication, June 1994).

THE CHALLENGING AND DYNAMIC ENVIRONMENT OF STATE ADMINISTRATION

How states implement programs and deliver services is in a state of flux that is unprecedented in the last half century. Robert Behn (1997a, 40) concluded that the decade of the 1990s "has been the 're' decade, as in reengineering, restructuring and retrenchment. That means it also has been a time for some other 're' phrases, such as reductions-in-force and early retirement." He went on to note the relevance of yet another "re" phrase, "reinventing government." Forces for change in the 1990s include the evolving state role in the American federal system, the increasingly blurred boundaries between the public and private sectors, and the emergence of new information and data processing technologies. These factors, combined with a public mood that is skeptical of government and resists higher taxes, have made the 1990s a period in which state administrative agencies have had to reconsider how to accomplish their goals.

Governors, state legislators, the courts, the federal government, and interest and clientele groups are but some of the external actors who are important elements of the environment of state bureaucracies. These actors seek to influence state administrative affairs, often vying among themselves for control. To this list must be added the nonprofit and for-profit entities that increasingly provide state services under contract. It is also argued that agencies must be more open to input from clients and others who have a stake in what those agencies are doing.

Today the states have administrative structures of considerable complexity. These structures reflect the emergence of new public problems and the consequent expanded range of responsibilities that states discharge. Jenks and Wright (1993) use the metaphor of "generations" to chart the evolution of state bureaucracies. A "first generation" of more than fifty agencies were present in at least thirty-eight states by the end of the 1950s. Many of these agencies have existed for decades and include those that discharge major, basic functions of state government such as corrections, education, health, higher education, highways, mental health care, tax collection, unemployment insurance, welfare, and workers' compensation. Other first-generation agencies are those with responsibilities in areas such as agriculture, banking, fish and wildlife management, insurance regulation, parks, and parole, along with units headed by elected executive branch officials such as secretaries of state, attorneys general, and treasurers.

The 1960s witnessed increased concern over issues of civil rights, environmental protection, consumer protection, poverty, and the problems of urban areas. The national government rather than state governments took the lead in addressing these concerns, however. The linkage of state and national administration noted earlier is clearly evident. Many states responded to these federal efforts, and to the federal dollars flowing into their coffers via federal grant-in-aid programs, by creating new organizational entities. Jenks and Wright have identified a dozen agencies that were present in most states at the end of the 1960s that were not commonly found at the beginning of the decade. National initiatives were largely responsible for the emergence of air quality, community affairs, criminal justice planning, economic development, and highway safety units.

The decade of the 1970s witnessed a resurgence in state efforts to deal with public problems at the same time that federal initiatives continued. During the 1970s, twenty-nine types of administrative entities not generally present before 1970 became common elements of state bureaucracies. Included were units dealing with civil rights, consumer protection, environmental protection, housing finance, workforce training, mass transit, medical care for the poor, occupational safety and health, and vocational rehabilitation.

The fourth generation of bureaucratic development occurring in the 1980s produced fewer offspring, with only nine new types of agencies becoming widespread. Limits on the revenue-raising capacities of state governments, stemming from the so-called "tax revolt," made it difficult for states to shoulder new responsibilities. Still, the continued severity of environmental problems prompted the creation of state hazardous waste and ground water management units. Yet another fourth-generation thrust expanded employment opportunities for workers in general, and for minorities in particular.

The scope of state administration is also reflected in the size of the state workforce. In 1995 the fifty states employed nearly 5 million people on either a full-time (3.5 million) or part-time basis (1.3 million), for a full-time equivalent (FTE) workforce of just under 4 million (see Table 8-1). More populous states have more employees, although the *ratio* of state employees to state population is generally lowest in these states. The relative balance of responsibilities between a state and its local governments also impacts state employment. In general, less populous, less densely settled, geographically smaller, and poorer states all tend to rely more heavily on state government for the delivery of services. Thus, although Arkansas ranks thirty-third in population, it ranks sixteenth in state government employees per 10,000 state residents. Some states have more employees simply because they do more in certain program areas. Although on average one-third of all state employment is in higher education, some states have more extensive higher education systems.

State employment increased by one-third from 1985 to 1995, but growth was uneven across the states, as revealed in Table 8-1. Spurts in employment are often followed by contractions. Half of the increase in employment during this period occurred from 1985 to 1986, as the financial circumstances of state governments improved following the severe economic recession of the early 1980s. Half a decade later, with their economies again in recession, a majority of the states laid off employees.

Employment growth in the past decade has also been uneven across functions. In most functional areas employment grew slowly, remained stable, or, occasionally, declined. In the area of corrections, however, employment exploded. Seeking to "get tough" on crime, states built and staffed more prisons. As a result, corrections-related employment grew by 77 percent. The other major growth area during this period was for instructional and other staff at state colleges and universities, with such staff growing by nearly 50 percent from 1985 to 1995.

PERSPECTIVE ON STATE BUREAUCRATIC PERFORMANCE

Although the bureaucratic "horror story" is a journalistic staple, the more *systematic* evidence suggests that such stories are the exception rather than the rule

Table 8-1 State Government Employment, 1995

State	Population rank	State employees, all functions (FTE, thousands)[a]		Percentage of work force in higher education	State employees, all functions, per 10,000 residents		Percentage change in employment, all functions, 1985–1995
		Number	Rank		Number	Rank	
Alabama	23	81	18	37	191	17	29
Alaska	49	22	39	18	366	2	5
Arizona	22	58	27	38	135	42.5	67
Arkansas	33	48	34	32	192	16	35
California	1	338	1	33	107	50	44
Colorado	25	57	28	55	153	35.5	56
Connecticut	28	63	26	24	193	15	28
Delaware	46	22	40	30	307	3	41
Florida	4	175	4	23	123	48	58
Georgia	10	115	11	31	159	31.5	43
Hawaii	40	51	31	14	436	1	42
Idaho	41	21	42	34	179	24	62
Illinois	6	141	8	37	119	49	28
Indiana	14	89	15	47	153	35.5	42
Iowa	30	53	29	46	187	20.5	35
Kansas	32	48	33	42	187	20.5	34
Kentucky	24	73	22	36	190	18	29
Louisiana	21	93	14	33	214	8.5	12
Maine	39	21	41	26	172	27	19
Maryland	19	81	19	22	161	29.5	18
Massachusetts	13	82	17	28	135	42.5	7
Michigan	8	141	7	45	148	38	39
Minnesota	20	73	23	51	157	33.5	53
Mississippi	31	50	32	30	186	22	25
Missouri	16	79	20	31	149	37	36
Montana	44	18	45	36	208	11	26
Nebraska	37	30	38	34	181	23	13
Nevada	38	21	43	29	134	44	63
New Hampshire	42	17	46	32	147	39	22
New Jersey	9	125	9	22	157	33.5	43
New Mexico	36	42	35	37	251	5	41
New York	3	257	3	17	142	41	0
North Carolina	11	115	12	37	159	31.5	33
North Dakota	47	16	47	44	257	4	34
Ohio	7	143	6	46	128	45	40
Oklahoma	27	68	24	35	206	12	27
Oregon	29	52	30	29	166	28	42
Pennsylvania	5	152	5	31	126	46.5	34
Rhode Island	43	20	44	29	203	13	15
South Carolina	26	78	21	31	213	10	31
South Dakota	45	14	48	36	194	14	26
Tennessee	17	84	16	43	161	29.5	35
Texas	2	268	2	32	143	40	51
Utah	34	42	36	50	214	8.5	51
Vermont	48	13	49	34	216	7	20
Virginia	12	116	10	36	175	25.5	31
Washington	15	96	13	38	175	25.5	46
West Virginia	35	35	37	35	189	19	-1
Wisconsin	18	64	25	44	126	46.5	22
Wyoming	50	11	50	29	227	6	14
Total	—	3,971	—	34	151	—	33

SOURCES: Bureau of the Census, 1995; Council of State Governments, 1986. Population data is estimated for 1995.

[a] Full- and part-time employees expressed as full-time equivalents (FTE).

when it comes to state bureaucratic performance. More than 80 percent of a sample of Wisconsin residents described their contacts with state transportation employees (highway patrol officers and driver's license examiners) as being either "good" or "excellent" as far as "courtesy of treatment" and "helpfulness of employees" were concerned (Goodsell 1985). Other client surveys paint a similar picture (Goodsell 1994, esp. 25–39; Michigan Department of Civil Service 1987). Recorded statistics on agency operations also suggest satisfactory performance. For example, a study of state unemployment compensation operations found that 90 percent of claims were paid within three weeks (Goodsell 1985). Judgments about bureaucratic performance may conflict because we apply differing, and sometimes contradictory, standards. Four standards of public bureaucratic performance are cost, efficiency, effectiveness, and political–public accountability. The first three standards can be applied to public, private, and nonprofit organizations alike. Cost is the least useful standard. Saving money by reducing the quantity or the quality of services is easy. The problem lies in our willingness to accept fewer or lower quality services in return for cost savings. Efficiency and effectiveness are more useful measures. An efficient organization gets the most out of a given amount of resources. If a greater volume of highway litter is collected at a comparable or a lower cost, efficiency has increased. Effectiveness is goal oriented. An effective organization gets the job done. It also asks the question, "So what?" However efficiently administered, does a program solve or ameliorate a problem? For instance, does vocational training for incarcerated felons improve their chances of securing jobs on release and reduce the likelihood that they will engage in future criminal activity?

A major problem with the "public bureaucracy is inefficient" argument is that efficiency is rarely the only standard that we want public bureaucracies to meet. Efficiency is to be pursued in the context of other values. One of the most important of these other values is accountability. Accountability has two dimensions. A *process dimension* is concerned with the constitutionality or legality of administrative actions—with honesty, observance of due process, impartiality, and decency in dealing with the public. More demanding expectations concerning this standard distinguish public from private administration. *Responsiveness* is a second dimension of accountability. *Whose* goals do state bureaucracies attempt to achieve? Because bureaucrats are not elected, their role in the political process troubles many. Specifying to whom administrators should be responsive is, however, difficult. Is primary responsibility owed to the governor or to the legislature? What about responsiveness to those served by an agency's programs? What if what a governor or the legislature wants done potentially conflicts with constitutional standards or professional norms?

IMPROVING STATE BUREAUCRATIC PERFORMANCE: RESHAPING OR REPLACING STATE ADMINISTRATIVE AGENCIES?

Although state bureaucracies typically perform better than their critics admit, their performance is not ideal. This section examines various efforts to improve the administration of state programs.

Improving State Administration with Organizational Redesign

The Bureaucratic Form of Organization. We have been using the term *bureaucracy* loosely, but it has a technical meaning as a particular type of formal organization, one that is common to all sectors of society. "Bureaucratic" characteristics include

• systematic division of organizational tasks: Bureaucracies emphasize division of labor and specialization of function.

• arrangement of organizational units in a hierarchy: Authority flows down from a single head at the top, and responsibility flows upward to this individual. Bureaucracy embodies the principle of *monocratic authority.*

• employment of persons based on their possessing technical competence relevant to an organization's tasks rather than considerations such as their political beliefs or family connections: Bureaucracy embraces the norm of "neutral competence." Employment decisions should not be based on "irrelevant" considerations such as a person's political beliefs or family connections. The goal is to employ those who possess the technical competence relevant to an organization's tasks and to ensure that they apply that expertise in a politically neutral way.

• an elaborate set of rules governing the operations of the organization.

What some today dismiss as the "old orthodoxy" of public management places a high premium on structuring organizations along bureaucratic lines to ensure administrative success. Organizations based on these principles supposedly are capable of delivering services reliably and consistently while treating citizens fairly. The ability of elected officials to hold public bureaucracies accountable is enhanced by the hierarchy of authority within them.

As state administrative systems evolved over the past 200 years they often deviated from this bureaucratic ideal. Organizational patterns sometimes embody the views of various and competing "political sovereigns" as to how certain arrangements may enhance their influence. Governors, legislators, and interest groups sometimes use organizational strategies to "stack the deck" to ensure that programs get implemented in ways that they prefer. As states took on new tasks, these were often assigned to new single-function agencies, further complicating the structure of state administration. By the 1950s, state bureaucracies often contained 100 or more units.

The Dynamics of Reorganization. The "orthodox" view favored organizing individual agencies along bureaucratic lines. It was also concerned to fit individual bureaucracies together as a system. One goal is to consolidate the responsibilities of numerous separate agencies into a small number of broadly functional units such as transportation, natural resources, or human services, to reduce wasteful duplication and uncoordinated service delivery. This, combined with the familiar pyramidal structure of higher level administrators closely supervising lower level units and employees, clarifies lines of responsibility and enhances the accountability of the bureaucracy as a whole. Not only is control by agency heads enhanced, but through them—when such heads are appointed by the governor—so is gubernatorial control. Orthodox reorganizers also argued that enhanced accountability to the governor required abandoning the practice of directly electing officials with administrative responsibilities—such as treasurers, secretaries of state, or superintendents of education. They also disliked the "plural executive"—the widespread practice of heading agencies with boards or commissions. Such arrangements limit gubernatorial control because the members of boards or commissions—whether directly elected or actually appointed by a governor—are insulated from gubernatorial control because they typically have long, staggered terms of office.

The tenets of traditional reorganization doctrine were so persuasive that twenty-six states accomplished major administrative restructuring in the quarter century after 1965 (Conant 1992). Some reorganizations resulted in as much as an 80 percent reduction in the number of agencies, and these agencies have often been combined into a smaller number of large, multifunctional, "cabinet" departments. Although monetary savings are often promised by proponents of traditional reorganization, reducing the number of agencies—although it may produce a tidier state organizational chart—often saves little money because many of the eliminated agencies had minuscule budgets or their functions continue to be performed by other agencies. More recent reorganizations stress gains in efficiency or effectiveness over dollar savings, and administrators generally believe that reorganization improves agency performance (Elling 1992). The clearest consequence of orthodox reorganization has been to increase administrative accountability, especially to the governor (Elling 1992; Hebert, Brudney, and Wright 1983).

New Strategies to Enhance Administrative Performance: TQM and REGO

Today there are those who dismiss reorganization of the bureaucracy (along with certain reforms of state personnel systems to be discussed later in this chapter) as being irrelevant to the realities that confront state governments as they seek to provide the services demanded by citizens now and into the twenty-first century.

Critics believe that the reliability of service provision offered by bureaucratic-style organization all too often turns into inflexibility and resistance to change. Old style bureaucracies are insufficiently "nimble" for the new age. Bureaucracy's emphasis on hierarchy and top-down management is also seen as a problem because the lower level employees most involved in delivering services, and who most directly interact with those whom an agency serves, have too little say in how services are delivered. The emphasis on hierarchy and close supervision supposedly results in unnecessary layers of organization between those at the top of the agency and those at the bottom, hampering communication and reducing the ability of the organization to respond to feedback from its environment. These maladies are magnified because public bureaucracies are monopoly providers of services not subject to the necessary "discipline" of market competition.

Total Quality Management (TQM) and reinventing government (REGO) are two manifestations of dissatisfaction with old ways of doing things. TQM emerged out of analyses of the supposed successes of Japanese private sector management. Key elements of TQM include

• a view that organizational ineffectiveness stems not so much from lazy or uncaring employees but from management processes that have been badly designed by higher level managers.

• a customer focus.

• elimination or redefinition of much of middle management.

• empowerment of employees by devolving authority downward in the organization.

• group problem solving and team management.

• an emphasis on measuring results, both in terms of "customer satisfaction" and other standards, to ensure "continual improvement" in product quality.

This logic was so persuasive that by the mid-1990s, thirty-two states had initiated statewide TQM efforts (Chi et al. 1997).

Proponents of TQM and REGO recommend "flatter" bureaucracies; that is, some of the layers of organization between top- and lower-level employees should be eliminated. This not only saves tax dollars, as supposedly superfluous middle-level managers are eliminated, but it simultaneously "empowers" lower-level employees who are now subject to less close supervision than before because those managers who remain must supervise more subordinates. Iowa, for example, sought to reduce the number of levels of management in state departments by 50 percent. In many agencies significant progress toward this goal had occurred by 1994 (Walters 1996).

Although some "flattening" of excessively "tall" bureaucracies is justified, caution is also advised. Morgan et al. have argued that pruning the ranks of middle managers must be done carefully because these managers perform important tasks unique to the public sector. One of these is "defining what good service means." This role is important because governments have more of a problem measuring their outputs and products than does the private sector. A second unique function for public sector middle managers is "dealing with a variety of accountability problems arising from our constitutional system of governance" (1996, 362). These problems include "making sense out of multiple sources of authority" and "representing the organization to constituency groups."

The debate over "flattening" bureaucracies flows over into the debate over "empowering" lower-level employees. Again, there is much good sense in this argument. Service quality may be improved if lower-level employees who are continually involved in implementing an agency's programs—and are often in an excellent position to know how best to do this—are given more freedom from "over the shoulder" supervision and second-guessing. Empowerment is facilitated by desktop computing and networked databases that give lower-level employees access to information for decision making previously available only to higher-level managers. Still, given continuing concerns about ensuring administrative fairness and due process in dealing with citizens, precisely how much freedom to do what they personally think is "best" for a client–customer do citizens want to grant to welfare caseworkers, state police officers, psychiatric hospital staff, tax auditors, or prison guards? Empowerment of "street-level" bureaucrats requires a degree of trust in them that is rare among either elected officials or the general public today.

The Dogma of "Reinvention"

Numerous states have undertaken highly publicized REGO initiatives. TQM is but one important source of inspiration for REGO. The "reinvention" movement is more skeptical of the utility of public bureaucracies in providing services than is TQM. Thus, books in the reinvention tradition speak of "breaking through" bureaucracy (Barzelay and Armajani 1992), if not actually "banishing" it (Osborne and Plastrik 1997). One key to reinvention is *catalytic government*, which is defined as a government that "steers but does not row" (Osborne and Gaebler 1993, chap. 1). Although governments must determine what is to be done, what services will be provided, and how they will be paid for, implementation of those policies should not necessarily be assigned to government bureaucracies. Closely related is the call by proponents of REGO for *competitive government*, for "injecting competition into service delivery" (Osborne and Gaebler 1993, chap. 3). Reliance on private or nonprofit organizations to deliver services is an obvious implication of these two principles taken together.

REGO and Contracting for Services

Various forms of privatization are consistent with the arguments of REGO, and states have made increased use of these. Here I examine the most commonly used form of privatization—contracting with private or nonprofit organizations for the provision of particular services. State governments contracting out the provision of services is not new, although the 1990s has featured more of it. Nearly three-fifths of the state officials surveyed in 1997 said that privatization activity had increased since 1992 (Chi and Jasper 1998). Contracting has expanded from various "hard" services—such as road construction or building maintenance—to "soft" services—such as adoption and foster care services, mental health services, child support enforcement, substance abuse treatment, Medicaid claims management, regulation of child care facilities, and employee training and placement. A few states have experimented with privately run correctional institutions. Still, privatization remains highly variable across the states. More than 100 programs or services have been privatized in California, Colorado, Florida, Iowa, Maryland, Michigan, and New Jersey. At the other extreme, fewer than forty services or programs have been privatized in Delaware, Idaho, Indiana, Massachusetts, Mississippi, New Mexico, North Dakota, Ohio, Rhode Island, Vermont, or Wyoming (Chi and Jasper 1998).

The most common justification for contracting out is that private or nonprofit organizations can provide services of equal or better quality more cheaply than can government bureaucracies, who are monopoly suppliers. Cost savings were cited as a reason for increased service privatization by almost half of state officials surveyed in 1997 (Chi and Jasper 1998). When a government has only a limited or short-term need for certain services, hiring a contractor to provide them makes sense. For-profit providers, in particular, may possess more modern technology or greater employee expertise. State officials may believe that services purchased from contractors can more readily be terminated or reduced if a state confronts fiscal difficulties than is the case when they are provided by traditional state employees. Other considerations also drive the process. Elected officials who have campaigned on platforms favoring the downsizing of the state bureaucracy may embrace contracting even when cost savings are minimal because it reduces the number of workers who are directly employed by the state. In many states the proportion of state employees that collectively bargain exceeds the proportion in the private sector. Hence, contracting may be a way to lower labor costs, if not also "bust the unions." Public sector unions contend that this is often the primary reason that jurisdictions shift from in-house to contracted service delivery.

An accumulating body of research indicates that contracting rarely works as well as its proponents assert. Costs have often declined, but sometimes this is so because the quantity or quality of service being provided has also declined. Although competition may cause contractors to deliver better services, the need to make a profit may tempt them to skimp on quality. A bigger problem is that competition among *qualified* providers is often absent, especially in less populated areas, and for specialized services. In their examination of the contracting out of substance abuse treatment services in North Carolina, for example, Smith and Smyth found that little competition existed for the contracts to provide these services and that "once created a contract tends to be renewed routinely" (1996, 286).

Corruption may also subvert the contracting process. Bid rigging, bribery, and kickback scandals are common in the history of contracting. Freedman (1994) has argued that some governors, whose traditional patronage powers have been limited by the courts, have embraced the "new patronage" based on steering government contracts to political supporters. Effective contracting requires that specific performance standards be written into contracts and that contractor performance be closely monitored. Writing precise performance criteria is difficult, however, especially when the services involved are complex. Monitoring of contractor performance and auditing contractor records is frequently limited or haphazard. Often effective monitoring occurs only after outrageous abuses have become public. Moreover, good monitoring is not cheap and may well exceed 10 percent of a contract's value. Hence, when effective monitoring systems are in place, the costs of such monitoring, combined with other contract administration costs, may largely negate any savings from contracting.

Finally, the use of contractors to provide state services raises accountability and liability concerns. Contracting complicates the chain of command. It runs not just from a governor or the legislature to an agency head and then down to the level at which services are delivered in an agency, but now to private or nonprofit entities charged with delivering certain services as well. The contracting agency may tell disgruntled citizens to contact the contractor; the contractor may refer citizens to the contracting state agency. Contracting also raises liability issues. Government's ultimate power is its ability to deprive an individual of his or her life, liberty, or property. Giving private actors such power is controversial and is why few states have contracted for the operation of maximum security correctional institutions, and remain doubtful about its suitability for other regulatory functions (Gormley 1996c). Cooper (1994) argued that demands for accountability in contract administration will ultimately come to exceed those that currently exist with respect to direct delivery of public services because of "the fear that contractors are not motivated by a public service commitment and are not subject to the range of accountability mechanisms applicable to public employees" (107).

In conclusion, contracting often works well and deserves to be among the tools available to state governments in achieving their goals. Nevertheless, the growing literature on contracting and other privatization options suggests that states should exercise caution in selecting candidates for privatization. Even for services that are good candidates for contracting, significant resources must be devoted to contract administration, especially the drafting of specific contract language and vigorous monitoring of contract compliance. Because an adequate supply of qualified private or nonprofit providers can not be presumed to exist in all program areas, a state government must "stay in the ring" by maintaining some service capacity of its own, both as a standard against which to judge the performance of private providers and to guard against interruptions in service delivery associated with their withdrawal.

MANAGING THE PERSONNEL OF STATE BUREAUCRACIES

Government is a labor-intensive service enterprise. Although contracting out may reduce the number of employees directly employed by state governments in service delivery, others will have to be hired to perform the tasks that ensure that a system of "catalytic" government works well. Moreover, many functions will continue to be performed by those who are directly employed by state governments. Hence, the performance of state bureaucracies will continue to be significantly affected by the ability of state governments to secure, motivate, and retain a competent, productive corps of administrative employees. This section of the chapter focuses on the human resources of state administration.

Throughout much of the nineteenth century, states (and other units of government) filled administrative positions via systems of political patronage. Getting and holding on to a government job was largely dependent on a person having the "right" partisan affiliation or political connections. In the late nineteenth century civil service reformers attacked political patronage and argued that effective government required the hiring and retention of public employees on the basis of *merit*—that is, on the basis of their education, experience, and actual job performance—rather than their political or family connections. Independent civil service commissions would ensure adherence to merit principles. The result would be a competent corps of politically neutral civil servants. Such a system is consistent with bureaucratic values. Today three-fourths of the states have comprehensive civil service systems. In many of the remaining states, however, only employees involved with federally aided programs may be covered because federal grants have long mandated such coverage.

State Personnel Processes: Competence, Organizational Effectiveness, and Accountability

Defenders argue that civil service ensures that "only the best shall serve the state." Critics charge that contemporary civil service systems often fail to achieve this goal. As I discuss criticisms of state civil service systems, keep one important point in mind, however. Civil service arrangements have clearly improved the quality of state administration. It is my judgment that no state can effectively meet the demands placed on it today using pure patronage arrangements. To be sure, some would disagree with my assessment. For those who are of such a mind, Anne Freedman's (1994) discussion of the corrosive effects of patronage-based practices in Illinois state government is instructive. Although the state has dedicated, hardworking, and competent individuals among its employees, these employees have been demoralized by the state's patronage practices.

> Conscientious employees find it very upsetting to have to work with some of the people that the system (the patronage system) has foisted upon their agencies. Managers have also complained about having to waste time interviewing applicants when the patronage office has already decided who will get the job. Some are bitter about having to negotiate with the patronage office over hires and of having to sacrifice some positions to the governor's patronage needs. Almost everyone resents the fact that the public so often sees them as lazy and unqualified patronage job holders. There are people who don't even admit publicly that they work for the state. And, needless to say, many employees have experienced frustration and anger at seeing jobs and promotions repeatedly go to the politically connected. . . . Because of the patronage system, countless citizens have opted not to work for the state or have left state jobs in disgust (103).

Not just "good government" civil service reformers have found the Illinois system wanting. Since the mid-1970s, no fewer than three U.S. Supreme Court decisions struck at the state's patronage-based practices. In the most recent of these rulings, the *Rutan et al. v. Republican Party of Illinois* (110 S. Ct. 729) decision in 1990, a majority of the court rejected the state's argument that those whom it hires must be supporters of the governor's party or else they will not be motivated to work effectively, or may try to subvert the governor's program. Instead, the Court maintained that the

> inefficiency resulting from the wholesale replacement of large numbers of public employees every time political office changes hands belies this justification. And the prospect of dismissal after an election in which the incumbent party has lost is only a disincentive to good work. Further, it is not clear that dismissal in order to make room for a patronage appointee will result in replacement by a person more qualified to do the job since appointment often occurs in exchange for the delivery of votes, or other party service, not job capability (quoted in Freedman 1994, 4).

Not that civil service arrangements invariably contribute to effective state administration either. Securing able employees is sometimes hampered by unimaginative recruiting and by examinations and other selection methods whose job relatedness has not been validated. Hiring practices may be so complex and slow that qualified applicants accept jobs elsewhere. Civil service systems struggle with how to limit patronage by protecting the competent from dismissal for inappropriate reasons while not making it too difficult to fire the objectively incompetent.

Developments in Wisconsin, a state with a well-established civil service system, illustrate how the states are responding to some of these problems. A survey conducted by the Wisconsin Department of Employment Relations (DER) disclosed that agencies were having difficulty recruiting sufficient numbers of qualified employees, in part because the length and complexity of the hiring process caused them to lose good applicants to competing employers. In response, the DER made several important changes. Via on-campus recruitment of college graduates for entry level professional positions, the time needed to hire an applicant was shortened by more than a month. The adoption of "walk-in testing" of more than 30,000 applicants per year for positions that require a written examination reduced by three weeks the time that elapsed between applying for a position and being certified as eligible for appointment. Finally, the DER replaced written notices of job vacancies with an on-line system that is accessed more than 500,000 times a year (Lavigna 1996).

Compensating State Government Administrative Employees. Levels of pay and benefits for government employees of all types are often controversial. Although some criticize supposedly excessive levels of compensation for state employees, state personnel directors believe that their states have had but average success in providing competitive salaries and benefits (Hays and Kearney 1992). In fact, assessing compensation, both among states and between the states and the private sector, is complicated. Public sector jobs often have no private sector equivalent. The value of "indirect compensation," such as health care and retirement benefits or annual leave, must also be considered. Interstate comparison requires that cost of living differences be taken into account.

With these complexities in mind, how does the compensation of state employees compare across the states and with that paid to private sector workers? Table 8-2 indicates that in 1995 the monthly pay of a full-time state employee not employed in education averaged $2725—or more than $32,000 annually. Average state pay varies greatly, however. Cost of living differences explain some of this variation. A study using 1989 noneducation state employee earnings data took cost of living into account. This changed the pay rankings in 1989 dramatically in some states (Gold and Ritchie 1993). Reflecting its high cost of living, Alaska's pay rank dropped from first to thirteenth. In contrast, Vermont emerged as the best-paying state even though it ranked twenty-second in unadjusted pay. Adjusting for cost of living narrows but does not eliminate interstate pay differences. Even when its low cost of living was factored in for 1989, West Virginia remained the state that paid its employees least well.

Table 8-2 Average Monthly Earnings, Full-Time Noneducation State Employees, October 1995

State	Rank	Average monthly earnings	State	Rank	Average monthly earnings
Alaska	1	$3,654	Vermont	27	2,385
California	2	3,547	Florida	28	2,383
New Jersey	3	3,435	Virginia	29	2,374
New York	4	3,382	Kansas	30	2,371
Michigan	5	3,285	North Carolina	31	2,368
Rhode Island	6	3,221	Montana	32	2,345
Minnesota	7	3,153	Alabama	33	2,314
Colorado	8	3,139	Arizona	34	2,284
Connecticut	9	3,096	Nebraska	35	2,270
Ohio	10	3,056	Tennessee	36	2,269
Massachusetts	11	3,022	Texas	37	2,262
Illinois	12	3,018	Kentucky	38	2,259
Washington	13	2,990	North Dakota	39	2,259
Wisconsin	14	2,916	Georgia	40	2,247
Iowa	15	2,902	South Dakota	41	2,216
Nevada	16	2,898	Indiana	42	2,214
Pennsylvania	17	2,798	Missouri	43	2,198
Maryland	18	2,663	Louisiana	44	2,189
New Hampshire	19	2,659	Arkansas	45	2,163
Oregon	20	2,655	Wyoming	46	2,158
Utah	21	2,573	Mississippi	47	2,143
Delaware	22	2,569	South Carolina	48	2,143
Hawaii	23	2,562	West Virginia	49	1,949
Maine	24	2,537	Oklahoma	50	1,885
Idaho	25	2,511			
New Mexico	26	2,400	50-state average		$ 2,725

SOURCE: U.S. Bureau of the Census 1996.

In addition to wages or salary, employee compensation includes important benefits, such as pensions, vacation and sick leave, and most important, health care coverage. The value of these benefits averaged 24 percent of salaries and wages for all states in 1987 (Stevens 1992). In general, states ranking high in regard to average monthly salary also rank high when the value of fringe benefits is considered, although a few states become either more or less competitive.

Inadequate compensation not only hampers the ability of state administrative agencies to attract good employees but their ability to retain them as well. This relationship is clear from my research on state employee turnover in twenty-one states from 1993 to 1995. Levels of aggregate turnover (stemming from voluntary resignation or "quitting," as well as death, dismissal, layoff, or retirement) of about 10 percent, and "quit" rates perhaps half that great, are considered "tolerable" by experts on the subject. Across these states, aggregate turnover for the 1993 to 1995 period averaged 9.5 percent but varied from less than 5 percent to nearly 17 percent. "Quit" rates averaged 6 percent, but varied from less than 3 percent in a few states to more than 9 percent in others.

Analysis clearly indicates that states that paid less well had more employees quitting. Using several different measures of employee compensation—including one that adjusted pay for cost of living and another that factored in the estimated value of fringe benefits—between 40 and 60 percent of the variation among these states in quit rates could be accounted for by compensation alone (Elling 1997). The six states with the lowest quit rates—California, Iowa, Michigan, Minnesota, Pennsylvania, and Wisconsin— all rank in the top twenty in pay in the listing in Table 8-2. Of the six states with the highest quit rates—Florida, Idaho, Kansas, Missouri, North Carolina, and Texas—all but Idaho rank in the bottom half in average pay.

Adequate pay for high-level state administrators is a particular problem. Although it was estimated in the 1980s that private sector administrators with responsibilities comparable to those of top state administrators earned between $230,000 and $600,000, the average annual salary of eight top-level administrators in each of the fifty states in 1989 only ranged from $49,602 in Arkansas to $105,164 in New York (Gold and Ritchie 1993). Americans tend to view private sector employment more positively than public sector employment and public employees as either less able or less hard-working than their peers in the private sector. Whether this is true or not, it means that higher-level state government executives will almost certainly never be paid salaries comparable to those paid to private sector executives, even when those jobs entail a similar degree of responsibility or difficulty. Nevertheless, many current and potential state employees do have employment options, and state governments must pay competitive salaries to attract and retain competent persons for these jobs.

Some critics argue that state pay systems do not sufficiently reward "high flyers" and penalize "drones." Whatever the attractiveness of so-called "merit" or "performance contingent" pay arrangements in theory, the experiences of those states that have used such arrangements has been mixed at best. Developing performance appraisal instruments that are perceived as fair by employees is but one of the problems. Another has been the reluctance of legislatures to provide sufficient funding for such systems so that bonuses to recognize superior performance are meaningful. TQM also fundamentally challenges the logic of "merit pay." With its stress on work teams, TQM finds individualistically oriented pay arrangements to be counterproductive. Although they are still rare, TQM favors "gain sharing" arrangements in which bonuses are shared by members of high-performing teams or units. Another approach that is consistent with TQM precepts that stress "empowerment" and "self-directed work teams" is one recommended by the National Commission on the State and Local Public Service (1993). In arguing for the creation of a "learning government," the Commission urges significant increases in funding for employee training and development combined with compensation arrangements that reward employees for acquiring new skills that either help them do their current jobs better or give them the knowledge needed to perform other tasks. Several states, including North Carolina and Virginia, have begun to use such skill-based pay systems in selected agencies.

Are State Employees Too Hard to Fire? Many citizens could not care less if state employees are poorly paid. They are more concerned about how hard it supposedly is to fire state employees who are not doing a good job. Data collected as part of my state turnover study indicate average annual dismissal rates for 1993–1995 in eighteen states that ranged from as low as three employees out of 1000, to a "high" of approximately two employees out of 100, with the annual firing rate for these states across this time period averaging about one dismissal for every 100 employees.

The fact that dismissal rates are quite low reflects a persisting dilemma for civil service systems. State personnel directors think that their state's personnel system does a good job of protecting employees from adverse personnel actions unrelated to their actual ability to perform and of ensuring the political neutrality of the state workforce (Hays and Kearney 1992). This is a valuable accomplishment of civil service. But it comes at the price of rules and procedures that make it difficult to discipline or discharge public employees who are performing poorly. In recent years numerous states have made it easier to discipline or dismiss employees to achieve a better balance between employee rights and the public's right to a productive workforce (Walters 1994). Whether it is wise to go as far as Georgia is debatable. In "reinventing" its civil service system in 1996, Georgia made all of its employees "at will" employees, which means that they have few of the protections against dismissal typically accorded to classified civil servants. This change seems premised on the belief that agency managers and governors in Georgia will consistently be motivated by concerns for high performance and effective management in deciding who to fire. Although guidelines promulgated by the governor require "agencies to make employment decisions free from political intervention or influence" (Tanner 1996), one can be forgiven for doubting that this will always, or even usually, be the case.

The Challenge of Equal Opportunity and Diversity

Civil service's stress on "objective merit" has reduced discrimination based on race, ethnicity, age, gender, and disability. Still, illegal discrimination exists, and state governments have been forced—in response to federal and state laws and court rulings—to address discriminatory practices or effects in their personnel systems. One can distinguish between employment *representation* and employment *stratification*. The former refers to the proportion of all jobs in a governmental jurisdiction or unit held by members of a particular group. Stratification refers to imbalances in the type and quality of jobs that are held by groups of employees in a given agency or jurisdiction.

The overall share of jobs in state government held by women and minorities has increased. From 1973 to 1989, African Americans as a proportion of all full-time state employees grew from 10 to 18 percent, the proportion of other ethnic minorities increased from 3 to 7 percent, and the proportion of female employees rose from 43 to 49 percent (Hebert, Wright, and Brudney 1992). The column on employment representativeness in Table 8-3 indicates that, although men continue to hold a disproportionate share of all state jobs, the difference is not great. Moreover, in terms of the *quantity* of state jobs held, African American women do better than any group, although white, Asian American, and Native American males also have ratios greater than 1.00. Using this measure, both Hispanic men and women do poorly.

Table 8-3 Representativeness and Stratification Ratios for the State Government Workforce, 1995

	Employment representativeness[a]	Employment stratification[b]
Men	1.04	1.52
White	1.14	1.75
African American	0.83	0.84
Hispanic	0.62	0.52
Asian American	1.03	1.29
Native American	1.02	1.75
Women	0.94	0.51
White	0.92	0.57
African American	1.24	0.35
Hispanic	0.67	0.18
Asian American	0.89	0.40
Native American	0.93	0.50

SOURCE: Constructed from data in Riccucci and Saidel (1997) and Center for Women in Government (1997).

[a] *Employment representativeness*—what Riccucci and Saidel term the baseline measure in their analysis—is the ratio of the share of all state government administrative positions held by members of a particular group, excluding top-level political appointees. These data are reported by states to the U.S. Equal Employment Opportunity Commission. These are data for 1995 and were collected from each state by Riccucci and Saidel.

[b] The *job stratification* measure is the ratio of the percentage of appointed policy leaders as of the summer of 1997, compared to proportion of residents in a state who are members of particular groups. *Appointed policy leaders* are heads of state departments, agencies, offices, boards, commissions and authorities, plus key members of the governor's office in each state. The statistics for Native American employees, in particular, should be interpreted cautiously given the relatively small number of Native American state employees nationwide. In the table, ratios greater than 1.0 indicate that a particular group holds a share of total jobs, or higher level jobs, that exceeds what would be expected based on its share of total population in a state.

Job stratification is the major problem today. To be sure, women and minorities hold a larger share of higher-level jobs that pay better and have more responsibility than ever before. Between 1964 and 1997 the proportion of female state agency heads grew from 2 percent to 24 percent. During the same period the proportion of African American agency heads increased from 1 percent to 7 percent. The proportion of all minorities combined was 8 percent in 1978 and nearly 14 percent in 1997 (Bullard and Wright 1993; Center for Women in Government 1997). These figures remain well below the proportion of women (51.2 percent) or minorities (24.5 percent) in the population as a whole, however.

Employment stratification is typically calculated by comparing the proportion of higher-level positions, or better-paying positions, held by members of particular groups as compared to the group's share of the population or the workforce. These data are not, however, readily available on a state-by-state basis.[2] Fortunately, a new

2. Although states report information that could be used to calculate such indexes to the U.S. Equal Employment Opportunity Commission (EEOC), the EEOC merges employment data for a particular state government with the data from all units of local government in that state. Although states are often willing to provide copies of the data that they have sent to the EEOC, securing such data requires contacting each of the fifty states.

data series produced by the Center for Women in Government (CWG) at the State University of New York at Albany provides insight on job stratification. This project focuses on a different group of high-level positions than have prior studies, however. In addition to looking at the number of positions as heads of departments, agencies, boards, or commissions, that are held by persons from varying backgrounds, the CWG project adds in a category of "top advisors" who are "appointees in governor's offices or executive chambers with policy developing, advising or influencing responsibilities" (1997, 1). Included are positions such as a governor's chief of staff, press secretary–communications director, and budget director. Although most individuals in these positions are not typically considered to be "civil servants," these are important positions, and, like agency head positions, are subject to gubernatorial appointment. This measure does not assess the share of jobs held by various groups in the upper reaches of the state civil service below the level of political appointees, and these positions are also important. The CWG data does, however, have the advantage of being available on a state-by-state basis. Moreover, because none of these top policy positions are subject to civil service or union seniority rules that often favor whites or men, we might expect women or minorities to have had greater success in reaching these positions than other higher-level administrative positions that are not filled through gubernatorial appointment. If members of particular groups are underrepresented in these positions, they very likely do even less well in achieving high-level administrative positions not subject to political appointment. Of some 1,806 positions in the Center's 1997 database, 29 percent are "top advisor" positions. Women filled a higher percentage of "top advisor" than "agency head" positions (40 percent versus 24 percent) although no significant differences existed by type of position so far as racial or ethnic group representation was concerned.

Overall, as the second column of Table 8-3 indicates, men held half again as many of these higher-level jobs as would be predicted based on their share of a state's population. Although white males are particularly advantaged, the stratification ratios for Asian American and Native American men are also greater than 1.0. Although, as we have seen, African American women hold a disproportionate share of all state jobs, they are severely underrepresented in high-level positions, as are Hispanic women.

Table 8-4 examines job stratification on a state-by-state basis. Women and minorities have clearly had more success in reaching higher-level positions in some states than others. The proportion of top positions held by women varies from as low as 7 percent in Oklahoma and 8 percent in West Virginia, to as high as 46 percent in Vermont and 49 percent in Nevada. In most states, between 20 percent and 30 percent of these top positions are filled by women. This results in ratios in the 0.40 to 0.60 range, far short of proportionality. Seven of the ten states in which women did least well in 1997 were southern or border states, although North Carolina and Virginia ranked in the top ten in appointing women to high-level administrative and policy posts.

Table 8-4 Representation of Women and African Americans in Top-Level Positions in State Government Appointed by Current Governors in 1997

State	Percentage of women in high-level positions [a]	Percentage of women in state population	Representation ratio (state rank) [b]	Percentage of African Americans in high-level positions [c]	Percentage of African Americans in state population	Representation ratio (state rank) [d]
Alabama	19.0	52.1	0.36 (47)	0.0	25.2	—
Alaska	32.1	47.3	0.68 (12)	0.0	4.1	—
Arizona	28.6	50.6	0.57 (24)	4.8	3.0	1.60 (9)
Arkansas	21.6	51.8	0.42 (42)	8.1	15.9	0.51 (30)
California	28.4	49.9	0.57 (23)	4.1	7.4	0.56 (28)
Colorado	25.0	50.5	0.50 (34)	6.3	4.0	1.56 (10)
Connecticut	19.4	51.5	0.38 (45)	9.7	8.3	1.17 (14)
Delaware	28.6	51.5	0.56 (25)	3.6	16.8	0.21 (35)
Florida	19.2	51.6	0.37 (46)	7.7	13.5	0.57 (27)
Georgia	14.0	51.5	0.27 (48)	14.0	26.9	0.52 (29)
Hawaii	25.9	49.2	0.53 (28)	0.0	2.4	—
Idaho	38.7	50.2	0.77 (8)	0.0	0.3	—
Illinois	25.8	51.4	0.50 (32)	9.7	14.8	0.66 (22)
Indiana	28.3	51.5	0.55 (26)	13.3	7.8	1.71 (7)
Iowa	32.3	51.6	0.63 (16)	3.1	1.7	1.79 (6)
Kansas	23.5	51.0	0.46 (37)	8.8	5.8	1.52 (11)
Kentucky	25.9	51.6	0.50 (31)	18.5	7.1	2.59 (3)
Louisiana	23.8	51.9	0.46 (38)	9.5	30.7	0.31 (34)
Maine	29.2	51.3	0.57 (22)	0.0	0.4	—
Maryland	39.0	51.5	0.76 (10)	22.0	24.8	0.89 (16)
Massachusetts	32.0	52.0	0.62 (17)	4.0	5.0	0.80 (18)
Michigan	26.1	51.5	0.51 (30)	8.7	13.9	0.63 (25)
Minnesota	32.3	51.0	0.63 (15)	1.7	2.2	0.78 (19)
Mississippi	30.8	52.2	0.59 (19)	11.5	35.5	0.32 (33)
Missouri	33.3	51.8	0.64 (14)	0.0	10.7	—
Montana	40.7	50.5	0.81 (5)	0.0	0.3	—
Nebraska	30.8	51.3	0.60 (18)	5.1	3.6	1.40 (12)
Nevada	48.6	49.1	0.99 (1)	2.9	6.5	0.44 (31)
New Hampshire	41.7	51.0	0.82 (3)	0.0	0.6	—
New Jersey	41.2	51.7	0.80 (6)	9.8	13.3	0.74 (20)
New Mexico	26.5	50.8	0.52 (29)	0.0	2.0	—
New York	22.7	52.0	0.44 (40)	3.0	15.6	0.63 (36)
North Carolina	41.7	51.5	0.81 (4)	13.9	21.9	0.63 (23)
North Dakota	26.7	50.2	0.53 (27)	0.0	0.6	—
Ohio	20.5	51.8	0.40 (43)	12.8	10.6	1.20 (13)
Oklahoma	6.9	51.3	0.13 (50)	6.9	7.4	0.93 (15)
Oregon	38.6	50.8	0.76 (9)	9.1	1.6	5.61 (1)
Pennsylvania	25.9	52.1	0.50 (33)	5.6	9.2	0.61 (26)
Rhode Island	22.7	52.0	0.44 (39)	9.1	3.9	2.35 (5)
South Carolina	20.0	51.6	0.39 (44)	10.0	29.8	0.34 (32)
South Dakota	34.8	50.8	0.69 (11)	0.0	0.5	—
Tennessee	30.0	51.8	0.58 (21)	10.0	15.9	0.63 (24)
Texas	24.4	50.7	0.48 (36)	10.0	11.9	0.84 (17)
Utah	24.2	50.3	0.48 (35)	0.0	0.7	—
Vermont	45.5	51.0	0.89 (2)	0.0	0.3	—
Virginia	40.0	51.0	0.78 (7)	13.3	18.8	0.71 (21)
Washington	32.6	50.4	0.65 (13)	9.3	3.1	3.03 (2)
West Virginia	7.7	52.0	0.15 (49)	7.7	3.1	2.45 (4)

Table 8-4 *Continued*

State	Percentage of women in high-level positions[a]	Percentage of women in state population	Representation ratio (state rank)[b]	Percentage of African Americans in high-level positions[c]	Percentage of African Americans in state population	Representation ratio (state rank)[d]
Wisconsin	29.7	51.1	0.58 (20)	8.1	5.0	1.62 (8)
Wyoming	21.4	50.0	0.43 (41)	0.0	0.8	—
50-state average	28.3	51.2	0.55	6.9	11.9	0.58

SOURCE: Center for Women in Government, Summer 1997.

[a] Percentage of positions as state department heads or top advisors in governor's office held by women. Total number of positions nationally is 1,806. The number of positions in particular states varies from thirteen (West Virginia) to ninety (Texas).

[b] Calculated by dividing the percentage of top positions held by women by the proportion of state residents who are women.

[c] Percentage of positions as department heads or top advisors in governor's office held by African Americans.

[d] Calculated by dividing the percentage of top positions held by African Americans by the proportion of state residents who are African American. States with no African Americans in these positions are not ranked.

Table 8-4 indicates that African Americans also do better in some states than others. Although there are no African Americans in high-level positions in fourteen states,[3] in another fourteen the proportion of African Americans in "top policy" posts exceeds the share of a state's population that is African American.[4] In none of these latter states are African Americans a significant proportion of total state population, however. The picture is quite different in states with the largest percentage of residents who are African American. Although one quarter of all Alabamians is African American, in 1997 there was no African American policy leader in the state. In both Louisiana and Mississippi, the share of top-level positions held by African Americans was less than one-third of what would be expected based on their presence in the state's population. Perhaps such statistics for former states of the Confederacy ought not to surprise us. Certainly, African Americans have been more successful in attaining high-level posts in other states with significant African American populations such as Ohio, Maryland, and New Jersey, along with the southern state of Texas.[5]

3. These states are Alabama, Alaska, Hawaii, Idaho, Maine, Missouri, Montana, New Hampshire, New Mexico, North Dakota, South Dakota, Utah, Vermont, and Wyoming.

4. These states are Arizona, Colorado, Connecticut, Indiana, Iowa, Kansas, Kentucky, Nebraska, Ohio, Oregon, Rhode Island, Washington, West Virginia, and Wisconsin.

5. Breakdowns by state for other racial–ethnic categories are not provided because there are few high-level state administrative officials from these groups in most states. To be sure, Hispanic, Native American, and Asian American individuals do fill some of these positions in some states, typically those in which they are a more significant presence in a state's population. California and Hawaii are the two states with the largest Asian American populations. In Hawaii, where 60 percent of the population is Asian American, Asian Americans are significantly overrepresented in top policy posts, with a representation ratio of 1.43. This is not true in California where fewer than 3 percent of appointees are Asian American in a state where nearly one in ten residents is Asian American. In the six states in which Native Americans are 5 percent or more of a state's population (Alaska, Arizona, Montana, New Mexico, Oklahoma, and South Dakota), Native Americans hold more than their proportional share of top positions only in Oklahoma, and hold a nearly proportional share in Alaska. In eight states His-

The less favorable employment circumstances of women and minorities in state government are by no means entirely a result of discrimination. But racism and sexism persist, especially in the promoting of employees to higher level positions. Stereotypes about the abilities of women and minorities are a key factor in explaining "sticky floors" (jobs with limited promotion potential) and "glass ceilings" that limit advancement.

Sexual harassment is a form of gender discrimination that may discourage women from pursuing opportunities in male-dominated occupations or may cause them to leave jobs to escape it. A five-state study found that the percentage of female employees who had experienced "requests for sexual favors" ranged from 11 to 24 percent; those reporting "offensive physical contact" ranged from 14 to 36 percent; and those encountering "offensive verbal behavior" ranged from a "low" of 33 percent, among female employees in Texas, to 60 percent in Wisconsin (Kelly and Stambaugh 1992).

Fortunately, by 1994, thirty-four states had adopted state employee sexual harassment policies (Bowman and Zigmond 1996). Unfortunately, these policies varied widely in their adequacy. Five requirements for a comprehensive sexual harassment policy were articulated in the 1991 *Robinson v. Jacksonville Shipyards* (760 F. Supp. 1486, M.D. Fla.) court decision. No state with a formal harassment policy in 1994 met all five of these standards, and only ten—California, Colorado, Florida, Michigan, Montana, New Hampshire, Oregon, South Dakota, Washington, and Wisconsin—had policies that met four of the five standards.

Efforts to improve the employment status of women and minorities have been controversial, especially when they have taken the form of affirmative action. Opponents charge that affirmative action unfairly discriminates against better qualified candidates who just happen to be white males. Although this may occasionally occur, there is little evidence that female or minority candidates for promotion are being systematically "leap-frogged" over better educated or more experienced white or male state employees, or that the women and minorities are otherwise less qualified for promotion (Bullard and Wright 1993; Olshfski and Caprio 1996). The slow increase in the proportion of minorities or women in higher-level public jobs suggests that affirmative action constitutes a *very* modest revolution. Still, the future of affirmative action policy is in doubt. In 1996 California voters approved Proposition 209, which ended state affirmative action efforts in education and employment. Proposals to restrict, repeal, or revamp affirmative action were introduced in eighteen states in 1995 and fifteen states in 1997 (Kellough, Selden, and Legge 1997). Still, no proposal affecting affirmative action practices passed in any state in 1997.

panics constitute 10 percent or more of the population. Although Hispanics are well represented in state government in some of these states, notably Arizona, Colorado, and New Mexico, in no state are Hispanics represented in high-level positions in proportion to their presence in a state's population. In California, with a Hispanic population of nearly 26 percent, only 7 percent of top posts are filled by Hispanics (Center for Women in Government 1997, 14).

The Challenge of Collective Bargaining

State employees in thirty-four states engage in some form of structured negotiations with their employer, although genuine collective bargaining (as opposed to "meet and confer" arrangements) exists in only thirty (Kearney 1992; NASPE 1996). Although approximately 40 percent of full-time state employees belong to an employee organization or a union, the percentage of state employees represented varies widely. In twenty-one states, 70 percent or more of state classified employees are covered by union contracts.[6] Most are states with a history of strong private sector unionization. With the exceptions of Florida and New Mexico, state employee unions are weak or nonexistent in states in the South, Southwest, or Mountain West. America's Pacific Rim states of California, Oregon, Washington, Alaska, and Hawaii, on the other hand, all have heavily unionized state workforces. Following rapid growth in the 1960s and 1970s, state employee unions today confront a less hospitable environment. Only New Mexico has adopted legislation permitting state employees to collectively bargain in the 1990s. Fiscal stringency has changed the contours of bargaining. The threat to contract out the provision of services sometimes has been used to wrest concessions from unions.

The consequences of collective bargaining for state administration are far from clear. The diversity of state laws on the matters that are subject to negotiation, and the differing political and economic environments in which collective bargaining occurs ensure highly variable effects. Although most states that authorize collective bargaining permit bargaining on wages, benefits, and working conditions, a few permit bargaining over just one or two of these subjects. Still, collective bargaining has affected the operation of civil service systems, the costs of state government, and administrative performance.

Collective bargaining and civil service practices often coexist. Unions join civil service advocates in opposition to patronage practices and support protections against dismissal for non–work-related reasons. Merit principles are compromised by unions' emphasis on seniority as the primary criterion for promotion, salary increases, or layoffs. This preference also hampers efforts to increase the diversity of the state workforce.

Some critics fear that wage and fringe benefit settlements resulting from collective bargaining inflate budgets and lead to tax hikes. Although most research suggests a modest impact on wage levels, Grady and Lane (1995) found that only state employees in highly unionized states have experienced real income growth over the past thirty years. Public sector unions—particularly those with many members who are women employed in health care and clerical jobs—are in the vanguard of "comparable worth" efforts. "Comparable worth" advocates argue that job classes that disproportionately employ women have lower rates of pay because "women's

---

6. These states are Alaska, California, Connecticut, Florida, Hawaii, Illinois, Indiana, Iowa, Maine, Massachusetts, Michigan, Minnesota, Nebraska, New Hampshire, New Jersey, New York, Ohio, Pennsylvania, Rhode Island, Vermont, and Wisconsin.

work" is systematically undervalued. In those states that have addressed such concerns, women in affected job classes have sometimes received substantial raises, with these adjustments affecting state budgets significantly in the short run. On the other hand, tight state budgets have prompted union flexibility on compensation, often in return for guarantees that there would be no layoffs. In 1991, for example, nearly all bargaining units in Connecticut gave up pay increases in order to save jobs (Kearney 1992).

Other critics fear that administrative performance will be impaired as unionized employees gain more say in decisions traditionally reserved for managers. This may sometimes be so, but even in highly unionized states such as California, Michigan, and New York few managers considered "limits on managerial authority due to collective bargaining" to be a serious impediment to effective management. In these same states, unions were seen, on average, to have only "some impact" on the conduct of daily operations (Elling 1992). Moreover, collective bargaining can be viewed as a vehicle for achieving the participative management and employee empowerment touted by TQM and REGO enthusiasts (Kearney and Hays 1994). Public unions sometimes defend inefficient work practices. But there is little systematic evidence that collective bargaining hampers productivity or reduces the quality of government services (Loney 1989). In Minnesota, for example, members of the American Federation of State, County, and Municipal Employees were key actors in restructuring the state's services for persons with developmental disabilities (National Commission on the State and Local Public Service 1993).

Unions are often suspicious of TQM or REGO initiatives, seeing them as just two more episodes in a long history of unilateral "managerialism." Union suspicions are heightened when such efforts occur in conjunction with budget cuts and contracting out (Hyde 1995b). Nonetheless, unions are supportive of efforts to expand employee training and development, to empower lower level employees, and often favor the "flattening of bureaucracies" by eliminating layers of middle management (Walters 1996).

The emergence of collective bargaining, just like efforts to increase the diversity of the state government workforce, has changed the contours of state administration. This may sometimes have been a change for the worse. At least as often, in my view, it represents a change for the better.

ADMINISTRATORS AND OTHERS: STATE ADMINISTRATIVE PERFORMANCE IN A POLITICAL CONTEXT

The dichotomy between politics and administration posited by Woodrow Wilson in the 1880s held that efficient and effective administration would result if trained professionals with considerable job security handled administrative tasks. For their part, elected officials were to establish agencies, authorize their programs, and specify the amounts of dollars and personnel to be made available to them. As a description of contemporary reality, such a dichotomy is seriously flawed. The difficulty of crafting complex policy in the modern era, combined with the fact that nonadministrators control resources crucial to administrative success, causes many administrators to believe that policy making cannot remain the sole preserve of elected officials. It is hardly surprising, then, that state administrators devote as much as one-fourth of their time to policy development activities (Elling 1992; Wright, Yoo, and Cohen 1991). At the same time, elected officials seek to influence agencies to ensure that policies are implemented appropriately. State agencies make too much difference in the lives of constituents for elected officials to allow them to function in splendid isolation.

State Bureaucrats as Policy Shapers

Bureaucratic influence in policy making stems from several sources. First, career bureaucrats often know best how to deal with problems. Public health officials, for example, know more than anyone else in state government about a state's health problems and its public health programs.

Second, state agencies possess discretionary authority. No law can be so precisely drafted as to eliminate completely the need for choice in applying it. Moreover, it is unwise for elected officials to limit administrative discretion unduly because policy implementation is often improved if administrators can respond to feedback and make adjustments according to the circumstances in individual cases. In deference to bureaucratic expertise, elected officials often grant agencies broad authority to develop the procedures and regulations necessary to implement programs.

Third, administrative influence in policy making increases to the extent that the beneficiaries of the programs an agency administers become supporters of those programs and the agency itself. Agencies sometimes develop constituencies that contribute to administrative influence in policy making.

The first row of Table 8-5 illustrates the policy-shaping role of state bureaucracies. Not only do administrators see their agencies as dominant actors in administrative realms, but many say that their agencies also importantly influence the content of major decisions that are formally made by political institutions. Indeed, 40 percent of these managers reported that they originated half or more of the legislation affecting their units. That so many managers see their agencies as the dominant player in making major policy decisions affecting their units is striking.

If the politics–administration dichotomy has been breached from the administrative side, does this mean that we are confronted with runaway state bureaucracies? Such a conclusion is as wrong as believing that state bureaucracies and bureaucrats leave policy making to elected officials while passively awaiting their marching orders. Every agency's situation is different. Administrative influence is also relational. As more nonadministrative players get into the game, the relative power of an agency itself declines. The knowledge possessed by administrative agencies is also less persuasive in an era of policy volatility when modest alternations in existing programs may seem insufficient (Rourke 1991). Moreover, bureaucrats are appointed officials in a political system in which popular election is a powerful source of legitimacy. Administrators taking unilateral action are likely to

Table 8-5 Impact of Selected Actors on Decisions Affecting, or Actions of, State Bureaucracies in Ten States

Influence actor	Determination of overall agency budget level	Budget levels for specific programs	Major policy or program changes	Content of rules and regulations	Establishing administrative procedures	Daily operations
Agency itself	2.8	2.9	3.1	3.3	3.5	3.7
Governor and staff	2.7[a]	2.6[a]	2.5[a]	1.7[a]	1.5[a]	1.1[a]
State legislature	3.2[a]	3.1	2.8[a]	2.2	1.7[a]	1.2
Federal agencies/Congress	1.6	1.5	1.6	1.4	1.1	1.1
Federal courts	0.8	0.7	1.0	1.1	0.7	0.6
State budget office	2.9[a]	2.8[a]	2.0[a]	1.0[a]	1.4[a]	1.4[a]
State personnel office	1.3[a]	1.0[a]	1.0[a]	0.8[a]	1.4[a]	1.3[a]
Other state agencies	1.0	0.9	0.9	1.1[a]	1.1[a]	1.0
Local governments	0.8[a]	0.7[a]	0.8	0.8[a]	0.6	0.8
Professional associations	0.7	0.7	0.8	0.9[a]	0.6	0.6
Agency clientele	1.2	1.2	1.4	1.4	1.1	1.6
State employee unions	0.8[a]	0.7[a]	0.6[a]	0.6[a]	0.7[a]	0.7[a]
Political parties	0.7[a]	0.6	0.6	0.4	0.3	0.3
Communications media	0.9	0.8	0.9	0.7	0.5	0.8
Interest groups	1.3	1.3	1.4	1.4[a]	1.0	1.1[a]

SOURCE: Elling (1992). Used by permission of Praeger Publishers, an imprint of Greenwood Publishing Group, Inc., Westport, CT.

NOTE: Each column shows the mean attributed impact for an actor on a given decision or activity based on responses in all ten states. Response options were (0) no impact, (1) some impact, (2) moderate impact, (3) great impact, (4) very great impact. Depending on an actor or the area of decision or activity, the number of respondents ranged between 780 and 821

[a] Statistically significant difference in the mean impact of influence actor across the ten states (F-test, .01 level).

be harshly criticized for exceeding their authority. Most administrative power is derivative power, exercised at the sufferance of others. The abolition of an agency or the transferring of some of its programs is rare. But both occur. More common is the narrowing of administrative discretion as a consequence of elected officials' displeasure with how that discretion has been used.

The data in Table 8-5 convey the complexity of state administrative influence relationships. State legislatures and governors significantly affect agency budgets. Although the governor is slightly less influential than the legislature, the governor's role becomes substantial when the influence of the budget office—which is highly attuned to gubernatorial interests—is factored in. The governor and legislature both have a significant voice in basic policy decisions affecting state bureaucracies. In addition, the federal government, agency clientele, and interest groups have moderate influence in these three arenas.

Nonadministrative actors have less say in the promulgating of rules and regulations, the determination of administrative procedures, or daily operations, although a few have moderate impact. The governor, legislature, federal agencies, state budget and personnel offices, other state agencies, agency clientele, and interest groups even have some effect on daily operations.

Footnote *a* in Table 8-5 also indicates that the impact of certain actors varies from state to state. This is particularly so for governors, legislatures, budget and personnel offices, and state employee unions. Within a given state the influence of nonadministrative actors may vary as a function of agency responsibilities or other factors. In the ten-state study, agencies that depended on the federal government for much of their funding reported substantially more federal agency or congressional influence. Federal and state courts importantly influence agencies with certain responsibilities. Agencies with criminal justice, environmental protection, transportation, and regulatory responsibilities report that state courts have greater impact on broad policies affecting them. The federal courts have forced states to increase funding for, and modify the operations of, correctional institutions and facilities for the mentally ill, developmentally disabled, and all children (O'Leary 1994). Federal and state courts have also affected state personnel systems through decisions relating to patronage practices, collective bargaining, sexual harassment, and affirmative action.

Having sketched the broad outlines of interaction between state agencies and other actors, I will now explore bureaucratic relations with the governor, the state legislature, and the public in various guises—organized interest groups, clients of agencies, and ordinary citizens—in greater detail.

The Governor as Chief Bureaucrat

To be successful, governors often need the bureaucracy. Although gubernatorial relations with state bureaucracies are sometimes conflictual, more often they are not (Elling 1992, chap. 7). Michigan's Republican governor John Engler is no fan of big government. Yet one of his aides had this to say about Michigan's bureaucracy: "The biggest surprise we faced when moving to the governor's office . . . was in working with the bureaucracy. We now had to recommend programs that could be effectively implemented and we needed state agency assistance on that. We were surprised at how many really good people were over there" (Elling and Kobrak 1995).

Until quite recently governors were often chief executives in name only. This is much less true today. Administrative reorganization is one reason. Governors in more than half of the states can initiate organizational changes that take effect unless the legislature objects within a specified time period (Rosenthal 1990). Personnel system reform has also enhanced gubernatorial leverage over the bureaucracy. Nearly every state has shifted personnel management responsibilities from a semi-autonomous civil service commission to a central personnel agency. In half of the states, the head of this unit is appointed by and reports directly to the governor. In another dozen states the personnel director is appointed by a department head who is, in turn, a gubernatorial appointee (NASPE 1996). Many states have also increased the number of higher-level positions subject to gubernatorial appointment. The justification for doing so is that officials in these positions are significantly involved in shaping policies as well as administering them. This argument has merit because in some states, such as Wisconsin and Michigan, all but a handful of high-level positions in state agencies are covered by civil service. But others worry that this change threatens excessive politicization and is but a veiled attempt to reintro-duce patronage practices into state administration (Freedman 1994).

Although governors are more powerful than ever in formal terms, vigorous gu-bernatorial direction of a state's bureaucracy remains the exception. Governors sometimes fail to exploit their formal resources. Governors must perform other tasks in addition to functioning as chief bureaucrat. These other obligations, such as providing policy leadership for the legislature, may be both more pressing and more interesting. The complexity of state administrative structure also discourages involvement. Moreover, many governors believe that an excessively intrusive man-agement style is ineffective. As former New Jersey governor Thomas Kean has ob-served,

> I am wary of governors who try to get too involved in the day-to-day details of man-aging a bureaucracy. We all remember the awful anecdote about President Carter wanting to know who was playing on the White House tennis courts. This is a real danger (quoted in Cox 1991, 59).

Given these realities, involvement with state bureaucracies is very much a matter of governors picking their spots. What prompts gubernatorial interaction with a state agency? Sometimes governors focus on agencies with the biggest budgets or those administering programs central to the goals of their administrations (Hebert, Brudney, et al. 1983). Governors may intervene only if a "crisis" arises in the ad-ministration of a particular program that has the potential for serious political fall-out (Weinberg 1977). Nearly two-thirds of the managers in my ten-state study felt this was true of gubernatorial involvement in their state. Although waiting for crises to occur may seem a risky management strategy, even governors with strong formal powers must often embrace such a strategy to function effectively as chief bureaucrat.

The Legislature as Bureaucratic Overseer

Although the role of most governors in state administration has grown, state legislative influence rivals that of the governor. Especially when different parties control the governorship and the legislature, battles between the two actors can be highly stressful for agencies (Gormley 1996a).

Legislatures can tap an impressive array of resources in seeking to influence bu-reaucracies. These include approving agency budget requests, modifying agency programs or organization, investigating agency practices, and confirming at least some of the governor's appointments to top administrative posts. Not all state leg-islatures are well-prepared for the task of overseeing the bureaucracy, however. State legislatures with longer sessions, with lower rates of turnover because legisla-tors are better paid, and with more extensive staff support are better able to provide direction to their state's bureaucracy. As chapter 5 indicates, however, state legisla-tures with these characteristics are not numerous. Moreover, the adoption of leg-islative term limits in twenty states is likely to reduce legislative influence over administrative affairs. Effective oversight requires a combination of persistence and knowledge. It is hard to see how term limits contribute positively to this capability.

Legislatures have some newer tools for impressing their will on state agencies. Although legislatures delegate authority to administrative agencies to promulgate the technically complex, specific rules or regulations giving operational effect to general statutes, they also fear that agencies may ignore or distort legislative intent. Forty states mandate legislative review of proposed rules and regulations before they take effect (Rosenthal 1990). Especially controversial are provisions in approximately one-third of the states that permit the legislature as a whole, a single house, or, in a few states, a legislative committee to invalidate an administrative rule or regulation (Gormley 1996a). Administrative agencies dislike such arrangements. Only 34 percent of the managers in the ten-state study saw the legislative veto of agency rules as having positive effects for agency performance (Elling 1992, 90). Nor are governors fond of the process. Fortunately for governors, state courts have frequently invalidated legislative veto arrangements on the grounds that they violate the separation of powers enshrined in state constitutions. Hence, the legislative veto may be in decline as a vehicle of influence.

Legislative auditors, now found in nearly every state, are another emerging resource for legislative oversight. What has made these offices increasingly influential is a shift from narrowly oriented financial auditing to performance auditing. Performance auditing moves beyond concerns for financial rectitude to questions of how well agencies are implementing programs and how successful those programs are in solving problems. Although audits shine the harsh light of legislative and public attention on agencies or programs, almost two-thirds of the managers in my ten-state study felt such audits had positively affected the performance of their units.

In assessing state legislative influence in state administration it is important to understand that legislators are especially interested in the *specific* actions of *specific* agencies as they affect *specific* individuals, groups, or interests. This is why oversight of the bureaucracy that occurs as a byproduct of handling the complaints and problems of constituents—referred to as *casework*—is so attractive to them. Among a sample of Minnesota and Kentucky legislators, at least half claimed that addressing casework matters alerted them to more general administrative problems (Elling 1979). Administrators surveyed by Abney and Lauth (1986) said constituent complaints relayed by legislators improved service delivery. Unfortunately, casework can compromise administrative impartiality. One quarter of the Minnesota administrators and almost half of the Kentucky administrators I interviewed felt that "most of the time legislative requests on behalf of constituents amount to asking for special favors or exceptions" (Elling 1980, 336).

State Bureaucracies and Organized Interests

State bureaucracies do things that make a difference in citizens' lives. These citizens, whether organized or unorganized, have a stake in how those agencies operate. Interest groups—which may be well organized but not broadly representative—can exert undue influence on state administration. Especially in the case of agencies created to regulate segments of the economy, the result has sometimes been a "captured" agency—one that is highly solicitous of the interests of the targets of regulation but neglectful of the interests of the broader public that is supposed to benefit from regulation.

Agencies and interest groups interact because each has resources useful to the other. In the ten-state study, I found that agencies often contacted groups to acquire information on the effects of their programs, to secure input on proposed regulations, and to gain technical information needed for agency operations. Groups contacting agencies often sought information about agency programs or tried to shape the content of rules and regulations. Such contacts may improve agency performance and help citizens to access services to which they are entitled.

Interest groups may also hamper administrative performance, however, or—more precisely—they may want agencies to do things that are not good for the rest of us. Groups may encourage bias in rule application or distort agency priorities (Abney and Lauth 1986). Such problems are especially likely if few groups contend for influence. Bureaucracies that interact with a larger number of groups are less likely to be beholden to any single one and can play one against another. This is more likely today because, as discussed in chapter 4, the state interest group universe has grown more diverse. My ten-state study revealed that half of the agencies interacted with six or more groups, and these groups varied in their support for agency policies and actions. Hence excessive interest group influence on state administration may be less common today than in the past. Certainly, as Table 8-5 indicates, the state managers I surveyed in the 1980s did not consider organized groups to be extremely influential. Other research paints a similar picture (Abney and Lauth 1986; Brudney and Hebert 1987).

Interest groups may also be less powerful today because many states have expanded public representation in administrative decision-making processes, especially in the case of regulatory agencies. Public access has been facilitated by requiring hearings on environmental issues and mandating the appointment of public members to state occupational licensing boards. By the early 1990s, thirty-eight states also had *proxy advocacy* units that represented citizens in the deliberation of state agencies that determine the rates that electric and gas utilities may charge (Gormley 1996b).

State Bureaucracies and the Public Encounter: Clients, Customers, or What?

One yardstick for judging an agency's performance is how well it meets the needs of those individuals or groups that are why it exists. One of the purported virtues of the bureaucratic model is that similar cases are treated similarly. Once an individual has satisfied the criteria for receiving services, the ideal bureaucrat draws on his or her professional skills to provide services irrespective of that individual's race, age, gender, social status, or political connections. This optimistic view is challenged by those who argue that a bureaucracy's emphasis on reliability and consistency causes bureaucrats to exaggerate the importance of formal rules. "Going by the book" becomes an end in itself so that the bureaucrat never forgets a single rule binding her action and, as a result is unable to assist many of her clients. Even worse, the ideal of equal treatment may get perverted so that bureaucrats treat all clients in an equally nasty manner.

Denunciations of client-hostile bureaucracies must be taken with a grain of salt, however. Table 8-5 indicates that state managers see clients as influential. An agency's clientele exerted more impact than any other nonagency actor on the daily operations of these units. Studies of citizens' contacts with bureaucracies, some of which were summarized earlier in this chapter, suggest that most citizens are treated well and that the bureaucrats with whom they deal are helpful. Moreover, those citizens who have been unfairly treated by a state agency can pursue various avenues of redress. The roles played by legislative casework and interest group intervention have already been noted. State agency actions are also regularly challenged in the courts, although the costs of and possibilities for delay inherent in the judicial process limit the judiciary's value as an avenue of appeal for the average citizen. All states have open records or freedom-of-information laws designed to facilitate citizen access to materials on which state agencies base their actions. A few states have adopted variants of the Scandinavian institution of the ombudsman—an official who investigates citizens' complaints about problems with government agencies.

Both TQM and REGO argue that improving governmental performance requires that agencies adopt a "customer orientation." Adopting such an orientation is, however, complicated by the slippery meaning of the concept of "customer" in the public sector. The private sector notion of a customer as someone who values a product or service enough to pay a certain price for it is clearly too narrow. Albert Hyde (1995a) has distinguished among those served or affected by public agencies in terms of how much choice or influence they have. *Customers* are service recipients who have the most choice and influence over the service process. An example might be students at a state university, or residents who select between different state parks for camping. Those citizens who have legal or contractual ties with agencies are *clients*—recipients of welfare benefits might be an example. Those with the least amount of choice or recourse are *captives*. This latter category is similar to Barzelay's and Armajani's conception of *compliers*. Because of the unique nature of what governments do, many of those "served" by state agencies are compliers–captives. Governments require that certain individuals or organizations behave in certain ways. If they do not, then various penalties may be imposed on them. Citizens, when asked to pay state taxes, are compliers. So are inmates in state correctional facilities; as are business firms who are subject to consumer protection, worker health and safety, environmental protection, and antidiscrimination laws. Many agencies have both customers and compliers, and how the former fare is related to how the latter are treated. Such agencies can not make compliers completely happy without perverting the reason that they exist in the first place: to collect taxes; to isolate lawbreakers from the general population;

to protect the health and safety of workers; to enhance the quality of a state's physical environment; or protect certain groups of citizens from unlawful discrimination. Environmental groups complain that environmental protection agencies worry too much about the needs of compliers—the individuals or firms who may be polluting—and too little about the needs of the broader public that benefits from a cleaner environment. My point is not to take sides in this debate. The point is that ambiguity regarding the concept of "customer" in these settings is one reason why controversy exists.

Battle and Nayak (1994) recommended that customer satisfaction for public sector agencies be replaced by a broader stakeholder analysis. In addition to those who may be directly benefited or otherwise affected by what an agency is doing, stakeholders include elected officials, professional associations, contractors, and taxpayers, among others. Agencies may be less customer-friendly than they could be because stakeholders send mixed messages. For example, via budget cuts, the governor or the state legislature is asking agencies to provide "good service" but to do it with fewer personnel or other resources.

Unless an agency carefully analyzes the nature of its customer base, determining how well it is serving that base is an exercise in futility. Barzelay and Armajani (1992) argued that for "true customers" the appropriate standards of performance are the amount of choice in services and satisfaction with services received. For compliers, the appropriate indicators are efficiency, accountability, and simplification. A business firm subject to environmental regulation, for example, may resent such regulation, but if the process is not excessively intrusive, if opportunities exist for the firm to air grievances, and if the process is not inordinately complicated, then the environmental protection agency may have "satisfied" the needs of this type of customer.

Despite complications such as these, many state agencies are seeking to gauge their performance. By the early 1990s, 83 percent of the state agencies that were engaged in TQM efforts were seeking to ascertain customer needs and 60 percent were monitoring customer satisfaction (Berman 1994). As part of Minnesota's STEP (Strive toward Excellence in Performance) program to improve agency performance, managers sit in the service areas of their offices to talk with "customers" and ask employees who regularly deal with them what they are hearing and how service delivery can be improved.

Numerous examples of state efforts to improve service can be cited. Arkansas, Minnesota, and Wisconsin provide their employees with customer service training (Osborne and Gaebler 1993). In New York, the Office of Vocational and Educational Services for Individuals with Disabilities of the State Department of Education reduced the time required to determine an applicant's eligibility for services from eighteen to three months (Chi et al. 1997). Pennsylvania's Department of Environmental Protection provides an example of how to provide higher quality service to compliers. The department has established shorter deadlines for issuing environmental permits to individuals, businesses, and local governments and guarantees that an applicant's permit fee will be refunded if a permit is not issued on time (Behn 1997b).

Computers and information technology offer important opportunities for agencies to provide better service. Massachusetts has simplified the lives of a huge group of compliers—those who pay state income taxes—by permitting the filing of tax returns by telephone. Under this program, refunds to taxpayers are mailed within four days of electronic filing (Chi et al. 1997). In Iowa, Maryland, Minnesota, New Jersey, New Mexico, Texas, and Wyoming, ATM-type systems are used to distribute welfare payments and Food Stamps to needy families. Recipients like the convenience of this arrangement and state welfare administrators like it because it is cheaper than mailing checks or stamps, minimizes lost or stolen checks, and makes fraudulent use of food stamps more difficult (Milward and Snyder 1996).

State bureaucracies must always be mindful of the needs of their customers. Sometimes a few easy or inexpensive changes may improve service quality. But administrators and their political sovereigns also need to think carefully about who exactly are the customers of various agencies. It must also be recognized that service improvements may occasionally demand something as old-fashioned as hiring more staff.

STATE BUREAUCRACIES AND ADMINISTRATION IN A CHALLENGING ERA: SOME CONCLUSIONS

Concerns about state government performance quickly become concerns about state bureaucracies and administration. This is why efforts to reinvent government and to install systems of total quality management are so attractive. Although I think these strategies are worth pursuing, this should be done cautiously and pragmatically. Proponents of TQM and REGO sometimes seem oblivious to the inappropriateness of their prescriptions in a public setting. The limits of a simplistic customer focus noted earlier is one example of this problem. Another is the almost knee-jerk hostility of proponents of REGO to traditional bureaucracies with their emphasis on hierarchy. Zajac and Al-Kazemi argued that, in its treatment of authority in public organizations, REGO has "misapprehended the political, legal, and constitutional context of public sector management reform. Reinventing government must recall that *public* sector hierarchies are as much accountability devices as management tools" (1997, 379, emphasis added). A final reason for caution is that evidence of the benefits of TQM and REGO is less compelling than often claimed. Because success has many parents and failure is an orphan (so goes the old chestnut), the successes of REGO and TQM are more likely to be reported than are the failures. Systematic assessment remains rare. The problems with contracting discussed in this chapter are an example of the mixed record to date.

State administrative employees continually seek and find new ways to do their jobs better to benefit both those who receive services and those who pay for those services with their tax dollars. If quality improvement and reinvention stimulate these efforts in important ways, then they will have made a difference for the better.

It is easy to claim too much for REGO and TQM. Yet it would be a mistake to dismiss either one as mere fads that are enthusiastically—but fleetingly—embraced by elected officials and others. My sense is that—as has been true of other past efforts to enhance state administrative performance—both TQM and REGO will have a lasting, positive legacy but that legacy will be more modest than advocates expect.

Concerns about the accountability of state bureaucracies may well increase in the twenty-first century. State administrators are important policy shapers who have breached any wall that may once have limited their involvement in the broader policy-making process. Still, the increasing complexity of the administrative influence matrix, combined with the efforts of governors, legislatures, the courts, and the public to exert greater influence over the affairs of state bureaucracies, suggest that runaway agencies are rare.

Policy making is improved by the involvement of bureaucrats and bureaucracies in it. We rightfully prefer that the governor and the legislature make major policy decisions. Still, elected officials are fallible. They find it hard to look beyond the next election. With greater security of tenure, and the benefit of professional expertise, administrators can broaden the horizons of elected officials and point out deficiencies in proposed policies that those officials may wish to ignore.

That state agencies operate on a short leash may be taken as good news. But the intervention of nonadministrative actors in administrative affairs raises the question of how much efficiency and effectiveness may have to be sacrificed in return for increased accountability or responsiveness. It is difficult to strike the proper balance between leaving an administrative agency alone to do its thing, on the one hand, and looking over its shoulder or putting handcuffs on its wrists, on the other.

Most of the time state programs are administered in a reasonably efficient and effective manner. Unfortunately, the greater scope of state administrative responsibilities means that even if bureaucracies perform better than in the past, the aggregate costs of inefficiency or ineffectiveness remain great. The incompatibility of the standards to which we hold state bureaucracies means their performance can never be good enough. Instead, changes will occur in the trade-offs that elected officials and citizens will accept. Sometimes improving efficiency and effectiveness will be emphasized. But often we will value accountability or responsiveness more highly.

REFERENCES

Abney, Glenn, and Thomas Lauth. 1986. *The Politics of State and City Administration.* Albany: State University of New York Press.

Barzelay, Michael, and Babak Armajani. 1992. *Breaking through Bureaucracy: A Vision for Managing Government.* Berkeley: University of California Press.

Battle, Byron, and P. Ranganath Nayak. 1994. "Going Public." *Spectrum: The Journal of State Government* 67(2):16–22.

Behn, Robert. 1997a. "Management." *Governing* (October):40–41.

———.1997b. "The Money-Back Guarantee." *Governing* (September):74.

Berman, Evan. 1994. "Implementing TQM in State Governments: A Survey of Recent Progress." *State and Local Government Review* 26:46–53.

Bowman, James, and Christopher Zigmond. 1996. "Sexual Harassment Policies in State Government: Peering into the Fishbowl of Public Employment." *Spectrum* 69 (Summer):24–36.

Brudney, Jeffrey, and F. Ted Hebert. 1987. "State Agencies and Their Environments: Examining the Influence of Important External Actors." *Journal of Politics* 49:186–206.

Bullard, Angela, and Deil Wright. 1993. "Circumventing the Glass Ceiling: Women Executives in American State Governments." *Public Administration Review* 53:189–202.

Center for Women in Government. 1997. *Appointed Policymakers in State Government: The Regional Profile, 1997.* Albany: State University of New York at Albany.

Chi, Keon, and Cindy Jasper. 1998. *Private Practices: A Review of Privatization in State Government (Executive Summary).* Lexington, Ky.: Council of State Governments.

Chi, Keon, Drew Leathersby, Cindy Jasper, and Robert Eger. 1997. *Managing for Success: A Profile of State Government for the 21st Century.* Lexington, Ky.: Council of State Governments.

Conant, James. 1992. "Executive Branch Reorganization in the States, 1965–1991." In *The Book of the States, 1992–93.* Lexington, Ky.: Council of State Governments.

Cooper, Phillip. 1994. "Reinvention and Employee Rights: The Role of the Courts." In *New Paradigms for Government: Issues for the Changing Public Service,* edited by Patricia Ingraham, Barbara Romzek, and Associates. San Francisco: Jossey-Bass.

Council of State Governments. 1986. *The Book of the States: 1986–87.* Lexington, Ky.: Council of State Governments.

Cox, Raymond. 1991. "The Management Role of the Governor." In *Gubernatorial Leadership and State Policy,* edited by Eric Herzik and Brent Brown. Westport, Conn.: Greenwood.

Elling, Richard. 1979. "The Utility of Legislative Casework as Means of Oversight." *Legislative Studies Quarterly* 4:353–379.

———.1980. "State Legislative Casework and State Administrative Performance." *Administration and Society* 12:327–356.

———.1992. *Public Management in the States: A Comparative Study of Administrative Performance and Politics.* Westport, Conn.: Praeger.

———.1997. "Slip-Slidin' Away? Patterns of Employee Turnover in American State Bureaucracies." A paper presented at the Ninety-third annual meeting of the American Political Science Association, Washington, D.C., August 28–31.

Elling, Richard, and Peter Kobrak. 1995. "The Bureaucracy: An Ambiguous Political Legacy." In *Michigan Politics and Government: Facing Change in a Complex State,* edited by William Browne and Kenneth Verburg. Lincoln: University of Nebraska Press.

Freedman, Anne. 1994. *Patronage: An American Tradition.* Chicago: Nelson-Hall.

Gold, Steven, and Sarah Ritchie. 1993. "Compensation of State and Local Employees: Sorting Out the Issues." In *Revitalizing State and Local Public Service,* edited by Frank Thompson. San Francisco: Jossey Bass.

Goodsell, Charles. 1985. *The Case for Bureaucracy: A Public Administration Polemic.* 2d ed. Chatham, NJ: Chatham House.

———.1994. *The Case for Bureaucracy: A Public Administration Polemic.* 3d ed. Chatham, N.J.: Chatham House.

Gormley, William. 1996a. "Accountability Battles in State Administration." In *The State of the States,* 3d ed., edited by Carl Van Horn. Washington, D.C.: CQ Press.

———.1996b. "Counterbureaucracies in Theory and Practice." *Administration and Society* 28:275–297.

———.1996c. "Regulatory Privatization: A Case Study." *Journal of Public Administration Research and Theory* 50:243–260.

Grady, D., and K. S. Lane. 1995. "State Employees Ride Roller Coaster of Wages." *State Trends Bulletin* 1 (February/March):4.

Hays, Steven, and Richard Kearney. 1992. "State Personnel Directors and the Dilemmas of Workforce 2000: A Survey." *Public Administration Review* 52:30–38.

Hebert, F. Ted, Jeffrey Brudney, and Deil Wright. 1983. "Gubernatorial Influence and State Bureaucracy." *American Politics Quarterly* 11:243–264.

Hebert, F. Ted, Deil Wright, and Jeffrey Brudney. 1992. "Challenges to State Governments: Policy and Administrative Leadership in the 1990s." *Public Productivity and Management Review* 16:1–21.

Hyde, Albert. 1995a. "Improving Customer Service Quality: Changing Concepts, Goals and Methods, An Afterword." *The Public Manager* (Fall):25–27.

———.1995b. "Total Quality Management: A Personnel Perspective." In *Public Personnel Administration: Problems and Prospects,* 3d ed., edited by Steven W. Hays and Richard C. Kearney. Englewood Cliffs, N.J.: Prentice-Hall.

Jenks, Stephen, and Deil Wright. 1993. "An Agency-Level Approach to Change in the Administrative Functions of American State Governments." *State and Local Government Review* 25:78–86.

Kearney, Richard. 1992. *Labor Relations in the Public Sector.* 2d ed. New York: Marcel Dekker.

Kearney, Richard, and Steven Hays. 1994. "Labor–Management Relations and Participative Decision Making: Toward a New Paradigm." *Public Administration Review* 54:44–51.

Kellough, J. Edward, Sally Selden, and Jerome S. Legge, Jr. 1997. "Affirmative Action under Fire: The Current Controversy and the Potential for State Policy Retrenchment." A paper presented at the Ninety-third annual meeting of the American Political Science Association, Washington, D.C., August 28–31.

Kelly, Rita, and Phoebe Stambaugh. 1992. "Sexual Harassment in the States." In *Women and Men of the States: Public Administrators at the State Level,* edited by Mary Guy. Armonk, N.Y.: M. E. Sharpe.

Lavigna, Robert. 1996. "Innovation in Recruiting and Hiring: Attracting the Best and Brightest to Wisconsin State Government." *Public Personnel Management* 25:423–437.

Loney, Timothy. 1989. "Public Sector Labor Relations Research: The First Generation." *Public Personnel Management* 18:162–175.

Michigan Department of Civil Service. 1987. *Public Perceptions of State Employment in Michigan.* Lansing: Michigan Department of Civil Service.

Milward, Brinton, and Louise Snyder. 1996. "Electronic Government: Linking Citizens to Public Organizations through Technology." *Journal of Public Administration Research and Theory* 6:261–275.

Morgan, Douglas, Kelly Bacon, Ron Bunch, Charles Cameron, and Robert Deis. 1996. "What Middle Managers Do in Local Government: Stewardship of the Public Trust and the Limits of Reinventing Government." *Public Administration Review* 56:359–366.

National Association of State Personnel Executives (NASPE). 1996. *State Personnel Office: Roles and Functions.* 3d ed. Lexington, Ky.: Council of Governments.

National Commission on the State and Local Public Service. 1993. *Hard Truths/Tough Choices: An Agenda for State and Local Reform.* Albany, N.Y.: Nelson A. Rockefeller Institute of Government.

O'Leary, Rosemary. 1994. "The Expanding Partnership between Personnel Management and the Courts. In *New Paradigms for Government: Issues for the Changing Public Service,* edited by Patricia Ingraham, Barbara Romzek, and Associates. San Francisco: Jossey-Bass.

Olshfski, Dorothy, and Raphael Caprio. 1996. "Comparing Personal and Professional Characteristics of Men and Women State Executives: 1990 and 1993 Results." *Review of Public Personnel Administration* 16:31–39.

Osborne, David, and Ted Gaebler. 1993. *Reinventing Government: How the Entrepreneurial Spirit Is Transforming the Public Sector.* New York: Penguin Books.

Osborne, David, and Peter Plastrik. 1997. *Banishing Bureaucracy: The Five Strategies for Reinventing Government.* Reading, Mass.: Addison-Wesley.

Riccucci, Norma and Judith Saidel. 1997. "The Representativeness of State-Level Bureaucratic Leaders: A Missing Piece of the Representative Bureaucracy Puzzle." *Public Administration Review.* 57:423–430.

Rosenthal, Alan. 1990. *Governors and Legislatures: Contending Powers.* Washington, D.C.: CQ Press.

Rourke, Francis. 1991. "American Bureaucracy in a Changing Political Setting." *Journal of Public Administration Research and Theory* 1:111–129.

Smith, Steven, and Judith Smyth. 1996. "Contracting for Services in a Decentralized System." *Journal of Public Administration Research and Theory* 6:277–296.

Stevens, Alan. 1992. "State Government Employment in 1990." In *The Book of the States, 1992–93.* Lexington, Ky.: Council of State Governments.

Tanner, Joe. 1996. "How Can We Fix the Merit System: Counterpoint." *State Government News* (June–July):6–7.

United States Bureau of the Census. 1996. *Public Employment in 1995.* Available at http://www.census.gov/govs/www/apes95.html.

Walters, Jonathan. 1994. "The Fine Art of Firing the Incompetent." *Governing* (June):35–39.

———.1996. "Flattening the Bureaucracy." *Governing* (June):20–24.

Weinberg, Martha. 1977. *Managing the State.* Cambridge: MIT Press.

Wright, Deil, JaeWon Yoo, and Jennifer Cohen. 1991. "The Evolving Profile of State Administrators." *Spectrum: The Journal of State Government* 64(1):30–38.

Zajac, Gary, and Ali Al-Kazemi. 1997. "Reinventing Government and Redefining Leadership." *Public Productivity and Management Review* 20:372–383.

SUGGESTED READINGS

Chi, Keon, Drew Leathersby, Cindy Jasper, and Robert Eger. *Managing for Success: A Profile of State Government for the 21st Century.* Lexington, Ky.: Council of State Governments. 1997. A wide-ranging review of state efforts to enhance government performance and service delivery via TQM and other initiatives.

Elling, Richard. *Public Management in the States.* Westport, Conn: Praeger, 1992. Drawing on a survey of administrators in ten states, this study explores the problems confronting state bureaucracies, how managers have sought to address those problems, and how a wide range of actors affect the state administrative process.

Gormley, William. "Accountability Battles in State Administration." In *The State of the States,* 3d ed., edited by Carl Van Horn. Washington, D.C.: CQ Press, 1996. Assessment of efforts to limit the discretion of state bureaucracies and the battles among political sovereigns for influence over them.

Thompson, Frank, ed. *Revitalizing State and Local Public Service.* San Francisco: Jossey-Bass, 1993. Noted experts explore challenges to effective management in states and localities and discuss how to meet those challenges. The book is a companion to the first report of the National Commission on the State and Local Public Service, *Hard Truths, Tough Choices,* which is reprinted in an appendix to that volume.

CHAPTER 9

The Politics of Taxing and Spending

RICHARD F. WINTERS

By any measure of public spending, the growth of American governments in the twentieth century is phenomenal. Government outlays have grown sixtyfold since the beginning of the century. Per capita spending has increased by a factor of twenty, and in relation to the size of the economy as a whole—probably the best overall measure of relative growth—federal, state, and local government spent 38 percent of the 1996 gross domestic product, five times the comparable figure in 1902.

Growth in government spending has meant increased taxes, and more taxes have led to heightened citizen concern and debate over the size and role of government. By the 1994 elections, four out of every five Americans with an opinion believed that American government "wastes a lot of tax money" and that "government was run for the benefit of a few big interests" (Stanley and Niemi 1998, Fig. 3-7).

If the public agrees on the wasteful size of American governments and that few benefit from such waste, how did we get into this situation? The argument in this chapter is that voters implicitly vote for larger budgets when they elect executives and representatives who promise goods and services. But factors other than voter preferences also contribute to growth in government, so the question still arises: If voters believe governments tax too much and spend wastefully, how can they exert control over taxing and spending policies that do not reflect public opinion? In fact, voters in the American states have taken many recent steps to control the growth of their govern-

Some of the material in this chapter comes from a series of interviews with New Hampshire and Vermont legislators and officials first begun in 1973.

ments, and these steps are often expressed in budgeting rules and practices that restrain government growth.

A CLOSER LOOK AT GROWTH OF GOVERNMENT

In 1902 federal, state, and local governments together spent about $374 per person. They now spend about $7,000 per person, an increase of almost 1,800 percent. Population, of course, grew during the past ninety years, but government grew five times faster during the same period. From another and more absolute perspective, at the beginning of the century barely 7 percent of all goods and services were provided by governments; that figure is now almost 40 percent. The most recent growth has been at the state and local levels. There are many explanations for why governments grow, some of them simple and straightforward.

Population Growth

Many services that state governments offer their populations—colleges and universities, health and hospital beds, welfare payments, and so forth—grow as the populations of college students, the sick, and the needy grow. But the figures on per capita spending data show that the provision of public goods and services grew much faster than population, so there must be other factors at work.

Increasing Income and Changing Preferences of Voters

Voters' appetites for public goods and services expand as their personal incomes and wealth grow. College and university education is an excellent example. Middle-class parents want their children to go to college. They argue that the benefits of a well-educated and better-skilled population accrue not only to the individual, but also to society as a whole, so colleges and universities ought to be at least partially supported from tax revenues. Even on issues such as welfare, it is now generally accepted that states with wealthier populations have been more generous with welfare benefits for their poor citizens because wealthier citizens prefer that their state be helpful to the poor (Plotnick and Winters 1985).

There is a second path from increasing income to growing governments: States with rapidly growing economies, and therefore rising personal incomes, are those with diversifying and industrializing economies. With economic development there is an "expanded need for law and order, regulation, etc., arising from the increased complexity of industrialized society" (Berry and Lowery 1987; Larkey, Stolp, and Winer 1981, 176).

Inflation

Several analysts argue that the costs of delivering government goods and services rise faster than the simple rate of inflation (Baumol 1967). Government must compete with the private sector for administrative personnel; thus, government wages and salaries for secretaries, laborers, and administrators must approximate the salaries and wages paid in private business. But, the productivity of public employees is harder to gauge because governments usually do not produce goods and services in measurable unit quantities with accompanying information about prices (Olson 1973). This makes productivity comparisons among government agencies difficult, and cost savings from heightened efficiency hard to achieve. By this logic, the cost of delivering even the same amount of government goods and services will rise inexorably, even after "controlling" for changes in inflation.

Behavior of Elected Leaders

The choices that politicians make and the way their choices are presented to voters shape the growth of government. Governors campaign on the basis of promises of new or expanded programs that benefit segments of the state populations. Legislators have local constituencies that seek help, support, and protection. Hence, political leaders couch campaign alternatives in ways that lead voters to choose the path of greater government spending (Riker 1986; Winters 1990). Political leaders face a powerful incentive to extol, if not exaggerate, the benefits of government spending while depreciating, delaying, or evading the tax costs of the benefits. Yet the costs cannot be avoided forever; taxes, fees, or charges must be levied sometime to pay the costs of government.

There is a further point to be made. State governments have grown as a result of decisions made by state legislators and signed into law by governors. When these elected officials seek reelection, voters usually return them to office. Contrary to what one might expect, voters reelect politicians who are "taxers and spenders" (Kone and Winters 1993). Since 1945, twelve states have instituted new income tax programs, and twenty states have instituted new general sales taxes. The fundamental lesson of budgetary politics is clear—taxing more and spending more does not necessarily lead to electoral defeat.

The Varying Effects of the Aggregate Economy: Booms Versus Busts

National economic performance is one of the most important factors shaping states' taxing and spending. When the economy falls into recession, as it did in the early 1980s and then again in the early 1990s, revenues fall and hard decisions about tax increases or expenditure cuts must be made (Lemov 1992, 22–26). What makes this decision-making particularly complex is that as the economy falters the demand for government help increases. Similarly, when the economy booms, as it has in the period from late 1992 to mid-1998, state treasuries benefit from revenue windfalls (Lemov 1997, 44–47). Revenue booms permit government growth; new programs can be started or old ones enlarged.

Some states have tax policies that magnify or dampen the boom–bust relationship. Oregon, Idaho, Montana, and Kentucky have revenue systems that respond strongly and positively to changes in the economy. In Oregon's case, for every percentage point increase in statewide personal income, state revenue increases by a little more than 1.04 percent. For these states, their treasuries grow slightly faster than do their states' economies. Even the lowest ranked states—Nevada and Washington—although reacting in a more tempered fashion (an increase of 1 percent in statewide personal income yields only .87 percent growth in state revenues [State Policy Research 1998, 17]) still have revenues that grow nearly apace with personal income. According to *State Policy Reports,* thirteen of the fifty states have elasticity coefficients equaling 1 or higher, which means that revenues in these states grow at least as fast as personal income. The typical state has a coefficient of .96, which implies that the average state budget grows larger at a rate only slightly less than growth in personal income. Thus, part of the explanation of government growth is that revenue growth is very closely built into the revenue system as it responds closely to simple growth in the economy.

This trait of varying revenue system elasticity—the responsiveness of a state's revenue system to changes in income—has important consequences. If Oregon does not cut taxes in times of economic growth, its budget will grow at a faster, compounded rate compared with the neighboring state of Washington with its smaller elasticity of revenue. As a result, the pressures to spend in Oregon will likely be greater compared with Washington. Oregon legislators, administrators, and beneficiaries of government exist in a more expenditure-favorable political environment; thus we would expect that they would behave in a more active, program-favoring fashion. Each constituency that benefits from the programs will endeavor to gain its share of rapidly growing revenue. Program support from beneficiaries will be reinforced, if not stimulated, by program administrators and sympathetic legislators (Winters 1980).

State political leaders have little control over the timing of economic booms or recessions, in part because they are subject to economic decisions made in Washington and elsewhere. Yet they must come to grips with the effects of recessions, namely diminishing revenue from sales taxes and from personal and corporate income taxes and increased demand for state services from the jobless or disadvantaged. Many states have "rainy day funds," monies that are set aside with special statutory limits. In a boom year such as 1997, the typical state socked away about 3 percent of the total amount that it historically spent as a hedge against bust periods (State Policy Research 1997, 14). Another response is to diversify revenue sources to reduce the effects of economic fluctuations. A third strategy is to be risk-averse—that is, legislators and governors resist the pleas of special interests for benefits because they may not always be able to finance those benefits, a lesson that state leaders have learned the hard way.

The 1990–1991 economic recession illustrates the variable effect of recessions across the states. For the country as a whole, the year-long recession saw a loss of about 1 percent in employment. But states in the West South Central region, such as Oklahoma and Arkansas, saw on average a 1 percent gain in employment, whereas the New England states averaged a 4.6 percent loss of employment. The recession experience hit California hardest of all, because it coincided with a series of earthquakes, mud slides, and rainstorms that damaged buildings, highways, and public facilities. This resulted in both a loss of revenue from diminished economic activity and a need for increased public outlays to rebuild the state's infrastructure.

California typically adds hundreds of thousands of jobs per year to its economic rolls, but the depression cost the state more than 700,000 jobs. Exacerbating these difficulties was the post–Cold War decline in defense spending and growth in population caused by illegal immigrants from Mexico and other Central American countries, all adding to the demand for public services (Barone 1994). The effects of the decline in defense spending were loss of jobs, personal income, taxes, and government grants. The cumulative effect of the immigration was to create great uncertainty among political leaders about how much revenue was needed or might be expected to satisfy increasingly difficult-to-predict public demands for government services. An increase in political conflict was the result. In the summer of 1991, California Governor Pete Wilson faced a shortfall of $14.3 billion, which was met by cutting $7 billion in current spending and increasing taxes by $7 billion. The budget was not passed until seventeen days after the beginning of the fiscal year; in the following year the budget was not passed until two months after the start of the new budget cycle (Purdom 1998b).

Leaders do not always behave in a cautious fashion; the economic boom of the mid-1990s illustrates different political reactions to the opposing conditions—when economic performance fills state treasuries. In 1998 California faced its best economy, jobs, and government revenue picture of the decade. California government revenue was so far up, running more than $1 billion ahead of forecasts, that Governor Wilson declared his state the "powerhouse of the Pacific" (Purdom 1998a). In spite of the good times, California again had no budget at the start of the 1998 fiscal year. The issue that deadlocked Republicans and Democrats was how to deal with a $4.4 billion surplus. The debate was rancorous and mirrored party and institutional differences. Republicans, including the governor, wanted to cut a highly visible, politically unpopular tax on the value of personal automobiles. Legislative Democrats, on the other hand, wanted to cut a fraction of a cent off the sales tax. The governor and his Republican colleagues wanted large permanent tax cuts, whereas legislators, especially Democratic legislators, wanted smaller absolute decreases in the size of California's revenues and more increases in spending on state government programs of direct benefit to their constituents, in this case spending on education (Purdom 1998b).

The net result of these causal factors is that over time substantial interstate variability in taxing and spending is created. Some states are consistently thrifty, others consistently generous, and some vary over time. How can we best explain this short-term variability? Is it that voter preferences differ—that is, some states' electorates are more willing to be taxed than other states' electorates—or that their preferences may change over time? Do some states have leaders who are more persuasive? Or is it that some states have put into place rules and practices that constrain and dampen spending and taxing?

VARIABILITY AND CHANGE IN STATES' TAXES

Levels of per capita taxation among the states at four different points in time are displayed in Table 9-1. Taxation by all of the states increased during this period. Even the least-taxed state increased its levies threefold between 1950 and 1970 and more than fivefold between 1970 and 1997. The lowest taxing state, New Hampshire, had the third lowest tax burden in 1950 and the lowest in 1970, 1990, and 1997 (for an explanation, see Winters 1980). Note, conversely, that some states have consistently high taxes. By 1950 Maryland, Massachusetts, Michigan, and Minnesota had settled into positions of well above average taxation levels and remain to this day among the most heavily taxed states.

Other states demonstrate substantial changes in their relative tax levels, and these may be the most interesting of all. Louisiana fell from the most heavily taxed state in the 1950s to the eleventh in burden by 1990. In part this is an artifact of tax policies in the 1950s, which relied on the oil and gas severance tax—a tax on natural resources as they are extracted—the largest part of which falls on consumers of oil and gas in other states. This is a classic case of a state exporting its tax burden, which many states do in one way or another. Frequently encountered examples are hotel and meal taxes (R. Fisher 1988, 20).

Other states that lightened their tax load in recent decades include Colorado, South Dakota, and Utah. States that experienced sharp increases in taxes between 1950 and 1990 include New Jersey, which went from the least taxed (first in rank) to thirty-seventh—followed by Connecticut, Massachusetts, Kentucky, and Maine. All of these states experienced at least one new major source of taxation during this period—new income taxes in Maine (1969), New Jersey (1976), and Connecticut (1991), and new sales taxes in Massachusetts (1966) and Kentucky (1960).

Some states bounced back and forth over the forty-year time span. Vermont started off in the middle of the pack in 1950 and then rocketed to forty-seventh in rank, becoming the fourth most heavily taxed state by 1970. Since then, it has settled into the middle. The rise and fall of its taxes parallel changes in its income and the institution of the sales tax in 1971. Since then, the tax code has remained fairly stable. Vermont is a moderate state ideologically and a relatively Republican state by conventional public opinion standards (see Erikson, Wright, and McIver 1993, Figs. 2.1 and 2.2). Neither the prevailing party attachments nor the moderate ideological stance of its population explain the radical changes in its tax structure. As we note later, the behavior of political leaders does explain taxing and spending choices.

AN ANALYSIS OF CAUSES OF CHANGING TAXES AND SPENDING

Three corollary questions arise when one asks why states have the taxing and spending policies that they do. First, what accounts for the origin of the policy? Second, once a tax policy is in place, what forces maintain it? Third, how is tax

Table 9-1 Per Capita Burden of Taxation in the American States, Selected Years

State	1950 taxes	1950 rank	1970 taxes	1970 rank	1990 taxes	1990 rank	1997 taxes	1997 rank
Alabama	36.84	2	191.09	11	945.29	7	1,269.78	5
Alaska	—	—	290.20	44	2,811.44	50	2,658.64	50
Arizona	67.00	39	273.04	41	1,194.13	31	1,500.29	19
Arkansas	46.10	14	183.72	8	961.80	9	1,496.86	18
California	78.48	44	278.91	42	1,459.98	42	1,911.08	40
Colorado	69.08	40	217.13	23	931.71	6	1,358.80	7
Connecticut	51.99	22	247.26	35	1,602.62	47	2,491.07	48
Delaware	81.57	46	362.31	50	1,695.59	48	2,381.47	46
Florida	63.82	35	213.99	22	1,027.17	14	1,438.52	12
Georgia	37.49	4	206.84	17	1,092.62	20	1,455.72	14
Hawaii	—	—	200.37	16	2,106.78	49	2,601.47	49
Idaho	52.72	23	220.49	26	1,131.11	26	1,620.25	28
Illinois	43.86	11	259.87	37	1,127.72	24	1,558.89	25
Indiana	51.26	21	194.91	13	1,100.55	21	1,551.99	24
Iowa	56.80	28	224.00	28	1,193.15	30	1,643.20	31
Kansas	62.00	32	192.74	12	1,077.26	19	1,629.95	30
Kentucky	37.69	5	219.84	25	1,156.13	27	1,744.88	36
Louisiana	91.45	48	231.77	29	968.42	11	1,297.39	6
Maine	46.10	15	209.29	20	1,271.14	35	1,626.00	29
Maryland	56.45	27	279.75	43	1,349.99	41	1,689.13	34
Massachusetts	49.54	20	246.66	34	1,557.26	44	2,174.80	45
Michigan	62.07	33	267.06	38	1,220.34	32	2,079.58	44
Minnesota	64.26	36	271.67	40	1,558.65	45	2,395.06	47
Mississippi	41.94	9	218.81	24	931.08	5	1,470.72	17
Missouri	41.79	8	176.91	5	965.23	10	1,446.87	13
Montana	52.99	24	185.62	9	1,073.36	18	1,432.57	11
Nebraska	41.52	7	177.28	6	958.53	8	1,537.82	23
Nevada	69.76	41	310.68	48	1,317.39	36	1,809.28	39
New Hampshire	37.18	3	130.89	1	536.67	1	779.92	1
New Jersey	30.25	1	187.77	10	1,349.76	40	1,789.99	37
New Mexico	79.30	45	270.49	39	1,329.34	37	1,793.16	38
New York	59.88	30	337.84	49	1,590.54	46	1,922.29	41
North Carolina	54.39	25	236.59	31	1,186.49	29	1,701.46	35
North Dakota	65.68	38	195.89	14	1,059.97	16	1,659.92	32
Ohio	47.59	17	161.19	2	1,054.32	15	1,467.96	16
Oklahoma	75.17	43	198.08	15	1,105.31	22	1,525.66	21
Oregon	69.76	42	208.87	19	980.15	12	1,525.22	20
Pennsylvania	42.29	10	236.57	30	1,112.61	23	1,612.10	27
Rhode Island	47.81	18	245.36	33	1,229.05	33	1,665.70	33
South Carolina	44.37	12	211.55	21	1,128.40	25	1,431.23	10
South Dakota	60.10	31	168.72	3	718.52	2	1,041.32	2
Tennessee	46.29	16	176.27	4	870.38	4	1,232.56	4
Texas	41.34	6	178.82	7	866.36	3	1,184.46	3
Utah	65.00	37	240.30	32	1,026.20	13	1,462.21	15
Vermont	55.35	26	309.33	47	1,183.00	28	1,526.59	22
Virginia	44.68	13	207.14	18	1,066.77	17	1,429.70	9
Washington	87.86	47	307.52	46	1,525.29	43	1,996.84	43
West Virginia	48.72	19	220.50	27	1,243.25	34	1,600.19	26
Wisconsin	58.26	29	304.42	45	1,340.57	38	1,970.36	42
Wyoming	63.77	34	256.76	36	1,349.39	39	1,379.90	8

SOURCE: 1950, 1970, and 1990 figures are from Tax Foundation 1992, table E21; 1997 figures are from state government tax collections, fiscal year 1996–1997, from the Census Bureau homepage at http://www.census.gov/ftp/pub/govs/www/sttax97.html.

NOTE: Figures are in current dollars; rankings are from the least to the most taxed.

policy altered or changed? In responding to the causal questions of origins, maintenance, and change, three levels of analysis are important: within-state causal factors, horizontal causal factors, and vertical causal factors.

Within-State Causal Factors

Most of us carry around in our minds the notion that politics in various states are largely determined by particular, idiosyncratic determinants that set states apart from one another. What accounts for Louisiana's apparent willingness to tax (especially other states' citizens), New Hampshire's thrift, and South Dakota's reluctance to tax is determined by political forces operating within the state. States, by this line of reasoning, are *sui generis,* one of a kind, and the peculiarities of each state's politics determine the adoption of certain tax policies. Each of us acts as both a citizen of the United States and of our own state, and we are aware of and sensitive to how our state differs from others within the Union.

Horizontal Causal Factors

All states exist within a horizontal set of across-state relations that affect the choices they make. Adoption of a policy by one state may make adoption of that policy by a nearby state easier or more difficult. Some states may be consistent leaders in sales taxation, for example, usually setting rates at a high level, yet not so high as to lose customers to adjacent states. Other states then set their rates at some fraction of the leading state's tax. The adoption of or increase in a general sales tax may ease or make more difficult a change in another state's tax policy. It is easier if a state is bordered by other states with sales taxes at least as high as the prospective new tax rate. Similarly the absence of a sales tax in an adjoining state may constrain a state's political choices in increasing its tax rate.

Vertical Causal Factor

Finally, states exist within a vertical arrangement of relations with the federal government. As discussed in Chapter 2, the federal government makes spending on some kinds of activities more attractive by altering the rate of matching funds. One dollar of state highway funds is often matched by $9 of federal funds, whereas in welfare $1 of state money will generate only $1 of federal aid for many states. When faced with a menu of federal matching rates, state officials must consider the flow of federal matching funds and the state appropriations that must be financed from state taxes.

Interactions among factors at the differing levels of analysis probably account for the largest fraction of tax changes (Winters 1990). Changing taxes is typically a two-step process. Leaders initiate costly new programs within a state, calculating that new spending will gain them votes and will be financed in the short-term by expected ordinary gains in revenue or through minor tax and revenue changes. As the full costs of new programs become apparent over time, it becomes obvious that

Table 9-2 Major Revenue Sources by Level of Government (in percentages)

Type of revenue	Federal	State	Local
Sales and gross receipts taxes	0	23	8
Federal intergovernmental revenue	0	22	3
Social insurance and other insurance	38	16	4
Individual income tax	44	15	2
Charges, fees, and miscellaneous	0	15	30
Corporation income taxes	9	3	0
Excise taxes	4	0	0
Customs duties	2	0	0
Property	0	1	39
Other	3	6	15

SOURCE: Calculated from data in U.S. Bureau of the Census 1993, tables 510 and 480.

other programs cannot be trimmed nor can minor revenue changes be found to finance increasing demands for spending. New taxes are needed to balance the budget. There is a changed political calculus: The political value of continuing already established programs outweighs the political costs of new taxes even in economically tough times.

HOW STATES COLLECT REVENUE AND SPEND

How do state governments finance their activities? Table 9-2 presents the percentages of the revenue obtained from the most important sources available to American governments. Distinctive patterns are clear. The federal government relies overwhelmingly on two sources of revenue: the individual income tax and individual contributions to the social security and Medicare programs. Together, revenues from these two programs constitute more than four-fifths of federal revenues.

About 40 percent of local government revenue comes from a single source, a levy on property, which is an easy-to-calculate tax on an immobile form of wealth. During the twentieth century a gradual division of revenue specialization occurred among the three levels of government, which ceded this source of revenue to local governments. In 1900 the property tax was the largest single revenue source for the states, but by 1993 it had shrunk to about 1 percent (Tax Foundation 1995, 179, 185). As property values declined during the Great Depression, states abandoned this taxing power to local governments. Because of the need for new sources of revenue, there were sixty separate state adoptions of the three major taxes during the Great Depression—the individual income tax, the corporation income tax, and the general sales tax. During the climactic two-year legislative period following the 1932 elections and at the height of the Great Depression, there were twenty-three adoptions of a new broad-based tax.

State governments rely on more and more evenly mixed revenue sources than the federal and local governments. This situation came about in part because the states gave up certain taxation powers—the property tax to local governments and

Figure 9-1   State Revenues, 1942–1995

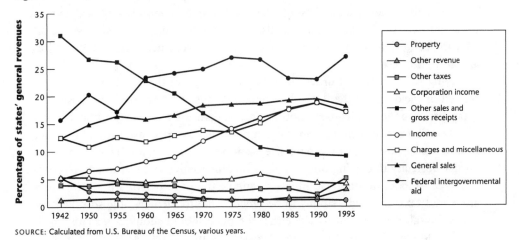

SOURCE: Calculated from U.S. Bureau of the Census, various years.

the bulk of the personal income tax to the federal government. There are other reasons as well. States rely on a broad mix of taxes to spread the burden of taxation to as many people and activities as possible. Lawmakers regard reliance on diverse revenue sources as desirable. One virtue of the diversity is that it insulates a state's total revenue from the vagaries of short-term economic fluctuations that affect some regions and not others. Spreading revenue sources spreads the risk of revenue fluctuations. In addition, lawmakers create a virtue from what voters see as multiple sins. Making numerous small changes in different tax programs to balance the state budget is proof to legislators that many citizens are fairly sharing the burden of the costs of government. Finally, because there are strong political imperatives for states to balance their budgets, the larger the number of revenue sources, the more evenly spread and the more difficult to detect will be the revenue changes that are required to bring taxes in line with required spending.

Raising Revenue to Meet States' Programmatic Needs

Sales taxes make up the largest single source of revenue for states, followed by intergovernmental aid, the bulk of which comes from the federal government, and the personal income tax. Like local governments, the states also rely on user fees and charges for substantial revenue.

Figure 9-1 is a chart of the changing revenue mix for the most important state revenue sources for 1942 through 1995. The largest (in 1995) of the various state revenue sources is at the bottom of the chart and the smallest is at the top. The "big four" sources in 1995—aid from the federal government; sales taxes; charges, fees, and licenses; and the personal income tax—account for almost 80 percent of state revenue. Note that this combined figure grew from about 50 percent forty-eight years earlier. The most dramatically shrinking revenue source is that of selective sales and receipts taxes, discussed later.

Evaluating Taxes

How shall we judge taxes? First of all, there is a state economic standard. Does a tax so burden the choices of individuals and businesses that citizens are worse off after the tax, even after the benefits of additional government goods and services are taken into account?

Asking who bears the burden of paying the tax poses the question of how the burden or incidence of the tax is distributed. If those who are best off, those with great wealth or high incomes, shoulder more than a simple proportional share, then taxation is considered *progressive*—a person's taxes rise faster than his or her income rises. Advocates of progressive taxation argue that poorer citizens have greater difficulty in carving out a share of income to give to government. Necessities of life—food, housing, clothing—dominate the poor person's budget. Others argue that taxation ought simply to be *proportional* to income—the so-called flat tax. Although it is difficult to argue that the poor should shoulder a share that is heavier than proportional, many state tax systems are, in fact, *regressive*—the share of a person's income given up in taxes actually rises as income falls, disproportionately burdening the poor.

Elastic taxes rise along with personal incomes in the state. Some would argue that state governments ought to share in the increasing income that citizens obtain. After all, costs for government go up, as does the demand for government services; thus more money is needed to satisfy these increasing demands. But as we noted earlier, elasticity varies about the unit value. Although some states' tax and revenue systems vary almost perfectly with personal income—a $1 billion increase in personal income yields a proportional increase in state taxes (West Virginia); others increase more rapidly (Oregon); and others increase more slowly than income (Nevada).

The issue of elasticity is closely related to *dynamic adequacy,* a new and emerging concern among state policy analysts (State Policy Research 1998, 13–14). Many state taxes, such as the taxes on liquor and cigarettes, tax parts of the economy that grow slowly. Most sales taxes do not tax fast-growing commercial transactions such as personal services. And as consumers purchase more and more services that crowd out goods such as liquor, goods-based sales taxes become less and less adequate.

State governments are also concerned with ease of administrative application and collection. Taxes ought to be easy to calculate and easy to collect. If a tax is costly to apply and collect, then governments have less money to spend—and they may have alienated citizens, too.

Finally, there is the judgment and assessment of the political costs of new taxation. As discussed later, because taxes come with direct costs to citizens, they have political and electoral costs for leaders in terms of diminished voter support. Let us review the major taxes in regard to the first four standards.

General Sales Tax

The general sales tax—that most familiar of all state and local taxes—is applied to consumer purchases of merchandise in forty-five of the fifty states. As was shown in Figure 9-1, the general sales tax is the states' major tax and has been so for the past half century. The data in Table 9-3 indicate that among the forty-five states, it accounts for a low of 21 percent of state tax revenue in New York to a high of 62 percent in Florida. In principle a sales tax is a general tax applied to a wide range of merchandise; it is a tax on consumption and on retail sales; and it is applied at an established rate. In practice, none of these statements generally holds. For example, the sales tax base is usually a general one only on some kinds of merchandise. In practice states exempt a wide range of items from the sales tax, food being the major exemption. Only a few states tax services, none taxes housing, and many exempt drugs.

The sales tax base is gradually eroded with the passage of time. Either the consumers of particular items or the purveyors of those goods pressure state legislators to exempt them. One compelling argument for exemption is that the item is not truly a "consumption" good, but rather it is an intermediate good used in the production of some other item. "Fairness" is a successful argument that has been employed to eliminate the sales tax on food. Over the past twenty-five years, eleven states have exempted food from taxation (Lemov 1996, 29). The net effect of the gradual erosion of the sales tax base is pressure on lawmakers to increase the rate on the remaining nonexempted items (Mikesell 1992). Recently, states have extended the sales tax to services such as advertising, legal advice, auto repair, and so on; however, such moves have been met by strong resistance from voters and service providers. The in-state, locational basis of sales taxation is also under attack. States cannot tax goods purchased by catalog across state lines and over the Internet.

To the extent that the sales tax is applied to some goods, and to goods but not services, it distorts economic performance and diminishes economic efficiency. Because the sales tax applies only to a fraction of all goods and services sold, consumers may substitute untaxed products or services for the taxed products. Still another distortionary effect is the time-consuming behavior of citizens who avoid the sales tax by shopping in a nearby state with a lower sales tax or none at all. Examples of tax migrations abound, most directly in customer travel to such sales-tax-free states as Delaware, New Hampshire, and Oregon.

The sales tax is regressive; it more severely affects low-income citizens (Fisher 1988, 187–188). Those with low incomes devote a larger share of their income to consumption—as opposed to saving or investing—and thus the tax falls more heavily on them. Regressivity can be diminished by not taxing food, drugs, and other necessities of life (Mikesell 1992, 85). A summary statistic of one estimate of the overall regressivity or progressivity of state tax systems can be found in Table 9-3.

The sales tax can better be thought of as cyclical and responsive as opposed to elastic. The revenue yield varies with business conditions; when times are good and consumers are flush with cash, sales tax coffers fill quickly. In recessionary times or in periods of economic and job anxiety, reluctant consumers do not spend and states do not collect. As the base of items that are taxable shrinks, the predictability of the sales tax revenue decreases, and elasticity increases as slow-growing sectors of

Table 9-3 States' Tax Distribution, Tax Regressivity, and Bond Ratings

	General sales	Selective sales	Personal income	Corporation income	Severance taxes	Overall regressivity[b]	Bond rating[c]
Alabama	27	25	29	5	2	194	AA
Alaska	—[c]	5	—	12	71	171	AA
Arizona	44	15	24	4	—	160	—
Arkansas	37	16	33	6	1	142	AA
California	31	8	39	11	—	111	A1
Colorado	27	17	44	4	—	150	—
Connecticut	46	20	12	13	—	193	AA
Delaware	—	14	40	10	—	87	AA1
Florida	62	18	—	5	—	328	AA
Georgia	37	12	41	7	—	148	AAA
Hawaii	50	13	30	4	—	94	A1(-1)
Idaho	34	15	35	6	—	121	—
Illinois	31	18	33	6	—	208	AA3(+1)
Indiana	42	13	34	6	—	179	—
Iowa	28	16	38	6	—	139	—
Kansas	33	15	32	8	3	161	—
Kentucky	26	19	28	7	5	137	AA
Louisiana	31	19	18	9	10	187	A3(+1)
Maine	33	17	37	4	—	106	AA
Maryland	24	18	44	5	—	111	AAA
Massachusetts	21	11	52	9	—	133	A1
Michigan	28	11	35	16	—	154	AA
Minnesota	27	16	42	7	—	101	AAA
Mississippi	45	20	18	5	2	162	AA
Missouri	38	12	36	4	—	174	AAA
Montana	—	21	33	9	11	99	AA
Nebraska	34	21	33	5	—	168	—
Nevada	51	35	—	0	1	327	AA
New Hampshire	—	46	7[a]	21	—	215	AA
New Jersey	32	21	28	1	—	132	AA1
New Mexico	42	15	18	3	15	134	AA1
New York	21	12	53	3	—	116	A2(+1)
North Carolina	23	18	43	8	—	117	AAA
North Dakota	34	22	16	7	12	172	AA
Ohio	31	19	36	6	—	124	AA1
Oklahoma	24	20	29	3	11	144	AA3(-1)
Oregon	—	14	66	5	2	102	AA2(+1)
Pennsylvania	32	18	24	1	—	211	AA3(+1)
Rhode Island	32	20	35	6	—	129	A1
South Carolina	37	18	35	4	—	117	AAA
South Dakota	50	31	—	6	2	308	—
Tennessee	55	22	2[a]	8	—	307	AAA
Texas	52	29	—	0	7	339	AA
Utah	40	12	37	5	2	147	AAA
Vermont	20	28	38	4	—	87	AA
Virginia	20	19	47	5	—	141	AAA
Washington	60	15	—	0	1	326	AA1(+1)
West Virginia	34	19	23	10	7	127	A1

Table 9-3 *Continued*

	General sales	Selective sales	Personal income	Corporation income	Severance taxes	Overall regressivity[b]	Bond rating[c]
Wisconsin	30	15	40	7	—	141	AA2(+1)
Wyoming	27	9	—	0	42	258	—
Average	33	16	32	7	2	—	

S O U R C E : Figures in the first five columns were calculated by the author from data drawn from *Facts and Figures on Government Finance, 1992,* Table E18, pp. 244–245.

"—" denotes no such tax program in that state.

[a] New Hampshire and Tennessee income taxes are on interest and dividend income only.

[b] Calculated by the author from data provided by Citizens for Tax Justice in "A far cry from fair" (April 1991, Washington, D.C.) The figures represent the percentage of income extracted in taxes from the lowest 40 percent of income earners as a percentage of the percent of income extracted from the top 5 percentage of income earners in each state. As the figure in the *overall regressivity* column gets larger and larger, it reflects a greater burdening of the lowest income classes.

[c] July 1998 Moody bond ratings for state government: rank from high to low is AAA, AA1, AA2, AA3, AA, A1, A, BAA1, BAA, BA1, BA, B1, B. Numbers in parentheses indicate the change in bond ratings from fourth quarter 1996 to July 1998.

"necessities and essentials" such as food and clothes are eliminated (Duncombe 1992, 308–309).

The sales tax is applied at the final stage of sales—at the retail level—so the ease of application of the tax is dependent on the efforts of the retail merchant community. A fraction of the sales tax that each retail merchant collects is returned to the merchant for administrative expenses.

Personal Income Tax

In 1942 the individual income tax accounted for about 5 percent of state revenues (see Figure 9-1). By 1995 it accounted for nearly 18 percent. Forty-three of the fifty states have some form of income tax. Alaska (which abolished its income tax in 1980), Florida, Nevada, South Dakota, Texas, Washington, and Wyoming do not have income taxes. New Hampshire and Tennessee tax limited forms of income and are not considered to have general income taxes (Tax Foundation 1992, 249).

As indicated in Table 9-3, states that rely heavily on the income tax include Oregon, New York, and Massachusetts, with 66 percent, 53, and 52 percent, respectively, of their revenue coming from the income tax.

Three different ways of assessing the state income taxes bear on the incidence of taxation. Four of the states (Colorado, North Dakota, Rhode Island, and Vermont) use the federal income tax form as a basis for the state income tax. In Vermont, for example, the state income tax liability is 25 percent of the federal tax liability. Because citizens with higher incomes fall into a higher federal tax bracket and thus pay a higher percentage of their income in taxes, the income taxes in these states are fairly progressive. Still other states—Connecticut, Illinois, Indiana, Massachusetts, Michigan, and Pennsylvania—levy a flat tax on personal incomes. In principle, this is a proportional tax, but with the large number of exemptions, deductions, and credits, the flat tax can take on progressivity, as it has in Massachusetts, or be almost perfectly proportional, as it is in Pennsylvania (Citizens for Tax Justice 1991).

Most states with income taxes adopt some form of the "ability to pay" principle. Steeply progressive income brackets exist in California, where a 1 percent rate is applied to those with less than $5,000 in annual income, whereas those with $215,000 or more in income pay taxes at an 11 percent rate. This is the highest rate and it is applied in Montana as well to residents who earn more than $62,000 (see Tax Foundation 1995, table E23). Note that the estimates of regressivity supplied by the Citizens for Tax Justice in Table 9-3 are strongly affected by a personal income tax and by the progressivity of such a tax.

The income tax tends to be responsive to changes in personal income in states; thus it is considered an elastic tax. Revenues in states with progressive income taxes that include several income brackets and increasing rates applied to increasing incomes tend to be more elastic, but they also tend to be more variable—that is to say, they rise rapidly in good economic times but fall rapidly in poor times. There seems to be a trade-off: States with steeply progressive taxes have tax systems that are highly responsive to economic change, but the yield is more difficult to predict (Dye and McGuire 1991).

The income tax may require substantial administrative costs of application at the government level and at the taxpayer level. Forms have to be prepared, information on personal income checked and verified by state revenue administrators, likely taxable amounts withheld from paychecks, and delinquents and malingerers pursued. Taxpayers also bear personal costs in time spent preparing the return and the use of accountants and tax services in assisting in preparation. Note that state income taxes that are calculated as a fraction of the federal income tax liability can, in principle, be collected by a very simple form at a low cost of preparation to the citizen.

There is disagreement about the economic efficiency of the income tax. Of particular concern to state politicians is the local efficiency—that is, how the income tax and its progressivity affect the residential choice of citizens and of businesses. States with high, punitive income tax codes may drive individuals and businesses with high taxable incomes into nearby or adjacent states with lower or no income taxes.

Selective Sales and Excise Taxes

Selectively taxing the sale of a set of particular items is jokingly labeled by state legislators as "taxing the five bees"—taxes on selective sales of "butts, beer, booze, bellies, and beds" (that is, cigarettes, beer, wines and liquors, restaurant meals, and room occupancy in hotels and motels). They are often referred to as "sin taxes" and are popular because they satisfy so many political interests. One important interest is efficiency. State legislators believe they can easily raise the tax rate on cigarettes or beer or wine without affecting consumption of the items. Even if consumption of cigarettes or beer slowly declines with ever-higher taxes (and at some point consumption must decline with ever-higher taxes), legislators believe that the resulting diminished consumption actually benefits the state. Higher taxes will lead to declines in "sinful" consumption, which will lead to less sickness, fewer drunk drivers, and so on.

One inefficiency in sin taxing derives from its interstate variability. Cigarette taxes are the best example: They vary from a low of 5 cents, 3 cents, and 2.5 cents per pack in the tobacco-producing states—North Carolina, Kentucky, and Virginia—to highs of twenty times more in non–tobacco-producing states (New York at 56¢ per pack). The difference in prices as a result of the higher taxes creates incentives for the illegal interstate smuggling of cigarettes.

Selective sales taxes are generally thought to be regressive. Most analysts believe that the reasonable way to figure out the burden of sin taxes is to assume that they are distributed by the consumption of the item taxed. Thus, motor fuels are thought to be regressive because the poor make heavier use of older, inefficient automobiles. Increases in liquor and wine taxation, however, may be relatively progressive because of the heavier consumption of these items by middle- and upper-income individuals.

Selective sales taxes are characterized as inelastic taxes. The consumption of beer, tobacco, and motor fuels, although responsive to changes in personal income, does not increase much more rapidly than personal income.

Selective sales are one of the best established bases of taxation in the states. States have cooperated with the manufacturers and wholesalers of items that are selectively taxed, most especially the tobacco and beer and liquor distributors, to ensure ease of administrative application. Even at the retail level of hotels, motels, and restaurants, vendors are easily detectable and procedures relatively straightforward. Very often consumers are not aware that selective sales taxes are applied to the goods that they purchase; gasoline and liquor are examples.

No analysis of taxing and spending in the states would be complete without a discussion of what is now a small but fast-growing source of revenue: a selective sales and gross receipts tax on gambling. The reasons for the rapid growth are increases in demand by consumers for gambling activities; enormous growth in the availability of gambling sites; the decline in opposition to legalized gambling on the part of lawmakers and voters; and, finally, a constitutional anomaly in American law. Gross revenues of gambling businesses increased by 300 percent per year to $30 billion from 1982 to 1992, whereas box office revenues in many other entertainment sectors barely budged. During the first six months of legalized gambling in Louisiana, gross business revenues from gambling went from zero to $100 million per month, and taxes paid to the state went from zero to nearly $20 million per month. Nevada has long relied on direct revenue from casino and other gambling to finance about one-sixth of its activities. Only two states, Utah and Hawaii, allow no gambling at all.

One proximate cause of the rapid growth in gambling is the federal courts' rulings on how state and local governments must treat lands held by recognized Native American tribes (Johnson 1993, 6). If a state—for example, Connecticut—allows some forms of gambling, such as bingo nights sponsored by charitable or nonprofit activities, then the semisovereign tribes gain even more general rights and can open up a casino. In one case, Connecticut authorities, recognizing the inevitable, allowed the Mashantucket Pequot tribe to open what is now the enormously successful Foxwood Casino in Ledyard, Connecticut. A large fraction of revenues from slot machines is given to the state in lieu of other tax payments. The success of the Mashantucket tribe has been emulated elsewhere. One important within-state effect of successful tribal gambling is to create internal pressures on other recognized tribes within the state to open competing casinos. Tribal gambling success also creates incentives for nontribal private entrepreneurs and local officials who see the economic development potential of local casino gambling operations.

Corporation Income Taxes

Although important sources of revenue for the states, corporation income taxes are neither large nor growing. This tax amounted to about 5 percent of state revenues in 1942 and about 4 percent in 1995. One possible reason why it is not a growing source of revenue is the complexity of the tax. Ordinarily, one would think of the corporate income tax as equivalent to the personal income tax and apply the appropriate tax rate much like the ordinary citizen does to personal income. In fact, this would be a gross receipts tax. However, if it is assumed, quite reasonably, that the greatest fraction of the total receipts that businesses receive for sales is used for the direct costs of production—for labor, materials, financing, and so on—then the company should not be taxed on its total receipts but rather on receipts less the costs of production, sales, and so on. Basing the corporate income tax on income net of costs, then, brings up the question of what is justifiably a cost of production? Still another complication is the following: If a business is headquartered in California but has half of its production operations in Nevada and half in Malaysia and sells only 10 percent of its goods in California, what state (or nation) taxes what?

State decision makers are faced with conflicting interests in assessing efficiency considerations of the corporation income tax. On the one hand, corporations are "good citizens" of states and therefore corporations ought to share in the financing of services that benefit them. On the other hand, to the extent that corporate taxes are low, a state will be seen as a more attractive place to continue to do business or to move one's business. Further, the profits of these companies are distributed to shareholders, employees, managers, and owners whose incomes can then be taxed. State legislators must ask themselves if, by lowering such taxes, more businesses with more jobs can be lured to the state and if the state's revenue picture is thus ultimately improved.

Are corporation income taxes progressive? Corporate taxation becomes another cost to the company, which hopes to shift that cost to the consumer. It may not be able to do so, however. For example, if a rival is in business in another state with low corporate taxation, a company may be constrained by the competitive market to pass on the tax cost to shareholders or to employees in reduced corporate benefits, pay, and so on. Corporation taxes ought to be elastic and probably are quite volatile as they track the economic performance of the state and nation. But such taxes pose profound problems of application and collection.

Charges, Fees, and Miscellaneous Revenues

A somewhat smaller rate of growth is seen in charges, fees, and miscellaneous revenues that are collected by the state for those activities for which it can reasonably expect users to pay. This category of revenue can be likened to government pricing its own goods and services. Well-known examples would be entrance fees to parks and museums, tuition at colleges, charges for drivers' and automobile licenses, water and sewer fees, and so on.

Such fees seem to be simple benefit taxes—those who benefit most from use pay for its provision. Even though everyone actually benefits from the provision of certain state and local services, those who are direct beneficiaries, such as park users and homeowners who have a hookup to the sewer system, ought to pay a fair share of the costs. It is often not possible, however, to price a government's goods and services directly and fully (Olson 1973). All citizens benefit from governments' provision of services such as parks and sewer systems through the parks' contributions to an attractive and beneficial environment and from the sanitary sewers' contribution to public health. In economic terms, these are positive externalities associated with these goods and services—positive effects of a service the benefits of which cannot reasonably be captured through a user fee or personal charge. Thus, there is no simple linkage between the cost of a service, its user fee as a price, and a tax on all beneficiaries.

The calculation of how progressive or regressive such fees are is difficult to assess. Although governments that charge for their services can be praised for allocating the costs of government to those who benefit, another task of government is to ensure that all citizens can obtain some fair share of public services regardless of wealth or income. Many states now require telephone companies, as state-regulated public utilities, to provide elementary "lifeline" phone service to all consumers at a price less than the cost of the service. In effect, all telephone users pay a higher fee for telephone service (a hidden user tax) to ensure that this service is available and distributed to all citizens.

Charges, licenses, and miscellaneous fees are not elastic. Fees are usually set by statute at a particular figure and remain unchanged until the law itself is changed. Revenue thus fluctuates as a function of the number of users, licensees, or beneficiaries. Administrative application of this source of revenue, however, is easy. Users and licensees are charged by formula.

Intergovernmental Aid

The largest source of revenue for state governments in 1995 was intergovernmental aid, 95 percent of it from the federal government (U.S. Bureau of the Census 1997, 309). In 1995 about $202 billion in federal monies were employed by states to advance their programs. About one-half of this supported welfare programs, 15 percent supported education, and 10 percent supported highway building.

Severance Taxes

Although severance taxes do not amount to much in the way of revenues in the fifty American states (at 1.5 percent of total taxes collected by the states), for a handful of states they loom large—51 percent of Alaska's revenues and 39 percent of Wyoming's. States with large oil and coal extractive industries rely on such a tax as a way of placing the burden onto the consumers of such resources, almost all of whom live in other states. From the perspective of the state's economy the burden is exported to out-of-state (nonvoting) citizens. Having other states' citizens finance their government is seen as a tax windfall by lawmakers. A major concern about the severance tax, however, is that it is a highly volatile source of revenue. Because the severance tax is levied as a percentage of the value of the resource extracted and sold, the amount the severance tax yields is a function of production and price. Oil, especially, has been highly volatile in both production and price. In 1970, Alaska earned $10 million in severance taxes; in 1980, $506 million; in 1986, $1.4 billion; and in 1987, $667 million. In effect, the Alaskan revenue system fluctuates just about as wildly as the world market price of oil.

DETERMINING HOW STATES SPEND THEIR TAX MONIES

The following chapters in this volume discuss spending for welfare, economic development, education, and environmental protection, showing how spending in these areas varies from state to state and exploring factors associated with greater or lesser spending. Figure 9-2 compares these programs across time, and sets out, for the period from 1940 to the mid-1990s, the fraction of total state government spending devoted to education, highways, public welfare, health and hospitals, natural resources, government administration and "other."

There is considerable variation over time in the relative shares of state spending devoted to these programs. In 1960 highway spending accounted for more than one-third of total spending; by 1994 it had shrunk to less than one-tenth. Relatively speaking, highway spending was displaced from the center of the state agenda to being one among many competing programs. Similarly, spending on natural resources such as state parks and forests shrank, relatively, by one-half over these same three decades. Although natural resource spending still remains large and important, its rate of growth, although positive over the three decades, has been lower when compared with fast-growing programs such as welfare. Conversely, programs of spending assistance for the poor took on the opposing pattern; accounting for 12 percent of spending in 1960; by 1994 it had almost tripled in size. However, although substantial variation in relative shares occur across time, there are important continuities. Education accounted for about 20 percent in 1960 and about the same in the 1990s; spending for health and hospitals shows similar stability.

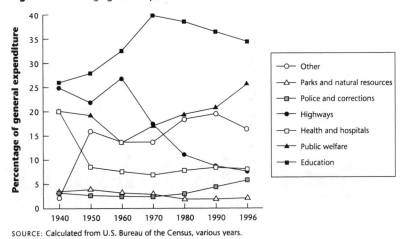

Figure 9-2   Changing State Expenditure Shares

SOURCE: Calculated from U.S. Bureau of the Census, various years.

Drawing on a conclusion from Chapter 2 of this volume, much of the historical variation in composition can be traced to the influence of changes in the national political agenda. The 1960s decade was marked by the importance of transportation and highway spending in the states. This concentration reflected the high point of the great period of expansion of the interstate highway system that had its origin in the federal spending programs of the Eisenhower administration and the incorporation of federal monies and new highway responsibilities into state budgets. Similarly, the expansion of spending for education in the late 1960s and the gradual rise of spending on welfare also reflected a national agenda more favorably inclined toward public education and direct assistance to the poor.

Nevertheless, programs also expand and contract as a function of voter preferences. The 1996 welfare reform act that is discussed in Chapter 10 has important state-level determinants. States—their governors and legislators—led the way in welfare reform largely because the program had become so costly, as Figure 9-2 illustrates, that reform was demanded by voters and their leaders. Welfare consistently ranked among the least popular of all spending programs and by the mid-1990s it had come to be the largest single program of state spending. The chapters that follow discuss in detail spending on these various policies. The political story of how this spending gets supported—via taxes and revenues—is the topic of the rest of this chapter.

HOW TAXES GET ADOPTED AND GET CHANGED

New taxes are adopted and existing ones increased to allow more spending in the states. We also know, however, that politicians are reluctant to tax, for "tax adoptions are nearly always unpopular and pose great risks for politicians hoping to win re-election" (Berry and Berry 1992, 716). Several studies have examined how new taxes get adopted or tax rates get changed. In brief, significant changes in tax

Figure 9-3   Adoptions of State Sales Tax Programs and State Income Tax Programs

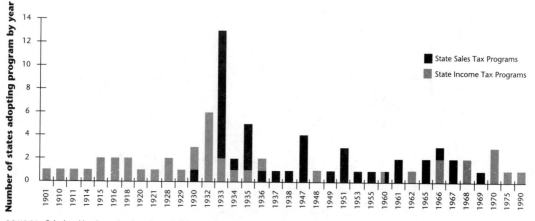

SOURCE: Calculated by the author from *Facts and Figures on Government Finance*, 1992, p. 249.

laws are more likely when fiscal woes hit the state; less likely late in the gubernatorial term; more likely in wealthy states; and more likely if a state is bounded by other states with similar programs (Berry and Berry 1992; Hansen 1983, 1990). But the story is more complicated and politically more interesting.

Let us narrow our focus on innovations to the most broadly based taxes, defined as new programs of general sales taxes, new personal income tax programs, or rate changes in either of these two existing taxes. These are the tax programs that are most likely to galvanize public sentiment. The dates and number of states adopting these two taxes can be seen in Figure 9-3. The figure shows tax innovations by year. New tax programs have been frequent, and all but a handful of states now have one or both of these programs. The data offer several lessons bearing on what causes innovations in the forty-one states with income taxes and the forty-five states with sales taxes (states with no sales or income tax programs are noted in Table 9-3).

The nonfederal income tax was first adopted by law when the then remote U.S. possession of Hawaii was first organized as a territory in 1901. Among the states, Wisconsin and Mississippi first adopted the tax in 1911–1912, and it slowly spread to other nonadjacent states over the next two decades. The pace of income tax adoptions rapidly accelerated during the Great Depression. In this time of great personal and governmental hardship, property taxes and selective sales and excise taxes were either hard to collect or did not amount to enough revenue to be useful. A new revenue source was needed, and states' leaders saw that the income tax had established itself as administratively workable. Also, burdening the better-off was a politically acceptable solution to revenue shortfalls in those difficult economic times. But as the years of the Great Depression drew to an end, so did adoptions of the income tax. Nevertheless, the data in Figure 9-3 reveal the most important factor in explaining tax changes: hard times.

The situation in which hard times and budgetary woes determine tax adoptions or rate changes is a classic within-state causal factor. Nevertheless, other budgetary choices are available to a state's political leaders. Governors and legislators could, after all, reduce expenditures. Thus, although the state's budgetary troubles are a necessary condition for tax increases, such troubles are not a sufficient condition to produce taxes. Leaders focus on how many votes will be lost because of the imposition of new taxes in relation to how many will be lost if expenditures for programs are cut (Downs 1957; Hansen 1983). New taxes are attractive if the vote loss from program cuts is formidable. The actions of the states' leaders during the Great Depression suggest that large gaps between expenditure needs and revenues lead to new tax programs. The most recent example of this phenomenon was the imposition of a new income tax in Connecticut in 1991 as noted in Figure 9-3.

The pattern of sales tax adoptions in Figure 9-3 also appears to be strikingly affected by difficult financial situations. Nearly one-half of the American states adopted the general sales tax in the years of the Great Depression. Politically competitive states that fell under the control of the Democratic party in the Roosevelt era were much more likely to be among those that adopted (Hansen 1990, 359). A second pattern found in sales tax adoptions differs from the pattern in income tax adoptions. Every four years or so, usually in the years immediately following the gubernatorial elections, new sales tax programs were adopted. Timing, defined as passing tax legislation early in a gubernatorial term, then, is a second general factor in adoptions, in addition to hard times and budgetary woes.

Berry and Berry (1992) argued that tax innovations are more attractive when they occur well before the next election. Politicians count on the short memories of voters to diminish the pain of increased taxes, and they also count on voters' myopic vision to put into sharp focus the beneficial stream of services present at election time and financed by the now-several-years-old "new" tax. As the term of a governor nears its end, not only do the incentives to put the state into budgetary balance diminish, but so does the will and capacity of the incumbent to mobilize legislators to balance the budget. The political will of states' governors and legislators to raise new taxes weakens as the election approaches because of the fear of voter wrath and because it is, therefore, easier to postpone the needed fiscal stringency until later, after the election. Gubernatorial incumbents reason that if they can hold off on new taxes for the next year and if they are reelected, they will be in a stronger position with the legislature; if they are not reelected, then their successors can bite the tax bullet.

Politicians avoid broad, general tax changes in an election year, but that may not be true for all taxing activities. Mikesell (1978) discovered that in the third and fourth year of a gubernatorial term, minor taxes are more likely to get changed, sin taxes increased, and the taxes not easily ascertainable by voters increased.

Vermont's adoption of a new 3 percent general sales tax in 1969 is a classic case of timing. In the 1968 Vermont gubernatorial election, a businessperson and long-time Republican activist, Deane Davis, succeeded the three-term Democratic incumbent, Philip Hoff, the first Democrat to be elected as Vermont's governor in 100 years. Hoff was responsible for many new expenditure programs and for the expansion of countless others, leaving his Republican successor with a large gap between expenditure obligations and expected revenues. In January 1969, nine minutes after being sworn in, Davis recommended in his inaugural address a 3 percent general sales tax as a solution to Vermont's fiscal problems. One analyst predicted that Davis began to lose the 1970 election in that ninth minute of his term. Davis's own view on the effects of the new sales tax on his reelection chances was more optimistic. He noted that former governor Hoff congratulated him on his sales tax message immediately after the inauguration, claiming that Davis "was doing the right thing" (personal communication with Davis, July 18, 1990). Davis obtained passage of his new 3 percent general sales tax; he also won reelection with a greater margin of victory than he had had in his first election.

The timing of tax legislation is further entangled in two other important determinants of adoption. Democratic party control, in the public's view, is related to increasing taxes. Democrats are seen as representing voters who favor larger government, which provides many more, and expensive, services (CBS-*New York Times* poll as reported in Oreskes 1988, 32). The Democratic party is also seen as the party more favorable to special interests in need of governmental assistance. All of these perceptions suggest upward pressure on spending that may require Democratic tax increases. But if party control is related to timing of tax increases, the effects of that control ought to manifest themselves early in the period of control, not later. A new Democratic governor coming into office with a newly Democratic legislature is under great pressure to produce programs that demonstrate the worth of the Democrats' control of government. If that entails a tax hike, then it will occur early to finance the noteworthy additions that the Democrats bring to the government establishment.

Several analysts of American state politics in reviewing the effect of party control of the governor's office on budgetary politics, have found it difficult to predict the direction and kinds of budgetary changes that occur when party control of the governorship switches (Garand 1985; Plotnick and Winters 1990). Hansen noted that change in party control and electoral realignments are associated with changing taxes (1983). An interesting example of timing, party control, and election consequences occurred in 1971, when Democrat John J. Gilligan replaced James A. Rhodes, the tough-minded, fiscally conservative Republican governor of Ohio. Gilligan campaigned and won, in part, because of his promise to put Ohio's fiscal house in order and his promotion of state assistance to programs aiding localities, the poor, and those with special needs. To finance these programs a large new tax source was needed, and Gilligan obtained passage of a brand-new income tax early in his term. Three years later, Gilligan lost his reelection bid. Many more examples of tax increases for programmatic ends occur in the states. New taxes for increased funding for education are particularly popular items. Two well-known examples resulted in more salutary outcomes for Govs. Terry Sanford of North Carolina and

Bill Clinton of Arkansas, each of whom increased their respective sales taxes for education programs and went on to win reelection.

Another factor related to timing is the public mood. In some eras voters want bigger government; it is as if there is a demand for government, which governors and legislators endeavor to satisfy. The adoption of new income and sales tax programs in the 1960s and early 1970s are examples of such a period. An outstanding example exists in the behavior of a former Republican governor of Massachusetts, John Volpe. In his reelection campaign for the governorship in 1964, Volpe signaled to the voters that he might proceed with a new sales tax. Volpe framed the new sales tax as a positive electoral issue by the time of his reelection. In recalling the sales tax fight, Volpe's lieutenant governor, Elliot L. Richardson, noted, "There was no fiscal crisis as such, we just wanted to be able to do more" (Black 1990, 21). Volpe highlighted the public benefits of new programs financed by the new sales tax, a strategy that was enormously successful. State legislators remember walking in Memorial Day holiday parades (in mid-spring when the legislature was still in session) with people shouting from curbside, "Pass the tax!"—puzzlingly quaint behavior by today's standards (Black 1990).

An important within-state causal factor that shapes gubernatorial and legislative receptiveness to new taxes is the income and wealth of the state. Richer states are more generous in their spending programs, partly because they can afford to tax more (Dye 1966; Plotnick and Winters 1985). The law of diminishing marginal returns suggests that voters are more generous when they have high incomes and that they are more willing to tax themselves in rich states; thus politicians may have less to fear at the polls. A parallel causal factor is that wealthy states are the most socially and economically diverse states and have the most closely competitive electoral systems. The net effect of wealth in combination with greater diversity of social and economic interests is an increase in political pressures on governors and legislators alike to help groups in need of assistance. As diversity increases in a competitive state, more and more groups can reasonably claim that each provided the last crucial voting bloc to the victor's winning coalition. "In the diverse states, party leaders will lack precise information on the validity of the claims of group influence and will become captive to the pleas of many of them" (Plotnick and Winters 1985, 463).

A within-state causal factor that helps to explain tax adoptions is that the new tax is an equilibrium outcome, one that is agreeable to more than a simple winning coalition. Republican fiscal conservatives such as Davis in Vermont and Volpe in Massachusetts advocated a new tax as the solution to the state's problems. By personally advocating the tax and pushing for it, they muted criticism from fiscal conservatives. But programs that are already in existence have many advocates for their continuation, such as government bureaucrats who deliver the services, those working in the private sector who benefit from a particular program (doctors, social workers), and the direct beneficiaries of the services (welfare clients, farmers, students). Governors can make this same argument to every group assisted by government: "Get on board with this tax now or put your program in peril." Threats of budgetary cutbacks mobilize a diverse coalition of groups. They may only agree on the desirability of new revenue, but that is all the governor needs.

A classic example of the equilibrium nature of new and expanded tax programs comes from the first term of Gov. Kenneth Curtis of Maine. The Democratic Curtis narrowly defeated the incumbent governor, John H. Reed, in the 1966 election, campaigning on behalf of his "Maine Action Plan." Two years later, some of the costs of action came due, and Curtis pushed for and won a general income tax. The tax passed the house and the senate by a margin of one vote; the crucial votes were cast by the Republican leadership in the two chambers. In effect, a bipartisan tax plan was passed in Maine. Curtis went on to win reelection, having mooted the ability of his Republican opponent to use the new taxes against him.

A final factor that eases the way for new taxes is the behavior of neighbors, a horizontal factor affecting state politics. Berry and Berry argued that information that voters get about the practice of a tax in a nearby state alleviates the "uncertainty" about possible consequences. A large number of nearby states with the same tax "should diminish the fear that adopting the tax would seriously hurt a state's ability to compete for business, thereby reducing the political costs of doing so" (1992, 722). Having many nearby neighbors with the tax, however, also works in the opposite direction—increasing the marginal value to states' leaders of being among the very last tax holdouts. Not having the sales or income tax when neighbors do is an important horizontal causal reason for not adopting them. The taxless state becomes more attractive as a residence and business location. Many states currently benefit from this tax-free situation: Florida, Nevada, New Hampshire, Texas, and Washington benefit from citizens fleeing the income taxes in other states. Delaware, New Hampshire, and Oregon, particularly, benefit from their sales-tax-free environment that lures shoppers from nearby states with its guarantees of saving 5 percent or more on each purchase.

Both propositions—emulating one's neighbors and holding out against them—are probably valid. In the early and midpoint of the diffusion of tax programs across the states, a nearby state's positive experience with a tax program probably counts in favor of its adoption and expansion. However, as the diffusion of tax adoptions proceeds, the value of not adopting the tax—of holding out—becomes more politically and economically profitable for a state. It is unclear what the final stages of this emulation process will look like in regard to adopting sales and income taxes among all fifty states. It is reasonable to speculate, however, that the five states now without sales taxes and the nine states without general income taxes face increasing difficulties in adopting these taxes. The longer the taxless state holds out, the more citizens and groups actively benefit from the taxless situation. States with no sales taxes have significant numbers of owners of small businesses who aggressively lobby to keep their state tax-free, and states with no income tax attract a sizable retired and wealthy population who are politically active in safeguarding the advantages of their tax-free residency.

VOTERS' REACTIONS TO UNPOPULAR TAXES

The political wisdom of activists and leaders says that the relation between new or increased state taxes and voting is direct and negative. The defeats of Gov. James Florio in New Jersey (1993) and the withdrawal of Lowell P. Weicker in Connecticut (1994) confirm the conventional wisdom of electoral vulnerability. The link between taxes and voting has strong informal and anecdotal evidence, as well (Beyle 1992; Sabato 1978). A study that merged aggregate data with exit polls of voters confirmed the voter–tax link (Niemi, Stanley, and Vogel 1995) The authors' conclusions are consistent with the image of discriminating voters who are sensitive about taxes and are knowledgeable about state officials who tax, especially those who increase the most objectionable taxes (Bowler and Donovan 1995).

Yet many political scientists share an earlier analyst's conviction that "contrary to the rules of political folklore, governors who lead in increasing taxes do not suffer at the polls significantly" (Pomper 1968, 133–134). Eismeier examined 389 elections between 1950 and 1980 and argued that "governors, gubernatorial candidates and state parties that urged higher taxes faced greater risks of electoral defeat," yet "these risks are not overwhelming in all cases" (1983, 379). In an examination of the tax–vote link, a colleague and I proposed a model of a rational electorate wreaking retribution against a party and its candidates for changes in tax policy— new or additional taxes—in which the party's incumbent chief executive was directly involved (Kone and Winters 1993). We included in the model factors that plausibly account for the vote received by the incumbent: changes in national economic indicators (income, unemployment) and changes in statewide economic indicators of income and unemployment that are also relevant to the plight of voters. Our results indicated that although passing new tax programs did have the predicted negative effects on electoral outcomes, the effects were quite modest. Further examination turned up only a few cases in which electoral defeats could reasonably be traced to new tax programs, and for every tax-related election loss such as those of Norbert T. Tiemann in Nebraska and John J. Gilligan of Ohio, there were equally powerful counterexamples of new tax programs put into place and election gains that followed; the reelections of Deane C. Davis of Vermont and Milton Shapp of Pennsylvania are examples (Winters 1990).

SPENDING AND TAXING AND THE BUDGETARY PROCESS

Every two years in about one-third of the states with biennial sessions, and every year in the remaining states, the appropriations bill is introduced into the states' legislative chambers. How a bill becomes a law is discussed in Chapter 5 of this volume, but the appropriations and tax bills differ in significant ways from an ordinary bill. More time and energy and more people's cumulative knowledge are devoted to the appropriations bill than to any other in state politics. Even though the size and sophistication of staffs of governors and legislatures vary across the states, both of them usually have their own staffs at work on their versions of the appropriations or budget acts. The companion revenue bill also receives close attention—sometimes, even closer attention—but generally by fewer people. The appropriations bill is closely scrutinized because so many important decisions are wrapped up in this one or handful of bills; it is presented to the legislature as the governor's program; it is considered by multiple subcommittees and committees of the states' legislative chambers, amended (at times, substantially so), and approved by the legislature. Once signed into law, the bill limits what can be spent by the state—program by program and agency by agency—for the coming fiscal year or two-year period. The revenue bill is subject to close scrutiny, as well, because of the dramatic impact simple changes in revenue codes can have on the activities of concerned individuals and groups.

The appropriations bill is an object of attention because the personal futures and well-being of so many are dependent on it. The livelihood of administrators depends on successfully defending or advancing the interests of their particular program (Clynch and Lauth 1991). Administrators believe in what they are doing, and they have a professional stake in promoting the goods or services they deliver. Additionally because the number, size, and benefits of state government activities have grown during the past several decades, legislators and their constituents have come to value what the state provides (Chubb 1985). One of the inevitable consequences of the growth of state government has been, then, the rise of groups attentive to changing government activities. These interest groups pressure legislatures and governors to avert cuts (in their worst case) and (better yet) to increase appropriations in beneficial programs (Winters 1980).

An important lesson is that the appropriations power is not simply divided between the governor and legislature; it is shared. Officials rarely have the power to act independently without the approval or consideration of the interests of other individuals or institutions. The degree of power sharing varies among the states. Some states, such as Illinois and California, have powerful governors with formidable powers of initiation, approval, and change. Other states, such as Florida, Mississippi, and South Carolina, have powerful legislatures that are active in budget formulation and action. Since the mid-1970s, legislative involvement and influence in budgeting have increased with the rising professionalism of those bodies (Squires 1992).

Preparing the Administrative Budget

In a typical budget year, six (or more) months before the legislature considers the budget and a year before the final budget takes effect, orders go out from the governor's office to begin preparing the administrative budget. The process begins at the front lines of each agency as officials document what is needed to provide the current level of goods and services for which they are responsible. This current-services budget level is the amount of monies calculated to deliver what the legislature has already ordered the agency to provide. The current-services budget is also supported by all of the work and analysis that goes into the current year's appropriation as the baseline budget. The current-services budget differs from the baseline budget in at least two ways. First, the costs of providing the same level of services will move upward incrementally because of changes in wages and salaries paid to government employees and because of upward (usually) changes in the cost of goods and services required for executing the policy as set out by law. Second, the demand for the government good or service may have changed for the forthcoming year. For example, if there is a downturn in the economy, the Department of Welfare (or its equivalent) will ask for more money to handle the greater expected demand for welfare assistance.

The head of the department or his or her budgetary staff collects the requests from lower-level administrators of agencies and assembles them as a draft of the department budget. This budget can be thought of as the administrators' and department heads' summation of the current-services budget—that is, the current year's budget adjusted by changes in costs and expected demand. Administrators are at the same time asking their departmental colleagues about new initiatives and programs that will likely catch the governor's or legislators' eyes as politically feasible and desirable (see Wildavsky 1980, chap. 3). We can speculate on what might determine how expansionary an administrator could be. In times of economic growth, bureaucrats in states with responsive revenue systems forcefully claim their "fair share" of the booming revenues. States with consistently growing revenues may attract individuals who could be termed bureaucratic entrepreneurs, individuals who are highly ambitious and who recognize that the fastest route to personal advancement in their chosen fields is to build programs that become nationally noteworthy among their peers (Winters 1980). Yet, the constraints on precisely how much to request are considerable on departmental officials. In states in which there is a balanced budget requirement, all participants recognize that in the end expenditures cannot exceed revenues, that their preferences for larger budgets must have limits. Administrators realize that it makes little sense to request an increase greatly in excess of the expected change in total revenues; bureaucrats are sensitive to the need for "political credibility" (Wildavsky 1980).

Nevertheless, each department's budget is calculated in the absence of knowledge of what other departments are doing. Given poor information, it is in the self-interest of each department head to scrutinize closely any new initiatives that might be attractive in light of the interests of the governor and legislators. This scrutiny is also in the self-interest of governors and legislators who rely on administrators to inform them of possible programmatic opportunities. Nevertheless, all elected officials realize the information provided by agency officials is biased in favor of the case for continued or greater appropriations for their program.

The vertical arrangement also affects bureaucratic budgetary behavior. Some agency officials may gain an advantage in their efforts to shape the budget by exploiting federal aid matching requirements. As noted in Chapter 2, the federal government matches state efforts in a variety of ways, from a match of dollar for dollar to a match of $9 of federal aid for every $1 of state appropriations. The bureaucrat who enrolls a larger federal match has an advantage in budgetary negotiations with governors and legislators. There are also across-state variations in acquiring federal aid. Some states have aggressively sought such aid. Other states have been more suspicious of federal entanglements in state policy making, fearing the strings that may accompany federal aid in the form of expensive or otherwise objectionable federal mandates.

Preparing the Executive Budget

In the fall, several months before the legislature gathers for the new year, the governor and his or her budgetary staff scrutinize the budget requests of department heads and their agencies. In many states, formal representations of the budget requests are made either to the governor or his or her budget staff and advisers. Much time is devoted to the budget because it is a key indicator of gubernatorial priorities and a signal to electoral supporters of the delivery of commitments. Ordinarily, the amounts in the executive budget are smaller than what was asked for by agency and department officials. Governors, like presidents, believe that agencies pad their budgets with requests that are not necessary and that agencies engage in acquisitive behavior (Thompson 1987).

When the budgets of states are examined closely, it appears that new administrations make few significant changes (Lowery, Konda, and Garand 1984). Governors, even those who may be hostile to particular programs, decide that it is not worth the political effort to reduce or abolish popular programs. Statutory commitments mandating the outlays of monies double the difficulties of legislative alteration—both the statute and the budget have to be changed. In addition, budgets are fixed because of strings associated with federal matching aid; because of the political commitments that legislators have made to various programs; and because new governors often get elected in times of economic distress, precisely when the demand for government assistance is the greatest. Thus, newly elected governors find budgets can only be changed incrementally because the political consequences of change are too costly. New endeavors, they often find, must be financed out of new taxing initiatives.

Profound changes do sometimes occur in taxing and spending policies following elections, as demonstrated by the election in 1990 of the Independent candidate Lowell Weicker in Connecticut and the election in 1993 of the Republican Christine Todd Whitman in New Jersey. Whitman, who succeeded Governor Florio, campaigned on the basis of rolling back the Florio tax increases. She interpreted her victory as a mandate for shrinking New Jersey's spending, which she and the Republican legislature immediately began doing. Whitman, who won reelection in 1997, is discovering, however, that it is more difficult than she anticipated to alter spending and taxing in New Jersey, even though significant changes have occurred (for a review of her successes and failures, see State Policy Research 1997, 4–11).

The Revenue Bill

A companion bill to the appropriations bill sets out changes in the tax and revenue code required to balance the state's budget. Revenue bills generally follow alongside appropriations bills because what the state needs in revenue is determined by the appropriations act. This act also establishes the bounds of what the state can expect in some revenue streams—for example, what can be expected in federal aid is often determined by how much is appropriated as the state's share. As the legislative session unfolds, the governor, the executive budgetary staff, and the legislative revenue committees have three crucial pieces of information before them. First, there are increasingly finer estimates of the revenue requirements that the final budget act entails. A clearer picture appears of the likely shape of the appropriations bill and, therefore, of what changes are required in the tax and revenue code. Second, a somewhat clearer picture is also obtained of what the present array of taxes, charges, and federal aid will produce in the way of revenue. Revenue estimation is part science and part art; the flow of funds depends on the performance of the national, regional, and state economies and on the public's reaction to economic news.

The final set of figures that governors and legislators have available to them is the likely yield of incremental changes to existing taxes and the yield that will accrue as a result of enacting new taxes or increasing present ones. Schedules prepared for the revenue and tax committees will, for example, note that a one-cent increase in the sales tax would yield so many millions in new revenue, whereas the extension of that same tax to the heretofore exempt "all retail grocery food" would yield other many millions. The committee might also consider smaller changes, such as an increase of one cent on cigarette packs or a new tax on, say, boat moorings and services. State legislative committees responsible for drafting the revenue have the ability to differentially inflict damage via raising one tax versus other taxes and for their ability to help citizens by granting exceptions to tax levies (Lemov 1989, 46–52).

One interesting device used by many states is to combine the appropriations and revenue committees and their bills. By linking the two actions directly, legislators are compelled to justify increased expenditures with the new taxes or revenues needed to finance them (Miller 1994).

Submitting the Budget

The final gubernatorial recommendation to the legislature can probably best be characterized by the calculus that governors will add expenditures up to the point at which the vote gain from the next expenditure just balances the vote loss of the new revenue programs needed to finance new spending (Downs 1957). But what is crucial for the budgetary process is that this electoral calculus—what makes sense politically in terms of taxing and spending—for the governor is not necessarily the same calculus that makes sense for state legislators. They have their own electoral interests, which may not be congruent with the governor's. Legislatures in the past two decades have increased their scrutiny of the executive budget and reshaped it for their own ends (Chubb 1985; Clynch and Lauth 1991, esp. chap. 9). State legislators see that their own electoral fortunes are affected by state taxing and spending; the institutional changes described in Chapter 5 of this volume, such as greatly increased staffing and computerized retrieval of appropriations and revenue data, strengthen them in bargaining with the governor about the budget (Squires 1992).

The Legislature Acts

The legislature receives the budget in the form of enormously detailed information about all government spending, including that of each department, agency, and program. How the legislature handles the budget varies from state to state, but the typical state legislature receives the budget by a letter or formal speech by the governor outlining his or her priorities as set out in the accompanying budget documents. The governor's budget is given a bill number by the leadership of the legislative chambers and is then assigned to the committees responsible for appropriations in the chambers. The house of representatives ordinarily begins earlier action, holding hearings with department heads on spending in their departments. Subsequent hearings with agency and program officials are often carried out at a subcommittee level, where the budget is parceled out to numerous smaller subcommittees for even more detailed scrutiny. Seats on committees responsible for appropriations are widely seen by legislators to be prestigious, yet time-consuming, legislative assignments. These ordinarily attract serious and committed legislators.

For a variety of reasons, then, the total of the many departmental and agency requests submitted to the appropriations committees are larger, on the average, than the current year's appropriations. If automatic revenue gains do not match the increases in requests, then the members of the committee begin considering strategies for cutting budgets. One observer has classified such typical, first-slice cuts as "soft" as opposed to "hard" (State Policy Research 1990, 9). Favorite soft cuts include freezes in hiring new personnel, thereby allowing the number of state employees to decline via normal retirement and resignation, freezes on out-of-state travel for state employees, deferring spending from one fiscal year to the next, and across-the-board cuts. The last strategy is an oft-encountered one because it appears so politically attractive—all share equally in the burden and no specific hard choices of penalizing one program and favoring another have to be made. Politically difficult cuts involve layoffs and specific benefit and program reductions.

Efforts are often made to fashion a broad, bipartisan consensus on the budget. Such efforts often fail because of significant party differences in spending and taxing priorities. In the typical state, each subcommittee sends back to the appropriations committee a majority report on its section of the bill (which is usually made up of majority party members), and the majority party on the committee is then charged with reconciling the sum of all subcommittee operations within the revenue constraint. Because each subcommittee attracts members with personal or constituency stakes in its appropriations, the appropriations figures, in the aggregate, may still be too large, thus entailing further cutting at the full committee level. The appropriations committee reports its bill to the full chamber, where it is voted on and often amended. More frequently, a series of opposing party amendments are dutifully voted down by the majority party, and the bill is sent on to the senate. In some states, to promote more regularized procedures, the house votes to bind itself to a particular date for the approved bill to "cross" to the senate.

The senate, with its smaller committees, often operates at a more leisurely pace than the house and without subcommittees. It is continually aware of progress in the other chamber, and it continuously refashions its hearings with agency officials in light of developing events in the house. It eventually has the house bill before it, and that bill focuses hearings in the senate on whether and where to depart from the house figures. The senate committee bill is usually in the form of amendments—either increases or decreases—to the house bill. The senate committee must finally come to agreement, an agreement made easier because the house vote settles many issues. Discussion and voting then occur at the floor level, and the final bill is sent to the governor for approval, veto, or some intermediate action.

When the two chambers disagree on the text of the appropriations bill or on the specific spending amounts, a conference committee comprised of majority and minority leadership and members of the house and senate appropriations committees meets to reconcile the conflicts.

The Governor Acts

In forty-two states, governors have some form of intermediate item veto that allows them to veto parts of bills, lines, or particular items in a bill. Governors with these powers often take some care in examining the budget bill and alter it in important ways. In principle, this ought to be a particularly powerful weapon in the hands of those governors because, as Fisher noted (1985, 7), most state budgets are written in highly specific line-item form that spells out spending for the most minute outlay. This is unlike the federal budget, where large items are budgeted in lump sums. As Chapter 6 of this volume notes, the veto powers of governors vary across the states. These differences from state to state—strong in Illinois and California, weak in New Hampshire and North Carolina—suggest that there may be rules, practices, and institutions that constrain spending, that dampen political impulses to spend. It turns out that this is only one of many budgetary institutions and traits that vary among the states.

CONTROLLING SPENDING AND TAXING: INNOVATION, CHANGE, AND VARIABILITY IN BUDGETING RULES AND PRACTICES

In an often-quoted dissenting opinion of the U. S. Supreme Court, Justice Louis Brandeis stated, "[I]t is one of the happy incidents of the federal system that a single courageous State may, if its citizens choose, serve as a laboratory; and try novel social and economic experiments without risk to the rest of the country" (New State Ice Co. v. Liebmann, 285 U.S. 262 at 311 [1932]). Over the past century and a half the American states have compiled a fascinating record of experimentation in the rules and practices that shape their spending and taxing. Innovations that are now commonplace—for example, the "executive budget"—were at their time of origin self-consciously designed experiments. Others, like the item veto, originated in nineteenth-century American constitutions. The item veto, interestingly enough, had its origin in the constitution of the Confederate States of America. Others arose almost spontaneously from initiative and referendum processes, which produced many tax and expenditure limitations.

Brandeis's acclaim for the power of states' experimentation was based on his belief that worthy innovations would diffuse and be adopted as practice or policy across the states. Worthy innovations among the states also create speculation about their likely effects if adopted nationally. Based on his California experiences, former governor Ronald Reagan repeatedly advanced his arguments on behalf of the item veto in Washington. After years of debate and bipartisan presidential recommendation, Congress granted just such authority to Bill Clinton in 1996 only to see it struck down by Supreme Court action in 1998 (Clinton v. City of New York, 118 S. Ct. 2091). Many state budgeting rules and practices also get adopted or considered for adoption by our national government. One example is the appropriate time period for budgeting. Some states budget annually; others write a budget every two years. Vice President Al Gore, who presided over the report of the National Performance Review (1993, as discussed in Fisher 1997a), advocated biennial budgeting for the federal government.

In addition to the executive budget, other innovative budget rules and practices include annual versus biennial appropriations, the line-item veto, the item-reduction veto, omnibus versus separate appropriations acts, separate capital and operating budgets; the constraining influence of external financing of state general obligation bonds; various forms of balanced budget rules in place; and tax and expenditure limitation rules or fiscal caps.

Annual Versus Biennial Appropriations

Historically, most states passed a budget that legislated spending for the two-year period that corresponded with the legislative session—the biennium. Over time, the number of states that budgeted biennially shrank from forty-four in 1940 to about ten or so in 1995 (ACIR 1995, 4–5; Kearns 1993, 42). But that figure may increase because the debate over the wisdom of biennial versus annual budgeting continues to flare in the states. It is an object of reform interest at the federal level, too (Fisher 1997a). Many argue that legislative consideration and passage of a two-year statute appropriating funds leads to smaller budgets. The logic is that biennial budgets are more certain and fixed, whereas annual budgets are more flexible, and "flexible" in budgeting invariably means "more money." If agency officials know they can plan for serial, annual rounds of budgeting, they will organize their agency's operations in such a way to increase pressure on legislators to approve increased spending. Pressures two years out are harder to organize and legislators are apt to react conservatively in the absence of these pressures, thus leading to lowered levels of spending.

Biennial budgeting would probably enhance executive influence at the expense of the legislature, another dampening effect on spending (Fisher 1997a, 93–94). In the more uncertain situation of biennial budgeting, legislators and governors are more likely to act in cautious, risk-averse fashion. Not knowing what the inflation rate will be, or how personal income or consumption spending will change—key determinants of the income and sales taxes—will lead political leaders to take safer, thrifty, more conservative courses of constrained spending. Finally, there should be some savings from smaller numbers of people involved and less effort required to produce one budget every two years versus one every year (Fisher 1997a; Kearns 1993). And, as predicted, there does appear to be some evidence that states with annual budgets spend more (Kearns 1990, 54).

However, the interesting and yet-to-be-resolved issue is the direction of causality. Is it that annual sessions lead to more spending, as the previous analysis suggests? Or is it that states with pressures to spend more "need" to have annual sessions to exert finer control over these spending pressures? The answer is probably a combination of both. Legislators in big states such as California, New York, and Massachusetts need annual sessions to ensure that administrative agencies serve their constituents well. Yet the very existence of regular, annual sessions sets up a hazard for legislators in that the more often they meet, the more constituent and administrative pressure they generate for themselves. From the legislators' perspective, this may be a positive (although barely so) trade-off; they may be willing to endure more constituent pressure as a necessary cost of gaining better control of state government. The net effects, though, are longer and more expensive legislative sessions and increased administrative and constituency pressures to spend, both of which result in enlarged budgets.

The Executive Budget

One of the earliest and most significant state innovations placed responsibility for the origination of the budget in the hands of the governor as chief state executive. At present, about forty of the fifty states employ a system (like that operating on the federal level) in which the chief executive has full responsibility for the initial budget document and the legislature increases or decreases the recommendation. But a few states exist at the outer limits of heightened gubernatorial power (see Chapter 6 of this volume for a discussion) in situations in which the governor recommends a budget and the legislature cannot increase spending, but can only decrease or cut it. There is an opposing pole of gubernatorial weakness: Two states have other officials sharing the power of budget formulation with the governor, and the legislature has the power to increase or decrease recommendations. The implication of these alternative rules is the prediction, for which there is weak but confirming evidence, that as power is centralized in the governor's office, there is diminished pressure to increase spending, and this will lead to smaller budgets (Crain and Miller 1990, 1041).

Omnibus Versus Multiple Budget Bills

About one-half of the states adopt a single operating budget, and the remaining have varying practices (Crain and Miller 1990). The conventional wisdom holds that as the number of budget bills handled by a legislature shrinks to one omnibus bill, it should be more and more difficult to amass a successful coalition to oppose this single bill. In most years, the budget bill is among the very last bills considered by the legislative chambers, usually right before the start of the new fiscal year. This leads to strong pressures mobilized on each legislator to pass the budget and the pressures multiply in enforcing support of a single omnibus act. From their point of view, legislators have before them a budget bill the bulk of which they approve, even though there may be some items of which they strongly disapprove. An all-or-nothing omnibus budget bill strategy, then, should lead to budget enlargement as more and more items that could not possibly win approval on their own or as part of a divided, smaller appropriation get inserted for this very reason and win approval as part of an omnibus act.

We would expect that as the number of appropriations bills considered shrinks in a state legislature, with the limit approaching the single omnibus act, the budget gets larger. On the other hand, there is a limit in the opposing direction. As the number of separate spending bills considered by the legislature increases, the amount of time and energy and coordination costs devoted to appropriations politics increases with associated political and personal costs. But the bottom line is still the fewer the number of appropriations bills, the larger the budget is in its total. Crain and Miller (1990, 1042) in their examination of the fifty states over the 1979–1986 period found weak but predictable effects of omnibus bill strategies and more spending.

The Capital Budget and the Operating Budget

The most common form of multiple budget bills found in the American states is the separation of the capital and the operating budgets. The operating budget is what we ordinarily think of in budgeting—how much to spend on welfare, how much we should aid colleges and universities, how much to maintain public health in local communities, and how many dollars for state police, courts, and prisons. But social workers counsel and give assistance in office buildings; students live in dorms; public health officials work in state laboratories; and the states' courts systems operate in courthouses, police stations, and prisons. How should long-lived buildings and equipment be financed?

At the federal level and in eight or so states, there is no distinction between the two—capital spending is merged into the operating budget. If the state needs a new prison, that becomes part of the operating budget. In six of the states with no capital budget, all capital expenditures are made on a pay-as-you-go basis—buildings and infrastructure proposals are budgeted in the current annual or biennial budget and form part of the ongoing taxpayers' burden of the cost of construction (Poterba 1995, 169). However, the bulk of the states separate spending on long-lived items such as buildings, roads, mainframe computers, and so on. Most of these states borrow in competitive bond markets to finance these capital expenditures on the theory that spending on a highway is not the same as spending in support of a state college faculty salary. The teacher receives her salary for services rendered in that period; the highway is built for her and all taxpayers' use as well as for future generations of beneficiaries. Borrowing and building now spreads the costs of construction over time so that each generation pays more or less proportionately for the government benefits that they enjoy (for a discussion of state debt, see Clingermayer and Wood 1995).

Let us consider the budget size consequence of the simple division of the budget into capital and operating versions. If there is a separate office or agency responsible for organizing, processing, and completing capital projects, this is an added expense and it puts into place an agency with stakes in more spending on capital projects. Also, a capital budget allows interest groups with stakes in the spending— for example, construction firms and bond-financing firms—to focus their efforts on one agency and one legislative committee, further pressuring spending upward (Poterba 1995, 170). Politicians are attracted to projects for which they can claim credit and capital projects such as a new highway or a new bridge are particularly useful in this regard (Mayhew 1974). But consider the contrary effects of pay-as-you-go. If capital projects are financed out of current tax revenues, they must compete with operating expenditures and be financed by levying taxes on current citizens so future generations of citizens can reap the benefits. The alternative is debt financing by borrowing.

There is a long-standing proposition that borrowing creates a fiscal illusion of diminished real cost for current taxpayers (see Mueller 1989, 342–343). Current taxpayers borrow today, finish the project, and enjoy the fruits of the borrowing while paying for only a fraction of the cost. Later generations of taxpayers will pay for much of the capital project—the road or the college dormitory—and the benefits are enjoyed by current taxpayers. Note the difficulty of making the opposing case: Is it reasonable for current taxpayers to pay for a long-lived project out of their current income? Why should not future beneficiaries of the new highway or dorm pay for part of the cost? The issue is further complicated because the borrowed-for project costs more. By debt financing, the state government borrows and obtains the principal to be used to finance the project but they must pay back both the principal as well as interest expenses. Overall, the total cost—principal plus interest—is much larger than the cost of the project financed pay-as-you-go.

Constraints on Borrowing and Debt

There is a long historical record documenting the propensity of state governments to engage in debt financing. To control the temptation to debt financing, all but a handful of states place new restrictions on the use of debt. Some states—for example, California—require that voters approve of debt financing via a referendum and that a supermajority of the legislature (in various states ranging from 60 percent to 75 percent) also approve. Only Connecticut, Maryland, New Hampshire, Tennessee, and Vermont have no popular or legislative restrictions (Kiewiet and Szakaly 1996, 65–67). Some require that the debt obligation of the states be limited to a certain fraction of the state's revenues or be limited to some percentage of some other key state trait. A number of states simply prohibit debt financing—Colorado and Nebraska are examples (Kiewiet and Szakaly 1996; Regens and Lauth 1992).

The borrowing behavior of the American states over the recent past is predictable. States with capital budgets tend to spend more on capital projects than those with single unified budgets. Further, debt financing also leads to more capital spending (Poterba 1995). Kiewiet and Szakaly (1996) discovered that states with some kinds of restrictions on incurring debt such as requiring approval in voter referendum borrow less. They discovered that states that only require a legislative supermajority do not seem to be constrained by this barrier—states that simply require a legislative supermajority put together that coalition and borrow as much as those without such a requirement. Further, restrictions on state borrowing often mean downward focusing pressures that will lead to more borrowing by local county, city, and town governments.

There is a further external limit on debt financing. Borrowing that is "guaranteed" by state governments and their taxpayers, the "general obligation bond," is sold at a rate of interest to lenders (for a useful discussion, see Lemov 1991, 32–36). The interest rate, which is the cost of borrowing, rises as the riskiness of the loan rises. Some states are seen as particularly good risks, as credit-worthy, whereas others are seen as poorer risks. Several bond firms rate the states as to their credit-worthiness. The mid-1998 rating by Moody's is set out in the last column of Table 9-3. Highly worthy states are rated as triple A (Georgia, for example), and the most risky state borrowers—Louisiana, New York, Hawaii—are rated lower at A3, A2, and A1. Changes up or down in the ratings over the past two years are indicated in parentheses. Note that both New York and Louisiana have improved their ratings, which will decrease their cost of borrowing, and Hawaii's rating declined, thereby upping the interest rate required to attract borrowers.

In an interesting study, Bayoumi and colleagues (1995) discovered that as the size of the states' debts rise, so does the interest rate charged. Lenders require a premium from highly indebted states, and the premium rises more steeply as debt increases. When the amount of state debt reaches somewhere between 8 percent and 10 percent of total state economic product, further borrowing is no longer possible. At that level of debt, the state literally loses credit. Today, Hawaii, Connecticut, and Massachusetts are nearing or at that limit (Perez-Pena 1998). Bayoumi et al. (1995) also confirmed that fiscal controls on debt lower the cost of borrowing. So do high tax rates. High tax rates indicate a willingness of politicians and voters to tax themselves to pay off debt, which gives confidence to lenders. The identical ratings of New Hampshire and Vermont (both at AA) indicate these contrasting effects. Debt is much higher in Vermont than in New Hampshire, thus the bond rating should be less than triple-A. New Hampshire has a much lower debt burden, but because the state has resolutely avoided either a sales or income tax the low level of "willingness to be taxed" creates doubts in lenders' minds about taxpayers' willingness to back debt. What makes one state fiscally upright and another suspect, then, are the estimates of their economic strengths and their fiscal—spending and taxing—reputations.

There are alternative strategies for states' leaders to the use of general obligation bonds. First, limits on the amount of debts that states can assume lead to the creation of "public authorities" such as tollroad authorities (for example, New York, Pennsylvania, and the New Jersey thruways or turnpike authorities) to borrow separately with revenues from the authorities' operations dedicated to paying off the debt (Bunch 1991; von Hagen 1991). Note the politicians' and voters' logic in creating these kinds of authorities. Present users (many are voters) benefit from the tollroad and share the costs of the tollways with future fellow citizens and travelers (and not-yet voters). Second, nonvoters will share in paying for these tollways that voters enjoy. Surely the bulk of tolls on the New Jersey Turnpike are paid by non-New Jersey citizens.

The Veto, the Item Veto, and the Item Reduction Veto

Of all the budgeting characteristics among the states, probably the structure and practice of gubernatorial vetoes has most interested citizens and scholars. In forty-three states, governors have some form of intermediate item veto. Several scholars have studied governors' use of the item veto in the American states in expectation of establishing evidence of its efficacy (Abney and Lauth 1985; Alm and Evers 1991; Berch 1992; Fisher 1997b; Nice 1988). The conclusion of most state studies, however, is that the item veto has a negligible impact on total or aggregate spending in the states. States in which the governor is empowered to burrow into the budget and selectively cut it do not seem to have appreciably smaller budgets than states with less-empowered governors. Alm and Evers (1991), generally confirming other studies, did note a very small effect—about 1 percent smaller than expected budget—when the governor was of one party and the legislature of the other. More supportive are Crain and Miller who noted that of the forty-three governors with item vetoes, ten of them have the power of the "item reduction veto," the power to "write in a lower spending level or veto the entire item" (1990, 1034). In their analysis of state spending, they discover significant impacts of the item reduction veto on the total size of state budgets (1041–1042).

The finding that the governor's general item veto had little or no overall impact and that it had only a small effect under divided control of government may be explained by the same causal process—the item veto sets up a situation in which governors and legislatures engage in sophisticated political games. For example, if the legislature prefers a larger amount of spending, it will pad, or increase, the amount it desires to allot to an item in an effort to preserve it from an item reduction veto. One sophisticated method of padding is to combine line items liked by the governor with line items that are not favored, which usually will mean that both items are preserved. Under the condition of divided partisan control of the government the stakes and sophistication of the games increase. Legislatures heighten their efforts to protect favored programs, and governors subject the budget to even greater scrutiny and broader excision, thereby reducing slightly the overall budget. Gamesmanship reached new heights (or depths) when Gov. Tommy Thompson of Wisconsin "vetoed words, including 'shalt' and 'not,' punctuation such as commas and periods, and 'then cobbled together the surviving words into whole new sentences—and new law'" (Beyle 1994, 44).

Balanced Budget Rules

The constitutions of twenty-four states require final legislative passage and gubernatorial approval of a balanced budget. In eight states the necessity for a final balanced budget is a weaker, statutory requirement (CSG 1992, 355–356). Although eighteen states do not require that the final budget signed by the governor be balanced, all states, except for Vermont, have some sort of statutory or constitutional budget requirement for balance at either the stage of the gubernatorial budget, the legislative budget, or on final passage. California, for example, constitutionally requires that the governor submit a balanced budget; it does not require that the final budget itself be balanced. Conversely, Colorado does not require gubernatorial submission of a balanced budget, but it does require that the budget passed by the legislature with final gubernatorial action be balanced. Note the logic of each position: For California lawmakers, requiring a balanced budget from the governor informs them of the basic priorities of the governor—what programs must be cut or what taxes raised to finance necessary programs. The legislature may, as the year unfolds, find a greater wisdom in a short-term deficit, depending on revenue performance. In contrast, Colorado's less constraining procedure allows that state's governor to inform the legislature of gubernatorial priorities regarding new initiatives and possible alternative policies and to leave the question of financing increased spending—balancing the budget—for later negotiation. Many states require that the budget be balanced at all three stages: submission of governor's budget, submission of legislative budget, and final passage with gubernatorial approval. This process forces revelation of spending and taxing preferences of the governor and legislature, and mandates that their preferences ultimately be reconciled.

In assessing various rules, Poterba (1994, 1995) concluded that as the balanced budget rules increased in stringency, the likelihood of borrowing dropped and expenditure cuts or tax increases were more likely to be employed to regain balance. The alternative hypothesis—that these rules could and would be ignored or circumvented—is unsupported by the evidence. In fact, Alt and Lowry found that budget rules were more effective when a Republican administration was in office. In their words, "institutions matter, and party control matters" (1994, 823).

Fiscal Caps, Tax and Expenditure Limitation Rules

After 1978, when the first tax revolt proposition was voted in California, states and localities across the country adopted devices meant to constrain the size of their governments (Hansen 1990; Lowery and Sigelman 1981; Sears and Citrin 1985). A cap on the size of the budget in relation to the size of the state economy or total personal income has been favored by many state electorates. Fiscal "caps are explicitly designed to restrict public sector size to some proportion of the size of the total economy" by the conservative political movement, which desires to constrain "excessive government growth" (Cox and Lowery 1990, 492).

In an interesting comparison of three states that had caps of varying degrees of porosity with three other states—matched in terms of region, population size, and wealth, with no fiscal caps—Cox and Lowery found no differences between the capped and uncapped states in various measures of taxing and spending (1990, 507). The most likely interpretation of this finding is that all states' economies grew fast enough in the period examined to allow for comparable government growth in the capped and uncapped states. Still, the caps do exist in many states, and it is possible that a prolonged decline in statewide personal income would force the budget up to the level of the cap. A later team (King-Meadows and Lowery 1996) updated the review of these six states to a time period with more severe economic constraints and slightly modified the earlier conclusions. As they put it, "we have found the first—albeit very weak and tentative—evidence that caps may actually act to restrict the growth of government" (109). Nevertheless, the overwhelming message of their newer study is that similar states react the same to similar economic stimuli—either booms or recessions—and that fiscal caps have a marginal impact on spending. The message of "no or very weak overall effects" is reflected in other research as well (for a review, see Mullins and Joyce 1996; alternatively, see Elder 1992).

In addition to the powerful effects of the economy driving state budgets, Cox and Lowery (1990) mentioned a more general process at work in the states that may dampen growth in tax revenues—a horizontal causal process. Although legislators in the states that have caps may be reluctant to increase revenues rapidly and thereby approach the limit of the cap, the restraint may constrain legislators in the nearby states that have no caps. After Tennessee adopted its cap, legislators in uncapped Kentucky may have learned two lessons. First, by constraining tax increases on their own, Kentucky legislators could reduce public pressure for imposing a cap in Kentucky. And second, constraint in revenue and tax rises might prevent Kentucky's losing businesses and other mobile residents to Tennessee.

Conclusion on the Effects of Budget Rules and Practices

There are no simple solutions for balancing budgets. Some studies support the effects of the item reduction veto or balanced budget rules or fiscal caps; others find little of value. It is clear though that under some reasonably ordinary conditions such as divided government or strong ideological predispositions, rules and practices can serve as useful ways to constrain government spending. What we do not know is how these rules might interact with one another and with relevant within-state characteristics. It should be no surprise that the most enthusiastic governor advocating enhanced executive veto powers is a veteran conservative Republican governor already possessed of the item reduction veto, and a governor who had long-standing state legislative experience prior to serving as governor, and who now governs what was once a highly taxed, expenditure-generous state: Gov. Tommy Thompson of Wisconsin.

FUTURE DIRECTIONS

The evidence concerning government growth is unambiguous. We have ever so slowly but significantly enlarged government. Citizens and voters have contributed to this growth by their demands for government goods and services. Also contributing to this growth are the very indirect and only tentative links between taxing and instruments of voter control. Elections are ordinarily the means by which voters control elected officials, but the links between taxing and voter disapproval in this modern era are imperfect and indirect. We may not like taxes, but we have not in the past disliked our legislators and our governors so much that we punished them directly at the polls when they tax us. And there is a certain logic to the weak electoral link. Only a handful of elected officials ever put themselves into the position of having their election become a referendum on a tax. Elected officials present more facets in their appeals to voters, and it is the complexity and diversity of determinants of voter choice that attenuates the link between taxing and voting. Nevertheless, the pressures of cutting spending and taxes appear inexorable.

There is a complementary argument, however, that voters can be presented with unambiguous choices of cutting taxes in referendums; California's Proposition 13 and the various tax caps installed by referendum in many states are examples. When faced with such direct and simple choices, voters often vote for direct rules such as caps or tax cuts—self-interest is direct and straightforward (Sears and Citrin 1985). When admonitions from politicians such as "Vote for this proposition and watch your property taxes get cut by two-thirds" are heard, it is difficult for voters to resist. What is much more difficult to achieve, however, is agreement on exactly which government program or service should get cut if the revenue-cutting proposition passes. In fact, no such agreement could ever be reached among voters on a list of cuts. Each of us would list the programs that we want untouched, and each voter's list would be slightly different from that of the next person; no agreement on spending cuts would ever be reached by a direct voting process.

The ordinary institutions of representative government in America are structured to make those kinds of decisions—reconciling the demands of those seeking government goods and services with the interests of those seeking to minimize the costs of government. Ultimately, if control of government taxing and spending is to occur, it will have to be by means of these representative institutions—the governors and legislatures. The control has been ragged and inefficient to this point, but we may be entering an era of heightened voter awareness of the limits of what government can do, heightened sensitivity to the costs of government action, and greater attention both to the rules and practices shaping politicians in institutions, as well as on ways and means of tightening or altering rules and practices to constrain political choice. Politicians, because of their vote-seeking natures, are sensitive to these signals from voters.

There is impressive evidence that budgets of the American states will continue to grow and possibly accelerate, regardless of voter pressure to cut taxes. Powerful voter pressure exists to increase spending on some items—corrections, transportation, and economic development programs, for example, that are discussed in the following chapters. Still other programs may well be forced on states. Several states are under state supreme court orders to equalize per pupil educational expenditures by reducing reliance on the local property tax. States continue to rely on aid from the federal government for a large part of their revenue. Yet all of the signals emanating from Washington, D.C., suggest further diminishing federal support. Cutting federal aid for state programs in welfare, highways, environmental protection, and law and corrections may reduce state revenues for such programs, but it will not diminish citizen interest in and pressures for program continuity. The next several years promise to be a particularly interesting period in the American federal system as states' political leaders wrestle with these dilemmas of the conflicting political interests of taxing and spending.

REFERENCES

Abney, Glenn, and Thomas P. Lauth. 1985. "The Line Item Veto in the States." *Public Administration Review* 45:372–377.

ACIR (Advisory Commission on Intergovernmental Relations). 1995. *Significant features of fiscal federalism*, Volume 1. Washington, D.C.: Author.

Alm, James, and Mark Evers. 1991. "The Item Veto and Government Expenditure." *Public Choice* 68:1–15.

Alt, James, and Robert C. Lowry. 1994. "Divided Government, Fiscal Institutions, and Budget Deficits: Evidence from the States." *American Political Science Review* 88:811–828.

Barone, Michael. 1994. *The Almanac of American Politics*. Washington, D.C.: National Journal.

Baumol, William J. 1967. "Macroeconomics of Unbalanced Growth: The Anatomy of Urban Crisis." *American Economic Review* 62:415–426.

Bayoumi, Tamim, Morris Goldstein, and Geoffrey Woglom. 1995. "Do Credit Markets Discipline Sovereign Borrowers? Evidence from the States." *Journal of Money, Credit and Banking* 27:1046–1059.

Berch, Neil. 1992. "The Line Item Veto in the States: An Analysis of the Effects over Time." *Social Science Journal* 29:335–346.

Berry, Frances S., and William D. Berry. 1992. "Tax Innovation in the States: Capitalizing on Political Opportunity." *American Journal of Political Science* 36:715–742.

Berry, William, and David Lowery. 1987. *Understanding United States Government Growth: An Empirical Analysis of the Postwar Era*. New York: Praeger.

Beyle, Thad, ed. 1992. *Governors and Hard Times*. Washington, D.C.: CQ Press.

———. 1994. "The Governors—1992–1993." *The Book of the States, 1994–95*. Lexington, Ky.: Council of State Governments.

Black, Chris. 1990. "The Sales Tax Revisited: Lessons from 1965." *Boston Sunday Globe*, May 27, A2:1.

Bowler, Shaun, and Todd Donovan. 1995. "Popular Responsiveness to Taxation." *Political Research Quarterly* 48:1.

Bunch, Beverly 1991. "The effect of constitutional debt limits on state governments' use of public authorities." *Public Choice* 68:57–69.

Chubb, John E. 1985. "The Political Economy of Federalism." *American Political Science Review* 79:994–1015.

Citizens for Tax Justice. 1991. *A Far Cry from Fair.* Washington, D.C.: Author.

Clingermayer, James C., and B. Dan Wood. 1995. "Disentangling Patterns of State Debt Financing." *American Political Science Review* 89(1):108–120.

Clynch, Edward J., and Thomas P. Lauth, eds. 1991. *Governors, Legislatures, and Budgets: Diversity across the American States.* Westport, Conn.: Greenwood Press.

Cox, James, and David Lowery. 1990. "The Impact of the Tax Revolt Era: State Fiscal Caps." *Social Science Quarterly* 71:492–509.

Crain, W. Mark, and James C. Miller, III. 1990. "Budget Process and Spending Growth." *William and Mary Law Review* (Summer):1021–1047.

CSG (Council of State Governments). 1992. *The Book of the States, 1992–93.* Lexington, Ky.: Author.

Downs, Anthony. 1957. *An Economic Theory of Democracy.* New York: Harper and Brothers.

Duncombe, William. 1992. "Economic Change and the Evolving State Tax Structure: The Case of the Sales Tax." *National Tax Journal* 45:299–313.

Dye, Thomas. 1966. *Politics, Economics, and the Public: Policy Outcomes in the American States.* Chicago: Rand McNally.

Dye, Richard, and Therese J. McGuire. 1991. "Growth and Variability of State Individual Income and General Sales Taxes." *National Tax Journal* 44:55–66.

Eismeier, Theodore. 1983. "Votes and Taxes: The Political Economy of the American Governorship." *Polity* 15:368–379.

Elder, Harold. 1992. "Exploring the Tax Revolt." *Public Finance Quarterly* 20:47–63.

Erikson, Robert S., Gerald C. Wright, and John P. McIver. 1993. *Statehouse Democracy: Public Opinion and Policy in the American States.* New York: Cambridge University Press.

Fisher, Louis. 1985. "The Line Item Veto: The Risks of Emulating the States." A paper presented at the annual meeting of the American Political Science Association, New Orleans, August 29–31.

———. 1997a. "Biennial Budgeting in the Federal Government." *Public Budgeting & Finance* (Fall):87–97.

———. 1997b. "The Line-Item Veto Act of 1996: Heads-up from the States." *Public Budgeting & Finance* (Summer 1997):87–97.

Fisher, Ronald. 1988. *State and Local Public Finance.* Glenview, Ill.: Scott, Foresman.

Garand, James C. 1985. "Partisan Change and Shifting Expenditure Priorities in the American States, 1945–1978." *American Politics Quarterly* 14:355–391.

Hansen, Susan B. 1983. *The Politics of Taxation: Revenue without Representation.* New York: Praeger.

———. 1990. "The Politics of State Taxing and Spending." In *Politics in the American States,* edited by Virginia Gray, Herbert Jacob, and Robert B. Albritton. Glenview, Ill.: Scott, Foresman/Little, Brown.

Johnson, Kirk. 1993. "Tribal Rights: Refining the Law of Recognition." *New York Times,* October 17.

Kearns, Paula S. 1993. "The Determinants of State Budget Periodicity: An Empirical Analysis." *Public Budgeting & Finance* (Spring):40–58.

Kiewiet, D. Roderick, and Kristin Szakaly. 1996. "Constitutional Limits on Borrowing: An Analysis of State Bonded Indebtedness." *Journal of Law, Economics and Organization* 12:62–97.

King-Meadows, Tysons, and David Lowery. 1996. "The Impact of the Tax Revolt Era [on] State Fiscal Caps: A Research Update." *Public Budgeting & Finance* (Spring):102–112.

Kone, Susan, and Richard Winters. 1993. "Taxes and Voting: Electoral Retribution in the American States." *Journal of Politics* 55:22–40.

Larkey, Patrick D., Chandler Stolp, and Mark Winer. 1981. "Theorizing about the Growth of Government: A Research Assessment." *Journal of Public Policy* 1:157–220.

Lemov, Penelope. 1989. "Sorry, I Can't Do That." *Governing* (September):46–52.

———. 1991. "Bad Times and Bond Ratings." *Governing* (March):32–36.

———. 1992. "The Decade of Red Ink." *Governing* (November):29–30.

———. 1996. "The Tastiest Tax Cut." *Governing* (November):44–47.

———. 1997. "Fiscal Tricks for the Fat Years." *Governing* (February):44–47.

Lowery, David, Thomas Konda, and James C. Garand. 1984. "Spending in the States: A Test of Six Models." *Western Political Quarterly* 37:48–66.

Lowery, David, and Lee Sigelman. 1981. "Understanding the Tax Revolt: An Assessment of Eight Explanations." *American Political Science Review* 75:963–974.

Mayhew, David. 1974. *Congress: The Electoral Connection.* New Haven, Conn.: Yale University Press.

Mikesell, John L. 1978. "Election Periods and State Policy Cycles." *Public Choice* 33:99–106.

———. 1992. "State Sales Tax Policy in a Changing Economy." *Public Budgeting & Finance* (Spring):83–91.

Miller, Penny. 1994. *Kentucky Politics and Government.* Lincoln: University of Nebraska Press.

Mueller, Dennis C. 1989. *Public Choice II.* New York: Cambridge University Press.

Mullins, Daniel R., and Philip G. Joyce. 1996. "Tax and Expenditure Limitations and State and Local Fiscal Structure: An Empirical Assessment." *Public Budgeting & Finance* (Spring):75–101.

Nice, David C. 1988. "The Item Veto and Expenditure Restraint." *The Journal of Politics* 50:487–499.

Niemi, Richard G., Harold W. Stanley, and Ronald J. Vogel. 1995. "State Economies and State Taxes: Do Voters Hold Governors Accountable?" *American Journal of Political Science* 39:936–957.

Olson, Mancur. 1973. "Evaluating Performance in the Public Sector." In *The Measurement of Economic and Social Performance,* edited by M. Moss. New York: National Bureau of Economic Research.

Oreskes, Michael. 1988. "The Republicans in New Orleans: The People in the Party." *New York Times,* August 14, 1:32.

Perez-Pena, R. 1998. "New York Debt Follows Economy: Up." *New York Times,* July 15, A1:5.

Plotnick, Robert D., and Richard F. Winters. 1985. "A Politico–Economic Theory of Redistribution." *American Political Science Review* 79:458–473.

———. 1990. "Party, Political Liberalism, and Redistribution: An Application to the American States." *American Politics Quarterly* 18:430–458.

Pomper, Gerald M. 1968. *Elections in America.* New York: Dodd, Mead.

Poterba, James M. 1994. "Capital Budgets, Borrowing Rules, and State Capital Spending." *Journal of Public Economics* 56:165–187.

———. 1995. "Balanced Budget Rules and Fiscal Policy: Evidence from the States." *National Tax Journal* 48:329–337.

Purdom, Todd. 1998a. "Budget Surplus Is Driving a Hole in California's Pocket." *New York Times,* January 19, A8:5.

———. 1998b. "California Budget Struggle Is Bitter Despite Surplus." *New York Times,* July 8, A12:6.

Regens, James L., and Thomas P. Lauth. 1992. "Buy Now, Pay Later: Trends in State Indebtedness, 1950–1989." *Public Administration Review* 52:157–161.

Riker, William H. 1986. *The Art of Political Manipulation.* New Haven, Conn.: Yale University Press.

Sabato, Larry. 1978. *Goodbye to Good-time Charlie.* Lexington, Mass.: Lexington Books.

Sears, David O., and Jack Citrin. 1985. *Tax Revolt: Something for Nothing in California.* Cambridge, Mass.: Harvard University Press.

Squires, Peverill. 1992. "Theory of Legislative Institutionalization and the California Assembly." *Journal of Politics* 54:1026–1054.

Stanley, Harold W., and Richard Niemi. 1998. *Vital Statistics on American Politics—1997–1998.* Washington, D.C.: CQ Press.

State Policy Research. various years. *State Policy Reports.* Alexandria, Va.: Author.

Tax Foundation. various years. *Facts and Figures on Government Finance.* New York: Author.

Thompson, Joel A. 1987. "Agency Requests, Gubernatorial Support, and Budget Success in State Legislatures Revisited." *Journal of Politics* 49:756–779.

U.S. Bureau of the Census. Various years. *Statistical Abstract of the United States.* Washington, D.C.: U.S. Department of Commerce, Bureau of the Census.

von Hagen, Jurgen. 1991. "A Note on the Empirical Effectiveness of Formal Fiscal Restraints." *Journal of Public Economics* 44:199–210.

Wildavsky, Aaron. 1980. *The New Politics of the Budgetary Process.* Glenview, Ill.: Scott, Foresman.

Winters, Richard F. 1980. "Political Choice and Expenditure Change." *Polity* 12:598–622.

———. 1990. ""Forget All about that 'Read My Lips' Stuff, OK!"—Gubernatorial Election and Re-election Strategies in the Face of New Tax Programs, 1957–1985." A paper presented at the annual meeting of the American Political Science Association, San Francisco, August 30–September 2.

SUGGESTED READINGS

Auerbach, Alan, ed. *Fiscal Policy: Lessons from Economic Research.* Cambridge: MIT Press, 1997. The chapters by Quigley and Rubinfeld and by Poterba are economic analyses of the political economy issues of federalism and budget rules discussed in this chapter.

Clynch, Edward J., and Thomas P. Lauth, eds. *Governors, Legislatures, and Budgets: Diversity across the American States.* Westport, Conn.: Greenwood Press, 1991. A survey of budgeting politics in thirteen states.

Fisher, Ronald C. *State and Local Public Finance.* Glenview, Ill.: Scott, Foresman, 1988. The standard public finance textbook presents the economist's view of taxing and spending in American state governments.

Hansen, Susan B. *The Politics of Taxation: Revenue without Representation.* New York: Praeger, 1983. The most comprehensive and interesting political science account of taxation in state politics.

Excellent regular reviews of state spending and taxing appear in the biennial volumes, the *Book of the States,* published by the Council of State Governments, in Lexington, Kentucky; in the monthly magazine *Governing,* published by Congressional Quarterly of Washington, D.C.; and in the biweekly *State Policy Reports,* published by State Policy Reports, of Alexandria, Virginia.

CHAPTER 10

Transforming State Health and Welfare Programs

MARK CARL ROM

State governments are increasingly taking responsibility for health and welfare programs. The states, moreover, are changing these programs' goals, their clientele, and the way their services are delivered. These changes create new opportunities and obstacles for those who administer the programs, those who are affected by them, and those who hope to study their causes and consequences.

This chapter focuses on the most important state programs that deliver medical services and economic support to the needy and the transformations affecting these programs. I attempt to answer several questions: What are the major health and welfare programs in our nation, and what roles do the states play in designing, funding, and implementing them? What are the main patterns regarding the state programs over time and across the states regarding recipients, benefits, and expenditures? What are the states now doing to reform their health and welfare programs? What are the politics of these programs? What are the states doing to promote personal health and economic independence so that these medical and income support programs will be less necessary in the future?

THE PROGRAMS

America's health and welfare are tightly connected. One of the classic research questions indeed is, "Are individuals prosperous because they are healthy, or healthy because they are prosperous?" Our health and welfare programs have not been closely coordinated, however, and they are becoming less so. Our health programs have delivered medical treatment, and our welfare programs have provided income support. Both types of programs have delivered treatment or income to well-defined, and often fairly narrow, groups. Government-sponsored medical services have gone, in particular, to the elderly and to those with low incomes, the same groups assisted by welfare programs. These programs have helped millions by staving off deprivation and disease, yet they have failed to ensure a nation of independent, prosperous, healthy individuals. And they have always sought to remedy problems rather than to prevent them.

The problem has not been a shortage of programs that affect our health and welfare; the United States has such programs beyond count. There are more than 85,000 units of government around the country, and almost anything these governments do influences the health and welfare of their constituents. When governments fund or regulate agriculture, the environment, or transportation, for example, they affect our food, our water, and our air, surely the basic factors on which our health is based. As governments fund or regulate education, housing, and commerce, they shape our knowledge, our shelter, and our jobs, all issues that determine our welfare.

Health and social welfare programs are the giants in our governments' budgets. In 1993 federal, state, and local governments spent more than $1.5 trillion on social programs, including more than $400 billion on medical programs (U.S. Bureau of the Census 1997, 372). (To help us to compare different years, all economic data have been converted into 1995 dollars unless otherwise stated.) State and local governments accounted for about 40 percent of these expenditures, with the federal government picking up the rest of the tab.

Social welfare programs either transfer income or provide services to individuals to improve the quality of their lives. The vast majority of social welfare spending is not aimed specifically at those in poverty, however, nor is all of it visible. For example, Social Security, the largest national social welfare program, paid more than half a trillion dollars to the elderly in 1997 (SSA 1998). Medicare, a purely national program that provides medical benefits to the elderly, cost the federal government more than $200 billion in 1996 (HCFA 1998a). Public education, the largest social welfare program funded by state and local governments, cost these governments almost $400 billion in 1994 (U.S. Bureau of the Census 1997, 300). Many additional billions of dollars are invisibly transferred through tax breaks for housing, education, medical care, and pensions (Howard 1997).

Yet these social expenditures are not what is commonly known as welfare. *Welfare* usually refers to those programs that provide public assistance only to the poor. Overall, American governments spend about one-fourth of their total social expenditures on these welfare programs. State and local governments, for their part, pay more than one quarter of these welfare expenditures. The most important federal, state, and local welfare spending categories (including medical programs that target the poor) are presented in Table 10-1.

Medical programs are the largest welfare programs, consuming almost half of the nation's welfare spending, with states paying more than 40 percent of this

Table 10-1 Cash and Noncash Benefits for Persons with Low Incomes, 1994
(in millions of 1995 dollars)

Program	Federal	State and local	Percentage of state and local welfare spending	Percentage change 1992–1994 state and local spending
Medical benefits	96,551	69,152	68	15
Medicaid	84,473	63,186	62	16
Veterans	8,393	0	0	0
General assistance	0	5,522	5	5
Indian health service	1,998	0	0	0
Maternal and child health	706	443	0	−1
Cash aid	63,218	22,903	23	1
AFDC	14,541	12,113	12	−2
SSI	24,211	3,873	4	−12
EITC	17,018	0	0	0
Foster care	2,826	2,479	2	18
Pensions for needy veterans	3,248	0	0	0
General assistance	0	3,342	3	−8
Food benefits [a]	37,259	1,920	2	22
Housing benefits [a, b]	14,989	403	0	NA
Education [a]	15,223	929	1	39
Social services [a, c]	6,928	5,394	5	55
Jobs and training [a]	5,008	680	1	31
Energy assistance [a]	1,889	35	0	−66
Total	253,214	101,414	100	13

SOURCE: U.S. Bureau of the Census 1997, 375; Bureau of the Census 1994, 373; U.S. House 1996, 1,293.

NOTES: AFDC = Aid to Families with Dependent Children; SSI = Social Security Insurance; EITC = Earned Income Tax Credit.

[a] Includes other programs not shown separately

[b] Undefined; states reported no housing benefits in 1992.

[c] Nonfederal expenditure is a rough estimate.

amount. Note, in particular, that more than two-thirds of state spending on welfare is devoted to medical care. The vast majority of this spending is channeled through the Medicaid program. Indeed, states spend more on providing medical services to the poor than they do on all other health and medical programs combined.

Cash assistance programs make up the second largest block of welfare spending, accounting for about one quarter of all welfare spending. The states, moreover, pay one quarter of this amount, and less than one quarter of state welfare expenditures goes to cash assistance programs, with the largest such programs being Temporary Assistance for Needy Families (TANF—before 1996, Aid to Families with Dependent Children, AFDC), Supplemental Security Income (SSI), and general assistance (GA). The states played a relatively minor role in all of the other welfare programs, as almost all state spending on benefits provided either medical or cash assistance. Notably, the states spent small amounts on such items as nutritional assistance, job training, or educational aid to the poor.

Table 10-1 illustrates trends in state spending on health and welfare, three of which are especially noteworthy. Medical programs, which already consume the bulk of spending, continued to grow vigorously through the 1990s. In contrast, programs that provide cash assistance have been rather flat and now are shrinking. Although the states were offering less income support to the poor, they were also raising (although from a relatively small base) the amount they spend on most other social services.

Medicaid, TANF/AFDC, SSI, and GA together soak up almost 90 percent of state welfare spending, with Medicaid and AFDC/TANF alone accounting for three-fourths of it. To understand state health and welfare programs, we must focus on these four programs—especially the biggest two.

Medicaid

Medicaid is the program that provides medical care to low-income persons who are aged, blind, disabled; to poor families with children; and increasingly to certain other pregnant women and children (for a discussion of Medicaid eligibility, services, and financing, see U.S. House 1996, 879–887). Medicaid, created during the Great Society efforts of the mid-1960s, is an entitlement program. In an *entitlement program,* any person eligible for benefits can obtain them; the government is obligated to provide the benefits necessary to fill all claims. (Compare this to a discretionary program, in which the government determines how much it will spend and so does not guarantee that all claims for assistance will be met.) The federal government and state governments share responsibility for Medicaid. The federal government establishes program guidelines (concerning eligibility, services, and financing), and the state governments design and administer the program. The state and federal governments split the cost of the program based on the federally established matching rate that requires the more affluent states to pay a higher share of the cost.

All states must provide Medicaid to individuals in *categorically needy* groups—for example, those eligible for SSI or who would have qualified under the AFDC program. This does not hold in Arizona, which since 1982 has been running a medical program for low-income residents as a demonstration project. States can also, at their option, provide coverage to those in *medically needy* groups—that is, those individuals who do not meet the income or resource standards of the categorically needy but otherwise meet the Medicaid standards. By the end of 1995, forty states offered at least some services to the medically needy. States are required to provide more extensive services to the categorically needy than the medically needy.

Medicaid eligibility historically has been linked to participation in other welfare programs, in particular AFDC or SSI. The federal government began gradually expanding coverage for other low-income pregnant women and children beginning in the mid-1980s. Starting in 1988, for example, states were required to provide Medicaid for an additional year to families that left AFDC because of rising income. By 1991 Congress had extended Medicaid to cover other poor, pregnant women and their children even if they were not eligible for AFDC. More recently, the State Children's Health Insurance Program (CHIP) created by Congress in 1997 further expanded eligibility for medical services to previously uninsured children in families with incomes above federal poverty level and, in some cases, children in families with incomes substantially higher. Still, eligibility for Medicaid is broadest for children in poverty. In 1994, for instance, seven out of ten poor children under five years of age received benefits, compared with only three of ten poor adults between the ages of forty-five and sixty-four (U.S. House 1996, 886).

The federal government requires that states provide a broad list of medical services within Medicaid, including inpatient and outpatient hospital services as well as physicians' services, to the categorically needy. States are allowed to offer additional services (such as the provision of drugs, eyeglasses, or psychiatric care), and they are also permitted to establish limits on recipients' use of the services (for example, on the number of hospital days reimbursed).

Medicaid does not have its own team of doctors. Instead, states reimburse private health care providers who have delivered services to Medicaid recipients. The states decide, within federal guidelines, the reimbursement rates. Because some states set these rates so low that few doctors wanted to take Medicaid patients, states are now required to set reimbursement rates high enough so that Medicaid services will actually be available to recipients, at least to the extent that they are available to other residents in the state. Health care providers cannot charge Medicaid patients additional fees above these amounts.

All individuals who are eligible for Medicaid are entitled to receive benefits, although many, in fact, do not claim these benefits. Federal and state governments are obligated to pay for the medical services obtained by eligible recipients. These governments thus can neither budget precisely how much they will spend on Medicaid each year nor limit expenses to a fixed amount. As a result, this open-ended entitlement program has become the biggest threat to state budgets.

Temporary Assistance to Needy Families

The welfare map was rewritten in 1996 when the federal government terminated the Aid to Families with Dependent Children (AFDC) program and established the Temporary Assistance for Needy Families (TANF) program in its place. To understand what TANF is, it is necessary first to understand first what AFDC came to be.

AFDC was created as a minor and uncontroversial element of the Social Security Act of 1935, with the intention that it would be a temporary program to provide income support to widows and their families. It did not turn out that way, however. Fifty years after its creation, AFDC provided assistance to more than 14 million Americans. The vast majority of the parents it assisted were not widows but parents who were divorced, separated, or never married. Only a small percentage of the mothers receiving AFDC had paid employment, even though now most other mothers do earn income by working. (AFDC did have a work element, the JOBS program, but only about 10 percent of AFDC adults actually participated in it.) At any given time, moreover, almost two-thirds of adults receiving AFDC had been "on the dole" for eight or more years. Finally, almost two-thirds of the recipients were nonwhite minorities (see U.S. House 1996, 473, 474, 505). In short, a large proportion of adult AFDC recipients were minority single mothers with little earned income who remained on the rolls for years. For these reasons, AFDC came to be seen as a program that discouraged marriage and work, encouraged out-of-wedlock childbearing and dependency, and primarily served people of color (Rom 1997a).

Presidents since Richard Nixon, and more recently congressional Republicans, consequently had vowed to get rid of this politically unpopular program. When the Republicans took control of the Congress in 1994 they pressured, and ultimately succeeded, in calling on President Clinton's campaign promise to "end welfare as we know it" (Rom 1997b). In 1996 the Congress approved, and Clinton signed, the bill to end AFDC and create TANF in its place.

TANF differs from AFDC in several important ways. One of the most noteworthy changes is that the states have much more power over TANF than they did over AFDC. The states now have the flexibility to determine who is eligible for TANF, what kinds of obligations recipients face and what benefits they receive, and how the programs will be designed, implemented, and evaluated. (The states must still submit reports to the U.S. Department of Health and Human Services detailing how they are spending federal funds.) States now can deny benefits to any family or category of poor family—and they are doing so with gusto. States can require certain behaviors in return for benefits; Wisconsin, for instance, effectively requires employment or community service as a condition for receiving TANF benefits. Some states have even decided not to run uniform TANF programs, delegating responsibility for program operation to the counties.

Another major change is that AFDC was an entitlement program and TANF is not. The federal government gives each state a set block of funds to pay for the program each year, with a state's grant based on the average amount it received from the federal government for AFDC. The states, for their part, are required to spend at least 80 percent as much as they had for AFDC in 1994; if they meet certain work requirement goals, they need spend only 75 percent as much. The states can, however, use a substantial portion of their funds for purposes other than providing cash benefits. What this means is that the states are spending less now on welfare than they have in the past.

A third important difference between TANF and AFDC is that whereas the main goal of AFDC was to provide income support to poor families, the main goal of TANF is to promote work. The states are required to enroll increasing shares of their caseloads in job-related activities; by the year 2002, 50 percent of the single parents and 90 percent of the two-parent families in the TANF caseload must be working or the state faces financial penalties. States with declining caseloads have lower work participation requirements. This suggests that the states can meet these requirements either by placing recipients in work activities or removing them from the welfare rolls (and which methods states choose is a matter of great interest). States that do not meet these targets will have the size of their federal grants reduced.

TANF is also much more concerned with changing recipient behavior than was AFDC. To discourage dependency, the federal government will not allow its funds to be used to provide benefits to families for more than five years, although a small portion of the recipients can be exempted from these time limits. The states are also allowed to cut benefits off earlier if they wish. To discourage childbearing, states may deny benefits to unmarried teenagers and their children or to children born while their mothers were receiving benefits. States may require school attendance by the parents if they have not completed high school. States may also require "personal responsibility" contracts as a condition of enrolling in TANF (NGA, NCSL, and APWA 1996). Although the states are not exactly Big Brother, they can increasingly be Stern Parent.

General Assistance

If you are poor and do not qualify for TANF, you are almost—but not quite—out of luck. Many states have their own general assistance programs to provide cash, medical assistance, and other services to low-income individuals who are not eligible for other welfare programs (Uccello and Gallagher 1998). (The term *general assistance* is a generic term for the entire group of purely state programs, which vary widely.) Some GA programs cover broad categories of people who are not eligible for federal assistance, such as able-bodied adults without children, certain two-parent families with children, and the not quite elderly or disabled. Other states provide benefits only to narrow groups (such as those who have applied for SSI but are not yet receiving benefits) or in special circumstances (as when a home is destroyed by a natural disaster). In 1996, forty-one states had some form of general assistance, with thirty-two offering statewide programs, and at least some counties in nine other states had GA programs. Eight states—Alabama, Arkansas, Louisiana, Michigan, Mississippi, Oklahoma, Tennessee, and Wyoming—have no GA programs at all (Thompson 1995). Only twelve states provide financial assistance to all financially needy persons who do not qualify for federal welfare programs.

As with state welfare efforts more generally, general assistance programs are now doing more to provide medical assistance than income support. In 1994 medical care made up nearly two-thirds of state GA spending, and states are gradually spending more for medical services and less for cash assistance.

Supplemental Security Income

Established by the federal government in 1972 to replace several other federal programs that provided grants to the states, the SSI program provides cash payments to elderly, blind, or disabled persons who are also poor. Maximum SSI benefits are available to these individuals who are without other resources, and so benefits are reduced as a recipient's earned income rises or if the recipient is living with another person. SSI recipients may also be eligible for Social Security, Medicaid, and food stamps; they may not, however, also receive benefits from TANF.

Although still the fourth largest state-supported welfare program, SSI is gradually becoming a more fully federal program. The federal government already establishes eligibility requirements, sets national benefit levels, and administers the program; states have the option of supplementing the federal benefit standard. All but seven states—Arkansas, Georgia, Kansas, Mississippi, Tennessee, Texas, and West Virginia—provide some form of supplemental benefits. The federal government pays for federal benefits and administration; the state governments fund the supplemental benefits and their administrative costs (for details, see U.S. House 1996, 257–326). In 1996 the federal SSI benefit standard for an individual with no other income was $470 per month; for a couple, $705 per month. State-supplemented benefits are much lower. In half of the states the neediest individual was eligible for only $27 and the couple $25 monthly. Federal SSI benefits are indexed to inflation, so recipients receive the same cost-of-living adjustments as do Social Security beneficiaries; state benefits are not indexed.

THE POLITICS

The Medicaid, TANF, SSI, and GA programs together spend more than $200 billion each year to assist about 30 million recipients. Except for GA, the programs are a complex mix of federal and state designs, funds, and administrations. What factors influence the design and operation of these programs? Although these elements include economic and demographic attributes, political factors ultimately dominate. The reasons for this are clear. Economic and demographic conditions provide policy makers with opportunities and constraints, but these conditions do not by themselves make policies: Politicians do. The politicians make program decisions based on their electoral concerns, their ideological beliefs, and their pragmatic judgments about what is best for their constituents, state, and country.

Federalism

Ours is a federalist country. Authority over health and welfare policy is thus shared—not always agreeably—among state and national governments. This has three main implications for state policies. First, states do not have sole jurisdiction over health and welfare policy: They are constrained by national laws. On the one hand, states must provide certain services and follow specific rules; on the other, they cannot adopt proposals they prefer if these conflict with federal law.

Second, state and federal governments often attempt to gain control over health and welfare programs while at the same time attempting to shift burdens to the other party. Efforts toward control can be seen in federal mandates on the states, in which the federal government requires the states to perform certain functions and state requests for waivers from these mandates, whereby the states seek to escape from these requirements and establish their own standards. States, moreover, are often tempted to play these programs in such a way that they obtain the maximum federal financial support at minimum cost to themselves. The states do have greater incentives to manipulate welfare financing than does the federal government. Unlike the federal government, the states' constitutions prohibit them from running budget deficits, so the states literally cannot afford to be as generous as the federal government.

Third, state governments compete and, at times, cooperate with each other. Some of the competition is political, as ambitious politicians strive to build their national reputations by developing innovative programs to address social problems. The competition can also be economic, as politicians seek to make their states more attractive for businesses and workers. Political and economic competition can lead in different directions; politicians have reasons for making their states distinctive, but not so distinctive that they scare away economic resources.

Internal Politics

In addition to these influences of federalism, state policy choices are influenced by political, economic, and demographic factors that can vary across the states and over time. The political cultures, ideologies, institutions, and public opinions of the states can all affect their policies for health and welfare. The economic conditions of the states, their wealth and the sources of it, can influence state politicians as they choose among policies. The states also differ in the age of their populations, the composition of their families, and the ethnicity of their citizens, each with potential significance for the states' policies.

Political culture is "the particular pattern of orientation to political action in which each political system is embedded" (Elazar 1972, 84–85). This orientation

> may be found among politicians and the general public, and it may affect their understanding of what politics is and what can be expected from government, influence the types of people who become active in politics, and influence the ways in which they practice politics and formulate public policy (Sharkansky 1969, 67).

In moralistic political cultures, "both the general public and the politicians conceive of politics as a public activity centered on some notion of the public good and properly devoted to the advancement of the public interest" (Elazar 1970, 174). Traditionalistic or individualistic political cultures, in contrast, view politics as a way of preserving the status quo or gaining personal enrichment, respectively, as explained in Chapter 1. Moralistic political cultures thus tend to be more activist and generous in their health and welfare programs than traditionalistic or individualistic states. A state's political culture changes only slowly, moreover, so it is the most stable of the political variables.

Political ideology involves the durable views of politicians about what the government should do and how it should do it. Most basically, Americans have either conservative or liberal ideologies regarding health and welfare programs; liberals are in favor of expanded benefits and more inclusive eligibility standards, and conservatives prefer more restrictive benefits and eligibility. Political culture is related to, but by no means identical to, political ideology. Moralistic states are not necessarily liberal, nor individualistic states invariably conservative, although traditionalistic states almost always are conservative. (For an excellent discussion of the relationship between ideology and political culture, see Erikson, Wright, and McIver 1993, 150–176.) Political conservatives in moralistic states might believe that governments best help the poor by making welfare difficult to obtain; liberals in individualistic states might seek to increase welfare spending merely to enhance their own political fortunes.

The political institutions of American governments—their legislatures, bureaucracies, political parties, interest groups, electoral systems—can also influence health and welfare policies. In general, governments with professional legislatures and competent bureaucracies are more active in developing programs and open-handed in supporting them. Interest groups are more involved, and more influential, in some states than in others and in some issues than others (Hrebenar 1997). States with more highly mobilized publics and more competitive elections are also more likely to support social welfare programs (Holbrook and Van Dunk 1993).

Policy makers pay attention to public opinion, and these opinions vary across the states, over time, and among health and welfare issues (Berry et al. 1998). It should come as no surprise that the citizens of Minnesota and Mississippi, for example, have different opinions about the appropriate role of their governments in social policy and that state policies in part reflect these opinions. Still, the sentiments of the nation as a whole also change over the years, with the public looking more favorably on the recipients of welfare in the 1960s than in the early 1980s and mid-1990s. The American public also appears typically to be more sympathetic to programs that provide goods and services (such as food and health care) to the poor rather than give them cash (Cook and Barrett 1992). Certain types of recipients are more politically popular. The "deserving poor" (for example, the disabled, children, and the elderly) are viewed sympathetically and provided greater support from health and welfare programs, whereas the "undeserving poor" (for example, young men and women bearing children out of wedlock) are scorned by the public (Katz 1986).

Interest groups are also active in welfare and, especially, health politics. Medical providers—doctors, nurses, hospitals, insurers—all have an interest in how health programs are designed, administered, and financed. Certain types of patients—particularly the elderly and disabled—also have organizations that routinely promote their claims (welfare mothers, in contrast, usually do not). Interest groups are less pronounced in welfare policy, where the main organizations are typically welfare officials, charities, and religious organizations.

ECONOMIC AND DEMOGRAPHIC FACTORS

The principal economic factors influencing health and welfare policies are both cyclical and structural. Whenever the economy goes into recession, for example, the number of individuals eligible for these programs increase (as more people become poor) and program costs rise; when the economy is growing faster, fewer individuals receive benefits and costs are reduced. This cyclical effect, however, is overshadowed by broader structural changes in the American economy and demography during the last couple of decades that have increased the prevalence of poverty within certain groups, especially women and children, even during times of prosperity (Blank 1997).

The causes for these economic and demographic changes are complex and hotly debated. They involve such issues as the decline in well-paying blue-collar jobs, the increase in temporary or part-time jobs lacking benefits, the increase in single-parent families through divorce and, particularly, childbearing out of wedlock, and the perceived rise in a more permanent underclass apparently locked in poverty. Nevertheless, it is important to note that the absolute wealth of the country—and so the potential resources available for health and welfare programs—has increased substantially every decade since the 1940s. These gains have not been shared equally by all groups or by all states, however.

The economic and demographic characteristics of the states provide the context in which the politicians operate. States that are richer have more resources to devote to health and welfare programs, if they wish to do so. States that have relatively fewer single-parent families or disabled elderly, for instance, have relatively fewer social welfare needs. But neither resources nor needs determine what policies will be chosen. Policy makers do.

INTERSTATE COMPETITION

Although the states are politically independent of each other, they are all part of a nationwide economic and political system. State politicians seeking to develop a national reputation accordingly have incentives to conduct bold policy experiments. When running for president, Bill Clinton pointed to the educational reforms he pioneered as governor of Arkansas. More recently, Wisconsin governor Tommy Thompson, Michigan governor John Engler, and New York mayor Rudolph Guiliani have gained notoriety—and mention as potential candidates for national office—for their welfare innovations. If they prove successful, or otherwise attractive politically, other states often imitate these innovations. This pattern of state innovation and diffusion is a well-recognized pattern in American politics (Walker 1969).

States are also engaged in economic competition with each other regarding finance, commerce, and labor. Politicians find it far easier to run for reelection, after all, if they can boast that under their direction the state has a booming economy, rising incomes, high employment rates, and low taxes. This interstate economic competition has led some scholars to conclude that states are ill-suited to have responsibility for redistributive programs (see especially Peterson 1995). The logic behind this claim is simple. Individuals, whether citizens or politicians, act in their own self-interest. If a state offers generous health and welfare benefits, it will become a "welfare magnet" attracting the poor who need these benefits and repelling the affluent who pay the taxes to support them. But politicians are more sensitive to the concerns of the affluent because they are more important politically. As a result, politicians have strong incentives to keep their states from becoming welfare magnets; indeed, the incentives are to have welfare programs that are less generous than the state's neighbors. If each state acts the same way, welfare benefits would become increasingly stingy and welfare eligibility increasingly stringent as the states "race to the bottom."

Whether states have been "welfare magnets" or will "race to the bottom" are unsettled questions. If generous states exert magnetic attraction to the poor, the pull is weak at most. Some scholars find evidence of welfare magnets; others do not (see for example Peterson and Rom 1990; Schram, Nitz, and Krueger 1998). But whether or not welfare magnets exist in fact, it is clear that many politicians find the phrase a useful rhetorical device to attack welfare generosity. And although state-provided welfare benefits have tended to decline in recent decades, it is not at all clear that states are racing to the bottom (Berry, Fording, and Hanson 1997; Rom 1998).

POLICY IMPLICATIONS

These political, economic, and demographic factors affect health and welfare policies in subtle and complex ways. All American governments are subject to their influence. But because the exact weight of each factor differs for each state, varies between state and national governments, and changes over time, there is no single pattern of evolution for health and welfare policies. Still, a few observations might be offered.

States have tended to be more parsimonious than the federal government in their efforts to restrain eligibility and benefits. The federal government, in contrast, has been more generous in expanding health and welfare eligibility criteria and benefit levels. The programs under more state control (such as TANF and GA) have tended to have smaller rolls that are more prone to shrink, whereas programs for which the federal government has primary responsibility for establishing eligibility criteria (such as Medicaid and SSI) have tended to have larger rolls likely to expand. This tendency is not absolute, of course; many states award benefits, especially medical care, to more residents than the federal government requires, and the federal government acted to restrict welfare eligibility in 1996.

Benefits tend to be higher in programs serving more politically felicitous constituencies. SSI benefits are higher than those in TANF and GA, for example, in part because SSI recipients (the elderly or disabled poor) are seen as more deserving of government support than are TANF or GA recipients (single parents incapable of adequately providing for their children, or able-bodied single men). These different perceptions of the relative merit of SSI, TANF, and GA recipients also probably contributed to the growing gap between the programs, as the public remains sympathetic to the idea of helping the ill while becoming increasingly hostile to the idea of supporting the indolent.

It also appears that programs that provide services to the poor are politically more popular than those programs that provide income. For example, public support is much higher for providing medical treatment to those who need it than for providing cash to those who lack it (Cook and Barrett 1992). Although it is now popular to "end" welfare, few politicians call for terminating health care for the poor.

Although the states in general are less willing and able than the federal government to support public assistance programs, there is nonetheless tremendous variation in the demand for and supply of these programs among the states. This variation again arises from economic, demographic, and political reasons. States differ in their economic circumstances. States also have diverse populations, with certain states having higher proportions of groups (for example, single-parent families, disabled individuals, and elderly individuals) typically in greater need of public assistance as a result of differences in racial composition in the population, as well as other factors; policy makers in these states undoubtedly face greater political pressure to restrain program costs and reduce the number of beneficiaries. The states that have moralistic political cultures, highly professional institutions, mobilized parties and publics, and generously inclined publics have shown greater support for health and welfare programs than those states that do not have these characteristics.

It is worth remembering, however, that state health and welfare policy choices are far more complicated than a simple tallying of economic, demographic, and political forces would suggest. Policies vary among the states for unique historical reasons. An unusually forceful leader, a public scandal, a temporary surge in public opinion, can all have lasting effects on policy choice.

THE PATTERNS

Let us now turn to the patterns—and the anomalies—in health and welfare policies. Let us first examine the broad trends since 1975 in recipients, benefits, and expenditures for AFDC/TANF, Medicaid, and SSI. Although comparable data do not exist for general assistance, those programs will be mentioned where appropriate.

Trends in Benefit Levels

Trends in benefits for the AFDC/TANF, Medicaid, and SSI programs are shown in Figure 10-1. The most important trend involves Medicaid. Annual medical expenditures per recipient increased by more than 150 percent between 1975 and 1995. While average Medicaid expenses were only somewhat less than AFDC benefits and much less than SSI benefits in 1975, by 1980 Medicaid costs per beneficiary exceeded AFDC and by 1990 they equaled SSI. Moreover, real per-recipient Medicaid costs grew every single year during this period, unlike SSI which fluctuated and AFDC which steadily declined. For AFDC recipients, it was belt-tightening time: Benefits have decreased by more than 30 percent from their peak in 1977 and under TANF continue to shrink. Although only nine states have thus far actually adjusted the benefits from those they offered under the AFDC program, inflation still chips away at their real value. Of the nine states that have altered their benefits, five have increased them and four lowered them (Gallagher et al. 1998, VI-1).

Figure 10-1   Annual Welfare Expenditures per Recipient

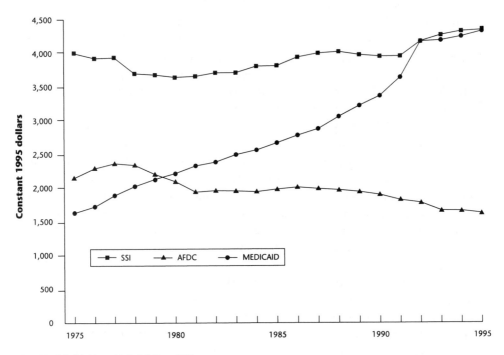

SOURCE: Calculated from data in U.S. House 1996.

Better to be poor and elderly than poor and a single parent, at least as far as welfare benefits go. Note that SSI benefits have been much larger than AFDC benefits for the entire period. In 1977, when the gap was narrowest, AFDC recipients received somewhat more than half as much as SSI recipients; by 1995 AFDC benefits were somewhat less than half as much. Moreover, SSI and AFDC benefits have moved in different directions, with SSI growing and AFDC shrinking.

The differences in benefits between state and federal governments are even more striking. Average SSI benefits per person are much more generous than AFDC benefits, in large part because the federal government sets and fully funds a minimum benefit level for SSI. These federal benefits have also been indexed to inflation since the mid-1970s (and indeed slightly overindexed). As a result, real federal SSI benefits grew at least slowly during these decades, whereas state supplements declined sharply. Twenty-three states have supplemented federal SSI benefits continuously between 1975 and 1996, yet real state-funded benefits for aged couples declined an astonishing 85 percent in the median state during that period, and benefits for aged individuals fell by nearly 70 percent (U.S. House 1996, 279–283). Only in Alaska and Minnesota did state-funded SSI benefits keep pace with inflation.

As with AFDC/TANF, benefits for general assistance programs have been declining. In no state have the benefits kept pace with inflation since at least 1992, al-

Figure 10-2 Welfare Recipients, 1975–1997

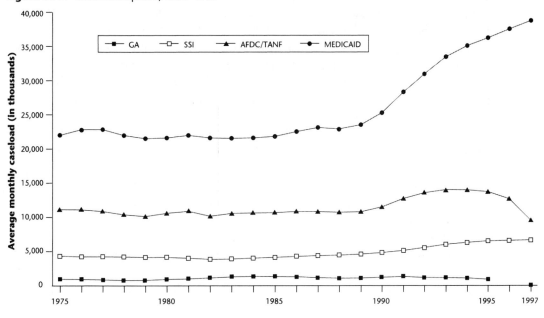

SOURCE: Calculated from data in U.S. House 1996; HCFA 1998; SSA 1997.

though eight states have enacted nominal increases. Six states have actually cut their GA benefits. In the extreme case, California gave its counties permission to lower their assistance levels, and Los Angeles chose to do so by one-fourth (Uccello and Gallagher 1998).

Several factors have contributed to these trends. Program benefits set by the federal government (such as Medicaid and, mainly, SSI) have grown; benefit levels set by the states (such as for AFDC/TANF and GA) have fallen. The states are clearly more eager to avoid paying for public assistance than is the federal government. Public opinion also supports these trends; hostility to providing cash to the "undeserving poor" (that is, AFDC/TANF and GA recipients) has grown, whereas furnishing services (for example, through Medicaid) to the needy has not. Inflation in medical fees has also contributed to the growth in Medicaid benefits. Finally, it must be noted, constituencies supporting higher benefits for SSI and Medicaid (for example, the elderly, the disabled, and doctors) have been more effective in voicing their support for these programs than have the supporters of AFDC and GA.

Trends in the Number of Recipients

The number of recipients in the AFDC, Medicaid, SSI, and GA programs annually between 1975 and 1997 are shown in Figure 10-2. Three trends are especially noteworthy. For the first fifteen years, program rolls were relatively stable, growing just slightly over time. Between 1990 and 1993, however, each program experienced strong growth, with the AFDC rolls growing fast, SSI faster, and Medicaid fastest. During the next four years the SSI and Medicaid rolls continued to grow as first AFDC and then TANF fell by almost one-third. The number of GA recipients, relatively stable through the 1980s, also fell by nearly one-third between 1991 and 1995 and is likely to have fallen further since then as states continue to restrict eligibility.

The last trend—strong growth in Medicaid rolls, sharp decline in TANF and GA caseloads—is especially important for state politics and policy. This trend was not caused purely by economic or demographic changes. It does reflect the clear preference of state and national politicians for providing medical care to the elderly, disabled, or children who are poor and for withholding income support from impoverished, working-age adults.

This trend also appears likely to continue for the next several years. The CHIP program, and related expansions, could add several million individuals to state medical rolls. It has been estimated that nearly five million children are eligible for Medicaid but not enrolled in it (Selden, Banthin, and Cohen 1998). Meanwhile, TANF rolls continue to shrink, falling nearly 40 percent between 1993 and 1998. No one knows, of course, how small the TANF rolls will ultimately become. But a bigger question concerns whether—and how much—they will again grow if the economy enters a prolonged recession that makes it difficult for workers with less experience and fewer skills to find and hold jobs.

Trends in Expenditures

Total real federal and state spending on AFDC, SSI, and Medicaid during 1975–1995 is shown in Figure 10-3. This figure illustrates the size of each program in relation to the others as well as the shares funded by federal and state governments. State and federal spending on Medicaid dwarfs expenditures by either level of government on SSI and AFDC. Although it did so even in 1975, the gap between it and other programs had become much wider by 1995: In that year, total spending on Medicaid was five times more than SSI and more than seven times more than AFDC. Real state and federal expenditures on Medicaid rose more than twice as rapidly as did spending on SSI, and AFDC expenditures actually fell. Comparable data are not available for more recent years, but state spending for Medicaid continues to rise, although not as rapidly, and state spending on TANF declined by an additional 20 percent between 1996 and 1998. If welfare spending is a threat to state budgets, the peril comes from Medicaid, not TANF.

State and federal governments both shared in the growth of Medicaid's spending, as the portion of the expense borne by each level of government was constant over the period, with the state governments carrying about four-tenths of the load. (The states will pay a smaller share of the costs for the new CHIP program.) Medicaid's extraordinary growth, fueled both by rising caseloads and benefits, was thus a burden to state and federal governments alike.

The distribution of AFDC costs was unchanged between 1975 and 1995, with the state governments picking up a little less than half of the cost every year. Ironi-

Figure 10-3   Welfare Spending, 1975–1995

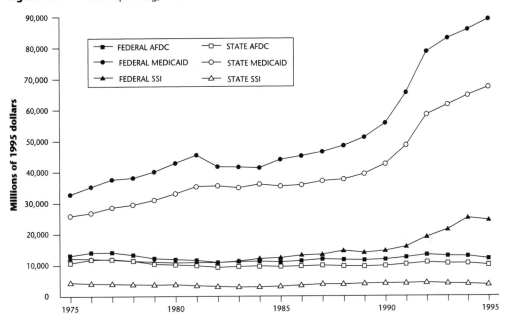

SOURCE: Calculated from data in U.S. House 1996. Data in constant 1995 dollars, adjusted according to the CPI-U index.

cally, although the states have more authority over the TANF program they thus far are bearing less of the cost of it. Each year between 1997 and 2002 each state receives a lump sum payment from the federal government, based on the amount the federal government spent in the state under AFDC. As the states are required to spend only 80 percent as much for the program as they did for AFDC—and it appears that many states are doing just that—the proportion of the program paid for by the states will decline. In this way TANF may more closely resemble SSI, for which the state governments' share of program costs declined by almost a half percent between 1975 and 1993.

The states now spend almost one quarter of their budgets on Medicaid and AFDC/TANF, much more than they did a decade ago. All of the increase can be attributed to medical care, as income support programs have gradually played a smaller role in state budgets.

The future trends in expenditures are hard to predict, at least for the health programs. Medical prices, relatively stable the past few years, appear poised to start rising more rapidly again. If caseloads continue to grow, total medical spending would rise yet more rapidly. Sharp increases in spending are less likely for TANF. As the states are no longer required to provide benefits to any category of recipients, nor required to provide any particular of benefits, the states could restrain spending even if needs grew.

State Welfare Benefits and Recipients

The national trends this decade have thus featured diverging recipient populations, program expenditures, and benefit levels, with Medicaid and SSI growing in each case and AFDC/TANF and GA shrinking. These trends have not affected all states equally, nor have all states responded in the same way to the changing times.

Benefits. Welfare benefits vary dramatically across programs and among the states (Table 10-2). The average annual Medicaid expenditure per recipient by the states in 1995 was $3,600; the average annual AFDC benefit was less than half this amount. In every state except California, AFDC benefits were lower than Medicaid expenditures—much lower in most states.

One must be careful to note the distinction between "benefits" and "expenditures," however. Cash benefits are one accurate indicator of a state's generosity to its needy; the higher the benefit, the more generous the state. This is not necessarily true for medical expenditures, however. It is possible for one state to deliver the same level of medical care as another state at a lower cost. States with higher Medicaid expenditures thus do not inherently offer better medical care to the poor.

It is worth noting how much benefits and expenditures vary across the states. In 1995 the most generous state (New York) paid AFDC recipients more than four times as much as did the least generous (Mississippi); New York's average Medicaid expenditures per recipient were also four times as large as in Tennessee, the state that spent the smallest amount. The state with the most generous GA cash benefits, Nebraska, offered benefits that could potentially bring a recipient up to the poverty line, whereas eight states offered no cash benefits at all (Uccello and Gallagher 1998). These differences are much greater than the cost-of-living variations in the states, and so indicate real differences in how the states treat their low-income residents.

States that offer more generous cash benefits generally, but not always, also spend more on medical benefits. Note, for example, that six of the ten states with the highest AFDC benefits also had Medicaid expenditures in the highest ten. Alaska, Connecticut, Hawaii, Massachusetts, Minnesota, and Rhode Island are among the most liberal states in terms of spending per AFDC and Medicaid recipient. Four of the ten states with the lowest AFDC benefits also had Medicaid expenditures in the lowest ten, however, with Alabama, Mississippi, Tennessee, and Texas near the bottom on both lists. The states with the greatest contrast between their programs include California and Washington, which were among the ten most generous in AFDC and ten lowest spenders in Medicaid, as well as Arkansas and Louisiana, among the most stingy in AFDC yet having relatively high Medicaid expenditures. Another way of showing the relationship between these variables is the correlation coefficient. When the coefficient equals 1 a perfect relationship exists; when it equals 0 the variables are not related at all. The correlation between cash and medical benefits across the states is 0.56.

As we have already seen, AFDC benefits have declined nationally since the mid-1970s. This trend toward lower real benefits has affected all states: Once inflation is taken into account, no state had a higher maximum in 1996 than in 1970. The de-

Table 10-2 Mean Annual Welfare Benefit or Expenditure per Recipient, Fiscal Year 1995

State	Medicaid		AFDC	
	Expenditure	*Rank*	*Benefit*	*Rank*
Alabama	2,698	40	700	48
Alaska	3,698	17	2,900	1
Arizona	NA	NA	1,332	30
Arkansas	3,893	15	775	46
California	2,097	48	2,287	6
Colorado	3,619	19	1,310	32
Connecticut	5,588	2	2,254	7
Delaware	4,128	12	1,456	23
Florida	2,768	39	1,236	35
Georgia	2,681	42	1,085	39
Hawaii	4,983	5	2,618	2
Idaho	3,129	30	1,317	31
Illinois	3,608	21	1,267	33
Indiana	3,359	24	1,040	42
Iowa	3,406	23	1,494	20
Kansas	3,250	28	1,420	24
Kentucky	3,035	31	971	43
Louisiana	3,449	22	602	49
Maine	4,965	7	1,685	14
Maryland	4,873	9	1,381	28
Massachusetts	5,460	3	2,132	4
Michigan	2,918	36	1,675	15
Minnesota	5,386	4	2,132	9
Mississippi	2,436	46	525	50
Missouri	2,932	34	1,085	38
Montana	3,300	27	1,464	22
Nebraska	3,609	20	1,383	27
Nevada	3,322	26	1,259	34
New Hampshire	4,880	8	2,032	11
New Jersey	4,828	11	1,613	17
New Mexico	2,491	45	1,482	21
New York	7,276	1	2,424	3
North Carolina	2,928	35	1,068	40
North Dakota	4,839	10	1,614	16
Ohio	3,644	18	1,387	25
Oklahoma	2,680	43	1,236	36
Oregon	2,937	33	1,738	13
Pennsylvania	3,766	16	1,518	18
Rhode Island	4,973	6	2,190	8
South Carolina	2,902	37	837	44
South Dakota	4,120	13	1,335	29
Tennessee	1,891	49	779	45
Texas	2,562	44	701	47
Utah	2,895	38	1,515	19
Vermont	3,210	29	2,293	5
Virginia	2,690	41	1,209	37
Washington	2,285	47	2,118	10
West Virginia	3,009	32	1,047	41
Wisconsin	4,118	14	1,828	12
Wyoming	3,328	25	1,387	26

SOURCE: Calculated from data in HCFA 1998; U.S. House 1996.

cline has also been large, and everywhere. In the median state, maximum benefits for a family of three fell by more than half during this period (U.S. House 1996, 448). The state with the smallest decline was California, where maximum benefits fell by almost 20 percent; in Texas, maximum benefits shrank by nearly 70 percent. The declines were not concentrated in the most generous states, either. Benefits in the most and least generous states fell by similar proportions.

The more affluent states support more generous social welfare programs than do their poorer peers, as noted earlier. In general, a state whose median income is $1,000 higher than that of another state offers annual maximum AFDC benefits that are $280 higher. This relation is not ironclad, however. Some states with higher incomes nonetheless have lower benefits, and vice versa. In Minnesota, for example, maximum AFDC benefits are $6,380 per year and median annual household income is $31,000; in Virginia, for example, median household income is more than $7,000 higher than in Minnesota and maximum AFDC benefits are more than $2,000 lower.

Yet the gap between AFDC benefits and typical household incomes grows larger as the benefits fall lower. In the most generous ten states, maximum AFDC benefits averaged about 20 percent of income in the median household (incomes averaged $36,500; benefits averaged $7,600), and in the stingiest ten states, maximum AFDC benefits averaged less than 10 percent of household income (incomes averaged $24,800; benefits averaged $2,400). The states with the highest (and lowest) incomes reveal a similar picture. In the ten states with the highest median incomes (averaging $38,700), mean AFDC benefits were $6,600, and AFDC benefits averaged 17 percent of median income. In the ten states with the lowest incomes (averaging $24,200), mean AFDC benefits were $2,900, and the average benefit was 12 percent of median income. In the wealthiest and most generous states, then, benefits are relatively high; in the poorest and least generous states, benefits are relatively low.

AFDC benefits are also as closely tied to a state's political ideology as to its income. States that are more liberal provide, on average, greater benefits. The correlation between ideology (as Erikson et al. [1993, 77] define it) and AFDC benefit is 0.75. Once again, there are strong exceptions. Delaware is much more liberal than its relatively low AFDC benefits would indicate; New Hampshire offers higher benefits than its conservative ideology suggests it would.

Ideology and income are not entirely independent of each other. In general, states with higher incomes were also more politically liberal (the correlation = 0.60). Yet income and ideology each are important influences on welfare. If you know both a state's income and its ideology, you could predict its welfare benefits better than if you knew only one of those factors. Together, income and ideology explain about 80 percent of the variation in AFDC benefits among the states.

Recipients. The differences in the size of the welfare populations across programs and time and among the states are remarkable (Table 10-3). First, consider TANF. On average, the states had 3 percent of their residents enrolled in TANF in 1997. Yet California has seventeen times more TANF beneficiaries, relative to its

population, than does Idaho: California has nearly 7 percent of its residents enrolled in that program while Idaho has less than half a percent. (The differences in
the absolute size of the rolls is of course much larger, with Idaho having fewer than
5,000 recipients and California 2.5 million.) Note, also, that the TANF rolls are
shrinking almost everywhere, with the average decline among the states more than
40 percent between 1993 and mid-1998; only in Hawaii did the rolls continue to
grow. These declines are not concentrated in the states with largest TANF programs, however. On average, the states with relatively smaller TANF rolls had relatively larger declines in their rolls during these years. Idaho, which already had the
smallest AFDC program in 1993, had the sharpest drop, with the size of its rolls
falling by an astounding 80 percent by mid-1998.

The Medicaid picture is more complex. The states have much larger Medicaid
caseloads than TANF caseloads, of course, but the interstate variation is also larger.
More than 20 percent of the residents of Tennessee are enrolled in the TennCare
program, for instance, and only 5 percent of Nevada residents receive medical care
from Medicaid. More puzzling are the trends. Between 1993 and 1997 Medicaid enrollment in the states, as a percentage of the population, increased by more than 1
percent a year. This modest increase masks the dramatic changes experienced in the
states. At the extremes, caseloads in Tennessee and Mississippi more than doubled,
whereas caseloads in Colorado and South Carolina fell by more than half.

GA programs tend to be much smaller but are more variable; the median state of
the thirty-nine for which data were available had about 4,000 GA recipients. New
York's GA program served almost 400,000 individuals each month in 1992. South
Carolina offered benefits to a mere five.

What is the relation between the generosity of a state's benefits and the size of its
welfare rolls? It might seem obvious that states that offered higher benefits would
have greater shares of their residents receiving welfare. Yet this has not been true for
every program and for all times. It does appear that the connection is tightening,
however. In 1997 there was a stronger statistical link between benefits and caseloads, suggesting that a state that offered $100 more in average benefits than anoth-
er state would have a very slightly higher TANF caseload. Again, there are exceptions, with some states offering relatively high benefits and having relatively low
caseloads, and vice versa. New Hampshire has the third smallest caseload with the
eleventh highest benefits; Illinois has the sixth largest caseload with the thirty-third
highest benefits. For Medicaid, there is no relationship between per recipient expenditures and caseload size. Paradoxically, the highest proportion of welfare recipients are found in the more affluent states with higher benefits (such as California
and New York) as well as in the poorer states with lower benefits (such as West Virginia and Mississippi).

The Transformations

During the 1960s and 1970s the federal government was the leading innovator
in social welfare policy. It is no more. The states, once again, are where the main

Table 10–3 Welfare Recipients as a Percentage of the Population, 1997

State	TANF percentage	Change, 1993–1997	1997 rank	Medicaid percentage	Change, 1993–1997	1997 rank
Alabama	1.6	–52.8	8	11.5	0.9	30
Alaska	5.4	–11.5	47	14.4	94.9	44
Arizona	3.0	–39.1	29	9.5	–15.0	18
Arkansas	1.7	–43.0	11	10.6	9.5	23
California	6.9	–12.7	50	14.8	45.4	46
Colorado	1.5	–56.0	5	5.9	–55.7	3
Connecticut	4.6	–6.1	44	11.0	–23.3	26
Delaware	2.8	–29.3	23	11.0	51.6	25
Florida	2.6	–49.2	20	9.6	–0.1	19
Georgia	3.2	–45.2	32	11.8	35.2	35
Hawaii	6.3	32.8	49	14.0	25.0	43
Idaho	0.4	–78.8	1	6.7	–46.7	5
Illinois	4.7	–20.5	45	11.5	35.0	31
Indiana	1.8	–51.2	15	6.9	–12.8	6
Iowa	2.6	–27.7	21	7.6	–32.0	9
Kansas	1.8	–49.5	14	7.1	–19.5	8
Kentucky	3.7	–37.0	39	13.5	36.1	41
Louisiana	2.9	–52.1	25	14.6	62.8	45
Maine	3.6	–34.4	37	12.5	–18.6	36
Maryland	2.9	–36.0	24	9.1	–44.1	17
Massachusetts	3.2	–41.3	33	11.7	–10.5	34
Michigan	4.3	–41.5	43	11.4	50.4	29
Minnesota	3.1	–26.9	31	8.6	–27.8	15
Mississippi	3.0	–53.8	28	19.9	121.4	49
Missouri	3.3	–34.5	35	11.4	–38.2	28
Montana	2.6	–36.4	22	8.1	–23.8	11
Nebraska	2.3	–23.6	18	8.7	21.7	16
Nevada	1.7	–33.9	10	5.3	–43.9	1
New Hampshire	1.4	–46.3	3	6.0	7.6	4
New Jersey	3.1	–31.0	30	8.5	34.8	14
New Mexico	3.3	–44.7	34	14.0	58.4	42
New York	5.4	–18.5	46	12.7	–3.5	37
North Carolina	2.9	–38.8	27	11.1	–20.9	27
North Dakota	1.6	–46.4	6	7.1	–37.5	7
Ohio	3.7	–42.0	40	9.8	9.0	20
Oklahoma	2.2	–48.9	17	13.2	1.4	39
Oregon	1.6	–58.5	9	11.6	4.2	33
Pennsylvania	3.4	–32.3	36	13.2	1.3	40
Rhode Island	5.5	–10.4	48	11.6	18.6	32
South Carolina	2.0	–50.1	16	10.5	–50.9	22
South Dakota	1.6	–44.0	7	8.2	–30.8	13
Tennessee	2.9	–51.8	26	22.1	147.4	50
Texas	2.4	–44.7	19	10.7	–30.5	24
Utah	1.5	–46.6	4	5.7	–48.8	2
Vermont	3.7	–25.2	38	16.5	21.6	47
Virginia	1.7	–43.3	12	7.8	–2.2	10
Washington	4.2	–23.1	42	13.0	20.2	38
West Virginia	4.1	–37.7	41	17.1	1.1	48
Wisconsin	1.7	–63.7	13	8.2	–6.3	12
Wyoming	0.8	–79.5	2	10.1	12.7	21
Mean	3.0	–38.4		10.9	5.7	

SOURCES: Population, U.S. Bureau of the Census, Web site at www.census.gov/population/estimates/state/st9097t1.txt; AFDC: U.S. Department of Health and Human Services, Administration for Children and Families, Web site at www.acf.dhhs.gov/news/caseload; Medicaid: HCFA 1998.

policy experiments are being conducted. The federal government is responsible for this by omission and commission: It failed to enact comprehensive health care reform in 1994, and it delegated substantial control over welfare to the states in 1996. The states, for their part, have been eager to gain control over these policy areas (as long as this control does not cost them too much) and willing to innovate to solve their problems.

HEALTH CARE REFORM

The states continue to be the leaders in health care reform—and they continue to have good reasons to be. State health expenditures, especially those for Medicaid, along with education remain the largest items in many states' budgets; at the extreme, New Hampshire spent nearly 40 percent of its 1997 budget on Medicaid (National Association of State Budget Officers 1998). Medical costs also continue to rise, though not as rapidly as in the past. Because virtually all state constitutions require balanced budgets, the states, unlike the federal government, are unable to finance health programs by running deficits. The number of Medicaid recipients has also been growing, in part as a result of factors such as federal mandates and also other measures beyond state control (such as the growing number of people without private health insurance). Meanwhile, public demand for health services continues to increase. The pressures of rising costs, rising demand, and rising numbers of the uninsured create powerful incentives for states to innovate in the way they deliver health care.

State health care reform proposals are usually built around three main goals. The first is to control costs, both for the state's citizens and for the state itself. The second is to provide access, so that the health care needs of the citizens—at least those citizens that state political systems determine are worthy of support—are met. The third goal, high-quality care, is also important but is more controversial and difficult to define.

To accomplish these goals, state policy makers have focused their efforts on four major types of reforms. They have sought to enroll Medicaid recipients in managed care programs, expand insurance coverage for children, control long-term health care costs, and make insurance more affordable and available to the small-business community (Sparer 1998). This section examines managed care and insurance for children (for the other topics, see Nichols and Blumberg 1998; Wiener and Stevenson 1998).

MEDICAID MANAGED CARE

Until recently Medicaid, like most private health insurance, was a fee-for-service program. Medical providers who treated individuals covered by Medicaid were reimbursed for the services they provided. State governments established the reimbursement rates for the various services, the federal government required the states to set these rates high enough that the services would actually be available to Medicaid recipients, and medical providers were required to accept the reimbursements as payment in full for their services. Although this fee-for-service system neither pleased medical providers, who generally believed that the rates were too low, nor guaranteed access to care for Medicaid recipients, who often found that the services they needed were not easy to obtain, it did allow total costs to grow rapidly as providers sought higher payments and recipients sought more care.

These features of fee-for-service insurance led private sector companies to experiment with managed care programs. Although a wide array of such programs exist, one important element in many programs is that they are *capitated*—that is, the program receives a fixed amount of money per enrolled person to provide them a set of services. If the program spends less than this amount per patient it will run a surplus; if it spends more, it will incur a loss. This creates incentives for the program to reduce medical costs by delivering care efficiently, by minimizing unnecessary care and, many fear, by withholding appropriate care. Managed care programs are rapidly coming to dominate the private health insurance market, with traditional fee-for-service plans now covering fewer than a quarter of privately insured individuals.

Until 1997 federal Medicaid law did not allow the states to experiment with managed care programs, or other administrative experiments, unless the states first obtained permission (through what were called Section 1115 or 1915 waivers) from the federal government. Since the 1970s states have sought waivers to try various innovations (Schneider 1997). Most of these Medicaid waivers had the dual purpose of controlling costs while expanding access to health care. For example, early waivers allowed states to offer medical care to the elderly in their homes, and to children in schools, rather than in nursing homes or medical clinics.

Arizona was the first state to receive a waiver (in 1982) to experiment with managed care with its Health Care Cost Containment System (indeed, Arizona has never had a traditional Medicaid program). The Arizona system, which covers both acute care and long-term care, has been shown to contain health care costs by developing a competitive Medicaid health care market (U.S. House 1996, 890). Still, until recently the federal government waivers were difficult to obtain. This changed with the Clinton administration, which streamlined the waiver process and gave greater weight to state proposals. This greater flexibility, together with increased state interest in health care reform, brought a surge in waiver applications: More were submitted and approved between 1992 and 1995 than in the entire history of the Medicaid program (Schneider 1997). The Balanced Budget Act of 1997 eliminated the waiver requirement, however, so states no longer need federal permission to move their Medicaid populations into managed care programs (Sparer 1998).

Virtually all states are now moving swiftly to enroll their Medicaid recipients in managed care programs (HCFA 1997a). By mid-1997 twelve states had at least three quarters of their recipients in such programs, and Washington and Tennessee had their entire caseload enrolled; only the two most rural states (Alaska and Wyoming) had no Medicaid recipients in managed care programs (Table 10-4).

Table 10-4 Medicaid Managed Care Programs, 1997

State	Medicaid enrollment	Managed care enrollment	Percentage in managed care
Washington	730,052	730,052	100
Tennessee	1,188,570	1,188,570	100
Montana	70,821	62,004	88
Oregon	376,345	312,345	83
Alabama	497,434	407,643	82
Hawaii	166,725	135,200	81
Arizona	431,813	349,142	81
Delaware	80,561	65,061	81
Colorado	228,558	184,000	81
Utah	118,343	93,785	79
Michigan	1,115,903	865,434	78
Maryland	465,136	347,640	75
South Dakota	60,412	41,542	69
Nebraska	144,238	93,085	65
Massachusetts	716,465	461,989	64
Connecticut	360,246	231,966	64
Georgia	881,632	560,771	64
Florida	1,410,881	896,559	64
Rhode Island	114,162	70,944	62
Arkansas	267,525	159,458	60
Virginia	522,080	306,804	59
New Mexico	242,445	139,337	57
New Jersey	684,880	384,644	56
Pennsylvania	1,585,807	870,365	55
Indiana	405,000	220,000	54
North Dakota	45,303	24,295	54
Oklahoma	437,161	222,818	51
Kansas	185,301	94,430	51
Kentucky	527,211	268,205	51
Wisconsin	422,870	205,523	49
Missouri	614,783	264,496	43
North Carolina	825,464	351,043	43
Minnesota	402,787	169,329	42
Iowa	217,668	88,282	41
West Virginia	310,710	125,521	40
Idaho	80,553	32,428	40
California	4,791,253	1,854,294	39
Ohio	1,095,268	352,833	32
Nevada	88,500	26,376	30
New York	2,296,479	660,725	29
Vermont	96,985	22,946	24
Mississippi	543,560	81,255	15
Illinois	1,370,354	187,048	14
Texas	2,079,297	275,951	13
New Hampshire	70,922	9,102	13
Maine	155,524	12,511	8
Louisiana	635,672	40,469	6
South Carolina	393,475	14,311	4
Wyoming	48,348	0	0
Alaska	87,475	0	0
Totals	30,813,957	14,643,252	48

SOURCE: HCFA 1998.

Nationally, only one in ten Medicaid recipients was in a managed care plan in 1991, yet now more than half are.

One prominent example of the state Medicaid managed care innovations is Tennessee's TennCare Program, implemented in 1994. TennCare was designed to cover Medicaid beneficiaries and also to expand coverage to those having preexisting health problems that left them uninsurable and those who did not have access to other employer- or government-sponsored insurance. (And expand it did—recall the growth in Tennessee's Medicaid program, illustrated in Table 10-3.) TennCare's medical benefits are more generous than the federal government requires, but participants with incomes above the poverty line are required to pay premiums, deductibles, and copayments based on their income. To encourage preventive care, however, all such services are free (HCFA 1997a).

It is too early to judge whether the move to managed care will improve health care delivery and at the same time reduce health care costs. Caution is in order, however. It looks like cost savings are likely to be less than anticipated, as most Medicaid–managed care beneficiaries are mothers and children, and most Medicaid expenditures go to the elderly and disabled (Holahan et al. 1998). Others have suggested that there is little care management in Medicaid managed care programs, as few beneficiaries are skilled at using these programs and few organizations adept at delivering them (Sparer 1998).

STATE CHILD HEALTH INSURANCE PROGRAM

The federal government created the Child Health Insurance Program (CHIP) in 1997 to help states create and expand programs providing medical care to low-income children. CHIP is hardly a new program dreamed up by the federal government and imposed on the states, however. The fact is that the states had already taken the lead in expanding medical care for poor children (in part through the Section 1115 waivers), and CHIP was established in large part because of the political efforts of state governments. Prior to CHIP's birth, thirty-four states were already offering care to more pregnant women and infants than the federal government required; twenty-four states were providing care to more children ages six and over; and eleven states had expanded care for younger children. Several states had established programs entirely funded from state revenues (NGA 1998; see also Bruen and Ullman 1998). During the 1997 legislative season, thirty-eight states had considered legislation to improve children's health. It is important to note that the proposals were not limited to the richest or most innovative states. Even states with relatively stingy Medicaid programs (such as Arkansas, Indiana, Ohio, and Oklahoma) approved expansions, as did states with more generous programs.

The big picture is simple. In CHIP the federal government provides block grants to the states based on their proportion of the nation's poor (in families with incomes less than 200 percent of the poverty line), and uninsured children. The states, in turn, must provide matching funds (at a lower rate than for Medicaid). The states can use these funds to expand Medicaid, create a separate program, or both. The states will spend about $10 billion in their own funds on CHIP in the program's first five years, with the federal government spending an additional $20 billion.

A close-up shows much more complexity (Bruen and Ullman 1998; Riley, Pernice, and Mollica 1998). Even though the program is quite new—in July 1998 only half the states had their plans approved—it is already clear that the states will use their discretion and design programs that vary substantially from place to place. Most states are deciding who they will cover under CHIP and how they will deliver services to them, as no final federal regulations exist to guide the states. Most of the states that acted early proposed to expand their Medicaid programs. A smaller number of the state programs were entirely outside Medicaid—and several states proposed a combination of Medicaid and non-Medicaid programs to deliver CHIP. Evidence suggests that this mix will be followed by other states. Note, however, that many proposals are still being evaluated by state legislatures, planning commissions, and the Health Care Financing Administration in Washington, D.C., so it is not possible to predict the final shape of this program.

The states do face a dilemma in deciding what kind of CHIP to offer. It will be faster and easier for states to expand their Medicaid programs, but by doing so they will be bound more tightly by federal law. States that create their own programs will have more flexibility but face more uncertainty in how well the program will work.

These state experiments—whether in Medicaid managed care, CHIP, small business insurance, or long-term care—remain controversial. The TennCare concept, for instance, was devised and actively promoted by Gov. Ned McWherter, and the proposal was swiftly adopted by the legislature and approved by the federal government. Yet health care providers strongly opposed the proposal and sought to block it, making implementation arduous and intricate (Bonnyman 1996; Schneider 1997). And the program will not expand care to all the uninsured, as the program is limited to covering almost 1.5 million individuals—but not all those who need insurance.

We need not even imagine that the state innovations are a panacea. Developing and implementing these experiments require administrative expertise and integrated data systems—traits that have often been in short supply. The programs might be more expensive than expected or permitted by the federal government. They will not cover all those who need coverage. And, after all, experiments do fail. State experimentation is no guarantee of state success (Sparer 1996a, 1996b, 1998; Sparer and Brown 1996). States will continue to face substantial barriers in their efforts to improve access, enhance quality, and contain costs (Sparer 1998; Thompson and DeIulio 1998). Still, the promise of medical coverage for our most vulnerable citizens is more nearly realized now than it was even a few years ago.

WELFARE REFORM

If the states are experimenting with health reforms, they are blowing up welfare programs. The termination of AFDC in 1996 and the creation of TANF might mark the states' declaration of independence from federal control but, in fact, the revolution had already been waged for several years.

Many matches lit this fire. The AFDC program was hated by policy makers, many members of the public, and even many of the welfare recipients. Many saw that the program did not help its beneficiaries to become economically self-sufficient and, indeed, that it encouraged them to behave badly by working less, avoiding marriage, bearing children out of wedlock, and becoming dependent on governmental support, even across generations (Rom 1997a). There was some truth to these perceptions—at least enough to put welfare defenders' backs to the wall (Weaver and Dickens 1996). But the political force of these views had a much larger impact on reform efforts than did their empirical validity, as policy makers grappled with designing welfare programs that would be seen as encouraging economic independence and other socially beneficial behavior (see Bryner 1998).

The Family Support Act of 1988, the federal law that prevailed during the early 1990s, had been a step toward such a reform, but no one really defended it. President Clinton, who came in to office on the promise to "end welfare as we know it," did not forcefully promote any welfare legislation during his first term and the Congress was not prepared to act on its own. A former governor, Clinton was nonetheless sympathetic to the desires of the states to conduct welfare experiments on their own.

As in Medicaid, the states were not permitted to innovate without limits. If a state proposed a welfare project that conflicted with federal law, the state had to obtain a waiver for this program from HHS. Although a trickle of waiver applications had been filed and approved before Clinton came into office, during his administration this trickle turned into a torrent—by the mid-1990s, most states had waivers (the exceptions were Alaska, Idaho, Kansas, Kentucky, Nevada, New Mexico, and Rhode Island). States were thus given the opportunity to begin trying "workfare" and "learnfare" programs (that is, programs that require welfare recipients to work or attend school or lose benefits) as well as "family caps" (programs that withhold additional benefits for AFDC recipients who had additional children; see Levin-Epstein and Greenberg 1992).

The states as a group were also beginning to demand more freedom to run their welfare programs. The National Governors' Association (NGA), having already played a central role in the development of the Family Support Act, petitioned the federal government for such freedom. In 1994, when the Republicans gained control of the Congress, the NGA gained a most sympathetic audience. (By that year Republicans also controlled the governor's office in the majority of the states, including virtually all of the largest ones.) The governors wanted more control over welfare and, by eliminating AFDC and creating TANF, the Congress and the president gave it to them.

Some states, such as Wisconsin, have used waivers and their new power to totally redesign their welfare programs (Kaplan 1998; Wiseman 1996). Other states have made much more modest changes. It is difficult to describe concisely how the states are using their new powers to design and implement TANF, in part because the states (or counties, in some states) are doing so many different things (see Gallagher et al. 1998 and NGA 1998 for summaries). But there are a few common elements in the state efforts to promote economic independence and other socially beneficial behaviors.

Work Requirements

TANF's goal is work. The federal government requires all adult recipients to participate in work activities within two years of entering the rolls, although it exempts various parents from these requirements. The states still have wide leeway to determine whom they will exempt from the work requirements, how soon work must begin, what counts as work, and what happens if a recipient does not comply with the rules.

Exemptions. States can decide how long they will allow a parent to stay at home with a young child before having to enter the workforce. Twenty-six states exempt parents with children under age one from their work requirements. Two states set the exemption age at six months, twelve states set it at three months, and five states do not provide an exemption based on the age of the youngest child. Only five states allow a single parent to remain with the child for more than a year before being required to work, and federal law gives the states incentives to set the exemption at one year or less. Eighteen states, moreover, set a cumulative time limit for how long a parent can be exempted from work. And although some states already had these policies in place prior to TANF, thirty-eight states have adopted them since that law's enactment (Gallagher et al. 1998, V-2).

Work Starts. Federal law requires that TANF recipients must begin work activities within twenty-four months, or sooner, at state discretion, unless they are exempted from these requirements. Most states have adopted this limit. Several other states require recipients to begin work activities earlier, but because these activities differ so much—they can include such tasks as job search, job "readiness," or job skill training—it is hard to compare these rules. Ten states require paid employment or unpaid work experience in less than two years. At the extreme, Wisconsin requires work immediately upon entry in the program in unsubsidized employment, trial jobs, or community service (Gallagher et al. 1998, V-10, V-11).

Sanctions. Federal law requires the states to penalize individuals who refuse to work, but the states can determine how big these penalties will be. Most states have adopted scaled penalties that become more intense (lasting longer or reducing benefits further) as the recipient resists complying. Fourteen states now cut off benefits entirely at the first offense, and the other states have withheld benefits as their most extreme penalty. Twenty-one states remove the sanction immediately when the individual starts complying, and the rest of the states withhold benefits until sometime after the individual starts playing by the rules. In seven states—a person judged to be continually out of compliance with the rules can never again obtain welfare benefits from the state (Gallagher et al. 1998, V-6).

Social Values

Under AFDC, eligibility for two-parent families was sharply restricted, although each additional child brought an enrolled parent (usually a single mother) additional cash benefits. This feature made possible the claim that welfare was antimarriage and pro-illegitimacy. Both provisions were eliminated by TANF.

States now have the flexibility to impose family caps, which reduce or eliminate additional benefits for children conceived while their mothers are on the TANF rolls. Twenty-two states have adopted some form of family caps, seventeen states offer no additional benefits, and five offer reduced benefits. In only two states, Wisconsin and Idaho, are benefits not related to the size of the family (Gallagher et al. 1998, VI-8).

States can also determine which, if any, two-parent families are eligible for support. Thirty-five states now treat such families the same as one-parent families. Eight states have retained the restrictive criteria that existed for AFDC. The remaining states established eligibility rules less restrictive than under AFDC but more restrictive than the states treating two-parent families the same as single-parent families (Gallagher et al. 1998, III-12, III-13).

The National Governors' Association has created a summary table of state TANF programs. This table (reproduced in Table 10-5) illustrates the broad range of policy options that states face under federal law as well as the variety in state TANF programs (Kaplan 1998). This table does not show other program details that the states have determined on their own initiative. If you want this information, check out the state Web sites listed in the suggested readings section at the end of this chapter.

Wisconsin

Wisconsin is the state most aggressively reforming its program (for discussions of welfare politics and policy in Wisconsin, see Corbett 1995; Kaplan 1998; Peterson and Rom 1990; Wiseman 1996). In 1993 the Wisconsin legislature, feuding with Gov. Tommy Thompson, voted to end AFDC and replace it with a wholly new system before 1999. Thompson used this opportunity to devise the W-2 program, which he unveiled in August 1995 and the legislature enacted with little change the following spring.

W-2 is almost entirely different from AFDC in its goals, structure, and administration (Kaplan 1998). Able-bodied parents are required to work; cash assistance is only provided to those who do. Participants are expected to succeed in the labor market; all cash benefits are available for only a limited time and come, like paychecks, only after work is performed. The government provides child care and health care assistance to the working poor, but participants have to pay a portion of the expense. Finally, the program is administered by organizations—whether governmental or private—that compete successfully for the right to administer it. Indeed, in eight of the seventy-one counties outside Milwaukee, private agencies already administer the program (Kaplan 1998).

Table 10-5 State TANF Plans

	Yes	No	Other
Is the time limit for receiving assistance shorter than sixty months?	20	34	
Is work required sooner than twenty-four months after first receive TANF assistance?	21	33	
Is community service required after two months?	5	49	
Does the state TANF program treat families who recently moved from another state differently than state residents?	14	40	
Does the state continue benefits at the same level if a family on TANF has an additional child?	21	32	1[a]
Does the state provide TANF to non-U.S. citizens legally in the state?	52	2	
Does the state deny TANF benefits to drug felons?	37	17	
Does the state require drug testing for TANF participants?	8	45	1[b]
Does the state provide transitional child care assistance for longer than twelve months?	29	25	
Does the state provide transitional Medicaid benefits for longer than twelve months?	12	42	
Does the state allow Individual Development Accounts?	27	26	1[a]
Does the state offer payments or loans to families diverted from participating in TANF?	30	24	
Does the state subsidize employers who hire TANF participants?	37	16	1[a]
Is the state continuing any AFDC waiver programs?	31	14	8[d], 1[a]

SOURCE: Derived from Kaplan 1998 summary of data at NGA Web site www.nga.org.

NOTE: Includes the 50 states, the District of Columbia, Guam, Puerto Rico, and the U.S. Virgin Islands.

[a] No information available
[b] Pending
[c] No wavier
[d] No waivers to continue

PREVENTION

We have state and federal health and welfare programs that, by definition, provide care to the sick and income to the poor, especially poor women with children. They do not work to prevent individuals from becoming sick or from needing public assistance. American health and welfare programs emphasize treatment rather than prevention.

There are good reasons for this from a political perspective. The most important ones are that there is too much to do and too little with which to do it. Policy makers usually face the situation in which people need immediate assistance, and there is not enough money both to help them with their needs and to prevent others from requiring the same assistance later. This is not unlike the situations most of us face every month with our own budgets: The roof is leaking and the furnace needs maintenance, but this month we have only enough money to choose one. We try to fix the roof first and let the furnace go until next month. Unfortunately, next month something else will need fixing. The dilemma is that something needs fixing every month—and so we often get around to fixing things when it is too late to do so easily.

Yet the maxim is true: A dime of prevention is worth a dollar of cure. It is cheaper—and easier—to keep people off welfare than to get them off, just as it is cheaper and easier to stay well than to become healed. Most observers, conservative and liberal alike, agree that well-designed health and welfare prevention programs can be more effective and cost less than treatment programs.

State health and welfare policies have, to their credit, tilted somewhat more to prevention in recent years. Medicaid managed care has a better chance to emphasize wellness programs (that is, prenatal care, well baby care, and routine screenings, among others) than traditional Medicaid. Offering better medical care to children can lead to healthier, and we hope economically more independent, adults. States are experimenting with ways to help keep TANF recipients in school or in jobs, and to help deter unwanted pregnancies, as ways of helping the beneficiaries become economically self-sufficient. As a matter of policy, however, federal and state governments typically spend far more on treatment than prevention, at least on matters of public health. In the late 1980s the federal Centers for Disease Control and Prevention estimated that U.S. investment in prevention was less than 5 percent of U.S. spending on health care (CDC 1992).

The dilemma that favors treatment over prevention can be overcome in certain circumstances. If a state is rich enough, it can afford to do both. Paradoxically, the states that need most to emphasize prevention often have the worst current problems and are least able to afford to look toward the future. At any rate, the richer the state, the better able it is to afford prevention. If a state is unified and committed enough politically—or if a political leader is able to persuade it that it should be—it might also decide to spend on prevention despite its pressing treatment needs. Unity and commitment are necessary, as there are never enough resources, so spending on prevention dictates that some constituents in need of treatment will be ignored. Ignoring constituents is possible to the extent that policy makers concur that it must be done—and stick to this concurrence.

The combination of unity and commitment is scarce in partisan politics. But even when both political parties are committed to prevention they may have strong differences about what real prevention is. Liberals (and Democrats) in general view prevention as a set of positive incentives offered by the government. To keep individuals healthy, programs must provide them education or services so that they will be willing and able to become physically strong and economically self-sufficient. Conservatives (and Republicans) usually reject this view, placing responsibility for physical and economic health more squarely on the individual citizens. Government, from the conservative perspective, mainly creates incentives for persons to become dependent and diseased by providing welfare and health benefits in the first place. Accordingly, government practices prevention best by ensuring that individuals bear the consequences of their own actions.

Nonetheless, it is worth considering three questions. Why do people become ill, and so in need of medical care? Why do families become needy, and so in need of welfare? What can states do to prevent illness and neediness? Although the answers to the first two questions no doubt involve social and even metaphysical elements, I will focus on behavioral answers: People need medical treatment and welfare in part because of the way they behave. State efforts at prevention therefore might need to address these behaviors.

The major behavioral factors contributing to premature death, and excessive need for medical care, have now been identified (McGinnis and Foege 1993). These behavioral risk factors are largely responsible for about half of all premature deaths each year. The big three—tobacco use, poor diet and lack of exercise, and abuse of alcohol—cause in part 40 percent of all deaths and 75 percent of premature deaths. The other major factors identified—microbial or toxic agents, firearms, sexual behavior, motor vehicles, and illicit drugs—account for the other 25 percent of premature deaths. (The other factors include such things as infections that individuals could have sought treatment for early on but did not.) Our public policies devote resources to controlling these risks in inverse proportion to the risks they cause to public health (Meier 1994). We spend far more to control illegal drugs than to encourage Americans to live healthier lives, even though far more die from legal but unhealthy lifestyles than from abusing illegal drugs.

The major behavioral factors that lead to welfare dependency are also clear. Families are most likely to spend long periods on welfare when children are born out of wedlock to young women who are poorly educated. At the end of the 1980s in the United States, the vast majority of the children living in female-headed families in which the mother was younger than twenty-one were poor; virtually all these families received public assistance. Our welfare policies spend much more on providing assistance to these families than on preventing the need for assistance in the first place.

The behavioral risks that damage public health or create the need for public assistance each have distinctive politics. None of these politics is simple or rational. All involve personal activities—smoking cigarettes, eating too much and exercising too little, drinking alcohol, shooting firearms, and having unsafe sex—that raise strong emotions in the political arena. Because they involve highly personal behaviors of millions of individuals, they are difficult for governments to control or change. Still, state governments have made at least temporary public health progress on some of these issues. Smoking rates are falling, as is the frequency of drunk driving. Other behaviors have been less susceptible to change. The public's willingness to adopt healthier diets and sexual behaviors has not been firmly established. And America has not proved capable of greatly reducing its gun violence.

Tobacco

Tobacco use, especially cigarette smoking, is by far the largest threat to public health. Each year tobacco use is responsible for approximately 430,000 deaths from a wide variety of causes, such as cancer, cardiovascular disease, lung disease, and burns (CDC 1997a). Although the federal government and most state governments treated the tobacco industry gently for decades, they now are taking an increasingly tough stance in regard to cigarette smoking.

There are many reasons for the shift toward tougher policies on tobacco use. First, the scientific evidence has become incontrovertible that smoking creates large health risks without producing any positive health benefits. Second, these health risks exist not just for the smokers themselves, but also for those who live or work with them, although scientific debate still exists regarding the effects of "environmental tobacco smoke" (see Sullum 1994). Third, economic and social elites—who are also typically those with the most political resources—have become more hostile toward tobacco use because they themselves smoke less. In the mid-1990s about four out of ten high school drop-outs aged twenty-five and older smoked, for example, whereas only one in ten with college degrees did (National Center for Health Statistics 1998). Fourth, blame for tobacco use has been clearly placed on the tobacco industry itself. Often depicted as the merchant of death, the industry denied that there was any link between smoking, addiction, and health problems long after it became unbelievable. The industry also targeted a particularly vulnerable and sympathetic group—children—in its advertising campaigns. Fifth, programs discouraging tobacco use need not cost much (through regulation) and indeed can raise substantial sums (through taxes). Sixth, various governments have decided that smoking-related health problems have imposed large costs on the public through the Medicaid and Medicare programs—and the states are increasingly suing the tobacco industry for compensation.

The tobacco industry and users are not without their own political resources, of course, as the Congress was reminded in 1998 when it considered legislation to tax and regulate cigarettes further. The industry's main resource is money. It spends far more to promote smoking than the government does to discourage it; for example, the tobacco industry spends millions every year on advertising, not including the advertising inherent in its sponsorship of sporting events (the Virginia Slims Tennis Tour, for example, or the Winston 500 automotive races) and other activities. Tobacco interests also contribute extensively to political campaigns to ensure that their voice is heard. The tobacco users' main political strength is in their numbers. Because more than a quarter of the American public continues to smoke, politicians who threaten this activity (especially through taxation) face repercussions at the next election. Still, despite the tobacco industry's millions of smokers and millions of dollars, political strength is moving toward those who want to raise the cost and difficulty of smoking cigarettes.

State governments have acted with increasing vigor and creativity to discourage smoking. Indeed, all fifty states have now obtained out of court settlements with the tobacco industry in which the industry will pay more than $230 billion to the states over the next twenty-five years. Four states (Mississippi, Florida, Minnesota, and Texas) successfully pressed their own claims individually before the industry reached a global settlement with the other states in November 1998 (Action on Smoking and Health 1998).

States are also using various other means to reduce tobacco-related risks, although the intensity of the effort varies from state to state. Virtually every state requires smoke-free indoor air in some places to some extent. Only Alabama, Kentucky, North Carolina, and Tennessee—major tobacco producers—either had no such laws or had state laws that preempted any local laws that would restrict smoking in public places. Forty-some states had laws restricting smoking in government work sites; more than thirty states regulated smoking in restaurants; more than twenty restricted smoking in private work sites; and some states regulated smoking in other locations, such as day care centers (for details, see CDC 1995).

The states also use policies to make it more difficult for youth to smoke. All states prohibited the sale and distribution of tobacco products to minors, and thirty-two states prohibited minors from buying, possessing, or using tobacco products. No state allows vending machine sale of cigarettes to minors, and thirty-two states again provided additional restrictions to make youth access to vending machines more difficult. Only nine states had laws restricting tobacco advertising, however, and most of these restrictions were quite modest (CDC 1995).

Laws do not necessarily mean results, of course, because state enforcement of tobacco laws is notoriously lax, particularly regarding sales to minors (see, for example, CDC 1995, for an analysis of the effect of state regulations on state smoking rates). Still, these laws do send a message concerning state priorities.

California has had the most ambitious smoking-control program. Beginning in 1988, when the state's voters approved Proposition 99, California raised cigarette taxes by twenty-five cents per pack and launched a high-profile television campaign (as well as education efforts by schools and doctors) financed by $80 million of the $780 million raised each year by the tax (Zamichow 1992). These policies, and changing social norms, caused California's smoking rate to fall farther and faster than the national average; the smoking rate in California dropped by 30 percent since the mid-1980s. And California continues to get tough. Beginning in 1998 California banned smoking in all public areas, including bars and restaurants.

Still, the American youth are not terribly impressed by all this. Smoking has become increasingly fashionable in middle and high schools, with smoking rates among ninth through twelfth graders rising substantially in the 1990s. As Donna Shalala, secretary of Health and Human Services, noted,

> Today, nearly 3,000 young people across our country will begin smoking regularly. Of these 3,000 young people, 1,000 will lose that gamble to the diseases caused by smoking. The net effect of this is that among children living in America today, 5 million will die an early preventable death because of a decision made as a child. (Shalala 1997)

Diet and Activity

Diet and activity (D&A) contribute to more than 300,000 premature deaths each year, according to McGinnis and Foege (1993). The problem is not too little food and too much work, but just the opposite: Americans in general eat too much fatty food and exercise too little. Yet state and federal policy makers have done much less to reduce the threats to public health from obesity than from smoking or drinking.

The political dynamics of obesity make it exceptionally difficult for policy makers to take effective action to reduce its risks. As is true of smoking, the evidence for the harmful effects of excessive fatty foods and lack of exercise is strong, and political elites are generally sympathetic to the need for healthier diets and more exercise. A moderate correlation exists between income, education, exercise, and weight. Those with more than twelve years of education are twice as likely as those with less than twelve years to exercise regularly (50 and 25 percent, respectively); those with incomes above $50,000 are much more likely to exercise than those with incomes below $10,000. Similarly, those with more education and higher income are less likely to be overweight than those with less education or income (U.S. Bureau of the Census 1997, 148).

Yet the other political liabilities associated with tobacco vanish as if in smoke. The risks obesity create do not directly influence the health of others, as smoking does, so no natural opposition to obesity exists from those who are more physically fit. The risks associated with obesity create few obvious villains. Unlike tobacco, virtually all foods can be part of a healthy diet, and no one food can be singled out as the culprit (there is no "smoking gun" in the food business). Nor is there an obvious (and cheap) way to regulate or tax foods or activity to induce better diets and more exercise. Even more than tobacco use, diet and exercise are regarded as purely personal activities that the government has no authority to regulate or tax. Of course, food is regulated in many ways (for example, for contaminants and truth in labeling), and sales taxes are often applied. But nowhere in the United States is food regulated or taxed on the basis of content. Moreover, purveyors of junk food spend opulently on advertisements, whereas advocates of healthier diets spend next to nothing. There is a large athletic products industry, of course, but it hardly need be mentioned that they have a greater interest in selling fashion than in improving body-fat indicators. The number of Americans who weigh too much and exercise too little exceeds even the number of smokers.

As a result, there is no political momentum for legislatures to restrict diets or mandate exercise, and little political interest in more positive incentives. Any policy activity that occurs comes from public health officials (or, for example, nutritionists), who understand the importance of improved physical fitness. Lacking regulatory authority, these officials have chosen to pursue an educational strategy to reduce the risks of obesity to public health. The one best place for state and local governments to intervene might be the schools, through the school lunch and physical education programs.

Still, the news is not promising. More Americans are overweight and fewer exercise vigorously than ever. More than one-third of adults are overweight in the late 1990s, and this problem is (literally) growing, as this represents a 10 percent increase over the late 1970s (National Center for Health Statistics 1998). Sixty percent of the adult population do not exercise regularly, and 25 percent do not exercise at all. More worrisome is the fact that about half of all youth (ages twelve to twenty-one) do not exercise, and participation in school physical education courses has been declining (NCCDP 1996).

Alcohol

Alcohol misuse accounts for 100,000 premature deaths annually. These deaths can occur through alcohol's effect on the body (for example, cirrhosis of the liver or fetal alcohol syndrome) and, more important, on behavior. When you go out this weekend, reflect on this: Half of all homicides, assaults, car and boat fatalities, drowning and fire fatalities, and the like can be attributed at least in part to alcohol consumption (McGinnis and Foege 1993).

There are old politics and new politics of alcohol. The (mainly religious) call for prohibition defines the old politics. The public health consequences or the costs and benefits of alcohol use did not enter into the debate; the debate was about whether drinking was a sin. These politics still prevail in many parts of the country. Although no states maintain prohibition, numerous dry counties dot the map (especially through the parts of the country known as the Bible Belt). It is no small irony that the Jack Daniels (a Tennessee bourbon) distillery is located in a dry county.

The new politics of alcohol are a hybrid of those for tobacco as well as diet and activity. One of the main differences is that there is no real elite opposition to alcohol, no doubt because those with more income and education drink as much as (if not more than) those with lower socioeconomic status. Alcohol use, moreover, is not seen (either medically or socially) as inherently harmful. Large portions of the public drink moderately, and medical research suggests that this might, in some circumstances, be healthful. The alcohol companies themselves urge their buyers to drink in moderation.

Although almost all tobacco use is politically vulnerable and almost no issues involving diet and activity issues are, the new politics of alcohol divides sharply between personal use and public misuse. In some central cities where personal alcohol consumption is itself seen as a major public health problem, there appears to be growing support for additional restrictions on the availability of alcohol (see, for example, Schneider 1994). In most places, however, additional policies to restrict purely personal use by adults have little political support. In contrast, public misuse—especially drunk driving—is being vigorously attacked around the country. Groups such as Mothers against Drunk Driving (MADD) and its offshoots (for example, Students against Drunk Driving, SADD) have mobilized much political and social support for their goal.

The states have led the way in these attacks, although not always willingly. The major impetus to state action was the 1984 federal law that required states to enact a minimum drinking age of twenty-one by 1986 or lose a portion of their federal highway funds (O'Malley and Wagenaar 1991). In 1982, for example, only fourteen states prohibited the purchase of alcohol by those under the age of twenty-one; all fifty states prohibited it by 1988. In a more recent victory for state autonomy, if not for public health, in 1998 the Congress considered but ultimately rejected a proposal requiring all states to adopt a uniform limit for the blood alcohol concentration (0.08 percent) at which an automobile driver is considered intoxicated. Theories of federalism had less to do with this decision than lobbying by the beverage and restaurant industries, however. Still, fifteen states have themselves adopted this lower limit; the others use a blood alcohol concentration of 0.10 as the legal limit. This combination of tougher drunk driving laws, increased penalties for violators, and expanded enforcement, together with changing social mores, has contributed to the substantial decrease in the rate of deaths, injuries, and accidents attributed to alcohol-influenced driving. Between 1980 and 1995, the proportion of traffic fatalities in which at least one person had a blood alcohol concentration of 0.10 or higher fell from 40 percent to 30 percent (U.S. Bureau of the Census 1997, 633).

Firearms

Violent crime has again been in the news, but for two very different reasons. The frequency of violent crime—homicides, rapes, robberies, assault—has been dropping around the country for the past several years. By 1996 the violent crime rate was at its lowest point in three decades and it has declined further since then (U.S. Department of Justice 1998). Still, there have been several highly publicized episodes of killings in the schools—most notably, the sniper attack by two students in Jonesboro, Arkansas, which killed five students and a teacher.

But whether we should be cheered by the trends or alarmed by the incidents, this much is clear: With firearms associated with more than 30,000 fatalities through homicides, suicides, and accidents each year, the toll taken on society by guns is unique among wealthy nations (Fingerhut and Kleinman 1990). Unique, also, is the widespread belief that gun ownership is a constitutionally protected citizen's right.

The politics of firearms are extraordinarily divisive (Spitzer 1995). No claim concerning the role of firearms in our society's violence goes unquestioned (for a summary of some of the controversies, see Witkin 1994). Support for stricter gun control is broad among elites and the public as a whole, but opposition to controls is intense among gun owners and suppliers. Supporters of gun control recite with horror the toll taken by intentional and accidental gunfire each year. Gun advocates, for their part, correctly note that most gun owners pose no threat to public health; the others, the advocates contend, will pose a threat whether controls exist or not. As a result of the divisiveness of the politics of firearms, at least at the national level, the public is at times subjected to embarrassing debates about banning "assault weapons," as if such bans either would protect the public health or pose a threat to constitutional rights.

The extent of firearm violence varies widely from state to state and over time. In general, the southern and western states have much higher levels of violence than states in the Northeast or Midwest. Louisiana, for example, had more than 400 firearm-related violent crimes per 100,000 residents in 1995, whereas North Dakota had fewer than 10 per 100,000; the 50-state average was fewer than 200 per 100,000 residents (U.S. Department of Justice 1996, 319).

The states also have a wide variety of policies to regulate and control the purchase, carrying, or ownership of firearms, and many states have attempted to strengthen these laws in recent years. (For a state-by-state summary of laws and regulations concerning handguns, see U.S. Department of Justice 1996) The impact of these policies is difficult to measure. Opponents of gun control argue that these results demonstrate that such control does not work to reduce violence. Supporters contend that in a society that so resembles an arsenal, the modest measures imposed by the states can hardly have much effect on reducing violence.

The largest current controversy concerns concealed-weapons laws. These laws generally allow any adult without a criminal record or history of mental illness to obtain a permit to carry (concealed) handguns virtually anywhere. In places that do not have these laws, a person must typically show a compelling reason to carry a concealed weapon. One scholar presents evidence that concealed-weapons laws reduce the frequency of violent crime by deterring criminals from attacking potential victims who may, after all, be armed and ready to retaliate (Lott 1997). This analysis has been widely, and convincingly, criticized (see, for example, Ludwig 1998a, 1998b; Webster et al. 1997).

The link between research and policy is always tenuous. But to the extent that the states are voting in this debate, it appears that they favor Lott's position. Thirty-one states now have concealed-weapons laws. Twenty-three of the states have enacted these laws since 1985, with nine states acting since 1995. In 1998 the Missouri legislature voted to place a concealed-weapons referendum on the state ballot, to allow its citizens to vote directly on this idea in 1999 (*Economist* 1998). The most popular form of gun control laws appear now to be the laws that allow individuals to carry and, it is hoped, control their own guns.

Sexual Behavior

Alas, one of life's greatest pleasures is one of its greatest problems. Unprotected sexual intercourse can kill, injure, and deprive—and not just by transmitting the virus that causes AIDS. The human immunodeficiency virus (HIV), sexually transmitted, did account for 33,000 deaths in 1996, and is the largest single cause of death for males aged twenty-five to sixty-four. But unprotected sexual intercourse also contributes to approximately 5,000 excess infant deaths (from unintended pregnancies), 4,000 extra deaths from cervical cancer (linked to certain sexually transmitted diseases), and 1,600 deaths from hepatitis B infection each year. In addition, some 12 million persons become infected with a sexually transmitted disease each year, and more than half of all pregnancies are unintended (McGinnis and Foege 1993). Whether or not one believes that the price of abortion is a human life, all should agree that the demand for abortion is far higher than we want.

The onset of AIDS has created special challenges for certain states' public health systems. Although every state has persons with AIDS (PWAs) as residents, AIDS is not spread uniformly across the country: California, Florida, and New York alone accounted for more than forty percent of total AIDS cases in 1996 (CDC 1997b, 7). Moreover, a large proportion—about half of all adults and nine out of ten children with AIDS—eventually receive Medicaid and thus become, at least medically, wards of the state (HCFA 1998b). Typically, PWAs become eligible for Medicaid if they lose their own private insurance, their jobs, or their personal resources; through their eligibility in SSI or AFDC; or through a state's "medically needy" category of Medicaid. The result is that much of the health care cost of AIDS is shifted to the public sector; the ugly term for this is the Medicaidization of AIDS (Green and Arno 1990). States with large numbers of PWAs, in particular, have thus been under tremendous pressure to contain the costs they have imposed on the public. A principal way states have tried to cope is to seek Medicaid waivers so that PWAs may receive home or community-based long-term care (rather than more expensive hospitalization).

The politics of sex has been characterized by the struggle between those who view sexual behavior as a moral issue and those who consider it a policy issue only to the extent that sexual behavior threatens public health (Nice 1994). The attitudes and policy preferences of those holding these views are fundamentally different. The former group believes that government policy should encourage or enforce only "moral" sex—that is, monogamous relations within a heterosexual marriage. The latter group argues that sexual relations between consenting adults are acceptable to the extent that they do not cause unintended pregnancies or spread disease; as a result, this group favors education concerning "safe sex" as the appropriate policy. State policies toward sexual behavior have to a large extent mirrored these divisions within their populations; more conservative states use less sex education; more liberal states rely less on moral messages.

The politics of sex have been especially unhelpful in regard to welfare policy. Unprotected sexual intercourse, of course, is literally the beginning of the nonmarital births to teenagers that put the family at special risk of needing public assistance. But prevention policies that tell teenagers either to "just say no" or "just be safe" apparently have little impact on teenage pregnancy rates. It is intriguing—a hopeful sign—that policies emphasizing both moral restraint and safer sex are more successful at reducing unwanted pregnancies and sexually transmitted diseases than either approach alone.

It is also apparent that youth who become pregnant, or who impregnate, often have academic, economic, and emotional difficulties before the conception occurs. Dropping out of school, living in poverty, and having little hope for the future help create the conditions that lead teenagers to become parents (Dryfoos 1990; Lawson and Rhode 1993). Research suggests that it is important to address teenagers' social conditions as a way to prevent teen pregnancies. Rather than focusing on pregnancy prevention by itself, public policy needs to improve the educational, economic, and emotional circumstances of adolescents most at risk. (For a discussion of how some local programs seek to prevent adolescent pregnancies, see Brindis 1993.) The best form of birth control is the realistic hope for a better future if childbearing is delayed. Providing such realistic hope for teenagers is not always an easy task even for parents. The states face even greater challenges in providing this hope.

CONCLUSION

Each year federal and state governments spend almost $300 billion providing health care and welfare to assist more than 30 million needy individuals in the United States. We should not underestimate the help this assistance provides. Without it, millions of Americans would face worse health and meaner poverty—and many would not survive.

Most government spending on health and welfare for the poor is channeled through just four programs: Medicaid, TANF, SSI, and GA. Contrary to the common wisdom, the greatest part of this welfare does not consist of giving cash to the poor; programs that provide cash assistance cost only about one-third as much as those that provide medical services, and the proportion of cash assistance is steadily declining.

Although Medicaid and TANF are federal programs, the states carry a heavy burden in financing and operating them, especially for Medicaid. During recent decades Medicaid benefit levels have grown, recipient rolls have expanded, and total expenditures have soared. TANF rolls, in contrast, are now rapidly falling, with expenditures also falling at a slower rate.

These trends have not affected all states equally. Tremendous variation exists among the states in welfare benefits, caseloads, and expenditures. State policy responses to their health and welfare problems have also varied as a result of the specific political, economic, and demographic conditions existing within each state. Still, all states face similar pressures: Their constitutions forbid them from running deficits, and economic competition with their peers restrains their abilities to raise taxes as well as their interest in redistributing income.

The states are now struggling with ways to design their health and welfare programs so that services are provided to those most in need without encouraging others to become dependent on governmental largesse. State governments are also striving to develop ways to deliver these services while controlling costs. In doing so, the states are entering a period of extraordinary policy innovation—especially now that the federal government has given them substantial flexibility to conduct their experiments.

We can hope that these policy experiments will go beyond assisting the sick and the poor to preventing sickness and poverty. The barriers to doing so are high, of course. It is difficult for states to focus on prevention when there are so many demands for treatment. It is difficult to change individuals' behavior so that they will become healthy and independent. Yet such prevention is essential. Healthy citizens are less likely to become dependent on government support. Prosperous citizens are likely to need fewer medical services from the government. The best way for states to control their health and welfare spending is for them to help create healthy and independent citizens.

REFERENCES

Action on Smoking and Health. 1998. Web site at http:\\ash.org.

Berry, William D., Richard C. Fording, and Russell L. Hanson. 1997. "Reassessing the 'Race to the Bottom' Thesis: A Spatial Dependence Model of State Welfare Policy." A paper presented at the 1997 American Political Science Association's Annual Conference, Washington, D.C., August 28–31.

Berry, William D., Evan J. Ringquist, Richard C. Fording, and Russell L. Hanson. 1998. "Measuring Citizen and Government Ideology in the American States." *American Journal of Political Science* 42:327–348.

Blank, Rebecca. 1997. *It Takes a Nation: A New Agenda for Fighting Poverty.* Princeton, N.J.: Princeton University Press.

Bonnyman, Gordon, Jr. 1996. "Stealth Reform: Market-Based Medicaid in Tennessee." *Health Affairs* 15:306–314.

Brindis, Claire. 1993. "Antecedents and Consequences: The Need for Diverse Strategies in Adolescent Pregnancy Prevention." In *The Politics of Pregnancy,* edited by Annette Lawson and Deborah L. Rhode. New Haven, Conn.: Yale University Press.

Bruen, Brian K., and Frank Ullman. 1998. "Children's Health Insurance Programs: Where States Are, Where They Are Headed." Washington, D.C.: Urban Institute.

Bryner, Gary. 1998. *The Great American Welfare Debate: Politics and Public Morality.* New York: W. W. Norton.

CDC (Centers for Disease Control and Prevention). 1992. "Estimated National Spending on Prevention—United States." *Morbidity and Mortality Weekly Report* 41 (July 24):529–531.

———. 1995. "State Laws on Tobacco Control—United States, 1995." *Morbidity and Mortality Weekly Report* 44:No.SS-6.

———. 1997a. "Facts about Cigarette Mortality." Fact sheet at Web site http:\\www.cdc.gov\od\oc\media\fact\cigmortl.htm.

———. 1997b. "HIV/AIDS Surveillance Reports." Web site at http:\\www.cdc.gov\nchstp\hiv-aids\stats\hasrlink.hta.

"Concealed-Weapons Laws: Can Hidden Guns Cut Crime?" 1998. *Economist.* May 30, 24–25.

Cook, Fay Lomax, and Edith J. Barrett. 1992. *Support for the American Welfare State: The Views of Congress and the Public.* New York: Columbia University Press.

Corbett, Thomas J. 1995. "Welfare Reform in Wisconsin: The Rhetoric and Reality." In *The Politics of Welfare Reform,* edited by Donald F. Norris and Lyke Thompson. Thousand Oaks, Calif.: Sage.

Dryfoos, Joy G. 1990. *Adolescents at Risk: Prevalence and Prevention.* New York: Oxford University Press.

Elazar, Daniel J. 1970. "The States and the Political Setting." In *Policy Analysis in Political Science,* edited by Ira Sharkansky. Chicago: Markham.

———. 1972. *American Federalism: A View from the States.* 2d ed. New York: Thomas Y. Crowell.

Erikson, Robert S., Gerald C. Wright, and John R. McIver. 1993. *Statehouse Democracy: Public Opinion and Policy in the American States.* Cambridge: Cambridge University Press.

Fingerhut, L. A., and J. C. Kleinman. 1990. "International and Interstate Comparisons of Homicide among Young Males." *JAMA,* June 27, 2210–2211.

Gallagher, L. Jerome, Megan Gallagher, Keven Perese, Susan Schreiber, and Keith Watson. 1998. *One Year after Federal Welfare Reform: A Description of State Temporary Assistance to Needy Families (TANF) Decisions as of October 1997.* Washington, D.C.: Urban Institute.

Green, Jesse, and Peter S. Arno. 1990. "The 'Medicaidization' of AIDS: Trends in the Financing of HIV-Related Medical Care." *JAMA,* September 12, 1261–1266.

HCFA (Health Care Financing Administration). 1997a. Web site at http:\\www.hcfa.gov\medicaid\ord-1115.htm.

———. 1997b. Web site at http:\\www.hcfa.gov\medicaid\tnfact.htm.

———. 1998a. Web site at http:\\www.hcfa.gov\stats\nhe-oact\tables\t18.htm.

———. 1998b. "Medicaid and AIDS and HIV Infection." Fact Sheet. Web site at http:\\www.hcfa.gov\medicaid\obs11.htm.

Holahan, John, Stephen Zuckerman, Alison Evans, and Suresh Rangarajan. 1998. "Medicaid Managed Care in Thirteen States." *Health Affairs* 17:43–63.

Holbrook, Thomas M., and Emily Van Dunk. 1993. "Electoral Competition in the American States." *American Political Science Review* 87:955–962.

Howard, Christopher. 1997. *The Invisible Welfare State: Tax Expenditures and Social Policy in the United States.* Princeton, N.J.: Princeton University Press.

Hrebenar, Ronald J. 1997. *Interest Group Politics in America.* New York: M. E. Sharpe.

Kaplan, Thomas. 1998. "Wisconsin's W2 Program: Welfare as We Might Come to Know It." A paper presented at the Midwest Political Science Association meeting, Chicago, April 23–25.

Katz, Michael B. 1986 *In the Shadow of the Poorhouse: A Social History of Welfare in America.* New York: Basic Books.

Lawson, Annette, and Deborah L. Rhode, eds. 1993. *The Politics of Pregnancy: Adolescent Sexuality and Public Policy.* New Haven, Conn.: Yale University Press.

Levin-Epstein, Jodie, and Mark Greenberg. 1992. *The Rush to Reform: 1992 State AFDC Legislative and Waiver Actions.* Washington, D.C.: Center for Law and Social Policy.

Lott, John. 1997. *More Guns, Less Crime.* Chicago: University of Chicago Press.

Ludwig, Jens. 1998a. "Guns and Numbers." *The Washington Monthly* (June):50–51.

———. 1998b. "Concealed-Gun-Carrying Laws and Violent Crime: Evidence from State Panel Data." *International Review of Law and Economics* 18:239–254.

McGinnis, J. Michael, and William H. Foege. 1993. "Actual Causes of Death in the United States." *JAMA*, November 10, 2207–2212.

Meier, Kenneth J. 1994. *The Politics of Sin: Drugs, Alcohol, and Public Policy.* New York: M. E. Sharpe.

National Association of State Budget Offices. 1998. Web site at http:\\www.nasb.org.

NCCDP (National Center for Chronic Disease Prevention and Health Promotion). 1996. *Physical Activity and Health: A Report of the Surgeon General.* U.S. Department of Health and Human Services, Centers for Disease Control. Web site at http:\\www.cdc.gov\nccdphp\sgr.

National Center for Health Statistics. 1998. Web site at http:\\www.cdc.gov\nchswww\fastats.

NGA (National Governors' Association). 1998. *Policy Positions, February 1998.* Washington, D.C.: Author.

NGA, NCSL (National Council on State Legislatures), and APWA (American Public Welfare Association). 1996. *Analysis of the Personal Responsibility and Work Opportunity Reconciliation Act of 1996.* Web site at http:\\www.nga.org\Welfare\WelfareDocs.

Nice, David C. 1994. *Policy Innovation in State Government.* Ames: Iowa State University Press.

Nichols, Len M., and Linda J. Blumberg. 1998. "A Different Kind of 'New Federalism'? The Health Insurance Portability and Accountability Act of 1996." *Health Affairs* 17:25–42.

O'Malley, Patrick M., and Alexander Wagenaar. 1991. "Effects of Minimum Drinking Age Laws on Alcohol Use, Related Behaviors, and Traffic Crash Involvement by American Youth: 1976–1987." *Journal of Studies on Alcohol* 52(5):478–491.

Peterson, Paul E. 1995. *The Price of Federalism.* Washington, D.C.: Brookings Institution.

Peterson, Paul E., and Mark C. Rom. 1990. *Welfare Magnets: A New Case for a National Welfare Standard.* Washington, D.C.: Brookings Institution.

Riley, Trish, Cynthia Pernice, and Robert Mollica. 1998. "How Will States Implement Children's Health Insurance Programs?" *Health Affairs* 17:260–263.

Rom, Mark Carl. 1997a. "AFDC's Fatal Flaws." A paper presented at the Southwest Social Science Association meeting, New Orleans, March 26–29.

———. 1997b. "Welfare in the Congress and the White House: A Brief History." A paper presented at the American Political Science Association meeting, Washington, D.C., August 28–31.

———. 1998. "What Race! To Where? A Critique of the 'Race to the Bottom' Slogan." A paper presented at the Wilson International Center for Scholars, Washington, D.C., April.

Schneider, Alison. 1994. "Booze City." *Washingtonian,* September, 83–84, 129–130.

Schneider, Saundra K. 1997. "Medicaid Section 1115 Waivers: Shifting Health Care Reform to the States," *Publius* 27:2, 89–109.

Schram, Sanford, Lawrence Nitz, and Gary Krueger. 1998. "Without Cause or Effect: Reconsidering Welfare Migration as a Policy Problem." *American Journal of Political Science* 42(January):210–230.

Seldon, Thomas M., Jessica S. Banthin, and Joel W. Cohen. 1998. "Medicaid's Problem Children: Eligible but Not Enrolled." *Health Affairs* 17:192–200.

Shalala, Donna. 1997. Testimony before the Senate Labor and Human Resources Committee. September 25. Web site at http:\\www.cdc.gov\nccdphp\osh\oshaag.htm.

Sharkansky, Ira. 1969. "The Utility of Elazar's Political Culture: A Research Note." *Polity* 2:67.

SSA (Social Security Administration). 1997. *Annual Statistical Supplement.* Web site at http://www.ssa.gov/statistics/ores_home.html.

———. 1998. Web site at http:\\www.ftp.ssa.gov\pub\statistics\1b1.

Sparer, Michael S. 1996a. "Great Expectations: The Limits of State Health Care Reform." *Health Affairs* 14:191–202.

———. 1996b. *Medicaid and the Limits of State Health Reform.* Philadelphia: Temple University Press.

———. 1998. "Devolution of Power: An Interim Report Card." *Health Affairs* 17:7–16.

Sparer, Michael S., and Lawrence D. Brown. 1996. "States and the Health Care Crisis: Limits and Lessons of Laboratory Federalism." In *Health Policy, Federalism, and the American States,* edited by Robert F. Rich and William D. White, Washington, D.C.: Urban Institute.

Spitzer, Robert J. 1995. *The Politics of Gun Control.* Chatham, N.J.: Chatham House Press.

State Tobacco Information Center. 1998. Web site at http:\\www.stic.neu.edu.

Sullum, Jacob. 1994. "Just How Bad Is Secondhand Smoke?" *National Review,* May 16, 51.

Thompson, Frank, and John DeIulio. 1998. *Medicaid and Devolution: The View from the States.* Washington, D.C.: Brookings Institution.

Thompson, Lyke. 1995. "The Death of General Assistance in Michigan." In *The Politics of Welfare Reform,* edited by Donald F. Norris and Lyke Thompson. Thousand Oaks, Calif.: Sage.

Uccello, Cori E., and L. Jerome Gallagher. 1998. *General Assistance Programs: The State-Based Part of the Safety Net.* Washington, D.C.: Urban Institute.

U.S. Bureau of the Census. 1997. *Statistical Abstract of the United States, 1997.* Washington, D.C.: U.S. Government Printing Office.

U.S. Department of Justice. 1996. *Sourcebook of Criminal Justice Statistics.* Washington, D.C.: U.S. Government Printing Office.

U.S. Department of Justice, Bureau of Justice Statistics. 1998. "National Crime Victimization Survey." Web site at http:\\www.ojp.usdoj.gov\bjs\.

U.S. House of Representatives, Committee on Ways and Means. 1994. *The Green Book, 1994.* Washington, D.C.: U.S. Government Printing Office.

———. 1996. *The Green Book, 1996.* Washington, D.C.: U.S. Government Printing Office.

Walker, Jack L., Jr. 1969. "The Diffusion of Innovation in the American States." *American Political Science Review* 63:830–899.

Weaver, R. Kent, and William T. Dickens, eds. 1996. *Looking before We Leap: Social Science and Welfare Reform.* Washington, D.C.: Brookings Institution.

Webster, Daniel W., Jon S. Vernick, Jens Ludwig, and Kathleen J. Webster. 1997. "Flawed Gun Policy Research Could Endanger Public Safety." *American Journal of Public Health* 87:918–921.

Wiener, Joshua M., and David G. Stevenson. 1998. "State Policy on Long-Term Care for the Elderly." *Health Affairs* 17:81–100.

Wiseman, Michael. 1996. "State Strategies for Welfare Reform: The Wisconsin Story." *Journal of Policy Analysis and Management* 15:515–546.

Witkin, Gordon. 1994. "Should You Own a Gun?" *U.S. News and World Report,* August 15.

Zamichow, Nora. 1992. "Anti-Smoking Effort Works, Study Finds." *Los Angeles Times,* January 15, Section 5.

SUGGESTED READINGS

Norris, Donald F., and Lyke Thompson, eds.. *The Politics of Welfare Reform.* Beverly Hills, Calif.: Sage, 1995.

Sparer, Michael S. *Medicaid and the Limits of State Health Reform.* Philadelphia: Temple University Press, 1996.

Thompson, Frank, and John DeIulio. *Medicaid and Devolution: The View from the States.* Washington, D.C.: Brookings Institution, 1998.

Urban Institute. "Assessing the New Federalism." Web site at http:\\www.newfederalism.urban.org, 1998.

Welfare Information Network. Web site at http:\\www.welfareinfo.org, 1998.

CHAPTER 11

The Politics of Education

DAN A. LEWIS AND SHADD MARUNA

The American states are at the center of a massive, decentralized, and fragmented system of public education in the United States. There is great debate about the states' precise role in this educational system, and considerable disagreement about how much influence state authorities should have on what is taught in public schools and how those schools should be financed and evaluated. There is even a movement to privatize parts of the public system.

The debate about the states' role is woven into a deeper and more fundamental national debate about how to improve public education in the United States. Although the national debate is as old as the republic, it has gained considerable intensity in the last generation as concern has shifted from equity to excellence. During the first Reagan administration (1980–1984), the secretary of education commissioned a review of national education policy. That effort resulted in the release of *A Nation at Risk* (National Commission on Excellence in Education 1983), and the assumption that excellence can be achieved within the current publicly funded and administered system has come under attack as national and state leaders vie for leadership in the race to define what a better system of public education should look like.

The role of states in this new system of education must be understood in the overall context of domestic policy development and policy implementation of the United States. American social and educational policy is made in a complex and fragmented environment. The constitutional relations between the various layers of government and the separation of powers at all levels of government create the legal and political divisions that make power sharing the very basis of collective action. Our democratic institutions and the cultural commitment to individualism limit the power of government and the faith we put in its operation. These factors combine with the regional variety of the country and its size to make educational policy variegated and complex.

It is on this stage that the education reform agenda has been played out since the 1960s. Beginning in the early 1980s, the issues of educational reform shifted temporarily away from the questions of equity and race that were dominant in the 1960s and 1970s to a renewed focus on excellence and international competition. The states and their governors assumed a primary position as this new approach gained momentum. In 1989 President Bush called an educational summit to which he invited all the governors of the American states and out of which came six national educational goals that have focused much of the attention of state educational administrations and legislatures over the past decade. The summit signaled a sea change in educational reform, shifting the focus from the federal government to the states.

Some commentators say that the states are wresting control of the enterprise from entrenched interests that seek to maintain the status quo. Most scholars look at the reform endeavor with a rather jaundiced eye, though, seeing more rhetoric than result. What is surprising is the lack of much empirical, comparative work on the states' educational activity and reform. It turns out that we know very little about the factors associated with different outcomes at the state level. Despite much anticipation about state-level educational improvement, we are still at a preliminary stage in our knowledge about improving the learning process.

Yet the lack of knowledge has rarely stopped legislators from making laws, and the momentum continues for state action to improve education. The states are legally responsible for the education of resident children. The 1990s have produced a whirlwind of activity in most states to improve that education.

GOVERNING EDUCATION

The education of young people in the United States is an enormous enterprise. In the fall of 1993, nearly 63.9 million students were enrolled in U.S. schools and colleges, and about 7.9 million individuals were employed as teachers, faculty members, and support staff (NCES 1997). In all, more than one in four Americans participate in formal education every year. Not surprisingly, education represents the largest single cost for both local and state governments and has become one of the central political issues of our time. We now spend more than $250 billion each year educating children in grades K–12.

Public schooling is not mentioned in the U.S. Constitution. The Tenth Amendment to the U.S. Constitution states, "The powers not delegated to the United States by the Constitution, nor prohibited by it to the States, are reserved to the States respectively, or to the people." This amendment, ratified in 1791 as part of the Bill of Rights, has been interpreted as effectively leaving the right to establish an educational system to the states. With the recent upsurge in conservative thinking in the United States, the Tenth Amendment has been used to justify the focus on education at the state and local levels of government, particularly as confidence in the federal government wanes.

The nineteenth century saw the development of state responsibility for education with much delegation to local communities. Now all fifty state constitutions authorize education as a public good and require compulsory school attendance of all young people. These often vaguely worded provisions usually guarantee a "thorough" or "efficient" system of public education for all the children in the state. States also have authority over the various tax systems that finance individual schools and provide the basic administrative structure of public schooling through local school boards.

Much of that power is delegated to local school districts created by the state government. This leads to a set of complex interactions between the fifty state governments and the more than 15,000 school districts that exist in the United States. When the federal and state judiciaries are added to this mix, we can predict heightened conflict over who should decide educational matters. Indeed, the current debates over charter schools and choice plans are good examples of these competing venues and overlapping jurisdictions.

The Federal Role

Education has been a state responsibility and a local function throughout the twentieth century. Yet the federal government has played a carefully defined, peripheral role as well. Article I, Section 8, of the U.S. Constitution gives Congress the power to collect taxes to "provide for the common Defence and general Welfare of the United States." This has been interpreted as authorizing federal investment in education. Most federal legislative power over school governance has been in the form of requiring states to comply with specific conditions to qualify for federal funding. In particular, the federal government has concentrated on areas of national concern such as equal access to schooling, special education, and special programs for disabled, non–English-speaking, and economically disadvantaged children.

Federal funding for public schools nearly doubled in the 1960s with the implementation of the Elementary and Secondary Education Act and the Bilingual Education Act, but the federal role still remains small. Federal funding of elementary and secondary education in the United States grew from 2.9 percent of school funding in 1950 to 9.8 percent in 1980 (NCES 1997). Then federal grants declined steadily under the administrations of Ronald Reagan and George Bush, bringing the federal share back to only 6.2 percent in 1991.

Whereas many countries feature versions of a "national curriculum," the diversity and social divisions within the United States have always made local control of school content the more politically feasible strategy. The only time the federal government has significantly ventured into the governance of curriculum was the *Sputnik*-inspired National Defense Education Act of the late 1950s, when Cold War rivalry permitted such a serious break with the ideal of local and regional control (James 1987). The Clinton administration's education plan, for example, though broad in scope, carefully focuses on national, quasi-governmental groups and voluntary national standards rather than a mandated national curriculum (Fuhrman 1994b). Goals 2000: Educate America Act was passed by the Congress and signed into law by President Clinton in 1994 and is seen by some as usurping too much power for the federal government, but it is too early in the implementation process to know for sure whether the balance between the states and the federal government has tipped in the latter's direction.

The federal government took a leading role in the movement to desegregate America's schools following the *Brown v. Board of Education* (347 U.S. 483 [1954]) decision. Individual states and school districts in both the North and the South challenged federal authorities on the issue. One notorious standoff involved the Chicago public school system in 1965. Calling Chicago "by far the best case in the North of de facto segregation," Francis Keppel, the U.S. commissioner of education, threatened to withhold federal aid to the Chicago public schools, jeopardizing almost $32 million, if efforts were not made to bring the schools in compliance with Title VI of the 1964 Civil Rights Act. Yet when Chicago's infuriated mayor Richard J. Daley flexed his political muscles on the issue, the administration of Lyndon B. Johnson immediately backed off and instructed the Department of Health, Education, and Welfare (HEW) to offer the mayor a face-saving compromise. Keppel found himself relieved of his education post and made the "assistant secretary of HEW in charge of nothing," as he put it (Lemann 1992, 197).

The Chicago fiasco effectively caused federal education authorities to retreat from pursuing northern school desegregation issues directly for the next thirty years (Lewis and Nakagawa 1995). By the 1980s there was no serious federal action on desegregation issues. During the Reagan presidency, neither the Education Department's Office for Civil Rights nor the Justice Department filed a single school desegregation suit, and no positive policy proposals supporting desegregation emerged from any branch of the federal government (Orfield 1993). In 1990 there were 256 school districts with student enrollments of more than two million operating under court supervision in school desegregation cases brought by the U.S. Department of Justice.

Ironically, Reagan did play a major part in the school reform movement of the 1980s. His initial interest in education was mainly to dismantle the federal education bureaucracy and decentralize the public system by supporting tuition vouchers for private schooling. In fact, Reagan reduced federal support to education by nearly 10 percent (Augenblick, Gold, and McGuire 1990). Nonetheless, the unwavering commitment of Terrel Bell, the secretary of education, to an "excellence in education" campaign eventually moved the president into a more proactive posture. Reagan's endorsement of Bell's *A Nation at Risk: The Imperative for Educational Reform* (National Commission on Excellence in Education 1983) lent the publication credibility with the public and brought immediate attention to the shortcomings of the nation's school system. Following Reagan, Presidents Bush and Clinton have similarly used the "bully pulpit" of the presidency to demand increased innovation and a commitment to quality among the nation's schools. All three presidents sought to influence the national debate without being accused of trying to grow the federal government. Clinton has championed the "Goals 2000: Educate America Act," mentioned previously, which has developed a series of mechanisms to give "national" leadership on educational issues without extending the reach of the federal government into local educational matters. The focus of this legislation is to develop standards that states would be encouraged to follow, a far cry from the federal involvement of the 1960s and 1970s, but nevertheless an attempt to lead on issues of curriculum and instruction.

The Tug of War between Local and State Governments

The values of equity and autonomy are frequently opposed in the endless tug of war between state educational agencies and local school districts. Some policy makers seek more centralized control over schools to guarantee students comparable educational opportunities, whereas others argue for decentralization to encourage innovation at the local level. Timar and Kirp (1988, 75) called this division a conflict between "hyperrationalists who believe that schools are infinitely manipulable" and "romantic decentralists" who believe the key to school improvement "lies in deregulation and local control of schools."

Each approach reflects competing views of politics and human nature. The first assumes that hierarchical control exists and that one level of government can dictate to another what it is to do. Commands are given and with the right mix of incentives they are executed. Get tougher and hold subordinates responsible and results will follow. Allow individual districts complete autonomy and some might flourish, but many will fail miserably. Proponents of local control, in contrast, assume that progress comes from freeing individuals and institutions to pursue their own goals and interests. Institutions have better chances of achieving their formal goals unburdened by state regulation.

Federal policy makers also move back and forth between these two perspectives, sometimes even combining them (see the section "Systemic Reform" later in the chapter) in what they hope will be practical and advance educational practice. The forces of centralization were very strong in the early 1980s, pushing through a variety of state reforms mandating more schooling and more academic classes for many states. Later in the decade, notions of decentralization and site-based management came into vogue. Timar and Kirp (1988) argued that only a balance between these ideals of state accountability and local authority can effectively bring about the type of results sought by policy makers. Achieving something like this middle ground, in fact, has become the reigning paradigm among education reformers, who in good democratic style seek a compromise between the competing positions.

The State's Role

Despite "hortatory preambles, vague constitutional articles, terse statutes [and] a feeble administrative apparatus," the earliest system of common schools was clearly governed exclusively through "local control" (James 1987). Individual schools were financed almost entirely through local property taxes and granted nearly complete autonomy. Therefore, schools developed unevenly across the states with few checks for preventing corruption or poor performance.

State regulation of schools, beginning in the 1920s in most states, first took the shape of sporadically enforced minimum standards for staff qualifications and facilities. Since that time, state governments have gradually taken a more assertive role in coordinating education to promote equity between school districts and provide higher quality services to overburdened districts. Fuhrman and Elmore (1990, 84) wrote, "[S]tate policy steadily escalated, with each new policy focus adding to rather than replacing previous laws, regulations and structures." By the mid-1980s, state regulation rose to unprecedented levels.

The post-World War II myth that a public school system could be managed by neutral, objective administrators was widely abandoned following the sometimes violent conflicts surrounding school desegregation. In the 1960s, education became highly politicized. Governors and state legislators, who once shied away from mingling in school affairs, now frequently make statewide reform agendas the central part of their campaign strategies. Kirst (1987, 161) wrote, "Now state government officials create education policies, and local groups react to them. Educators lost control of the state agenda quite a while ago." In fact, the Texas Supreme Court in its 1989 decision in *Edgewood v. Kirby* (777 S.W.2d 391, 397) decided that local control of the schools had become a relic of the past:

> Most of the incidents in the education process are determined and controlled by state statute and/or State Board of Education rule, including such matters as curriculum, course content, textbooks, hours of instruction, pupil–teacher ratios, training of teachers, administrators and board members, teacher testing, and review of personnel decisions and policies (quoted in Wise and Gendler 1989, 16).

The reasons that states assumed such power over schools included increased judicial activism, the growing power of social movements demanding change, increasing education costs, and a recognized need for more efficient use of school resources. Some federal initiatives, such as Title V and VI of the Elementary and Secondary Education Act, also broadened the role of individual states because state education departments are charged with enforcing these national laws. Some observers suggest that states have merely filled the void left when the Reagan administration scaled back federal education programs in the 1980s (Clark and Astuto 1986).

Proponents of centralization view the coordinated control of schools as a means of overcoming the fragmentation, inequities, and inefficiency of the traditionally decentralized system of public education. Citing the multiple failures of urban school districts in particular, those hoping to reform education frequently rely on state-level policies to make schools more accountable to accepted standards of performance. Furthermore, Hochschild (1984) and others have called for continued centralization of control to combat rampant school segregation by race and social class.

On the surface, this growth in top-down governance would appear to reduce the freedom and control of individual schools and districts. Frymier (1987, 9) has argued that such creeping centralization "neuters" educators. Kagan (1986, 64) has called it "regulatory unreasonableness." Nonetheless, Fuhrman and Elmore (1990, 89) have cautioned that critics should not "mistake volume for significance" when assessing a state's control over the education system. Many new state reforms and regulations are merely symbolic in nature and do little to shift the balance of authority away from schools and local school districts. Enforcing severe sanctions for noncompliance with state standards can be costly and politically dangerous, so compliance is generally achieved more through bargaining and negotiation than top-down decree.

In fact, research by Tyree (1993) and Fuhrman and Elmore (1990) indicates that even successful state activism has done little to reduce local control and may have even increased local initiative. Fuhrman (1994b, 83) wrote, "State reforms appear to have exerted a multiplier rather than a depressive effect on local policies." In particular, researchers point to several state policies specifically designed to promote decentralization and site-based management. The centralizing tendency has supporters from the left and the right who are intent on redistributing power away from local school boards, administrators, and teachers to other constituencies who have more leverage at the state level than they do competing at the local school district level. The irony of the centralizing tendency is that in the hands of certain groups it can lead to more autonomy for local districts as the costs, both political and economic, of oversight and accountability schemes become prohibitive.

Local Control

Every state except Hawaii has a long tradition of local control of the school system in the form of school districts and local school boards. The striking differences in content and quality that exist between even neighboring school districts in America are the result of this uniquely American system of local control. States continue to delegate considerable regulatory authority to these districts, governed by boards of lay citizens, although states have assumed a more centralized role since the 1970s.

School districts are quite separate from municipalities, even when their borders are the same. Whether elected or appointed, local school boards are essentially state agencies (Russo 1992). School board members hold office by virtue of legislative enactment, and the state has the authority to increase or diminish their powers. Although boards hold executive, legislative, and judicial power over the schools in their district, they are ultimately responsible to the state, and the only authority they hold is vested in them by the legislature. To facilitate increased coordination, the number of school districts across the country has been substantially consolidated, from 119,000 in 1938 to only about 15,000 today (NCES 1997).

Moreover, the role and influence of the local school board seems to be giving way to increased "building-level" decision making that gives individual school administrations control over much of the school board's former domain. Odden (1992) has called this a move toward education systems that are "focused at the top" and "loose at the bottom." These initiatives empower educators and principals but substantially neglect the district school board. In Chicago, for instance, the legitimacy of the district school board had been called into question because independent local school councils, made up of parents, teachers, and student representatives, performed most of the functions once reserved for the district. In 1995 the Illinois legislature passed a significant reform that gave back to the mayor of Chicago much of the authority that was passed to the local school councils by the earlier reform in 1988. Finn (1992), arguing that traditional district school boards have become dysfunctional and superfluous, even calls for the abolition of these "middle managers" in favor of a completely site-based system of control. The role of school districts and their elected boards are very much in question at this point in time. Pressures are emanating from both the state and local schools for a redistribution of authority either up to the state or down to the school building. These pressures merge in the call for both charter schools and choice programs.

Behind the Classroom Door

State governments have assumed an unprecedented role in the finance and regulation of America's schools, yet they are still limited in what they can accomplish once the classroom door closes. This interplay between policy, administration, and the actual practice of education can be both complicated and rather frustrating for observers. Reform efforts in the last few years have focused more and more on improving instruction and learning in the classroom and have to some extent shied away from governance issues.

Analysts such as Weatherly and Lipsky (1977) have suggested that "street-level bureaucrats"—in this case, individual teachers—rather than federal or state authorities, make the key decisions in implementing education policies. It is hard to describe, much less analyze, what these teachers do or how they do it. As Hanushek (1981, 20) said, "Our understanding of what makes for effective performance in schools is astonishingly primitive." Patterns of teaching and their correlates are even harder to know. Teachers can fill out surveys about what they do and students can be tested on what they know, but how those two phenomena are related is difficult to assess.

Therefore, despite the growing role of states in the governance of education, many observers suggest that local control of schools is absolutely inevitable, in some aspects at least. Researchers have shown that the actual effect of state policies on the daily practice in the classroom is weak and inconsistent at best (Cuban 1990). Moreover, very little systematic evidence links state policies with improved educational outcomes (Berger and Toma 1994; Hanushek 1986).

In sum, states may play a large role in financing and governing education, but individual teachers and school administrators are still far more important to educational outcome than state policies. Reformers on the state level have only a limited range of policy options, and it seems very difficult to affect the poorly understood aspects of "good teaching" with topdown mandates.

THE STATE POLICY-MAKING PROCESS

The education policy landscape has become increasingly crowded with groups competing to set the agenda. Policy initiatives can originate from the grassroots agendas of individual schools or districts, from academic researchers, from teachers' lobbies, from the business community, or from top-down reform efforts of state leaders. Firestone (1989, 23) called this education policy-making structure an "ecology of games" to emphasize the "messiness and discontinuities" of the multifaceted process.

Regional Diversity

Every state has its own constitutional language describing the purposes and goals of its educational system, as well as its own system and structure for implementation. State policy makers also work under the constraints of regional variations in political cultures and traditions that affect the character of school governance. A state's political culture has a traceable history and distinct continuities over time. Still, these cultures are malleable to change as states are confronted with new challenges from the larger environment. Changes in resources, demographic shifts, national movements, lessons from other states, accidents, and unexpected catastrophes all lead to such political evolution. This counterpoint between continuity and change is difficult to understand and predict, although in retrospect stories can be told about why things happened.

Several scholars have tackled the complicated question of the social and cultural base of state educational politics. Marshall, Mitchell, and Wirt (1989) have looked carefully at the variations in the problem-solving techniques that develop in states as a function of the power of interest groups and government officials. They concluded that interest groups relate to each other depending on the skills of those in the groups and, more important, the distinct systems of meaning and political cultures that have developed in the states over time. In other words, state policy makers bring to the table various "assumptive worlds" or subjective understandings of what is appropriate in the prevailing political and cultural ethos of the state. For instance, Marshall and colleagues (1989, 376) found that in West Virginia, labor associations such as the School Service Personnel Association have to adjust their style of bargaining to survive the state's political traditions. Unlike other states, West Virginia's personnel association has taken an anti–collective-bargaining position and affiliates itself instead with key education lobbies.

From a series of interviews with policy makers and insiders, these researchers attempt to identify and describe the key influences on the formulation of state education policy. Marshall and colleagues (1989) found considerable variation among states concerning which groups and individuals were allowed special control of the process (see Table 11-1).

Table 11-1 Order of Importance of Policy Actors in Selected States

	Six-state ranking	Arizona	West Virginia	California	Wisconsin	Pennsylvania	Illinois
Individual legislators	1	1	3	2	4[a]	1	3
State legislature as a whole	2	2	5[a]	1	6[a]	4	3
Chief state school officer	3	4	2	7[a]	1	3	12[a]
Education interest groups	4	9[a]	8[a]	3	5	6	4
Teachers' organizations	5	12[a]	6	4	2	7	1[b]
Governor and staff	6	13[a]	9	6	3	2[b]	5
Legislative staff	7	7	11[a]	5	9	5	6
State board of education	8	3[b]	4[b]	16[a]	NA	9	14[a]
Others	9	10	7	8	13[a]	18[a]	7
School board association	10	6[b]	15[a]	11	7	11	8
Administrators' association	11	15[a]	12	9	8	8	13
Courts	12	11	1[b]	10	14	12	11
Federal policy mandates	13	8[b]	10	13	11	10	9
Noneducational groups	14	5[b]	13	12	10	13	10
Lay groups	15	14	16	15	12	14	15
Education research groups	16	16	14	17	15	15	17
State referenda	17	18	18	14	17	17	16
Education materials producers	18	17	17	18	16	16	18

SOURCE: Adapted from Mitchell, Marshall, and Wirt 1986, 351.

[a] Much lower than average.

[b] Much higher than average.

Although the state court system is rated one of the least influential policy actors in five of the six states in the survey, the courts play a leading role in West Virginia (Table 11-1). Similarly, although the chief state school officer (CSSO) fills an important role in most of these states, in Illinois the position is rated quite low in influence. These differences are rooted in personalities, local histories, traditions, and politics, and can change over time.

Major Policy Actors

No longer the exclusive domain of powerful school lobbies, education reform and policy initiatives are now the product of many different institutions competing for resources and cooperating in efforts to achieve values such as equality, efficiency, and excellence.

State Legislatures. State legislatures have emerged as the supreme policy makers in American education (James 1987). In fact, Marshall and colleagues (1989) found that individual legislators who specialize in education issues and lead various reform committees with the legislature are ranked as the most influential policy entrepreneurs by most of the states in their sample (see Table 11-1). These elected officials delegate responsibility for actual governance and administration of schools to various bodies, but they have been the primary impetus for changes in education policy since the early 1970s.

Governors. With the assistance of more specialized staffs, as well as the National Governors' Association and the Education Commission of the States, many governors began to take the lead in educational policy making in the early 1980s. Governors traditionally have had little interest in educational matters beyond fiscal concerns. Yet governors such as Tennessee's Lamar Alexander and Arkansas's Bill Clinton gained national prominence by taking activist roles during their respective states' reform periods in the 1980s. Moreover, the National Governors' Association report *A Time for Results* (1986) urged policy makers to focus their attention on school-based change rather than increasing state regulation. This document played nearly as influential a role in initiating the second wave of education reform as *A Nation at Risk* (National Commission on Excellence in Education 1983) did in the first.

Governors, however, seem to deal more in imagery than specifics with regard to educational issues. Mazzoni (1993, 364) said that governors rarely act as innovators in the policy arena; instead, they "pick up, package and promote options formulated by others." Moreover, since governors are the most likely to be held directly accountable for the condition of a state's schools by voters, they inevitably favor reforms that can show clear and immediate effects, especially in election years. For this reason, James (1987, 198) suggested that governors are "drawn irresistibly to bold and unrefined ideals" and are likely to abandon their demands for immediate reform if the political landscape suddenly shifts.

Chief State School Officers. Marshall and colleagues (1989) found that the CSSO was actually ranked as being more influential than governors in the design and implementation of reform in most states. In fact, the CSSO was rated as the most important single player in the policy process in Wisconsin. Still, the role and importance of the CSSO varies considerably from state to state, as indicated in Table 11-1. In some states the CSSO is appointed by the governor and merely acts as the executive officer's spokesperson. In others, the State Board of Education selects the chief. In still other states, such as California, the CSSO runs for elective office.

Education Department. State departments of education and state education bureaucracies have the function of implementing and administering state policies. Departments of education primarily play a regulatory role, ensuring that schools comply with state and federal law and assisting them in meeting state standards, but some departments have also begun providing incentives (money or services) for improvements in student outcomes as well (Lusi 1994). Traditionally, these highly structured and hierarchical education departments perform the routine, administrative work of licensing teachers, performing site visits, regulating building codes and accreditation requirements, and compiling educational statistics and school evaluations. For this reason, they were not included among the primary shapers of state education policy in the survey represented in Table 11-1.

Still, these once "mostly innocuous and invisible" agencies have tripled in size since the 1960s as a result of substantial federal aid (Murphy 1980, 2). Today, departments of education are actively involved in establishing curriculum standards, selecting texts, and appropriating funding for individual schools. Lusi (1994) argued that these departments have been fundamentally reinvented as part of systemic or coherent reform efforts on the state level.

State Boards of Education. State boards of education, almost always appointed by the governor, tend to be rather minor players in the policy process. Although the board is charged with the general supervision of education for the state, chief state school officers tend to be more visibly influential in this regard. Marshall and colleagues (1989, 22) wrote, "No doubt it is an honor to be appointed, but it certainly does not signify high influence." State boards of education do have considerable power in a few states, such as Arizona and West Virginia, however, and are sometimes charged with the important task of selecting the state's chief school officer. Wisconsin is the only state that does not have such a board.

Teachers' Union. Teachers' unions play an important role in state educational politics. Both the National Education Association and the American Federation of Teachers have considerable political power at the state level. The National Education Association has political action committees in many states, and its members are organized to influence legislators and appointed officials. The late Albert Shanker, president of the American Federation of Teachers, played a key part in the national reform debate since the mid-1970s. He identified the need for educational reform in the early 1980s and challenged union members to think beyond the industrial union approach in formulating a perspective on reform. The adversarial approach to union management relations and the emphasis on work rules and bread-and-butter issues of pay and seniority led to an attitude that ranges from cautious to hostile toward reform efforts in many communities.

Like traditional labor unions, teachers' unions work to secure the most favorable work conditions for their members. These conditions include not only pay scales but class sizes, length of workdays and school terms, curriculum content, and certification requirements—all of which have been debated in state legislatures. The power of these unions is evidenced not only by their strength in lobbying for favorable reforms but by their ability to influence the practice of education. Strikes by public school teachers increased from twenty-five in the years between 1960 and 1965 to more than 1,000 between 1975 and 1980 (Toch 1991).

Much of the conservative critique of education over the past twenty years has been a less-than-veiled attack on teachers' unions and the federal government. Conservative critics have been very successful at painting the teachers' unions as the primary impediment to educational reform in the states—and with much justification. The unions have fought reforms across the United States, seeing many of them as undermining the integrity of the collective bargaining process. In taking this tack, the unions have lost much credibility with the American public and have failed to take seriously the public's real dissatisfaction with public education. As a result, teachers' unions are on the defensive in many states, often fighting rear guard actions to protect union prerogatives. There recently has been serious discussion between the American Federation of Teachers and the National Education Association about merging the two groups. If such a merger is successful, the resulting organization will play a very powerful role at both the state and national levels in further discussions of reform.

Other Interest Groups. Formal and informal networks of experts and citizens' groups also are influential in pushing for changes in laws concerning educational practices. Such lobbying organizations as school board associations, civic and community groups, and parent organizations frequently have agendas for state policy. Although often hidden from the spotlight, these groups can exert considerable pressure on policy makers.

Business groups are credited with inspiring many of the excellence-in-education reforms of the early 1980s. Linking higher educational standards with increased productivity, business leaders such as H. Ross Perot in Texas played instrumental roles in both encouraging and developing various reform efforts. Prior to his first bid for the presidency in 1992, Perot chaired a school reform development committee and hired his own staff of lobbyists to promote the legislation. Similarly, powerhouse business lobbying groups turned their focus and considerable influence to school politics and helped shape important legislation. The Minnesota Business Partnership helped draft the Minnesota Plan, for example, which became the basis for the public school choice program in that state (Mazzoni 1993).

Finally, independent issue constituencies and "policy entrepreneurs" have since the 1950s acted as full-time advocates for various policy alternatives (Kingdon 1984). These policy and research organizations have also emerged on the state scenes. Often supported by national foundations, these organizations are the source of many reform ideas in the 1990s. The groups provide both analysis and innovative ideas for policy makers, often favoring legislators with whom they share ideological common ground with legislation and supporting materials. Frequently these organizations are supported by business or labor interests.

State Court. The state judiciary plays an active, if reluctant, role in state education policy. Beyond the landmark school desegregation decision in *Brown v. Board of Education,* the U.S. Supreme Court has fairly consistently stressed the need for local control and maintained that education matters should be left to the states (Combs 1984). State court systems therefore have assumed a large role in nearly every aspect of the educational process.

State courts generally do not interfere with decisions made by a school board or educational administrators unless the action is deemed an abuse of power (Russo 1992). Still, courts now hold the final authority on such issues as the constitutional rights of students, which would have been considered strictly private matters for individual schools until the mid-1950s. Beckham (1993) identified nearly fifty important state judicial decisions made between July 1992 and July 1993 alone, including the legality of dress codes, locker searches, loitering policies, teacher competency tests, graduation prayers, special education placements, and recitation of the Pledge of Allegiance.

Still, the most obvious and dramatic role of the state court system since 1970 has been in determining the legality of school financing schemes, school desegregation policies, and school district consolidation plans. The state court system has intervened in these politically charged and difficult issues in part because legislators have been unwilling to risk the public disapproval that accompanies such divisive problems without at least the threat of court action.

In many states the courts have in fact taken the lead in educational policy. The Kentucky Supreme Court actually declared the state's entire public education system unconstitutional. The court essentially required the state to redesign its entire school system by enacting comprehensive educational and financial reforms. An Alabama ruling recently followed this remarkable precedent, dramatically raising the stakes for education litigation and perhaps signifying an impending wave of judicial activism to spur failing systems of education. The focus of many of these suits has been the educational adequacy of the public school systems.

Universities. University departments (and schools) of education play a considerable role in determining the credentials for state educators and shaping the nature of teacher education. Also, university-level researchers, backed by government support and foundation grants, have assumed considerable influence in the design and implementation of school governance systems. From the Reagan era to the Clinton administration, education scholars have been recruited to fill high-ranking positions atop the federal bureaucracies. For instance, before being named under secretary of education for the Clinton administration, Marshall S. Smith was one of the key academic theorists behind the concept of school effectiveness and systemic reform. Many of the reform initiatives of the last generation have emerged from the minds of university researchers, and some of the most successful programs for improving education are housed in universities. There is considerable interest in having university faculties play a larger role in improving K–12 schooling, and many faculty members have gotten involved with programs to make such improvements.

EDUCATIONAL FINANCE

Education accounts for the single largest cost in most state and local budgets. For 1992–1993 expenditures were estimated at more than $375 billion for all public schools and colleges (NCES 1997). In general this money comes from a combination of local taxes and state and federal grants-in-aid, but the balance between these sources has shifted considerably over the years. Local tax revenues consist almost entirely of property taxes except in states such as Louisiana, where local sales taxes are common. The composition of state tax revenues was described in Chapter 9. Increasingly, states are also earmarking for the schools funds generated through state lotteries.

Fiscal Responsibilities of States

During World War I, 83 percent of school financing was provided by local districts, and state governments provided only about 17 percent (Wong 1989). In the 1970s and early 1980s, however, state governments began to assume the primary responsibility for educational funding (see Figure 11-1). The state share of total edu-

Figure 11-1   Sources of Revenue for Public Elementary and Secondary Schools

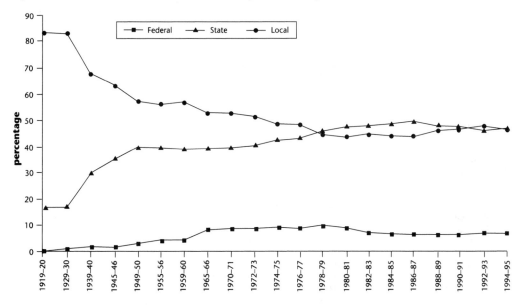

SOURCE: Adapted from National Center for Education Statistics 1997, 157.

cational funding increased from 41 percent in 1968 to about 50 percent in 1986, whereas local contributions to school expenses fell from 50 percent in the late 1960s to about 43 percent by the mid-1980s (Wong 1989).

Elementary and secondary education expenses now consume nearly a quarter of the average state budget, and postsecondary schools account for another 12 percent (Farrell 1988). Finance and governance of education have not gone hand in hand, however. As Fuhrman and Elmore (1990, 89) wrote, "[C]ontrol does not necessarily follow the dollar." States began assuming primary responsibility for educational finance nearly a decade before the increased regulation and centralization of the 1980s.

Several explanations are possible for this shift. For instance, states have a broader revenue base than individual localities and have been better able to absorb the growing costs of education. In addition, a widespread revolt by taxpayers led to Proposition 13 in California, Measure 5 in Oregon, and Proposition 2 1/2 in Massachusetts. These and similar laws elsewhere put restrictions on property tax increases and limit the ability of local districts to maintain fiscal control of their schools. Still, the most important factor has been the movement to equalize school expenditures across various school districts.

State Diversity. Wong (1989) pointed out that even though states are generally assuming most of the burden of school funding, considerable interstate differences persist. Firestone, Fuhrman, and Kirst (1991, 242) found that "the local property tax is still alive and well" in many states. Although schools in Hawaii are funded al-

Table 11-2 States with the Highest Percentages of Local and State School Funding, 1994–1995

State and funding source	Local	State	Federal	Private
Locally funded schools				
New Hampshire	87.3	7.3	3.1	2.3
Illinois	63.3	28.0	6.5	2.2
Vermont	63.2	29.8	4.6	2.4
Nevada	61.1	30.1	4.9	3.9
South Dakota	60.5	26.5	10.0	3.0
Virginia	59.1	31.8	5.7	3.4
Massachusetts	56.0	36.3	5.4	2.3
New Jersey	56.0	38.0	3.3	2.7
Nebraska	55.8	32.4	5.8	6.0
Maryland	54.9	37.0	5.0	3.1
State-funded schools				
Hawaii	0.5	90.2	7.4	1.9
New Mexico	11.6	74.4	11.8	2.2
Washington	22.3	68.7	6.0	3.1
Alaska	19.4	67.5	10.8	2.3
Michigan	24.6	67.3	6.2	1.9
Kentucky	24.1	65.8	9.3	0.8
North Carolina	24.6	65.1	7.5	2.8
West Virginia	26.8	63.6	8.1	1.5
Delaware	26.8	64.3	7.2	1.6
Idaho	29.3	61.2	7.7	1.8
U.S. average	43.8	46.8	6.8	2.7

S O U R C E : Adapted from National Center for Education Statistics 1997, 158.

most entirely at the state level, some states, such as Oregon and Virginia, provided less than a third of school funding, and in New Hampshire, state funds accounted for less than a tenth (see Table 11-2). Moreover, although state spending in Minnesota and California rose by nearly 69 percent between 1983 and 1987 (Toch 1991), in twenty states the state share in education spending actually dropped (Firestone, Fuhrman, and Kirst 1991).

Wong (1989) identified several factors associated with whether state governments engineered a shift from "parity to dominance" in the responsibility of education financing. States that did not substantially shift the burden of education funding frequently had no legal suits brought against the state system, were not subject to pressure to lower property taxes, had restrictions on state taxation, and often contained a large population of African American students. Several of the states in his study, such as Michigan, however, have since experienced major shifts away from reliance on local taxes.

Wealth Disparity. Like school governance, the issue of financing America's schools is characterized by conflict between the ideals of local control and equal opportunity. In virtually every state, there is a wide range between school districts in taxable wealth and tax rates. Some school districts have far lower expenditures per pupil than others within the same state (see Table 11-3). Even when these poor-

Table 11-3 Range of Annual School Funding per Pupil, 1990

State and rank	Poorest districts	Richest districts	Gap
Largest gaps			
Alaska	6,115	19,155	13,040
Massachusetts (secondary)	4,595	11,653	7,118
New York	5,439	11,725	6,286
Illinois (secondary)	3,796	9,484	5,688
Maine (elementary)	2,664	6,640	3,976
Illinois (elementary)	2,665	6,240	3,575
Montana (elementary)	2,720	5,593	2,873
Arizona (elementary)	2,419	5,014	2,595
Smallest gaps			
Hawaii	4,288	4,288	0
West Virginia	3,160	4,023	863
Kentucky	2,509	3,520	1,011
Alabama	2,674	3,741	1,067
Iowa	3,593	4,700	1,107
Georgia	3,000	4,322	1,322
California	3,669	5,079	1,410
South Carolina	3,369	4,852	1,483

SOURCE: Adapted from Walters 1993, 750.

er school districts tax themselves at higher rates than other districts, they may be able to spend only a third as much per student as areas with higher property values (Darling-Hammond 1994). Wealth disparity between districts is further exacerbated by the imbalance in the distribution of commercial, industrial, utility, public, tax-free, and residential property as well as an uneven distribution of school-aged children.

Critics claim that this uneven distribution of educational funding magnifies social inequalities by leaving the children who have the fewest educational resources at home with the fewest resources in their schools. Many studies have indicated that uneven school financing has a racial element as well. For instance, Berne and Stiefel (1992) found that in New York, districts with greater proportions of minority students had larger class sizes, less qualified and less experienced teachers, and fewer state and local expenditures per student than other districts.

First-Wave "Equity" Reforms

During the early 1970s a wave of school reforms addressed these disparities. Coons, Clune, and Sugarman (1970) were among the first educational researchers to push for the principle of "fiscal neutrality" in public schooling. Appealing to the notion of equity in education, salient at least since *Brown v. Board of Education* (1954), they argued that the quality of public education should be a function not of the wealth of a child's parents or neighbors but of the state as a whole.

This notion of equalizing educational expenditures across districts within a state guided several court cases in the early 1970s. After losing lawsuits in Illinois (1968) and Virginia (1969), proponents of fiscal neutrality won a resounding victory in

California. In *Serrano v. Priest* (5 Cal.3d 584, 585 [1971]), the California Supreme Court ruled by a six-to-one margin that the state's system of financing its schools "invidiously discriminates against the poor" and therefore violated the equal protection provisions of the state constitution. In this case, commonly called *Serrano I,* a group of parents from the Baldwin Park district of Los Angeles brought a class action suit against the state, charging that children in the neighboring Beverly Hills district were receiving far better educational services. Despite paying a tax rate that was less than half that of Baldwin Park, Beverly Hills residents were able to spend twice as much per student as the residents of Baldwin Park.

Following the court's decision, California adopted the first of several school financing reform plans in an effort to correct these disparities. Other state legislatures followed California's lead and pushed through reforms without court orders. In fact, in 1973 alone thirteen states changed the way schools were financed in hopes of creating more equity across districts (Wong 1989).

Still, that same year the U.S. Supreme Court strongly challenged the *Serrano I* precedent with its critical five-to-four decision in *San Antonio Independent School District v. Rodriguez* (411 U.S. 1 [1973]). Justice Lewis F. Powell, Jr., wrote that education is not "a fundamental interest" protected under the Constitution and that differences in per pupil expenditures cannot be shown to be directly related to the quality of education a district offers. State supreme courts in other states—for example, Arizona (1973), Idaho (1975), and Ohio (1979)—followed suit. Citing *Rodriguez,* these courts supported the need for local control and suggested that the proper arena for educational matters is the state legislature.

Although one might have assumed that this decision would have marked the end of the surge in school financing reform, the issue showed remarkable resiliency. In fact, only one month after the *Rodriguez* verdict, the New Jersey Supreme Court found that the state's system of financing its public schools should be invalidated for failing to meet constitutional requirements (*Robinson v. Cahill,* 62 N.J. 473 [1973]). The *Robinson* plaintiffs used the same argument concerning wealth disparity that was employed in *Serrano I,* but they focused on the specific language about education found in the New Jersey Constitution. Every state constitution includes an education clause, and usually there is some mention of a "thorough and efficient" or "equitable" system of schooling. Following *Robinson* and their defeat in *Rodriguez,* reformers generally concentrated on this state constitutional language rather than making appeals to the Fourteenth Amendment.

Roughly a third of the lawsuits of the 1970s concerning the financing of schools were successful in leading to equalization legislation, including those in Connecticut (1975), Washington (1977), Wyoming (1980), West Virginia (1982), and Arkansas (1983). Yet even the threat of such a suit led many states to act independently in this regard. In all, about half of the states enacted school financing reform measures between 1971 and 1983 (see Table 11-4). Court-ordered reforms (the "strong reform") tend to limit local discretion and result in considerable reductions in the magnitude of interdistrict spending disparities. "Weak reforms," however, are

Table 11-4 Timing of Finance Reforms

State	Weak reform	Strong reform[a]
Iowa	1972	
Colorado	1973	
Florida	1973	
Illinois	1973–1980	
Kansas	1973	1976
Minnesota	1973	
Wisconsin	1973	
New Mexico	1974	
Ohio	1975–1982	
Virginia	1975	
Utah		mid-1970s
New Jersey		1976, 1990
California	1977	1978
Missouri	1977	
South Carolina	1977	
Tennessee	1977	
Connecticut		1978
Idaho	1978	
Maine	1978	
Washington		1978
West Virginia		1979
Arizona	1980	
Arkansas		1983
Wyoming		1983
Texas	1984	1989
Massachusetts	1985	
New Hampshire	1985	
Rhode Island	1985	
Georgia	1986	
South Dakota	1986	
Oklahoma	1987	
Vermont	1987	
Louisiana	1988	
Kentucky		1989
Montana		1989
Michigan		1993

SOURCE: Adapted from Downes and Shah 1994, 22, table 1.

[a] Courtordered reform.

generally legislative reforms that tend to preserve substantial local discretion and result in smaller reductions in interdistrict disparities (Downes and Shah 1994).

Second Wave Reforms

During the 1980s, momentum toward more equitable financing was considerably overshadowed by the so-called excellence movement. Although states continued to tinker with their funding schemes, finance litigation all but disappeared. Still, the issue reemerged in the 1990s with considerable success for reformers.

Augenblick et al. (1990) offer two general reasons for this resurgence of litigation and legislation concerning finance reform. First of all, the conditions to which finance systems must be sensitive, such as land values, student enrollments, and population demographics, have changed considerably since the 1970s, when many of the funding schemes were created. Second, the decade of attention to school quality and excellence in education raised the important question of how these reforms were to be funded. Moreover, many observers suggest that the reforms of the 1970s did not adequately accomplish what they set out to do. Many state reforms were merely temporary or partial solutions, in which legislatures targeted a little money for poorer districts but failed to alter the fundamental design of their states' financing schemes. In fact, funding inequalities between school districts did not substantially change between 1970 and the mid-1980s, despite the number of reforms (Odden 1992).

In the past six years, courts in Massachusetts, Montana, New Jersey, and Texas have ruled those states' systems of school financing unconstitutional, and litigation is pending in dozens of other states. Even in states in which reformers seemed to win decisive victories in the 1970s, the equity of school-funding schemes continues to be a major issue. In fact, nearly every new legislative reform plan is sent back to the courts for protracted rounds of litigation. Although most state courts have tended to uphold existing school financing systems (Darling-Hammond 1994), recent court decisions have signaled possible new directions for innovation in finance reform.

Texas. Nowhere has the battle over finance reform been so contentious and protracted as in Texas. For twenty-five years, legal challenges against the Texas school system have flooded state and federal courts; yet achieving a legislative solution that appeals to voters in the aggressively antitax state has been nearly impossible. After losing their bid for finance reform in the landmark Supreme Court case *San Antonio v. Rodriguez,* parents from the Edgewood School District filed a second lawsuit, this time through the Texas state court system, in 1984. By a ruling of nine to zero, the Texas Supreme Court ordered the state to design a more equitable funding system for the state's schools (*Edgewood v. Kirby* [777 S.W.2d 391, 397, 1989]).

Yet the battle did not end with the *Edgewood* ruling. The first proposal offered by the legislature would have raised the funding levels for all school districts but would not have significantly reduced the disparities between districts. The court deemed this plan unacceptable (Rocha and Webking 1992). A second plan that would have redistributed $400 million to poorer districts was successfully derailed by representatives from wealthy districts on the grounds that the reform represented an illegal statewide property tax. Under the latest compromise, adopted in 1993, the wealthiest districts have to limit their taxable property to $280,000 per student and the excess will go to poorer districts.

New Jersey. New Jersey has also experienced numerous school financing reform plans since the *Robinson v. Cahill* (62 N.J. 473 [1973]) decision in 1973. Representatives from disadvantaged districts took the state to court a second time in the 1980s, alleging that the state's reforms have not done enough to help these predominantly minority areas. The state supreme court agreed and ordered the state to enact additional finance reform. This landmark decision (*Abbott v. Burke,* 575 A.2d 359, 400 [1990]) was unique in that it focused not on statewide disparities but rather on twenty-eight specific, disadvantaged urban districts, and the state's educational system was found unconstitutional only for those districts.

Two weeks after the decision, the Quality Education Act was passed by New Jersey's Democrat-controlled legislature, making a substantial amount of compensatory aid to poorer districts a constitutional requirement. The accompanying tax increase led to a tremendous popular backlash, however, and Republican majorities were elected to both houses of the state legislature in 1991. The new legislature amended the original reform bill to spread targeted spending throughout the state, not solely to urban areas, and reduced the total amount of redistribution.

Michigan. In some states, finance reform has not been quite so contentious. Michigan and Nebraska, in fact, have moved independently to reform funding distributions in recent years with innovations that might signal a new direction for legislative efforts. In 1993, with widespread fiscal disparity and several poorer school districts facing the real possibility of bankruptcy, Michigan's legislature and governor implemented one of the most radical reforms of the new wave. The state repealed roughly $6.9 billion in local property taxes without designating an alternative source of funding. This essentially denied to the state's school system what had been its primary funding source for the past 100 years and the source of more than two-thirds of its budget the year before. The shock of losing most of the school system's budget was intended to force the state to design a more equitable method of funding schools than using local property taxes. Michigan citizens responded by overwhelmingly voting in support of a 2 percent sales tax increase and a tripling of cigarette taxes to fund the schools.

Under the plan, every school in the state will operate with a budget of between $4,200 and $6,500 per student in 1994 dollars (Pierce 1994). The Michigan strategy also includes reforms dealing with a core curriculum for the state and an extension of the school day. States such as Wisconsin are already moving in a similar direction.

Kentucky and Alabama. Finally, large disparities in educational funding and quality exist between entire states as well as local districts, and state courts are beginning to see this as similarly unfair to the children of these poorer states. For instance, although some states, such as Alaska, Connecticut, and New Jersey, all spent more than $7,500 per student in 1992, Alabama, Idaho, Mississippi, and Utah spent less than half that amount that year (NCES 1997).

In Kentucky the courts declared the entire educational system in the state unconstitutional for failing to meet the constitutional requirement of providing a "thorough and efficient" school system. The court even required the legislature to enact comprehensive educational reform in addition to new finance measures. Relying on the latest research and policy analysis, the court ordered the state to set achievement standards, complete with fiscal incentives and sanctions, increase teacher training, and create new compensatory programs for disadvantaged students. The incredibly ambitious, five-year strategy that was eventually enacted required much higher spending per pupil across the state but preserved local control in the form of increased site-based management.

In Alabama, where student achievement is among the lowest in the nation, circuit court judge Eugene Reese ruled in 1993 that schools need to be made more "adequate" as well as more equitable. The ruling provides specific criteria necessary for meeting the state's constitutional requirement for a quality education. This includes achieving educational outputs comparable to national and international standards.

The two decisions symbolize a possible new direction for finance reform litigation. It may be that courts will now, when warranted, order states not only to level the playing field for schools but to raise the entire floor and bring all schools within certain standards of excellence.

Achieving Equity

Achieving equity in school financing is anything but easy. Often these equity reforms lead to some aggregate increase in education spending for the state but little equity. With education in direct competition with the increasingly expensive health care and corrections expenses, raising school spending across the board can be difficult without proposing politically unpopular tax hikes such as those in New Jersey. Moreover, Robin Hood strategies that involve the redistribution of tax revenues from wealthy districts to poorer districts can raise the ire of voters from the wealthier districts, who feel that their children are being unnecessarily punished by the reforms. In Kansas voters from wealthy districts have fought reforms both at the ballot box and through the state court system, and every state legislature is wary of the type of backlash that followed the New Jersey reform. Still, many states have tried to put explicit spending caps on wealthier districts and sold the measure as "property-tax relief," rather than a redistributional plan.

Furthermore, equity in education is not simply translated into the reality of fair school district funding across a state. Wise (1967, 133) cautioned,

> In the first place, price levels differ from one part of a state to another; this variation implies that equivalent services cost more in some parts of a state than in other parts. Second, sparsity and density of population generate diseconomies in the operation of schools. Third, the needs of different students vary, thus creating complications.

Other salient equity concerns frequently overlooked by reformers include the distribution of funds among individual schools within a district, among subject areas of the curriculum, among tracks and categories of students, and among levels of schooling (Darling-Hammond 1994).

Odden (1992) pointed out another problem of definition. If financial inequity is defined as variation in the tax base of local districts, this would lead to the enactment of a guaranteed tax base. Yet when the problem is seen as differences in spending per pupil, the remedy is to mandate equal spending across all school districts. Although states differ in their interpretation, Odden observed that most are leaning toward the equal per pupil expenditures and away from equal access to property tax bases.

Finally, in many arguments for equity, school quality is casually used as a synonym for dollar expenditures. Yet the relation between school spending and student output has been called into question at least since the highly influential report *Equality of Educational Opportunity* (HEW 1966). In the report, Coleman and his associates suggested that schools "bring little influence to bear on a child's achievement that is independent of his background and social context" (HEW 1966, 72). More recently, Hanushek (1981, 1986, 1162) surveyed nearly 150 studies of the effects of school financing and similarly found "no strong or systematic relationship between school expenditures and student performance." Hanushek (1986) accepted that teachers and schools "differ dramatically" in their effectiveness, but he argued that these differences have more to do with autonomy and innovation than school funding. The question for those interested in equity is what money for education actually buys. Studies seem to show that increases in spending do not necessarily correspond to increases in student achievement (Odden and Picus 1992).

To this line of argument, Coons et al. (1970, 30) replied, "If money is inadequate to improve education, the residents of poor districts should at least have equal opportunity to be disappointed by its failure." In addition, Card and Krueger (1992) have uncovered something of a paradox in this field. Their research suggests that even though student performance, as measured by test scores, does not clearly correlate with the amount of money spent per student, other positive correlations can be found. For instance, adult males who were educated in schools with lower pupil–teacher ratios and higher teacher salaries have a higher monetary "return to education" than other males. In other words, their post-high school earnings are higher than those of similar individuals educated in less affluent schools. This measure may be both more reliable and more valuable than test scores as a measure of the importance and efficiency of school funding. Moreover, a demonstrably strong link between expenditures and achievement is probably not necessary to justify finance reform. The goal of most court decisions and state reforms after all is not to guarantee improved outcomes but rather to provide an equal opportunity for educational success.

THE FUTURE OF SCHOOL FINANCING

Because more than half of the fifty states are currently involved in litigation with regard to school financing plans, it seems clear that the issue will continue to dominate state politics into the new millennium. In fact, probably as long as the educational system is composed of semiautonomous local centers of control, concern that the distribution of educational funds is inequitable will linger. Verstegen (1990, 222) argued that "given the persistence of rich schools and poor schools . . . it may only be that states will cease to invidiously discriminate by wealth inside their borders when the federal government provides incentives, sanctions, or mandates that call for equal opportunity in the states." Indeed, there have been Senate subcommittee hearings on this possible course of action, but the financial and political costs of such a move are probably too high for such measures to be taken seriously.

Increasingly, it is likely that the future of litigation concerning school financing will center on outcomes as well as inputs (Odden 1992). Disparities in student achievement and in the way in which schools use tax dollars are beginning to be seen as more important criteria for judging the constitutionality of school systems than dollar expenditures. Many states are considering the use of fiscal incentives for raising student performance as well. Finance reform that is tied into a package of education reforms, such as curriculum standards or choice proposals, is more likely to win the support of business and community groups.

REFORMING EDUCATION

A Nation at Risk (National Commission on Excellence in Education 1983), with its warning of a "rising tide of mediocrity" in the nation's schools, inspired and legitimized an unprecedented wave of state reform. Between 1984 and 1986, especially, education was the dominant issue in many state legislatures nationwide. Special sessions were called specifically to address reform issues—for example, in Arkansas and Florida in 1983 and Tennessee in 1984 (Toch 1991).

Critics warned that such rediscoveries of educational shortcomings frequently involve a type of collective amnesia, wherein recycled versions of earlier panaceas return as solutions to timeless problems of student discipline and apathy (S. Clark 1993). Still, reformers' concerns were substantiated by a growing body of research that showed that spending on schools was increasing while student performance was sliding downward. For instance, from 1963 to 1980, scores on the Scholastic Aptitude Test (SAT) steadily dropped from an average of 478 to 424 on the verbal section and 502 to 466 on the math (Murnane 1985).

Furthermore, when reports tied educational outcomes to the nation's economic competitiveness, state action seemed all the more critical. In *Making the Grade,* the Twentieth Century Fund (1983, 4) warned, "The skills that were once possessed by only a few must now be held by the many if the United States is to remain competitive in an advancing technological world." The probusiness stance of the Reagan administration combined with the weakened position of the United States in the world economy opened the door for a reform posture that was opposed to federal spending but in favor of improvement in educational outcomes. In fact, many of these reforms were endorsed by social conservatives as well as traditional progressives. Reagan's New Federalism approach deemphasized the role of the federal government and emphasized volunteer activities, state actions, and a strengthening of standards.

Although the costs of most popular reforms were low, states still pumped vast amounts of new revenue into these efforts. Fortunately, many of the more sweeping reforms coincided with periods of considerable economic expansion in many states. Although not all of the activist states benefited from this financial growth (Firestone et al. 1991), a strong correlation between a state's economic expansion and its education reform efforts exists. Toch (1991, 37) wrote, "The reform movement was lucky. Had the nation's economy not rebounded as dramatically as it did from the 1981–1982 recession, leaving 37 states with budget surpluses and only 3 with deficits, there would have been much less money available to pay for education reforms."

The Excellence-in-Education Reforms

The first wave of reform in the 1980s concentrated on raising standards and requirements in an effort to achieve educational excellence. The movement was highly regulatory in nature, consisting mostly of mandates, laws, and state prescriptions to be enforced through various mechanisms. Sometimes fiscal incentives were used to encourage districts to increase standards for teachers and students on a voluntary basis. Other reforms focused on the need to create mechanisms to monitor student progress and performance better.

Student-Focused Reforms. The most popular educational reform in the excellence movement was raising graduation requirements. Forty-five states modified high school graduation requirements in the 1980s, usually requiring more credits in science and mathematics (Fuhrman 1994a). This was a low-cost, manageable reform with clear results (students did take more core coursework) and therefore greatly appealed to legislators and governors eager to show their commitment to excellence. In many states, however, most school districts already met or surpassed state requirements in their graduation policies, so the state law did nothing to improve these programs (Firestone et al. 1991).

Led by the reform movement in Florida, many states have also moved toward new assessment techniques that measure the progress of students in multiple academic fields. Often these assessments take the form of "minimum competency tests," which determine whether students are qualified for graduation or promotion. These tests also link funding to measurable improvement in educational output. Other popular reforms include No Pass, No Play, which places restrictions on extracurricular activities, and statewide attendance policies. States have also experimented with comprehensive reform programs such as Robert Slavin's Success for All and James Comer's School Development Program and have mandated additional classes for advanced students and students with special needs.

Many recommendations prompted by the excellence movement, especially those that were rather expensive, were not widely implemented. For instance, suggestions for increasing the school year to 200 or more days were considered by thirty-seven states in the mid-1980s. Yet, only nine actually lengthened school terms, and no state lengthened the year beyond 180 days (Firestone et al. 1991). Costly recommendations to lengthen the school day, provide public preschooling, and establish state homework policies also were largely ignored.

Educator-Focused Reform. States have even entered the once purely local domain of teacher compensation, which makes up more than 70 percent of a typical school budget (Hanushek 1986). Prior to 1980, only a few, predominantly southern, states got involved in teacher salaries, but during the 1980s Darling-Hammond and Berry (1988, v) found, nearly every state enacted legislation to improve teacher compensation: "In all, over 1,000 pieces of legislation regarding teachers have been developed over the course of the decade, and a substantial fraction have been implemented." Some of the strategies include raising teachers' salaries across the board, raising the base pay for full-time faculty, and creating performance-based incentives, such as career ladders and merit pay programs. The career ladder program allows qualified educators to move through a progression of jobs, with increases in pay and responsibility.

Still, as the data in Table 11-5 make clear, states have moved at different rates in raising teacher salaries. Although the average teacher salary in Connecticut grew by more than $3,000 between 1989 and 1991, salaries dropped in South Dakota and Mississippi during this time. Generally, as can be seen in Table 11-5, the salary increases of the first wave of education reform simply brought teacher salaries back to the level of twenty years earlier in most states.

Also, the first wave of the reform movement included often contradictory reforms in the area of teacher certification requirements. Some states increased subject-specific credentials and added teacher competency and certification testing. Similarly, many states required certain teachers to obtain advanced degrees or generally tightened entrance requirements for state teacher education programs. In contrast, other states purposely opened alternative routes to teacher certification in an effort to attract increased numbers of applicants who were graduates of programs outside of the traditional education programs. Although some states decided to make it easier to become a teacher, others sought to make it more difficult, although both hoped for similar results.

The Restructuring Movement

The first wave of school reform lasted approximately from 1982 to 1986, when several critics began pronouncing the incremental reforms ineffective. For instance, Chubb and Moe (1986) argued that any reform that leaves the basic structure of the public education bureaucracy intact, as these reforms did, will "tend to be assimilated and neutralized." Thus, beginning in the late 1980s this regulatory phase had been increasingly replaced by a movement that seeks to change the fundamental structure of the educational system by encouraging bottom-up improvements at the school site. More centralized excellence-in-education reforms, although no longer as faddish, continue to be enacted in some states, alongside decentralization efforts.

This second wave of reforms emphasizes "learning for understanding," teaching higher order thinking, and improving the depth—rather than the quantity—of student coursework. This restructuring mostly translates into seed money to encourage local experimentation and a shift toward school site autonomy, shared decision making, school choice programs, and the professionalization of teaching. In essence, although outcome goals are increasingly being set from the state, individual schools are being given fuller responsibility for administering the reforms (Lewis 1993).

Table 11-5 Highest and Lowest Average Annual Salaries of Teachers in Public Elementary and Secondary Schools, 1969–1970 to 1995–1996 (in constant 1996–1997 dollars)

	1969–1970	*1979–1980*	*1989–1990*	*1995–1996*
Highest paid				
Connecticut	38,962	33,219	50,637	51,688
Alaska	44,423	55,697	54,006	51,036
New York	43,480	40,553	48,714	49,488
New Jersey	38,407	35,127	44,648	49,277
Pennsylvania	37,263	33,805	41,722	47,402
Michigan	41,335	40,248	46,395	46,074
Massachusetts	36,867	35,315	43,442	43,470
California	43,392	36,885	47,554	43,465
Rhode Island	36,918	36,849	45,125	43,363
Maryland	39,471	35,940	45,453	42,334
Lowest paid				
South Dakota	26,935	25,275	26,657	27,098
Louisiana	29,565	28,166	30,411	27,565
North Dakota	28,168	27,148	28,804	27,738
Mississippi	24,390	24,256	30,401	28,482
Oklahoma	28,950	26,829	28,872	29,214
New Mexico	32,795	30,472	30,982	29,904
Arkansas	26,532	25,175	27,973	30,159
Montana	31,996	29,756	31,389	30,202
North Carolina	31,525	28,896	34,895	31,279
Utah	32,156	30,517	29,643	31,461
U.S. average	36,287	32,689	39,256	38,632

SOURCE: Adapted from National Center for Education Statistics 1997, 85.

School site autonomy means providing schools with more decision-making authority through reallocating budgeting, curriculum, and personnel decisions from district offices to individual schools. Seven of the eight largest urban school districts in the United States, as well as, for example, the states of California, Florida, and Minnesota, are implementing various versions of decentralized, site-based management. Based on research on effective schools, these programs aim to increase school productivity, accountability, and student performance.

Closely related to site-based management is the concept of teacher professionalism. The Carnegie Task Force on Teaching as a Profession (1986, 55) and other groups urge that bureaucratic authority be replaced by "schools in which authority is grounded in the professional roles of teachers." In general this means giving teachers a clearer role in the making of policy and the administration of the schools in which they teach. In Pennsylvania, for instance, teacher participation in staff development programs is mandated by the state.

Parents, too, are being given more power in the schools during this wave of reforms. Several states have made intentional efforts to enfranchise parents through school–parent councils such as those implemented in Georgia (Firestone et al. 1991). A dozen states even implemented reforms that give voters the opportunity to remove school administrators and school board members of low-achieving school systems (Toch 1991). In this movement toward local control, parents, educators, and community members are seen as agents of change with a common interest in the operation of schools that is somehow different from that of other groups who have controlled education in the past (Lewis and Nakagawa 1995).

School Choice

The final link in this notion of decentralization is school choice and the empowerment of parents as consumers. Nearly a dozen states have experimented with public school choice plans. These plans, although varying widely in content, all attempt to give parents an expanded choice (throughout either the state or a district) about where their children attend school.

There are literally dozens of approaches to expanding the options open to students and their parents when it comes to selecting schools they wish to attend. Some of these options are the direct result of desegregation litigation and are attempts to reduce racial isolation by offering students schooling in buildings that are in neighborhoods outside their own. Some involve magnet schools, or district-wide programs developed to attract and retain quality students in the public school system and promote voluntary racial integration by offering specialized curriculum to qualified students. Some involve interdistrict plans, and others are intradistrict. Most try to balance concerns about equity with attempts to improve quality.

All depend on serious implementation efforts and able personnel to administer the programs for their success. Implementing school choice programs is a problem that confronts many school boards and superintendents as districts expand the options they wish to offer students. To understand how well any program is implemented and what its effects are, one must look at the interaction between the people administering the plan and those who are supposed to change their behavior and choose to go to a new school (Lewis 1990).

School choice plans have captured the imagination of many state legislatures and governors. Minnesota, led by Gov. Rudy Perpich (1976–1979 and 1983–1991) and powerful business lobbies, has been a pioneer in this effort and has experienced considerable success. During the 1992–1993 school year, more than 100,000 of Minnesota's 786,000 students took advantage of the state's choice program and attended a different school from the one they attended the previous year, and polls show that about 75 percent of Minnesota residents support the choice program (Nathan and Ysseldyke 1994). Besides open enrollment, Minnesota's choice package also features a Postsecondary Enrollment Options program, which provides tax funds to enable eleventh and twelfth graders to attend classes at colleges or universities, and a Second Chance program, which allows school dropouts to transfer to new schools.

Minnesota also implemented a program of charter schools in 1991. Charter schools are largely autonomous public schools that draw students from throughout a school district. Groups of interested teachers, parents, or community members can open these schools by signing a contract or charter with the local school board or state agency agreeing to follow various guidelines and quality standards. Like magnet schools, charter schools are intended to promote innovation and reinvigorate public school systems losing students to private schools. A dozen other states have already followed Minnesota's lead and have begun experimenting with charter school programs.

Private School Choice

Including private and parochial schools in these choice strategies is a quite different and much more controversial issue, although several states have experimented with such plans. Wisconsin, for instance, enacted a voucher program in Milwaukee for low-income and minority students to choose between public and private schools. Proponents of private school choice would like to see private school tuition vouchers offered across entire states, allowing students at all socioeconomic levels to attend private schools for reduced or no tuition.

Research by Chubb and Moe (1986, 1990) has been used extensively in support of this cause. Chubb and Moe have shown how centralized, bureaucratic authority over schooling reflects the needs and desires of the bureaucracy and politicians rather than those of students, parents, and educators. Public schools, they have suggested, are "captives of democratic politics" and "subordinates in a hierarchic system of control," thus making institutional goals "heterogeneous, unclear and undemanding" (1986, 28):

> The fundamental causes of poor academic performance are not to be found in the schools, but rather in the institutions by which the schools have traditionally been governed. Reformers fail by automatically relying on these institutions to solve the problem—when the institutions are the problem.

> The key to better schools, therefore, is institutional reform. What we propose is a new system of public education that eliminates most political and bureaucratic control over the schools and relies instead on indirect control through markets and parental choice. These new institutions naturally function to promote and nurture the kinds of effective schools that reformers have wanted all along. (1990, 5)

The attack on the bureaucracies and the dispersal of authority and control are the hallmarks of choice plans. The community and family are often contrasted favorably with the "heartless" institutions and bureaucracies. Bureaucratic power is seen as the problem, and family choice is the solution. It is believed that if schooling is left to the professionals insulated in their bureaucracies, then it will surely fail (Bastian et al. 1986; LaNoue and Smith 1973).

On the other hand, critics of vouchers contend that in the name of community and family, reforms have been introduced that remove equity and racial fairness from the policy agenda. Family and community can be stand-ins for race and class in the allocation environment. If we leave education to the family and community, pathology, discrimination, and personal income may dictate who gets ahead and who stays behind. Reliance on the community and family is the policy mechanism to replace the status quo, for education and economic power will dictate who gets what. Under a system of choice, wealthy communities and interested parents still have an advantage over poor communities and uneducated parents; indeed, their advantage may be increased by the shift of authority outside the bureaucracy. Privatization and the blurring of boundaries between the state and parochial education are the result (Lewis 1990, 1993).

School choice may be about shifting parent power and redistributing educational values. It is also about the basic nature of how the state regulates the poor, as it improves the lives of the middle-class. It is about creating new markets for private industry with the state serving as the provider of capital, and it is about legitimizing that social control function in the name of democratic values. Choice of schools as an institutional reform plays on the economic metaphor in policy making and may increase polarization of our society. Recent studies (Levin, 1998) suggest that choice programs may not produce the outcomes they have promised, or if they do, the costs of such improvements come with too high a price tag both socially and economically.

Systemic Reform

In the most recent wave of reform, the states are being asked by the federal government to create curricular frameworks that outline goals and techniques for achieving high standards in different subjects. These state efforts are to be driven by national guidelines that give the country as a whole ways to achieve common goals. The Clinton education policy, represented in Goals 2000, centers on "systemic reform." This would be a coordinated effort to raise standards and educational achievement uniformly across the country and overcome the fragmentation of the current education system. California began implementing curriculum standards similar to those put forth in Goals 2000 as far back as the mid-1980s, and even states traditionally strong on local control, such as Minnesota, New Jersey, and Vermont, have enacted versions of this "coherent" reform in recent years (Fuhrman 1994b).

According to the proponents of this national standards movement, existing policies, despite their rhetoric about excellence, drive curricula toward mediocrity because of their fragmentary and occasionally contradictory nature. A systemic national education policy would hold all students to a common high set of standards and encourage educators of students who are at risk of failing and disadvantaged students to create more ambitious instruction to meet the standards (Fuhrman 1994b). Furthermore, all states receiving federal assistance would have to establish assessment, professional development, and curriculum standards consistent with the unifying aims of the Goals 2000 plan, thus further improving the coherence among federal and state efforts. Finally, new achievement-based state assessments will augment and eventually replace standardized basic skills tests that primarily measure low-level abilities. The result will push teachers and schools toward improving educational outcomes.

Criticism of the proposals for systemic reform is just beginning to emerge. Clune (1993) argued that national curriculum standards may impede the process of matching curricula to diverse student needs and that high-stakes national examinations will lead to a highly prescriptive curriculum of "teaching to the test." He wrote, "Low-income schools and students do not need a curriculum that is identical to a curriculum somewhere else in the state or country; they need a curriculum that is well adapted to produce dramatic gains in learning for their particular students" (1993, 237). Clune also warned that implementing such systemic reforms under the current system of school governance would be nearly impossible. Schools in the United States, he suggested, can probably achieve a common curriculum "in name only."

Fuhrman (1994b, 89) countered such fears: "[W]e already have an informal national curriculum—a basic skills national curriculum." The proposed national standards are designed specifically to replace the emphasis teachers place on preparing students for standardized tests that measure only basic skills. Moreover, its proponents are quick to point out, systemic reform policy would encourage local experimentation by providing support and flexibility for innovative local programs. The Clinton administration is trying to combine national leadership with state responsibility to improve educational outcomes, but history suggests the combination is not viable.

Charter Schools

The charter school provides a middle ground between a complete rejection of public schools as suggested by the choice advocates and the cumbersome Clintonian bureacratization of the standards movement reflected in the systemic reform initiative. Charter schools began in the early 1990s in Minnesota, and at the close of 1998 twenty states had "chartered" about 700 schools that enroll 170,000 students. Charter schools are authorized by the state and have a great deal of autonomy in the selection of staff and curriculum, although in most cases they are required to abide by federal civil rights law. States often delegate to local school districts the selection of organizations to operate the individual schools, and there is much excitement nationally about the potential of charter schools to lead the way to improved learning because they are not hamstrung by the bureaucratic rules and regulations (including union contracts) that limit what public schools can do.

There is much anecdotal evidence that students at charter schools outperform their counterparts in public institutions, but there have been no systematic studies that substantiate these claims with rigorous comparative studies of the charter schools. Still the attraction is there for state policy makers. Charter schools in principle unleash the creativity that many conservative critics of public education suggest will be found if bureaucratic constraints are lessened, comforting powerful liberal forces by not destroying the political architecture of public education. Both sides can see what they want to see about the effectiveness of the charter movement because there have been no serious evaluations of the charters by state officials.

Charter schools are either the harbinger of innovative trends in education or the misguided and peripheral challenges to a school system that can easily weather another reform that is going nowhere.

The Success of Reforms

Studies have shown that most of the 1980s reforms have been successful in achieving their desired immediate effects (Fuhrman and Elmore 1990). Odden (1991) found that local response to top-down initiatives was "swift, positive and in several instances enthusiastic." For example, students in states with increased graduation requirements are in fact taking more academic courses (Clune, White, and Patterson 1989). Still, little is yet known about whether these additional courses affect learning or improve educational outcomes (Cuban 1990), and our knowledge about the comparative success of these efforts is rudimentary at best.

Reports by the states on their own schools tend to magnify successes, and because many of these efforts are relatively new and not very well funded, it is difficult to assess systematically their impact on the classroom. School districts and individual schools have a great deal of autonomy in developing teaching and learning strategies, and although compliance can be achieved superficially, it is difficult to ascertain how deep that compliance runs. Courses can have their titles changed and administrators can write reports that attest to compliance, but those claims are of dubious value.

Hierarchical approaches have produced mixed results when it comes to measurable improvements in learning. For instance, comparative studies have failed to show significant correlation between improvement in student test scores and the teacher's experience or education (Murnane 1985). Neither specific college training in education nor obtaining a master's degree seems to correlate with the ability to improve student outputs (Hanushek 1981, 1986). Furthermore, Hanushek (1986) reviewed nearly 150 studies of educational outcome and could not find any evidence that indicated that smaller class sizes were correlated with positive student outcomes.

Following the first round of reforms, students did show some improvement in basic skills, measured by standardized tests, but this success was short-lived. SAT scores increased by sixteen points between 1980 and 1985 but declined by ten points again between 1987 and 1991 (Fuhrman 1994a). Toch (1991) attributed this lack of consistent improvement to the movement's failure to address the critical issue of alienation and apathy among students and educators. Other research suggests that, to be effective, state policies must be sensitive to local conditions and appealing to educators.

Besides ineffectiveness, critics also fear that school reforms will have unintended consequences. Possible examples include an increase in dropout rates following increased graduation standards and an increase in "teaching to the test" pedagogy in response to high-stakes examinations (Murnane 1985). Berger and Toma (1994) illustrated how in one instance excellence-in-education reforms seem to have actually led to lower student achievement. Using SAT scores as a measure of student performance and holding student background characteristics constant, they found that students in states that required a master's degree for teacher certification actually performed worse than students in states without the reform.

HIGHER EDUCATION

McGuinness (1988, 11) called state coordination of higher education "the most complex, difficult balancing act in state government." Colleges and universities, approximately half of which are publicly operated and governed, are historically decentralized and notorious for their aloofness and outright opposition to outside intervention. Newman (1987, 1) wrote, "It is not unusual to hear, within the university walls, the argument that the state has no proper role with regard to the university beyond providing adequate funding." Yet seeking a balance between autonomy and accountability in higher education, state governments have assumed increasingly centralized control over the realm of higher education, even in sensitive areas such as admissions policy and curriculum requirements. In fact, Newman suggested, "It is no longer simple to describe where the state ends and the university begins" (1987, 12).

Governance of Higher Education

In 1950 only sixteen states featured strong, centralized coordinating boards to oversee college and university policy decisions; this number had more than doubled twenty years later (Berdahl 1975). At the end of 1998 all states assign some degree of responsibility for coordinating the state's higher education system to one or several governing bodies. These boards, usually called a board of trustees or board of regents, are charged with some level of planning, policy making, fiscal, and management functions for a state's postsecondary institutions. They are designed to coordinate the program selection among schools to serve better the needs of the state. For the most part these state agencies regulate public institutions, not private ones. Zumeta (1992) made the case, however, that states will need to pay increasing attention to private and independent universities to maintain the quality of state higher education.

The emergence of state boards has made the higher education system appear more like other parts of state government—dealing with a governing board is easier for governors and legislators than working directly with individual university presidents (Newman 1987). Therefore, it is no coincidence that the 1970s and early 1980s also saw increasingly sophisticated governors, legislators, and their staffs become directly involved in higher education policy development. In addition, boards give the university system a clearer mission and buffer campuses from inappropriate intrusion from the state by improving the communication procedures between legislatures and campuses (Newman 1987).

In general, states feature one of the following types of intermediate agencies between the legislature and its public campuses: a consolidated governing board, a coordinating board, or a planning agency (Skolnick and Jones 1992). Although variations exist, these groupings describe differences in the formal authority of the board.

Usually a governing board has authority over most if not all state colleges and universities. The members usually appoint and evaluate campus presidents and have the authority to intervene in the governance and budget decisions of individual campuses, including establishing admission standards, tuition costs, and campus organizational structures (Hines 1988). A coordinating board, in contrast, merely acts as a liaison between campus governing bodies and the state legislature. Whereas many governing boards function as advocates for the colleges and universities they govern, coordinating boards more often reflect the interests of the state government. Both typically have the authority to review and recommend the appropriation of funds, approve degree programs, and formulate a master plan for the state's higher education system (Millett 1984). Finally, planning agencies—found in Delaware, Michigan, Nebraska, and Vermont—have more limited authority. Colleges governed by planning agencies have the most autonomy because state education policy tends to be determined predominantly by individual university presidents.

Many individual colleges and universities feature a board of trustees, charged with selecting the college's president, managing the school's budget, evaluating staff and assessing legal matters, and enhancing the school image (Hines 1988). These trustees are usually appointed by the governor, but the board of trustees for the University of Illinois and a handful of other schools are popularly elected in statewide elections.

The Increasing State Role

Several explanations exist for the increasing centralization of control over colleges and universities. Higher education has grown rapidly in America since World War II, making policy decisions increasingly complex. Today, higher education frequently represents the greatest item of discretionary spending in a state's budget (Zusman 1986).

The G.I. Bill, enacted at the end of World War II, allowed millions of veterans to attend college. The bill created considerable growth in the size and scope of the postsecondary education system in the late 1940s and 1950s. The expansion of community colleges, federal financial aid, and student loans during the 1960s and 1970s further contributed to the burgeoning size of higher education. Enrollment grew by 41 percent between 1970 and 1980 and another 20 percent between 1980 and 1992 (NCES 1997). In one striking example, the University of California system grew from 41,925 students and a $135 million annual budget in 1957 to 150,065 students and a $4.2 billion budget only thirty years later (Newman 1987). Today, college enrollment in the United States has risen to a record level of more than 14 million and is expected to grow to nearly 15.5 million by fall 2000 (NCES 1997).

Furthermore, state legislatures are increasingly concerned about the link between higher education and state economic growth. A study conducted for the Joint Economic Committee of the U.S. Congress found, "In an extraordinary number of cases, a university played a major role in the history of the companies that have chosen to relocate" (Newman 1987, 4). State policy makers therefore see control over higher education as a tool for economic development.

Reformers in the 1950s and 1960s also argued that a strong centralized coordinating board would be more effective and equitable than a patchwork of autonomous units in planning and developing higher education policy (Hearn and Griswold 1994). "Left totally to its own," Newman (1987, 8) wrote, "the university will evolve toward self-interest rather than public interest." State boards seek to improve the coordination of courses offered by two-year and four-year universities and prevent so-called turf wars between campuses, vying for the role atop the state pyramid as the research university.

Finally, some federal legislation also inspired more centralized state oversight. Congress even provided funds to assist states in establishing coordinating boards and stipulated the character these boards should take (Skolnick and Jones 1992).

Criticism of this creeping centralization has been widespread among university scholars and administrators concerned about a loss of autonomy (Millett 1984; Mingle 1983). Critics suggest that the most damaging state intrusion occurs in the affairs of nonresearch institutions and community colleges (Hines 1988). Although it is difficult to prove systematically, Newman (1987) even suggested that an inverse relation probably exists between state intervention in the affairs of a university and that university's perceived quality. As a result, several states, such as Colorado in 1981, have moved to "deregulate" their system of higher education and transfer the responsibility for financial management back to the individual university boards.

Reforming Higher Education

The surge of reform initiatives in primary and secondary education has caused many states to consider similar changes in the postsecondary education system. In fact, some of the most important state higher education reforms have been directly related to improving state elementary schools and high schools. For example, to improve the caliber of teachers, several states raised graduation requirements for college students majoring in education. Other higher education reform proposals, such as raising admission standards and creating outcome assessment programs for college students, nicely mirror reforms in state high school programs. In many ways, these developments in higher education have emerged somewhat in tandem with primary and secondary school reforms. Despite considerable differences in structure, the two systems are intimately connected. The fate of one level has immediate and obvious consequences for the other.

The main focus of postsecondary reforms has been on better defining the mission of the university system and linking that to the goals and needs of the state. For instance, many reformers perceive that state resources are being wasted on duplicative and repetitive programs at neighboring campuses. They therefore advocate increased "distinctiveness" and "mission differentiation" among college programs (Hines 1988).

Furthermore, many reformers have called for increased attention to the problem of insufficient minority enrollment and completion rates in state four-year colleges. After a rapid increase in access to higher education in the late 1960s and early 1970s, minority participation in colleges and universities has suffered a puzzling and dramatic stagnation and even decline (Carter and Wilson 1992). In 1990, 32.5 percent of all white 18- to 24-year-olds were enrolled in college, but only 25.4 percent of all African Americans and 15.8 percent of all Latinos in this age group were similarly enrolled (Carter and Wilson 1992).

Stabilizing and reducing tuition costs have been another area of concern. Between 1982–1983 and 1992–1993, the cost of a public university education rose by nearly 83 percent, substantially surpassing the rise in the consumer price index of 45 percent for that same period (NCES 1997). To promote equal opportunity and competition within the schools, California and other states have passed legislation to keep these costs to a minimum for applicants from within the state.

Governors and legislators usually instigate these reforms, as they do other school reforms, but state coordinating boards are emerging as key players in negotiating and designing statewide postsecondary policy. Hearn and Griswold (1994) have tried to account for the variation across states in the amount of postsecondary reform by determining specific characteristics common to activist and nonactivist states. Among other factors, they found that states with considerable postsecondary reform, such as Iowa and Texas, often have more centralized and powerful governing boards than less activist states, such as Mississippi and New Mexico.

In general, higher education has not embraced the reform agenda nearly as readily or completely as the primary and secondary education systems (Hines 1988). Despite increasing centralization, colleges and universities expect and demand far more autonomy from state interference. Although states are developing more elaborate oversight mechanisms to increase accountability, colleges and universities are not likely to give up this considerable independence.

CONCLUSION

The delivery of educational services depends on coordinating activities between many organizations. Teachers are hired, textbooks are purchased, students show up for class, and something called learning happens more than occasionally. School boards are elected, taxes are collected, and proms are chaperoned. These activities require many people working together.

State politics play a role in all of this, but not in the day-to-day business of schooling. The state affects that business at a considerable distance. From a political perspective, governors and legislators present the appearance of movement and reform, but the need to show improvement within an electoral time-frame makes them less sensitive to the long-term effectiveness of reforms. The real world of state politics has to do primarily with the distribution of resources and symbols. Educating young people is the business of schools and teachers. It is the task of future scholars to tie these two levels together into a meaningful synthesis.

The politics of education—that is, the process through which resources are distributed to learning institutions and the students who attend them—must be understood if we are to make this effort intelligently and effectively. There have been politics around public education since the states began taxing their citizens to pay for schooling. Those politics have been about money, authority, and content: who pays for the education, who controls the education, and what gets taught.

Until recently, this political discourse has been dominated by school district personnel, local politicians, state politicians, and state bureaucrats, although public-spirited reformers occasionally got into the fray. Since 1980, however, several new and powerful actors have been added to the mix, and the salience of educational issues has risen for the public. Many of the new faces active in the state capitols challenge the conventional models that political scientists use to explain state politics. For example, the demand for privatization and more choice in schooling has become a highly contentious issue in many states, and in most states litigation about it has occurred. Yet the conventional institutional actors of a generation ago—superintendents, school boards, teachers' unions, and federal officials—do not dominate these struggles. Rather, national think tanks, advocacy groups, and business organizations define much of this agenda, and much of the agenda is played out at the state level. Similarly, the push for higher academic standards, more accountability, and improved outcomes also originates from groups other than the traditional policy actors.

In the terrain of state education politics, the mix of political forces and actors varies, as does their relative strength. But the power to make things happen has shifted to a set of actors that either did not exist until the mid-1970s or was relatively uninvolved and quiescent. Governors are taking political chances and committing themselves to reform agendas that were unheard of just a short time ago. National policy entrepreneurs are shaping state debates with concerted efforts to make a political impact. National movements to cut state spending shape the debate about financing.

Political scientists are challenged by these changes to think about state educational politics in new ways. Old frameworks and ways of conceptualizing political behavior are inadequate to the task of understanding what is happening in education. New frameworks are needed to account for the power of these new actors and to explain how decisions are being made about the distribution of resources. Furthermore, although the federal government and the school district were once thought to be the sites of political activity in past decades, today the state is primarily where these issues will play themselves out. Therefore, to understand the profound and exciting changes taking place in schools across the country, one must understand the push and pull of competing interests on the state level.

REFERENCES

Augenblick, John, Steven D. Gold, and Kent McGuire. 1990. *Education Finance in the 1990's*. Washington, D.C.: Education Commission of the States.

Bastian, Ann, Norm Fruchter, Marilyn Gittell, Colin Greer, and Kenneth Haskins. 1986. *Choosing Equality: The Case for Democratic Schooling*. Philadelphia: Temple University Press.

Beckham, Joseph C. 1993. *School Officials and the Courts: Update 1993.* Arlington, Va.: Educational Research Service.

Berdahl, Robert O. 1975. "Problems in Evaluating Statewide Boards." In *Evaluating Statewide Boards,* edited by Robert O. Berdahl. Washington, D.C.: American Council on Education.

Berger, Mark C., and Eugenia F. Toma. 1994. "Variations in State Education Policies and Effects on Student Performance." *Journal of Policy Analysis and Management* 13:477–491.

Berne, Robert, and Leanna Stiefel. 1992. *The Relationship between School Resources and Racial/Ethnic Status of Students in New York State Public Schools.* New York: New York State Education Department.

Card, David, and Alan B. Krueger. 1992. "Does School Quality Matter? Returns to Education and the Characteristics of Public Schools in the United States." *Journal of Political Economy* 100:1–40.

Carnegie Task Force on Teaching as a Profession. 1986. *A Nation Prepared: Teachers for the 21st Century.* New York: Carnegie Forum on Education and the Economy.

Carter, Deborah, and Reginald Wilson. 1992. *Minorities in Higher Education: Tenth Annual Status Report.* Washington, D.C.: American Council on Education.

Chubb, John E., and Terry M. Moe. 1986. "No School Is an Island: Politics, Markets, and Education." *Brookings Review* 4(4):21–28.

———. 1990. *Politics, Markets, and American Schools.* Washington, D.C.: Brookings Institution.

Clark, David L., and Terry A. Astuto. 1986. *The Significance and Performance of Changes in the Federal Educational Policy 1980–88.* Bloomington, Ind.: Policy Studies Center of the University Council for Educational Administration.

Clark, Shirley M. 1993. "Higher Education and School Reform." *Review of Higher Education* 17:1–20.

Clune, William H. 1993. "The Best Path to Systemic Educational Policy: Standard/Centralized or Differentiated/Decentralized?" *Educational Evaluation and Policy Analysis* 15:233–254.

Clune, William H., Paula White, and Janice Patterson. 1989. *The Implementation and Effects of High School Graduation Requirements.* Princeton, N.J.: Rutgers University, Center for Policy Research in Education.

Combs, Michael W. 1984. "The Federal Judiciary and Northern School Desegregation: Judicial Management in Perspective." *Journal of Law and Education* 13:345–399.

Coons, John E., William H. Clune, and Stephen D. Sugarman. 1970. *Private Wealth and Public Education.* Cambridge, Mass.: Harvard University Press.

Cuban, Larry. 1990. "Reforming Again, Again, and Again." *Educational Researcher* 19(1):3–13.

Darling-Hammond, Linda. 1994. "Inequality and Access to Knowledge." In *The Handbook of Multicultural Education,* edited by James A. Banks. New York: Macmillan.

Darling-Hammond, Linda, and Barnett Berry. 1988. *The Evolution of Teacher Policy.* Santa Monica, Calif.: RAND.

Downes, Thomas A., and Mona P. Shah. 1994. "The Effect of School Finance Reforms on the Level and Growth of per Pupil Expenditures." A paper presented at the annual meeting of the Association for Public Policy Analysis and Management, Chicago, October 27–29.

Farrell, Kenneth A. 1988. *State Expenditure Report, 1988.* Washington, D.C.: National Association of State Budget Officers.

Finn, Chester E. 1992. "Reinventing Local Control." In *School Boards: Changing Local Control,* edited by Patricia F. First and Herbert J. Walberg. Berkeley, Calif.: McCutchan.

Firestone, William A. 1989. "Education Policy as an Ecology of Games." *Educational Researcher* 18(7):18–24.

Firestone, William A., Susan H. Fuhrman, and Michael W. Kirst. 1991. "State Educational Reform since 1983: Appraisal and the Future." *Educational Policy* 5(3):233–250.

Frymier, Jack R. 1987. "Bureaucracy and the Neutering of Teachers." *Phi Delta Kappan* 69:9–14.

Fuhrman, Susan H. 1994a. "Legislatures and Education Policy." In *The Governance of Curriculum,* edited by Richard F. Elmore and Susan H. Fuhrman. Alexandria, Va.: Association for Supervision and Curriculum Development.

———. 1994b. "Intergovernment Relations in Education in the1990's." *Publius* 24(3):83–98.

Fuhrman, Susan H., and Richard F. Elmore. 1990. "Understanding Local Control in the Wake of State Education Reform." *Educational Evaluation and Policy Analysis* 12:82–96.

Hanushek, Eric A. 1981. "Throwing Money at Schools." *Journal of Policy Analysis and Management* 1(1):19–41.

———. 1986. "The Economics of Schooling: Production and Efficiency in Public Schools." *Journal of Economic Literature* 24:1141–1177.

Hearn, James C., and Carolyn P. Griswold. 1994. "State-Level Centralization and Policy Innovation in U.S. Postsecondary Education." *Educational Evaluation and Policy Analysis* 16:161–190.

HEW (U.S. Department of Health, Education, and Welfare), Office of Education. 1966. *Equality of Educational Opportunity,* by James S. Coleman, Ernest Q. Campbell, Carol J. Hobson, James McPartland, Alexander M. Mood, Frederic D. Weinfeld, and Robert L. Yonk. Washington, D.C.: U.S. Government Printing Office.

Hines, Edward R. 1988. *Higher Education and State Governments. ASHEERIC Higher Education Report No. 5.* Washington, D.C.: Association for the Study of Higher Education.

Hochschild, Jennifer. 1984. *The New American Dilemma.* New Haven, Conn.: Yale University Press.

James, Thomas. 1987. "State Authority and the Politics of Educational Change." *Review of Research in Education* 17:169–224.

Kagan, Robert A. 1986. "Regulating Business, Regulating Schools: The Problem of Regulatory Unreasonableness." In *School Days, Rule Days: The Legalization and Regulation of Education,* edited by David L. Kirp and Donald N. Jensen. Philadelphia: Falmer Press.

Kingdon, John W. 1984. *Agendas, Alternatives, and Public Policies.* Boston: Little, Brown.

Kirst, Michael W. 1987. "The Crash of the First Wave." *Bacharach* 85:20–29.

LaNoue, George R., and Smith, Bruce L. 1973. *The Politics of School Decentralization.* Lexington, Mass.: Lexington Books.

Lemann, Nicholas. 1992. *The Promised Land.* New York: Vintage Books.

Levin, Henry M. 1998. "Educational Vouchers: Effectiveness, Choice, and Costs." *Journal of Policy Analysis and Management* 17(3):373–392.

Lewis, Dan A. 1990. "Implementing Choice." In *Choice and Control in American Education,* edited by William H. Clune and John F. Witte. New York: Falmer Press.

———. 1993. "Deinstitutionalization and School Decentralization: Making the Same Mistake Twice." In *Decentralization and School Improvement,* edited by Jane Hannaway and Martin Conroy. San Francisco: Jossey-Bass.

Lewis, Dan A., and Kathryn Nakagawa. 1995. *Race and Educational Reform in the American Metropolis.* Albany: State University of New York Press.

Lusi, Susan F. 1994. "Systemic School Reform: The Challenges Faced by State Departments of Education." In *The Governance of Curriculum,* edited by Richard F. Elmore and Susan H. Fuhrman. Alexandria, Va.: Association for Supervision and Curriculum Development.

Marshall, Catherine, Douglas Mitchell, and Frederick Wirt. 1989. *Culture and Education Policy in the American States.* New York: Falmer Press.

Mazzoni, Tim L. 1993. "The Changing Politics of State Education Policy Making: A 20-Year Minnesota Perspective." *Educational Evaluation and Policy Analysis* 15:357–379.

McGuinness, Aims C. 1988. *State Postsecondary Education Structures Handbook.* Denver, Colo.: Education Commission of the States.

Millett, John D. 1984. *Conflict in Higher Education: State Government Coordination versus Institutional Independence.* San Francisco: Jossey-Bass.

Mingle, James R., ed. 1983. *Management Flexibility and State Regulation in Higher Education.* Atlanta, Ga.: Southern Regional Education Board.

Mitchell, Douglas, Catherine Marshall, and Frederick Wirt. 1986. "The Context of State-Level Policy Formation." *Educational Evaluation and Policy Analysis* 8:347–378.

Murnane, Richard J. 1985. "An Economist's Look at Federal and State Education Policies." In *American Domestic Priorities: An Economic Appraisal,* edited by John M. Quigley and Daniel L. Rubinfeld. Berkeley: University of California Press.

Murphy, Jerome T., ed. 1980. *State Leadership in Education: On Being a Chief State School Officer.* Washington, D.C.: George Washington University, Institute for Educational Leadership.

Nathan, Joe, and James Ysseldyke. 1994. "What Minnesota Has Learned about School Choice." *Phi Delta Kappan* 75(9):682–688.

NCES (National Center for Education Statistics). 1997. *Digest of Education Statistics.* Washington, D.C.: Office of Educational Research and Improvement.

National Commission on Excellence in Education. 1983. *A Nation at Risk: The Imperative for Educational Reform.* Washington, D.C.: National Commission on Excellence in Education.

National Governors' Association. 1986. *Time for Results: The Governors' 1991 Report on Education.* Washington, D.C.: Author.

Newman, Frank. 1987. *Choosing Quality: Reducing Conflict between the State and the University.* Denver, Colo.: Education Commission of the States.

Odden, Allan R., ed. 1991. *Education Policy Implementation.* Albany: State University of New York Press.

———. 1992. "School Finance and Education Reform: An Overview." In *Rethinking School Finance,* edited by Allan R. Odden. San Francisco: Jossey-Bass.

Odden, Allan R., and Larry O. Picus, eds. 1992. *School Finance: A Policy Perspective.* New York: McGraw-Hill.

Orfield, Gary. 1993. *The Growth of Segregation in American Schools: Changing Patterns of Separation and Poverty since 1968.* Alexandria, Va.: National School Boards Association, Council of Urban Boards of Education.

Pierce, Neal R. 1994. "How a Bit of Brinkmanship Paid Off." *National Journal,* April 9, 851.

Rocha, Gregory G., and Webking, Robert H. 1992. *Politics and Public Education:* Edgewood v. Kirby *and the Reform of Public School Financing in Texas.* Minneapolis, Minn.: West.

Russo, Charles J. 1992. "The Legal Status of School Boards in the Intergovernmental System." In *School Boards: Changing Local Control,* edited by Patricia F. First and Herbert J. Walberg. Berkeley, Calif.: McCutchan.

Skolnick, Michael L., and Glen A. Jones. 1992. "A Comparative Analysis of Arrangements for State Coordination of Higher Education in Canada and the United States." *Journal of Higher Education* 63(2):121–142.

Timar, Thomas B., and David L. Kirp. 1988. "State Efforts to Reform Schools: Treading between a Regulatory Swamp and an English Garden." *Educational Evaluation and Policy Analysis* 10:75–88.

Toch, Thomas. 1991. *In the Name of Excellence.* New York: Oxford University Press.

Twentieth Century Fund. 1983. *Making the Grade.* New York: Author.

Tyree, Alexander K. 1993. "Examining the Evidence: Have States Reduced Local Control of Curriculum?" *Educational Evaluation and Policy Analysis* 15:34–50.

Verstegen, Deborah. 1990. "Invidiousness and Inviolability in Public Education Finance." *Education Administration Quarterly* 26(3):205–234.

Walters, Jonathan. 1993. "School Funding." *CQ Researcher* 3:747–762.

Weatherly, Richard, and Michael Lipsky. 1977. "Street-Level Bureaucrats and Institutional Innovations: Implementing Special Education Reform." *Harvard Educational Review* 47:171–197.

Wise, Arthur. 1967. *Rich Schools, Poor Schools: The Promise of Equal Educational Opportunities.* Chicago: University of Chicago Press.

Wise, Arthur, and Tamar Gendler. 1989. "Rich Schools, Poor Schools: The Persistence of Unequal Education." *College Board Review* 151:12–18.

Wong, Kenneth. 1989. "Fiscal Support for Education in American States: The 'Parity-to-Dominance' View Examined." *American Journal of Education* 97:329–357.

———. 1989. "Fiscal Support for Education in American States: The "Parity-to-Dominance" View Examined." *American Journal of Education* 97(4):329–357.

Zumeta, William. 1992. "State Policies and Private Higher Education." *Journal of Higher Education* 63(4):364–417.

Zusman, Ami. 1986. "Legislature and University Conflict: The Case of California." *Review of Higher Education* 9:397–418.

SUGGESTED READINGS

Chubb, John E., and Terry M. Moe. *Politics, Markets, and American Schools.* Washington, D.C.: Brookings Institution, 1990. Chubb and Moe provide an evocative analysis of the effects of institutions on school effectiveness. They recommend a new system of education based on parent–student choice and school competition.

Elmore, Richard F., and Fuhrman, Susan H., eds. *The Governance of Curriculum.* Alexandria, Va.: Association for Supervision and Curriculum Development, 1994. This collection provides a broad overview of the politics of curriculum reform and policy development. It includes thorough discussions of the interaction between policy actors on the district, state, and federal levels.

Marshall, Catherine, Douglas Mitchell, and Frederick Wirt. *Culture and Education Policy in the American States.* New York: Falmer Press, 1989. This important analysis focuses on the ways in which values affect state education policy. Drawing from data collected on six states, the researchers provide a cultural framework for studying state policy and describe the differences between states in terms of these varying cultural influences and regional values.

Smith, Marshall S., and O'Day, Jennifer A., eds. *Politics of Education Association Yearbook.* Vol. 4. New York: Falmer Press, 1990. This collection offers a groundbreaking analysis on how to improve education in the United States. Smith and O'Day's work focuses on setting national standards in curriculum content and creating incentives for school districts and states to meet these standards.

Wirt, Frederick W., and Michael W. Kirst. *Schools in Conflict: The Politics of Education,* 3d ed. Berkeley, Calif.: McCutchan, 1992. Wirt and Kirst analyze public education as a political system and provide valuable insight into the political behavior of individuals within this system and the ways in which institutions function.

CHAPTER 12

Economic Regulation and Environmental Protection

BRUCE A. WILLIAMS

Government regulation has long been the scapegoat of American politics. Although the scope of regulatory policy dramatically increased in the 1960s and early 1970s, by the late 1970s both Democratic and Republican politicians made cutting "unnecessary" and "wasteful" regulations a priority. The general condemnation of government regulation originated with the claim by conservative academics and politicians that government interference in the economy was imposing a significant drain on productivity and was a prime cause of economic decline. During the administrations of Presidents Ronald Reagan and George Bush, efforts were made to cut back severely on regulations by subjecting them to the most stringent cost–benefit review possible.

Following the 1994 election the new Republican congressional majority made regulatory reform a centerpiece of its legislative agenda. This focus has come to be shared by most liberal politicians as well. Vice President Al Gore's National Performance Review, issued in September 1993, noted, "Many federal regulations impose too many constraints on individuals and businesses (such as by unnecessarily using command-and-control structures that tell regulated parties precisely what to do) while still failing to accomplish the goals for which they were imposed" (Office of the Vice President 1993, 3). Public opinion polling finds that "while Americans dislike regulations as a general matter, when asked about specific programs, such as for health and safety, they respond favorably" (Office of the Vice President 1993, 7). So, although there is support for individual regulations, overall the general reputation of government regulation has fallen on hard times.

One of the main strategies for regulatory reform has been the devolution of regulatory responsibility from the national level to state governments. The Republican Party's Contract with America, which served as the campaign platform for the 1994 congressional elections, embraced devolution of regulatory responsibility on the grounds that state and local governments are closer to the people, more responsive, efficient, and innovative than the federal government. As a result of this "devolution revolution," in a variety of areas states have replaced the national government as leaders in regulatory innovations. Although the national government has had a difficult time regulating the tobacco industry, the attorneys general of states as diverse as Minnesota, Mississippi, and Florida have sued the tobacco industry to recoup state medical expenditures on cigarette-related illnesses. Entering the realm of antitrust regulation, a number of states have sued the software giant Microsoft over its monopolistic practices. Some states have even used banking regulations to enter the realm of international relations by threatening sanctions against Switzerland for failing to pay back savings deposited during World War II by Holocaust victims. Reflecting the diversity of state politics, some states have been extending the regulatory reach of government, other states have been at the forefront of limiting regulation. The Wise Use Movement in many southwestern states has challenged the right of government to regulate the way individuals choose to use their own lands.

In this chapter, I examine the ways in which regulatory policy affects and is affected by state governments. Focusing especially on environmental protection and economic regulation, I attempt to clarify the concept of regulation; dispel some myths about its history and operation; and examine the reasons for the persistent attacks on it. The discussion of regulation is guided by three themes.

First, I emphasize the inevitability of government interference in the private market economy. Although some politicians and scholars harken back to a golden age when the private market was allowed to operate unhindered by the actions of government, in fact, such a laissez-faire age never existed. Indeed, it is government that must define the legal rights associated with private property itself. Throughout American history, the question has never been whether government will intervene in the market; rather, it has always been what specific policies will be pursued and which levels of government will be responsible for them. Less federal activity in this policy area means greater policy-making responsibilities for states and localities. For example, the failure of the federal government to enact new regulations in an area such as health care, as happened in 1994, does not mean that the health care system is made free from government interference. Rather, it means that the burden falls on state governments to manage the health care system.

The second theme involves the significance of federalism in understanding the different options facing regulators at different levels of government. Federalism imposes two types of limits on the regulatory process: constitutional and structural. Because the U.S. Constitution reserves for the federal government the right to regu-

Table 12-1 Developmental and Redistributive Public Policies

	Policy arenas	
	Developmental	*Redistributive*
Characteristics	Policies that increase resources available to government by expanding the tax base	Policies that shift income from one group to another, especially policies that benefit those who pay proportionately less in taxes at the expense of those who pay proportionately more
Examples	Economic development (for example, tax credits, enterprise zones, venture capital programs)	Welfare policy and many types of economic and social regulation (for example, air pollution controls, hazardous waste regulation)

SOURCE: Adapted from Peterson 1981, 1995.

late interstate commerce, states have very limited ability to regulate the flow of capital across their borders.

Constitutional limitations combine with features of a capitalist economy to constrain further the options open to states. In a capitalist economy, the private businesses that ultimately control investment decisions are free to shift their resources between states. State policy makers must therefore compete with one another to attract the investment on which their economic well-being depends (see Chapter 13). To the extent that the demand by states exceeds the supply of factories, retail stores, high-technology research centers, and so forth, the terms of this competition are defined by the business interests that states try to attract. This dynamic is much less a factor at the federal level because the ability to shift investment between countries is far more constrained than the ability to shift between states. That is, the exit costs of moving between states are far lower than the exit costs of moving between countries. Understanding the limits on state policy makers in this regard is essential for analyzing regulatory policies in the states.

Of particular importance is the argument developed by political scientist Paul Peterson (1981, 1987, 1995), which emphasizes the significant policy-making differences between federal, state, and local governments. Peterson has built his theory around two different types of public policies: developmental and redistributive (see Table 12-1). Developmental policies are aimed at economic growth and "strengthen[ing] the local economy, enhanc[ing] the local tax base, and generat[ing] additional resources that can be used for the community's welfare." Redistributive policies "help the needy and unfortunate and . . . provide reasonably equal access to public services" (Peterson 1981, 41, 44).

In a federal system, Peterson has argued, state and local governments tend to pursue developmental policies and avoid redistributive policies. The former are in what he defines as the general interests of the community: increasing the tax base—without increasing tax rates—provides more resources for improving the state or community. Redistributive policies are avoided because they tend to provide services for those who pay proportionately less in taxes by taking from those who pay proportionately more. Such policies provide an incentive for the latter to leave the state and relocate in an area where they will receive a higher level of services for their taxes. A central consideration for states is that relatively low exit costs for capital and labor make such movement a real possibility. An exodus of those who pay proportionately more in taxes would work against the overriding goal of economic development. Thus, although developmental policies are the province of state governments, redistributive polices are the province of the national government.

To illustrate his arguments, Peterson (1995) analyzed changing state welfare policies, the purest example of redistributive policy. In an analysis of Aid to Families with Dependent Children, one type of welfare policy, he found that states with more expansive benefits became a magnet for poor people who moved across state lines to gain those benefits. The result was a "race for the bottom" with "each state trying to shift the cost of welfare to its neighbors" (1995, 127). However, as is discussed in Chapter 10, other political scientists disagree with Peterson, finding little evidence of either welfare magnets or a race to the bottom. Whether or not scholars can demonstrate why people move to other states, it may still be the case that state legislators fear the magnetizing effect and do not want to be overly generous in granting welfare benefits. We will explore these arguments when we examine the redistributive impacts of various kinds of state regulatory policies.

Peterson's arguments are deterministic, leaving little room for variation in state policy making, at least when it comes to the most redistributive policies. In his view, redistributive polices are simply the province of the federal government and development policies are best pursued by states and localities. Other scholars, however, have focused on the very different ways that political actors within states and localities respond to the economic constraints they face. The proponents of "regime theory" argue that different states and localities, depending on the interest group structure, political history, culture, and so forth (in other words, the regime), produce very different policies that respond to the same economic competition (Elkins 1987; Ferman 1997; Stone 1989). We shall see that "regime theory" is very useful in explaining the growing diversity in state responses to the "devolution revolution," which continues to shift regulatory responsibility from the federal to state and local governments.

The third theme of the chapter, following from the second, is that the impact of shifting regulatory policy-making responsibilities between levels of government is not neutral. Rather, such shifts systematically and predictably present advantages and disadvantages to various groups in society. Reducing federal responsibility and increasing the state role in various types of regulatory activities, depending on the specific characteristics of that regulation and the states within which they are promulgated, changes the formulation and implementation of these policies. In particular, the redistributive aspects of many regulatory policies often make them difficult for states to enforce effectively.

GOVERNMENT REGULATION

A general discussion of regulatory policy is first necessary to set the discussion of state environmental and economic regulatory policies within the broader context of the overall themes of this chapter: the inevitability of government interference in the private market; the structural limitations imposed by federalism; and the effect of changes in the level of government responsible for various economic policies.

Regulations are adopted on the assumption that their benefits will outweigh their costs. Indeed, the explicit or implicit justification for most regulation is that its benefits—usually defined in terms of an overriding public interest—justify the imposition of costs on specific groups or on the entire population. Benefits, however, are usually difficult to calculate. Consider the seemingly simple question of where to locate traffic lights. The benefits of safe street intersections are obvious and significant. However, determining an optimal level of even obvious benefits is often quite difficult. Where do we place the traffic lights? How many should we buy? If we place lights at every intersection, travel will be very safe but quite slow: increasing benefits usually increases costs. The question then becomes, how many traffic lights are we willing to pay for and how much inconvenience are we willing to subject ourselves to in exchange for how many avoided accidents? Determining an optimal answer to this question is complicated by the fact that one's response will depend on whether one is a motorist in a hurry, a pedestrian trying to cross the street, a harried politician attempting to minimize local taxes, or the owner of a company that manufactures traffic lights. What this example illustrates is that even in the case of regulations that are clearly in the interest of almost the entire public (imagine intersections without traffic lights!), individuals' and groups' costs and benefits vary quite dramatically. Regulation becomes a difficult political issue to the extent that, with little regard to collective costs or benefits, people attempt to influence the decisions of government either to raise their individual benefits or to lower their individual costs.

ENVIRONMENTAL PROTECTION AND ECONOMIC REGULATION

Most of the regulations imposed by government are, like traffic laws, noncontroversial. This chapter deals, however, with more controversial regulation: the regulation of economic activity and environmental protection.

At first glance, it might seem that regulation of the private market by government is unnecessary. One of the supposed advantages of a private market economy is that the behavior of individuals pursuing their own self-interest is aggregated through the invisible hand of the market into a social good. The prices determined by the free and competitive interaction of supply and demand most efficiently allocate the resources of a society. Thus the public interest is seemingly served by the private market *without* the heavy hand of government interference.

Economists have long realized, however, that the market often fails to aggregate individual greed into a social good. They suggest that even in a private market society, government interference is justified in such instances of market failure.

There are three general conditions under which markets fail in this context. First, markets fail when there are significant *externalities* involved in transactions. Externalities are significant costs or benefits from a transaction falling on individuals who are not involved in the buying or selling of the goods produced. Because they are not involved in the transaction, the costs or benefits to such individuals are ignored in the exchange of goods and services. For example, the production of industrial goods is often accompanied by environmental pollution. Many of the costs of this pollution fall on those who live near the polluting factory, however, and are not included in the price of the good. The commodity is thus produced and sold for less than it actually costs—its selling price does not include the cost of pollution borne by the affected public. Hence the good—along with the pollution that accompanies its production—is underpriced and overproduced. Because it imposes costs on consumers that are not determined by the costs of production, monopoly is considered an example of a market failure involving significant externalities.

Market failures that produce significant externalities cannot be readily solved by the market itself. The competition between producers to produce goods at the lowest possible price prevents even civic-minded producers from raising the cost of their goods to cover the cost of pollution controls. In a truly competitive market, such well-meaning entrepreneurs would quickly be driven out of business by their less-public-minded competitors. In such a case, government is justified in interfering in the market to ensure that the externalities are somehow accurately reflected in the price of the good. In the example, government might require that all producers install pollution control equipment; this would force all producers to include the costs of their pollution in the price of the good.

The second kind of market failure is the market's inability to provide public goods. Public goods are those goods and services that, when provided, are not divisible—that is, those who do not pay for the goods cannot practically be excluded from their consumption. National defense is the classic case of a public good. If the state of Iowa were to stop paying its share of the cost of national defense, it would be impractical to exclude that state from enjoying the benefits of the defense protection provided for the rest of the states. Because individuals cannot be excluded from consuming a public good once it is provided, they have every incentive to avoid paying for it—becoming what economists call "free riders." Because individuals will seek to avoid paying for public goods, such goods are unlikely to be provided in the private market. To the extent that specific public goods are deemed necessary or desirable (for example, defense or parks), government must intervene in the private market either to produce the goods themselves or to create incentives for their production by the private sector.

The third kind of market failure occurs when consumers cannot obtain accurate information about the quality of a product. In these cases, individual consumers will be either unable or unlikely to acquire the information needed to make informed choices in the market. Thus government may justifiably intervene to ensure that their choices will not result in disaster: for example, it requires that all foodstuffs be demonstrated to be safe for human consumption. Lack of accurate information leads to poor or even dangerous decisions in the marketplace.

There are three categories of this type of market failure: Individuals are often unaware of the risks associated with their jobs; individuals are often unable to make informed choices about the competencies of professionals that they might hire (for example, doctors); individuals are sometimes unable to judge the safety of products that they might purchase, such as electrical appliances or processed foods. Government intervention in the private market is justifiable to ensure safety, competence, and quality of products.

We can distinguish between two broad kinds of regulation that address market failures. Economic regulation addresses natural monopoly; social regulation deals with "the externalities and impacts of economic activity" (Vogel 1981, 238). In areas such as environmental protection, health care reform, occupational safety, and consumer protection, these externalities and impacts often include "quality of life" issues that are difficult to define, requiring regulators to "affect the economy in nonmarket dimensions" (Litan and Nordhaus 1983, 10).

For example, price closely captures the full value of an airline ticket, train ride, or kilowatt hour of electricity. The challenge for economic regulation is to attach accurate price tags to such commodities when markets fail to do so. In contrast, price is less appropriate for capturing the full value of a healthy environment or avoiding cancer. Although their value certainly has a component that is captured by money, they are not traded on the market, and estimating their price becomes a political rather than an economic determination. Social regulation, then, raises fundamental questions about the relation between technological progress, capitalism, and democracy.

Various conditions exist that seem to mandate the government regulation of economic activity: Sometimes, markets fail to produce socially beneficial outcomes. The conditions under which most economists would concede that government regulation is necessary, however, are frequently not the same conditions under which government regulation is enacted and implemented: The rationale for and the reality of economic regulation can be quite disparate. Political factors, rather than economic logic, often govern policy making. Studies of the creation and activities of regulatory agencies have revealed that regulation is not always guided by a consideration of market failure and the public interest. Rather, government regulation often serves the interests of those groups that are being regulated (Stigler 1975). Market failure may establish the preconditions for "government failure" (Weisbrod, Handler, and Komesar 1977). Indeed, most of the classic scholarly work on regulation focuses on the capture of regulatory agencies by the groups that they are charged with regulating (Bernstein 1955; Huntington 1952)—that is, rather than speaking in the interest of the public, regulatory agencies serve the narrow interests of the regulated. One reason for current discontent with economic regulation is the contention that we have it where we do not need it, and need it where we do not have it. Such arguments have fueled deregulation efforts in fields such as transportation and communications (Derthick and Quirk 1985).

A second reason for the discontent with regulation centers on the way its costs and benefits are distributed across organized interests even when government action is successfully remedying market failures: Many environmental protection measures serve as examples. In such cases, those adversely affected by regulation, such as industrial polluters, attempt to alter regulations to reduce the costs they must bear. Even when the purpose of the regulation is being achieved—for example, when pollution is effectively reduced—it still generates opposition from those who must bear the costs.

Costs, Benefits, and Controversy

This discontent with regulation has resulted in an explosion of interest in the actual effect of government regulations. If they are not remedying market failure, then what are they doing? If they are remedying market failure, then why is there so much opposition to regulation? Attempts to answer these questions have fueled the controversy surrounding economic and social regulation.

Increasingly, scholarly attention has turned to an analysis of the costs and benefits of regulation. This focus has led to the unpleasant recognition that difficult trade-offs must be made between economic growth and social goals such as safe jobs and clean air. If, for example, we decide that a safe workplace is a desirable social goal, we pass regulations that require employers to spend money to make factories safer. In turn, this results in higher production costs and prices, which presumably slow economic growth. Increasingly, such difficult choices must be faced. How much are we willing to spend to save the lives of workers in dangerous jobs? Such decisions are even more difficult to make because there is enormous uncertainty about the relationship between exposure to any particular toxic substance and actual disease in human beings. How much productivity are we willing to forgo to preserve clean air and water? How much risk are we willing to endure for cheap energy? Moreover, there is moral resistance to attaching any price tag to such items that lie outside "the domain of dollars" (Okun 1976, 137). The very act of establishing a "price" for human life or clean water in regulatory calculations remains distasteful for many people.

Because decisions about regulation involve implicit or explicit answers to such questions, regulation generates controversy. That controversy is further fueled by the fact that preferences about such trade-offs are not randomly distributed throughout the population. Rather, persons' preferences depend on whether they stand to gain or lose from a particular policy decision. In addition, the people who reap the benefits are usually not the same people who bear the costs. Workers in a chemical company are likely to value a safe workplace, even at the cost of increased prices; in contrast, the owners and customers of the company are likely to prefer a lesser degree of safety and its attendant lower prices or greater profits.

A final reason for the controversy surrounding regulation is that underlying this controversy is the conflict between an economic system presumably built on the unfettered use of private property and a government philosophy that limits the free use of that property for the sake of the public interest. The public interest, however, is not readily and objectively defined. Understandably, its invocation in constraint of private property is controversial. For example, many northern industrial states have seen movements to pass bills limiting the ability of companies to move their plants to other states or out of the country. Is the public interest best served by maintaining jobs in the state, or by allowing owners the freedom to exercise control over private property? Do the benefits of such regulations outweigh and justify the costs imposed on owners, as well as the costs that might flow from interfering in the private market? Clearly, no objectively correct definition of the public interest can be found for this case. A person's definition will likely be determined by whether he or she is a factory worker in Youngstown, Ohio, or a stockholder in United States Steel.

Trends in State Regulation: The Myth of Laissez-Faire

Most popular and scholarly attention has focused on the federal government's activities, but states were actively involved in regulating market relations, often in minute detail, long before the federal government became involved. As noted at the beginning of the chapter, the myth of a laissez-faire era is sustainable only if we ignore the role of states. State regulations, in fact, created many precedents for later activities by federal regulatory officers. It is certainly true that federal regulation was largely nonexistent prior to the creation of the Interstate Commerce Commission in 1887. In the states, however, the regulation of commerce had been attempted before the commission was established. As in other areas of early federal regulation, actions by the states—in this case, Illinois, Iowa, Minnesota, and Wisconsin—paved the way for federal action. Throughout the post-Civil War period, states were also increasingly active in the regulation of banks and the rapidly growing insurance industry. As the American economy became national in scope, the federal government became an increasingly important source of regulatory authority. Still, it tended to supplement—rather than supplant—the states' regulatory efforts. Clearly, states have historically maintained an enduring involvement in a great deal of regulatory activity.

Nevertheless, for good reasons most scholarly and popular attention over the past few decades has focused on the actions, or inactions, of regulators at the federal level. Throughout the twentieth century it is at the national level that government regulatory activity expanded most rapidly in areas such as consumer protection, antitrust, environmental protection, and so forth. However, the enthusiasm for devolving regulatory responsibilities to the states, especially during the Reagan and Bush administrations and the 104th Congress are in many ways turning back the clock to an earlier style of regulation that places states at the forefront.

For three reasons, state regulatory activity is likely to become increasingly important in the future. First, there is intense competition between states to attract investment (see Chapter 13). To the extent that businesses attend to the costs of regulation, states are likely to compete with one another for industries by lowering such costs. To attract businesses, states can be expected to reduce their regulatory burdens, even at the expense of the benefits of such regulation to the general population. Indeed, the lack of regulatory activity in many southern states has already been used as a means to attract businesses. The outcome of such competition will, along with economic development policies, determine the economic health of many states and, in some cases, both the physical and economic health of their citizens. We shall return to this issue when we explore state environmental regulation.

Second, the devolution of regulatory responsibilities leaves states with important decisions about whether or not to assume full responsibility for the regulation of areas such as air and water pollution control, consumer protection, and occupational health and safety. In short, the focus of many political battles over regulation has shifted from the federal to the state level.

Third, the responsibility and costs for enforcing many regulations passed by Congress fall on the states in the form of unfunded mandates. Unfunded mandates are the reason that the old theme song of state and local officials "Give Me Money!"—a favorite throughout the lean years of the Reagan and Bush administrations—has finally given way to a new tune, "Leave Me Alone" (Stanfield 1994, 726). Consider the revisions made in 1994 to the 1974 Safe Drinking Water Act. The act requires local governments to build state-of-the-art water treatment facilities and to monitor drinking water for a wide variety of contaminants in an effort to regulate the safety of America's drinking water. As originally passed, the act seemed to be a program entirely consistent with a model of "picket-fence" federalism. It linked environmental officials in Washington with officials in states and localities responsible for drinking water by establishing technical requirements that had to be met in all localities. Given the widespread concern of most Americans with drinking water safety, the goals of the act had wide public support. In the twenty years between the act's passage and its revisions in 1994, however, much had changed in the dynamics of federalism. Concern about rising federal deficits made it increasingly difficult for Congress to provide the money for localities to carry out its mandates. Yet public support for environmental protection remained strong. The result was that the cost of complying with federally mandated standards fell on state and local governments. This brought howls of protest from organizations representing local governments. As a consequence, revision of the Clean Water Act became a highly charged and controversial topic as conservatives in Congress, already opposed to stringent federal environmental standards, joined forces with state and local officials who opposed additional federal burdens without additional federal funds to pay for them. As Mayor Sharpe James of Newark, a city required to build a $41 million water treatment facility that would be paid for out of an already severely stretched city budget, explained, "If I only have $1 and I'm trying to pay for police, fire, education and cleaning up the street, and the federal government says take 50 cents of that to build this water treatment plant . . . we can't function" (Kriz 1994, 947).

Past research on regulatory activity identifies the factors that are likely to shape the outcome of a state's regulatory decision making: political perceptions of the regulation's costs and benefits (in particular, perceptions of its redistributive implications); the degree to which those affected by the regulation are mobilized and powerful; the ability of affected parties to manipulate multiple decision-making arenas; and the limited ability of states to enforce regulations with redistributive effects.

First, because regulation always involves the government imposition of costs and benefits on various segments of the population, the distribution of these must be identified. Any interference by government inevitably alters the status quo of the market, bettering the condition of some actors and worsening the condition of others. If affected segments of the population recognize the costs or benefits of the regulation to them, they will pressure the government to recognize their interests in making regulatory decisions. The "proper" calculation of regulation's costs and benefits becomes a highly political issue. Furthermore, many types of costs and benefits are inherently difficult to measure: For example, what is the actual benefit of a given reduction in air pollution? Combined, these two factors make it difficult—if not impossible—to render an "objective" cost–benefit measurement in most cases.

Second, because regulation bestows costs and benefits on groups, regulatory decision making is usually determined by the interplay of interest groups. As Bernstein (1955, 18) noted, "[R]egulation is largely a product of the clash of organized private economic interests seeking to utilize governmental powers for the enhancement of private interests." The attention accorded a particular group's costs and benefits is usually a function of the group's political clout in relation to other interested and active groups. As Olson (1965) has observed, however, different kinds of individuals have widely different potentials for organizing into formal interest groups. In regulation, it is frequently the case that large numbers of unorganized individuals are each only slightly affected by the actions of government: For example, a consumer of a regulated product is usually only marginally affected by regulation's effect on the price of that product—even though the total costs to all individuals may amount to a huge sum. Because the cost imposed on each individual is small, no one individual has an incentive to spend the resources in time and money required to organize all of those similarly affected into a formal interest group. Even if such "latent groups" (as Olson called them) manage to organize around a particular regulatory issue, they are unlikely to stay organized for very long. The size of the benefit that will accrue to each individual member is, quite simply, too small to induce people to bear the cost of organization for very long.

In contrast, when regulations impose large costs on a small number of individuals, such "privileged groups" (as Olson [1965] called them) tend to form strong and well-maintained organizations to represent their interests. It is for this reason that, in the long run, interest groups representing business interests are better organized and more powerful than those representing consumers. For example, consider the individual businesses in a regulated industry such as insurance. Because each insurance company has such a high stake in the outcome of regulatory decision making, all of the affected companies are willing to invest their resources in organizing to pursue their interests in the regulatory process.

Once organized, different groups have vastly different levels of resources that can be translated into political influence. The outcome of regulatory politics will change as the balance of power among competing groups changes, therefore. As regulatory issues move off of and onto the political agenda, the groups mobilized and the resources committed to influencing policy change. In certain areas, past regulation may have been as predictable as it is portrayed by those who speak of the capture of regulatory agencies. But currently, at the state level, regulation is a dynamic area of public policy making.

A third determinant of the outcome of state regulatory decision making is the diversity of regulatory arenas provided by our federal system of government. Business corporations can choose the state in which their headquarters will be located and thereby select the state that will be their primary regulator. In some cases, an industry can seek to be subject to federal regulation rather than a plethora of individual states' regulations.

There are two ways that those adversely affected by state policies can try to escape the costs of regulation (Williams and Matheny 1995, chap. 4). One way is to make a geographic move within the same level of government. Businesses often move, or threaten to move, from one city to another or one state to another. I call this *horizontal exit*. Another way is to shift the level of government that has authority over regulatory decisions. For instance, the insurance industry, unhappy with the prospect of coming under the regulatory authority of the federal government, supported passage of the McCarran–Ferguson Act, which delegated regulatory authority to the states. I call this *vertical exit*.

The effect of federalism on regulation, as characterized by the ideas of both horizontal and vertical exit, is illustrated by controversies in the regulation of savings and loan institutions (S&Ls). Such thrift institutions had the option of operating under either federal or state charters; they could shift their charters from one level of government to another ("Many Harried S&Ls" 1981, 1). In the 1970s and 1980s, state-chartered S&Ls claimed that state regulators were overly sensitive to the wishes of consumer groups and that they artificially depressed the interest rates on home mortgages. To escape such restrictions, many S&Ls threatened to shift to the federal charter system. Given the probusiness climate and the corresponding weakness of consumer groups in Washington at the time, these S&Ls believed that federal regulators would grant them greater latitude to set adjustable interest rates; such rates, the bankers argued, were necessary to ensure adequate levels of profit. When a financial institution shifts its charter to the federal system, however, the state loses more than the power to regulate: It also loses substantial tax revenues. The mere threat of such a shift has created tremendous pressures for the states to align their regulations with federal standards.

Table 12-2 Categories of Regulatory Policy

	Perceived benefits of regulation	
	Diffuse	Concentrated
Perceived costs of regulation		
Diffuse	Majoritarian politics: social security	Client politics: insurance regulation
Concentrated	Entrepreneurial politics: environmental protection, hazardous waste regulation	Interest group struggle: health care reform, medical malpractice regulation

SOURCE: Adapted from Wilson 1980.

The pressures on state regulators, however, resulted from more than intergovernmental competition for regulatory powers and revenues. Interstate competition for these resources is always fierce. Several pioneering states—notably Texas and Virginia—attracted banks to their state systems by eliminating many restrictions on home mortgage interest rates. The inability or unwillingness of states to regulate these institutions effectively resulted in the S&L crisis of the 1980s, when thrifts across the country collapsed under the weight of bad investments and outright fraud (Sherrill 1990).

FRAMEWORK FOR STUDYING STATE REGULATORY POLICY AND POLITICS

Scholarly work on regulatory politics has increasingly incorporated the four determining factors in state regulatory decision making discussed previously. In a synthesizing work, Wilson (1980) argued that regulatory politics is best understood through an analysis of a regulation's perceived costs and benefits. Costs and benefits may be either concentrated on a specific group or more widely dispersed throughout the entire population. Taxes on income, for example, are costs of regulation that are widely distributed. The benefits of price supports for a particular farm crop—tobacco, for example—are concentrated. Although many people may be affected by the higher prices that can result from such supports, they are affected only slightly, whereas a small group of people are deeply affected by the structure of such supports—the farmers themselves. Because the concentration or dispersion of costs and benefits affects the probability of interest groups forming to represent those who are so deeply affected, this concentration or dispersion will determine the type of politics that surrounds each type of regulation. Based on an analysis of the dispersion of costs and benefits, Wilson identified four major types of regulatory politics (Table 12-2).

When both costs and benefits are widely dispersed, regulatory politics will be majoritarian. The passage in 1935 of federal Social Security legislation is a prime example of majoritarian politics. All—or at least all of those covered under the act—expected to gain something: the provision of Social Security benefits on retirement, disability, or death. All expected to pay some sort of cost: Social Security taxes, regularly deducted from paychecks. Because costs and benefits were so widely dispersed, no strong and long-lived interest groups formed around the issue. The possible benefits or losses to individuals were not sufficiently great to persuade them to mobilize for political action. Majoritarian politics is an important part of a full understanding of regulatory policy in the United States. However, it is a form of regulatory politics that generally occurs at the federal rather than the state level. Because of the problem of mobilizing such majorities of the whole, and the general absence of interest group agitation concerning such issues, instances of majoritarian politics are exceedingly rare in state regulatory politics, and we shall not deal with this category in this chapter. Indeed, the examples Wilson used—Social Security, wartime drafts, the Sherman Antitrust Act—are all federal issues.

In client politics, the benefits of a policy affect a concentrated group, and the costs are dispersed throughout the population. In such cases, the former group has much motivation to organize and pressure the political system to provide the benefit. Because the costs of the policy are widely distributed and most likely inconsequential for any one individual, opposition groups have little incentive to form. Price subsidies are a prime example of this type of regulation: When they are granted, subsidized producers profit quite handsomely. In large part, the cost of the subsidy is found in higher prices for the subsidized product. Each individual consumer, however, may pay only a few cents more than the unsubsidized good would have cost. The cost of such a subsidy is a matter of indifference to those who pay but is of great importance to those receiving the subsidy. Those who pay will be unlikely to spend the time and money necessary to stop the subsidy. Client politics fit well with the classic capture model of regulation: Where government regulation originally was intended to serve the public interest, it ends up serving the interests of the small organized group. In the states, it is well illustrated by certain aspects of insurance regulation.

When both the costs and benefits of regulation are narrowly concentrated in their effect on particular groups, Wilson suggested that interest group struggle will dominate the politics of the issue. Some categories of actors will clearly be dramatically affected by the regulation; this realization precipitates their mobilization; mobilization leads to active and competitive lobbying efforts. In such cases, the policy that is eventually adopted is likely a function of the ability of such groups to gain organizational strength and of the relative strength of the competing groups. Recent conflicts arising in regard to the regulation of certain types of insurance (for example, medical malpractice and liability), provide excellent examples of this type of regulatory policy.

Finally, regulations may provide widely dispersed benefits while imposing concentrated costs on a particular group. Attempts to regulate pollution provide the best example of such policy. Such regulations are passed when political entrepreneurs can mobilize latent groups and can act as the "vicarious representatives of groups not part of the legislative process" (Wilson 1980, 370). The benefits (cleaner air) affect anyone who lives in the area in which pollution is reduced—and beyond, if one takes into account acid rain, the Greenhouse effect, and so forth. At the same time, the costs of cleaner air are borne by the industries that must pay for pollution control devices—unless, of course, they can manage to pass these costs on to consumers in the form of increased prices. As Wilson noted, the emergence of entrepreneurial policies is difficult to explain. "Since the incentive to organize is strong for opponents of the policy but weak for the beneficiaries, and since the political system provides many points at which opposition can be registered, it may seem astonishing that regulatory legislation of this sort is ever passed" (Wilson 1980, 370). This seeming puzzle is explained by the ability of political entrepreneurs, such as the consumer advocate Ralph Nader, to use a crisis or scandal as the means for mobilizing public opinion. Their ringing denunciations of some offensive condition put the offending group on the defensive and render elected officials unwilling to ally themselves with the denounced party. Hence, governors and state legislators will often support regulations that impose heavy costs on concentrated interests. Indeed, many politicians have seized on such issues and used them to generate media attention and to build constituencies for election to public office.

Although elected officials will often support the passage of stringent entrepreneurial regulations, enforcement of such legislation is usually difficult. Although entrepreneurs may manage to mobilize a public outcry on specific issues, such mobilization is apt to be transitory. For example, the groups organized to protect consumers' rights formed a powerful political coalition at both the state and federal level during the early 1970s, but the coalition then drastically declined in size and power (Nadel 1975). In contrast, the groups organized to protect the interests of those who bear the concentrated costs of consumer protection regulation—that is, the industrial and retail trade associations—tended to maintain their organization and power. Thus, although entrepreneurial regulation has frequently been passed in the states, the enforcement of such legislation has fallen far short of the laws' goals after the public outcry and media attention have faded away. As the groups that pressed for its passage dwindled in strength and as entrepreneurs moved on to other issues, only the concentrated interests remained organized and active. Under their relentless pressure, enforcement weakened. This process is even more severe at the state level, where the threat of exit is a powerful club in the hands of industries unwilling to bear the costs of regulation.

An analysis of regulatory politics must include more than the relative power of competing groups at a given moment in time: It must also include the relative staying power of those groups. Coalitions operating on behalf of large latent interests are notoriously unstable and transitory. In the long run, they can succeed only by institutionalizing regulatory procedures that will protect the interests of their members even after the organized groups have faded away.

In the rest of the chapter while I examine state regulatory policies that fall within the three relevant cells of our typology, I spend the most time on environmental regulations, an example of concentrated costs and diffuse benefits. In contrast to the more stable client and interest group politics, the entrepreneurial politics of environmental protection are quite dynamic and subject to change, depending on the ways in which various political actors define the issues at stake. Although insurance regulation, for example, changes relatively slowly, environmental regulation has been changing quite dramatically. It is at the center of the devolution revolution in regulatory policy. At the state level, the movement for environmental justice has reordered the way the issue is defined and the perception of costs and benefits across various groups. Hence, state environmental policies illustrate better than most other regulatory policies the issues raised by the differences between Peterson's deterministic approach to federalism and the more fluid predictions of regime theory. Finally, over the past few years we have witnessed an intensifying debate about worldwide environmental issues such as global warming, ozone depletion, and the disproportionate use of global resources by the developed nations, especially the United States. At a time when such debates raise the possibility that humans are altering the very nature of life on earth and seem to call for national and global approaches to regulation, it is especially important to examine the implications of the American trend to devolve responsibility for environmental regulations to lower levels of government.

CONCENTRATED COSTS AND DIFFUSE BENEFITS: ENVIRONMENTAL PROTECTION AND THE MOVEMENT FOR ENVIRONMENTAL JUSTICE

Environmental protection is a type of regulatory policy that bestows benefits on a diffuse group and imposes costs on a concentrated interest.[1] The areas of regulation that fall within this category are among the most controversial regulatory policies of federal and state governments: land-use management, in which government attempts to control the use and development of public and private lands; consumer protection, in which costs are imposed on businesses to benefit the unwary consumer; and environmental protection, in which frequently considerable costs are imposed on polluting industries to benefit those who might be affected by such pollution. These areas are especially controversial when, as is often the case, costs are imposed on concentrated interests in the present for the benefit of future generations. Needless to say, organized interest groups representing those who must pay now are generally better represented than latent interest groups composed of those who are not yet born.

Since 1970, major pieces of environmental protection regulation have been passed at the federal level. The federal attention to environmental regulation was brought about, in large part, by organizations representing the interests of previously unorganized or poorly organized latent groups. This first wave of the environmental movement emerged in the late 1960s and early 1970s, its appearance highlighted by Earth Day 1970 and formalized by the organization of new public

---

1. This section was written with help from Gail D. Taylor.

interest groups, primarily at the federal level, dedicated to protecting our natural resources. Environmental groups such as the Natural Resources Defense Council and the Environmental Defense Fund pressed for new, strong federal laws and regulations. Many states had established agencies to deal with resource management in the 1950s, but they paid little attention to environmental protection until the passage of federal legislation such as the Clean Air Act and Clean Water Act in the 1970s (Switzer 1994, 67–68). This legislation relied on states to implement federal regulations and provided much of the money that funded the creation of state environmental protection agencies. At least initially, federal attempts to impose redistributive regulatory policies were backed up by federal budgetary commitments.

However, this initial commitment did not last. Over the entire course of the development of environmental regulation, federal commitments—either to funding or to attempts to overcome the fragmentation of state efforts—have been only sporadic and often ineffective (Rabe 1986). Indeed, as state environmental agencies grew in their ability and competence, so too did business resistance to state environmental regulation. Exercising what we have called *vertical exit*, "[t]hey turned to the federal government for regulatory relief and federal preemption of state authority" (Switzer 1994, 67). This strategy of regulatory relief was particularly effective during the Reagan administration, when arguments about getting government off the backs of the people found an especially receptive ear in Washington.

Richard Harris and Sydney Milkis discussed a specific case of the granting of regulatory relief in the area of environmental protection. Despite general support for reducing federal regulatory control and increasing state autonomy, the Reagan administration reversed its position when the state of Washington pressed for more stringent enforcement standards in the cleanup of the Department of Energy's nuclear facility in Hanford. They note the "impressive irony" of what they call the "heavy-handed intervention of the Department of Justice in favor of enforcing federal standards and limiting the autonomy of state officials." Harris and Milkis concluded that, "At a minimum it shows that the concerns of a state received relatively short shrift when they conflict with conservative principles" (Harris and Milkis 1989, 317).

In 1995 the Republican majority in Congress took up the task of devolution anew. Supporters argued for these policies on familiar democratic grounds. Allowing states and localities to determine their own levels of enforcement better reflects the differences between regions. Taking advantage of the possibilities for diversity inherent in federalism, such decentralization would be both more democratic and more efficient. However, the symbolic language of greater democracy is not all that is operating in the play of federalism. The economic competition, also created by federalism, meant that many states found it difficult to pay for increased enforcement. That is, funding effective enforcement mechanisms would have required raising taxes or imposing costs on industry that because of the possibility of horizontal exit by these same industries would run counter to the goal of economic development. The end result was that many states that were hard-pressed economically were unable to enforce federal environmental regulations (Williams and Matheny, 1984).

One result of the devolution of environmental regulation has been great variability between states, as regime theory would predict. Table 12-3 provides comparative information about state environmental policies and the severity of environmental pollution. Taken from Goetz, Ready, and Stone (1996), the column labeled "Environmental Policies" summarizes the degree to which states have adopted proenvironmental regulatory policies. The number for each state is a sum of the ratings each state received across seventeen different policy areas such as air pollution, hazardous waste management, groundwater protection, and so on. The higher the number, the more proenvironmental are a state's regulations. So, for instance, California with a score of 134 ranks first among the states in environmental regulation, and Wyoming, with a score of 46 ranks last.

Also taken from Goetz et al. (1996), the column labeled "Environmental Conditions" in Table 12-3 provides some comparative information on pollution levels. The numbers for each state are a composite of numerous measures of environmental quality across a wide range of media: air pollution, water pollution, land pollution and so forth. Positive values indicate better than average environmental conditions, negative numbers indicate lower-than-average conditions. There is considerable variation among the states, with Nevada ranking first with a composite score of 4.77 and Indiana ranking last with a score of -5.28.

At least two intriguing questions are raised by this variation among the states. First, are stricter state regulations effective? That is, do states with stricter environmental regulations actually enjoy a cleaner environment? Answering this question is complicated because strict regulations may be undertaken as a result of severe environmental problems and only produce improved conditions over the long term. Rinquist (1993) explored the dynamic relationship between state environmental regulations and actual environmental quality. He found that over a twelve-year period stricter environmental regulations did lead to significantly improved air quality, but that there was no connection between regulatory action and water quality.

A second question raised by devolution of regulatory responsibility to the states is the impact of environmental regulation on economic growth. Are states punished economically for strict regulation? Goetz et al. (1996) indicate that, as regime theory would suggest, states are increasingly diverging in their approaches to environmental policy. Some states with higher per capita incomes, higher growth rates, and a more educated work force have managed to protect their environment and maintain strict environmental regulations. For these states (California, Wisconsin, and Oregon are good examples), environmental quality becomes part of economic development strategy and is used as a tool for attracting nonpolluting enterprises. However, states with lower per capita income and less educated workforces have pursued an economic development strategy that depends on attracting industrial facilities with more severe environmental impacts that are attracted by less stringent environmental oversight (Louisiana, Alabama, and Mississippi are good exam-

Table 12-3 Selected State Environmental Characteristics

State	Environmental conditions	Rank	Environmental policies	Rank	Toxic chemical releases	Rank
Alabama	−2.98	46	53	46	102,765,046	5
Alaska	1.94	13	56	44	6,960,305	41
Arizona	0.66	20	72	31	35,832,635	22
Arkansas	−1.66	35	48	48	34,681,977	24
California	0.57	23	134	1	42,727,076	19
Colorado	4.12	5	75	29	4,565,426	42
Connecticut	−0.73	27	117	5	8,764,089	38
Delaware	−0.81	28	78	28	4,510,435	43
Florida	−1.03	30	114	8	83,972,862	8
Georgia	−1.86	36	80	23	55,523,894	13
Hawaii	3.96	6	79	24	469,968	50
Idaho	3.19	9	68	34	8,188,036	39
Illinois	−2.74	44	97	15	99,753,258	6
Indiana	−5.28	50	79	27	79,777,978	9
Iowa	0.58	22	107	11	34,765,080	23
Kansas	−1.32	32	74	30	22,816,324	29
Kentucky	−2.06	38	66	35	41,925,203	20
Louisana	−2.54	42	52	47	172,259,192	2
Maine	2.52	11	103	13	10,167,855	37
Maryland	1.22	18	101	14	13,321,893	34
Massachusetts	−0.35	26	123	4	8,141,053	40
Michigan	−2.14	40	107	12	75,263,953	11
Minnesota	0.88	19	116	7	22,459,624	30
Mississippi	−1.56	34	47	49	56,755,254	12
Missouri	−0.98	29	79	25	49,646,866	17
Montana	2.83	10	73	32	43,891,840	18
Nebraska	1.46	16	70	33	10,957,989	36
Nevada	4.77	1	56	43	3,559,408	44
New Hampshire	1.63	15	92	18	2,563,072	46
New Jersey	−1.97	37	125	3	14,645,356	33
New Mexico	3.31	8	61	40	18,706,252	32
New York	0.57	24	113	9	36,573,059	21
North Carolina	−2.08	39	111	10	86,160,483	7
North Dakota	4.44	2	61	39	2,561,837	47
Ohio	−4.59	48	88	22	121,870,567	3
Oklahoma	0.63	21	65	37	24,953,463	28
Oregon	3.33	7	116	6	21,194,711	31
Pennsylvania	−2.85	45	91	21	54,260,053	15
Rhode Island	1.64	14	95	16	2,782,799	45
South Carolina	−1.15	31	79	26	54,339,031	14
South Dakota	4.19	4	63	38	1,913,006	48
Tennessee	−4.75	49	60	41	111,182,899	4
Texas	−2.25	41	66	36	283,932,143	1
Utah	0.53	25	57	42	76,321,734	10
Vermont	4.37	3	91	19	552,845	49
Virginia	−2.60	43	95	17	52,913,332	16
Washington	1.28	17	91	20	26,450,970	27
West Virginia	−3.65	47	56	45	27,357,393	26
Wisconsin	−1.53	33	131	2	31,177,744	25
Wyoming	2.01	12	46	50	11,002,562	35

SOURCES: Adapted from Goetz, Ready, and Stone 1996, Environmental Defense Fund 1998.

ples). Among these states, at least, devolution of regulatory responsibility leads to a kind of "race for the bottom" in environmental protection.

As the locus of authority over environmental protection has alternated between state and federal levels, the relative strength of contending groups has also changed at these two levels of government. State governments, many scholars argue, are beholden to industrial interest groups in a way that makes adequate land-use, consumer, or environmental regulations impossible. In consequence, first-wave environmental groups initially concentrated their efforts at the federal level; through legislation at this level, they forced the reluctant states to act on their behalf—as, for example, in the implementation of the federal Clean Air and Clean Water acts and their more recent amendments.

Reflecting growing disenchantment with the federal government, whose commitment to the effective implementation of environmental regulations was waning, a second wave of environmentalism developed in the late 1970s. The paradigmatic group was the Love Canal Homeowners Association, but an array of other local groups also formed early on, notably FACE (For a Clean Environment), organized to fight against contaminated groundwater in Woburn, Massachusetts, and the citizens of Times Beach, Missouri, who protested against dumpings of dioxin near them. The focus of these groups was, of necessity, state and local governments (Tesh and Williams 1996).

Most second-wave environmental disputes centered on exposure to hazardous waste. Most industrial processes result in the production of large amounts of waste. When hazardous waste first became defined as an environmental problem, the Environmental Protection Agency estimated that 344 million metric tons were produced each year (Raloff 1979). A hazardous waste, according to Congress, is any waste that "may cause an increase in death, serious irreversible illness or incapacitating ailments, or pose a substantial present or potential hazard to human health or the environment when improperly treated, stored, transported, disposed of, or otherwise managed" (quoted in Raloff 1979, 348). Although only dramatic cases such as Love Canal make headlines, the problem of the safe disposal of hazardous wastes is widespread.

State regulation of hazardous waste disposal is guided by the 1976 Resource Conservation and Recovery Act (RCRA). The act required the EPA to establish criteria for treatment, disposal, and storage facilities, and to create a system for tracking hazardous wastes from their manufacture to their disposal sites. Like many other pieces of regulatory legislation at both the state and the federal level, RCRA was written in a vague and general manner; therefore, EPA personnel found it difficult to delegate the responsibility for its implementation. In fact, the actual rules for implementing RCRA were not finished until May 1980, four years after the passage of the act. During this period, as the federal government struggled to write the rules, state regulators waited for the federal government to provide guidelines for actions. This lag provided an opportunity for many companies to dispose of their wastes before implementing stringent new rules. Often this "midnight dumping" occurred in poor communities. As finally written, the regulations govern 501 specific wastes, waste processes, and waste sources—or approximately 40 million of the 57 million metric tons of hazardous wastes produced each year ("CMA Says States Can Handle Chemical Waste" 1980).

Although the federal government has been passing and trying to implement comprehensive legislation, state governments have also been attempting to deal with the problem of hazardous wastes. Indeed, RCRA is a good example of the trend in social regulation, beginning during the administration of Jimmy Carter and accelerating during the Reagan and Bush years, to devolve authority to the states. RCRA's Subtitle C recognizes that the states are the appropriate level for developing specific plans for dealing with waste disposal. It allows the EPA to authorize a state to operate a hazardous waste program in lieu of federal operation if the program meets standards established by the EPA. Forty-two states administer their own hazardous waste programs.

Although most states have assumed the responsibility for administering RCRA, the redistributive implications of such activities pose serious obstacles to effective state implementation. Producers of hazardous wastes seek to minimize their costs by disposing of such wastes in the least expensive manner. Often this is accomplished unsafely, posing long-run health threats to the community at large. Because the purpose of regulation is to force such producers to dispose of their wastes safely, regulations, presumably, lead producers to factor into their production costs the "true" expense of safe disposal. Furthermore, the purpose of programs such as the Superfund (Comprehensive Environmental Response, Compensation, and Liability Act—also known as CERCLA), which deal with the cleanup of abandoned and leaking hazardous waste sites, is to force those responsible for the sites to pay for cleanup, either by locating and charging the actual firms that abandoned the sites or by taxing the chemical and petroleum industries to pay for cleanup when responsible firms cannot be located. These regulations have the effect of raising producers' costs, and thus the prices that consumers must pay for their products. This increase in costs to producers and consumers is imposed to raise the income of the community at large (in the form of lowered health care costs, increased property values, and so forth); thus one effect of such regulation is the redistribution of income from producers and consumers to the general public. To the extent that the industries that bear the costs of regulation are well organized and significant to a state's economy, states may have a difficult time enforcing hazardous waste regulation.

According to quantitative analyses by Williams and Matheny (1984, 1995), states respond to these cross-pressures in an interesting fashion. Where the problems of hazardous waste disposal are severe, states tend to pass more stringent regulations. However, neither the severity of the problem nor the stringency of the laws increases the regulatory burden on the industries that produce the wastes. Rather, funding for the proper disposal and regulation of hazardous wastes is drawn from the state treasury, where this policy area competes with other issues for a share of the state budget.

So when state environmental groups are strong, more state resources flow to the enforcement of hazardous waste regulations. However, this group pressure does not lead to increased spending by private industry. Such increases would constitute the sort of redistributive policy that state policy makers try to avoid. In fact, Williams and Matheny find that the more significant polluting industries are to a state's economy, the less industry spends on pollution abatement. This is a result of the pressure on state and local government to foster economic development: The more important an industry is to a state's economy, the less able are state policy makers to impose increased costs on that industry because of fear that these costs might lead that industry to migrate. As a result, the most significant determinant of state effort is the size of the state budget, rather than the severity of the problem, quality of the laws, or any other factor (Williams and Matheny 1995, 148).

Overall, then, the dynamics of environmental regulation in a federal system made it quite difficult for many states to effectively address the problem. However, the emergence of strong citizen groups characteristic of second-wave environmental concerns had two significant impacts on state environmental regulation. First, in large part a result of citizen pressure, the EPA enacted a Community-Right-to-Know program in 1984, with a mission of providing the public with basic information about hazardous chemicals in their communities. A part of this program is the Toxic Release Inventory (TRI), which requires companies to publicly report the amount and types of toxic chemicals that they release into the environment. Table 12-3 provides the 1997 data on toxic chemical release by state. As with environmental pollution, in general there is much variability depending on the state's economic structure (for example, the extent of polluting industries) and regulatory regime (for example, how strict the laws are and how well are they enforced). In 1995 Texas led the states with 283,932,143 pounds of hazardous chemicals released into the environment (land, air, and water combined). Hawaii was last with 469,968 pounds released. This database, available on a county-by-county basis (and easily accessible on the World Wide Web at http://www.epa.gov/envirofw/html) allows local groups to find specific information about industrial operations within their communities. Coupled with other data now available to the public for the first time (such as the National Tumor Registry, which tracks cancer across the country), citizens have at their disposal much more powerful data for determining the environmental risks they are facing and using this information as a resource in their attempts to influence policy (Steingraber 1997).

Another result of second-wave environmental activity is that the siting of new hazardous waste facilities, either for production or disposal, is increasingly difficult, if not impossible. The rise of local groups opposed to the siting of unwanted and environmentally risky land uses, often called the NIMBY (Not-in-My-Backyard) movement, leads many observers to say that policy making approaches "gridlock." An unanticipated consequence of this political shift is that the costs of producing and disposing of hazardous wastes has dramatically increased. As a consequence, industries and governments now devote more effort than before to reducing, through source reduction and recycling, the amounts of hazardous wastes actually produced. Another result of NIMBY pressure is that unwanted facilities tend to be located in states and localities that are either less powerful or more economically distressed and thus unable to resist the siting of dangerous industrial activities. One response to this process that exposes these communities to greater environmental hazards than their more powerful and prosperous neighbors is the movement for environmental justice.

ENVIRONMENTAL RACISM AND THE MOVEMENT FOR ENVIRONMENTAL JUSTICE

Sometimes called the third wave of the environmental movement, a new coalition has developed between civil rights and environmental groups. This third wave focuses on the disproportionate exposure to environmental hazards of low-income communities, especially communities of color: Such exposure is particularly disproportionate for African American, Hispanic, and Native American communities. For a number of reasons, when it comes to operations that cause air, water, and land pollution, businesses follow the "path of least resistance" by locating polluting facilities in or near poor communities, often populated by people of color. Land is cheaper, the communities are likelier than wealthy neighborhoods to accept the risks in return for the jobs that may be created, and poorer neighborhoods are assumed to be poorly organized and unlikely to protest effectively. As a result, most inner-city and poor rural communities have dirtier air, water, and land than do their suburban and wealthy neighbors. There is a good deal of controversy over whether this differential exposure is the result of racism or other factors, such as the lower average incomes of nonwhite populations (Ringquist 1998; Tesh and Williams 1996).

Whatever the causal mechanisms, the EPA has found that low-income citizens, and quite often minorities, are more likely than other groups to live near landfills, incinerators, and hazardous waste treatment facilities; low-income and African American children consistently have higher than normal levels of lead in their blood; 80 percent of Hispanics, 65 percent of African Americans, and 57 percent of white Americans live in communities that fail to meet some EPA air quality standards; and low-income, especially minority communities, use fish as their sole source of protein and are not well-informed about the risks associated with eating contaminated fish from polluted lakes, rivers, and streams (EPA 1998). Again, although this data is disturbing, it is unclear as to the causal connections between environmental racism, exposure to hazards, and actual health effects (Tesh and Williams 1996). As I argued previously, scientific and technical uncertainty are characteristics of social regulation that make it so difficult politically.

Benjamin Chavis (who went on to become briefly executive director of the NAACP) coined the term *environmental racism*, which he defined as "racial discrimination in environmental policy making and enforcement of regulations and laws, the deliberate targeting of communities of color for toxic waste facilities, the official sanctioning of the presence of life-threatening poisons and pollutants in communities of color, and the history of excluding people of color from leadership of the environmental movement" (Chavis 1994, x–xi).

Concern about environmental racism and the development of the movement for environmental justice illustrates the dynamics of social regulation in a federal system. First, it highlights the difficulties faced by state policy makers as they attempt to balance environmental group pressures against the redistributive effects of regulation. For many states with the worst hazardous waste problems, officials respond to environmental groups with vigorous laws but lax enforcement. Second, the movement for environmental justice illustrates the conclusions of regime theory, which focuses on the very different political capacities of states and localities to define and respond to the same economic constraints. In several states, by redefining environmental disputes as civil rights issues, the movement for environmental justice has mobilized new organizations and created new alliances that have disrupted established patterns of policy making.

A 1982 protest over the siting of a hazardous waste disposal facility in Afton, a predominantly black town in Warren County, North Carolina, is widely cited as the first nationally significant protest against environmental racism. Grassroots groups were joined by national civil rights leaders in protesting the disposal facility designed to store PCBs that had been illegally dumped on North Carolina roadways. More than 500 protesters were arrested, including several nationally prominent civil rights leaders and black elected politicians. One of the latter, Rep. Walter E. Fauntroy (D-NC) requested a Government Accounting Office study of the racial demographics of hazardous waste siting. The resulting 1983 report, which found that disposal facilities are disproportionately located in African American communities in the EPA's southeast region, became a central document in the struggle to include civil rights considerations in environmental decision making.

The question raised by environmental justice is, should the racial impact of environmental regulations be part of the calculations used by policy makers? At the federal level, the EPA had resisted such an expansion of its mandate throughout the Reagan and Bush administrations. EPA administrators argued that environmental policy should be guided by technical and scientific concerns and not issues of social justice and racial equity. However, the Clinton administration was persuaded otherwise. In 1994 President Clinton issued Executive Order 12898, which directed all federal agencies to ensure compliance with the nondiscrimination requirements of Title VI of the 1964 Civil Rights Act in all federally funded programs and activities that affect human health or the environment. The EPA was assigned as the coordinating agency for this effort.

As with most regulatory policies, the actions or inactions of the federal government had immediate implications for state policy makers. Because many state environmental programs, including hazardous waste regulations, operate under a system of federal oversight and delegation, Title VI complaints have been brought against state permitting decisions that involve pollution sources near minority and low-income communities. In 1997, for example, cases brought by groups in Texas,

California, and Louisiana challenged state-approved hazardous waste facility siting on the basis of claims of environmental racism and Title VI violations. As a result, state-level policy makers and the organizations that represent them at the national level have opposed the Clinton administration's Executive Order and subsequent environmental justice policies.

The National Governors' Association, for example, has taken the position that recent federal court and EPA actions threaten state environmental programs by delaying the permitting process; requiring states to perform assessments well beyond the scope of environmental laws (EPA now requires that environmental equity criteria be included in environmental impact statements); and reducing or eliminating the federal funds available to state environmental agencies and revoking state permits that have been issued in compliance with environmental laws. Similarly, the Environmental Council of States, which brings together each state's top environmental official, voted in March 1998 to reject EPA's implementation of Executive Order 12898, arguing that the policy intrudes on state and local land use policies (Cushman 1998).

To understand why President Clinton's Executive Order has been resisted so strongly by the states and how the development of the movement for environmental justice has altered state environmental policy making, we turn to a specific dispute: attempts to site a large chemical manufacturing facility in a predominantly black town in Louisiana. The controversy that swirls around the Shintech plant illustrates the economic constraints faced by states as they try to both attract industry and regulate the environment as well as the significance of allowing Title VI claims under environmental laws.

ECONOMIC COMPETITION, ENVIRONMENTAL RACISM, AND SHINTECH

Although its license plates declare it a "sportsman's paradise," the state of Louisiana is economically dependent on the petrochemical industry. With the collapse of the sugar plantation system after World War II, Louisiana became a prime location for the petrochemical industry. Consistent with the arguments of Peterson about the pressures on states to attract industry, especially poor states with faltering economies, this economic growth was driven by generous tax exemptions and other inducements offered by the state. One of these inducements was lax environmental regulation, which drew industrial investment from more environmentally conscious states—such as New Jersey, for example, which lost much of its petrochemical industry to Louisiana (Williams and Matheny 1995). By the 1970s, an 85-mile stretch along the Mississippi River from Baton Rouge to New Orleans was producing 60 percent of the nation's vinyl chloride and nitrogen fertilizer and 26 percent of its chlorine (Bullard 1994). In 1996 the petrochemical industry accounted for almost 15 percent of the state's gross state product (Crombie 1997).

This economic boom has not been without its environmental costs. The 85-mile Mississippi corridor where the petrochemical industry is located has been dubbed

"Cancer Alley" because of the health risks imposed on the residents by the many known carcinogens that are released daily into the environment by polluting industries. The Toxic Release Inventory indicates there were 172,096,225 pounds of toxic materials released by industry into the air, water, and ground of Louisiana (see Table 12-3). In 1995, the last year for which data is available, Louisiana ranked second among the states in toxic releases of chemicals. When we control for population size, Louisiana residents are exposed to toxic chemical releases at about four times the national average (Kuehn 1998). As we would predict, the state's economic dependence on this industry makes it quite difficult for state officials to strictly regulate its environmental impacts. The state ranks forty-seventh in the proenvironmental character of its regulations (see Table 12-3).

These regulatory dynamics made it unsurprising that in 1996 Shintech Inc. would propose to build one of the largest polyvinyl chloride (PVC) and ethylene dichloride (EDC) production facilities in the United States in St. James Parish, Louisiana. First, location near other similar facilities made economic sense, as well as proximity to raw materials, railroads, and the Mississippi River. Second, the facility qualified for many of the economic incentives that Louisiana offers to attract and maintain petrochemical industry investment. Shintech's site was located in one of Louisiana's six Foreign Trade Zones, which make it possible to import materials into and export goods out of the United States without paying duties. The company also qualified for a ten-year state property tax exemption, low-cost electricity (granted to large industrial users), a tax credit of $2,500 for each job created (the facility was expected to create 250 permanent jobs), a rebate of state sales/use taxes on building materials and operation equipment. At the local level, St. James Parish offered $129.9 million in tax rebates and savings. Third, Shintech's production facility, which would empty 3.6 million gallons of waste water per day into the Mississippi and emit 600,000 pounds of toxic emissions into the air every year (the maximum allowable by law) would operate in the lax system of Louisiana environmental regulation (Templet 1997).

Ordinarily we would expect the Shintech facility to be environmentally troubling but expected given the dynamics of interstate competition and the political regime in Louisiana. However, the growing influence of the movement for environmental justice and Executive Order 12898 has cast the facility's future into doubt. The dispute also reveals the troubling conflicts between economic, environmental, and racial equity values that arise at the state level.

St. James Parish currently ranks third in the state for its total TRI (Toxic Release Inventory) releases. It is also a predominantly poor and black parish. The proposed site for the Shintech facility, Convent/Romeoville (the town is also known as Freetown because it was founded by former slaves) is even poorer than the rest of the parish: Unemployment is 62 percent, half the residents lack a high school diploma, and the per capita income is $7,259. Further, although the black population of St. James Parish as a whole is 50 percent (compared to 31 percent for the state of Louisiana), Convent/Romeo is 84 percent black (Kuehn 1998). Figure 12-1 graphs

Figure 12-1   Percentage of Nonwhite Population
in Communities with EDC/VC Facilities

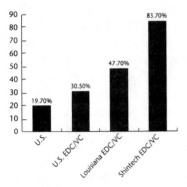

SOURCE: Adapted from Kuehn 1998.

the percentages of nonwhite residents in the communities surrounding facilities
that produce the same products as the Shintech plant. It illustrates that both for the
country as a whole, the state of Louisiana, and especially the area proposed for the
Shintech site, nonwhites are disproportionately exposed to the dangers of these
plants.

The conflict between environmental risk and economic opportunity has split residents of the parish and citizen groups have formed to support and oppose the facility. Although the state and local NAACP support plant construction, the NAACP
sponsored Environmental Justice Summit held in July 1997 opposed the plant. Gov.
Mike Foster, the Louisiana Department of Economic Development, and many state
leaders strongly support the plant on economic development grounds. Ordinarily,
the controversy would have ended when the Louisiana Department of Environmental Quality approved permits for the facility in May 1997.

However, citizen groups opposed to the facility had a new and powerful tool at
their disposal to challenge such decisions. With the aid of the Tulane Environmental Law Clinic, local groups petitioned the EPA to revoke the Shintech permits because of violations of Title V of the Clean Air Act (which requires all facilities that
emit toxic air pollution to receive a permit) and Title VI of the Civil Rights Act.
These petitions were granted by EPA Administrator Carol Browner, and Shintech
siting will now be adjudicated by the EPA under its new Title VI process. The decision was significant because it was the first time the EPA made a ruling based on violations of environmental justice standards. Browner wrote, "It is essential that
minority and low-income communities not be disproportionately subjected to environmental hazards" (cited in Payne 1997). So, although in the past only technical
mistakes would have triggered EPA intervention, Executive Order 12898 means that
the failure to consider racial equity is now sufficient grounds to halt the Shintech
siting process.

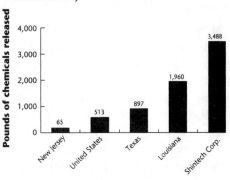

Figure 12-2 Toxic Releases per Job in the Chemical Industry

Although the outcome of this dispute is in doubt, the aftermath of the EPA intervention further illustrates the dynamics of state environmental regulation we have been exploring. As Peterson's arguments suggest, in a state such as Louisiana, which has chosen to pursue polluting industries as part of its economic development strategy, elected officials fear that they will be held accountable for any economic downturn that may result from attempts to regulate these industries. Governor Foster and several state legislators denounced both the Tulane Environmental Law Clinic's involvement and the EPA decision as hampering industrial development and going against the "public will." Shintech, although remaining committed to the St. James Parish site, is threatening horizontal exit by revealing it is being "courted" by other states and localities that want the facility built in their jurisdictions. Figure 12-2 provides a graphic view of the trade-offs made by states such as Louisiana in their pursuit of economic development. It shows that, on average, in the United States there are 513 pounds of toxic chemicals released into the air for each job in the chemical industry. In contrast, in New Jersey, a state that has lost petrochemical investment to Louisiana, the figure is much lower—65 pounds. Texas and Louisiana, states that have pursued the chemical industry, at least partially through a cooperative environmental regulatory regime, had 897 and 1,960 pounds per job.

At the same time, by creating new alliances between civil rights and environmental groups, the movement for environmental justice has increased the strength of latent groups who oppose risky and potentially inequitable developmental policies. The result is likely to be increasing contestation of environmental regulations at the state and local level, especially in states such as Louisiana with both fragile economies dependent on industrial manufacturing and sizeable minority populations who have been the victims of environmental racism. We now turn to considerations of the two other kinds of state regulatory policies described in Table 12-2.

CLIENT POLITICS IN THE STATES: STABILITY
AND CHANGE IN GOVERNMENT REGULATION

Most "traditional" areas of state regulation fall into the client politics cell of Wilson's typology (Table 12-2). In this section I focus on policies such as those involved in the licensing of professions, the regulation of the insurance and banking industries, and various forms of economic promotions and subsidies designed to improve the position of a state's industries. Although some benefits of this type of regulation are enjoyed by the general public (for example, protection from incompetent doctors or lawyers), most affect a concentrated group, such as a particular industry (for example, banking) or profession (as in the licensing of pharmacists). Such benefits can come in the form of direct subsidies, limited market entry for rivals and substitute products, or direct price fixing to ensure a profit. The costs fall on the general public in the form of higher prices, limited competition, lack of alternative producers, and, of course, higher taxes to pay for the maintenance of the government's regulatory apparatus. Every state has at least ten professional licensing boards, and some have as many as forty. These boards regulate a wide range of professions: television repairs, midwives, lightening rod sales people (in New Hampshire), and tattoo artists (in Hawaii). In addition, many states prohibit advertising of the prices of prescription drugs, eyeglasses, or hearing aids. The result is that consumers in many states pay higher prices for these regulated goods and services: "In Texas, where price advertising is allowed, single-vision eyeglasses sell for $20; in California, where a price blackout exists, the same glasses cost $60" (Weidenbaum 1977, 163).

Well-organized groups can readily obtain beneficial regulation. Although professional licensing is one of the oldest forms of regulation (the average state licenses thirty-seven occupations) and despite many states' attempts to limit the number of licensed occupations, the number of groups requesting—and receiving—this type of regulation is actually on the increase (Roederer 1980, 480–481). Opposition to such regulation is unlikely to be felt by legislators and regulators, because each individual usually bears only a small portion of the overall cost and thus has no incentive to organize against it.

State regulation of the insurance industry provides excellent examples of the dynamics of client politics and the ways in which a changing balance of interest group power can sometimes alter the basic structure of state regulation. The 6,000 companies that make up the insurance industry constitute one of the most economically significant industries regulated by the states (Warren 1992). State agencies oversee the financial soundness of companies, the fairness of the industry's trade practices, and the rates charged for insurance. Life insurance companies have assets of more than $200 billion. The investment of these assets provides one quarter of all nonfarm mortgages, one-third of all farm mortgages, and nearly three-quarters of all outside capital borrowed by American industry (Orren 1974, 15). Like the banking industry, life insurance has been regulated since the early nineteenth century. Initially, state governments attempted to control the use of the enormous resources of the insurance companies. Strict regulation of company investments was a common feature of early state control over the industry. By such regulations state governments sought to ensure that the profits generated by state-chartered insurance companies would remain within the state.

The insurance companies eventually rebelled at states' interference with what they regarded as a private area of corporate activity. Organizing into powerful trade associations (for example, the Chamber of Life Insurance, created in 1866), the industry pressed, as early as the 1860s, for federal regulation of the industry. In the opinion of trade association organizers, the federal government was more likely than state governments to be sympathetic to and easily influenced by the insurance industry. Although this threat of vertical exit failed to change the industry's regulatory arena, it did manage to establish the practice of exploiting the system of federalism. This strategy is based on the idea that states would prefer to moderate their regulations than lose the tax revenue and state jobs created by state regulation. Thus, the industry has been astute at taking advantage of the peculiarities of regulation in a federal system.

The industry's strategy of threatening to move the locus of regulatory authority was endangered in 1944 when the Supreme Court ruled that insurance was, in fact, interstate commerce and therefore subject to federal regulation. If allowed to stand, such a ruling would have made it impossible for the insurance industry to continue to take advantage of the system of federalism. This seeming setback for the industry, however, was reversed in 1949 by congressional action in the McCarran–Ferguson Act. This act—strongly supported by the industry—returned the regulatory authority to the states. As the political scientist Karen Orren (1974) pointed out, the situation has provided a good deal of political leverage for the industry. She noted that "the simple existence of a federal alternative creates an immediate vulnerability of state officials to the strictures and demands of the industry—in this case a vulnerability enhanced by the long history of constitutional uncertainty and the present probationary status of state regulation" (1974, 35).

As long as regulation remains at the state level, insurance companies are able to prevent the passage of onerous legislation in a particular state by threatening to move. Indeed, companies have done more than simply threaten to move from a state. Twenty-nine insurance companies left Texas after regulations were passed that restricted their freedom of investment. After the passage of reforms in Wisconsin, twenty-three companies left (Orren 1974, 36); combined, they held almost half of the life insurance in these states. Such interstate mobility also pressures states to adopt the favorable regulations passed in other states: If they do not, they risk corporate moves to more permissive states.

According to Orren, despite early attempts by states to control the life insurance industry, the industry and its representatives have used the threat of mobility to hinder effective regulation and to capture the regulatory process. In such a regulator–regulated relationship, the much-vaunted benefits of regulation disappear. A study by the General Accounting Office (GAO) analyzed the costs and benefits of state regulation of the insurance industry, concluding that regulations make very little difference in the behavior of insurance companies. The report stated that "the type of regulatory laws does not appear to be related to the aggregate cost of insurance" (GAO 1979, 79). The reason is simple: The regulated industry has captured the regulatory agencies, despite the formal imposition of "regulation in the public interest," so the industry is indistinguishable from its unregulated equivalents in other states. The regulators' capture was comprehensive. Only two of the seventeen states in which the GAO did extensive fieldwork (Massachusetts and Texas) actually did their own independent analyses to determine if industry requests for rate increases are justified. In the other fifteen states that were examined, requests for increases were routinely approved—solely on the basis of the insurance companies' own analyses (U.S. Senate 1980, 13–14).

Not only do captured state regulatory agencies fail to guard against unjustifiable rate hikes, they similarly fail in fulfilling other aspects of their mandates. For example, one of the traditional rationales for industrial regulation is to compensate for consumer ignorance. Despite this, the GAO concluded, "Most state insurance departments do not actively attempt to correct the problems of consumers' lack of information" (GAO 1979, 95). They found that state departments generally do not act to protect consumers from arbitrary termination or denial of insurance, nor do they assist in comparison shopping, nor do they effectively analyze and act on consumer complaints about insurance companies.

Little was done in response to the 1979 GAO report, however, and the issue of lax regulation surfaced again in the 1990s, following the failure of several large companies (Quint 1994; Warren 1992). As in the past, one response to lax state regulation was the threat of federal regulatory preemption. Legislation introduced by Rep. John D. Dingell (D-Mich.) called for the federal government to assume regulatory authority, but strong industry opposition led to its defeat. In response to the threat of federal takeover and the consequent loss of regulatory autonomy for the states and industry, the National Association of Insurance Commissioners developed a set of model laws that states would have to adopt to receive accreditation for their regulatory structure. Although supposedly a way to ensure more effective regulation, there is much question about the model laws' effectiveness and purpose. The Center for Insurance Research accuses the commissioners of doing very little in their model laws to improve the practices of insurance companies (Quint 1994, D1). Indeed, fifteen states remain unaccredited, including Connecticut and New Jersey, the homes of several of the nation's largest insurance companies. New York, long recognized as the leader in effective regulation, was stripped of its accreditation in 1993. According to a new GAO study, the National Association of Commissioners has used inconsistent standards for its accreditation process, and there remain large questions about whether this approach can work to regulate the industry effectively.

On the basis of the available evidence, we must conclude that state regulation— at least in many of the "traditional" regulatory arenas—is remarkably ineffective. In the words of the acting deputy insurance commissioner of Texas, who resigned because of the state's inability to discipline the industry in an effective manner: "We do not regulate the insurance companies, the companies regulate us" (quoted in Hayes 1989, 25).

Overall, then, we find that state regulation of the traditional regulatory arenas is remarkably ineffective and seemingly as expensive as federal regulation would be. The expense and apparent shortcomings raise two significant questions. First, why isn't state regulation more responsive to the interests of consumers? Second, given the shortcomings of state regulation, why has federal regulation failed to take its place? Both questions may be answered by examining the dynamics of state regulatory policy making in regard to the insurance industry.

The absence of change in the regulation of insurance and the generally proindustry outcomes of regulatory politics are explained by the intimate relationship between the regulators and the regulated that is at the heart of client politics. First, many individuals move back and forth between jobs in the insurance industry and the office of the insurance commissioner. This "revolving door" is a classic attribute of the captured regulatory agency. Although such an exchange of personnel is not necessarily pernicious, individuals who have worked (or plan to work) for the insurance industry are likely to learn the insurance business from a proindustry perspective and take that perspective to their positions in the regulatory agency. Second, the insurance commissioner's office, because of a generally small budget and staff, must rely on the insurance industry itself for the information necessary to its regulatory decisions. Third, the insurance industry is a potent lobbying force in most state legislatures and a source of large campaign contributions. In addition to its economic clout, its influence is undoubtedly strengthened by the large number of legislators whose backgrounds are in insurance. In fact, as discussed in Chapter 4, the insurance industry was ranked sixth in strength among forty interests at the state level. This is up seven ranks since 1990. Fourth, the avowedly technical nature of many regulatory decisions affecting insurance regulation makes participation in decision making extremely difficult for anyone not familiar with the industry. Hence those with insurance backgrounds tend to dominate the process. Fifth, although the industry is a well-organized lobbying force, no organized opposition usually exists. When such organized opposition does emerge, insurance regulation can change quite dramatically.

If insurance regulation is truly captured, all the state's citizens may consequently pay higher insurance rates, lack necessary information about policies, and be subject to inaccurate actuarial decisions. However, these costs are not readily calculable by the consumer and are not strikingly large for the average person. Hence, although the aggregate costs may be extremely large, individuals have little incentive to spend the requisite time and money to organize insurance consumers. Furthermore, even if such an organization were founded, it would be unlikely to have the resources of the interest groups representing the insurance industry.

Client politics are not, however, always stable. The relationship between captured regulator and captor regulatee may be changed if the costs imposed on the general population increase to the point at which organizations representing their diffuse interests are formed or if some specific event such as a political scandal focuses public attention on the costs of regulation.

This is exactly what happened to automobile insurance in California and New Jersey during the 1980s. Dramatically escalating rates for automobile insurance increased the costs to consumers to the point that client politics gave way to entrepreneurial regulatory activity. Consumer groups did form, and the costs of insurance were so substantial that public consciousness reached a high-enough level to pass a ballot initiative forcing a substantial rollback of automobile insurance rates. This occurred despite expensive efforts by the insurance industry to discredit consumer efforts and confuse the issue by placing many of their own initiatives on the ballot in November 1988. However, the long-run effect of this consumer victory is in doubt: Insurance companies have both challenged the initiative in court and exercised the threat of exit by refusing to write or renew policies in other states that adopt such laws. After several years, there is evidence that California may, nevertheless, be able to succeed in controlling costs because of its large market and the consequently high exit costs for insurance companies ("Write-off" 1992). However, as long as the locus of regulatory authority is the states, the available options for smaller states are much more limited. This episode illustrates how difficult and rare it is to break out of the hold of client politics when the costs of regulation are imposed on a large latent group.

A far more serious challenge to the client politics of insurance regulation results from emerging conflicts between other powerful interest groups—especially those representing the legal and medical professions—involving the reform of health care, in general, and the costs of medical malpractice insurance, in particular.

INTEREST GROUP STRUGGLE: MEDICAL MALPRACTICE INSURANCE

When regulation bestows costs and benefits on concentrated and organized groups with conflicting interests, the dynamics of policy making differ from those of client politics. Because the interests of both kinds of groups are similarly affected by the decisions made by regulatory agencies, both kinds of groups can be expected to pressure legislators, governors, and regulators. As a consequence, in contrast to client politics, no single interest group is likely to capture the state agency. Moreover, because such groups tend to remain mobilized around issues directly and continuously affecting them, the pattern of policy making in such areas is one of persistent group struggle. Such ongoing and routinized conflict also contrasts sharply with the long periods of stable capture—broken only occasionally by an outburst of entrepreneurial activity—that are typical of client politics.

The analysis of regulatory politics involving interest groups is more complicated at the state than at the federal level. As in all regulatory politics, the outcome of regulatory decision making reflects the relative strength of the competing groups. Unlike the case of client politics, however, the potential for organizing competing groups affected by regulation is fairly equal. Thus interstate differences in the relative power of the groups determine the outcome of regulatory decision making.

To illustrate the interest group style of regulatory politics, I discuss debates about state regulation of medical malpractice insurance. This regulatory arena pits against each other powerful interest groups representing the medical profession, the legal profession, and the insurance industry.

Although the failure of Congress to enact sweeping national health care reform in 1994 was the focus of most media and popular attention, it is important to remember that this simply meant that the states would remain major players in such reform. Indeed, efforts funded lavishly by the insurance industry and medical profession to defeat health care reform (a much analyzed series of nationally shown advertisements—the "Harry and Louise" ads—that lampooned the supposed consequences of federal preemption) can be seen as a conscious attempt by these powerful interests to maintain the leverage they have in a system of state-controlled regulation. As would be expected, given the diversity of interest group strength among the major players in this arena, states have adopted a wide variety of programs and "virtually every state has looked at some type of reform in the early 1990s" (Buerger 1994, 568).

Although none of the health care reforms debated in Washington addresses the issue specifically, malpractice laws are an important reason for the rising costs of health care. Indeed, although most health care reform proposals aim to control costs by regulating the supply of and demand for health care services, "this ignores the body of medical malpractice law that will exist no matter how supply and demand are structured, and could result in more malpractice litigation as doctors will be forced to be cost-conscious in their treatments" (Frankel 1994, 1297).

During the 1980s, increasing jury awards for malpractice suits, dramatically escalating premiums for medical malpractice insurance, and the refusal of insurance companies to write policies in several states gave rise to what has been called a crisis in this line of insurance. My purpose in choosing this issue is to contrast the ways in which this insurance crisis differs from both the normal client politics of insurance regulation and the entrepreneurial politics of attempts to lower rates for auto insurance. Unlike the latter two cases, in which the costs of regulation fall on a diffuse latent group of difficult-to-organize consumers, in this case the potential costs and benefits of regulation fall on highly organized and powerful interests. In fact, as Chapter 4 reveals, these interests are among the most powerful at the state level: doctors (rated tenth), represented by the American Medical Association; lawyers (rated fourth), represented by bar associations; health care organizations, such as hospitals (rated fifth); and the insurance industry (rated sixth). The difference in the distribution of costs and benefits results in a very different style of state regulatory politics. Because interest groups are organized and sustained, regulation of malpractice insurance rates has become a visible and active arena of legislative action. The response to rapidly increased auto insurance rates was an isolated ballot initiative in California, but the crisis in medical malpractice insurance moved to the legislative agenda in many states: "Medical malpractice emerged as the most visible and probably most serious area of concern with the tort and insurance systems" (Blair and Makar 1988, 427).

When powerful interest groups bear the concentrated costs and benefits of regulation, it is to be expected that such issues will conform to the dynamics of pluralist politics. They will be placed on the legislative agenda, and outcomes will be a function of the relative power of the groups involved. Furthermore, because the balance of interest group power is likely to remain relatively constant, policy will be much more stable than when regulatory issues conform to the dynamics of entrepreneurial politics (as in the case of the ballot initiatives concerning auto insurance rates in California, in which the potential for dramatic policy change is present).

It is important to emphasize that there is no objectively correct explanation for, or solution to, the crisis of medical malpractice insurance. Indeed, there is no consensus that there even is a crisis. Although serving the public interest is often piously invoked as the goal of regulatory legislation, this is a difficult standard to define and of little use to regulators. The absence of such a standard makes policy making in this area a fully political exercise. The three organized interests involved offer differing and plausible explanations for the changes in malpractice insurance.

Both the legal and medical professions, in addition to blaming each other, criticized the insurance industry. Angoff (1988), a lawyer, argued that increased premiums are the result of collusion on the part of the insurance industry. Since the early 1980s, insurance companies have drastically cut premiums below actuarially sound levels. This was done to generate liquid assets that could be invested by insurance companies for high returns. Such premium cutting occurs, Angoff suggested, because insurance companies know that, through the collusive practices allowed under the McCarran–Ferguson Act, they will be able to raise rates above actuarially sound levels at some future date. This allows them to make up whatever short-falls may result from periods of declining premiums. The net result is that McCarran–Ferguson's antitrust exemptions (while limited in scope) serve to guarantee the profits of the industry and also lead to extreme swings in insurance premiums.

The insurance industry denied that collusion or the McCarran–Ferguson Act played any role in the crisis in medical malpractice. Clarke et al. (1987), for example, showed that this line of insurance behaved quite differently from almost any other line of property–casualty insurance: The increase in payouts because of increasing jury awards and the resulting increases in premiums were constant since the 1970s and did not vary with any swings in the business cycle. Clarke et al. (1987, 383–384) also showed that, despite dramatic increases in premiums, profits on this line of insurance have not risen. Hassan (1991, 74), in a study for Blue Cross-Blue Shield, found that "from 1978 through 1986 . . . medical malpractice insurance ranked medium in underwriting profitability compared with other lines of insurance, and during 1985–86 it was the least profitable insurance business." Finally, both Clarke et al. and Hassan argued that the low barriers to entry in the insurance industry make it unlikely that any sort of collusive pricing could long be effective (see also Blair and Makar 1988; Lefkin 1988).

Instead, the insurance industry argued that the true problem was increased litigation and dramatically escalating jury awards. The solution is tort reform: The industry continues to support state and federal laws that specify awards for certain kinds of injuries and cap awards for pain and suffering. In support of such reform, an insurance trade association ran an advertisement in the *Washington Post* under the banner headline "There's a Price to Be Paid for Excessive Liability Awards in Our Courts. Guess Who's Going to Pay It?" In part the answer was as follows:

> The word "tort" means any civil wrong. And once our tort laws protected anyone injured by the negligence of another. But over the years courts have eroded the definition of negligence to the point that it's almost meaningless. The result is a landslide of litigation that costs society billions but adds nothing to our gross national product. And as the tort system recycles its enormous costs among all of us, they'll show up in the prices we pay for products, in medical bills and insurance premiums, in taxes and inflation. We may see a day when doctors can't afford to treat the sick, municipalities won't be able to provide needed services and manufacturers won't be able to make critical products. ("There's a Price" 1985, A16)

It is not surprising that the medical profession has agreed with this assessment of the causes of the rise in malpractice premiums, and the American Medical Association has pushed for reforms of the tort system; also not surprising, these reforms have been rejected by the American Bar Association ("Malpractice Mess" 1986, 74). To complete the picture, both the insurance industry and the legal profession have blamed the rise in premiums on the medical profession, which, they say, has been unwilling to regulate itself by imposing more effective procedures for rooting out the small percentage of incompetent physicians ("Malpractice Mess" 1986, 74).

This issue has been fought out in the legislatures of several states with varying results. Responding to pressure from the insurance industry and the medical profession, Colorado, Florida, and Washington enacted extensive tort reform in 1986. These states capped noneconomic damages and otherwise dramatically limited the ability of plaintiffs to collect damages. Still, despite such reforms premiums did not decline in these states (Angoff 1988). Indeed, after reforms were enacted, the Hartford Insurance Company announced that it would no longer issue medical malpractice policies in Colorado. Angoff (1988, 398 n.10) further supported the case for collusion on the part of insurance companies when he noted that extensive reforms in municipal liability laws during the late 1970s in Iowa, New Mexico, and Pennsylvania failed to reduce premiums for governments in these states.

In 1986 West Virginia, responding to a coalition of interest groups, enacted legislation that both reformed the tort system (by capping damage awards) and increased regulatory oversight of insurance premiums (by requiring disclosure of certain types of financial information by insurance companies and prohibiting midterm cancellation of policies). Reaction to this reform is instructive in evaluating the relative power of the contending interest groups. Unlike California in the case of automobile insurance regulation, West Virginia is not so large a market that companies cannot exercise the horizontal exit option. Three carriers of malpractice insurance announced that, because of the weakness of tort reform and severity of the new regulations, they would cancel all policies in the state the day before the new law was to go into effect. Responding to this threat of exit, the state legislature came back into session and both strengthened tort reform and lessened the amount of financial disclosure required. Interestingly enough, West Virginia sued to prevent such a boycott and the courts ruled that McCarran–Ferguson did not protect such behaviors and that, therefore, collusive attempts to withdraw from a state were violations of the Sherman Antitrust Act (Angoff 1988, 402–403). Nevertheless, the threat of exit was still credible enough to force modification of the reform legislation.

Based on our identification of the costs and benefits of regulation as the critical determinant of state policy, we would expect that regulatory reform would be dependent on the balance of interest group power in each state. We would also expect that attention to this issue would be more sustained and incremental than is the case with the entrepreneurial politics of automobile rate reform. By 1988, fourteen states had adopted some form of damage cap on malpractice suits (Javitt and Lu 1992). However, only two states, Florida and Virginia, went further by adopting no-fault medical compensation systems, although similar systems have been proposed in the legislatures of New York and Utah (Jost 1994).

As the West Virginia case illustrates, the insurance industry has an advantage not held by the medical and legal professions—a credible threat of exit. It is much easier for a national insurance industry to refuse to write policies in a specific state than it is for doctors or lawyers to pick up their practices and move to another state. This gives the industry the same sort of advantage when dealing with state policy makers as seen in the case of state efforts to attract industrial development in Chapter 13. In both cases, state governments must provide a favorable climate for businesses that can choose to locate in any of several states.

CONCLUSION

Although the locus of policy making has often shifted between levels of government, political interference in the economy has been an important feature of American political life since the founding of the Republic. And although specific regulatory policies differ considerably from one state to the next, three factors that seem to determine variation in the content of these policies have been identified. First, regulatory policy is a function of the ability of the individuals affected by regulation to organize. The propensity of individuals to organize—to become an interest group—is determined by their perceptions of the magnitude of the costs and benefits bestowed on them by regulation. In turn, the configuration of the interest groups that mobilize around an issue determines the resultant style of regulatory politics: interest group struggle, regulatory capture, or entrepreneurial crusading.

Second, both the enactment and the implementation of regulations are affected by the political power of organized groups and by their ability to stay organized.

Considerable interstate variation exists in both the political clout and the staying power of interest groups. Regulatory politics in a particular area may shift between styles as the perceived costs or benefits of regulation change and as groups wax and wane in strength.

Third, the redistributive implications of regulatory policies constrain the ability of state regulators to enforce those policies. To the extent that the trend continues of delegating regulatory authority to the states, enforcement will be compromised, especially in the most economically hard-pressed states.

Fourth, the balance of regulatory responsibility between state and federal governments has important implications for the kinds of policies we are likely to see. As the federal role declines, interstate variability in policy will increase. Of course, this variation will be a partial function of the constellation of political and economic forces in specific states. However, the outcomes of state policies are constrained, in ways that federal policy is not, by the structural reality of the increased interstate competition for economic growth. Thus states are limited by the need to foster developmental policies and avoid redistributive policies. The balance between these two imperatives at the state level will increasingly determine the economic and physical well-being of most Americans.

REFERENCES

Angoff, Jay. 1988. "Insurance against Competition: How the McCarran–Ferguson Act Raises Prices and Profits in the Property–Casualty Insurance Industry." *Yale Journal on Regulation* 5:397–416.

Bernstein, Marver H. 1955. *Regulating Business by Independent Commission.* Princeton, N.J.: Princeton University Press.

Blair, Roger D., and Scott D. Makar. 1988. "The Structure of Florida's Medical Malpractice Insurance Market: If It Ain't Broke, Don't Fix It." *Yale Journal on Regulation* 5:427–454.

Buerger, Elizabeth. 1994. "State-Health-Care Reform Initiatives." *Book of the States, 1994–95.* Lexington, Ky.: Council of State Governments.

Bullard, Robert D. 1994. "Environmental Justice for All." In *Unequal Protection: Environmental Justice and Communities of Color.* Edited by Robert D. Bullard. San Francisco: Sierra Club Books.

Chavis, Benjamin F., Jr. 1994 "Preface." *Unequal Protection: Environmental Justice and Communities of Color.* Edited by Robert D. Bullard. San Francisco: Sierra Club Books.

Clarke, Richard C., Frederick Warren-Boulton, David D. Smith, and Marilyn J. Simon. 1987. "Sources of the Crisis in Liability Insurance: An Economic Analysis." *Yale Journal on Regulation* 5:367–396.

"CMA Says States Can Handle Chemical Wastes." 1980. *Chemical and Engineering News* 58:7.

Crombie, Paul. 1997. *Tax and Business Incentives.* Baton Rouge: Louisiana Department of Economic Development.

Cushman, John. 1998. "Environmental Racism Not the Issue at This Point, Legislators Say." *New York Times,* March 2, A1.

Derthick, Martha, and Paul J. Quirk. 1985. *The Politics of Deregulation.* Washington, D.C.: Brookings Institution.

Elkins, Stephen L. 1987. *City and Regime in the American Republic.* Chicago: University of Chicago Press.

Environmental Defense Fund. 1998. *The Chemical Scorecard.* New York: Author.

Environmental Protection Agency. 1998. *Environmental Justice Fact Sheet.* Washington, D.C.: Government Printing Office.

Ferman, Barbara. 1997. *Challenging the Growth Machine.* Lawrence: University of Kansas Press.

Frankel, Jonathan J. 1994. "Medical Malpractice Law and Health Care Cost Containment: Lessons for Reformers from the Clash of Cultures." *Yale Law Journal* 103:1297–1331.

General Accounting Office. 1979. *Issues and Needed Improvements in State Regulation of the Insurance Business.* Washington, D.C.: U.S. Government Printing Office.

Goetz, Stephan J., Richard C. Ready, and Brad Stone. 1996. "U.S. Economic Growth vs. Environmental Conditions." *Growth and Change* 27:97–110.

Harris, Richard A., and Sidney M. Milkis. 1989. *The Politics of Regulatory Change.* New York: Oxford University Press.

Hassan, Mahmud. 1991. "How Profitable Is Medical Malpractice Insurance?" *Inquiry* 28:74.

Hayes, Thomas C. 1989. "Texas Insurance Regulator Quits, Calling System Lax." *New York Times,* January 17.

Huntington, Samuel P. 1952. "The Marasmus of the ICC: The Commission, the Railroads, and the Public Interest." *Yale Law Journal* 61:467–509.

Javitt, Gail, and Elaine Lu. 1992. "Capping the Crisis: Medical Malpractice and Tort Reform." *Law, Medicine, and Health Care* 20:258–261.

Jost, Kenneth. 1994. "Fault-free Malpractice: Two More States Propose Testing the Waters in a Controversial Approach to Medical Injury Claims." *ABA Journal* 80:46.

Kriz, Margaret. 1994. "Cleaner Than Clean?" *National Journal,* April 23.

Kuehn, Robert. 1998. *The Shintech Case.* Unpublished manuscript, Tulane Environmental Law Clinic, New Orleans.

Lefkin, Peter A. 1988. "Shattering Some Myths on the Insurance Liability Crisis: A Comment on the Article by Clarke, Warren-Boulton, Smith, and Simon." *Yale Journal on Regulation* 5:417–426.

Litan, Robert E., and William D. Nordhaus. 1983. *Reforming Federal Regulation.* New Haven, Conn.: Yale University Press.

"The Malpractice Mess." 1986. *Newsweek,* February 17.

"Many Harried S&L's, Irked by States' Rules, Seek Federal Charters." 1981. *Wall Street Journal,* August 13.

Nadel, Mark V. 1975. "Consumerism: A Coalition in Flux." *Policy Studies Journal* 4:31–35.

Office of the Vice President. 1993. *Accompanying Report of the National Performance Review.* Washington, D.C.: Government Printing Office.

Okun, Arthur. 1976. *Equality vs. Efficiency: The Big Tradeoff.* Washington, D.C.: Brookings Institution.

Olson, Mancur. 1965. *The Logic of Collective Action.* Cambridge, Mass.: Harvard University Press.

Orren, Karen. 1974. *Corporate Power and Social Change: The Politics of the Life Insurance Industry.* Baltimore: Johns Hopkins University Press.

Payne, Henry. 1997. "'Environmental Justice' Kills Jobs for the Poor." *Wall Street Journal,* August 16.

Peterson, Paul E. 1981. *City Limits.* Chicago: University of Chicago Press.

Peterson, Paul E. 1995. *The Price of Federalism.* Washington, D.C.: Brookings Institution.

Quint, Michael. 1994. "A Battle over Regulating Insurers." *New York Times,* July 29.

Rabe, Barry. 1986. *Fragmentation and Integration in State Environmental Management.* Washington, D.C.: Conservation Foundation.

Raloff, Janet. 1979. "Abandoned Dumps: A Chemical Legacy." *Science News,* May, 348–351.

Roederer, Doug. 1980. "State Regulation of Occupations and Professions." *The Book of the States, 1980–81.* Lexington, Ky.: Council of State Governments.

Ringquist, Evan. 1993. *Environmental Protection at the State Level.* Armonk, N.Y.: M. E. Sharpe.

———. 1998. "Equity and the Distribution of Environmental Risk: The Case of TRI Facilities," *Social Science Quarterly,* forthcoming.

Sherrill, Robert. 1990. "The Looting Decade." *Nation,* October 27.

Stanfield, Rochelle L. 1994. "Thanks a Lot for Nothing, Washington." *National Journal,* March 26.

Steingraber, Sandra. 1997. *Living Downstream : An Ecologist Looks at Cancer and the Environment.* New York: Addison-Wesley.

Stigler, George. 1975. *The Citizen and the State.* Chicago: University of Chicago Press.

Stone, Clarence N. 1989. *Regime Politics: Governing Atlanta, 1946–1988.* Lawrence: University of Kansas Press.

Switzer, Jacqueline Vaughn. 1994. *Environmental Politics.* New York: St. Martin's Press.

Templet, Paul. 1997. "Industrial Development in Louisiana: Shintech Case Study." *People First: Developing Sustainable Communities* (March):27–32.

Tesh, Sylvia, and Bruce A. Williams. 1996. "Identity Politics, Disinterested Politics, and Environmental Justice," *Polity* (Spring):285–305.

"There's a Price to Be Paid for Excessive Liability Awards." 1985. *Washington Post,* December 17.

U.S. Senate, Committee of the Judiciary. 1980. *Hearings before the Subcommittee on Antitrust, Monopoly and Business Rights on State Insurance Regulation.* 97th Cong. Washington, D.C.: U.S. Government Printing Office.

Vogel, David. 1981. "The 'New' Social Regulation in Historical and Comparative Perspective." In *Regulation in Perspective,* edited by Thomas K. McCraw. Cambridge, Mass.: Harvard University Press.

Warren, William T. 1992. "Wrestling over Insurance Regulation." *State Legislatures* 18:35–39.

Weidenbaum, Murray L. 1977. *Business, Government, and the Public.* Englewood Cliffs, N.J.: Prentice-Hall.

Weisbrod, Burton A., Joel F. Handler, and Neil K. Komesar. 1977. *Public Interest Law: An Economic and Institutional Analysis.* Berkeley: University of California Press.

Williams, Bruce A., and Albert R. Matheny. 1984. "Testing Theories of Social Regulation: Hazardous Waste Regulation in the American States." *Journal of Politics* 46:428–458.

———. 1995. *Democracy, Dialogue, and Social Regulation: The Contested Languages of Environmental Disputes.* New Haven, Conn.: Yale University Press.

Wilson, James Q. 1980. "The Politics of Regulation." In *The Politics of Regulation,* edited by James Q. Wilson. New York: Basic Books.

"Write-off: Insurance in California." 1992. *Economist,* July 11, 76.

SUGGESTED READINGS

Bullard, Robert D., ed. *Unequal Protection: Environmental Justice and Communities of Color.* San Francisco: Sierra Club Books, 1994. Excellent collection of writings, by academics and activists, that chronicle the movement for environmental justice. The book contains case studies of environmental justice disputes, overviews of the history of the movement, and suggestions for policy making.

Hartz, Louis. *Economic Policy and Democratic Thought: Pennsylvania, 1776–1860.* Cambridge, Mass.: Harvard University Press, 1948. The classic study of the relation between the development of capitalism and democratic government in the early republic.

Rabe, Barry. *Fragmentation and Integration in State Environmental Management.* Washington, D.C.: Conservation Foundation, 1986. An excellent overview of the development of state environmental regulation with a particular emphasis on state attempts to develop more coherent approaches to the interaction between different types of pollution.

Steingraber, Sandra. *Living Downstream: An Ecologist Looks at Cancer and the Environment.* New York: Addison-Wesley, 1997. A well-written and completely engrossing study of the effects that local environmental hazards are likely to have on human health. Steingraber shows how the latest nationwide data (TRI and Tumor Registry) available through Citizen-Right-to-Know legislation increases our understanding of the implications of environmental pollution. She also provides excellent material on how to compile this information for your own community.

Szasz, Andrew. *Ecopopulism: Toxic Waste and the Movement for Environmental Justice.* Minneapolis: University of Minnesota Press, 1994. This book explores the ways in which the shift of focus in the environmental movement to the state and local level has helped to radicalize and reinvigorate this movement. The author is especially strong on demonstrating the connection between local environmental activism and broader issues of political participation and democracy.

Williams, Bruce A., and Albert R. Matheny. *Democracy, Dialogue, and Social Regulation: The Contested Languages of Environmental Disputes.* New Haven, Conn.: Yale University Press, 1995. The authors examine the dynamics of environmental disputes, primarily at the state and local levels, and the competing languages used by citizens, policy makers, experts, and interest groups as they struggle over public policy. They also analyze the ways in which issues of race and gender affect the ability of various groups to influence environmental policy.

CHAPTER 13

Economic Development and Infrastructure Policy

MARTIN SAIZ AND SUSAN E. CLARKE

Not long ago, national borders protected state and local economies from the challenges of global capitalism. Today, with the help of free trade agreements and advanced by a revolution in worldwide communications, global competition is transforming the economy of the United States. Industries that were thought of as state or national assets commonly migrate across borders and oceans. Parts suppliers and production subcontractors to domestic industries are often located in faraway lands. During the past decade, states with mature industries, such as those in the Northeast and Great Lakes regions, experienced an increasing number of plant closings. From a national perspective, such changes need not be worrisome. If economic growth means that one region prospers while another languishes, the result is merely short-term unemployment. What really matters is the ability of the economy as a whole to absorb displaced workers into new or growing industries. But from the perspective of state and local government, plant closings can be devastating. The loss of a single manufacturer can result in the collapse of an entire commercial network because the service and ancillary industries were extensions of the base enterprise and depended on it. If the lost jobs are not replaced, the wealth and social health of the community will soon erode. Given such prospects, it is no wonder that each year the state and local governments spend billions of dollars on economic development programs designed to grow, attract, and retain business.

Yet there is little agreement among scholars that economic development programs actually work—meaning that they save industries from failing, keep businesses from moving, or cause stagnant economies to grow (for a recent review see Donahue 1997).

Thus there is some controversy about whether economic development programs are good public policy. Some scholars argue that offering subsidies to businesses leads to competition among state and local governments and results in bidding wars that soon spiral out of control. Others argue that a focus on local economic development leads to the efficient production of public goods such as roads and other services.

Scholars do agree that the mere existence of such policies creates a dilemma for public officials. Even if local officials suspect that economic development policies are not particularly effective, it can be difficult for elected officials to ignore the pleas of a distressed community to offer subsidies when a locally established company is threatening to relocate. Similarly, it is difficult to resist pressures not to offer incentives and miss the chance to claim credit for creating, retaining, or attracting a significant economic enterprise. Although it is not clear that economic development policies work, it is equally unclear that such expenditures are a waste. Considering the uncertainties together with the political benefits, it is likely that public officials will feel compelled to support economic development programs. The challenge for governments and policy analysts is to find a way for public officials to respond to the dilemma of economic development with fiscal integrity.

The sheer diversity and complexity of recent state economic development programs and the emergent global marketplace in which states must compete prompt us to rethink our assumptions about this policy arena. Four dimensions merit special attention in this chapter: (1) the significance of federalism and globalization in shaping state economic development options; (2) the changing definitions of the problems that emphasize investment in the infrastructure, locational incentives, and entrepreneurial solutions to state economic development issues; (3) periodic shifts in orientation of state policy among conventional cost-reduction, smoke-stack-chasing strategies, and more entrepreneurial policy approaches; and (4) the enduring debate over the effectiveness of state economic development policies in influencing state growth and development. These issues signal realignments in the politics of making state economic development policy in the coming decade.

FEDERALISM, GLOBALIZATION, AND STATE ECONOMIC DEVELOPMENT POLICY

The goal of national economic policy is to promote aggregate employment, production, and purchasing power. In contrast, the objective of state economic development policy is to promote investment in a particular location. Unlike national governments, individual states cannot control the movement of raw materials, capital, or workers across their borders. They cannot affect the supply of money or the rate of interest on borrowed funds. Most important, state governments cannot command business to invest. They can only hope to induce investment by offering businesses subsidies or other incentives. The incentives, it is hoped, can stimulate new investment that would otherwise not be made in that location. In theory a modest stimulus on the part of the state government can be of consequence to a local economy if the investment sets in motion a multiplier effect—creating new jobs in the subsidized and other businesses, diversifying the local economy, and ultimately increasing the economic well-being of state citizens.

Federalism and State Policy Choices

When analyzing state policies designed to promote economic growth, most scholars emphasize the constraints on policy making imposed by the system of federalism. The decentralized American federal system places many responsibilities on state and local governments but provides few national resources to help meet these responsibilities. As a result, American states compete with each other for private investment, bringing jobs and tax revenues to the state. Given this dependency on local sources of revenue and interstate economic competition, many analyses of state economic development policies reflect the themes best articulated by Paul Peterson (1981). Peterson argued that business and residents are attracted to places with the most favorable ratio of taxes paid to services received. In Peterson's view, states have a common interest in policies that promote economic activity to employ residents and to generate tax revenues. States need these revenues to provide good services at reasonable cost to create attractive locations for businesses and households. States thus enact development policies to enhance their economic position relative to other states and they do so under the implicit threat that residents and firms will leave if they perceive that the benefit–tax ratio is no longer favorable.

When states offer incentives to retain and attract companies, they do so under conditions of uncertainty. State governments are uncertain of the deals being offered by other states as well as the needs of the firms they are trying to attract or keep from leaving. This puts every state government in the position of having to act without sufficient information. Because most state governments pursue this strategy and few dare disengage from the competition, they often promise more than is wise or necessary to secure the deal, often with no guarantee that the benefits will outweigh the costs. State incentive packages ratchet upward because only the firm knows what it really needs, and states do not want to make a bid that is too low to attract the firm (Jones and Bachelor 1986). As a result, businesses can play states off each other to get the best deal; state and local governments take part in this bidding war because there are political advantages to winning the investment competition with other states (Wolman 1988; Wolman and Spitzley, 1996). This competitive environment of bidding up incentives across states sometimes resembles the spiral of decisions in an arms race (Hanson 1993; Peretz 1986). More than thirty-five states, for example, competed in 1993 to be the site for Mercedes-Benz's new sports-utility vehicle plant. With Mercedes-Benz in the "auctioneer's" seat, states presented custom-tailored incentive packages to entice the German firm to bring an estimated 1,500 jobs to their state. Alabama's $300 million winning package included tax breaks, promises to buy the vehicles for the state fleet, payments to workers while in training, commitments to develop the new site, and construction of a welcome center for visitors to the plant, as well as more traditional infrastructure development. The estimated price tag of $169,000 per job dwarfs Tennessee's $26,000 per job costs in winning the famous thirty-state bidding war over the Saturn automotive plant in the 1980s and Kentucky's $50,000 per job costs in attracting a Toyota plant (Mahtesian 1994).

Periodically, public officials grow weary of the competition and attempt to establish truces in these bidding wars. In 1993 the National Governors' Association adopted voluntary guidelines on tax breaks and subsidies aimed at winding down the bidding for private investment (Wyatt 1994). More recently, the Maryland legislature attached a "cease-fire" provision to a job-creation tax credit bill directing the governor to negotiate an agreement with his counterparts in Delaware, North Carolina, Pennsylvania, Virginia, and West Virginia (Mahtesian 1996). Several attempts have been made to get the U.S. Congress to intervene. The Federal Reserve Bank of Minneapolis published a report urging Congress to exercise its regulatory authority over interstate commerce to end competitive business recruitment. As of September 1998, eleven states have passed resolutions urging Congress to do something about states luring businesses from other states. Representative David Minge (D-Minn.) introduced the Distorting Subsidies Limitation Act in 1997, but the bill failed to attract the minimum number of sponsors. Truces between states are likely to be unstable and calls for congressional action are often short-lived. With few incentives for cooperation, governors continuously sacrifice collaborative strategies to respond to pressures to compete in a globalized economy.

Globalization and State Policy Choices

The emergent global economy challenges conventional assumptions about state development processes. It is clear that economic growth and development processes now must be considered in the context of larger trends. Growth no longer can be captured within politically bounded and relatively closed economies. Investment flows and decision makers are international rather than local or national. The most salient features of globalization include the greater mobility of capital, a new international division of labor with many production jobs moving outside the United States, the elimination of national trade barriers, new information and transportation technologies, and global competition increasingly driven by innovation rather than the costs of land, labor, and capital (Reich 1991). These features alter the investment priorities of firms and the policy options of states.

State policy makers are faced with the need to make their communities competitive in a global arena, in which increasingly mobile capital and new telecommunications technologies make locations appear interchangeable to firms. The traditional interjurisdictional competition for investment takes on a new dimension when the costs of production are lower outside the United States and all states are potential losers. Even regional economic recovery does not necessarily solve these problems. In the recent resurgence of the old manufacturing states, neither the number of new jobs nor their wage rates match those lost during the earlier decline. Today, regional recovery creates "islands of success" (Stokes 1994) but leaves behind communities and workers not able to find a niche in the global marketplace. In the absence of a national industrial policy, states have been compelled to craft their own responses to the diverse effects of globalization trends.

CHANGING PROBLEM DEFINITIONS:
ECONOMIC DEVELOPMENT AS A POLICY PROBLEM

Almost any policy initiative can be justified in terms of its economic development potential. When public school officials argue for a new bond issue, they often point out that improvements to the educational system will help local employers find more productive employees. Likewise, efforts to reduce air pollution or even programs designed to fight crime are justified by assertions that resolving these community problems will improve the local business climate. This reasoning has broad political appeal, but it makes economic development policy seem vague and overly inclusive. It may be true that solving community problems will enhance economic conditions, but an analysis of economic development policy requires a more precise definition.

To this end, we define economic development policy as those policies intended to encourage new business investment in specific locations in the hopes of developing the local economy by producing jobs and enhancing and diversifying the local tax base (Eisinger 1988, 4). This definition allows us to consider the full range of problem definitions states use to diagnose their development needs and identify appropriate solutions, from infrastructure programs to efforts to affect firms' locational decisions to more process-oriented strategies to encourage indigenous growth.

States as Economic Policy Activists

The American states are not newcomers to the practice of economic development. They have tried to promote economic growth since the first days of the Republic. The current array of economic development policies is only the latest stage in a continuing, albeit wavering, process of state intervention in economic activities. Prior to 1800 most of the U.S. population lived and worked on small, self-sufficient farms. Commercial farming was insignificant because the cost of transporting crops was overwhelming. For example, the overland journey between Boston and New York took more than a week; between Philadelphia and Pittsburgh, more than twenty days (Fainsod, Gordon, and Palamountain 1959, 54). The cost of transporting a ton of goods thirty miles overland was roughly equivalent to transporting them 3,000 miles overseas from Boston to London (Takaki 1990, 75). States supported commercial development by building infrastructures (ports, roads, bridges, and so forth) to facilitate the movement of goods to the coasts and then to other eastern cities or overseas. As competition developed between eastern seaports the states rushed to build canals. Cumberland (1971) estimated that the public investment in canal building was $432 million, of which $300 million was paid by the states and $125 million by local governments. The federal government contributed only $7 million (North, Anderson, and Hill 1983).

Within two generations, the American economy changed from a simple agrarian–commercial pattern to a complex industrial economy characterized by interregional specialization. By 1860 the Northeast, West (Illinois, Indiana, and Ohio), and South were economically integrated. Both the Northeast and the South depended on the West for the production of foodstuffs. The Southeast specialized in cotton production and supplied the textile factories in the Northeast. The South and the West purchased manufactured goods from the East (North 1966). This transition was spurred in large part by technological improvements that enabled, then led to demands for, an integrated transportation system, setting in motion the forces leading to what Taylor (1977) called the transportation revolution. The economic role of the states did not end with financing harbors and canals. The states contributed 48 million of the 179 million acres allocated to railroads for development of rail systems (North et al. 1983). After the railroads came highways with automobiles, then air transportation, all of which involved state government financing and improved the movement of goods and information and further stimulated economic growth.

Formal state economic development responsibilities, however, have a sporadic history. State economic development policy as an activity separate from transportation policy became a formal function of state government in Alabama, Florida, Maine, and North Carolina in the 1920s. In other states, economic development planning was adopted as an aspect of participation in the New Deal economic recovery programs in the 1930s and 1940s or as a way to coordinate industrial production in World War II. But except for a few in the South, all states had phased out their economic development agencies by the 1950s (Eisinger 1988).

Only in the 1980s and 1990s has economic development policy resurfaced as a major concern among the states' governors (Herzik 1983). Prior to the 1980s, Herzik described economic development as a "cyclical" policy—one that grows in concern, peaks, and then steadily declines. But since the mid-1970s the issue of economic development has been a perennial state issue. Throughout the 1980s, state governors ranked economic development with education, highways, corrections, welfare, and health care as enduring state policy issues. Today, every state recognizes economic development as an integral part of state government.

Variations in State Problem Definitions

Each state, however, differs in how they define their economic development problems and thus their policy solutions vary as well. These problem definitions correspond to theories of economic growth that policy makers draw on in diagnosing state development problems. These notions help policy makers pinpoint what causes development problems and what the appropriate solutions might be (Rochefort and Cobb 1994).

Policy making for state economic development is especially intriguing in the 1990s because of the competing problem definitions. The traditional "smokestack-chasing" strategies reflect a theory of economic growth that emphasizes the importance of low costs for basic production factors—land, labor, raw materials, and capital—in attracting investment. Some states pass laws hindering the formation of labor unions in order to keep state labor costs low relative to other states. In the wake of global competition, however, a different economic model is emerging. According to this new theory, state development problems stem not from production factors but from inflexible environments not receptive to new and innovative technologies and business activities. State officials persuaded by this new perspective are experimenting with policies that emphasize flexibility, risk taking, and market structuring on the part of state government to encourage innovation and to minimize barriers to innovation (Clarke and Gaile 1998). This activist state role can take many forms. For example, the Minnesota Partnership Initial Product Assessment Program helps businesses or individuals develop new products by offering grants to evaluate, test, or build a prototype of a new product or production process. More than seventeen states have established state venture capital programs that use public funds to provide high-risk equity capital for investment in new businesses. From the perspective of this theory, the costs of policy failure are not loss of investment to another locale but relegation to a global backwater while wealth is generated by centers of innovation elsewhere.

At this point, the variety of incentives states offer for business investment is impressive. As of 1994, the states offered 912 separate economic development programs not including programs funded primarily by the federal government; basic state taxes such as income, sales, and property taxes; and subsidies offered to induce compliance with environmental regulations. These policies range from programs offered by all states, such as industrial revenue bonds and tax incentives for the purchase of industrial machinery, to more innovative programs such as Arkansas's Beginning Farmer Loan Program, which gives tax breaks for direct loans made to small first-time farmers, or Iowa's Self-Employment Program, which offers low-interest loans to persons currently receiving welfare to start small business ventures. All states offer direct financial assistance through direct loans, grants, loan guarantees, or other interest subsidies. States also subsidize firms indirectly through tax breaks, by providing the infrastructure needed to support a new or expanded enterprise, by offering information or technical assistance, and by regulating the business environment through land-use controls or determining permissible employment practices (for a comprehensive list of policy instruments, see Sternberg 1987). Although there are many ways to classify state economic development policies, we discuss these various strategies in terms of their infrastructure investment objectives and their business promotional objectives; we characterize the latter as incentives aimed at influencing locational decisions or at facilitating entrepreneurial growth processes.[1]

ALTERNATIVE STRATEGIES FOR ECONOMIC DEVELOPMENT

We discuss three major policy strategies: infrastructure strategies, locational incentives, and entrepreneurial strategies. *Strategies for infrastructure* emphasize the

---

1. Our state program data are drawn from *The Directory of Incentives for Business Investment and Development in the United States for 1983, 1986, 1991, and 1994 (Directory of Incentives, various years).*

construction and maintenance of physical infrastructure such as roads and highways to encourage and support development. *Locational incentives* seek to reduce the costs of production factors in relation to other locations to attract businesses that wish to relocate, retain those tempted by other states to leave, or encourage existing businesses to expand in place. *Entrepreneurial strategies* emphasize facilitating growth processes rather than influencing particular firms in their choice of location. Each of these policy paths implies distinctive strategies that reflect different understandings of the logic underlying economic development processes. In addition, policy makers must also be pragmatists and seek orientations that accord with the dispositions of state voters. Although these investment and promotional strategies do not entail mutually exclusive choices, each state nevertheless exhibits a distinctive economic development policy profile. We compare these state policy profiles by developing a standardized index of policy attributes for each of the three policy orientations: the infrastructure investment approach, the locational incentive approach, and the entrepreneurial approach.[2]

The Infrastructure Development Approach

Although traditional infrastructure strategies center on providing seemingly prosaic fixed assets such as highways, sewers, and waste treatment plants, there is a sense of crisis surrounding infrastructure policy, and the very term itself is subject to debate. Perry (1994a) traced the evolving taxonomy from a focus on internal improvements in the early nineteenth century, to the concern with public works projects in the Great Depression era, to the more inclusive and systemic view of infrastructure systems in the 1980s. In contrast to a specific focus on bridges or roads, the term *infrastructure* now signifies a concern with both the technological systems

The directory presents the state programs in a narrative format that includes a description of the incentive, its terms, conditions, and eligibility criteria. The program information is self-reported by the states in a standardized format. Another frequently used data source, the *Industrial Development and Site Selection Handbook* ("the Conway data"), is also based on self-reporting but is more oriented toward industrial recruitment strategies. It slights entrepreneurial programs and reports merely the presence or absence of programs rather than the narrative detail included in the *Directory of Incentives*. State economic development policy efforts continue to expand. As reported by the *Directory of Incentives* (various years), between 1983 and 1994, the number of economic development programs rose from 465 to 912. In all, the states nearly doubled the number of incentive programs in ten years.

2. To construct our indexes, we coded the 2,756 program descriptions from the 1983, 1986, 1991, and 1994 editions of the *Directory of Incentives for Business Investment and Development in the United States* (*Directory of Incentives*, various years). We gave the programs one point for each attribute identified and then divided the number of attributes found by the number of programs the state offers. Our standardized index scores are simply the ratio of attributes to programs for each state for the infrastructure, locational, and entrepreneurial incentive approaches. For example, we found thirty-one locational attributes among Illinois's ten economic development programs in 1983; accordingly, their locational economic development policy score is 31/10, or 3.10. Our indexes appear to be reliable measures of the different policy orientations. A factor analysis confirms that the attributes loaded onto three underlying factors corresponding to the three economic development approaches and that the pattern became more distinctive over time. Cronbach's alphas were all greater than 0.75. Our entrepreneurial index correlates positively with other empirical measures of state economic development policy: Gray and Lowery's (1990) state industrial policy measure ($r = 0.48$ in 1983, 0.54 in 1986) and Berman and Martin's (1992) measures of state economic development policy ($r = 0.24$ in 1983, 0.23 in 1986, and 0.35 in 1991).

of physical facilities and the roles, particularly the economic role, these assets play in future growth and development. This link between infrastructure and development became prominent in the 1970s, when economic development needs displaced historical concerns with health, safety, and environmental needs as the primary justification for infrastructure investment (Felbinger 1994). In the absence of national infrastructure policy initiatives, however, there is a concern that there will be continued underinvestment in public infrastructure, with potentially negative effects on national and subnational policies.

Federalism and Infrastructure Investment. In the early 1980s Choate and Walter's report (1981) on public capital infrastructure, *America in Ruins,* galvanized public attention. Choate and Walter argued that local economic development was hampered by obsolete and deteriorating public facilities. Their diagnosis of an infrastructure crisis demanded a national policy response. Federal participation in infrastructure provision, however, has been erratic and reluctant. The national government has perceived most public works projects as having primarily local impacts and has thus been averse to taxing or borrowing for such purposes (GAO 1993; Rivlin 1995). This aversion has only been overcome in the past by framing infrastructure issues as national problems: Politicians justified the 1956 National Highway Act for defense purposes and claimed the Water Pollution Control Act of 1972 would ensure national standards for water quality.

The federal government's responsibilities in financing and regulating development of infrastructure continue to be in question. Federal capital spending for the nation's infrastructure peaked in the 1960s. Since 1970 there has been a precipitous decline in federal support for state and local infrastructure—a loss in constant dollars of more than 60 percent in federal grants-in-aid between 1970 and 1990. This left state and local governments in a dilemma: Their existing infrastructure was deteriorating, and they needed to invest in new facilities to retain their economic competitiveness. State and local governments now account for 90 percent of all public works spending, with a growing share (43 percent) of those expenditures by special purpose governments such as public authorities and special districts (Leigland 1994). By the mid-1980s, federal efforts were characterized as an ad hoc federal infrastructure strategy that emphasized aid for transportation programs; trust fund financing rather than grants-in-aid; and support for research, management, training, technical assistance, and demonstration projects (Man and Bell 1993, 19).

Despite numerous proposals for new funding to invigorate state infrastructure investment, there has been little resolution of the national policy gridlock (U.S. Congress 1984, 1990). One important exception to this stalemate was the passage of the Intermodal Surface Transportation Efficiency Act of 1991 (ISTEA), authorizing expenditures of $155 billion over six years for addressing "mobility needs" through intermodal transit—highways, mass transit, and safety and research programs—as well as non-roadway enhancements such as greenways, bike paths, and historic preservation (U.S. Department of Transportation 1993). It gives the states a prominent and flexible policy role in exchange for providing 20 percent of transportation funding while the federal government pays the remaining 80 percent. ISTEA transformed the historical federal–state transportation partnership by bringing new interests into the transportation policy arena and by requiring states to share planning for new transportation projects with metropolitan planning organizations (MPOs) (Kincaid 1992).

When ISTEA came up for reauthorization in 1998, the spending caps agreed to in the 1997 balanced budget agreement threatened any potential increases in spending. In addition, the "donor" states—mostly states in the Sunbelt and West, receiving less than $1 of highway and mass transit funding for each $1 their residents pay in federal gasoline taxes—rebelled over subsidizing transportation improvements in other states. They demanded a guarantee of a more equitable return on their tax contributions. Speaking for the donor state of Mississippi, Senate Majority Leader Trent Lott (R-Miss) declared, "We want some asphalt. . . . I also want more asphalt for my buddies in Florida, Texas and Alabama" (quoted in Ota 1998a). Negotiations over the successor legislation to ISTEA encompassed not only asphalt but also high-speed rail, drunk driving prevention programs, bridge replacement, surface transportation, new light-rail projects, and a host of other programs. The final version (now known as TEA-21) signed by President Clinton in June 1998 retained many of the innovative aspects of ISTEA but also signaled a return to more traditional debates on funding formulas and earmarked federal gas tax revenues as well as to congressional largess for special transportation projects in nearly every state.

State Infrastructure Policy Agendas. Infrastructure investment is the most traditional state investment and development tool and a good gauge of state involvement in economic development. This was especially so in the early part of the nineteenth century, when states and cities introduced a host of debt-financing mechanisms in support of aggressive public works projects. The dire consequences of many of these speculative financing gambits, however, led most states to limit their debt-financing powers and those of local government (Sbragia 1996). This created a later need for circumventing these debt limits through establishment of special authorities that allowed public works to be financed through "the back door" (Perry 1994b); it also made states more dependent on federal financing for large-scale public works.

Whether by default or design, since the mid-1980s infrastructure policies have become increasingly decentralized. State and local governments rarely debate whether infrastructure investment and maintenance are necessary; rather, the central issues are how to provide and pay for them. Even where the national government pays significant infrastructure construction costs, as in the highways programs, states and localities are responsible for the continued maintenance of these facilities. This stewardship is expensive, and it is tempting to defer maintenance; indeed, until recently the incentives of federal capital grants for replacement and renewal activities perversely encouraged delays on maintenance until deteriorating structures became eligible for federal funds (Perry 1994a). The 1991 federal highway law was created to channel money to states to maintain and improve highways that receive the greatest use. The law devolves significant authority to state transportation officials (rather than congressional committees) to decide when, where, and how much to spend, and Washington puts aside at least 30 percent of all federal highway dollars for these improvement projects (Rapp 1994a).

Historically, most of state public works activities were supported by taxes and bond financing, but the financing has become increasingly complex. In passing the National Highway System Designation Act of 1995, Congress encouraged states to come up with new financing approaches such as organizing infrastructure banks and experimenting with toll roads (Ota 1998b). California offers several prototypes of public–private partnerships, technological innovations, and private financing to construct transportation infrastructure. The state Department of Transportation, for example, entered into franchise agreements with private investors to construct transportation facilities that otherwise faced political stalemates. One project involved construction of four express toll lanes on the median strip of state route 91, which links Orange County and Riverside County; the private partners provided most of the financing, which is to be repaid by tolls collected electronically as cars enter the express lane with debit card transmitters on the cars' dashboards.

In today's competitive context, many state and local officials see sports stadiums as infrastructural assets with important revenue generating potential. Although some sports stadiums are privately financed (for example, the San Francisco Giants' Pacific Bell Park or the Boston Celtics' Fleet Center), most rely on substantial public subsidies. In the 1980s, cities spent $750 million on sports arenas' financing; since 1992, more than $1 billion in public funds has been spent on sports arenas, with another $7 billion earmarked for future construction (Barringer 1997). Teams often threaten to leave town if they do not get new stadiums and public subsidies to support them. Although relocation is rare, cities are hostage to these cyclical threats, because sports leagues enjoy a monopoly: National leagues create an "artificial scarcity" of teams by limiting the number of teams and controlling where they will be placed. By continually threatening to leave if cities do not meet their demands, sports teams create their own version of the arms race described previously. St. Louis and the state of Missouri, for example, paid the full costs (estimated at $300 million) of the new TransWorld Dome football stadium in St. Louis to attract the Rams from Los Angeles, throwing in a new practice facility and a $29 million relocation fee to sweeten the deal. When St. Louis later unsuccessfully sued the National Football League for conspiring against the city over the franchise price, the city attorney described it as "the worst sports deal in history" (Mahtesian 1998).

As in other economic development deals, the costs and benefits seem skewed toward private interests. Team owners and players clearly gain from the subsidized stadiums but the state and local benefits are less obvious. The usual taxpayer share in stadium construction is 80 to 100 percent, mostly for construction but governments often pay for land and street improvements (Barringer 1997). To raise these funds, supporters draw on state and local sources that might be used for other projects and place financial burdens on many who have neither the interest nor the ability to attend sporting events. In Detroit, for example, the city is providing 50 percent of the construction costs for the new stadium, but voters approved a 1 percent tax on hotels and a 2 percent tax on car rentals to generate nearly $5.5 million a year to support the $80 million in bonds issued (Barringer 1997). Funds from Indian casino revenue, city agency budgets, and the team owners are also part of the deal.

Although most citizens enjoy sports, polls, referenda, and elections consistently show few are willing to pay for sports stadiums with public funds. They see little reason to do so because most economic assessments fail to show increases in per capita income, wages, or even net employment associated with stadium development (Baade and Dye 1988; Rosentraub et al. 1994). Furthermore, fairness issues take on a clarity in sports financing that is often missing from other economic development debates. Despite the post-Super Bowl euphoria in Denver, the Denver Bronco's demands for a new stadium prompted one official to ask, "What about Mrs. Martinez?" The imaginary Mrs. Martinez may be unable to pay the ticket prices at the new stadium and will never see a game but will have to pay increased taxes to raise public funds for the stadium. In a sense, such arrangements transfer dollars from people who pay sales taxes—especially middle- and lower-class citizens—to owners and players who spend it elsewhere. When tax-free bonds are issued, all federal taxpayers end up subsidizing sports stadiums.

To gain a more precise sense of state infrastructure policy agendas, we examined state programs that offered incentives either to communities or private companies to develop infrastructure. In 1983 no state offered an infrastructure assistance program, but by 1994 twenty states did, and some now have more than one program. The Gund Foundation, for example, worked with Ohio to draw up a comprehensive infrastructure development plan for Cleveland, carried out by the Build Up Greater Cleveland public–private partnership (Licate 1994). We also considered incentives targeted to the transportation sector more generally. The number of transportation-sector incentives offered by the states—such as the tax preferences given to the trucking, railroad, and shipping industries—have remained relatively stable throughout the 1980s. Currently, twenty-eight states offer such incentives. On the basis of infrastructure incentives and targeted transportation incentives—we create an infrastructure index by summing attributes across programs. (See note 2.)

Our index of state infrastructure programs (Table 13-1) measures the commitment of states to infrastructure policies in relation to their overall economic development policy effort. The higher the score, the higher the states' commitment to infrastructure. An examination of infrastructure index scores shows that despite the increase in the number of infrastructure-related programs, the magnitude of the index scores remains about the same over time. This is because the number of programs highlighting transportation or infrastructure incentives adopted by the states is low in relation to the total number of incentives the state offers. In 1994 there appears to be a slight upward trend in infrastructure programs as a share of

Table 13-1 Infrastructure Economic Development Policy Indexes

State	1983	1986	1991	1994
Alabama	0.00	0.00	0.08	0.12
Alaska	0.00	0.00	0.00	0.00
Arizona	0.00	0.00	0.00	0.00
Arkansas	0.00	0.00	0.00	0.04
California	0.22	0.20	0.25	0.25
Colorado	0.11	0.14	0.08	0.08
Connecticut	0.00	0.00	0.00	0.00
Delaware	0.00	0.00	0.00	0.00
Florida	0.00	0.00	0.11	0.05
Georgia	0.00	0.00	0.00	0.04
Hawaii	0.08	0.07	0.07	0.14
Idaho	0.00	0.00	0.00	0.00
Illinois	0.00	0.00	0.08	0.04
Indiana	0.19	0.15	0.16	0.16
Iowa	0.00	0.00	0.00	0.00
Kansas	0.00	0.00	0.08	0.12
Kentucky	0.20	0.33	0.27	0.27
Louisiana	0.00	0.00	0.00	0.00
Maine	0.00	0.00	0.00	0.13
Maryland	0.00	0.00	0.00	0.00
Massachusetts	0.00	0.00	0.00	0.00
Michigan	0.07	0.06	0.13	0.20
Minnesota	0.15	0.06	0.10	0.10
Mississippi	0.00	0.00	0.08	0.12
Missouri	0.00	0.17	0.13	0.07
Montana	0.13	0.05	0.05	0.00
Nebraska	0.00	0.00	0.00	0.00
Nevada	0.00	0.00	0.00	0.00
New Hampshire	0.29	0.14	0.40	0.11
New Jersey	0.27	0.13	0.14	0.09
New Mexico	0.00	0.00	0.11	0.08
New York	0.06	0.06	0.08	0.12
North Carolina	0.00	0.00	0.00	0.00
North Dakota	0.00	0.00	0.00	0.00
Ohio	0.00	0.00	0.00	0.14
Oklahoma	0.00	0.00	0.00	0.00
Oregon	0.43	0.33	0.27	0.00
Pennsylvania	0.17	0.23	0.27	0.32
Rhode Island	0.10	0.07	0.08	0.08
South Carolina	0.13	0.09	0.06	0.30
South Dakota	0.00	0.00	0.00	0.00
Tennessee	0.30	0.33	0.40	0.36
Texas	0.40	0.40	0.08	0.14
Utah	0.33	0.25	0.11	0.00
Vermont	0.33	0.00	0.00	0.00
Virginia	0.00	0.00	0.05	0.00
Washington	0.20	0.20	0.20	0.11
West Virginia	0.00	0.00	0.00	0.00
Wisconsin	0.14	0.11	0.07	0.08
Wyoming	0.00	0.00	0.00	0.00

SOURCE: Computed from program descriptions in *Directory of Incentives,* various years.

overall economic development effort; in some states, such as Texas, this reflects a resumption of previous efforts, but in states such as South Carolina, Ohio, Maine, and Hawaii, it represents a marked increase in infrastructure initiatives.

Infrastructure for the Future State Economy. Recent information technology changes are likely to reshape state infrastructure agendas by the end of the century. Technological changes provide new ways of communicating and producing, but they also transform social and political dynamics in unanticipated ways. Into the next century state infrastructure politics are likely to reflect the changing nature of global competition, persistent tensions in intergovernmental relations, the continual question of public finance, as well as the particular social and economic conditions in each state. The effects of these contextual changes are already evident in struggles to define policy for the information highway.

As in the broader infrastructure debate, the concept of an information highway is elusive. Most definitions emphasize the connecting of technologies through networks that can carry voice, video, data, and imaging. The channels, or "pipes," carrying these different forms of information must be connected with each other and eventually linked into local-area networks and wide-area networks. In 1994, state and local officials ranked network integration as the most important emerging information technology (Richter 1994a, 78). The value of an integrated information technology stems both from its contribution to the information-intensive work of state government operations and from its facilitation of service delivery to citizens, such as verification of unemployment benefits or renewal of drivers' licenses at kiosk terminals. This spreading information web depends on a statewide fiber-optic grid. Linking these state and regional networks to national networks brings together an information highway. The analogy of an information highway similar to the federal interstate highway system, however, is somewhat imperfect. In contrast to the interstate highway program, the fiber-optic networks supporting the information highway generally are funded by private sector capital.

But many states are taking the lead in developing innovative information infrastructures. Iowa, for example, is financing and building its own fiber-optic network to ensure universal service and maintain public control; in addition to plans for public access, Iowa hopes to lease the use of its information superhighway to private firms. North Carolina, in contrast, formed a public–private partnership with twenty-eight state telephone firms in 1993 to develop a statewide information highway. In return for the commitment to be an early and large user of the computer network, the state government hopes to induce private companies to wire more than 3,000 public institutions to the statewide interactive system (Fulton and Newman 1993; Rapp 1994b, 84). Rewiring the state is part of North Carolina's economic development strategy: Officials anticipate that the existence of a statewide information highway will attract businesses to North Carolina because they will not have to build their own private networks (Richter 1994b, 68). They also anticipate that the network will add nearly $3 billion to the state economy and 44,000 jobs between 1994 and 2003 (Richter 1994b, 68).

The prospects for a national information superhighway became brighter with passage of the 1996 Telecommunications Act (S652, Pub. L. No. 104-104). This bill promised to overhaul the outdated 1934 Communications Act by deregulating telecommunications companies, opening up telecommunications markets to competition, and creating incentives for private sector development of the superhighway. Yet the initial impact appears less promising: rising cable and telephone rates and mega-mergers of telecommunications firms rather than competition. Furthermore, troubling governance issues stem from the tensions of public and private interests in telecommunications (Richter 1994b). One issue centers on the level or type of technological access constituting the "universal service" provided for in earlier regulations on telephone service. The 1996 Telecommunications Act directed the Federal Communication Commission (FCC) to ensure universal service with a program providing discounts for Internet hookups to schools, libraries, and rural health care centers and costs to be covered by all competing telecommunications firms in a market. The FCC's attempts to collect and distribute these Internet subsidies prompted an intense debate on how big the program should be, what it should pay for, who should benefit, and whether other residential consumers should bear the costs of the subsidies through increased rates (Gruenwald 1998a). Electronic commerce is creating another vexing governance issue. As on-line and Internet shopping activities increase, state officials fear shrinking sales tax bases and imperiled local businesses. By 1998, eight states were taxing Internet access and sales. To the Internet industry, this is a significant intrusion, but to many state officials it is a necessary step to protect the sales tax base that provides nearly half of all state revenue (Gruenwald 1998b). As the information superhighway emerges in the next decade, these governance issues will be increasingly salient.

The demand for these new kinds of infrastructure, in which information is a critical economic resource and distance is overcome by communication technology, will change the politics of scale in state politics. In many ways the implications parallel the political consequences of sewer developments in the nineteenth century. To be economical, sewer extensions transcended existing political jurisdictions and required new financing arrangements to amass sufficient capital. This led to unanticipated governance and financing issues that demanded innovative responses. Similarly, the emergence of statewide information highways as development strategies will require state governments to address issues of access, popular control, public financing, and jurisdictional boundaries (Schwarz 1990).

The Locational Incentive Approach

Locational economic development policies aim at improving a community's ability to compete with other locations for industry, jobs, and economic growth. This policy orientation is grounded in economic location theory, which suggests that, other things being equal, firms will seek those locations where the combined costs of land, labor, capital, energy, and transportation are minimal (Weber 1984). Thus, the state seeking a competitive advantage over other states must create an advantageous price structure for these "production factors," thereby creating a comparative locational advantage.

Common tools used in making locational policy include low-interest financing (frequently offered in the form of industrial revenue bonds), tax credits, abatements, deferments and exemptions, subsidized employee training, and assistance with site selection and preparation (Fosler 1988). The rubric of locational economic development policy also includes the notion of creating a "positive business climate" or a probusiness atmosphere. These are vague concepts, but the associated policies often include low taxes and regulatory policies designed to keep production costs low, such as right-to-work laws and relaxed environmental legislation (Plaut and Pluta 1983).

Attributes of Locational Policy Orientations. We assess the degree to which states pursue a locational economic development approach by measuring the extent to which their policies reflect key attributes of the locational orientation. First, we distinguish programs whose primary purpose is to reduce costs by offering direct financial subsidies to businesses. Second, we include policies that indirectly reduce costs to business such as when states offer tax relief or accelerated depreciation on capital expenditures. Third, from these programs we eliminate programs that target specific areas or economic sectors (other than manufacturing), leaving only nontargeted, administratively passive programs that require little initiative on the part of a governmental agency to implement. Thus the attributes of locational economic development policies show an acceptance of prevailing economic forces; other than attempting to lower costs within the state, the economic role of state governments remains subordinate to private sector decisions (Eisinger 1988; Fosler 1988).

Changes in Locational Orientations. The locational policy index measures the degree to which state governments have adopted policies with locational attributes in relation to the state's overall economic development policy effort. States with the higher index scores (as shown in Table 13-2) reveal greater commitments to a locational policy orientation than the other states. In 1983 states with the strongest locational policy orientations were Arizona, Nevada, South Dakota, Utah, and Wyoming. Only Arizona maintained this relative emphasis on locational strategies through 1994; in 1994, Idaho, Tennessee, Delaware, and Colorado also emerged as giving priority to locational strategies. Table 13-2 suggests no obvious regional pattern to these locational policy orientations, although less densely populated, less urbanized states and southern states with historical usage of locational policies appear to be the most prominent adopters of this strategy.

Although these states increased their locational policy orientations, most states do not seem to be pursuing locational approaches as single-mindedly as in the past. The average value of the locational indexes dropped 8.1 percent between 1983 and 1986, 10.5 percent between 1986 and 1991, and 21.5 percent between 1991 and 1994, despite increases in the total number of state economic development programs in each of these periods. In all, the average value of the locational index decreased 45 percent in the ten years. Between 1991 and 1994 only three states in-

Table 13-2 Locational Economic Development Policy Indexes

State	1983	1986	1991	1994
Alabama	2.40	2.40	2.15	1.82
Alaska	2.25	2.75	1.36	1.11
Arizona	2.50	2.67	2.67	2.00
Arkansas	2.50	2.33	1.56	1.19
California	1.67	1.70	1.58	1.58
Colorado	2.56	2.43	1.92	1.83
Connecticut	2.00	1.88	1.65	1.37
Delaware	2.00	2.13	1.46	2.09
Florida	2.27	2.10	1.47	1.05
Georgia	2.33	1.29	1.29	1.50
Hawaii	2.17	2.14	1.93	1.79
Idaho	2.50	2.43	2.43	2.22
Illinois	2.30	1.89	1.31	1.38
Indiana	1.88	1.80	1.79	1.74
Iowa	2.10	2.00	1.56	1.45
Kansas	2.50	1.91	1.25	1.64
Kentucky	1.60	2.00	1.91	2.00
Louisiana	1.83	1.93	1.53	1.67
Maine	1.85	1.71	1.92	1.63
Maryland	1.57	1.63	1.42	1.20
Massachusetts	1.77	1.79	1.38	1.45
Michigan	2.21	1.56	1.33	1.65
Minnesota	1.46	1.76	0.90	0.85
Mississippi	1.83	1.83	1.92	1.77
Missouri	2.00	1.54	1.40	1.46
Montana	2.25	1.53	1.60	1.39
Nebraska	2.00	1.63	1.73	1.73
Nevada	2.50	1.17	1.17	1.22
New Hampshire	2.43	2.43	2.60	1.21
New Jersey	1.91	1.63	1.36	1.30
New Mexico	1.80	2.20	2.00	1.38
New York	2.13	1.72	1.19	1.12
North Carolina	2.20	1.22	1.50	1.36
North Dakota	1.91	2.00	1.69	1.56
Ohio	1.69	1.50	1.46	1.71
Oklahoma	2.29	2.22	2.10	1.92
Oregon	1.86	1.44	1.36	1.35
Pennsylvania	1.67	1.27	1.05	1.32
Rhode Island	2.10	1.79	2.00	2.00
South Carolina	2.13	2.09	2.39	2.09
South Dakota	2.75	2.20	2.13	1.89
Tennessee	2.10	2.33	2.30	2.36
Texas	1.60	1.60	1.83	1.24
Utah	2.67	2.75	1.67	1.78
Vermont	2.00	1.75	1.71	1.71
Virginia	2.13	1.79	1.60	1.57
Washington	2.40	2.40	1.80	1.68
West Virginia	2.00	2.00	2.06	1.54
Wisconsin	1.86	1.44	1.27	1.08
Wyoming	0.00	0.00	0.00	0.00

SOURCE: Computed from program descriptions in *Directory of Incentives,* various years.

creased their locational index scores (Delaware, Georgia, and Michigan), whereas the scores in forty-five states declined. New state programs are more likely to include more entrepreneurial attributes.

Entrepreneurial Economic Development Policy Approaches

Entrepreneurial policies are grounded in a theoretical model of economic development processes that emphasize the wealth-generating capacities of innovative activities as the engine of economic growth. Rather than attempting to influence business locational decisions, state policy makers use public resources and authority to encourage new markets and economic ventures. This sometimes requires public officials to act like business entrepreneurs by taking risks and creating opportunities in hopes of generating a more vibrant state economy (Clarke and Gaile 1998; Eisinger 1988).

These entrepreneurial policies are recent additions to the states' economic development policy arsenal, most having been adopted during and after the recession of the early 1980s (Sherman, Wallace, and Pitney 1995). This entrepreneurial approach generates new roles for state governments, particularly a more central role in efforts to create jobs and facilitate growth processes (Osborne 1988, 249). It also often requires new institutional arrangements to carry out these new roles. Although economic development processes are still driven primarily by private sector decisions, the states, it is thought, can support these processes through public–private institutions. These new organizations, generally outside the governmental arena and staffed by development professionals, provide a means of coordinating investment decisions. They often also furnish means for overcoming the historic restrictions on state debt capacity still in place in many states. They often have independent financing authority and can leverage private sector investments with public funds in ways not available to state agencies. For example, quasi-public state organizations may supply seed money to stimulate new business formation or to fund the research needed to bring technological innovations to the market. These state organizational innovations allow state governments to be more flexible and versatile than bureaucratic structures normally permit; advocates claim they permit the state to anticipate, specialize, experiment, evaluate, and adjust to changing economic forces (Fosler 1988, 4).

Attributes of Entrepreneurial Economic Development Orientations. Four core attributes of entrepreneurial economic development programs distinguish them from more conventional locational economic development approaches. First, following Bowman (1987), we distinguish state efforts to create an environment in which innovative firms can flourish by increasing a firm's capacity to take advantage of, or adjust to, new production processes. Second, we single out programs that target high-technology and small businesses. Third, we isolate new organizational arrangements such as public–private partnerships such as local development corporations that attempt to shape markets by leveraging private capital with public, thereby increasing the pool of local investment funds. These programs also attempt to control the spatial relations of firms to markets and promote the economies of juxtaposition and agglomeration (Sternberg 1987, 159). Fourth, we identify programs that fund business at high-risk stages such as startup, new product, and research stages of business development. In Table 13-3, we present an index of state entrepreneurial policy approaches based on these attributes.

Changes in Entrepreneurial Orientations. The index score reflects the degree to which state governments adopted policies with entrepreneurial attributes in relation to their overall economic development policy effort. The higher the value, the greater the state reliance on this approach. A clear trend can be seen in Table 13-3 toward adoption of state policies with more entrepreneurial attributes. Index scores increased an average of 22 percent between 1983 and 1986 as thirty-three states changed their programs to reflect more entrepreneurial attributes. Between 1986 and 1994 the average index increased again by 27 percent, and forty-three states showed greater use of entrepreneurial approaches. In the mid-1990s, Arkansas, Florida, Minnesota, Massachusetts, New York, and North Carolina placed the greatest emphasis on entrepreneurial approaches. These states ranked high in the early indicators and maintained their positions by consistently adding programs with entrepreneurial attributes. New Hampshire recently became a new leader in this area by adding sixteen new programs with entrepreneurial attributes.

In line with Eisinger's contention (1988) that states will maintain a mix of traditional and entrepreneurial economic development policies, our indexes show that states continue to combine approaches. Some states take a leadership role in adoption of entrepreneurial economic development strategies, and other states, such as California, Indiana, Iowa, and Michigan, consistently fall in the middle range of both indexes for any given year.

This apparent balancing act is not surprising when we consider the political context of policy adoption. Although states increasingly are adopting new approaches with entrepreneurial attributes, these new policies are an overlay on previously adopted development programs characterized by locational attributes. Given the difficulty of terminating programs with influential beneficiaries, the shift toward entrepreneurial orientations is likely to be slow, partial, and uneven. Some analysts would argue that it could even be reversed. Tennessee's Saturn deal, Alabama's Mercedes-Benz package, and other such mega-deals could signal the return of smokestack-chasing (Guskind 1993; Mahtesian 1994). A careful state-by-state analysis of the full array of state development policies, however, indicates that even states caught up in these bidding wars continue to lay the groundwork for more entrepreneurial approaches. Rather than a dramatic shift in policy orientations, these indexes reflect continued policy evolution as state policy makers reassess the changing context.

Explaining the Adoption of Entrepreneurial Economic Development Policies. Although rising levels of state economic development activism can be interpreted in terms of the incentives embedded in decentralized federalism structures, the reasons why states favor one orientation rather than another are less clear. The logic of competitive federalism may be sufficient for explaining conventional cost-reduc-

Table 13-3 Entrepreneurial Economic Development Policy Indexes

State	1983	1986	1991	1994
Alabama	0.30	0.30	0.54	0.59
Alaska	0.75	1.00	1.36	1.39
Arizona	0.00	0.00	0.00	0.45
Arkansas	0.30	0.33	1.63	2.27
California	0.56	0.50	0.58	0.58
Colorado	0.11	0.14	0.42	0.33
Connecticut	0.93	0.76	0.90	1.05
Delaware	0.40	0.50	1.00	0.45
Florida	0.64	0.80	1.26	1.91
Georgia	0.50	1.64	1.47	1.19
Hawaii	0.25	0.21	0.50	0.64
Idaho	0.38	0.14	0.14	0.22
Illinois	0.50	0.61	1.00	1.00
Indiana	0.56	0.70	0.84	0.79
Iowa	0.30	0.50	0.78	0.75
Kansas	0.38	0.45	1.21	1.12
Kentucky	0.90	1.00	0.91	1.00
Louisiana	0.50	0.53	0.68	0.95
Maine	0.77	0.86	0.77	0.81
Maryland	1.07	1.00	0.92	1.20
Massachusetts	1.23	1.29	1.57	1.77
Michigan	0.64	0.94	1.08	1.15
Minnesota	0.85	0.59	1.81	1.90
Mississippi	0.08	0.50	0.58	0.62
Missouri	0.58	1.25	1.40	1.32
Montana	0.38	1.00	1.10	1.35
Nebraska	0.38	0.63	0.91	0.91
Nevada	0.00	0.92	0.92	0.78
New Hampshire	0.57	0.57	0.40	1.89
New Jersey	0.73	0.75	1.50	1.64
New Mexico	0.60	0.40	0.22	0.85
New York	0.69	1.11	1.76	1.67
North Carolina	0.40	2.11	1.90	1.82
North Dakota	0.73	0.75	1.00	0.94
Ohio	1.19	1.29	1.31	1.07
Oklahoma	0.29	0.33	0.30	0.85
Oregon	1.00	1.33	1.45	1.47
Pennsylvania	0.92	1.77	1.77	1.29
Rhode Island	0.30	0.79	0.62	0.62
South Carolina	0.38	0.64	0.56	0.57
South Dakota	0.25	0.40	0.38	0.56
Tennessee	0.70	0.44	0.40	0.36
Texas	0.60	0.60	0.50	0.95
Utah	0.67	0.25	1.00	1.00
Vermont	1.00	1.08	1.21	1.29
Virginia	0.63	0.79	0.75	1.13
Washington	0.20	0.40	0.70	1.42
West Virginia	0.63	0.67	0.71	1.23
Wisconsin	0.86	1.00	1.00	1.28
Wyoming	0.00	0.67	0.38	0.78

SOURCE: Computed from program descriptions in *Directory of Incentives,* various years.

tion strategies, but the use of state authority to shape market structures, to create public–private partnerships, or to pursue strategies involving higher risk and longer-term investments are less obvious. The growing reliance on entrepreneurial orientations suggests that state officials may be reframing their definitions of economic development problems in terms of the global rather than federal context.

Several analysts (Eisinger 1988; Osborne 1988) interpret these new state roles and entrepreneurial approaches as responses to a globalizing economy. But entrepreneurial policies are not simply rational, technical responses to new economic conditions. Changing economic conditions and a competitive federal context do provide constraints and opportunities for state decision makers, but these conditions are interpreted and mediated by political actors such as voters, interest groups, political parties, and public officials themselves. This underscores the political nature of state economic development policy making, a dimension confirmed by empirical analyses of the conditions associated with state adoption of entrepreneurial policy orientations.[3]

In trying to sort out this puzzle of state policy choice, Gray and Lowery (1990) found that states with more structured and integrated political relationships are more likely to pursue entrepreneurial policy options, or what they refer to as *industrial policy activism*. Although they show that economic conditions are important to the rise of economic activism, Gray and Lowery contend that these integrative institutions structure the resolution of economic and social issues between interests in ways that allow coordinated and cooperative action on development issues. Similarly, Berman and Martin (1992) found that political institutional features, such as the level of interparty competition and well-developed interest groups, and changing economic conditions are important factors in the adoption of entrepreneurial strategies. Elkins, Bingham, and Bowen (forthcoming) also claim that political variables such as professional legislatures, governmental capacity, and private labor union strength distinguish *programmatically rich* states employing diverse, entrepreneurial approaches from *programmatically lean* states relying on market forces and limited government intervention. It also appears that state political culture shapes the types of strategies states select: States with moralistic political cultures are more likely to rely on entrepreneurial strategies, although traditionalistic states are now less wedded to locational approaches (Boeckelman 1991; Hanson 1991; and see Chapter 1 of this volume).

MEASURING POLICY EFFECTIVENESS

The maturation of economic development policy is evident in the growth of economic development agencies and their budgets. Reports by state officials on

---

3. In empirical analyses of the determinants of entrepreneurial policies (Clarke and Gaile 1992; Saiz 1991), we test for the effects of deindustrialization, fiscal stress, socioeconomic environment, state political culture, interparty competition, state public opinion liberalism, policy liberalism, interest groups, gubernatorial turnover, the formal power of the governor, general state partisanship, and policy innovation.

Figure 13-1   Average State Expenditures for Economic Development Operations

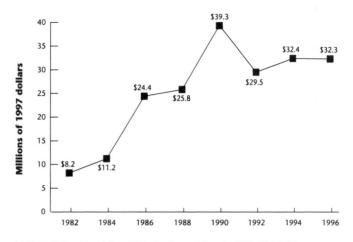

SOURCE: National Association of State Development Agencies 1992, 1994, 1996.

spending for economic development operations are collected by the National Association of State Development Agencies (NASDA) and shown in Figure 13-1. Although the data capture the value of some financial incentives such as the capitalization of revolving loan funds, venture capital, or other financing programs, it is primarily reflective of operating costs for program operations, including job training, advertising, and technical assistance programs. Notably missing are the costs of tax subsidies given to businesses and financing granted from loan pools created in past years or from off-budget sources such as pension funds. As such, the data reflect trends in the more active economic development programs in the 1980s and 1990s and provide some indication of the level of policy effort in different states. As interjurisdictional competition intensified in the early 1980s, states established economic development programs as full-fledged agencies often consolidating job training, tourism development, community development, and international trade programs in the process. By the mid-1980s states' programs became more diverse. Agency budgets climbed rapidly in the 1980s, showing a near fivefold increase in constant dollars by 1990. During this time, real expenditure growth averaged more than 50 percent per year. But the rate of growth began to slow after 1986, and with the exception of the period between 1988 and 1992 reflects slow but steady growth in real dollars.

The most serviceable explanation for the slowing rate of operations expenditures is that some states have chosen to reexamine their economic development strategies in response to the rising costs of business recruitment. As the costs of incentives rise, the projected return from state investment declines. The slowing rate of spending may show that interstate competition is approaching equilibrium—or at least a cost threshold some states are not willing to cross. Also, since the late 1980s recruitment strategies have come under increasing criticism. Articles appearing in the popular press characterized state attempts to lure industry as "a blood sport" (Barrett and Schwartz 1992) or a "new war between the states" (Guskind 1993). Indeed, some of the more visible competitions are also the most egregious examples of incentive abuse. The $300 million incentive package Alabama offered to Mercedes-Benz became a source of controversy soon after its inception. The controversy began when the teachers' union sued the state to keep it from raiding funds earmarked for education to help finance the deal. After the state missed a $43 million payment to the auto company, state officials were forced to borrow from the state's pension fund. The state even used its National Guard troops to clear the site for construction. The controversy became serious enough to be a major factor in the electoral defeat of James Folsom, the governor who originally claimed credit for the deal (CFED 1996). The slowing rate of appropriations to economic development agencies correlates with increased skepticism about economic development programs.

Yet, seen in another light, the slow but steady budget increases since 1992 show the durability of economic development appropriations in the face of widespread state budget reductions. In the first half of the 1990s states faced a general fiscal crisis fueled by a national recession, explosive growth in Medicaid expenditures, and increases in school enrollment. Some states faced court rulings that forced them to spend more on mental health programs or on prisons to reduce overcrowding. Others were ordered to equalize their school financing systems. In still other states, citizens passed initiatives cutting taxes, limiting spending, and otherwise restricting budgetary flexibility (Gold 1995). In this cautious environment any real growth in operations expenditures should be regarded as an indicator of continued commitment to economic development agendas.

THE POLICY EFFECTIVENESS DEBATE

Do state economic development policies make a difference? Evaluating whether these policies bring about net increases in employment, tax revenues, or long-term growth is a complex task. Even economic development officials admit they see only a weak relationship between their efforts and economic improvement (Rubin 1988). Given the political context and uncertainty about the effectiveness of their tools, policy makers are tempted, in Rubin's words, to "shoot anything that flies; claim anything that falls." Needless to say, this temptation to hedge casts doubt on the credibility of in-house program evaluations.

A similar problem exists when researchers ask corporate managers how economic development policies affect their business decisions. The early survey work showed that surprisingly few employers mentioned taxes or other inducements as a primary reason for choosing to invest (Bridges 1965). After interviewing officials from companies that accepted state incentives, Harrison and Kantor (1978) found that in every case "the company took actions according to its own plans, then learned about the existence of the tax credits and applied for them, often at the explicit urging of the state officials in charge of the program" (265). However, later research reveals that executives in relatively technology-intensive industries view taxes as an increasingly important cost factor. For these companies, traditional location factors matter less when high-value, low-weight products make it possible to serve distant markets (Blair and Premus 1987). But we should be skeptical about the claims of businesses as to the importance of economic development incentives. As Donahue (1997, 175) pointed out, "business officials might amplify their true importance in hopes of bluffing officials into sweetening incentives or deterring burdens."

The other approach to assessing whether economic development programs make a difference is through the use of statistical techniques to analyze the observed relationship between state incentive programs and various economic outcomes. Unfortunately, as Clarke and Gaile (1992, 193) concluded, attempts to assess the effects of economic development are "a quagmire of good intentions and bad measures." The problem is one of complexity. As dependent variables (the outcomes to be explained) should we consider general aggregate indicators such as employment, income, and capital investment, or should we include particular measures such as the movement, expansion, or creation of firms and jobs? If we focus on the latter, what about questions of quality or type? These choices are amplified when one considers independent variables (the factors hypothesized to explain economic outcomes) because the statistical models require that all plausible alternative explanations be considered. This is rarely possible. Another problem, as we have demonstrated previously, is that states combine several economic development approaches in making policy. Some approaches may be more effective than others, but the combined effect obscures the contribution of any particular policy. Lastly, measures of policy effectiveness become normative questions. Is it good policy if employment growth in Ohio comes at the expense of employment loss in Michigan?

The bulk of statistical studies examine the effect of basic tax structures—not specific economic development strategies—on economic growth. The results of the initial studies generally showed that state taxes have little to do with higher rates of economic growth (for reviews, see Ledebur and Hamilton 1986; Wasylenko 1981, 1984). Other elements, such as proximity to markets, labor supplies, transportation, and utility costs, tended to be more important than taxes. Later work has refined this conclusion. In an extensive review, Bartik (1991) found that studies produced since the 1980s suggest that lower taxes generally lead to more business activity. At the metropolitan level, taxes may have more influence on location decisions because the larger cost differences that exist between major economic regions are less relevant (Peretz 1986). International competition may revive the salience of tax differences as firms move beyond national borders to scan the globe seeking the best combination of services and taxes for their investment.

Early studies of state locational incentives showed they were ineffective (Bridges 1965), but recent studies are more ambivalent (Peirce 1994). McHone (1984) found that local communities offering industrial bond programs, tax abatements, and accelerated depreciation are somewhat better off economically than their metropolitan counterparts. Kale (1984) reported industrial development incentives actually decreased employment growth in the 1960s and early 1970s but increased growth in the later 1970s. Yet Hansen (1984) found that incentives reduce employment growth but increase the rate of business start-ups. Similarly, Brace's (1993) study of economic development policy activism in four states reveals a negative relationship between high policy usage and income growth. Nevertheless, Bartik (1991) concluded that these incentives can have positive effects on long-term business growth and labor market conditions, including prospects for African Americans and less educated workers. His arguments are open to challenge (Accordino 1994) but have prompted a reconsideration of the potential effects of state incentives.

Two recent studies suggest that higher expenditures on economic development operations fosters the creation of manufacturing jobs. Both studies found that higher general investment in economic development programs had a positive and significant statistical relationship to manufacturing employment growth (de Bartolome and Speigel 1995; Koropeckyj 1997). However, both studies urge caution in interpreting their findings. Most important, they use the data compiled by NASDA and thus do not consider tax expenditures, the single largest source of economic development spending.

Studies of entrepreneurial policy approaches are more limited, but the results, although tentative, are more optimistic. Eisinger's research (1988) shows that entrepreneurial policies do stimulate new investment and create jobs. Lowery and Gray assess the impact of state industrial policy activism on gross state product measures; their initial analyses (1992) reveal positive but not robust effects on state growth, leading them to argue that state economic conditions would have been worse but for the policies. In measuring impacts over a longer time period (1982–1989), they find there is little long-term economic benefit from such policies (Lowery and Gray 1995). Hansen (1984, 1989) also found limited effects from more activist, targeted policies. Discerning long-term impacts of any policy initiative is difficult.

Oregon, a leader in entrepreneurial approaches, devised a benchmark strategy for measuring its policy effectiveness. Because the policy goals center on improving the standard of living, rather than more narrow job creation goals, the state identified benchmarks, or standards to be achieved, for a wide range of economic and social goals—from economic diversification to babies born to drug-free mothers—that would reflect true state development (Mattoon 1993). Establishing benchmarks to measure program performance on a regular basis, and tying performance to budget decisions as in Oregon, is a basic but still uncommon evaluation tool.

THE NEW POLITICS OF STATE ECONOMIC DEVELOPMENT POLICIES

In a paradoxical turn of events, states and regions may become the new arenas for global competition. As firms scan the globe for the locations best fitting their needs, their menu of possible locations is less likely to be defined by national boundaries and more likely to reflect specific configurations of features and amenities sought by the firm. California's strongest competitors for investment, for example, may be provinces or regions in Europe or Latin America rather than other states in the United States. This means that the decision context for state officials is now broader than state or national boundaries. These changing politics of scale are exemplified by the formalization of regional markets superseding national boundaries, such as those created by the North American Free Trade Agreement. Although our decentralized federal structure historically encouraged bidding wars among the states, globalization forces appear to encourage a different type of competition. The issue is whether states can adjust to this turbulent environment and capture these new sources and forms of growth and wealth.

This new context forces us to reconsider our assumptions about state economic development policies. Although federalism still fosters interjurisdictional competition, globalization trends are altering locational calculations. State officials are caught up in interpreting what these trends and conditions mean for economic development in their states. As our data show, their policy responses vary widely. This indicates that these trends affect states in different ways, but also suggests that states with similar features are choosing different solutions to their development dilemmas. Many states continue to emphasize the need to be competitive with other states in attracting firms and investment with locational incentives. Given our decentralized federal system, it is hard to imagine this interstate competition disappearing completely. But it is also true that the changing nature of global competition is prompting more attention to state incentives that support innovation and growth processes rather than subsidies for specific firms.

Thus we continue to find evidence of a shift over time toward more entrepreneurial approaches even as states seek to balance this new orientation with more traditional approaches. State officials are taking a new look at infrastructure policy as well. States are increasingly responsible for infrastructure investments in an era in which technological changes have radically altered the costs of production as well as the costs of overcoming distance. In contrast to the segmented infrastructure programs of the past, these new state policies emphasize integration of infrastructure systems, competition rather than regulation, and complex financing arrangements.

Overall, these strategy shifts and different mixes of policy orientations over time may be in response to changing state political conditions or the waxing and waning of state commitments to activist, expensive economic development initiatives (Eisinger 1995). It is also possible they reflect an intentional, evolutionary effort to adjust and adapt state economic development strategies to a fluid and uncertain context. In particular, the escalating costs of industrial recruitment are fueling an increasingly critical view of the use of business incentives. Critics claim they create windfalls for business, fail to create net job increases, promote inequities among firms and industries within a state, and reduce the opportunities for state action on other programs—such as education and transportation—important for economic growth (CFED 1996). Groups opposed to the use of incentives to lure businesses have begun to pursue legal action to prevent their use. Others have called on the U.S. Congress to use the federal interstate commerce clause to limit interstate competition for industry.

More than ever, states are being asked to justify program dollars. In 1989 only two states had standards to ensure that benefits produced by economic development policies outweigh their costs; today more than twenty-nine states have such laws (CFED 1996). Several states now are using performance-based incentives whereby companies assisted must reach agreement on employment and revenue goals if they are to enjoy the full value of incentives. Louisiana, Ohio, and Texas pioneered the use of "clawbacks" for reclaiming some of the value of incentives when job goals are not achieved or a company leaves the state prematurely.

Models of state development policy making centered on assumptions about federalism slight the political changes associated with globalization. For many American communities, globalization brings increasing inequalities and social polarization between those benefiting from these economic changes and the many with less certain futures (Kanter 1995). It is possible that these deteriorating social conditions might serve as grounds for political action to challenge state economic development policy responses that overlook these new realities (Goetz 1993). But the logic of interstate competition and the pressures of globalization imply that directing policy attention to those seen as less productive and less competitive in a global era will not be in a state's long-term interest. Although Hwang and Gray (1991) found that redistributive policies were more prevalent at the state level than anticipated by this argument, their analysis predated widespread awareness of globalization trends and, especially, the impacts of welfare devolution.

The recent devolution of welfare responsibilities to the states exacerbates the implicit trade-off of state development and redistribution priorities built into our decentralized federal structure. With more control over determining who receives what level of welfare benefits and under what conditions, states may shun redistributive policies out of fear they will become welfare magnets (Peterson 1995; Peterson and Rom 1990) and discourage future private investment. Whether this era of welfare devolution will mean a race to the bottom of the benefits scale, as critics charge, or the successful use of workfare schemes to return welfare beneficiaries to productive employment is still unclear. The new politics of economic development and welfare are now intertwined in unanticipated and highly visible ways in state policy-making circles.

In short, the state context is more politicized and the organization of state politics is more amenable to political negotiation in regard to economic development issues than previously assumed. But the state political conditions—such as coherent party structures and interparty competition—that Hwang and Gray reasoned might encourage the mobilization of broad constituencies and the articulation of alternative economic and social agendas are less predictable in the face of globalization and devolution. Furthermore, state political institutions are evolving as well and often feature new organizational approaches to carrying out development policies (Clarke and Gaile 1998). Increasingly, state development politics are characterized by nonelected public and private actors as well as organizations and partnership arrangements that cannot be labeled as belonging to either the public or private sector. This trend includes the growing prominence of foundations and nonprofit organizations, as well as the privatization of some state economic development functions. For example, the Economic Development Corporation of Utah, a statewide, nonprofit, public–private organization formed in 1987, provides a privately run business development marketing program in tandem with the state's Department of Community and Economic Development. Similar privatization initiatives are under way in other states, including Arizona, Florida, Kentucky, Minnesota, and Wisconsin. In each instance, the objective is to find new institutional and organizational arrangements with sufficient scope, responsiveness, and flexibility to provide the foundation for economic development. These new arrangements allow state officials to think "outside the box" and to circumvent established interests and outdated ideas in considering policy options. Whether these new arrangements will represent the voices of those often adversely affected by globalization trends or encourage state officials to address their needs remains to be seen.

REFERENCES

Accordino, John J. 1994. "Evaluating Economic Development Strategies." *Economic Development Quarterly* 8:218–229.

Baade, R., and R. Dye. 1988. "Sports Stadiums and Area Development: A Critical Review." *Economic Development Quarterly* 2:265–275.

Barrett, Todd, and John Schwartz. 1992. "Can You Top This?" *Newsweek,* February 17.

Barringer, D. 1997. "The New Urban Gamble." *The American Prospect* (September–October) 28–34.

Bartik, Timothy J. 1991. *Who Benefits from State and Local Economic Development Policies?* Kalamazoo, Mich.: W. E. Upjohn Institute for Employment Research.

Berman, David R., and Lawrence L. Martin. 1992. "The New Approach to Economic Development: An Analysis of Innovativeness in the States." *Policy Studies Journal* 20:10–21.

Blair, John P., and Robert Premus. 1987. "Major Factors in Industrial Location: A Review," *Economic Development Quarterly* 1:78–85.

Boeckelman, Keith. 1991. "Political Culture and State Development Policy." *Publius* 21(2):49–61.

Bowman, Ann O'M. 1987. *Tools and Targets: The Mechanics of City Economic Development. A Research Report of the National League of Cities.* Washington, D.C.: National League of Cities.

Brace, Paul. 1993. *State Government and Economic Performance.* Baltimore: Johns Hopkins University Press.

Bridges, Benjamin. 1965. "State and Local Inducements for Industry, Part II." *National Tax Journal* 18(1):1–14.

CFED (Corporation for Enterprise Development). 1996. "Is Growth Tied to State Incentive Programs?" *Innovations Newsletter* 3 (July).

Choate, Patrick, and Susan Walter. 1981. *America in Ruins: Beyond the Public Works Pork Barrel.* Washington, D.C.: Council of State Planning Agencies.

Clarke, Susan E., and Gary L. Gaile. 1992. "The Next Wave: Local Economic Development Strategies in the Post-Federal Era." *Economic Development Quarterly* 6:187–198.

———. 1998. *The Work of Cities.* Minneapolis: University of Minnesota Press.

Cumberland, John H. 1971. *Regional Development Experiences and Prospects in the United States of America.* The Hague: Mouton.

de Bartolome, Charles A. M., and Mark M. Spiegel. 1995. "Regional Competition for Domestic and Foreign Investment: Evidence from State Development Expenditures." *Journal of Urban Economics* 37:239–259.

Donahue, John D. 1997. *Disunited States.* New York: Basic Books.

Eisinger, Peter. 1988. *The Rise of the Entrepreneurial State: State and Local Economic Development Policy in the United States.* Madison: University of Wisconsin Press.

———. 1995. "State Economic Development in the 1990s." *Economic Development Quarterly* 9:146–158.

Elkins, David R., Richard D. Bingham, and William M. Bowen. (forthcoming) "Patterns in State Economic Development Policy." *State and Local Government Review.*

Fainsod, Merle, Lincoln Gordon, and Joseph C. Palamountain, Jr. 1959. *Government and the American Economy.* New York: W. W. Norton.

Felbinger, Claire F. 1994. "Conditions of Confusion and Conflict: Rethinking the Infrastructure–Economic Development Linkage." In *Building the Public City,* edited by David C. Perry. Newbury Park, Calif.: Sage.

Fosler, R. Scott, ed. 1988. *The New Economic Role of American States.* New York: Oxford University Press.

Fulton, William, and Morris Newman. 1993. "Who Will Wire America?" *Governing* (October):28–30.

Goetz, Edward. 1993. *Shelter Burden.* Philadelphia: Temple University Press.

Gold, Steven D. 1995. *The Fiscal Crisis of the States.* Washington, D.C.: Georgetown University Press.

Gray, Virginia, and David Lowery. 1990. "The Corporatist Foundations of State Industrial Policy." *Social Science Quarterly* 71:3–23.

Gruenwald, Juliana. 1998a. "FCC Votes to Shrink Internet Subsidies Program; Two Bills Would Shift Costs." *Congressional Quarterly,* June 13, 1610.

———. 1998b. "Governors Offer Alternative to Hill's Internet Tax Bills." *Congressional Quarterly,* February 28, 483.

Guskind, Robert. 1993. "The New Civil War" *National Journal,* April 3, 817–821.

Hansen, Susan B. 1984. "The Effects of State Industrial Policies on Economic Growth." A paper presented at the annual meeting of the American Political Science Association, Washington, D.C., September 2.

———. 1989. "Targeting in Economic Development: Comparative State Perspectives." *Publius* 19(2):47–62.

Hanson, Russell L. 1991. "Political Cultural Variations in State Economic Development Policy." *Publius* 21(2):63–81.

———. 1993. "Bidding for Business: A Second War between the States?" *Economic Development Quarterly* 7:183–198.

Harrison, Bennett, and Sandra Kantor. 1978. "The Political Economy of State Job-Creation Business Incentives." In *Revitalizing the Northeast,* edited by Richard Sternlieb and Roger Hughes. New Brunswick: Rutgers University Center for Urban Policy.

Herzik, Eric. 1983. "The Governors and Issues: A Typology of Concerns." *State Government* 51:58–62.

Hwang, Sung-Don, and Virginia Gray. 1991. "External Limits and Internal Determinants of State Public Policy." *Western Political Quarterly* 44 (June):277–298.

Jones, Bryan, and Lynn Bachelor. 1986. *The Sustaining Hand.* Lawrence: University Press of Kansas.

Kale, Steven. 1984. "U.S. Industrial Development Incentives and Manufacturing Growth during the 1970s." *Growth and Change* 15(1):26–34.

Kanter, Rosabeth Moss. 1995. *World Class: Thriving Locally in the Global Economy.* New York: Simon and Schuster.

Kincaid, John. 1992. "Developments in Federal–State Relations, 1990–91." *The Book of the States, 1992–93.* Lexington, Ky.: Council of State Governments.

Koropeckyj, Sophi. 1997. "Do Economic Development Incentives Matter? Regional Financial Associates." http://www.rfa.com/samp/ecodev.stm

Ledebur, Larry, and Walton Hamilton. 1986. *Tax Concessions in State and Local Economic Development*. Washington, D.C.: Aslan Press.

Leigland, James. 1994. "Public Infrastructure and Special Purpose Governments: Who Pays and How?" In *Building the Public City: Politics, Governance, and Finance of Public Infrastructure*, edited by David C. Perry. Newbury Park, Calif.: Sage.

Licate, Jack. 1994. "Cities Can Take Back Their Infrastructure." *Governing* (July):68–71.

Lowery, David, and Virginia Gray. 1992. "Holding Back the Tide of Bad Economic Times: The Compensatory Impact of State Industrial Policy." *Social Science Quarterly* 73:483–495.

———. 1995. "The Compensatory Impact of State Industrial Policy: An Empirical Assessment of Mid-Term Effects." *Social Science Quarterly* 76: 438–446.

Mahtesian, Charles. 1994. "Romancing the Smokestack." *Governing* (November):36–40.

———. 1996. "Saving the States from Each Other: Can Congress Dictate an End to the Great Smokestack Chase?" *Governing* (November):15.

———. 1998. "The Stadium Trap." *Governing* (May 11):22–26.

Man, Joyce Y., and Michael E. Bell. 1993. "Federal Infrastructure Grants-in-Aid: An Ad Hoc Infrastructure Strategy." *Public Budgeting and Finance* 13:9–22.

Mattoon, Richard H. 1993. "Economic Development Policy in the 1990s—Are State Economic Development Agencies Ready?" *Economic Perspectives* 17:11–23.

McHone, Warren W. 1984. "State Industrial Development Incentives and Employment Growth in Multi-State SMSA's." *Growth and Change* 15(4):8–15.

NASDA (National Association of State Development Agencies). 1992, 1994, 1996. *Economic Development Expenditures Survey*. Washington, D.C.: Author.

North, Douglass C. 1966. *The Economic Growth of the United States, 1790 to 1860*. Englewood Cliffs, N.J.: Prentice-Hall.

North, Douglas C., Terry Anderson, and Peter Hill. 1983. *Growth and Welfare in the American Past*. Englewood Cliffs, N.J.: Prentice-Hall.

Osborne, David. 1988. *Laboratories of Democracy*. Boston, Mass.: Harvard Business School Press.

Ota, Alan K. 1998a. "Governors' Pleas Nudge Senate into Action on Highway Bill." *Congressional Quarterly*, February 28, 481–482.

———. 1998b. "American Hits the Highways, and Congress Must Navigate." *Congressional Quarterly*, May 16, 1266–1272.

Peirce, Neal R. 1994. "The When, How, and Why of Wooing." *National Journal*, February 26, 488.

Peretz, Paul. 1986. "The Market for Incentives: Where Angels Fear to Tread." *Policy Studies Journal* 5:624–633.

Perry, David C. 1994a. "Introduction: Building the Public City." In *Building the Public City: Politics, Governance, and Finance of Public Infrastructure*, edited by David C. Perry. Newbury Park, Calif.: Sage.

———. 1994b. "Building the City through the Backdoor: The Politics of Debt, Law, and Public Infrastructure." In *Building the Public City: Politics, Governance, and Finance of Public Infrastructure*, edited by David C. Perry. Newbury Park, Calif.: Sage.

Peterson, Paul E. 1981. *City Limits*. Chicago: University of Chicago Press.

———. 1995. *The Price of Federalism*. Washington, D.C.: Brookings Institution.

Peterson, Paul E., and Mark C. Rom. 1990. *Welfare Magnets: A Case for a National Standard*. Washington, D.C.: Brookings Institution.

Plaut, Thomas, and Joseph Pluta. 1983. "Business Climate Taxes and Expenditures, and State Industrial Growth in the United States." *Southern Economic Journal* 50 (September): 99–119.

Rapp, David. 1994a. "Route 66 Gets a Federal Fix." *Governing* (March):100.

———. 1994b. "The Digital Democrats." *Governing* (June):84.

Reich, Robert. 1991. *The Work of Nations*. New York: Alfred A. Knopf.

Richter, M. J. 1994a. "A Guide to Emerging Technologies." *Governing* (May):65–80.

———. 1994b. "Let the States Help Pave the Information Superhighway." *Governing* (November):72.

Rivlin, Alice. 1995. *Reviving the American Dream*. Washington, D.C.: Brookings Institution.

Rochefort, David A., and Roger W. Cobb. 1994. "Problem Definition: An Emerging Perspective." In *The Politics of Problem Definition*, edited by David A. Rochefort and Roger W. Cobb. Lawrence: University Press of Kansas.

Rosentraub, M., D. Swindell, M. Przybylski, and D. Mullins. 1994. "Sport and Downtown Development Strategy: If You Build It, Will Jobs Come?" *Journal of Urban Affairs* 16:221–239.

Rubin, Herbert J. 1988. "Shoot Anything that Flies; Claim Anything that Falls: Conversations with Economic Development Practitioners." *Economic Development Quarterly* 2:236–251.

Saiz, Martin. 1991. "Determinants of Economic Development Policy Innovation among the U.S. States." Ph.D. diss., University of Colorado at Boulder.

Sbragia, Alberta M. 1996. *Debt Wish. Entrepreneurial Cities, U.S. Federalism, and Economic Development.* Pittsburgh, Penn.: University of Pittsburgh Press.

Schwartz, Gail Garfield. 1990. "Telecommunications and Economic Development Policy." *Economic Development Quarterly* 4:83–91.

Sherman, Don Grant II, Michael Wallace, and William D. Pitney. 1995. "Measuring State-Level Economic Development Programs, 1970–1992," *Economic Development Quarterly* 9:134–145.

Sternberg, Ernest. 1987. "A Practitioner's Classification of Economic Development Policy Instruments, with Some Inspiration from Political Economy." *Economic Development Quarterly* 1:149–161.

Stokes, Bruce. 1994. "Out of the Rubble." *National Journal,* October 15, 2398–2403.

Takaki, Ronald. 1990. *Iron Cages.* New York: Oxford University Press.

Taylor, George R. 1977. *The Transportation Revolution, 1815–1860.* New York: M. E. Sharpe.

U.S. Congress, National Infrastructure Advisory Committee. 1994. *Hard Choices: A Report on the Increasing Gap between America's Infrastructure Needs and Our Ability to Pay for Them.* Prepared for the Subcommittee on Economic Goals and Intergovernmental Policy of the Joint Economic Committee. 98th Cong., 2d sess. Committee print.

U.S. Congress, Office of Technology Assessment. 1990. *Rebuilding the Foundations: Public Works Technologies, Management, and Financing.* Washington, D.C.: U.S. Government Printing Office.

U.S. Department of Transportation, Federal Highway Administration. 1993. *Intermodal Surface Transportation Efficiency Act of 1991: Selected Fact Sheets.* Washington, D.C.: U.S. Government Printing Office.

U.S. General Accounting Office (GAO). 1993. *Federal Budget: Choosing Public Investment Programs.* Washington, D.C.: U.S. Government Printing Office.

Wasylenko, M. 1981. "The Location of Firms: The Role of Taxes and Fiscal Incentives." In *Urban Government Finance: Emerging Trends,* edited by Roy Bahl. Beverly Hills, Calif.: Sage.

———. 1984. "Disamenities, Local Taxation, and the Intra-Metropolitan Location of Households and Firms." In *Research in Urban Economics,* edited by Robert Ebel. Greenwich, Conn.: JAI Press.

Weber, Melvin. 1984. *Industrial Location.* Beverly Hills, Calif.: Sage.

Wolman, Harold. 1988. "Local Economic Development Policy: What Explains the Divergence between Policy Analysis and Political Behavior?" *Journal of Urban Affairs* 6:19–28.

Wolman, Harold, with D. Spitzley. 1996. "The Politics of Local Economic Development." *Economic Development Quarterly* 10 (May): 115–50.

Wyatt, Cathleen Magennis. 1994. "Zero-Sum Games." *State Government News* (April):28–32.·

SUGGESTED READINGS

Bartik, Timothy J. *Who Benefits from State and Local Economic Development Policies?* Kalamazoo, Mich.: W. E. Upjohn Institute for Employment Research, 1991. Bartik asks three questions: whether state and local development policies affect growth, whether local growth helps the unemployed and low-income families, and whether interjurisdictional competition is a zero-sum game or actually helps the economy? He presents a cogent argument that development incentives may raise business activities as well as help disadvantaged workers.

Brace, Paul. *State Government and Economic Performance.* Baltimore: Johns Hopkins University Press, 1993. Brace examines the "mystery of state political economy" and finds that despite previous evidence, state governments can influence their economies. Using both case studies and rigorous quantitative analyses, he emphasizes the importance of national economic conditions in determining the success of particular state economic development strategies. He shows that state governments willing and able to invest in their economies are in a better position to endure national hard times.

Eisinger, Peter. *The Rise of the Entrepreneurial State: State and Local Economic Development Policy in the United States.* Madison: University of Wisconsin Press, 1988. Eisinger develops an analytical framework for comparing "supply-side" state policies designed to reduce the costs of land, labor, capital, and taxes with "demand-side" entrepreneurial strategies aimed at facilitating growth processes through the active intervention of state governments. He traces the evolution of these approaches and surveys evidence for the effectiveness of specific strategies in contributing to growth.

Peter S. Fisher and Alan H. Peters. 1998. *Industrial Incentives: Competition among American States and Cities.* Kalamazoo Mich.: W. E. Upjohn Institute. The authors examine a range of incentives in the twenty-four most industrialized states and in a sample of 112 cities in those states to assess the extent to which incentive policies target distressed areas and particular types of firms, subsidize competition between cities, and provide discretionary implementation opportunities. They use quantitative and descriptive analyses to determine the redistributive effects of various state and local incentive programs.

Hal Wolman with D. Spitzley. 1996. "The Politics of Local Economic Development." *Economic Development Quarterly* 10 (May):115–150. This article, written as the tenth anniversary essay for *Economic Development Quarterly*, assesses the local economic development policy literature. As such, it summarizes its findings and indicates its shortcomings.

CHAPTER 14

The Politics of Family Policy

SUSAN WELCH,

SUE THOMAS,

AND MARGERY M. AMBROSIUS

State legislation regulating family formation is as old as the Republic. Setting up conditions for marriage, ensuring that newborns are duly registered, and regulating divorce and child support are state actions that long preceded contemporary interest in "family policy." Even today, family law is dominated by state action, although the federal government has, in this arena as in others, increased its regulatory and financial scope.

Despite government oversight of a myriad of family concerns, political scientists have traditionally been disinterested in family policy, content to relegate the topic to the preserve of sociologists, demographers, and anthropologists. Recently, however, interest has grown, paralleling and reflecting the concern of public policy makers.

THE CHANGING FAMILY

Several factors explain the increased attention to family policy.[1] Families have changed for numerous reasons. The transformation of women's roles has led to a later age of marriage and parenthood and a greater participation in the work force, even after the birth of children.

Other shifts in societal norms have produced transformations of the family as well. Divorce is at a high level, and 40 percent of all children will have parents who divorce (Amato and Booth 1997, 10). Many children are born into families without fathers.

---

1. Much of the discussion here and in the following section is drawn from Aldous and Dumon (1990) and Moen and Schorr (1987).

Teenage pregnancy is higher than in any other industrial nation in the world. More than half of all children can expect to live in a single-parent household sometime during their childhood. As a consequence, poverty rates for children have increased. Twenty percent of American children are poor, and most of these live in families with one or no wage earner.

Families consisting of partners of the same gender and those who are of the opposite gender but unmarried are increasing too, giving further evidence of changing norms. "Blended" families, those with children from previous marriages, are common. As many as one-third of all children will live with a stepparent sometime before they are 18. Lifespans have become longer, leading to more elderly couples and more elderly people living alone.

It is hard to find a common thread in these changes except that families are becoming more diverse and their functions are shrinking. At frequent intervals, journalists trumpet that fewer than one quarter of all American families are "traditional" families of a husband, a wife who works in the home, and minor children. Single-parent families, step-families, elderly couples with grown children, couples without children, and unmarried couples all are part of what we define as families. As families become more diverse, expectations of family obligations are also becoming more disparate. Sociologists and demographers appear to agree on the trends, but they disagree on their implications and the extent to which we should be concerned about the changing family. Many fear that the family is in danger and that "widespread family breakdown is bound to have a pervasive and debilitating impact not only on the quality of life but on the vitality of the body politic as well" (Levitan, Belous, and Gallo 1988). And there is relatively little agreement about the stance government should take in supporting families.

The weakened traditional family ties, as measured by the increased number of single-parent families and the concomitant impact on the economic and sometimes emotional well-being of children, have led many people to argue that the federal government, and the states, should have policies to try to assist families, especially children. Support for family policies comes from diverse sources and for different reasons. For example, liberals and women's rights advocates support policies to ease the burden of working parents through parental leave, flextime, shared jobs, and subsidized day care. Conservatives favor reforming welfare to encourage families to stay together and tax breaks to encourage women to stay at home with their children. Both liberals and conservatives favor policies to mandate that fathers support their children.

DEFINING FAMILY POLICY

The variety of these policies raises the question, "What exactly is *family policy?*" This common term has many different meanings. Some define it as all legislation that affects the family (Bane 1980, 156), but that definition would include most social and economic legislation, even if the word *family* is not mentioned. After all, minimum wage laws affect the family, as do housing, welfare, health, and most labor policies. Other definitions focus more specifically on policies affecting children (Aldous and Dumon 1990; Lynn 1980).

Still others believe that family policy is that focusing on a "widely agreed-on set of objectives for families" (Moen and Schorr 1987, 795). And many observers implicitly define family policy as something that is directed toward poor families or other specific kinds of families.

The problems with these definitions are obvious. There are few widely agreed on objectives for families. Some argue, for example, that family policy should be directed toward restoring the two-parent family; others disagree. Some believe that family policy should be targeted toward providing income security for families; others believe this is not the job of government. Nor do most observers believe that family policy is something focused only on poor families, problem families, or other specific types of families.

In this discussion, we will take a broader view of family policy, defining it, as did Aldous and Dumon (1990), as policy specifically directed toward family well-being. We focus on several aspects of family policy: regulations of marriage and divorce, family planning, abortion, and helping parents balance work and child rearing through parental leave and day care regulation.

THE ROLE OF THE STATES IN FAMILY POLICY

States have been making family policy since the nation began. Traditionally, state family policy was regulatory, setting conditions for marriage, divorce, adoption, abortion, and removal of children from parental homes; defining spousal and children's rights in inheritance; and overseeing other such matters. Much of what states do is still of that nature.

Since about 1940, and especially since the mid-1970s, states have become much more active in promoting child welfare, protecting women in violent relationships, and aiding poor families. Some of this activism still comes in the form of regulation, such as enforcing standards for child care facilities, whereas other policies are distributive, providing services for families. Several states have given family policy a priority. For example, Mario Cuomo, then governor of New York, announced that 1988–97 would be the Decade of the Child. Other states have set up special task forces or committees to study how the state could better preserve families (Wisensale 1990).

We are concerned with the many family policies states have implemented. We are interested both in common trends and in the ways that states diverge in their adoption of policies designed to help the family. In explaining differences among states, we look at the impact of diverse political cultures and socioeconomic conditions. For example, people from states with individualistic political cultures are less likely than others to agree that government shares with families the responsibility for meeting the needs of children and the elderly and that government should allocate more money for these needs (Zimmerman 1992, 69; see Chapter 1 of this volume). Case studies of Minnesota, Nevada, and South Carolina also illustrate that

Minnesota, the most moralistic state by some definitions, had the most family policies, whereas Nevada, a prototypic individualistic state, had the least (Zimmerman 1992, chap. 5).

REGULATING MARRIAGE AND DIVORCE

Marriage

Traditionally, states have regulated marriage in mostly unexceptional and not very interesting ways, except perhaps to young couples below the minimum age requirement who want to elope. Rates of marriage have not changed much since the 1920s, averaging about ten marriages per 1,000 people, although the rates were somewhat lower in the 1940s and 1960s and higher in the 1950s (see U.S. Bureau of the Census 1994, table 90). The marriage rate has declined slightly in the 1990s, reaching a low of nine marriages per 1,000 people in 1993 (U.S. Bureau of the Census 1997, table 88). Perhaps the most controversial issue surrounding the regulation of marriage is the status of same-gender partners, discussed in a later section of this chapter.

Several states have recently attempted to find ways to strengthen marriage and to reduce divorce. Since 1997, Louisiana has offered two marriage options. A couple could choose to enter into a "covenant marriage" or a "regular" marriage governed by preexisting laws. The covenant option requires the couple to obtain premarital counseling and to seek further counseling when difficulties arise during the marriage. Under a covenant marriage, divorce would be more difficult to obtain than under previous law. The only legal grounds would be adultery by one of the partners, a felony conviction, abandonment, physical or sexual abuse, or a two-year separation.[2] Supporters argued that these restrictions would cause couples to work harder to reconcile any differences; opponents worried that the availability of a covenant marriage would apply considerable psychological pressure to choose this option with no guarantee that the differences in legal rights were clearly understood.[3] By 1998, several other states were considering legislation to allow covenant marriages.

Divorce

Whereas marriage rates and marriage laws have changed little, divorce rates have skyrocketed during the past century, and divorce laws have changed dramatically since the mid-1960s. Obtaining a divorce has traditionally been difficult in Western society. Until the past century, the Christian idea that marriage is a permanent bond made divorce a rare occurrence. Even in the early part of the twentieth century, the grounds for divorce were narrow and the social consequences of divorce often devastating. Couples could divorce only when one of the spouses was proved to be unwilling or unable to uphold his or her part of the marriage because of antiso-

2. See text of Louisiana House Bill 756 at www.lafayetteparishclerk.com\covenantmarriage.html.
3. See ABC News, Nightline, August 20, 1997.

cial behaviors, such as desertion, cruelty, adultery, and drunkenness. Only in a few states was it possible to divorce even after a prolonged separation that indicated the marriage was dead (Jacob 1988; Marvell 1989). Moreover, spouses filing for divorce had to be without blame; they could not be guilty of any acts that might have led their partners to engage in cruelty, desert the family, or commit another of the justifiable grounds for divorce.

Beginning in the 1960s, state legislatures began writing laws making divorce relatively easy. The legislation, labeled "no fault," permitted divorce when the couple could show "irretrievable breakdown" of the marriage. No longer did one partner have to prove that the other committed some act of cruelty, desertion, or worse. These legal changes both reflected and shaped more relaxed societal views toward divorce, and reflected a trend throughout the Western world that resulted in liberalized divorce laws.

By 1985, when South Dakota adopted some no-fault grounds, all states had no-fault divorce statutes. Nineteen states had only no-fault statutes; the rest retained some fault statutes alongside the no-fault grounds (Glendon 1987). No-fault grounds include such criteria as incompatibility, irreconcilable differences, and irretrievable breakdown of the marriage.

The Impact of No-Fault Statutes on Divorce Rates

At the time no-fault laws were passed, some argued that these laws would make divorce easier and thus more frequent by removing legal barriers that had previously forced couples who wanted to divorce into untruthful accusations of wrongdoing. Other observers argued that the new laws were likely to have little effect on divorce rates, because previous divorce laws were flouted. Parties to divorces under the old rules committed perjury and colluded with each other to make their case for divorce (Jacob 1988).

Overall divorce rates in the United States have increased tenfold in the past 100 years. Much of this increase long preceded no-fault divorce, as rates crept up from 0.4 per 1,000 people in 1880 to 2.5 in 1950. In the era of no-fault divorce, these rates doubled to 5.2 people in 1980 but have declined since (U.S. Bureau of the Census 1997, table 88).

Most social scientists who have examined divorce rates before and after the adoption of no-fault laws have found that these laws have had little effect on the rates of divorce (Jacob 1988; Sweezy and Tiefenthaler 1996; White 1991; for a summary see Marvell 1989). These findings support the argument that the no-fault laws brought laws in line with widespread practice. However, the implementation of no-fault rules clearly increased the divorce rate in eight states, and may have increased it in seven others. There was little effect in the remaining states (Marvell 1989). The laws seemed to affect the rate of divorce more in the eastern states and southeastern states. One possible explanation might be that the northeastern states have large populations of Catholics, and the Church has been very opposed to divorce; individuals may not have wanted to lie to the civil authority and flout the authority of the church at the same time. Similarly, many southeastern states have large populations of fundamentalist Protestants, whose religious training also is very much opposed to divorce.

Alimony and Property Division

In a pathbreaking analysis, Weitzman (1985) has argued that the replacement of fault divorce with no-fault standards has dramatically worsened the lives of divorced women. In particular, she has argued that women are, on average, financially worse off under no-fault laws than they were under the traditional divorce laws. She has maintained that no-fault laws improved men's economic conditions because no-fault standards meant that men who left the marriage were not obligated to pay alimony and thus no-fault divorce widens the income gap between men and women.

Weitzman's book has been influential in the debate about divorce and women's status in the 1980s and 1990s (see also Peters 1986). Her conclusion that after divorce women are financially worse off and men financially better off has been replicated in other studies, although other scholars suggest that her estimates of the magnitude of those effects are exaggerated. Some of her analyses of the particular effects of no-fault divorce are flawed in that they contrast the actual situation during the era of no-fault laws with an idealized vision of divorce in the era before them. It is divorce, not just no-fault divorce, that widens the economic gender gap.

Women have benefited from new legislation governing the division of property in divorce settlements. Most states now allot women half of all marital property, and federal law gives them claim to half of their husband's vested pension funds. Such laws have particularly aided middle-class women, who, with their husbands, are likely to have accumulated significant property during the marriage (Jacob 1988, 1989).

Child Custody

In most divorces, the parents agree on who is to have custody of the children, but in about 10 percent of divorces involving children, litigation is necessary to solve the custody issue (Buehler 1989). Some reformers believed that no-fault divorce would lead to more diversity in child custody arrangements. Husbands might win custody more frequently, if they were not charged with being the guilty party in a divorce. This does not seem to be the case, however. A study of child custody settlements over time, before and after the switch to no-fault divorce, showed the patterns of awarding custody unchanged. Women won custody about 90 percent of the time under the fault system and under the no-fault rules (McEvoy 1978).

Nevertheless, some changes in child custody policies have occurred. As more women have entered the workforce and more men become involved in their parenting role, legal doctrine has shifted from the presumption that the mother's preference should be honored to the assumption that custody should be for "the best interests of the child." Evidence from the late 1980s shows a slight increase in custody awards to fathers (Buehler 1989). Joint custody agreements, in which both parents share physical custody, have increased. Whereas joint custody provisions were nearly unheard of until the mid-1960s, most states now have such provisions (Jacob 1988). Some women's groups have opposed this trend toward joint custody, fearing that it would give men an excuse to argue for less child support, although some evidence suggests that joint custody arrangements seem to improve compliance with child support orders (Seltzer 1991).

Gay and lesbian rights issues have entered into the debate on child custody. Currently, no state excludes evidence in divorce cases regarding the sexual orientation of a parent. In California, Indiana, Ohio, Washington, Massachusetts, Michigan, and New Mexico, however, the appellate courts have ruled that sexual orientation of a parent by itself cannot be grounds for denying custody. On the other hand, in Arkansas, Tennessee, and Kentucky, courts take the opposite point of view. In almost every state, though, the standard for placement of the child is the best interests of the child (Achtenberg and Moulding 1994, 1–11).

A related issue is visitation for the noncustodial parent. Most state statutes strongly favor visitation, and in cases in which that has been denied, the goal is to eventually reunite parent and child. Some restrictions for visitation have been applied across the states, most often placing prohibitions on having the parents' partner present during visitation.

Child Support

Half the children now born in the United States will be part of a single-parent household at some time in their lives. Some are born to single mothers; others experience the divorce of their parents. In 1993, 29 percent of all children were currently living with only one parent or neither parent; of those, about 30 percent were living with mothers who had never married; about the same percentage lived with divorced mothers; and the rest were divided between those living with their mothers separated from husbands, those living with fathers (about 10 percent), those living with widowed mothers, and those living with neither parent (about 10 percent; U.S. Bureau of the Census 1994, table 80). By 1996, only three years later, the proportion of children living with only one or neither parent had increased to 32 percent (U.S. Bureau of the Census 1997, table 81).

Children in single-parent families have much higher probabilities of living in poverty and much lower family incomes than children in two-parent families. About 50 percent of young children living with single parents live in poverty, compared with 11 percent of children living in two-parent families (U.S. Bureau of the Census 1997, table 742).

Inadequate or absent child support is a major contributor to this situation. When parents divorce, the custodial parent is usually entitled to some amount of child support. However, as many as one-fifth of divorced women with children are not awarded support at all (Teachman 1990). A significant portion of noncustodial divorced parents do not meet their child support commitments. Most recent data indicate that only slightly more than half of divorced women with children received the full amount of child support owed them in any given year (U.S. Bureau of the Census 1994, table 605). A quarter received only some; and another quarter received none.

Unwed mothers are also entitled to child support, but they have a much lower probability of receiving it than do divorced mothers. In 1991, for example, only about 20 percent received it (U.S. Bureau of the Census 1996, table 605).

Inadequate child support, whether from delinquency in payments or lack of ability to pay, plays a major part in explaining the high levels of poverty among single-parent families and the prevalence of female-headed families among those who receive federal welfare assistance (Meyer 1993). Child support seems crucial to helping single mothers enter the labor market. Female-headed families are only about one-sixth of all families, but they make up about one-half the families under the poverty line (see Teachman 1990).

Some changes are being made in the awarding of child support and its collection, but the laws have changed faster than the willingness of states to implement them. Traditionally, state laws required support but left it to local courts to decide whether and how much support should be paid. Local judges had wide discretion to set the amount of support. In only a few jurisdictions were formal guidelines or formulas used to set child support.

Enforcement of these awards was lax, although absent fathers were sometimes jailed for failing to pay support. Inequities in levels of support abounded, but generally awards were too low to keep children out of poverty and often were far lower than the absent father could have afforded (see Garfinkel 1994; Garfinkel, Oellerich, and Robins 1991; Josephson 1997).

Increased concern over children in poverty and escalating costs of supporting families on welfare led the federal government and the states to change this traditional system. In 1974 legislation created a federal Office of Child Support Enforcement and required all states to establish such offices, with significant financial assistance from the federal government. At first, priority was given to AFDC cases, but in 1980, all cases were included.

The federal government moved further in 1984 when it required states to adopt child support guidelines or formulas that could be used by judges to determine child support levels. Four years later, federal legislation made the guidelines the presumptive child support level (Garfinkel 1994). Judges can deviate from the guidelines only with a written justification. Moreover, states are required to withhold child support obligations from wages.

Federal legislation also mandated states to increase their efforts to establish paternity and trace absent fathers by requiring their social security numbers before issuing birth certificates to their children, and requiring all parties in a contested paternity case to take genetic tests (largely paid for by the federal government). In 1995 states located 4,950,000 absent parents, established 659,000 paternities, and established 1,051,000 support obligations (U.S. Bureau of the Census 1997, table

611). Each of these activities is growing substantially (for example in 1990, the states located only 2,100,000 absent parents).

Although states have established support guidelines, and although they are required to have statewide monitoring systems for child support enforcement, only twenty-one states had met federal standards by February 1998. In 1996 the federal welfare reform law threatened penalties against states that did not move to track down "deadbeat dads" (some of the deadbeats are women, but most are men). As of 1998 no state had been penalized, even though only about half had complied with the law. Spending to create these systems is not a high priority of many state legislatures, where the representatives of those who pay child support are considerably greater in number than those who receive it. Although awarding and collecting child support are hardly panaceas for the high rate of children living in poverty, even greater state efforts toward increased enforcement would clearly contribute to an amelioration of poverty in many families.

FAMILY PLANNING POLICY

No family policy is more controversial than that concerning family planning. The conflict is visible not only in the heated public struggle over adult access to abortion but also in the political battles related to minors' access to both birth control and abortion.

The reasons behind the intense and sustained controversy over family planning policy, particularly abortion, are numerous. First, religious beliefs clash on several issues related to family planning. For example, Catholic Church doctrine teaches that the purpose of sex is for procreation, thus making illegitimate the use of artificial birth control devices. Many Catholics and fundamentalist Christians, among others, believe that human life begins at conception and that abortion is therefore murder. Many other religious groups, particularly liberal Protestant denominations and reform Judaism, disagree heatedly with both these assumptions and maintain that each woman must make her own decision.

Different perspectives on "family values" also provide fuel to these debates about family planning. Allowing minors access to contraception and abortion services stands in direct contradiction to the maintenance of parental control over children.

Political issues are almost as starkly defined. Prochoice forces focus on whether the government has any right whatsoever to intrude on the decisions a woman makes about her body. Prolife forces argue that the issue is not that clear. Two lives are at stake, they assert, and the pregnant woman's control over her own body is not the only or the overriding issue.

Abortion is also one of the primary symbolic issues separating feminists from antifeminists, and advocates of gender equality from advocates of traditional women's roles. If women have the sole right to make the decision to terminate their pregnancy, their other choices in life are more plentiful. They are less dependent on their husbands. Their freedom to move between traditionally male and female worlds increases. Traditionalists believe that the abandonment of a woman's unique role is not just problematic for individual women, and not just important to the issue of abortion, but has implications that go to the very fabric of society, affecting marriage, child rearing, the nature of families, and the social and economic composition of the work force.

BIRTH CONTROL

Although access to birth control is often taken for granted in the United States, such nonchalance about the topic was not always possible. Before the 1870s, a variety of birth control methods was widely used, although the use of them was often controversial. In fact, some thought discussions of birth control devices and techniques were obscene, and some communities suppressed information about them (Stetson 1991b; see also Gray 1979; Sapiro 1994).

Just beyond the middle of the nineteenth century, a political and social movement that focused on purity and moral rectitude aimed to place birth control advocacy, availability, and use directly into obscenity law. In a mere month in 1873, the antiobscenity and anticontraception crusader Anthony Comstock of Pennsylvania successfully lobbied the U.S. Congress and saw passed (with no opposition and only fifteen minutes of debate) the Comstock Law, which prohibited the use of the U.S. mails for distribution of any "obscene" materials, specifically labeling as obscene "the dissemination of any pornography, abortion devices, and any drug, medicine, article or thing designed, adapted, or intended for preventing conception" (McGlen and O'Connor, 1998, 208). Within twenty-five years, about half of the states had passed "Little Comstock laws." As a consequence, it became almost impossible for women to legally obtain information about contraception or abortion.

Opposing political activists such as Margaret Sanger advocated removal of private reproductive matters from the realm of criminal activity, whether in state or federal law. As public sentiment grew more permissive, advocates such as Sanger did find ways to disseminate some types of information. They began challenging the Comstock laws in court, and in the 1930s several federal court decisions held that contraceptives were no longer considered obscene. Federal prosecutions for the sale of contraceptives ended. State courts subsequently made similar decisions with respect to the Little Comstock laws. Then, in 1965 the U.S. Supreme Court in *Griswold v. Connecticut* (381 U.S. 479) held that a Connecticut law prohibiting contraceptive use by married persons was unconstitutional. The majority opinion noted that inherent in the Bill of Rights was the right to privacy. In 1972 in *Eisenstadt v. Baird* (405 U.S. 438) the Court held that the right to have a child was a private decision regardless of marital status and therefore contraceptives could not be denied to adults. In what was by then a largely symbolic move, Congress finally repealed the Comstock law in 1971 (Garrow 1994).

Today, neither federal nor state laws attempt to regulate birth control decisions for adults, whether married or unmarried. Choice and ability to pay regulate access to a variety of available devices. Ability to pay is less of an obstacle than it might otherwise be because federal programs assist the indigent, and family planning clinics offer prescriptions and medical services at reduced rates (Stetson 1991b). Free or low-cost contraceptive services for poor individuals are provided at clinics in all fifty states and are available in 85 percent of U.S. counties (Alan Guttmacher Institute 1997).

The access of minors to birth control information and devices still engenders much controversy. It has been the rule rather than the exception in state law for minors to be disallowed medical treatment unless a parent has consented. Certain exceptions, such as medical emergencies, have been allowed, however. Birth control has not traditionally been one of the few exceptions to parental consent. Only in 1977 did the U.S. Supreme Court, in *Carey v. Population Services International* (431 U.S. 678 [1977]), hold that minors too have a constitutional right to privacy, which includes the right to obtain contraceptives. Subsequent to *Carey,* some states passed laws that allow "mature" minors (those demonstrating the mental acuity and maturity to understand the type of treatment and its potential consequences) to seek medical treatment without parental consent. Other states have laws that allow minors to get medical treatment related to sexual activity, among other conditions.

Of course, allowing minors access not only to birth control, but also to information about sexuality remains highly controversial for all the religious and political reasons suggested earlier. Numerous local school board and state legislative races have highlighted issues such as whether and at what ages minors ought to be given information about sex and birth control. Proponents of the view that teaching teenagers about contraception encourages increased sexual activity vie with others who believe that sexual activity among teenagers will take place whether or not safe sex is taught in the schools. The latter group argues that teenagers also need good information about protection from HIV infection and AIDS. The federal government has also weighed in on this debate. The 1996 federal welfare reform reflects the congressional view that the best message to teenagers about birth control is abstinence from sexual activity. The legislation offers funds to support educational programs for teenagers about abstinence as a way to prevent pregnancy and sexually transmitted diseases, such as AIDS. Programs that qualify for these funds must teach teens that they should abstain from sexual activity until marriage.

ABORTION

The Early Era

Not unlike the situation with contraceptive access, in general abortion was not legally prohibited in the United States up through the late 1820s. Prior to that time, the United States followed English common law, which held that abortion was not a criminal act if performed before quickening (the time when the movement of the fetus could be felt in the mother's womb). In fact, in 1821 Connecticut passed the first U.S. law on abortion, and it followed common law precepts (Sapiro 1994, 368–369). Furthermore, as early as 1809, the Supreme Court of Massachusetts dismissed an indictment for abortion because the prosecution had not reliably proved that the woman was "quick with child" (Luker 1984, 15).

From 1828, when New York passed a law criminalizing abortion for unquickened fetuses, a movement to outlaw abortion grew. The American Medical Association (AMA) passed a resolution in the late 1850s that condemned abortion and urged state legislatures to pass laws prohibiting it. The AMA may have been concerned about the danger to women of improper abortions, or it may have been more concerned about professionalizing their occupation and monopolizing services. The Roman Catholic Church was also among those in the forefront of the movement to criminalize abortion; until the 1860s, Church policy ignored early abortions, but after that time, the church condemned all abortions (Luker 1984). By 1900 every state in the nation had passed legislation prohibiting abortion throughout pregnancy unless necessary to save the life of the mother. Penalties were imposed, usually on doctors, but in some states on the women themselves.

The Modern Era

In the 1960s, in part influenced by the civil rights movement and the feminist movement, political activists began advocating state legalization of abortion. They cited the vast number of illegal abortions that risked the health and lives of women and the right of women to control their procreation choices. With a model state law developed by the American Law Institute, several states, such as California, Colorado, Hawaii, New York, and North Carolina liberalized their abortion laws to allow the procedure when a women's life or health were endangered or when the pregnancy was the result of rape or incest. A 1970 New York law went the farthest and allowed abortion for any reason during the first six months of pregnancy (Luker 1984; Mezey 1992; Sapiro 1994; Stetson 1991b).

Activists were pressing state legislatures in many places to follow the lead of New York and others when the issue was addressed at the national level. These actions culminated in 1973 when, in *Roe v. Wade* (410 U.S. 113), the Supreme Court struck down a Texas law that prohibited abortion and held that a women's right to privacy (as established in *Griswold*) included the right to end a pregnancy. The Court, however, did not make this an absolute right. Rather, it held that in the first trimester (three months) of a pregnancy, the decision was solely up to a woman and her doctor. In the second trimester, states were allowed to regulate abortion to protect maternal heath. In the third trimester, the states, said the Court, had an interest in potential life and at the point of fetal viability could prohibit abortion altogether.

State legislatures across the nation began challenging the *Roe* decision by passing legislation that sought to limit its scope. In fact, within two years sixty-two laws were passed in thirty-two states to regulate consent requirements, recordkeeping and reporting, the location where abortions could be performed and who could perform them, funding, advertising, fetal protection, and to allow medical personnel whose conscience forbade them to participate not to be required to do so. A great many of these laws were immediately challenged by women's organizations; subsequent court decisions made clear that most of the regulations were inconsistent with the holding in *Roe*. Until 1989, only funding laws and laws related to parental notification and consent were ultimately upheld (Mezey 1992, 22).

Although the abortion policy arena changes continually, currently thirty-four states restrict public funding in various ways. Three states (Alabama, Mississippi, and South Dakota) allow funding only if the woman's life is endangered. Twenty-eight states allow funding if the woman's life is endangered or if the pregnancy results from rape or incest. Another three states (New Mexico, Virginia, and Wisconsin) provide funding for termination in these cases plus if the woman's health is poor. In sharp contrast, seventeen states allow public funding of abortion for all or most circumstances. These states are Alaska, California, Connecticut, the District of Columbia, Hawaii, Idaho, Illinois, Maryland, Massachusetts, Minnesota, Montana, New Jersey, New York, Oregon, Vermont, Washington, and West Virginia (NARAL Foundation/NARAL 1996) and four states have passed legislation to affirm explicitly the right to abortion (Connecticut, Maryland, Nevada, and Washington; Alan Guttmacher Institute 1997). California, Colorado, Kansas, Maine, Maryland, Massachusetts, Minnesota, Nevada, North Carolina, Oregon, Washington, and Wisconsin plus the District of Columbia have laws to protect clinic workers and women seeking abortions (NARAL Foundation/NARAL 1993b).

The states' role in abortion policy has been accentuated as a result of two U.S. Supreme Court cases. First, in 1989 in *Webster v. Reproductive Heath Services* (492 U.S. 490), the Court upheld a Missouri law that, among other things, required tests of fetal viability before abortions were performed, banned public funds to counsel women to have abortions if their lives were not in danger, and prohibited use of public facilities and public employees to perform abortions unless the woman's life was at issue. Though the Court did not explicitly overturn *Roe*, it allowed these restrictions on abortion and left open the question of what other restrictions could be imposed. In 1992, the Court ruled in *Planned Parenthood of Southeastern Pennsylvania v. Casey* (505 U.S. 833) that although women still retained the right to choose abortion, it was no longer a fundamental right. Abortion could be restricted as long as the nature of those restrictions did not constitute an undue burden, defined as "a substantial obstacle in the path of a woman seeking abortion." The precise operational definition of the phrase is not yet clear; however, the spousal consent requirement in the Pennsylvania law was deemed an undue burden. Nevertheless, the Court allowed parental consent for minors and a twenty-four-hour waiting period.

The *Casey* ruling, of course, opens the door to the states to impose a variety of regulations. Since *Casey*, eighteen states have adopted a mandatory waiting period before an abortion can be obtained (Delaware, Idaho, Indiana, Kansas, Kentucky, Louisiana, Massachusetts, Michigan, Mississippi, Montana, Nebraska, North Dakota, Ohio, Pennsylvania, South Carolina, South Dakota, Tennessee, and Utah). In seven states, the waiting period law is enjoined by the courts until review is complete (Delaware, Indiana, Kentucky, Michigan, Mississippi, Montana, and Tennessee; NARAL/NARAL Foundation 1996).

Another tactic to limit abortions has been to restrict what has variously been called the "partial birth," "late-term," or— the medical term—the "intact dilation and extraction abortion procedure." This procedure has been used in various forms for more than 100 years to perform abortions later in pregnancy, usually because of severe fetal defect or a life-threatening condition for the woman. Congress has twice passed a bill to outlaw intact dilation and extraction, the first time that a specific type of procedure was targeted, but President Bill Clinton vetoed both laws. By 1998, however, nineteen states had banned the procedure. At this writing, judges have blocked enforcement in eleven states, no one has yet contested the laws in six of them, and in the others, various types of action have been or are being taken to limit their applicability (Donnelly 1997; Garrow 1998). Challengers of intact dilation and extraction bans contend that the laws passed by the states may be void because they are vague and because they violate the *Roe* guidelines (though the *Roe* guidelines do allow states to prohibit abortion in the third trimester).

In the post-*Webster* era, state laws differ greatly from one another, with some states doing their best to limit abortions and others to protect women's rights to them. For example, New York funds about twenty times as many abortions per 1,000 women as does Wisconsin (Meier and McFarlane 1993, 251). Political and socioeconomic factors influence these state laws. Socioeconomic variables were the best predictors of state action in the pre-*Webster* era, but political factors were also related to abortion restrictiveness in the post-*Webster* era (Strickland and Whicker, 1992). The strength of citizen action groups and the distribution of partisanship were important determinants of policies toward funding abortions (Meier and McFarlane, 1993). State political culture matters too. The moralistic states, largely those of the Northern Plains, Northwest, and New England have the fewest restrictions.

Public opinion is another key element in assessing the future of abortion restrictions in the states. Since *Roe,* public opinion has reflected a general prochoice stance. In 1990, for example, public opinion in two states was predominantly pro-life (Kentucky and South Dakota), and in another four states (Alabama, Arkansas, Nebraska, and West Virginia), it was evenly split. In all other states, a majority was prochoice, including a landslide prochoice position in nineteen states (Cohen and Barrilleaux 1993). These conclusions are based on attitudes about abortion in general and not on specific types of procedures (Goggin and Wlezien 1993). Polls on the intact dilation and extraction abortion procedure, however, show the public overwhelmingly against its use (Balz, 1998).

When there is no clear public opinion majority, organized interest groups may prevail. Even when opinion is overwhelmingly on one side, interest groups on the other side win about half the time. Organized interests usually triumph unless opinion is nearly consensual (Cohen and Barrilleaux 1993, 214; for information about the effect of abortion on state electoral races, see Goggin 1993; Dodson and Burnbauer with Kleeman 1990).

The demographic makeup of state legislatures also has an effect on the types of abortion policies. As we discuss later in the chapter, a greater proportion of women in state legislatures generally leads to less restrictive action on this issue (Berkman and O'Connor 1993). The religious affiliation and party composition of state legislators are also strongly correlated with voting behavior (Witt and Moncrief 1993).

Minors' Access

Minors' access to abortion continues to be a highly charged political and social issue. As soon as the Court decided *Roe v. Wade,* state legislatures across the nation began passing parental consent and parental notification laws. *Consent* refers to the express permission of one or both parents for the minor girl to obtain an abortion. *Notification,* however, refers to simply informing one or both parents that the procedure is about to take place.[4]

Legal challenges to state consent and notification laws began soon after their passage and, starting in 1976, the U.S. Supreme Court began deciding these cases. In that year, in *Planned Parenthood of Central Missouri v. Danforth* (428 U.S. 52), the Court ruled that states cannot give parents absolute veto power over a daughter's decision to have an abortion. In other cases,[5] the Court further refined the scope of parental involvement, allowing states to require a minor to get consent of one or both parents, but only if there is an alternative provided to girls who believe they cannot inform their parents. This alternative usually consists of a judicial bypass, which means that a minor may go before a judge for a ruling on whether or not she is mature enough to make her own decision. If the girl is found too immature, the judge can also order an abortion for her if it is considered to be in her best interest. The Court ruled that a state may require a doctor to notify one or both parents of abortion plans.

Most states have adopted laws requiring parental consent or notification for minors. Thirty-one states have requirements for consent by one parent, and five (Arkansas, Massachusetts, Minnesota, Mississippi, North Dakota) require both to consent, although twenty-nine states do have a judicial bypass. In addition, twelve states have a mandatory waiting period and two (Connecticut and Maine) have mandatory counseling for minors (NARAL Foundation/NARAL 1996).

Public Policy and Abortion Rates

There are vast differences among the states in abortion rates (the ratio of abortions to women of child-bearing age), ranging from four per 1,000 in Wyoming and seven in South Dakota and Idaho to forty-six per 1,000 in Hawaii and New York. Almost one-third of all abortions take place in California, New York, and

---

4. Many prochoice activists argue that notification is interchangeable with consent because of the parent's considerable ability to prevent the procedure. And requiring permission or notification of both parents is an especially heavy burden because for many minors, only one parent may be in the home or even in contact with the child, or a parent may be abusive or have even fathered the child.

5. *Bellotti v. Baird* (443 U.S. 622 [1979]), *City of Akron v. Akron Center for Reproductive Health* (462 U.S. 416 [1983]), and *Planned Parenthood Association of Kansas City, Missouri, Inc. v. Ashcroft* (462 U.S. 476 [1983]).

Texas, although Texas is not among the states with the highest ratio of abortions to women of child-bearing age. California currently has the highest rate of all the states.

The most recent data available suggest that abortions have declined from around 1.5 million done annually in the 1980s and early 1990s to about 1.2 million in 1995 (U.S. Bureau of the Census 1997, table 114, provides annual data through 1992). The abortion rates (per woman of child-bearing age) have decreased in all but seven states, though more recently have increased in some states.

Declining abortion rates are a result of several factors, including the decrease (in 1990 down by 3 million from 1980) in the number of women in the 15- to 24-year-old age group, increased teenage use of contraception, and decreased access to abortion services (Vobejda 1997). More than half of all abortions are performed on women 15 to 24, so the dramatic population decrease certainly affects the numbers of abortions performed. Moreover, fewer teenagers are becoming pregnant, either because of better contraceptive practices, increasing rates of abstinence, or both, lessening the need for abortion (National Center for Health Statistics 1998). Aside from demographic factors, decreased access certainly limits abortion rates. The *Washington Post* reported that "more than 500 U.S. hospitals and clinics have stopped offering abortions since the early 1980s, and the number of young physicians who learn abortion techniques as part of their training has plummeted" (Goldstein 1995). Not surprisingly, the rate of abortion is lower in states with reduced provider access and more restrictions (Matthews, Ribar, and Wilhelm 1997).

Threats, intimidation, and violence against patients, providers, and clinics may also play some role in reducing the number of abortions. "Since 1989, there have been five deaths, over 25,000 clinic blockades, nearly 200 death threats, and 1,000 incidents of bombing, vandalism and burglary" (Rodgers 1997).

To combat these activities, states and the federal government have enacted legislation to protect clinics, providers, and patients. The 1993 murder of an abortion provider, Dr. David Gunn in Pensacola, Florida, spurred the U.S. Congress to pass The Freedom of Access to Clinic Entrances Act (FACE), signed by President Clinton in 1994. That act prohibits the use, attempt, or threat of force or physical obstruction to interfere with providers or reproductive services or the ability of patients to obtain services (McGlen and O'Connor 1998). Some states and municipalities have also passed legislation to protect clinic workers (California; Colorado; Kansas; Maryland; Massachusetts; Minnesota; Nevada; North Carolina; Oregon; Washington; Wisconsin; and Los Angeles, California). The laws have had an effect. As reported in *Ms.* magazine, after FACE, violent protests at abortion clinics dropped to fewer than 400 in 1996 (up to November) from 1,800 in all of 1995 (*Ms.* 1997).

Academic studies have sought to detect a relationship between violence and reduced rates of abortion. Neither funding cutbacks nor violence directed at clinics produced any declines in abortion rates in the 1980s (Hansen 1993). More recently, antiabortion violence has been associated with conservative abortion rights climates, but violence did not decrease the abortion rate, at least in three recent years studied (Doane and Meier n.d.). Instead, the presence or absence of public funding, the proportion of females in the labor force, and urbanism predicted abortion rates.

In sum, this very contentious issue of abortion is in a state of political flux. The ideological proclivities of legislatures, the willingness of the Supreme Court to allow additional state regulation of abortion with respect to specific abortion procedures, violence against providers and patients, and the availability of medical discoveries such as the abortion pill RU-486 (mifepristone) as an alternative to surgical abortion will all affect the future of abortion law and availability of abortions.

CHILD CARE AND CHILD PROTECTION

Government assistance to help families with child care and to prevent child abuse is not nearly as publicly controversial as abortion, yet disputes about the extent of government involvement have placed the United States at the bottom of the industrial world in the help it gives families. Indeed, as former Rep. Patricia Schroeder (D-Colo.) once remarked, "There's no capital city in the world that talks more about family and does less" (quoted in Roemer 1988, 188).

Still, states are increasingly active in a variety of child protection and child care activities. For example, one author estimated that between 1987 and 1990, forty-seven states strengthened their child abuse and neglect laws, forty-one fortified their child support enforcement bills, and seventeen passed laws designed to preserve and protect families, including laws regulating foster care (Wisensale 1991). We examine three types of policies: parental leave, day care regulation, and child abuse prevention.

Family Leave

Family leave policies are those guaranteeing employees a minimum benefit that would entitle them to keep their jobs even if they had to take a few days, weeks, or possibly months off to care for a new child, disabled parent, or other family member. The impetus for these laws was the massive numbers of women who have entered the labor market. By 1996 women were 46 percent of the American labor force (U.S. Bureau of the Census 1997, table 624). Many of these women have primary responsibility for the care of their children and for elderly relatives. More than half of all mothers with children under 1 year of age work outside the home, and more than 60 percent of all mothers with children under 6 are in the labor force (U.S. Bureau of the Census 1997, table 631). Nevertheless, the U.S. society often operates as if working mothers did not exist (Lenhoff and Becker 1989, 405). If a family member quits work or leaves a full-time job to work part-time in order to meet a home crisis, the economic well-being of the family is often sacrificed, and the family's stability shattered.

The History of Family Leave Policy. Family leave policy grew out of earlier policies on maternity protection and pregnancy leave. Some early feminists considered work to be harmful to women. Sweatshops and factories with poor ventilation, noxious fumes, and inadequate or too much heat were difficult for everyone, but reformers thought these conditions were particularly hard on women and their ability to bear children. Thus the reform movement of the 1890s advocated protective labor legislation for women (see Stetson 1991a). Legislatures passed and the Supreme Court upheld, in *Muller v. Oregon* (208 U.S. 412 [1908]), state policies barring women entirely from positions considered dangerous (which often happened to be higher paying jobs); dismissing women when they married, presumably because they were then entering their child-bearing years and because they no longer needed to work to support themselves; and limiting their benefits and their hours of work (thereby keeping them at home).[6]

Others, including feminist groups such as the National Woman's Party, believed that motherhood was not incompatible with work and that workers who were pregnant had rights, including the right of prenatal and postnatal leave (Stetson 1991a, 409). In 1942 Rhode Island became the first state to incorporate into law the idea of pregnancy as a covered disability. But other states excluded pregnancy from coverage, as they noted the cost to Rhode Island's employers for this provision. This exclusion garnered support from the federal Equal Opportunity Commission, which in the 1960s told employers that it was not a violation of civil rights to exclude pregnancy benefits because pregnancy was a disability unique to women. The Supreme Court continued to rule that failure to include pregnancy under temporary disability benefits was not sex discrimination, although the justices also ruled that mandatory maternity leave and deprivation of seniority protection after a childbirth leave were discriminatory.[7]

The status quo changed in 1978 when, prompted by support from unions, feminist groups, and civil rights groups, and recognition that more than 40 percent of the work force was made up of women (Gelb and Palley 1982, 157), Congress passed and President Jimmy Carter signed the Pregnancy Discrimination Act. Pregnancy was now defined as a temporary disability, and employers were obligated to provide the same fringe benefits for pregnancy and childbirth as for other medical disabilities. By 1982, 89 percent of employees with medical insurance had some form of maternity benefits, as opposed to only 57 percent in 1977. However, this federal law did not require employers to provide any disability benefits at all, and only five states (California, Hawaii, New Jersey, New York, and Rhode Island) had acted to do so (Kamerman 1991; Stetson 1991a, 413).

Current Family Leave Policies. The entrance of mothers of small children into the work force was dramatic during the 1980s. In 1977, the year before the Pregnancy Discrimination Act was passed, 32 percent of mothers of children 1 year old or younger were in the workforce; by 1988, 52 percent were (Kamerman 1991). Yet the supply of child care facilities had not grown proportionally to this striking so-

---

6. Much of this discussion is drawn from Stetson 1991b.

7. See *Geduldig v. Aiello* (417 U.S. 484 [1974]); *General Electric v. Gilbert* (429 U.S. 125 [1976]); *Cleveland Board of Education v. La Fleur* (414 U.S. 632, 1973); and *Nashville Gas Co. v. Satty* (434 U.S. 136, 1977).

cial change. Demand therefore increased for the federal government and the states to do more to help working parents. One of those demands was that states should guarantee that working women could take maternity leave without risking their jobs.

Montana in 1972 was the first state to adopt a maternity leave act. This act made it unlawful to terminate a woman's employment or to refuse to grant a reasonable leave of absence because of pregnancy. This maternal leave policy went much further than previous legislation because it mandated protection for pregnant employees and recognized women's maternal as well as employee role.

After Montana had done so, many other states adopted maternal or parental leave policies. By 1995, two-thirds of the states had such policies. Family leaves potentially benefit most families, not just low-income families. However, many employees are not able to take advantage of these leaves. Family leave guarantees only leave; employers are not obligated to provide any pay, and most do not. Family leave policy likely affects middle- and upper-income workers, then, much more than lower-income ones, and two-earner families more than single-parent households.

The issue of who should be covered has at least two important dimensions. One is whether the state should mandate parental leave only for its own agencies or whether it should mandate it for all employers. Only twenty-one states cover both private and state employees. In twelve other states, only state employees are covered (Makuen 1988). Another issue of coverage is whether the act should apply to men and women or only women. Gradually, maternal leaves evolved into parental leaves that could be taken by men or women.

Early versions of family leave bills covered only care for a newborn, but later policies extended this coverage to adoption, to care of elderly parents, sick children who were not newborns, spouses, and other family members. Currently, most state parental leave laws include both childbirth and adoption, and some provide leave for a family member other than a child or dependent.

Despite the opposition of many business organizations, such as the U.S. Chamber of Commerce and the National Federation of Independent Businesses, federal parental leave legislation was passed by Congress and signed by President Clinton in 1993. Employees throughout the nation are now covered if they work for firms having more than fifty employees, even if their own states do not have parental leave laws.

The federal law requires employers of fifty or more workers to allow employees to take up to twelve weeks of unpaid leave during any twelve-month period for the birth or adoption of a child, serious illness in the family, or the employee's own health. In addition to the unpaid leave provision, the bill also prohibits the loss of employment benefits during the leave and requires the employer to maintain health care benefits for employees on leave. These criteria obviously were the result of substantial compromises. For example, the larger the minimum number of employees in firms to be covered, the less opposition from small business interests but the fewer workers who would be covered. The threshold of fifty workers covers only

60 percent of all employees and applies to only 5 percent of employers (Lenhoff and Becker 1989). In contrast, a threshold of fifteen employees would cover 71 percent of employees and would apply to 82 percent of all firms.

Still, employees in firms covered by the federal bill have broader coverage than under many state laws; for example, the twelve weeks exceed the guarantee in all but nine states, and the federal guarantee of leave in the event of serious illness in the family or for the employee's own health is found in only a minority of states. Some state legislation, however, covers firms smaller than those included in the federal mandate.

The presence and scope of family leave laws do reflect cultural and economic differences among the states. We would expect states with moralistic political cultures to be more active in promoting ways to reconcile women's maternal and work roles, and, as expected, family leave laws are indeed significantly more likely to be found in states with moralistic political cultures. For example, fully 69 percent of moralistic states have parental leave laws covering both private and public employers. Only 40 percent of individualistic states and a mere 21 percent of traditionalistic states have such laws.

Day Care

Family leave policies help families with emergencies and special needs, but day care assists parents with the routine and essential day to day care of young children. States and localities have long been involved in regulating certain kinds of day care, specifically in licensing, inspecting, and setting minimum standards for child care facilities. But regulatory activities in child care are increasing, partly because of the massive increase of women in the workforce.[8]

Increasing Accessibility. The day care services that do exist are generally filled to capacity and have long waiting lists. State and federal legislation have addressed the issue in an effort to increase access to high-quality day care services. For example, in the late 1980s, seven states adopted policies encouraging employers to support child care. Oregon and Rhode Island, for example, created employer tax credits for child care assistance. Six states passed policies improving day care availability for low-income families, and four others did so for children with special needs.

The federal government has also stepped into the child care policy arena. In 1990 Congress passed and the president approved the ABC bill, the Act for Better Child Care Services. Although the act sounds broad in its impact, it is largely aimed at low-income families. It gives tax credits to low-income families to help pay for child care, and it gives grants to the states to help provide child care.

Who Is Regulated? There are many types of day care facilities, but the two basic regulatory categories are day care homes, where children are cared for by an individual, and group day care centers. The latter may be run by a business for profit;

---

8. This section relies heavily on Wisensale 1990; Gormley 1990, 1991a, and 1991b; and Gormley and Peters 1992.

by a business as a service for its own employees; or by a church, university, or other type of nonprofit organization. All states regulate group day care centers, and all states but Louisiana regulate family day care facilities.

However, regulatory coverage is far from complete. Twelve states, for example, exempt church-run day care centers from all or most regulations. In those states, this removes about one-third of all group day care centers from serious regulation (cited in Gormley and Peters 1992). Some states exempt other sorts of day care facilities as well, such as summer day camps or day care centers run by colleges and universities.

Some day care facilities are exempt because they serve only a few children. For example, thirty-six states exempt family day care homes serving three or fewer children from mandatory regulation and inspections (Adams 1990).

States typically require less of family day care homes than group day care centers. Group day care centers are typically required to have sprinkler systems, family homes only fire extinguishers; group centers might be required to have safe surfaces for jungle gyms, family homes only a fenced backyard; group homes need general liability insurance, family homes only access to a car in case of emergencies (Gormley 1990).

What Is Regulated. Day care facilities are increasingly regulated. States and localities regulate the physical facilities of the day care centers, the program personnel, and the health status of the children. The average number of pages of state regulations for family day care homes is about seventeen, those for group day care centers about thirty. Each page typically contains more than one regulation, so centers are covered by dozens. Connecticut's nineteen-page handbook includes 133 regulations (Gormley 1990).

There are at least three kinds of important program regulations, child-to-staff ratios, maximum group sizes, and the amount of training required of staff. Having many staff members in relation to the number of children, serving relatively few children, and having highly trained staff all contribute to the quality of care offered (Vandell, Henderson, and Wilson 1988). States in the Northeast and Midwest have much stricter child-to-staff ratios than do states in the South and West. Fewer differences are apparent in the size of group allowed (Gormley and Peters 1992).

Training requirements vary widely among the states. Nearly half require little or no training or experience, but more than one-third require a high school diploma or some college training. Compared to day care workers in other nations, those in the United States tend to be very poorly paid, reflecting the lack of qualifications needed. It is not surprising, perhaps, that annual turnover of personnel in group day care facilities is 40 percent (Gormley 1990; Gormley and Paters 1992).

Some regulations decrease the availability of day care facilities (Gormley 1995). In particular, requiring lower child–staff ratios depresses the number and increases the cost of group day care facilities, and strict inspection diminishes the numbers of family day care facilities. Training requirements, although they are found in only a minority of states, appear to improve the quality of the program and are not opposed by most day care operators (Gormley 1990, 1991b, 1995).

Enforcing Regulations. In contrast to the large number of regulations that day care providers must follow, the number of officials available to inspect facilities to ensure that the regulations are being followed is small. Many regulations are simply not enforced (Gormley 1990).

The primary regulators are state human service agencies, which license and inspect day care facilities. Local governments and other state agencies are usually involved, however. For example, building inspections are sometimes the jurisdiction of local or state building inspection departments; health inspections are sometimes done by local, county, or state health agencies. Local governments usually have jurisdiction over the zoning regulations that determine where day care facilities may be placed.

The Future. William Gormley, the political scientist who has studied child care regulation most intensively, has argued that both the federal government and the states need to modify their stance toward regulating child care services. He recommended that the federal government provide more financial support for low income families' day care needs and increased incentives for employers to help fund day care for their employees' children. He also recommended that states need to lighten the hand of regulation, especially for family day care centers, making it less onerous on a family to provide day care services, and he urged states to look carefully at the impact of some kinds of regulations, especially the child–staff ratio, on limiting access and driving up costs. On the other hand, he has argued that states should not exempt large classes of day care providers from regulation. He has maintained that care provided by churches and universities should be subject to state regulation just as much as that provided by nonprofit and for-profit agencies.

With some modifications of their approach, and without substantial subsidies, then, states may be able to increase the access to, and lower the cost of, quality day care services. These reforms and increased federal financial help have the potential to provide access to a substantially greater number of parents.

Child Abuse. Reports of child abuse and neglect have grown rapidly. More than 500,000 abused and neglected children are living in foster homes and residential institutions, but this is only a fraction of the estimated 2.5 million to 3 million children abused or neglected each year. The number of children in foster care has doubled since 1980 (McCurdy and Daro 1994; Russakoff 1998). Federal spending on foster care is nearly $4 billion annually, an increase of seven-fold since 1980.

Experts disagree about whether abuse and neglect are increasing or whether increases in reported numbers reflect increased attention to the problem, better reporting standards, or changing standards of appropriateness in how children should be treated (Straus and Gelles 1990, chap. 7). Reports indicate that about half the cases of child abuse concern neglect, another 30 percent physical abuse, 10 percent sexual abuse, and 10 percent other forms of abuse, including emotional (McCurdy and Daro 1994).

We do not have an exact estimate of the extent of child abuse even now. Although federal legislation of 1974 (the Child Abuse Prevention and Treatment Act) mandated uniform operating standards for the identification and management of child abuse cases, in practice these uniform standards do not exist. States vary in how they count instances of abuse (by family, by incident, or by number of children affected), how they classify different types of abuse, who should handle abuse cases (police or child protective services), and other dimensions of processing abuse cases (Berger 1992; McCurdy and Daro 1994; Wells 1988).

State and local agencies dealing with child abuse are extremely fragmented. Police services, child welfare agencies, schools, mental health agencies, and other agencies all play a role. Abusive families often have other problems, which contribute to abuse problems, such as drug or alcohol abuse or poverty and unemployment (Daro and Cohn 1988). Many are single-parent families.

New state initiatives are focusing on prevention of abuse by trying to provide services for families beset by multiple problems. Home visiting services are being implemented in most states to help new parents learn parenting skills and are especially directed to at-risk families. Currently, some states are experimenting with family preservation services, designed to help families with multiple problems that could lead to removal of children from their homes. Washington's Homebuilders program offers intensive services. The program provides a family with one worker for an average of ten to fifteen hours per week, to be available twenty-four hours a day every day, but for a short term (Farrow 1991). The Federal Family Preservation and Support Services Program of 1993 provided increased funding for such services, although even before this legislation, most states had increased funding for child protective services.

These preventive measures do not deal with those children already abused. Two generations ago, most states closed their orphanages, believing that foster care would serve the welfare of children better than large institutions. Foster care, however, has brought with it its own problems—in particular finding families who are willing and capable of being good foster parents.

The possibility of opening new orphanages has recently been introduced into the debate about welfare reform. Most experts agree that large institutional orphanages would not improve the lives of many abused youth, although smaller group homes might be an improvement for many. The costs of establishing appropriate group homes, however, would probably dwarf any savings from taking such children off the welfare rolls. Whatever the outcome of the orphanage debate, states must confront the breakdown of the foster care system.

GAY AND LESBIAN ISSUES IN FAMILY POLICY

The rights of lesbians and gay men who want to be married or to be parents are among the most controversial issues in family policy. Because the notion of family often evokes nostalgic images of the popular, idealized circumstance of a mother, father, two children and the family dog, no set of issues is more highly charged than the rights provided gays to adoption and foster care, custody of children, same-gender marriage, and consensual sex.

The religious and political symbolism surrounding many other controversial family issues extends to the legal protection for gay and lesbian families. Some religious believers hold that sexual relations between persons of the same gender, and, therefore, claims to family status, violate the dictates of God and must not be sanctioned in civil law. Other religious groups take a more neutral stand on homosexuality, arguing that biblical interpretation is ambiguous on this issue.

In the political arena, advocates of gay and lesbian rights have squared off against conservative politicians and activists over a variety of issues. For example, proponents of gay rights argue that constructed families are every bit as capable as biological families of contributing to society and ensuring positive socialization of children, and that one's sexual orientation should have nothing to do with legal rights in private life. Many conservatives believe that legal tolerance of alternative lifestyles threatens the perpetuation of traditional family structures and only the restoration of traditional family values will rescue society from a downward moral spiral.

Legally, the issue of the rights of gay and lesbian couples stems from the gay rights movement ignited by a 1969 police raid of a gay bar in New York City. That raid touched off protests known as the Stonewall Riots and awakened the consciousness of many gays and lesbians and their supporters about their subordinate legal status. Subsequent political action has focused on securing civil liberties to gays and lesbians at both the state and federal levels.

STATE LAWS

Consensual Sex

Adult consensual sex is one family-related issue affecting gays and lesbians. Sodomy is illegal for all citizens in Alabama, Arizona, Florida, Georgia, Idaho, Louisiana, Massachusetts, Michigan, Minnesota, Mississippi, North Carolina, Rhode Island, South Carolina, Utah, and Virginia. In addition, sodomy is illegal for homosexuals only in five states including Arkansas, Kansas, Maryland, Missouri, and Oklahoma (ACLU 1996). The states have a basis for these laws in a 1986 U.S. Supreme Court case, *Bowers v. Hardwick* (478 U.S. 186 [1986]) in which the majority held that the right to privacy does not cover "homosexual sodomy."

Domestic Partnerships and Same-Gender Marriages

Several other family rights that heterosexual couples take for granted are also circumscribed or banned for homosexuals. These include the legal right to marry, the extension of health insurance and other employment benefits to one's family, family leave, the right to adopt children and serve as foster parents, the power to transfer property to a family member after death, bereavement leave, guardianship, and, in the case of a divorcing couple, rights to custody and visitation of children. No state currently provides this range of rights enjoyed by heterosexual people to homosexuals. A few states, however, provide nontraditional families the ability to register their status. California was the first state that allowed nontraditional families to register as nonprofit associations. Since that time, similar laws have been passed in Oregon, Michigan, New Jersey, Virginia, West Virginia, and Wisconsin. However, it is not clear there are legal benefits from this registration (Achtenberg and Moulding 1994, 1–92.13).

As a response to political advocates on both sides of the issue, in July 1997 the Hawaii state legislature passed a partnership law not limited to same-gender couples that afforded sixty types of protection such as hospital visitation, guardianship, joint property ownership, insurance benefits, and inheritance. This law made Hawaii the first state to extend such broad protections to domestic partners (Cabaj and Purcell 1998).

The Hawaii Supreme Court was the first to rule on an issue related to gay marriage. In 1993, in *Baehr v. Lewin* (74 Haw. 530 [1993]) the court held that a Hawaii law that defines marriage between heterosexual couples only is a gender-based classification and deserves heightened scrutiny under the law. The court remanded the case to the trial courts and a final ruling by the Supreme Court is still pending.

In 1996, in response to the possibility that same-gender marriage would eventually become law in Hawaii, thereby necessitating recognition of Hawaiian marriages in other states, the federal government passed the Defense of Marriage Act, declaring that no state has to recognize a same-gender marriage granted by another state (Havemann 1997). Further, twenty-five states have passed laws barring same-gender marriages, and legislation is currently pending in additional states (Human Rights Campaign 1997).

No other states have gone as far as Hawaii in recognizing same-gender partners. Some states, cities, private businesses, and universities have allowed same-gender couples (and unmarried heterosexual couples) to register as domestic partners, and some of these entities allow domestic partners to obtain employment benefits along the lines of married couples. To date, one state (Massachusetts) and twenty-five cities offer domestic partnership registries. Further, four states (Massachusetts, New York, Oregon, and Vermont), along with fifty-six cities, offer some form of health insurance coverage for domestic partners of eligible employees.

Other sorts of protections for lesbian and gay partners are dependent on court interpretations of state and local legislation and, therefore, specific to individual jurisdictions. For example, in 1989, the New York Court of Appeals held in *Braschi v. Stahl Associates Co.* (74 N.Y.2d 210 [1984]) that a gay man's partner could take over his rent-controlled apartment after the man died. The court noted that the partner of the deceased was indeed a family member given a host of evidence, including a long-term relationship and the community recognition of the couple. In addition, in 1991 the Minnesota Court of Appeals allowed a woman to be named the legal guardian of her severely disabled lesbian partner after the disabled woman's parents fought against this for years and tried to obtain guardianship for themselves. The case, *In Re Kowalski* (478 N.W.2d 790 [Minn. Ct. App. 1991]), which received a great deal of national attention, is looked to as a model for legal acknowledgement of partner status (Achtenberg and Moulding 1994).

GAY FAMILIES

The number of gay families is unknown, but scholars and advocates believe that between 6 million to 14 million children live with at least one gay parent (Kantrowitz 1996). Political opponents and advocates of civil liberties for gay families spar about the effect of gay parents on children's development. Scholarly studies of the subject suggest that children of gay parents do equally well on measures of psychological adjustment and are no more likely to be gay than children of heterosexual parents (Patterson 1992).

Adoption and Foster Care

Adoption and foster care are also issues of growing importance for lesbians and gay men. The state is involved whether one adopts privately or through a public agency. As is the case with domestic partner benefits, the family law status of lesbians and gays is a patchwork of legislation and court decisions. Thus rights of homosexual parents and couples are highly dependent on the state and city of residence.

Adoption issues for lesbians and gays arise in several kinds of situations. For example, the partner of a lesbian who gives birth to a biological child must seek to adopt the child of her partner (second-parent adoption). Further, one partner may wish to adopt extant children of a partner. A single lesbian or gay man may seek to adopt a child, or lesbian or gay partners may wish to adopt a child who is biologically unrelated to either of them. Currently, no state has a law that affirms the right of lesbians or gay men to adopt, and Florida and New Hampshire ban the adoption of children by lesbians and gays (Havemann 1997). However, in December, 1997, with settlement of a class-action lawsuit, New Jersey became the first state to allow gay partners to jointly adopt children. Because the case dealt with children in foster care in the state, the ruling technically applies only to adoption of children in custody of the state. As an opposite example, in Arizona a bisexual male was denied the right to adopt a child by an appellate court because his homosexual conduct was illegal under Arizona law (Achtenberg and Moulding 1994).

Public Opinion

One of the reasons that lesbians and gays have fewer rights in family matters than heterosexuals have may have to do with public opinion. A national survey found that about 65 to 75 percent of Americans believe that homosexual relationships are always wrong, and this proportion has remained remarkably stable for the past twenty years (see the site for the Inter-University Consortium for Political and Social Research at the University of Michigan at www.icpsr.umich.edu/gss/subject/s-index.htm). On the other hand, one 1989 Gallup Poll indicated that "by a 47 to 36 margin (with the remainder undecided), Americans prefer legalization of homosexual relations between consenting adults" (as quoted in Horowitz 1991, 180).

Following a U.S. Supreme Court decision denying political jurisdictions the right to pass constitutional amendments barring local legislation protecting lesbians and gay from discrimination (*Romer v. Evans* [517 U.S. 620, 1996]), a *Newsweek* poll found that 58 percent of respondents said they believed gay marriages should not be legal (Kaplan and Klaidman 1996). However, other survey results indicate only a small minority (less than 15 percent) say they believe that homosexuals should have the right to marry ((www.icpsr.umich.edu/gss/subject/s-index.htm). The large difference in these results no doubt reflect the different question wording and the ambiguous feelings that many Americans have about homosexuals—disapproving the practice but not wanting government intruding on individuals' sex lives.

The Future

Since about 1970, support has increased for providing lesbians and gays with civil rights protection afforded to other groups in society. The AIDS epidemic, the increase in hate crimes, controversies about gays in the military, the 1996 Defense of Marriage Act passed by Congress, and the reintroduction of the Employment Non-Discrimination Act (which failed in the U.S. Senate by one vote in 1996), have heightened attention to the issue. Polls suggest that most American do not wish to endorse homosexuality, but they also do not want to see gays and lesbians discriminated against. Although family law in the states is still largely silent or even opposed to expanding definitions of family to include homosexual unions, legal recognition and acceptance of homosexual partnerships and families are increasing.

MAKING FAMILY POLICY

Changes in the policy-making environment have the potential to affect policy outcomes generally and family policy in particular. For example, different types of policy makers produce different policies (Tatalovich and Schier 1993; Witt and Moncrief 1993). For example, the increased presence of women in state legislatures affects the policies that are made (Thomas 1994; Thomas and Welch 1991; Welch and Thomas 1991). In state legislatures women, more than men, have an affinity for and promote legislation dealing with issues of women, children, and families. Men are more likely to promote business and economic issues.[9]

First, women were more likely than men to consider representing women in the constituency a very important part of their job. Fifty-seven percent of women state legislators agreed with that statement compared to only 33 percent of men. Second, women were more likely than men to take pride in bills passed concerning women, children, and families. Third, and perhaps most important, compared to men's, women's priority bills were more likely to pertain to children's issues, such as child care, family leave, child support enforcement, and early childhood education, and to women's issues, such as such as domestic violence, sexual harassment, and com-

9. These findings are from the Welch and Thomas study (1991) of women and men in state legislatures in these twelve states: Arizona, California, Georgia, Illinois, Iowa, Mississippi, Nebraska, North Carolina, Pennsylvania, South Dakota, Vermont, and Washington.

parable worth (Thomas 1994). Looked at another way, 42 percent of women had at least one priority bill dealing with issues of women, children, and families compared to only 16 percent of men (Thomas 1994).

Bill introduction without passage is little more than symbolic, so it is important to compare success rates of bills. The ratio of introduction to passage of women's, children's, and family issues was higher for women state legislators than men (27.1 percent for women compared to 11.1 percent for men). Similar if not more dramatic patterns are evident with respect to obtaining gubernatorial signatures. Women legislators' average ratio of introduction to signature of these types of bills was 25.6 compared to men's average of only 8.0.

Women's presence in state legislatures across the nation currently stands at 22 percent; however, in some states, women are as many as 40 percent of the legislature whereas in a few states there are fewer than 10 percent. This proportion affects women's ability to introduce and pass legislation that interests them. Women in states with higher proportions of female membership tend to introduce more priority legislation dealing with women, children, and families than the men in their states, and are more successful passing these bills. In addition, the proportion of women in a state legislature can affect the overall passage of family policy. States with either a very high proportion of women (in the relative, not absolute sense) or a formal women's legislative caucus had the highest rate of introduction and enactment of such legislation (Thomas 1991, 1994; Welch and Thomas 1991; see also Saint-Germain 1989).

Regardless of the proportion of women in the legislature, women state legislators were more likely than men to have worked on bills dealing with women's issues and are much more likely to give top priority to bills focusing on women's issues (Dodson 1991; Dodson and Carroll 1991).

Committee memberships of women state legislators have an impact on family policy. Women have been significantly more likely than men to be assigned to a health and welfare committee, and are also more likely to chair such committees (Carroll and Taylor 1989).

Research on abortion policy also helps make the case that the composition of legislatures matters to policy outcomes. The religious composition of the population, the proportion of hospital providers, a history of state policy liberalism, and previous abortion restrictions are all associated with subsequent state policies (Hansen 1993). Most important, the states with the least restrictive abortion laws tended to have a higher percentage of women in the state legislature.

Having more women in legislatures moves abortion policy in a prochoice direction. When women legislators reach a critical mass, they have a discernable effect on parental notification policy. Further, women's presence on committees charged with decisions on abortion policy proposals is key. This influence included strategic blocking of legislation as well as endorsement. The blocking strategies were especially evident in states with low proportions of women and in states with tendencies to introduce prolife legislation (Berkman and O'Connor 1993).

Policy outcomes are not the only way women influence family and other policy arenas. Women and men state legislators conceptualize public policy problems differently. One example concerns crime. Whereas male officeholders tend to view the problem as individual flouting of legal mandates, women are more likely to search for social antecedents of criminal activity. Hence, women's proposed solutions were more likely to address the roots of the problem rather than its most recent symptoms (Kathlene 1995)

Taken together, these studies suggest that, as new groups join public life, policy outcomes are affected. Of course, personal characteristics of legislators are not the only factors exerting influence on policy making in the states. Public opinion, the activity of interest groups, court decisions, the actions of the executive, and those of federal and local governments are all critical. However, broadening the range of individuals in state government does make a difference in general. The increase in the number of women state legislators and their consequent influence on family policy illustrates well that difference.

CONCLUSION

Government has always been involved in making family policy, but this activity has greatly increased since the mid-1960s. Traditionally, state governments dominated family policy, through their regulation of marriage, divorce, and certain kinds of relations between parents and children. Although the federal government provided some benefits to widows and orphans after the Civil War, it had little role in family policy until the New Deal. Then federal policies were aimed at low-income families, through the Aid to Families with Dependent Children program.

The flood of women into the workforce and the increasing poverty level of America's children have prompted considerably more family policy activity. The federal government's activity is largely directed to low-income families, although the Family and Medical Leave Act is a significant exception. States are engaged in a wide variety of activities designed to aid families, and especially children, at all income levels.

Action, however, lags far behind the profamily rhetoric so prominent in both federal and state political discourse. States do little to provide incentives for marriage or disincentives for divorce. Despite a decade of "getting tough" on fathers who do not pay child support, collection rates are shockingly low, and states are reluctant to make enforcement a priority. Working parents in the United States have far fewer child care services available than do those in most other industrial nations, and they have far fewer services that make it easier to combine the roles of bread-winning and parenting. Abused and neglected children pose a different challenge, and politicians and social welfare experts wrestle with the dilemmas of when to remove children from their homes. And many families must struggle to meet even their basic needs for food, clothing, shelter, and medical care.

There are important reasons for the failure of America's family policies. One is the lack of consensus about the appropriate role of government in aiding families.

Not everyone agrees that government should support day care or garnish wages to enforce child support payments, let alone promote family planning efforts, protect the right to abortion, or help same-gender couples obtain rights offered to married partners. People disagree strongly about the conditions under which it is appropriate to remove children from their parents to protect their health and safety. Family issues do not just have to do with the size and scope of government, about which compromise is difficult; family issues have to do with religion and morality, about which compromise is sometimes nearly impossible.

Another impediment to a comprehensive family policy is federalism. As in almost every other policy arena, our federal system has created a set of family laws and services that are byzantine in their complexity. National, state, and local courts, legislatures, and executives all play a role in family policy. These overlapping jurisdictions, coupled with the fact that many people do not want government to play a role at all, sometimes make for large gaps in the family safety net that are slow to be mended.

States are at the nexus of these issues. And they are beginning to move beyond their traditional roles in regulating families and child welfare. In many states, more comprehensive services are springing up that seek to tie together families, schools, and communities to provide increased support to families, especially those at risk. Minnesota's Early Childhood and Family Education Program, Connecticut's family resource centers, Maryland's family support programs, and Kentucky's family resource and youth service center, for example, all illustrate the attempts of states to bring together schools and social services to provide more comprehensive assistance to families. Given that the deterioration in family ties bodes poorly for community and societal ties, the challenge to the states in their key role is awesome indeed.

REFERENCES

ACLU. 1996. "Briefing Paper on Lesbian and Gay Rights," Number 18.

Achtenberg, Roberta, and Karen B. Moulding, eds. 1994. *Sexual Orientation and the Law.* San Francisco: National Lawyers Guild, Lesbian, Gay, Bisexual Rights Committee.

Adams, Gina. 1990. *Who Knows How Safe? The Status of State Efforts to Ensure Quality Child Care.* Washington, D.C.: Children's Defense Fund.

Alan Guttmacher Institute. 1997. "Issues in Brief, Contraception Counts: State-by-State Information." Washington, D.C.: Author.

Aldous, Joan, and Wilfried Dumon. 1990. "Family Policy in the 1980s: Controversy and Consensus." *Journal of Marriage and the Family* 52:1136–1151.

Amato, Paul R., and Alan Booth. 1997. *A Generation at Risk: Growing up in an Era of Family Upheaval.* Cambridge, Mass.: Harvard University Press.

Balz, Dan, "Abortion: A Staple of U.S. Politics," *Washington Post,* January 18, 1998.

Bane, Mary Jane. 1980. "Toward a Description and Evaluation of United States Family Policy." In *The Policies and Programs of Family Policy: United States and European Perspective,* edited by Joan Aldous and Wilfried Dumon. Notre Dame, Ind.: Center for the Study of Man, University of Notre Dame, and Leuvan Press.

Berger, Brigitte. 1992. "On the Limits of the Welfare State: The Case of Foster Care." In *The American Family and the State,* edited by Joseph Peden and Fred Glake. San Francisco: Pacific Research Institute for Public Policy.

Berkman, Michael B., and Robert E. O'Connor. 1993. "Do Women Legislators Matter? Female Legislators and State Abortion Policy." *American Politics Quarterly* 21 (January):102–124.

Buehler, Cheryl. 1989. "Influential Factors and Equity Issues in Divorce Settlements." *Family Relations* 38 (January):76–82.

Cabaj, Robert P., and David W. Purcell, eds. 1998. *On the Road to Same-Sex Marriage*. San Francisco: Jossey-Bass.

Carroll, Susan J., and Ella Taylor. 1989. "Gender Differences in the Committee Assignments of State Legislators: Preferences or Discrimination?" Paper presented to the annual meeting of the Midwest Political Science Association, April 13–16, Chicago.

Cohen, Jeffrey E., and Charles Barrilleaux. 1993. "Public Opinion, Interest Groups, and Public Policy Making: Abortion Policy in the American States." In *Understanding the New Politics of Abortion*, edited by Malcolm L. Goggin. Newbury Park, Calif.: Sage.

Daro, Deborah, and Anne Cohn. 1988. "Child Maltreatment Evaluation Efforts." In *Coping with Family Violence*, edited by Gerald T. Hotaling, David Finkelhor, John T. Kirkpatrick, and Murray Straus. Newbury Park, Calif.: Sage.

Doane, Alesha E., and Kenneth J. Meier. n.d. "Violence as a Political Strategy: The Case of Anti-Abortion Activists." Unpublished manuscript.

Dodson, Debra L., ed. 1991. *Gender and Policymaking: Studies of Women in Office*. New Brunswick, N.J.: Center for the American Woman and Politics.

Dodson, Debra L., and Susan J. Carroll. 1991. *Reshaping the Agenda: Women in State Legislatures*. New Brunswick, N.J.: Rutgers University Center for the American Woman and Politics.

Dodson, Debra L., and Lauren D. Burnbauer with the assistance of Katherine E. Kleeman. 1990. *Election 1989: The Abortion Issue in New Jersey and Virginia*. New Brunswick, N.J.: Rutgers University Center for the American Woman and Politics.

Donnelly, Sally B. 1997. "The Real Partial-Birth War," *Newsweek*, October 20, 50.

Farrow, Frank. 1991. "Services to Families: The View from the States." *Families in Society: The Journal of Contemporary Human Services* 72 (May):268–276.

Garfinkel, Irwin. 1994. "The Child Support Revolution." *American Economic Review* 84 (May):81–85.

Garfinkel, Irwin, Donald Oellerich, and Philip K. Robins. 1991. "Child Support Guidelines." *Journal of Family Issues* 12:404–429.

Garrow, David. 1994. *Liberty and Sexuality: The Right to Privacy and the Making of* Roe v. Wade. New York: Macmillan.

———. 1998. "Abortion Foes Are Losing in Court," *Washington Post*, January 18.

Gelb, Joyce, and Marian Lief Palley. 1982. *Women and Public Policies*. Princeton, N.J.: Princeton University Press.

Glendon, Mary Ann. 1987. *Abortion and Divorce in Western Law*. Cambridge, Mass.: Harvard University Press.

Goggin, Malcolm L. 1993. "Introduction: A Framework for Understanding the New Politics of Abortion." In *Understanding the New Politics of Abortion*, edited by Malcolm L Goggin. Newbury Park, Calif.: Sage.

Goggin, Malcolm L., ed. 1993. *Understanding the New Politics of Abortion*. Newbury Park, Calif.: Sage.

Goggin, Malcolm L., and Christopher Wlezien. 1993. "Abortion Opinion and Policy in the American States." In *Understanding the New Politics of Abortion*, edited by Malcolm L. Goggin. Newbury Park, Calif.: Sage.

Goldstein, Amy. 1995. "U.S. Abortion Services Drop," *Washington Post*, January 22.

Gormley, William T., Jr. 1990. "Regulating Mr. Rogers' Neighborhood: The Dilemmas of Day Care Regulation." *Brookings Review* 8(4):21–28.

———. 1991a. "Day Care in a Federal System." *Social Service Review* 65: 582–596.

———. 1991b. "State Regulations and the Availability of Child-Care Services." *Journal of Policy Analysis and Management* 10:78–95.

———. 1995. *Everybody's Children*. Washington D.C.: Brookings Institution.

Gormley, William T., and B. Guy Peters. 1992. "National Styles of Regulation: Child Care in Three Countries." *Policy Sciences* 25:318–399.

Gray, Madeline. 1979. *Margaret Sanger: A Biography of the Champion of Birth Control*. New York: Richard Marek.

Hansen, Susan B. 1993. "Differences in Public Policies toward Abortion: Electoral and Policy Context." In *Understanding the New Politics of Abortion,* edited by Malcolm L. Goggin. Newbury Park, Calif.: Sage.

Havemann, Judith. 1997. "N.J. Allows Gays to Adopt Jointly," *Washington Post,* December 18.

Horowitz, Carl F. 1991. "Homosexuality's Legal Revolution." *Freeman* (May):173–181.

Human Rights Campaign. 1997. "Same-Sex Marriage: Where the Issue Stands."

Jacob, Herbert. 1988. *Silent Revolution: The Transformation of Divorce Law in the United States.* Chicago: University of Chicago Press.

Josephson, Jyl J. 1997. *Gender, Families, and State: Child Support Policy in the United States.* Lanham, Md.: Rowman and Littlefield.

Kamerman, Sheila B. 1991. "Parental Leave and Infant Care: U.S. and International Trends and Issues, 1978–1988." In *Parental Leave and Child Care,* edited by Janet Shibley Hyde and Marilyn J. Essex. Philadelphia: Temple University Press.

Kantrowitz, Barbara. 1996. "Gays Come Out," *Newsweek,* November 4, 51–57.

Kaplan, David A., and Daniel Klaidman. 1996. "A Battle, Not the War." *Newsweek* (June 3):25–30.

Kathlene, Lyn. 1995. "Alternative Views of Crime: Legislative Policymaking in Gendered Terms," *Journal of Politics* 57 (August):696–723.

Lenhoff, Donna, and Sylvia M. Becker. 1989. "Family and Medical Leave Legislation in the States: Toward a Comprehensive Approach." *Harvard Journal of Legislation* 26:402–451.

Levitan, Sol, R. S. Belous, and F. Gallo. 1988. *What's Happening to the American Family.* Rev. ed. Baltimore: Johns Hopkins University Press.

Luker, Kristin. 1984. *Abortion and the Politics of Motherhood.* Berkeley: University of California Press.

Lynn, L. E. 1980. "Fiscal and Organizational Constraints on United States Family Policy." In *The Policies and Programs of Family Policy: United States and European Perspective,* edited by Joan Aldous and Wilifried Dumon. Notre Dame, Ind.: Center for the Study of Man, University of Notre Dame, and Leuvan Press.

Makuen, Kathleen. 1988. "Public Servants, Private Parents: Parental Leave Policies in the Public Section." In *The Parental Leave Crisis: Toward a National Policy,* edited by Edward F. Zigler and Meryl Frank. New Haven, Conn.: Yale University Press.

Marvell, Thomas B. 1989. "Divorce Rates and the Fault Requirement." *Law and Society Review* 23:543–567.

Matthews, Stephen, David Ribar, and Mark Wilhelm. 1997. "The Effects of Economic Conditions and Access to Reproductive Health Services on State Abortion Rates and Birthrates," *Family Planning Perspectives* 29 (March/April):52–60.

McCurdy, Karen, and Deborah Daro. 1994. *Current Trends in Child Abuse Reporting and Fatalities.* Chicago: National Center on Child Abuse Prevention.

McEvoy, Lawrence T. 1978. "The Impact of No-Fault Divorce: The Missouri Experience." *State Government* 5 (Spring):95–105.

McGlen, Nancy E., and Karen O'Connor. 1998. *Women, Politics, and American Society,* 2d ed.. Upper Saddle River, N.J.: Prentice-Hall.

Meier, Kenneth J., and Deborah R. McFarlane. 1993. "Abortion Politics and Abortion Funding Policy." In *Understanding the New Politics of Abortion,* edited by Malcolm L. Goggin. Newbury Park, Calif.: Sage.

Meyer, Daniel. 1993. "Child Support and Welfare Dynamics: Evidence from Wisconsin." *Demography* 30:45–62.

Mezey, Susan Gluck. 1992. *In Pursuit of Equality: Women, Public Policy, and the Federal Courts.* New York: St. Martin's Press.

Moen, Phyllis, and Alvin L. Schorr. 1987. "Families and Social Policy." In *Handbook of Marriage and the Family,* edited by M. Sussman and S. Steinmetz. New York: Plenum Press.

Ms., January/February 1997:15.

NARAL Foundation/NARAL. 1996. *Who Decides? A State-by-State Review of Abortion Rights,* 5th ed.

National Center for Health Statistics. 1998. Data cited in "Teen Moms," *Wall Street Journal,* May 8, A14.

Patterson, Charlotte J. 1992. "Children of Lesbian and Gay Parents," *Child Development* 63:1025–1042.

Peters, Elizabeth. 1986. "Marriage and Divorce: Informational Constraints and Private Contracts." *American Economic Review* 76 (June):437–454.

Peters, H. Elizabeth, Laura M. Argys, Eleanor E. Maccoby, and Robert Mnookin. 1993. "Enforcing Divorce Settlements: Evidence from Child Support Compliance and Award Modifications." *Demography* 30:719–735.

Planned Parenthood Fact Sheet. 1995. "Protecting Women and Their Health Care Providers from Violence and Harassment" (August).

Rodgers, Kathryn J. (Executive Director, NOW Legal Defense Fund). n.d. Letter to supporters.

Roemer, Julie. 1988. "Democrats Lining up behind 'Family' Banner." *Congressional Quarterly Weekly Report,* January 30, 183–188.

Russakoff, Dale. 1998. "Mother of Last Resort," *Washington Post National Weekly Edition,* February 22, 6–7.

Saint-Germain, Michelle A. 1989. "Does Their Difference Make a Difference? The Impact of Women on Public Policy in the Arizona Legislature." *Social Science Quarterly* 70 (December):956–968.

Sapiro, Virginia. 1994. *Women in American Society: An Introduction to Women's Studies.* 3d ed. Mountain View, Calif.: Mayfield.

Seltzer, Judith. 1991. "Legal Custody Arrangements and Children's Economic Welfare." *American Journal of Sociology* 96:895–929.

Stetson, Dorothy McBride. 1991a. "The Political History of Parental Leave Policy." In *Parental Leave and Child Care,* edited by Janet Shibley Hyde and Marilyn J. Essex. Philadelphia: Temple University Press.

———. 1991b. *Women's Rights in the U.S.A.: Policy Debates and Gender Roles.* Belmont, Calif.: Brooks/Cole.

Straus, Murray, and Richard Gelles. 1990. *Physical Violence in American Families.* New Brunswick, N.J.: Transaction Books.

Strickland, Ruth Ann, and Marcia Lynn Whicker. 1992. "Political and Socioeconomic Indicators of State Restrictiveness toward Abortion." *Policy Studies Journal* 20:598–617.

Sweezy, Kate, and Jill Tiefenthaler. 1996. "Do State-Level Variables Affect Divorce Rates?" *Review of Social Economy* 54:47–65.

Tatalovich, Raymond, and David Schier. 1993. "The Persistence of Ideological Cleavage in Voting on Abortion Legislation in the House of Representatives, 1973–1988." In *Understanding the New Politics of Abortion,* edited by Malcolm L. Goggin. Newbury Park, Calif.: Sage.

Teachman, Jay D. 1990. "Socioeconomic Resources of Parents and Award of Child Support in the United States: Some Exploratory Models." *Journal of Marriage and the Family* 52:689–699.

Thomas, Sue. 1991. "The Impact of Women on State Legislative Policies." *Journal of Politics* 53 (November):958–976.

———. 1994. *How Women Legislate.* New York: Oxford University Press.

Thomas, Sue, and Susan Welch. 1991. "The Impact of Gender on Activities and Priorities of State Legislators." *Western Political Quarterly* 44:445–456.

U.S. Bureau of the Census. 1994, 1997. *Statistical Abstract of the United States.* Washington D.C.: U.S. Government Printing Office.

Vandell, Deborah, V. Kay Henderson, and Kathy Shores Wilson. 1988. "A Longitudinal Study of Children with Day-Care Experiments of Varying Quality." *Child Development* 59:1286–1292.

———. 1997. "Abortion Rate in U.S. off Sharply," *The Washington Post,* December 5.

Weitzman, Lenore. 1985. *The Divorce Revolution: The Unexpected Social and Economic Consequences for Women and Children in America.* New York: Free Press.

Welch, Susan, and Sue Thomas. 1991. "Do Women in Public Office Make a Difference?" In *Gender and Policymaking Studies of Women in Office,* edited by Debra L. Dodson. New Brunswick, N.J.: Center for the American Woman and Politics.

Wells, Susan. 1988. "Factors Influencing the Response of Child Protective Service Workers to Reports of Abuse and Neglect." In *Coping with Family Violence,* edited by Gerald T. Hotaling, David Finkelhor, John T. Kirkpatrick, and Murray Straus. Newbury Park, Calif.: Sage.

White, L. K. 1991. "Determinants of Divorce: A Review of the Research in the Eighties." In *Contemporary Families: Looking Forward, Looking Back,* edited by Alan Booth. Minneapolis, Minn: National Council on Family Relations.

Wisensale, Steven K. 1990. "Approaches to Family Policy in State Government: A Report on Five States." *Family Relations* 39 (April):136–140.

————. 1991. "State Initiatives in Family Policy." In *The Reconstruction of Family Policy,* edited by Elaine Anderson and Richard Hula. New York: Greenwood Press.

Witt, Stephanie L., and Gary Moncrief. 1993. "Religion and Roll-Call Voting in Idaho: The 1990 Abortion Controversy." In *Understanding the New Politics of Abortion,* edited by Malcolm L. Goggin. Newbury Park, Calif.: Sage.

Zimmerman, Shirley. 1992. *Family Policies and Family Well-Being: The Role of Political Culture.* Newbury Park, Calif.: Sage.

SUGGESTED READINGS

Aldous, Joan, and Wilfried Dumon. "Family Policy in the 1980s: Controversy and Consensus." *Journal of Marriage and the Family* 52 (November 1992):1136–1151. Provides a review of the state of the family and family policies at the beginning of the 1990s.

Garrow, David. *Liberty and Sexuality: The Right to Privacy and the Making of Roe v. Wade.* New York: Macmillan, 1994. An engaging but encyclopedic account of the history, personalities, and issues leading up to the Supreme Court's landmark abortion rights decision.

Glendon, Mary Ann. *Abortion and Divorce in Western Law.* Cambridge, Mass.: Harvard University Press, 1987. Compares U.S. abortion and divorce policies with those of several western European nations.

Gormley, William T., Jr. 1995. *Everybody's Children.* Washington D.C.: Brookings Institution. A thorough account of the state, federal, and local politics of child care policy in the United States.

Jacob, Herbert. *Silent Revolution: The Transformation of Divorce Law in the United States.* Chicago: University of Chicago Press, 1988. Analyzes the dynamics of the dramatic change in divorce law in the United States from the 1960s through the 1980s.

Zimmerman, Shirley. *Family Policies and Family Well-Being: The Role of Political Culture.* Newbury Park, Calif.: Sage, 1992. Examines the family policies of the states, with a specific look at Nevada, Minnesota, and South Carolina.

Epilogue

For the third time in history the United States is entering a new millennium. The first two times were politically momentous: In the "revolution" of 1800 Thomas Jefferson was elected president, and power was transferred from the Founding Party to its political successor—peacefully and without incident, apart from the last-minute judicial appointments that spawned *Marbury v. Madison.* A comparable shift in power occurred after the critical election of 1896, which ushered in an era of Republican dominance in national politics that lasted until the New Deal. Both events marked sea changes in American politics. Thus we may well wonder how the political tide is running as we approach the twenty-first century.

In fact, sweeping changes are underway, and they are not confined to alternations in party control of the national government. The changes are the result of a devolution revolution that is shifting power from the national government to the states—a shift that is occurring partly because budget deficits have until recently limited policy initiatives emanating from Washington, D.C. The main reason, though, is political. In 1994 Republicans won control of Congress after signing the Contract with America, which promised to reduce the overall size of government and shift its domestic center of gravity to the states. The idea appealed to many citizens, and the corresponding attack on "big government" still wins votes. Not to be outdone, many Democrats endorsed devolution in key policy areas.

The welfare reform of 1996 is an outstanding example of devolution. Aid to Families with Dependent Children, an entitlement program created in 1935, was eliminated in favor of Temporary Assistance to Needy Families, a block grant that allows states enormous discretion in public assistance programming. This "end to welfare as we know it" was historic, but the political impetus for devolution extends to many other policy areas, including educational reform, environmental regulation, and health care. Devolution is also a prominent feature of policies involving social regulation, including abortion restrictions, gay rights, and recreational drug use or the use of marijuana for medicinal purposes. Many believe that devolution will continue well into the next decade, although the pace of devolution seems to be slowing (Conlan 1998).

For the most part states are using their newfound authority to address politically important problems. The architects of Ronald Reagan's New Federalism thought devolution would mean less government, because they assumed many states would choose not to exercise powers that once belonged to the national government. These hopes were dashed, however, and early experiences with devolution suggest that state policy makers are quite eager to use their new powers on behalf of political constituents. Now that they have wrested power from the national government, state governors and legislators will not hesitate to use it when citizens clamor for relief from a variety of state and local problems. The political incentives make it almost impossible for elected officials to refrain from acting.

Devolution empowers states from above, so to speak, but pressures from below are also augmenting states' power. A number of policy areas long dominated by local governments are becoming more centralized as state policy makers assert themselves. Economic development and closely related policies governing land use and environmental protection are good examples of this trend; regional and even statewide policies are now common, and the autonomy of local governments in these policy areas is clearly shrinking. Centralization is also evident in the increasingly important role of states in public education, particularly with respect to financing, but also in certifying teachers, setting curriculum standards, and expanding options to include charter and home schools. This centralization or upward gravitation of power is largely independent of devolutionary impulses, although the two developments will begin to reinforce each other in the twenty-first century. Devolution will free states from federal constraints, and as state policy makers exercise their authority they are bound to encroach even further on local prerogatives.

This convergence of responsibility from above and below is a political phenomenon in the sense that it has its roots in public opinion. Citizens now expect state governments to do more, and they have confidence in state officials' willingness and ability to solve problems that defeated other levels of government. Welfare reforms were enacted because federally dominated programs failed to provide effective work incentives, despite numerous reform efforts to accomplish that objective. State-level policy experiments showed greater promise in moving families off welfare rolls and into the workforce and were attractive for that reason. Similarly, school financing and other aspects of public education were centralized when it became obvious that many local school systems were incapable of improving educational outcomes on their own, and governors began to offer statewide remedies that promised better results. Voters responded positively, reinforcing state politicians' willingness to act.

The convergence of power in state capitals presents new opportunities for leadership. These new opportunities are attracting a new breed of politicians to the state capitals. Patronage-minded politicians and "good-time Charlies" have been displaced by professionally oriented men and women with ambitious programs for economic development, educational reform, environmental protection, and social regulation. In pursuit of these objectives the new breed of politicians is seeking election to statewide office, and their success has made the governor's mansion a staging area for domestic policy innovation in the United States. Recognizing this development, several members of the U.S. House of Representatives and the Senate recently abandoned safe positions in Washington, D.C., for the chance to lead their home states. The usual direction of career mobility is being reversed as politicians pursue power in its new locale.

Similar changes have affected state legislatures. Full-time representatives now fill the chambers of many state assemblies, which are better staffed and more technologically advanced than ever before. Many representatives have become policy specialists by virtue of their ideological commitments and long tenure in office. At the same time many voters are alarmed by the sense of professionalism and tendency toward political careerism in state legislatures. Voters in almost two dozen states have imposed term limits on state politicians, forcing them to leave office after their allotted time expires. These term limits create regular opportunities for political newcomers to enter state government and make a difference. As a result many new candidates are being drawn into state politics by the chance to reshape important policies.

Bureaucracies are being modernized, too. Governors and legislatures are reinventing, or in some cases privatizing, executive agencies of state government to improve the delivery of public goods and services. They are broadening and strengthening civil service laws, and professional norms now permeate the executive branch in most state governments. Most important, the caliber of civil servants is improving because highly qualified administrators who once aspired to serve in Washington now see attractive opportunities at the state level. They want to be where the action is, and in domestic policy making the action is now in the state capitals.

Across the board there is heightened interest in policy leadership at the state level. Officials no longer defer to the national government; they are initiating ambitious policies. The recent settlement with tobacco companies is a case in point. State policy makers took the lead in seeking additional curbs on advertising by cigarette manufacturers and reimbursement for health care expenses incurred by smokers under Medicaid and related state programs. This bold undertaking was first pursued in court, then in Congress, and finally in direct negotiations with the four largest tobacco companies. In the end, the states succeeded where Congress failed, effectively forging a national settlement on a contentious issue. Twenty years ago this sort of outcome was inconceivable; ten years ago it was highly improbable. Now it seems to be the natural expression of state politicians' desire or will to lead the way in domestic policy making.

States are not only willing to assume the lead in domestic policy making, they are now able to do so, at least in certain areas. The policy-making capacity of state governments has increased significantly during the past twenty-five years, for several reasons (Hedge 1998). A succession of new federalism initiatives has gradually strengthened the administrative underpinnings of state governments, enabling them to devise and implement policy on a large scale. In support of these initiatives, state legislators have become much more proficient in raising—and spending—money for popular programs and policies. Governors have mobilized public support for these undertakings, and they have placed new ideas on the agenda of state politics. Finally, a "cleaner" (but still quite contentious) form of politics and political decision making is taking shape as states institute public financing of elections and seek curbs on unethical lobbying. The progress is uneven, to be sure, but it is also undeniable.

There are many examples of effective policy making at the state level. Some states have already enacted comprehensive health care reforms, and others developed welfare programs that became models for national reform in 1996. Many states function as entrepreneurs in attracting new industries and retaining old ones, using sophisticated economic development strategies to accomplish their objectives. These states have improved business conditions by building bridges, funding new "information superhighways," and training workers for industry. States have been very active in education reform, too, where they have formulated numerous policies to improve the quality of instruction and learning and to equalize educational opportunities for all students.

States often serve as laboratories for developing and testing ideas for national policy makers to consider. Several notions currently being considered in Washington have their origins in the states. For example, the line-item veto, which was recently declared unconstitutional at the federal level by the Supreme Court, could have changed national politics dramatically, although it has been used in most states for many years. Similarly, states have experience in balancing their budgets and in separating operating expenses from capital outlays, ideas that are regularly floated in the nation's capital. And many states have successfully privatized some of the functions of government.

Certainly states have not solved all of the problems facing them. One is the continuing pressure on the budget, driven primarily by explosive growth in spending for corrections, health care, and elementary and secondary education. The growth of expenditure in these areas derives from demographic trends, which show increases in immigration, poverty, homelessness, family disruption, and the aging population, all of which push social service spending higher. The devolution of responsibility from the national government, and the inability of local governments to meet these needs on their own, will only intensify the challenge facing state policy makers.

Tough problems demand innovative solutions, but innovation at the state level gives rise to its own set of political challenges. As states innovate, they tend to adopt different policies. This is especially likely to happen when policies involve social regulation. States take different stances on controversial issues, reflecting their different political compositions. Some adopt conservative policies on abortion or gay rights, and others pursue liberal options that enjoy political support from their electorates. The inevitable result of these differences is a patchwork of policies, such that citizens' rights and privileges vary from state to state, as do the public goods and services they are entitled to receive. Occasionally, these interstate disparities grow large enough to generate calls for national legislation to establish greater uniformity. Such calls typically come from interest groups—liberal and conservative alike—who are unable to carry the day in every state and for whom the need for uniformity takes precedence over states' rights to determine their own affairs.

In other policy areas, innovative state policies diffuse rather quickly to other states, producing uniformity even in the absence of national policy. Interstate competition is the principal mechanism of this sort of policy diffusion. Thus there is pressure on every state to lower its taxes to match its neighbors, to lower welfare or health benefits to avoid becoming a magnet for poor individuals seeking higher benefits, and to relax its pollution regulations to retain or attract businesses. Some scholars believe this competition among states could generate a "race to the bottom" in which political leaders converge on policies that do not adequately meet the needs of some constituents. According to this line of thought, no state official wants to offend powerful interests. That sometimes requires policy makers to downplay or ignore the interests of the weak or powerless, for example, if serving those interests would harm the state's business climate.

Interstate competition rarely generates complete convergence, but it does produce calls to level the playing field by enacting national standards to keep competition within acceptable political bounds. The Environmental Protection Agency, for example, sets minimum standards for air and water quality, although it permits states to adopt more stringent standards if they so choose. Similarly, the advocates of programs for children and the elderly argue for minimal standards of public assistance, and proponents of minority rights seek uniform protection for basic rights and liberties. In each case, the argument is that states' authority must be limited to ensure that policies will be adequate for meeting widely shared political objectives.

It is therefore possible that devolution will prove to be self-limiting. Devolution allows for innovation at the state level, but the results of innovation will not satisfy everyone. There will be winners and losers, as there always are in politics. Those who are unhappy with state policies may very well seek remedies at the national level. If they succeed, the cycle of centralization, followed by subsequent calls for devolution, will begin anew and the rhythms of American politics will be repeated in the new millennium.

Russell L. Hanson

REFERENCES

Conlan, Timothy. 1998. *From New Federalism to Devolution: Twenty-five Years of Intergovernmental Reform.* Washington, D.C.: Brookings Institution.

Hedge, David M. 1998. *Governance and the Changing American States.* Boulder, Colo.: Westview Press.

Name Index

Subject Index